T0344208

Virtual Mentoring for Teachers:

Online Professional Development Practices

Jared Keengwe
University of North Dakota, USA

Lydia Kyei-Blankson
Illinois State University, USA

Managing Director: Lindsay Johnston
Senior Editorial Director: Heather A. Probst
Book Production Manager: Sean Woznicki
Development Manager: Joel Gamon
Development Editor: Myla Merkel
Assistant Acquisitions Editor: Kayla Wolfe
Typesetter: Nicole Sparano
Cover Design: Nick Newcomer

Published in the United States of America by
Information Science Reference (an imprint of IGI Global)
701 E. Chocolate Avenue
Hershey PA 17033
Tel: 717-533-8845
Fax: 717-533-8661
E-mail: cust@igi-global.com
Web site: http://www.igi-global.com

Library of Congress Cataloging-in-Publication Data

Virtual mentoring for teachers: online professional development practices / Jared Keengwe and Lydia Kyei-Blankson, editors.
     p. cm.
  Includes bibliographical references and index.
    ISBN 978-1-4666-1963-0 (hardcover) -- ISBN 978-1-4666-1964-7 (ebook) -- ISBN 978-1-4666-1965-4 (print & perpetual access) 1. Mentoring in education--Computer networks. 2. Teachers--In-service training--Computer networks. 3. Professional learning communities. I. Keengwe, Jared, 1973- II. Kyei-Blankson, Lydia.
  LB1731.4.V57 2013
  371.102--dc23
                         2012009704

British Cataloguing in Publication Data
A Cataloguing in Publication record for this book is available from the British Library.

All work contributed to this book is new, previously-unpublished material. The views expressed in this book are those of the authors, but not necessarily of the publisher.

Editorial Advisory Board

Table of Contents

Section 1
Professional Development Models for Faculty in Online Environments

Chapter 1

Designing Effective Online Instructor Training and Professional Development 1

Jennifer R. Banas, Northeastern Illinois University, USA

Angela Velez-Solic, Indiana University Northwest, USA

Chapter 2

Professional Development with Graduate Teaching Assistants (TAs) Teaching Online 26

Denice Ward Hood, University of Illinois, Urbana-Champaign, USA

Wen-Hao David Huang, University of Illinois, Urbana-Champaign, USA

Chapter 3

Multi-Modal Professional Development for Faculty 43

Sheri Anderson, University of North Carolina Wilmington, USA

Beth Oyarzun, University of North Carolina Wilmington, USA

Chapter 4

The Networked Learning Framework: A Model for Networked Professional Learning Utilizing
Social Networking Sites 66

Nathaniel Ostashewski, Athabasca University, Canada

Doug Reid, Wayfinder Education Group, Canada

Section 2
Understanding E-Learning and Best Practices in Teaching and Learning in Online
Environments

Detailed Table of Contents

Section 1
Professional Development Models for Faculty in Online Environments

Chapter 1

Jennifer R. Banas, Northeastern Illinois University, USA
Angela Velez-Solic, Indiana University Northwest, USA

There are many ways to deliver engaging, effective, and efficient online instruction, but most higher education instructors do not know how. So while the demand for online learning has drastically increased, the efficacious training of instructors into how to deliver online courses lags far behind. In this chapter, the authors demonstrate how adult learning and instructional design principles, coupled with known best practices for online teaching, can facilitate the design of effective training and professional development for online instructors. Case study examples are used to illustrate key concepts, and a sample outline for training is offered. Administrators and trainers of online instructors will form the primary audience; other stake holders in online education will benefit as well.

Chapter 2

Denice Ward Hood, University of Illinois, Urbana-Champaign, USA
Wen-Hao David Huang, University of Illinois, Urbana-Champaign, USA

As the number of online courses offered continues to increase, teaching online will become a standard expectation and responsibility for graduate teaching assistants (TAs). For TAs who will seek faculty positions, experience and self-efficacy teaching online are critical to their future career. The current and future university landscape and the higher education world these TAs will embody will require qualified individuals to be well trained in online course development and delivery. Of equal importance is the quality of teaching TAs provide for the large number of online undergraduate courses for which they have sole responsibility or provide instructional support. Colleges and universities need to develop professional development for TAs that reflects best practices in online teaching and learning and engages TAs in the instructional design as well as delivery process. The purpose of this chapter is to explore the literature on teaching assistant professional development and the implications for TAs teaching online.

This chapter describes a multi-modal faculty professional development program designed using the Analyze, Design, Development, Implement, and Evaluation process (ADDIE) and the Community of Learners model. The program includes a general training series, one-on-one trainings, on-demand training, as well as social events. The general training series is offered synchronously via face-to-face and webinar formats simultaneously. This training series is also offered asynchronously via training videos and slides that are published to a website. Additionally, the professional development program encourages faculty to support one another and share their experiences through social events and colloquiums. This multi-modal approach creates an adaptable and flexible environment that allows the professional development program to meet the needs of a diverse group of faculty.

This chapter describes the Networked Learning Framework (NLF), a networked learning model utilized in the development of a networked teacher professional development (nTPD) program. The NLF is a model which combines the use of social media tools found in common social networking sites with guided online activities to deliver innovative and engaging learning opportunities. One implementation of the NLF, the nTPD Courselet, delivered in a social networking site for Alberta teachers, is described in detail. Teachers report that the sharing of resources, reflective blogs, and collegial discussions are the most valuable outcomes of nTPD Courselets. Design principals and factors for designers of faculty PD developers to follow when using the Networked Learning Framework, as well as descriptions of two other NLF implementations, are presented in the chapter. Further research to identify effective supports for social networking novices and ways to build online facilitator capacity are needed.

The purpose of this chapter is to outline how pre-service teacher education can be adapted to the emergence of virtual educational structures and processes that complement traditional classes. The chapter is based on research conducted in rural schools in the Canadian province of Newfoundland and Labrador that links in-service and pre-service teachers to provide insights for the latter into real-life, networked classrooms, particularly those located in communities located beyond major centres of population, to which most students were likely to be appointed. Face-to-face groups of pre-service teachers were able to include virtual practicing teachers in their discussions. The significance of this study will be judged by the extent to which professional discourse between pre-service and in-service teachers reflects the virtual challenge of intranets to the physical isolation of traditional schools.

Chapter 6

Vassiliki I. Zygouris-Coe, University of Central Florida, USA

Online learning is a popular learning option for millions of students in US colleges and universities. Online facilitation plays an important role in student learning. With a growing number of courses offered online, there are many challenges associated with the quality of online instruction. This chapter presents information on a large-scale online project for preK-12 educators. The author presents detailed information on a model for training, support, professional development, and monitoring of online instructors. The author also discusses implications for further development and monitoring of online instructors' knowledge, skills, and dispositions that promote successful online experiences and learning for students.

Chapter 7

Richard B. Speaker, Jr., University of New Orleans, USA
Greg Levitt, University of Nevada, Las Vegas, USA
Steven Grubaugh, University of Nevada- Las Vegas, USA

The virtual world Second Life (SL) can be part of professional development deployment and mentoring using online learning. This chapter provides a portrait of professional development and teaching in SL. While SL requires a more extensive learning curve than might be expected, the virtual campus becomes a functioning instructional site for all disciplines, supplementing personal and text-based asynchronous learning in various other platforms with synchronous voice and text, enhancing the interactions in virtual professional development settings. In addition to regular face-to-face professional development meetings, the virtual campus allows faculty and staff to meet for professional development, mentoring, discussion groups, committees, and virtual academic conferences. Key ideas for operating educational sites in SL include training prospective faculty, staff, and instructors, mentoring, dealing with appropriate presentations of self as avatar, tracking activities and behaviors in SL, choosing modes of communication, and moving from lecture to discussion to immersive learning in media rich constructed spaces.

Chapter 8

Linda W. Wood, The Art Institute of Atlanta, USA

Higher education institutions are constantly challenged with the task of educating a technology savvy generation of students. Colleges must be able and ready to meet the needs of these digital-age students. What are the perceptions of college faculty of using virtual world technology as a teaching tool in the classroom? The purpose of this chapter is to explore how virtual world environments can be used as a faculty development tool in order to encourage the use of virtual worlds as a teaching tool in the classroom. This chapter references research from a mixed methods study exploring college faculty perceptions of the adoption of virtual world technology into the classroom, which in turn, provides insight to the willingness of higher education faculty to adopt this type of technology. In addition, the final section of the chapter includes a suggested guide on how to create a virtual world faculty development workshop based in Linden Lab's Second Life.

Professional development (PD) assessment is an ongoing, integral activity in order to improve results at individual, training, program, and institutional levels. Principles of assessment are outlined, and the general processes of assessment design, delivery, and analysis are explained. Technology greatly expands the possible data that can be collected for assessment purposes. Emphasis is placed on online environments, noting the issues that are unique to that environment.

Section 2
Understanding E-Learning and Best Practices in Teaching and Learning in Online Environments

There exists a consensus on the importance of teacher professional development. This chapter provides a knowledge base for environments, describes the benefits, best practices, and sources for quality online professional development. The attributes associated with online professional development can be examined within the framework of web conferencing, web cast, and online teaching and learning. An annotated bibliography and extensive glossary related to online professional development are included in this chapter.

A professional development program for online faculty members can be difficult to create, implement, and sustain. Its components will vary depending on the location of the online faculty, the institutional budget, and who is administering the program. A professional development program is essential if institutions wish to keep instructors up-to-date on technological advances and pedagogical shifts as online classrooms change. Today's online faculty members are inundated with information overload due to the internet and because information is increasing exponentially, which results in pressure to keep up. Because of this pressure and the proliferation of learning tools, institutions need to help faculty filter and use the information available to them. This chapter will focus on essential components of professional development programs, issues and potential solutions, examples from successful programs, and future trends in online professional development.

Kate Thornton, Victoria University of Wellington, New Zealand
Brenda Service, Victoria University of Wellington, New Zealand
Louise Starkey, Victoria University of Wellington, New Zealand

The shift to teaching online is not straightforward, and faculty new to online teaching needed to be adequately prepared and supported to ensure quality courses and successful student learning outcomes. This chapter outlines both the theoretical and practical influences that informed the teaching of a successful online course. These elements are reflected on and analysed in order to provide recommendations for future professional learning programmes. These recommendations include encouraging faculty members to reflect on their beliefs and values, helping motivate them to make the necessary changes to their teaching practice, ensuring that they are informed about digital age learning theory, and providing ongoing support for both the pedagogical and practical aspects of online teaching.

Lex McDonald, Victoria University of Wellington, New Zealand
Allie McDonald, University of Canterbury, New Zealand

The study of motivation in E-learning is an emerging field but there is a paucity of data about what learners and facilitators believe are the important factors involving and sustaining the interest of the learner. It is emphasised that more prominence needs to be given to the key players' perspectives in balancing what is known about E-learning motivation. In this literature review, consideration is given to how E-learning evolved and impacted upon learners. Theoretical approaches to understanding learning and motivation are discussed and the importance of instructional design as a motivating factor identified. Research concerning the motivational matrix of the E-learner, facilitator, and educational environment is then detailed to provide a context for understanding E-learner motivation. Following this, phenomenologically-oriented research related to learner and facilitator perspectives on what motivates the E-learner is discussed and links to the social cognitive theory are acknowledged. Implications and an exploratory model of E-learners' motivation are detailed followed by recommendations for future research.

Karen Skibba, University of Wisconsin-Whitewater, USA

This qualitative study describes opportunities, challenges, and lessons learned by instructors who transitioned face-to-face courses to online courses to meet the needs of adult learners. This study found that experienced faculty members needed to learn anew and rethink pedagogical strategies when designing and teaching online delivery formats. Faculty members who are learning to teach are also adult learners who learn through experience and by conducting experiments. The instructors learned how to teach adults online through the interrelated interactions between the five themes that emerged from the research data: (1) Adapted to Market Demand, (2) Anchored by Adult Learning Strategies, (3) Experimented in Online Laboratory, (4) Evolved from Trial and Error to Collaboration, and (5) Rethought Pedagogical Possibilities. This study confirmed that faculty members need guidance on how to use technology and also seek pedagogical strategies to increase both student and faculty success. Implications for online professional development practices are discussed.

With diverse options for teaching and learning, continued professional development is requisite for instructors in order to meet the needs of a growing online population of students. In online learning settings, if students are not engaged through various instructional techniques, students become easily distracted and miss valuable content necessary for learning. In traditional classroom settings, instructors can easily check for levels of engagement via a visual scan of the class. In an online environment, without the use of video, a visual scan is not possible. As a result, a productive way to ensure student engagement in asynchronous or synchronous courses is for instructors to implement modeling, graphic, manipulative, and simulation strategies into the online environment. This chapter reviews a variety of best practice strategies for engaging students in an online learning environment as part of faculty professional development to improve their teaching and learning. These practice strategies will be discussed, along with examples of how they can be implemented.

Young people will have to change their names in order to escape their "cyber past," prophesized Eric Schmidt (Google's CEO) in August 2010. This provocative thought from the principal opponent of Facebook may be considered a strategic maneuver, but it also highlights the deep societal changes coming with the continuing development of social media. From the instructors' perspective, people may wonder if online education could help students develop their communication skills in the era of web 2.0. But others may contend that a priority has to be given to the class content, not to another use of the media, which simply provides a new channel to enhance the learning experience. This chapter proposes a first step to reconcile the two perspectives and shows that improving students' communication skills and awareness when teaching in an online environment can enhance student learning and help personal branding, i.e. developing the ability to package their skills and to showcase their distinctive attributes. To help demonstrate this, results from the authors' courses are provided.

Foreword

by Mimi M. Lee

As educators in the 21st century, we are well aware of the growing prevalence of and subsequent focus on online education in recent years. Regardless of one's view on the rapidly increasing employment of digital technologies in various learning environments, we have come to a point where every educator has to recognize the possibility of offering some form of online instruction. Today's young generation is growing up in an information age where the lines between online and offline are constantly crossed and frequently blurred. From K-12 to college and beyond, learners are demanding quick and flexible access to multimodal ways of teaching and learning. K-12 schools and institutions of higher learning are responding, in part, by making greater numbers of classes and classroom experiences available online. So how much do we know about providing effective, meaningful online instruction and experiences, both for such a wide range of learners and their instructors? This volume offers more than a dozen perspectives of successful online professional development practices today with glimpses of where such training is headed tomorrow.

While there has been a significant amount of discussion addressing various issues of online learning, not enough has been researched about two questions tugging at the heart of anyone involved in online learning environments. First, how do teachers learn how to teach online? Second, what can their institutions and surrounding professional development programs and initiatives do to support effective online teaching and learning environments? To this end, the issue of professional development that includes training should be explored in depth with research results disseminated in myriad outlets including momentous edited volumes like this one. When discussing professional development for teachers, especially those that teach online courses, additional questions emerge. For example, just who are the people teaching millions of children and adults who either prefer to learn online or have no other choice but online course outlets? Are they experienced teachers who are brand new to online teaching or have they been experimenting with online technologies for some time? Alternatively, are they teaching assistants who are assigned to teach online courses without the full organizational support available to fulltime faculty members? What are the content of the professional development and the delivery format of the training for such teaching populations? Will they experience online or face-to-face training about teaching online? Or will they be offered online training about teaching face-to-face?

With each new delivery format springing to life, there are increasingly complex options and challenges. Part of the solutions will depend on the unique characteristics of these adult learners. At the same time, the types of online professional development will vary for teachers in rural area schools where the impact of such personalized training may be quickly noticeable and impactful.

The contributors to *Virtual Mentoring for Teachers: Online Professional Development Practices* provide models and real-life cases that are crucial to answering these questions. From Las Vegas to Atlanta to Wisconsin to New Zealand, the authors detail the evolution and refinement of their respective professional development models. Best practices find their way in online case scenarios, Second Life experiences, social networking exchanges, asynchronous support group discussions, and various other experimental as well as more traditional online technology tools and support structures. This is a timely and informative work for any educator who is interested in improving one's practice online as well as helping students and other educators. These contextualized stories of lessons learned provide situated knowledge using theoretical frameworks such as experiential learning and adult learning theory. They become a key component of a collective dialogue that is essential in helping us understand the current issues related to online professional development while simultaneously providing us with new models of online professional mentoring that will be pervasive in the near future.

Mimi Miyoung Lee *is an Associate Professor in the Department of Curriculum and Instruction at the University of Houston. She received her Ph.D. in Instructional Systems Technology in 2004 from Indiana University at Bloomington. Her research interests include theories of identity formation, sociological examination of online communities, issues of representation, and critical ethnography. Recently, she was a co-investigator on a five year, $3 million grant project from the Greater Texas Foundation, iSMART (Integration of Science, Mathematics and Reflective Teaching), an online Master's program for middle school mathematics and science teachers in the state of Texas.*

Foreword
by Punya Mishra

As a Professor of Educational Technology and one who teaches and conducts research on online learning environments, I am often asked, "Can online learning be as good as face to face learning?" The assumption here, of course, is that face to face learning is the "gold standard" against which we must measure every technologically mediated pedagogical innovation. For instance, an article in the *New York Times* about the rise of online learning due to higher gas prices included a series of quotes from students that implied that they perceived learning online as being inferior to the "real thing." One student said, "I don't feel I get as much out of an online class as a campus course... but I couldn't afford any other decision." I also remember a higher-education delegation from Pakistan I met a few months ago – where the inferiority of online learning was just taken as a matter of fact.

There are multiple responses to the question of whether online learning is as good as face to face. My quick response is that the data we have seem to indicate that there is indeed not much difference between student performance in online and face to face contexts. I could argue that we, as a species, are averse to change – and often feel threatened when we are asked to do things in new or different ways. I could also argue that some online learning is mediocre but so are many face to face classes (a special case of science-fiction writer Theodore Sturgeon's eponymous law: Ninety percent of everything is crap). With experience and time, however, I have come up with a response that I feel might be productive i.e. moves the conversation away from simple comparisons of face to face vs. online towards a more thoughtful discussion of the strengths and weaknesses (what as an academic one would call the "affordances and constraints") of each.

I, therefore, respond to a question such as "can online learning be as good as face to face learning?" by flipping it around and asking "can face to face learning be as good as online learning?" I then follow that up with examples of sound, effective, creative pedagogical moves one can make in online contexts that would be difficult or maybe even impossible in face to face contexts. For example, consider how technology can afford new forms of pedagogy in the case of Moodle's (courseware) method of structuring online conversations. One option, called a "Q and A forum" requires students to post before they can see any other postings. Using this type of discussion, different pedagogies are afforded than are traditionally unavailable. Of course, this can help instructors avoid the "me too" phenomena or the various forms of the "I agree" posting. The authors have used it to have students share their ideas of how a computer does a "magic" trick – in this activity, it is important for students to think about (and post) their ideas, and not simply provide answers by reading other students' posts. Ideally, pedagogy could be advanced in any instance in which teachers want to ensure that students share their own unique perspectives, free from the influence of prior responses. For example, brainstorming sessions require ideas to flow freely, instead of following the first few (or most vocal) ideas. Additionally, some activities require conversations wherein different interpretations of an event or material are important.

The point here is that pedagogical decisions do not exist in a vacuum. They are intimately constrained by the content to be covered and the technology being used (once again face to face classrooms with their use of whiteboards and over-head-projectors and papers and pencil are hardly devoid to technology). I have written (mostly with my colleague Matthew J. Koehler) about the TPACK framework. The Technological Pedagogical Content Knowledge (TPACK) framework attempts to identify the nature of knowledge required by teachers for instructional technology integration, while addressing the complex, multifaceted, and situated nature of teacher knowledge. At the heart of the TPACK framework is the complex interplay of three primary forms of knowledge: Content, Pedagogy, and Technology. The intelligent use of technology in teaching content requires understanding and negotiating the relationships between these three components of knowledge. A teacher capable of negotiating these relationships represents a form of expertise different from and greater than the knowledge of a disciplinary expert (say a mathematician or a historian), a technology expert (a computer scientist), and a pedagogical expert (an experienced educator). Effective technology integration for pedagogy around specific subject matter requires developing sensitivity to the dynamic (transactional) relationship among all three components.

The TPACK framework argues that the key issue of technology use is not whether one technology or the other is better per se but rather whether the technology is used appropriately for a given content and pedagogical style. There is a significant amount of research showing that teachers do not develop TPACK by themselves – but rather it has to be developed through carefully crafted curricula and professional development experiences. Thus the key to effective use of technology for teaching (whether face to face or online) is teacher development and teacher education. Research shows that moving to an online context requires more than merely shifting course materials online. It often requires completely over-hauling the content and pedagogical approaches to best fit this new medium. This is because, as I never tire of saying, good teaching lies at the intersection of content, technology, and pedagogy – and there is no one solution that would work for all contexts. Changing any one of the three forces would impact the remaining forces and consequently affect the right balance in attaining effective pedagogy.

This book *Virtual Mentoring for Teachers: Online Professional Development Practices* seeks to showcase a variety of research-based online professional development programs and best practice models that enhance effective teaching and learning. In my perspective, this book is a valuable addition to the literature on teacher professional development and mentorship, and will enhance our understanding of how new models of pedagogy need to be developed (along with re-visioned content) to best meet the potential of emerging ubiquitous and powerful technological tools.

Punya Mishra *is Professor of Educational Technology at Michigan State University where he directs the Master of Arts in Educational Technology program. He has worked extensively in the area of technology integration in teacher education which led to the development (in collaboration with Dr. M. J. Koehler) of the Technological Pedagogical Content Knowledge (TPACK) framework, described as being "the most significant advancement in the area of technology integration in the past 25 years." Dr. Mishra has received over $4 million in grants, and published over 45 articles and book chapters, and edited two books. He is also an accomplished visual artist and poet.*

Preface

Twenty-first century learning is a paradigm that is most often connoted with technology-integration instruction and online education. According to the most recent statistics on online learning, over six million students in higher education are enrolled in at least one course online (Allen & Seaman, 2011). Similarly, the number of online courses continues to grow at the K-12 level; a growth of about 47% was reported for K-12 online learning between 2005-2006 and 2007-2008 (Picciano, Seaman, Shea, & Swan, 2011). In addition to the expansion in enrollment, the general perception of online learning continues to improve among stakeholders across all levels of education. Given the ubiquitous presence of information technology, and the constant growth of enrollment in online courses, today's teachers are expected to be able to leverage learning among all students (traditional and non-traditional) with the appropriate use of educational technology and in a variety of learning environments that are mainly digital and virtual. As a result, most teachers are required to participate in professional development opportunities that enhance effective pedagogies using Information and Communications Technology as well as best practices for developing and delivering online instruction.

The fundamental success of instructors in technology-integrated classrooms and in online courses requires a major investment in professional development. While different models of professional development are in place, the typical format thus far consists of one day, one-size-fits-all workshops with no follow-up activities. Additionally, these "generic" workshops are led mostly by experts or skilled individuals who are not working in the organization and the meetings taking place in the traditional face-to face settings. However, given the scarcity of financial resources, faculty development occurring in online mode is gradually becoming an accepted approach among administrators and educators. Many online professional learning models are comprised of readings, and peer-to-peer discussions. Treacy, Kleiman, and Peterson (2002) list the benefits of professional development online as 1) increasing access to meet individual learning goals, 2) lending experience with the use of technology as a learner, 3) giving educators a chance to experience the power of technology while learning in a supportive environment, and 4) providing new opportunities for follow-up activities. Additionally, online professional development presents the opportunity for anytime and anywhere learning, the generation of communities of learners, and the opportunity for faculty to experience the online educational environment first hand as a student (Barczyk, Buckenmeyer, & Feldman, 2010). Also, this format of faculty development ensures cost saving and an increased access to professional learning opportunities for instructors while they direct their own development. Overall, recent findings suggest that online, self-paced, and just-in-time learning and mentoring have positive impact on faculty use of technology as well as faculty performance (Brill & Park, 2011).

Besides the benefits of online professional development, the steady growth of online workshops for instructors raises an urgent need for dialogue regarding the planning, design, development, and assessment of online professional development. Each of these processes, especially instructional design, is essential for the effective training of faculty in best practices in teaching and learning in online environments and to ensure the development and delivery of high quality online instruction. Therefore, *Virtual Mentoring for Teachers: Online Professional Development Practices* offers peer-reviewed essays and research reports contributed by an array of scholars and practitioners in the field of instructional technology and online education. The objective of this scholarship is to highlight research-based online professional development programs and best practices models that have been shown to enhance effective teaching and learning in a variety of environments. In addition, instructor experiences are discussed to raise awareness concerning challenges and successes in online teaching and learning. The text is organized around the following two primary themes: *Professional Development Models for Faculty in Online Environments and Understanding E-Learning and Best Practices in Teaching and Learning in Online Environments.*

The first theme: *Professional Development Models for Faculty in Online Environments*, highlights the need for instructor training in instructional design. According to Barczyk, Buckenmeyer, and Feldman (2010), instructors design courses based on how they were instructed as well as around their own lectures and therefore lack training in instructional design. This deficiency is especially present at the higher education level. As such, to ensure quality instruction, instructor training in instructional design and instructional design models is needed. Writing on this theme, Jennifer Banas and Angela Velez-Solic describe best approaches in designing effective training for online instructors that incorporate instructional design principles. Banas et al. also stress the need to center faculty training on two other important principles and practices; adult learning principles and best practices in online teaching. Next, Denice Hood and David Huang present a variety of online professional development (PD) models documented in the literature. Similarly, Sheri Anderson and Beth Oyarzun discuss a professional development program which is based on the concept of community of learners and modeled after the Analyze, Design, Development, Implement, and Evaluation (ADDIE) instructional design method.

Anderson and Oyarzun point out how such models of online professional development can be used to best serve and engage faculty from diverse backgrounds and disciplines while Nathaniel Ostashewski and Doug Reid offer a professional development model based on a networked learning framework approach. The unique feature of the Ostashewski-Reid model is that it is administered through social networking sites – using social media tools to deliver innovative and engaging learning opportunities. Given the current ubiquitous use of social networking and social media tools, one can see how such models can be easily adapted to in faculty training and mentoring. Subsequently, Ken Stevens reveals two approaches to professional development that can be used to support collaboration among instructors in virtual environments. Vassiliki Zygouris-Coe's paper shares a model for training, supporting, and monitoring online educators on a large scale and specifically at the K-12 level. What is distinct about this model is the fact that virtual learning is expanding at a very fast pace in the K-12 setting and, as Zygouris-Coe points out, teacher knowledge, skills, and dispositions are very necessary for promoting successful teaching and learning experiences in K-12 online environments. Linda Wood, Richard Speaker, Greg Levitt, and Steven Grubaugh demonstrate how a well-known social networking site, Second Life, was used to mentor and train faculty. While Wood provides perceptual evidence on faculty acceptance and adoption of virtual technology for the purposes of professional development, Speaker et al. discuss using Second Life in conjunction with traditional professional development workshops. This option is very appealing since it provides faculty the opportunity to engage socially and academically with each other both in a face-to-face format as well as on a virtual campus. Ideally, faculty development goes beyond the familiar or well-known traditional space. Finally, Lesley Farmer details professional development processes and unique assessment designs that are applicable for teaching and learning in online environments.

Contributors to the second theme of *Understanding E-Learning and Best Practices for Teaching and Learning in Online Environments* generally look at factors that influence or detract from successful online professional development and best online teaching experiences. First, Carol Brown presents a knowledge base necessary for understanding online environments in general and describes the benefits, best practices and sources for quality online professional development. Next, Angela Velez-Solic and Jennifer Banas point out how factors such as differences in location, departmental and institutional budgets, and departmental and institutional leadership may cause difficulty in the development, implementation, and sustenance of online professional development programs and offer solutions for dealing with such differences. Kate Thornton, Brenda Service, and Louise Starkey then discuss the challenges of training faculty to deliver quality online courses and outline both theoretical and practical influences that inform successful online teaching. An important follow up issue, Lex McDonald and Allie McDonald examine the issue of motivation among e-learners and discuss how this challenge may be eliminated with professional development. McDonalds' paper emphasizes the need for faculty training in online education. McDonald et al. also present theoretical approaches to understanding learning and motivation by way of instructional design. This is followed by Karen Skibba's discussion on the pedagogical and philosophical transformations and challenges that arise when faculty prepare to train and are trained to teach online. Next, Kim Hyatt, Michaela A. Noakes, and Carrie Zinger discuss a variety of best practice strategies for engaging students in an online learning environment which instructors should investigate as part of their professional development to improve teaching and learning. Finally, Nicolas Lorgnier, Shawn O'Rourke, and Patricia Coward present a model that is applicable to the development of instructors and discuss how information developed from the use of online professional models could be used to facilitate the learning of communication skills that are essential and desirable for all students.

The hope is that each of the scholarly works presented under the two themes generated will help forward the agenda and discussion on the significance and the need for training and mentoring faculty online. Overall, this book provides very useful information for administrators and educators who are interested in the planning, design, and implementation of online professional development and virtual mentoring.

Jared Keengwe
University of North Dakota

Lydia Kyei-Blankson
Illinois State University

REFERENCES

Allen, I., & Seaman, J. (2011). *Going the distance: Online education in the USA 2011*. Wellesley, MA: Babson Survey Research Group.

Barczyk, C., Buckenmeyer, J., & Feldman, L. (2010). Mentoring professors: A model for developing quality online instructors and courses in higher education. *International Journal on E-Learning, 9*(1), 7–26.

Brill, J., & Park, Y. (2011). Evaluating online tutorials for university faculty, staff, and students: The contribution of just-in-time online resources to learning and performance. *International Journal on E-Learning, 10*(1), 5–26.

Picciano, A. G., Seaman, J., Shea, P., & Swan, K. (2011). Examining the extent and nature of online learning in American K-12 education: The research initiatives of the Alfred P. Sloan Foundation original research article. *The Internet and Higher Education, 15*(2). Retrieved from http://dx.doi.org/10.1016/j.iheduc.2011.07.004

Treacy, B., Kleiman, G., & Peterson, K. (2002). Successful online professional development. *Learning and Leading with Technology, 30*(1), 42–47.

Acknowledgment

I would like to express my sincere gratitude to my friend and co-editor, Dr. Lydia Kyei-Blankson (Illinois State University). Thank you Lydia for your wonderful collaboration and the true commitment you showed throughout the entire review and editing process.

I would also like to acknowledge the considerable time and effort put forth by all the chapter contributors. Thank you for your gracious and timely responses to the reviewers' comments, and for your strong commitment to submit high quality revised chapters.

I would specially acknowledge the unconditional love of my parents (they taught me life's most valuable lessons: to smile, laugh, and stay positive), and close pals whose friendship and moral support were priceless during the, sometimes tedious, process of editing this book. I am forever indebted to all my entire family. Thank you for your trust in me and inspiration to believe that I can accomplish anything if I just put my heart in it.

Thanks to the wonderful staff at IGI Global who participated in the overall development and successful completion of this project. Finally, I am very grateful to the Editorial Advisory Board (EAB) team. Their incredibly quick turnaround time in providing invaluable feedback, precise advice, and detailed review notes on the chapters submitted is greatly appreciated. In particular, I would like to thank the EAB members.

Jared Keengwe
University of North Dakota

Section 1
Professional Development Models for Faculty in Online Environments

Chapter 1
Designing Effective Online Instructor Training and Professional Development

Jennifer R. Banas
Northeastern Illinois University, USA

Angela Velez-Solic
Indiana University Northwest, USA

ABSTRACT

There are many ways to deliver engaging, effective, and efficient online instruction, but most higher education instructors do not know how. So while the demand for online learning has drastically increased, the efficacious training of instructors into how to deliver online courses lags far behind. In this chapter, the authors demonstrate how adult learning and instructional design principles, coupled with known best practices for online teaching, can facilitate the design of effective training and professional development for online instructors. Case study examples are used to illustrate key concepts, and a sample outline for training is offered. Administrators and trainers of online instructors will form the primary audience; other stake holders in online education will benefit as well.

INTRODUCTION

Despite the growing popularity of online learning, there is still a large body of criticism regarding its ability to substitute for the brick and mortar higher education institution. This criticism has long been misdirected and we often find that technology has served as the scapegoat. As early as 1983, Clark pointed out we are missing an opportunity to improve the quality of education when we do this. In 2010, the U.S. Department of Education mirrored these sentiments. Technology is simply the vehicle by which education is delivered and it is unlikely to affect the quality of learning (Zhang, Zhou, Briggs, & Nunamaker, 2006). McCormick (as cited in Forum, Chronicle of Higher Education, 2010) stated, "The truth is that we know astonishingly little about the 'quality' of nearly all collegiate programs, whether face-to-face or

DOI: 10.4018/978-1-4666-1963-0.ch001

online. In fact, we don't even have a generally accepted understanding of what quality means in this context" (p. 42).

Despite the criticism, distance education, defined as "planned learning that normally occurs in a different place from teaching" (Moore & Kearsley, 2005, p.2), affords options both to potential students and higher education institutions that otherwise would not be possible. Many of these options benefit society as a whole. For example, distance education can provide developing countries with an opportunity to establish productivity and to compete globally by eliminating disparities related to education (Van Hook, 2006). Via e-learning networks, educational gaps are lessened by bringing the classroom to students who otherwise would go without education or only receive minimal schooling. Providing a different kind of benefit, the Massachusetts Institute of Technology offers free online public access to the learning materials from all of its courses. These materials can and have been downloaded by people throughout the world for self-study. Similarly, but via a different medium, Stanford University offers free Apple Computer iTunes podcasts of many campus lectures both to students as well as the general public (Van Hook, 2006). Such opportunities would not exist without the assistance of technology. (Author note: the terms *distance learning* and *online learning* may be interchanged in this chapter to mean the same thing, particularly when the terms are part of an original quote.)

Kurubacak and Yuzer (2004) approached the benefits of distance education and its associated technologies from a different perspective. More so than an opportunity to bridge educational gaps or a means to offer alternative forms of education, they regarded distance education technology as force that is eliciting an educational paradigm shift. Similarly, Wiley (2000) pointed out, "Technology is an agent of change, and major technological innovations can result in entire paradigm shifts" (p. 2). For example, McDermon (2005) described

the supplemental learning benefits of distance education. Using a video conferencing system, she "transported" her North Carolina elementary school students to locations that would otherwise be a dream field trip. Virtual field trips gave her students access to tours, interactive lessons, and experts offered by Colonial Williamsburg, NASA, the North Carolina Museum of Natural Science and other public institutions across the country. The system also had been used to "attend" professional conferences and to connect with students and teachers from other schools. While there is something to be said about actually attending a conference, a museum, or other locale, it appears that the video conferencing system opened doors to a whole gamut of learning experiences.

And finally, one last example of distance education technologies pushing a paradigm shift was Duke University's iPod program. In 2004, incoming freshman were given iPods at the beginning of the school year. The iPods were preloaded with the freshman orientation schedule, the academic calendar, messages from administration, advice from current students, athletic schedules, and more. Once classes began, students were also able to access classroom lectures, course content, field recordings, study support, and file storage/transfer. In this regard, not only did the iPods enhance and support student learning but also the student campus-living experience (Flanagan & Calandra, 2005). Programs like this demonstrate how distance education technologies can improve the quality of, access to, and face of education, while also meeting the needs of today's learners.

The lifestyles of today's learners demand more readily accessible learning environments and the rate of enrollment into online courses reflects that demand. According to the 2006 Sloan Consortium Survey of Online Learning, enrollment in one or more online courses increased from 1.6 million students in 2002 to 3.2 million in 2005 (Allen & Seaman, 2006). According to the 2010 survey, enrollment hovered at 5.6 million students. This represents thirty percent of all college students!

Moreover, the 2010 report revealed a twenty-one percent growth rate for online course enrollment compared to less than a two percent growth rate in higher education as a whole (Allen & Seaman, 2010). What is not mentioned in these reports is the increase in number of online instructors or that the source of much of online learning's criticism lies with the instructors (U.S. Department of Education, 2010). Lack of or poor quality training and professional development is often the cause.

In light of the increasing demand for and the rapid expansion of distance education, there is a parallel need for qualified online instructors who are prepared to teach from a distance. The same instructional techniques used to engage learners in on-campus courses are difficult or impossible to replicate in an online learning environment. It is like wearing running shoes instead of ice skates to get around an ice rink. One will eventually get all the way around, but there will be slips and falls along the way. Enough slips and falls, and one may choose to not get on the rink again! In this chapter, the authors (one, a former administrator of online instructors, and the other, a current director of online learning at a higher education institution), will demonstrate how both adult learning and instructional design principles can help administrators and trainers of online instructors to design effective training and professional development. (Author note*:* the term *training* is used to describe initial instruction of online instructors; whereas, the term *professional development* is used to describe their continuing education.)

BACKGROUND

As new technologies continue to be developed, the virtual "classroom" may become more common than not. Lao and Gonzales (2005) warned, however, that distance education programs should not be implemented just to meet the demand from students or to compete with other colleges and universities. Doing so often leads to haphazard

course development and poor training of instructors. Studies reveal that many instructors are ill-prepared to make the shift from the traditional face-to-face classroom to the online academic forum. Much of this is due to a general lack of understanding about what is entailed to teach a course online (Allen & Seaman, 2009; Care & Scanlan, 2001; Palloff & Pratt, 2001). Wood (2005) stated there is a persistent opinion that instructors who have never taught online can jump in and teach an online class. Ehmann and Hewett (2005) contended, "Instructors cannot directly transplant their understandings, strategies, and skills from face-to-face to online teaching environments" (p. 10). As colleges expand their online programs, institutions need to prepare instructors so that they can deliver courses online with the same integrity and effectiveness as traditional face-to-face courses (Carnevale, 2000). (Author note: the term *instructor* will be used to include both higher education faculty and instructors.)

Successful online instructors require a unique set of skills. Many of these skills are the same as those for any successful instructor: good communication and classroom organization skills (Roblyer & McKenzie, 2000). In addition, Anderson (2004) denoted the importance of being knowledgeable in one's content area and its pedagogy, and possessing both sufficient technological skills and tenacity. As a former dean of an online college, one of the chapter's authors (Banas), would also include the following qualities: resourceful (knowing how to find answers to questions), supportive and patient (many online learners lack confidence using technology), efficient (many tasks performed in online learning are repetitive, so they can be streamlined), adaptable and innovative (technology changes often and sometimes does not work), and a community leader (rich online learning communities are the product of effective and enthusiastic planning). In emulating these qualities, an online instructor's students eventually will come to model them, too.

In spite of what may be known about essential qualities of online instructors, less is known about the best ways to train them or what to offer in professional development. According to the report *Learning on Demand: Online Education in the United States* (Allen & Seaman, 2009), nearly one-fifth of all institutions do not even provide training or even informal mentoring for online faculty. Those institutions who do train their faculty often rely on untested assumptions about the skills that are most important (Taylor & McQuiggan, 2008; Velez, 2010). However, one should not assume that these training disparities are due to apathy, but rather that many higher education institutions have not grasped the differences between teaching on-campus and teaching online.

The pace of technology has often outrun the development of a new pedagogy, thus online instructors default to teaching the same way they would in the classroom. This usually means they take a teacher-centered approach to instruction instead of learner-centered. Barrett, Bower, and Donvan (2007), in a survey of 292 online instructors at twenty-eight community colleges, found that most (82%) online instructors teach from a teacher-centered versus learner-centered approach. Teaching this way disserves the students and ignores the potential for new ways of learning. Veletsianos (as cited in Forum, Chronicle of Higher Education, 2010) declared, "We need to think of online education as an experience and the instructor as the designer of that experience" (p. 46). Failure to train instructors in a way that helps them to adopt and practice new ways of teaching denies the opportunities afforded by technology as discussed in this chapter's introduction. So where to begin?

In today's economic times, higher education institutions cannot afford to rely on guesswork training approaches that leave instructors feeling unprepared. While there is not a one-size-fits-all prescription for training online instructors, there are recognized adult learning and instructional design principles that can be applied to develop effective training and professional development. The remainder of this chapter will focus on introducing those principles and describing means by which they can be used to prepare online instructors to meet the needs of their students.

APPLICATION OF ADULT LEARNING AND INSTRUCTIONAL DESIGN PRINCIPLES

Much as online learning is still relatively new, even newer is training online instructors. Fortunately, there is much that the fields of adult learning and instructional design can offer to trainers seeking best practices. This section, *Application of Adult Learning and Instructional Design Principles and Models*, provides the trainers with the "ingredients" (i.e. the principles) and "recipes" (i.e. models) for designing effective online instructor training and professional development.

The first part of this section provides a historic overview of adult learning, characteristics of adult learners, and commonly recognized principles and theories of adult learning. The theories and principles include andragogy, experiential learning, and transformative learning. The second part of this section introduces the field of instructional design, including principles and models such as cognitive-load, problem-based learning, scaffolding, the Smith and Ragan instructional design model, the nine events of instruction, and the first principles of instruction. Throughout the section, the authors provide examples of how both adult learning and instructional design principles can be applied to the design of training and professional development.

Before going a step further, it must be clarified that there *is* a distinct difference between teaching and learning, and that those differences are recognized in this chapter. The terms *teaching* and *training* will be used interchangeably to describe the activities performed to influence one's understanding. *Learning* will be used to describe the act or process by which behavioral change, knowledge, attitude, or skills are acquired (Knowles, Holton, and Swanson, 2005). Ideas in this chapter might refer to instructors who are teaching students and instructors who are being taught by trainers. The principles and models that follow refer to both of these activities.

Adult Learning

Since online instructors *are* adults, the design of training and professional development should heed basic principles of adult learning (Berge, 2007). The concept of adult learning was contrived by a German teacher in the early 1800's, reintroduced by German social scientists in 1920, and then brought to the United States shortly thereafter (Merriam, 2001; Thoms, 2001). Early American publications by John Dewey, Eduard C. Lindeman, and Edward L. Thorndike launched scientific research into and fostered interest in adult learning. Such research uncovered that adults *could* learn and *how* they learned (Knowles, Holton, & Swanson, 2005). Most importantly, the research demonstrated the differences between adult learning and child learning (i.e. pedagogy). Per Lindeman (1926), "The highest value of adult education is the learner's experience. If education is life, then life is also education" (p. 9-10). Through his research, Lindeman established five assumptions of adult learners:

1. Adults are motivated to learn as they experience needs and interests that learning will satisfy.
2. Adults' orientation to learning is life-centered.
3. Experience is the richest source for adult learning.
4. Adults have a deep need to be self-directing.
5. Individual differences among people increase with age (as cited in Knowles et al., 2005, p. 40).

Lindeman's work served as a foundation for the development of the field and elements of his assumptions can still be found throughout the current literature.

While there is no one theory that encompasses everything one should know about adult learning, elements from each can be used to develop effective training and professional development for online instructors. Per Frey and Alman (2003), "Adult learning theory helps faculty to understand their students and to design more meaningful learning experiences for them" (p. 8). The next part of this section introduces the theory of andragogy, and then reviews two other popular adult learning theories — experiential learning and transformative learning.

Andragogy

Perhaps most well known in the literature of adult learning is Malcolm Knowles and his development of the theory of andragogy. The term *andragogy* was first coined by adult educator Dusan Savicec in 1967 to differentiate youth education from adult education (Knowles et al., 2005). (The term "andra" meaning "man" or "adult", differentiating from "ped" as in *pedagogy*.) Though Savicec introduced the term, it is Knowles, founder of the Adult Education Association, whose work has become most associated with its use.

While some contend that andragogy is not truly a theory (Merriam & Caffarella, 1999), Knowles' six principles of andragogy provide a prescription for the design of adult education, and thus, also the training and professional development of online instructors. These principles are:

1. The learners' need to know - adult learners need to know *why* they need to know what they are learning something, *what* it is, and *how* they will go about doing it.
2. The learners' self-concept - adult learners wish to be autonomous and self-direct their learning.

3. The role of prior experiences of the learner – adults bring many experiences to the table that can serve as resources and mental models for new learning.
4. Readiness to learn – adults are ready to learn that which they need to know to deal with life situations.
5. Orientation to learning - adults are life- and problem-centered learners who seek contextual knowledge.
6. Motivation to learn – adults are responsive to both external and motivators including better jobs and higher salaries, as well as improved quality of life, job satisfaction, and self-esteem. (Knowles et al., 2005, 62-63).

One may note that many of these principles are similar to those cited by Lindeman in 1926. Together, these principles should remind trainers of online instructors about the differences between andragogy and pedagogy, particularly because pedagogical methods are still too commonly used to design education for adults. A brief summary comparing andragogy (adult education) to pedagogy (youth education) appears in Table 1 – Pedagogy versus andragogy orientations.

Andragogy: Solutions and Recommendations

The theory of andragogy offers many insightful elements for the design of online instructor training and professional development. Incorporating these elements can lead to effective outcomes. For example, McNamara, Duncan, McDowell, and Marriott (2009) studied a continuing education program offered to pharmacists via teleconference. The program design was based on Knowles' (1984) adult learning principles and adapted for medical educators (Kaufman, 2003). Participant focus groups revealed that convenience (time and access) and relevancy were facilitating factors in choosing the teleconference course; being required to complete the course was a barrier. Participants

Table 1. Pedagogy versus andragogy orientations

Orientation	Pedagogy	Andragogy
Learner's need to know	Teachers decide what learners need to know	Learners expect to know what they will learn, how they will learn, and why they should learn
Learners' self-concept	Dependent	Self-directed and competent
Role of experience	Little	Experiences serve as resources and mental models
Readiness to learn	Teachers dictate when learners should learn	Learners eager to learn life coping skills
Orientation to learning	Subject- centered	Life or task- centered, contextual
Motivation	External	Personal payoff (external) and intrinsic (internal)

indicated with positive emotions that the course was interactive, presented real-life problems, adjusted for existing knowledge, provided opportunities for reflection, and was self-directed. They also indicated positive emotions towards the evidence-based approach to the content. Based on the results, researchers felt that the intentional design of the course to meet adult learning needs was successful.

Regarding which andragogy elements to incorporate and in what way, Knowles (1984) iterated that the theory can be adopted in whole or in parts, and strategies for application will vary depending on the situation. The authors of this chapter suggest using them as a checklist to design and evaluate training and professional development. These elements are:

1. Identify means by which participants can self-direct their learning.
   a. Build in accommodations for a variety of learning styles, opportunities to pursue additional (but not require) learning, and flexibility in support and pacing.

2. Identify means to recognize the experiences participants bring to the training.
    a. Build in opportunities for participants to share and apply personal and professional experiences.
3. Identify means to foster intrinsic motivation.
    a. Build in opportunities to pursue self-selected goals and to monitor progress.
4. Identify means to demonstrate the need to learn what is being presented.
    a. Build in opportunities for participants to self-assess their need to learn and reflect on the outcome of their learning.

As a checklist, these elements offer trainers a quality control measure to guide both development and evaluation of trainings. Experiential learning, presented next, can offers additional insight.

Experiential Learning

Experiential learning is based on the premise that the richest source of learning for an adult is his/her own experiences and reflections about them (Brookfield, 1995; Kolb, 1984). These experiences provide a basis for self-identity and help to shape the learning. They also vary greatly from one adult to the next and can create bias that *inhibits* learning (Knowles et al., 2005). For all these reasons, attention to experience in the design of adult learning is an important consideration.

There are many theories describing how adults' experiences impact learning. Two popular and related cognitive theories are schema theory and information processing theory. *Schema theory* suggests that cognitive structures are built, accumulated, and bundled as learning experiences occur. Per Merriam and Caffarella (1999), these bundles become the basis from which new information is assimilated. New learning takes place when these bundles are deconstructed and rebuilt. *Information processing theory* suggests that one's prior experiences act to filter information. One tends

to pay more attention to that which is relevant or in line with one's current way of thinking (Bee & Bjorkland, 2004; Petty & Cacioppo, 1981, Zull, 2002). This concept is closely aligned with constructivist theory which suggests that learning is cumulative and new information must be relevant in order for a learner to retain and use it.

Building in relevant learning experiences and helping adults to connect to past experiences is an important aspect of designing adult education. Hanna (2010), for example, studied the impact of an experience-rich, adult literacy instructor training program that placed trainers on-site with the instructors instead of having the training offsite. The trainers demonstrated instructional methods that the literacy instructors practices, as learners, before trying the methods out with their own students. Participants described the training as "effective, engaging, and enlightening." (p. 177). They commented that after previous trainings, they were much less likely to employ new techniques; however, with this on-site, experiential training, they were eager to use what they had learned. The primary difference between the two trainings was that instead of postulating techniques that might work, they did them! Also, the instructors (as learners) were able to build off of existing experiences to help construct new ways of thinking.

Experiential Learning: Solutions and Recommendations

According to Cercone (2008), experiential learning is composed of three components: (a) knowledge of concepts, facts, information, and experiences; (b) prior knowledge applied to current, ongoing events; and (c) thoughtful analysis and assessment that contributes to personal growth. This means designers of adult learning should create a wide range of learning activities that require the application of prior knowledge to current and future implications, as well opportunities for reflective analysis and assessment.

In training online instructors, this might mean comparing how online learning *is* similar to classroom teaching, before explaining how it is not. Creating mock online classrooms in which online instructors take on roles both as a student and then later as an instructor could provide an experiential learning environment in which online instructors test out ideas and practice new skills. Critical to this experience would be reflective activities which require the participants to draw connections to their previous experiences and assumptions, and to identify how their thinking has changed as a result of the experiential learning. Finally, assessments should be included to evaluate progress towards preparedness to teach online. Such activities would help to transform their way of thinking and doing. The next and last adult learning theory in this section, transformative learning theory, emphasizes this concept.

Transformative Learning

Transformative learning theory is the process of "becoming critically aware of one's own tacit assumptions and expectations and those of others and assessing their relevance for making an interpretation" (Meizrow, 2000, p. 4). In this theory, frame of reference provides structure to one's point of view, influencing their thinking, beliefs, and actions. The revision of these frames is the transformative process (Taylor, 2008). The most current approach to understanding transformative learning is neurobiological. Per Janik (2007), the brain actually changes during transformative (discovery-based, curiosity-driven) learning as new neural pathways are created. In order for these changes to occur, learning should be rooted in needs and interests; and strengthened with emotive, sensory, and kinesthetic experiences. The goal is to make sense of one's understanding of the world and to negotiate one's own values and meanings rather than relying on those of others (Brookfield, 1995; Cercone, 2008). Ample op-

portunities for reflection are a critical piece in this process.

Reflection helps individuals to make sense of experiences and support knowledge construction (Jonassen & Reeves, 1996). In other words, reflection helps individuals to transform their current way of thinking to a suggested other. Adult learning environments, by nature, are rich with such activity. Dobrovlny (2006), for example, found that adult learners partaking in a corporate training frequently considered past and present experiences as a way of learning. Similarly, Guldberg (2008), in a study of 256 students working online towards a university certificate specializing in autism disorders, found the discussion boards to be rich with conversations about both current and past experiences. She contended this type of learning activity provides the self-evaluation and reflection necessary to assimilate new and accommodate old knowledge.

Transformative Learning: Solutions and Recommendations

Transformative learning requires opportunities for learners to make sense of their experiences and to reflect on their new roles (Wittrock, 1972). Learning occurs when learners are active participants in the learning process and construct their own knowledge about the content. For the design of online instructor training and professional development, this means participants should be given the opportunity to reflect on new learning. This reflection should require participants to identify existing beliefs and feelings about teaching in online learning environment, to consider new belief systems, and to debrief on feelings regarding any changes made. Using the same example for experiential learning theory, authentic learning experiences that place trainees into a mock online classroom to take on both student and instructor roles would foster the discovery-based, curiosity-driven type of learning to develop new neural pathways. The goal of such activities would be to help online instructors adopt a frame of reference that incorporates new teachings, but is uniquely their own.

Summary of Adult Learning Theories

If educational institutions intend to improve the quality of online education, online instructors need to be trained well to deliver it. Understanding and employing adult learning principles can guide trainers to develop more effective and engaging training and professional development. Andragogy, experiential learning, and transformative learning theories each offer research-driven insight into the adult learner and best ways to train them. Such concepts include providing occasions for self-directed learning, using authentic learning tasks, building on learner's experiences, and building in frequent opportunities for self-reflection and assessment. The second half of this section introduces instructional design principles and models that can provide practical guidelines for applying these concepts to the design and development of online instructor training and professional development.

Instructional Design Principles and Models

As a field, instructional design is primarily concerned with "deciding what methods of instruction are best for bringing about desired changes in student knowledge and skills for specific course content and a specific student population" (Reigeluth, 1983, p.7). Without calling it as such, Dewey (1900), an early advocate for research-based educational practices, saw instructional design as a necessary science to link theory and instruction. Since Dewey's time, much research has been devoted to instructional design as a means of improving learner effort and performance. This research includes strategies to implement at the macro level, such as an entire training program,

and the micro level, such as individual lessons or modules (Banas, 2007).

Principles from the field of instructional design can provide administrators and trainers of online instructors with guidelines for selection, development, sequencing, and presentation of content. Instructional design principles relevant to the development of online instructor training include cognitive load, problem-based learning, and scaffolding; as well as instructional systems designs (ISD) such as the Smith and Ragan instructional design model, the nine events of instruction, and first principles of instruction. Each of these concepts will be described next, beginning with cognitive load. In the section that follows, the authors will demonstrate how to combine adult learning and instructional design principles in order to create an outline for an effective and engaging online instructor training.

Cognitive Load

Knowledge and awareness of long-term memory, working memory, and cognitive load is essential for the effective design of training and professional development (Banas, 2011). *Long-term memory* is the large, central location in which information is stored, managed and retrieved for later use; *working memory* is the conscious locus of short-term information processing; and *cognitive load* is the burden placed on working memory during instruction (Sweller, 2003, 2004). Cognitive load can be affected by the mental effort necessary to process new information (intrinsic cognitive load), the manner in which the material is presented (extraneous cognitive load), and the effort required for activating schema (germane cognitive load) (Sweller, 1988).

Cognitive load influences both the efficiency and effectiveness of one's learning experience. "Limited working memory is one of the defining aspects of human cognitive architecture, and accordingly, all instructional designs should be analyzed from a cognitive load perspective"

(Sweller, Van Merriënboer, & Paas, 1998, p. 262). Additionally, as one grows older, the capacity of his/her working memory decreases (Cercone, 2008). This means that an older learner compared to a younger leaner will have reduced ability to retain large quantities of new information.

Cognitive Load: Solutions and Recommendations

In a multimedia environment, "a number of task characteristics, including format, complexity, use of multimedia, time pressure, and pacing of instruction…..have been identified by…. research to influence cognitive load" (Paas, Ayres, & Pachman, 2008). This means that the training of online instructors should not only consider the content of training, but also the amount of content and the familiarity of the medium by which the content is accessed. Because online instructor training and professional development may take place online, trainers need to consider the short-term memory tax placed on a learner who is unfamiliar with the electronic learning environment. When this is the case, part of the training should include learning how to navigate the learning environment.

As a general rule, "chunking" (i.e. grouping) information into smaller bundles helps learners to acquire information more efficiently by placing less strain on the working memory. For example, it is easier to remember this set of numbers "23, 65, 72, and 36" than it is to remember "2, 3, 6, 5, 7, 2, 3 and 6." Similarly, grouping instructional content together into meaningful bundles would help new online instructors to retain a greater quantity of information. For the trainers, this means taking the time to outline the desired training content and grouping tasks and/or information together for presentation. For example, grouped tasks for teaching online could include: (a) how to develop a syllabus for an online course, (2) how to develop online assessments, (c) how to engage learners in online discussion boards, or (4) how

best to manage time. One strategy for chunking online instructor training tasks would be to create a problem-based learning scenario. A description of and suggested application for problem-based learning appears next.

Problem-Based Learning

Problem-based learning (PBL) is instruction that places learners into authentic situations which require an ethical, policy, or process problem to be solved as a means of teaching content and skills (Hmelo-Silver & Barrows, 2006; Jonassen, 1997, 2000). In the process of solving the problem, learners are required to gather information and consider others' perspectives as they develop a solution. This process strengthens their ability to propose and to develop a solution in a real setting (Choi and Lee, 2008; Jonassen, 1997, 2000). This type of learning is aligned with constructivist learning theory. Constructivists believe that "learning is an active process of constructing rather than acquiring knowledge" and "instruction is a process of supporting that construction rather than communicating that knowledge" (Duffy & Cunningham, 1996, p. 170). Constructivists abide by one of five strategies for using PBL as a means of instruction:

1. **The Problem as a Guide**: The problem serves as a concrete reference point. Learners are told to think of the learning materials (e.g. readings, videos, demonstrations, etc.) in the context of the case presented; i.e. the case gives meaning to the reading assignment.
2. **The Problem as an Integrator or Test:** The problem is presented after the assigned learning materials are completed. The goal here is to apply the knowledge from the learning materials to the case.
3. **The Problem as an Example**: The problem is integrated into the learning materials and the case becomes the principle, concept, or procedure illustrated in the problem.

4. **The Problem as a Vehicle for Process**: The focus is on critical thinking skills, not just solving the problem.

5. **The Problem as a Stimulus for Authentic Activity:** The focus is on developing the skills that to solve a problem and others similar to it (Duffy & Cunningham, 1996, p. 190).

These five strategies demonstrate a variety of ways to make content meaningful to the learner. He or she must consider the information presented in a way that is meaningful in the real world.

Adult learners prefer authentic tasks to which they can apply existing knowledge and experiences. PBL fits this bill nicely while also providing ample opportunities for scaffolding (discussed next), and the type of critical reflection needed to adopt new belief systems.

Problem-Based Learning: Solutions and Recommendations

In order to prepare online instructors for the challenges associated with using technology in the online classroom, they should be exposed to situations they will encounter in the online environment. According to Wittrock (1974), learning occurs when learners are active participants in the learning process and construct their own knowledge. This means that content should be built around authentic learning tasks which require the learners to identify a problem, identify and select solutions, and evaluate outcomes. Constructing online instructor training around the skills needed to be an effective instructor will prepare them for the wide variety of situations they will face.

An online instructor trainer can use one or more of the five PBL strategies to construct a variety of learning activities for professional development learning modules. For example:

1. **The Problem as Guide:** Prior to assigning a reading about how to develop an online course syllabus, the trainer presents the online instructors with the scenario of having students with poor self-regulated learning behaviors.

2. **The Problem as an Integrator or a Test**: After online instructors watch a video about today's generation of digital learners, the trainer presents the challenge of engaging younger learners.

3. **The Problem as Example:** The trainer shares a news article about the rise in plagiarism in online courses. Next, the trainer asks the online instructors to design a sample learning assignment that would be difficult to plagiarize.

4. **The Problem as a Vehicle for Process**: The trainer presents online instructors with the problem of students not participating in online discussion board chats. Next, the trainer challenges the online instructors to identify why this might be happening.

5. **The Problem as a Stimulus**: The trainer presents the online instructors with the content for a mock course and challenges them to "chunk" the content into learning modules.

In performing such activities, the online instructors in training are prepared for situations they will likely encounter in their online classroom. PBL also helps to scaffold the learning process. Scaffolding, as an instructional design principle, is described next.

Scaffolding

In the early 1900's, social constructivist and psychologist Lev Vygotsky coined the terms *zone of proximal development* (ZoPD) and *scaffolding*. ZoPD is the difference between what a learner can do with and without help. *Scaffolding* refers to strategies or structures that nurture development and help move an individual beyond this zone. These strategies and structures reduce cognitive load and are gradually removed as learners' expertise increases (Kester, Kirchner, & Corbalan, 2007; Vygotsky, 1978). Strategies may include, but are not limited to, showing parts of a problem a little at a time, removing extraneous or distracting factors, asking guiding questions, providing feedback at regular intervals, modeling the end results (Tharp & Gillmore, 1988). The ultimate goal is for the learner to develop an automated response and to be able to perform the activity on his/her own.

Salden, Paas, and Merrienboer (2006) suggested *shared control* as a way to scaffold learning for adults. Shared control is a two-part process in which an instructor (or intelligent computer agent) first selects a set of subtasks that match the skills and needs of the individual learner. Then, from this set, the learner self-selects which task best meets his or her needs. The idea is the learner eventually comes to select subtasks in a way best suited to him/her, until he/she can master the whole task. In complex PBL tasks, the instructor can identify and breakdown the skill sets for the learners to develop and present these as subtasks, with the goal of the learner eventually being able to perform successfully the whole task.

Scaffolding: Solutions and Recommendations

Preparing for and teaching an online course consists of many complex problems which require a wide array of skills to perform. Trainers of online instructors should identify ways to chunk large skill sets into small skills and present them to online instructors using shared control. The self-directed nature of adult learners warrants providing them with choices of skills to master and varying degrees of support. This could be accomplished by allowing learners to "pass" onto another section or problem after demonstrating mastery. Those who need more time could continue to practice

the skill. Frequent assessment by way of progress monitors and reported self-assessment can help trainers identify online instructors who is ready to move onto the next level, or who is in need of more support (i.e. scaffolding).

How often should one assess? How should tasks be ordered? What is the best ways to present instruction? As stated earlier, instructional design pertains to "deciding what methods of instruction are best for bringing about desired changes in student knowledge and skills for specific course content and a specific student population" (Reigeluth, 1983, p.7). The final part of this section succinctly introduces three instructional design (ID) models –Smith and Ragan model, nine events of instruction, and first principles of instruction—that can provide a framework or model for building training and professional development. Application examples are shared within the content of their description. The section that follows, *Future Trends*, will provide a larger example that incorporates several of the principles and models introduced in this chapter, while also making a call for additional research.

Smith and Ragan Model

According to Mager (1984), the instructional designer's job is to answer three major questions: (a) where are we going? (I.e. the instructional objectives), (b) how will we get there? (i.e. the instructional strategies and instructional medium), and (c) how will we know when we have arrived? (i.e. formative and summative evaluation). One might recall seeing similar questions posed by adult learners, as per the theory of andragogy, earlier in this section. Most ID models provide a framework to address these questions and are a variation of these four primary steps: (a) determine the needs of the learner, (b) define the end goal of instruction, (c) create an instructional intervention, and (d) evaluate results (Baturay,

2008). One such ID model that is easily adaptable to and incorporates the adult learning and instructional design principles in this chapter is the Smith and Ragan instructional design model (Smith & Ragan, 1993).

The Smith and Ragan instructional design model helps instructors effectively and efficiently to design instruction. The model is divided into four stages and eight sub-steps.

1. Instructional analysis:
    a. Analyzing the learning context
    b. Analyzing the learners
    c. Analyzing the learning task
    d. Writing assessment items
2. Selecting Strategy
    a. Determining organizational, delivery and management strategies
    b. Writing and producing instruction
3. Developing Evaluation
    a. Conducting formative evaluation
    b. Conducting summative evaluation
4. Revising instruction

Using the development of online instructor training or professional development as a basis for example, the *analysis* stage is when the trainer would assess the context by which he/she has come to develop training. Questions asked may include, but are not limited to, any of the following: (a) Has the educational institution mandated training for all online instructors? (b) What are the abilities and attitudes of the online instructors? (c) What skills do they need to be taught? and (d) How will their ability be assessed? Answers to these questions can help the trainer to formulate the learning objectives.

The *strategy selection* stage of the Smith and Ragan instructional design model prompts the trainer to seek answers to questions such as: (a) How long will the training be? (b) When will the training be conducted? (c) What are the best means to teach skills (e.g. problem-based learn-

ing, experiential learning, etc.)? and (d) What instructional materials should be used? Answers to these questions help the trainer to thoughtfully plan for instruction.

The *evaluation* stage is when the trainer assesses learner performance to evaluate learner "readiness." He/ she would also evaluate the delivery method, instructional materials, scheduling, and other logistical factors. This evaluative phase helps the trainer to identify areas in need of revision.

While the Smith and Ragan model can used as a model to facilitate the design of online instructor training as a whole, it does not provide ideas about how to develop a learning module (i.e. lesson). The nine events of instruction, presented next, provide that sequence.

Nine Events of Instruction

Gagne (1985) believed that the most important elements of teaching were presenting the knowledge or demonstrating the skill, providing practice with feedback, and providing learning guidance. The nine events of instruction (Gagne, 1985; Gagne, Briggs, Wager, 1992) prescribe a sequence for instruction that abides by these elements. The premise for this sequence is what Gagne (1985) refers to as *conditions of learning*. Broken down into internal and external conditions, internal conditions pertain to the learner's existing knowledge and skills; external conditions pertain to the stimuli inherent to the individual learner.

The nine events of instruction afford a means by which to organize external stimuli in an order that makes use of the internal conditions. A description of these events and potential applications for designing training and professional development are as follows:

1. Gain attention.
    a. Helps to ground the lesson and motivate the learner to learn.

b. e.g. Presenting online instructors with a common online teaching problem or providing a sample completed online course syllabus.

2. Describe the goal.
   a. Helps learners to frame the information presented.
   b. e.g. Telling online instructors what they will accomplish by completing the training or professional development and how they will do it.

3. Stimulate recall of prior Knowledge.
   a. Helps learners to connect new information with existing knowledge and to assess skill level.
   b. e.g. Asking online instructors to discuss elements of good teaching and to predict what that looks like in an online learning environment.

4. Present the material to be learned.
   a. Helps learner know what tools will help them to learn.
   b. e.g. Presenting to online instructors the readings, videos, podcasts, images etc. from which information will be obtained.

5. Provide guidance for learning.
   a. Helps to scaffold learning.
   b. e.g. Having online instructors develop practice online discussion board questions, while providing question starters, step-by-step directions, and feedback until they can do it on their own.

6. Elicit performance.
   a. Helps learner to practice the skills.
   b. e.g. Requiring online instructors to create an online quiz.

7. Provide informative feedback.
   a. Helper learner to identify progress in relationship to goal.
   b. e.g. Providing feedback to online instructors that indicates when they are on target, their areas in need of improvement, and means by which to improve.

8. Assess performance.
   a. Helps learners (and trainers) know whether or not the goal has been obtained.
   b. e.g. Assessing online instructors' ability to build a shell for a course and break the course content into 3-5 learning modules.

9. Enhance retention and transfer (Gagne, 1985; Gagne, Briggs, Wager, 1992).
   a. Helps learners make connection to similar or "real world" situations.
   b. e.g. Providing online instructors with opportunities for professional development boosters throughout the teaching term.

In following these nine events, trainers can be assured that they are comprehensively addressing intended learning outcomes and maximizing the likelihood that learners obtain them.

The nine events are easily adaptable to developing and delivering both small and large learning modules. Sometimes, however, it is difficult and/or unpractical to address all nine events for singular learning tasks. The first principles of instruction provide a compact formula for doing just that and are presented next.

First Principles of Instruction

Merrill's (2002) first principles of instruction, and its respective instructional design model, are the product of a systematic review of instructional design theories, models and research. From these sources, Merrill abstracted a set of interrelated, prescriptive instructional design principles. To be included into this set, the principle had to appear in most instructional design theories; had to promote effective, efficient, or engaging learning; and had to be both design-orientated and supported by research.

According to the first principles of instruction, effective learning occurs when the following five principles are recognized:

1. Instruction is presented in the context of real world problems.
2. Instruction attempts to activate relevant prior knowledge or experience.
3. Instruction demonstrates what is to be learned rather than merely tell information about what is to be learned.
4. Learners have an opportunity to practice and apply their newly acquired knowledge or skill.
5. Instruction provides techniques that encourage learners to integrate the new knowledge or skill into their everyday life (Merrill, 2002).

These first principles of instruction offer much in the way of developing an effective training or learning module. The first principle reminds trainers that desired outcomes should be identified in the context of real world problems. In training online instructors, for example, this could be accomplished by showing a video case study, highlighting important findings in a journal article, or requiring learners to identify a desired outcome in their own environment. According to the second principle, instruction should activate relevant prior knowledge or experience. Earlier in this chapter, the authors discussed the information processing theory and the importance of relevancy. One pays more attention to that which is relevant or in line with one's current way of thinking (Bee & Bjorkland, 2004; Petty & Cacioppo, 1981, Zull, 2002). This means instruction should make connections with either past lessons taught or prior experiences.

The third and fourth principles are closely tied. The third principle indicates instruction should *demonstrate* what is to be learned rather than just telling learners; the fourth principle indicates instruction should offer students with opportunities to practice parts of the whole task. This means trainers should provide examples of the final product or performance. When training online instructors, this demonstration could be a

mock online course or sample course syllabus. Following the demonstration, learners would practice and then eventually apply fully their new knowledge and/or skills.

The fifth and final principle indicates instruction should encourage learners to integrate new knowledge and skills into their everyday life. This also aligns with Knowles, Holton, and Swanson (2005) who indicated adult learners are motivated to learn that which satisfies needs and interests, is life-centered, and allows them to be self-directed. Trainers of online instructors should afford opportunities to practice and apply both real and relevant learning tasks that relate to teaching online.

So what might these principles look like as an instructional model? Merrill (2002) suggests a four-phase model for implementing the first principles of instruction. The four phases are *activation, demonstration, application,* and *integration.* Each phase directly relates to the principles and is centered on a real world task. Using the example of training online instructors how to develop a discussion board, the phases are:

*   **Phase 1:** Activate relevant knowledge.
    *   e.g. Asking online instructors to describe qualities of effective in-classroom discussion and to provide examples of questions that would engage a wide variety of learners.
*   **Phase 2:** Present a demonstration of skills to be learned.
    *   e.g. Presenting the discussion board questions for a sample online course and sample student responses.
*   **Phase 3:** Practice and apply acquired knowledge and skills.
    *   e.g. Asking online instructors to develop the shell for an online discussion board and two online discussion board questions. Next, have them reply to fellow online instructors' discussion board questions. Finally,

15

provide feedback and discuss modifications for improvement.

- **Phase 4:** Integrate new skills.
    ◦ e.g. Requiring online instructors to develop online discussion board questions for their in-classroom course. Next, have them reflect on the outcomes.

The length of time devoted to each phase will vary depending on the complexity of the skill and the number of subtasks. As a whole, however, these four phases offer trainers a quick means to develop efficiently a learning module that is effective and engaging.

The first principles of instruction wrap up this section's overview of adult learning and instructional design principles and models. A summary of primary concepts appears in Tables 2 and 3. The next section, *Future Research Directions,* presents suggestions for training and professional development that abide by several of the adult learning and instructional design principles presented in this chapter.

FUTURE RESEARCH DIRECTIONS

While adult learning and instructional design principles provide guidance on *how* to design training and professional development, they do not provide guidance on the *content.* This is an area in need of research and development. In this section, the authors suggest such content based on current trends, while also indicating when and how the adult learning and instructional design principles and models presented in this chapter could be used.

Earlier in the chapter, qualities of an effective online instructor were mentioned. How does a trainer transform those qualities into online instructor training and professional development? Recalling that "chunking" is a means to reduce cognitive load, a trainer could consolidate the primary roles of an online instructor into separate learning modules. Berge (2007) neatly organized these roles into four categories:

1. **Pedagogical Role:** Act as an educational facilitator, using questions and probes to steer students in a way that helps them to focus on critical components, principles, and skills.
2. **Social Role:** Create a friendly, social environment that promotes human relationships, group cohesiveness, and collaborative learning.
3. **Managerial Role:** Set the agenda for the course, the objectives for instruction, the timetable, and the procedural rules; and manage interactions.
4. **Technical Role:** Assure that learners are comfortable with the LMS (or other technology), with the goal of making the technology transparent to the user. The closer to reaching this goal, the more the learner can focus on the learning goals and objectives.

These roles could be flushed out into four unique learning modules offered as separate professional development workshops, or as part of a larger, multi-module training. It is likely, too, that the four modules could be subdivided into even smaller modules. For example, the social role could be subdivided into: (a) designing assignments that foster collaborative learning, (b) creating and supporting group cohesiveness at a distance, (c) developing online discussion boards that build communities of learners. The managerial role could be subdivided into: (a) writing the syllabus for an online course, (b) managing your time as an instructor, (c) supporting student's development of self-regulated learning behaviors, (d) identifying and writing essential policies and procedures, etc. One can continue to subdivide the other roles in separate skills and even subdivide the skills, too. It all depends on the level of expertise administrators and trainers would like

Table 2. Adult learning concepts applicable to the design of training and professional development

Theory	Applicable Concepts
Andragogy	1. Adults want to know why they need to learn something, what it is, and how they will go about doing it. 2. Adults wish to be autonomous and self-directing in their learning. 3. Adults bring many experiences to the table that can serve as resources and mental models for new learning. 4. Adults are ready to learn that which is needed to deal with life situations. 5. Adults are life- and problem-centered learners who seek contextual knowledge. 6. Adults are responsive to both external and internal motivators.
Experiential learning	Authentic learning experiences help learners connect new experiences to existing knowledge and experiences, while also validating self-identity. Reflection and evaluation are critical component of the learning process.
Transformative learning	Changes in frame of reference occur when learners are given opportunities to make sense of their experiences and to reflect critically on new roles. Authentic learning opportunities allow for adults to test out new ideas and roles help to foster the transformation.

Table 3. Instructional design concepts applicable to the design of training and professional development

Theory	Applicable Concepts
Cognitive load	Cognitive load is the burden placed on working memory during instruction; working memory is the center for short-term information processing. To reduce cognitive load, new information and skills taught should be "chunked" into learning modules. Scaffolding also can reduce cognitive load.
Problem-based learning	Instruction that places learners into authentic situations which require an ethical, policy, or process problem to be solved as a means of teaching content and skills. The task requires learners to gather information and to consider others' perspectives as they develop a solution. This process strengthens learners' ability to propose and develop solutions for real problems. Problems can be introduced in any of the following ways: (a) as a guide or reference point, (b) as an integrator or test, (c) as an example, (d) as a vehicle for process, or (e) as a stimulus for authentic activity.
Scaffolding	Strategies or structures nurture development and help move learners to the point where they can perform a task on their own. Strategies may include: showing parts of a problem a little at a time, removing extraneous or distracting factors, asking guiding questions, providing feedback at regular intervals, or modeling the end results.
Smith and Ragan instructional design model	The primary stages are of instructional development are: (a) determine the needs of the learner, (b) define the end goal of instruction, (c) create an instructional intervention, and (d) evaluate results.
Nine events of instruction	The most important elements of teaching are presenting the knowledge or demonstrating the skill, providing practice with feedback, and providing guidance. The nine instructional events to carry out these elements. 1. Gain attention. 2. Describe the goal. 3. Stimulate recall of prior knowledge. 4. Present the material to be learned. 5. Provide guidance for learning. 6. Elicit performance. 7. Provide informative feedback. 8. Assess performance. 9. Enhance retention and transfer.
First principles of instruction	Effective learning occurs when the following five principles are recognized: 1. Instruction is presented in the context of real world problems. 2. Instruction attempts to activate relevant prior knowledge or experience. 3. Instruction demonstrates what is to be learned rather than merely telling what is to be learned. 4. Learners have an opportunity to practice and apply their newly acquired knowledge or skills. 5. Instruction provides techniques that encourage learners to integrate the new knowledge or skill into their everyday life.

their online instructors to have. So what might a highly integrated, online instructor training that addresses all of the roles look like?

At the higher education institution where both authors currently serve, one of the authors (Velez-Solic) has developed an online instructor training that is divided into two, multi-week courses that prepare faculty members to be proficient in online education. The first area of training is using the learning management system (LMS) and getting used to the technology. This also includes the basics of teaching online. The four-week long, completely online training supports faculty by assisting them in the paradigm shift necessary for transforming from face-to-face teaching to online or hybrid teaching. This training has been offered by the institution's Center for Teaching and Learning since fall 2009. At the time of this chapter's writing, the Center has graduated more than 115 faculty members.

The second area of training offered by the authors' institution is in course design and development, which includes teaching faculty members how to create interactive learning modules. The goal of the training is to set the stage for quality online instructional development, evaluation, and future mentoring by those who participate in this course. This training was offered for the first time as a nine-week, hybrid course during the summer of 2011. The objectives for the course were as follows:

- Design a basic course shell with easy and consistent navigation.
- Use a rubric grounded in research to conceptualize and evaluate course design.
- Design and deliver instructional modules based on solid pedagogical evidence for online teaching.
- Use innovative technology to implement course delivery of educational material.
- Develop mentoring skills to support incoming online faculty members in the areas of online teaching and course design.

Upon completion of this course, faculty members developed a complete online course. The outline for the training appears in Table 4.

Table 4. Sample outline for an online instructor training

Week #	Content
1	• Introductions/sharing of course that will be created • Discussion of quality control measures • Course navigation and components of course shell
2	• Writing learning objectives • Designing content around objectives and outcomes • Mapping out the course
3	• Designing assignments and assessment • Fostering peer sharing and collaboration on assignments and assessments
4	• Nurturing community and having online presence • Discussion boards and collaboration
5	• Writing the course syllabi • Developing directives/course outlines
6	• Understanding and applying online instructional pedagogy • Practicing basics of copyright
7	• Loading content into the LMS
8	• Peer mentoring: components, guidelines, best practices • Trouble-shooting common problems
9	• Using a research-driven rubric to review a course

Applying the adult learning and instructional design principles shared in the chapter, future, similar implementations of this nine-week training could be enhanced in many ways.

- **Andragogy:** Inform online instructors about the over-arching goal of the training. Allow them to develop a course they will eventually use, and to personalize it. Point out how completing the training will not only improve their teaching skills, but increase their marketability as a professional. Allow them to share experiences and knowledge about online teaching and learning.

- **Experiential Learning:** Direct online instructors to adopt and act out both the roles of instructor and learner at various times to enhance perspective. Allow time for reflection on these role plays.

- **Transformative Learning:** Enlist the use of reflection journals (ideally online) to foster reflective practice as a means of monitoring and supporting changes in belief systems.

- **Cognitive Load and Scaffolding:** Subdivide content into learning modules in which online instructors can practice and progressively develop skills. Provide feedback, guided prompts, and modeling.

- **Problem-Based Learning:** Introduce skills in the context of situations that online instructor will face when they teach online. The situations can be used to guide readings, discussions, project development, and other course activities.

- **Smith and Ragan Instructional Design Model:** In designing the training, determine the needs of the learner, define the end goal of instruction, create an instructional intervention, and evaluate results.

- **Nine Events of Instruction:** Develop the training and individual lessons using the nine events of instruction as a guide. Use the nine events as a way to tell the "story" of teaching online.

- **First Principles of Instruction:** Present content in the context of real situations, make links to previous experiences, demonstrate desired end products, provide opportunities for practice, give feedback, and encourage learners to integrate their new skills.

These suggested applications of adult learning and instructional design principles are not meant to be inclusive of all possible applications, but should give starting points for the implementation of best practices. Additionally, continued rigorous research into these areas is warranted.

CONCLUSION

The quality of the online learning experience is only as good as an institution's instructors. The better an institution prepares its instructors to teach online, the more positive the learning experiences will be for students (Muirhead & Betz, 2002; Velez, 2010). While there is no one specific model to guide the design of online instructor training and professional development, applying principles of adult learning and instructional design can aid the process. Inclusion of andragogy, experiential, and transformative learning theories will facilitate meeting the needs of adult learners. Using instructional design principles to facilitate the sequencing and method of presenting content will improve the effectiveness of the design.

Adult learning theory and instructional design principles applied to the design of online instructor training and professional development remain theoretical, however, without the evaluation of online instructor training and professional development. Sharing of training outcomes, both successful and unsuccessful, are needed to further the field and improve the quality of online learning. This responsibility is shared by all. As the paradigm of education today shifts into the paradigm of education tomorrow, educational institutions can choose to be on the cusp of that change, or let the change happen to them.

REFERENCES

Allen, I., & Seaman, J. (2009). *Learning on demand: Online education in the United States, 2009. Sloan Consortium Group.* Needham, MA: Sloan-C.

Allen, I. E., & Seaman, J. (2006). *Making the grade, 2010. Sloan Consortium Group.* Babson Park, MA: Babson Research Group.

Allen, I. E., & Seaman, J. (2010). *Online education in the United States, 2010. Sloan Consortium Group.* Babson Park, MA: Babson Research Group.

Banas, J. R. (2007). *The impact of a tailored lesson introduction on learners' motivation and cognitive performance.* (Doctoral dissertation). ProQuest Dissertations and Theses. (3272141).

Banas, J. R. (2011). Standardized, flexible design of electronic learning environments to enhance learning efficiency and effectiveness. In Kitchenham, A. (Ed.), *Blended and mobile learning across disciplines: Models for implementation* (pp. 66–86). Hershey, PA: IGI Global. doi:10.4018/978-1-60960-511-7.ch004

Barrett, K. R., Bower, B. L., & Donovan, N. C. (2007, March). Teaching styles of community college instructors. *American Journal of Distance Education, 21*(1), 37–49. doi:10.1080/08923640701298738

Baturay, M. (2008). Characteristics of basic instructional design models. *Ekev Academic Review, 12*(34), 471–482.

Bee, H. L., & Bjorkland, B. R. (2004). *The journey to adulthood* (5th ed.). Englewood Cliffs, NJ: Prentice Hall.

Berge, Z. (2007). Motivate and manage: Key activities of online learners. In Spector, J. M. (Ed.), *Finding your online voice: Stories told by experience online educators* (pp. 73–82). Mahwah, NJ: Lawrence Erlbaum and Associates.

Brookfield, S. D. (1995). Adult learning: An overview. In Tuinjman, A. (Ed.), *International encyclopedia of education.* Oxford, UK: Pergamon Press.

Care, W. D., & Scanlan, J. M. (2001). Planning and managing the development of courses for distance delivery: Results from a qualitative study. *Online Journal of Distance Learning Administration, 4*(2).

Carnevale, D. (2000, February). Assessing the quality of online courses remains a challenge, educators agree. *The Chronicle of Higher Education, 46*(24), A59.

Cercone, K. (2008). Characteristics of adult learners with implications for online learning design. *AACE Journal, 16*(2), 137–159.

Choi, I., & Lee, K. (2008). A case-based learning environment design for real-world classroom management problem-solving. *TechTrends, 52*(3), 26–31. doi:10.1007/s11528-008-0151-z

Chronicle of Higher Education. (2010, November 5). Forum. Chronicle of Higher Education, (pp. B42-46).

Clark, R. E. (1983). Reconsidering research on learning from media. *Review of Educational Research, 53*(4), 445–449.

Clark, R. E. (1994). Media will never influence learning. *Educational Technology Research and Development, 42*(2), 21–29. doi:10.1007/BF02299088

Dobrovolny, J. (2006). How adults learn from self-paced, technology-based corporate training: New focus for learners, new focus for designers. *Distance Education, 27*(2), 155–170. doi:10.1080/01587910600789506

Duffy, T. M., & Cunningham, D. J. (1996). Constructivism: Implications for the design and delivery of instruction. In Jonassen, D. H. (Ed.), *Handbook of research for educational communications and technology* (pp. 170–198). New York, NY: Simon & Schuster Macmillan.

Ehrmann, C., & Hewett, B. L. (2005). Designing a principles-based online training program for instructors. *Distance Learning: A Magazine for Leaders, 2,* 9-13.

Flanagan, B., & Calandra, B. (2005). Podcasting in the classroom. *Learning and Leading with Technology, 33*(3), 20–22.

Frey, B. A., & Alman, S. W. (2003). Applying adult learning theory to the online classroom. *New Horizons in Adult Education, 17*(1), 4–12.

Gagné, R. M. (1985). *The conditions of learning* (4th ed.). New York, NY: Holt, Rinehart, and Winston.

Gagne, R. M., Briggs, L. J., & Wager, W. W. (1992). *Principles of instructional design.* Fort Worth, TX: Harcourt Brace Jovanovich.

Guldberg, K. (2008). Adult learners and professional development: Peer-to-peer learning in a networked community. *International Journal of Lifelong Education, 27*(1), 35–49. doi:10.1080/02601370701803591

Hanna, M., Salzman, J. A., Reynolds, S. L., & Fergus, K. B. (2010). Engaging teachers as learners: Modeling professional development for adult literacy providers. *Adult Basic Education and Literacy Journal, 4*(3), 173–177.

Hmelo-Silver, C. E., & Barrows, H. S. (2006). Goals and strategies of a problem-based learning facilitator. *Interdisciplinary Journal of Problem-based Learning, 1,* 21–39.

Janik, D. S. (2007). *What every language teacher should know about the brain and how it affects teaching.* Paper presented at Wikipedia 2007 Conference on Foreign Language Pedagogy, University of Helsinki, Finland.

Jonassen, D. H. (1997). Instructional design models for well-structure and ill-structured problem-solving learning outcomes. *Educational Technology Research and Development, 45*(1), 65–94. doi:10.1007/BF02299613

Jonassen, D. H. (2000). Toward a design theory of problem solving. *ETR&D, 48*(40), 63–85. doi:10.1007/BF02300500

Jonassen, D. H., & Reeves, T. C. (1996). Learning with technology: Using computers as cognitive tools. In Jonassen, D. H. (Ed.), *Handbook of research for educational communications and technology.* New York, NY: Simon & Schuster Macmillan.

Kaufman, D. M. (2003). ABC of learning and teaching in medicine: Applying education theory in practice. *British Medical Journal, 326,* 213–216. doi:10.1136/bmj.326.7382.213

Kester, L., Kirschner, P. A., & Corbalan, G. (2007). Designing support to facilitate learning in powerful electronic learning environments. *Computers in Human Behavior, 23,* 1047–1054. doi:10.1016/j.chb.2006.10.001

Knowles, M. S. (1984). *Andragogy in action.* San Francisco, CA: Jossey-Bass.

Knowles, M. S., Holton, E. F. III, & Swanson, R. A. (2005). *The adult learner: The definitive classic in adult education and human resource development* (6th ed.). Burlington, MA: Elsevier.

Kolb, D. A. (1984). *Experiential learning: Experience as the source of learning and development.* Upper Saddle River, NJ: Prentice-Hall.

Kurubacak, G., & Yuzer, T. (2004). The building of knowledge networks with interactive radio programs in distance education systems. In G. Richards (Ed.), *Proceedings of World Conference on E-Learning in Corporate, Government, Healthcare, and Higher Education 2004* (pp. 2360-2367). Chesapeake, VA: AACE.

Lao, T., & Gonzales, C. (2005). Understanding online learning through a qualitative description of professors and students' experiences. *Journal of Technology and Teacher Education, 13*(3), 459–474.

Lindeman, E. C. (1926). *The meaning of adult education.* New York, NY: New Republic.

Mager, R. (1984). *Developing attitude toward learning.* Belmont, CA: David S. Lake Publishers.

McDermon, L. (2005). Distance learning. It's elementary. *Learning and Leading with Technology, 33*(4), 28–34.

McNamara, K. P., Duncan, G. J., McDowell, J., & Marriott, J. L. (2009). Community pharmacists' preferences for continuing education delivery in Australia. *The Journal of Continuing Education in the Health Professions, 29*(1), 52–57. doi:10.1002/chp.20006

Merriam, S. B., & Caffarella, R. S. (1999). *Learning in adulthood* (2nd ed.). San Francisco, CA: Jossey-Bass.

Merrill, H. S. (2003). Best practices for online facilitation. *Adult Learning, 14*(2), 13–16.

Merrill, M. D. (2002). First principles of instruction. *Educational Technology Research and Development, 50*(3), 43–59. doi:10.1007/BF02505024

Moore, M. G., & Kearsley, G. (1996). *Distance education.* Wadsworth Publishing Company.

Palloff, R., & Pratt, K. (2001). *Lessons from the cyberspace classroom: The realities of online teaching.* San Francisco, CA: Jossey-Bass.

Petty, R. E., & Cacioppo, J. T. (1981). Epilog: A general framework for understanding attitude change processes. In *Attitudes and persuasion: Classic and contemporary approaches* (pp. 255–269). Dubuque, IA: William C. Brown Company.

Salden, R. J. C. M., Paas, F., & van Merriënboer, J. J. G. (2006). Personalised adaptive task selection in air traffic control: Effects on training efficiency and transfer. *Learning and Instruction, 16*, 350–362. doi:10.1016/j.learninstruc.2006.07.007

Smith, P., & Ragan, T. (1999). *Instructional design* (2nd ed.). New York, NY: John Wiley & Sons, Inc.

Snyder, M. M. (2009). Instructional-design theory to guide the creation of online learning communities for adults. *TechTrends, 53*(1), 45–57. doi:10.1007/s11528-009-0237-2

Taylor, A., & McQuiggan, C. (2008). Faculty development programming: If we built it, will they come? *EDUCAUSE Quarterly, 3*, 29–37.

Taylor, E. W. (2008). Transformative learning theory. *New Directions for Adult and Continuing Education, 119*, 5–15. doi:10.1002/ace.301

Tharp, R. G., & Gallimore, R. (1988). *Rousing minds to life.* New York, NY: Cambridge University Press.

Thoms, K. J. (2001, April). They're not just big kids: Motivating adult learners. *Proceedings of the Annual Mid-South Instructional Technology Conference, Murfreesboro, TN.* (ERIC Document Reproduction Service No. ED463720)

U.S. Department of Education. (2010). *Evaluation of evidence-based practices in online learning: A meta-analysis and review of online learning studies.* Retrieved from http://www2.ed.gov/rschstat/eval/tech/evidence-based-practices/finalreport.pdf

Van Hook, S. R. (2006). *Access to global learning: A matter of will. University of California – Santa Barbara.* Extension Language and Culture Program.

Velez, A. M. (2010). *Creating and sustaining virtual communities of practice by operationalizing constructs of preparation, collegiality, and professional development.* (Doctoral dissertation). Retrieved from ProQuest Dissertations and Theses. (3409364).

Vygotsky, L. S. (1978). *Mind and society: The development of higher mental processes.* Cambridge, MA: Harvard University Press.

Wiley, D. A. (2000). Connecting learning objects to instructional design theory: A definition, a metaphor, and a taxonomy. In D. A. Wiley (Ed.). *The instructional use of learning objects.* Retrieved from http://reusability.org/ read/

Wittrock, M. C. (1992). Generative learning processes of the brain. *Educational Psychologist, 27*(4), 531–541. doi:10.1207/s15326985ep2704_8

Wood, C. (2005). Highschool.com. *Edutopia, 1*(4), 32–37.

Zhang, D., Zhou, L., Briggs, R. O., & Nunamaker, J. F. Jr. (2006). Instructional video in elearning: Assessing the impact of interactive video on learning effectiveness. *Information & Management, 43*(1), 15–27. doi:10.1016/j.im.2005.01.004

Zull, J. E. (2002). *The art of changing the brain: Enriching teaching.* Sterling, VA: Stylus.

ADDITIONAL READING

Boettcher, J. V., & Conrad, R. M. (2010). *The online teaching survival guide: simple and practical pedagogical tips.* San Francisco, CA: Jossey-Bass.

Bowdon, M. A., & Carpenter, R. G. (Eds.). (2011). *Higher education, emerging technologies, and community partnerships: Concepts, models and practices.* Hershey, PA: Information Science Reference. doi:10.4018/978-1-60960-623-7

Calbraith, D., & Dennick, R. (2011). Producing generic principles and pedagogies for mobile learning: A rigorous five part model. In Kitchenham, A. (Ed.), *Blended and mobile learning across disciplines: Models for implementation* (pp. 26–48). Hershey, PA: IGI Global.

Clark, R. C., & Mayer, R. E. (2007). *Electronic learning and the science of instruction: Proven guidelines for consumers and designers of multimedia learning.* San Francisco, CA: John Wiley & Sons.

Clark, R. E. (1994). Media will never influence learning. *Educational Technology Research and Development, 42*(2), 21–29. doi:10.1007/BF02299088

Garmire, E., & Pearson, G. (Eds.). (2006). *Tech tally. Approaches to assessing technological literacy.* Washington, DC: The National Academies Press.

Garza Mitchell, R. L. (Ed.). (2010). *Online education.* San Francisco, CA: Jossey Bass.

Hannafin, M., & Spector, J. M. (Eds.). (2005). *Educational technology research and development.* New York, NY: Springer.

Hannafin, M., West, R., & Shepard, C. (2009). The cognitive demands of student-centered, web-based learning: Current and emerging perspectives. In Zheng, R. (Ed.), *Cognitive effects of multimedia learning* (pp. 194–216). New York, NY: Information Science Reference.

Jonassen, D. H. (Ed.). (2003). *Handbook of research on educational communications and technology* (2nd ed.). Mahwah, NJ: Lawrence Erlbaum.

Jonassen, D. H. (2005). *Modeling with technology: Mind tools for conceptual change* (3rd ed.). Prentice Hall.

Lehman, R. M., & Conceição-Runlee, S. (2010). *Creating a sense of presence in online teaching: How to "be there" for distance learners.* San Francisco, CA: Jossey-Bass.

Mayer, R. (2005). Cognitive theory of multimedia learning. In Mayer, R. (Ed.), *The Cambridge handbook of multimedia learning* (pp. 31–36). New York, NY: Cambridge University Press.

MERLOT. (n.d.). *Multimedia educational resource for learning and on-line teaching website.* Retrieved from http://www.merlot.org/

Merrill, M. D. (in press). Converting e3learning to e3learning: an alternative instructional design method. In Carliner, S., & Shank, P. (Eds.), *Electronic learning: Lessons learned, challenges ahead.* San Francisco, CA: Pfeiffer/Jossey-Bass.

Mezirow, J. (2000). *Learning as transformation: Critical perspectives on a theory in progress.* San Francisco: Jossey Bass.

Morrison, G. R., Ross, S. M., & Kemp, J. E. (2004). *Designing effective instruction* (4th ed.). San Francisco, CA: Wiley.

O'Lawrence, H. (1999). A profile of postsecondary technical education students at Northampton Community College in Pennsylvania. *Workforce Education Forum, 26*(2), 42–53.

O'Lawrence, H. (2007). An overview of the influences of distance learning on adult learners. *Journal of Education and Human Development, 1*(1). Retrieved from http://www.scientificjournals.org/journals2007/articles/1041.htm

Reigeluth, C. M. (Ed.). (1983). *Instructional design theories and models: An overview of their current status.* Mahwah, NJ: Lawrence Erlbaum Associates.

Reigeluth, C. M. (Ed.). (1999). *Instructional-design theories and models: A new paradigm of Instructional theory.* Mahwah, NJ: Lawrence Erlbaum Associates.

Reigeluth, C. M., & Carr-Chellman, A. A. (Eds.). (2009). *Instructional-design theories and models: Building a common knowledge base.* Mahwah, NJ: Lawrence Erlbaum Associates.

Reiser, R. A., & Dempsey, J. V. (Eds.). (2006). *Trends and issues in instructional design and technology* (2nd ed.). OH: Prentice Hall.

Rovai, A. P., Ponton, M. K., & Baker, J. D. (2008). *Distance learning in higher education: A programmatic approach to planning, design, instruction, evaluation, and accreditation.* New York, NY: Teachers College Press.

Shapiro, A. (2008). Hypermedia design as learner scaffolding. *Educational Technology Research and Assessment, 56,* 29–44.

Simonson, M., & Schlosser, C. (n.d.). Quarterly Review of Distance Education. *Nova Southeastern University.*

Spector, J. M., Merrill, M. D., Van Merrienboer, J., & Driscoll, M. P. (Eds.). (2007). *Handbook of research on educational communications and technology* (3rd ed.). Mahwah, NJ: Lawrence Erlbaum.

Tomei, L. A. (2010). *Lexicon of online and distance learning.* Lanham, MD: Rowman & Littlefield.

Uden, L., & Beaumont, C. (2005). *Technology and problem-based learning.* Hershey, PA: Information Science Publishing. doi:10.4018/978-1-59140-744-7

Wang, M. J. (2007). Designing online courses that effectively engage learners from diverse cultural backgrounds. *British Journal of Educational Technology*, *38*(2), 294–311. doi:10.1111/j.1467-8535.2006.00626.x

Wang, M. J., & Kang, J. (2006). Cybergogy of engaged learning through information and communication technology: A framework for creating learner engagement. In Hung, D., & Khine, M. S. (Eds.), *Engaged learning with emerging technologies* (pp. 225–253). New York, NY: Springer Publishing. doi:10.1007/1-4020-3669-8_11

KEY TERMS AND DEFINITIONS

Andragogy: The art and science of helping adults to learn. "Andra" means "man" or "adult."

Cognitive Load: Working memory is the center for short-term information processing. Cognitive load is the burden placed on working memory during instruction

Experiential Learning: Experiential learned is a theory based on the premise that the richest source of learning for an adult is his/her own experiences and his/her reflections about them. These experiences provide a basis for self-identity and help to shape the new learning.

Instructional Design: Decisions about best methods of instruction for bringing about desired changes knowledge and skills for specific content and a specific learner.

Pedagogy: The study of teaching processes and strategies for instruction. (In this chapter, "pedagogy" was used to distinguish between the study of teaching adults from the study of teaching children.)

Problem-Based Learning: Instruction that places learners into authentic situations which require an ethical, policy, or process problem to be solved as a means of teaching content and skills. In the process of solving the problem, learners are required to gather information and consider others' perspectives as they develop a solution.

Scaffolding: A specific of strategies or structures that nurture development and help move an individual beyond this zone

Transformative Learning: Transformative learning is a theory based on the premise that learning is a process in which one becomes critically aware of one's own assumptions and expectations and those of others, and assessing their relevance. This as assessment helps them to abandon an existing frame of reference for a new one.

Zone of Proximal Development (ZoPD) and Scaffolding: ZoPD is the difference between what a learner can do without help and what he or she can do with help.

Chapter 2
Professional Development with Graduate Teaching Assistants (TAs) Teaching Online

Denice Ward Hood
University of Illinois, Urbana-Champaign, USA

Wen-Hao David Huang
University of Illinois, Urbana-Champaign, USA

ABSTRACT

As the number of online courses offered continues to increase, teaching online will become a standard expectation and responsibility for graduate teaching assistants (TAs). For TAs who will seek faculty positions, experience and self-efficacy teaching online are critical to their future career. The current and future university landscape and the higher education world these TAs will embody will require qualified individuals to be well trained in online course development and delivery. Of equal importance is the quality of teaching TAs provide for the large number of online undergraduate courses for which they have sole responsibility or provide instructional support. Colleges and universities need to develop professional development for TAs that reflects best practices in online teaching and learning and engages TAs in the instructional design as well as delivery process. The purpose of this chapter is to explore the literature on teaching assistant professional development and the implications for TAs teaching online.

INTRODUCTION

Many years ago, one of the authors sat in a classroom for a Rhetoric and Composition course, excited on the first day as a college freshman at a large, public, Research University. She overheard a classmate mention that a teaching assistant (TA) would be teaching the class. She had only the sketchiest notion of what a "TA" was but that did not diminish her enthusiasm for the class. She had loved English in high school and anticipated the "professor-in-training" would help make the subject challenging yet interesting. This zeal was soon replaced with puzzlement when the TA greeted the class with a mixture of disdain and

DOI: 10.4018/978-1-4666-1963-0.ch002

boredom. He explained the syllabus, announced that he did not care much for teaching freshmen, informed the students of the minimum requirements needed to pass the course and dismissed the class. The author wishes she could report that subsequent class meetings were an improvement but, unfortunately, the students in this course soon realized that the TA seemed satisfied to do the minimum required.

As this incident occurred well before the advent of online courses, the authors can speculate that this lack of engagement might have been perceived as exponentially *more* troubling had the students encountered this TA in an electronic learning environment (ELE). This reminiscence is not shared to suggest that all TAs meet their responsibilities with such ennui and detachment. To the contrary, subsequent undergraduate experiences with excellent TAs proved to be enlightening and helped shaped the author's decision to pursue graduate degrees. Still, in the years since this incident, the author has reflected back on that semester in English 101 and that first TA. Arguably, the TA's attitude, pedagogical approach and teaching style were the result of several conflated factors including his personality but as the authors' interest in the scholarship of online teaching and learning has evolved, we considered the extent such incidents were related to the professional development the TA received, or the lack thereof.

The purpose of this chapter is to explore the literature on Teaching Assistant (TA) professional development (PD) and specifically, the implications for professional development related to teaching online courses.

The following questions guided this investigation into professional development for TAs who teach online:

- Why do graduate students teach?
- What are TAs' roles and responsibilities in online courses?
- What do TAs need in order to be effective online instructors?

- In what ways does effective professional development benefit TAs, faculty, departments and students?
- What is the theoretical grounding/perspective of the training?
- What are the best practices for online teaching and are these communicated to TAs?
- How are TA professional development programs evaluated?

BACKGROUND

Online Education

Online education has become a viable and a frequently-chosen option for students in the United States. By surveying more than 2,500 colleges and universities, Allen and Seaman (2010) reported that 30% of students in higher education now are taking at least one online course, which indicates a 21% growth rate of online enrollment. At the same time the enrollment growth rate of higher education institutions in general remains below 2%. In the fall of 2009, there were 5.6 million students taking courses online; a nearly one million user-increase from the previous year. Approximately 1/3 of all students in higher education now take at least one course online (Allen & Seaman, 2010). Clearly the trajectory of online education expansion is trending upward and is not showing any sign of retrenchment.

While some may be skeptical about the quality and consistency of online education across and within institutions, the fact is that more and more college students (full-time and part-time) are considering online education as a feasible option for them to realize their academic goals. As a result, there are increasing demands placed on instructional staff to design and teach high quality online courses. As these data suggest, a large section of instructional faculty are now or soon will be providing at least some (if not all) of their course content in an online format. A review of faculty advertisements will attest that new faculty will be expected to teach online and this will involve skills in addition to those required to teach face-to-face (Austin, 2002).

One metric of course quality is student and instructor satisfaction. Satisfaction, while a complex construct to measure, is a common indicator of performance and participation in online education evaluation efforts. Factors that influence the perceived satisfaction levels from online instructional staff and online students vary. For online instructors, being able to teach a diverse group of students and having more opportunities to encounter intellectual challenges contribute to their satisfaction (Bolliger & Wasilik, 2009). For online students, the interaction levels between instructors and students, the clarity of course expectations and structures, and student autonomy during online learning all contribute to perceived online learning satisfaction (Benson & Samarawickrema, 2009; Palmer & Holt, 2009; Dennen, Darabi, & Smith, 2007).

Prior research in online learning satisfaction mostly focused on three areas. The first was on how to increase online learners' satisfaction levels by identifying and attending to a host of student characteristics and instructional variables (e.g., learning styles, gender differences, motivational strategies) (Dron, 2005; Keller, 2008; Selwyn, 2007). The second aspect emphasized the importance of providing relevant training opportunities for in-service online faculty and instructors (Fang, 2007; Littlejohn, 2002). The third aspect of online learning satisfaction research expanded its focus to institutional support (Bollinger & Wasilik, 2009; Orr, Williams & Pennington, 2009). While all three aspects interconnect and should work together to increase both online faculty and learners' satisfaction levels, current research is deficient in developing comprehensive and sustainable curriculum frameworks for training future higher education faculty (graduate teaching assistants) who will teach online.

Some researchers have proposed professional development models for faculty who teach online (e.g., Fang, 2007; Littlejohn, 2002). The implementation of those professional development interventions, however, only addresses faculty's on-the-job needs. Faculty in many cases might not have had to teach online when they were initially employed but due to the recent expansion of online education and its increased legitimacy as a valuable instructional format, their teaching loads now include both face-to-face and online courses. The nature of their PD, as a result, falls into the category of on-the-job training (OJT) (Jacobs & Osman-Gani, 1999), which has been argued against on the grounds that OJT lacks long-term effectiveness and sustainability (Van der Klink & Streumer, 2002).

Considering that online teaching has become an expected activity for faculty and TAs, relying only on short-term OJT is not a prudent course of action. Although beyond the scope of this volume, it is acknowledged that instructional faculty would also benefit from professional development based on pedagogical best practices for online teaching and learning. This chapter proposes that graduate programs in colleges and universities should consider online teaching and designing online courses as essential competencies for all graduate teaching assistants to acquire.

Theories of Effective Online Teaching

While many higher education institutions provide professional development activities to help TAs acquire and hone their instructional skills (e.g., face-to-face teaching, designing courses, providing faculty support), existing programs and workshops are insufficient to address a different set of skills that are uniquely associated with effective online teaching. This section presents two theoretical frameworks on online course design and delivery that speak to the requisite skills. First, effective online teaching requires an accommodation to the changing roles of instructors, learners, and learning environments. The Transactional Distance Theory (Moore, 1993) explains this dynamic relationship from the viewpoint of online interactions. Considering the lack of engagement in some online learning environments, Keller (2008) further proposed principles of learning motivation to provide a rationale for motivational strategies in online learning. Second, this new constellation of skills that consists of online instructional design, delivery, and management cannot be effectively developed and sustained via short-term OJT. A common practice at some institutions is for TAs to learn by trial and error. Very limited formal professional development is provided per se; however, TAs pick up strategies, methods, tips and technical skills through experimentation on their own and informal sharing with other TAs.

Transactional Distance Theory

Since online instructors and learners communicate via computer-based interfaces, pedagogical models derived from face-to-face environments cannot fully address the needs of TAs teaching online. That is, while some intersection of instructional skills exists, a one-to-one transfer of proficiency from the traditional classroom to online instruction cannot be assumed. The characteristics and materials that comprise good face-to-face teaching ability do not automatically translate into the online instructional environment (Goodyear, 2002). As an example, when teaching face-to-face, being *present* involves entering the classroom.

In online teaching and learning, the Transactional Distance Theory describes the learner-perceived gap with online instructors. Such a gap is often a self-evaluated outcome of students' cognitive, affective, and behavioral learning upon participating in the online learning process. A smaller perceptual gap, or a shorter transactional distance, should lead to better learning outcomes (Moore, 1993). Moore (1989; 1993) described the concept of transactional distance (TD) as the

learners' perceived proximity to their instructor, regardless of actual physical and temporal distance between the learner and the instructor. In effective online learning, both the learner and the instructor should strive to decrease the transactional distance via such multilateral interactions as dialogs, structure of the course content and delivery, and the instructor facilitating the learner's autonomy. High levels of dialog can decrease the transactional distance. A low level of dialogue, on the other hand, might increase the transactional distance (Benson & Samarawickrema, 2009). The course structure can directly impact the level of dialog instead of the overall transactional distance (Gorsky & Caspi, 2005), thus implying a layered relationship between dialog and structure and reinforcing the importance of sound instructional design principles. The level of learner autonomy, however, could either positively or negatively impact the perceived transactional distance, depending on the context of online learning and learners' skills in planning and autonomous learning (Benson & Samarawickrema, 2009).

In electronic learning environments, productive interaction has been regarded as an essential characteristic for enhancing dialog, thus improving online learning quality (Gunawardena & McIsaac, 2003; Moore, 1993; Wagner, 1994; Vrasidas & McIsaac, 1999) since high levels of interaction between Learners and Learners as well as Learners and Instructors contributes to satisfactory online learning experiences (Arbaugh, 2000). Interaction, in the context of online teaching and learning, is a process in which shared events take place between learners, instructors, and learning environments to help learners achieve intended learning goals (Arbaugh & Benbunan-Fich, 2006; Wagner, 1994). Three types of interaction affect the level of dialog: Learner-Content, Learner-Instructor, and Learner-Learner (Moore, 1989). As online learning is mediated via technologies, Hillman, Willis, and Gunawardena (1994) added the fourth interaction: Learner-Interface. Kearsley (2000) further argued that there should be a distinction between synchronous/immediate interaction and asynchronous/delayed interaction. Therefore interactions in online learning can be extended to several forms: Mediated synchronous discussion (e.g. audio/video conferencing), mediated asynchronous dialogue (e.g. e-mail, discussion postings), and getting feedback from systems (e.g. interactive computer programs) (Anderson, 2003).

FIRST PRINCIPLES OF MOTIVATION TO LEARN AND E³-LEARNING

Motivation drives and sustains learning processes. In online learning, however, leaner motivation can be difficult to assess and manage due to the lack of face-to-face observations. While multiple modalities are available for instructors to interact with online learners, it remains rather difficult to detect signs of changes in learners' motivational level based on learners' text messages, online discussion postings, frequency of online activities, and audio responses. Even with a webcam and video conferencing applications instructors can still miss cues or gestures that might express the students' engagement or frustration. Consequently online instructors can face challenges to effectively motivating their students. To address the critical motivation issue, Keller (2008) proposed a Motivation-to-Learn design framework with five principles. First, motivation to learn must be aroused by a knowledge or skill gap perceived by learners. Learners' attention level increases when they feel curious about the content and interactions in online learning environments. Online instructors or online learning designers should devise and implement instructional activities that arouse learner's interest. Using multimedia in the online learning environment could also be effective in increasing learners' attention. Second, learners are better motivated when they perceive a higher level of relevance toward online learning content

and processes. The intended learning goals must be meaningful to their personal or professional aspirations. However, it is not always an easy task for online instructors to effectively convey the value of learning outcomes to online learners. The third principle deals with learners' confidence in online learning environments. The online environment must provide opportunities and support for learners to successfully develop the intended knowledge or skills. Learners also need to feel in control of their learning processes to enable their sense of confidence. Confident online learners are more likely to focus their efforts on the intended learning goals. The fourth principle emphasizes the importance of developing learners' sense of satisfaction as the result of online learning, which is crucial for the sustainability of the online learning process. This principle consists of providing extrinsic rewards and recognitions, enabling learners to apply newly acquired knowledge and skills and developing a sense of equality among learners. The fifth principle advocates for learners' volitional control in order for them to be motivated. That is, learners must be allowed to plan, manage, and execute their learning processes in the online learning environments. With this design principle online learners are enabled to translate their motivation to learn into actions of learning.

The Transactional Distance Theory and the First Five Principles of Motivation-to-Learn clearly focus on the design aspect of online learning environments and they imply a changing instructional delivery process. Such change consists of restrictions caused by the lack of face-to-face interactions and allowances enabled by new information and communication technologies. To help instructors and TAs migrate face-to-face courses to ELEs or enhance existing online courses, professional development opportunities should be made available by the educational institutions. The effectiveness of these PD interventions, however, remains inconclusive.

Why do Graduate Students Teach?

Graduate students teach for a variety of reasons. TA positions provide financial support in the form of a stipend and/or a tuition and fee waiver and many students would be unable to complete a doctoral program without this funding. Gaining experience as a TA may be of particular interest to graduate students planning to pursue a faculty teaching position upon completion of their degree. TAs taking note of the increased demand for faculty with online course design and e-learning expertise may surmise that they will need this skill set to enhance their marketability (Sierra, 2010). A deep commitment to their students and to their identity as an effective educator motivates many doctoral students to teach (McDaniels, 2010). The TA is an emerging teaching professional who is gaining valuable skills she will utilize regularly in her future faculty career. As anyone who has done it can attest, teaching online involves synchronizing multiple complex tasks and it can be a much more time-consuming endeavor than teaching face-to-face. However, for a graduate student interested in a future faculty career, an online TA position is a valuable investment (Hardré, 2008). Referred to by McDaniels (2010) as "one of the developmental milestones" of a doctoral career, cultivating an identity as a future faculty member is facilitated by sound PD and increasingly more comprehensive and demanding instructional experiences.

TA Instructional Roles and Responsibilities in Online Courses

The roles and responsibilities assumed by an online TA are dynamic and multidimensional (Lewis & Abdul-Hamid, 2006). The extent of their role depends on several factors including individual faculty preference, departmental policies, and the TA's prior teaching experience. Five key roles have been identified that an instructor occupies in relating to learners in an online environment.

These roles are social, managerial, communicator, technical, and pedagogical (Berge, 2009; Dennen, Darabi & Smith, 2007). Each role emphasizes a distinct skill set, best practices, evaluation criteria and training approach. For example, these tasks can include grading papers and exams, uploading the graded papers into the Learning Management System (LMS), monitoring discussion forums, responding to student queries about course content troubleshooting technical issues, helping students learn to navigate the LMS, working with students in a tutorial capacity in laboratory and recitation groups, course management tasks (e.g., entering grades into the LMS electronic grade book), developing writing assignments and assessments, preparing course material, and facilitating video conferencing or synchronous chat sessions. The communicator role may involve utilizing tools such as text messages, e-mail, tweets, wikis, blogs, video and podcasts to interact with students. A TA may be the primary instructor for the online course section. In this circumstance she/he may have more autonomy with course content and the practice of teaching but also total responsibility and accountability as the instructor-of-record.

Research universities in particular rely heavily on TAs to teach introductory, undergraduate courses (Border & von Hoene, 2010). With TAs being responsible for a great deal of undergraduate instruction, they are often the first teacher these students encounter at their college or university. Consequently, they can influence students' perceptions of the university and ultimately higher education. TAs often teach and/or provide instructional support for many of the introductory level 'gate keeper' courses that determine if students are able to continue in their pursuit of some majors. These high stakes further illustrate the need for appropriate PD for graduate TAs. If a TA is the primary instructor, she may have an expanded curriculum/instructional design role and the added responsibility to situate that introductory course in the context of the discipline and the departmental curriculum (Nyquist & Wulff,

1996). In addition to the scholarly structure of their discipline, TAs must learn how to convey that structure to their students (Ronkowski, 1998 in Marincovich, 2010). Depending on their role in the course, TAs may have substantial contact and interaction with students or they may be relatively 'invisible' to those enrolled if their role is one of instructional support. Despite being behind the scenes, TAs can contribute (or detract) from the overall course effectiveness.

In electronic-learning environments (ELEs), TAs can play a substantial role in promoting and facilitating engagement and individual reflection, helping create courses that are student-centered and leveraging the unique affordances of ELEs. There has been little attention paid to TA online instruction in the published research. Much of what is available on campuses for faculty PD would have relevance for TAs; however, there are professional development needs unique to the role and context of a graduate student TA that should be addressed. Because they are not full-time faculty, the availability PD related to teaching may be limited. The unit/party responsible for this PD may range from the academic department, the graduate college, a center for teaching excellence, or the faculty supervisor. It could be everyone or no one. Faculty may have more scrutiny and more opportunities: annual reviews, peer coaching, and on-going assessment of the extent to which they are meeting their goals for teaching. None of this may be available for a graduate student employed as a TA. for Even if a TA has K-12 or higher education teaching experience, it should not be assumed that she/he needs little beyond technical training in the LMS in order to be successful in the online classroom.

Literature on the transition process of novice-to-expert is helpful in understanding some of the characteristics of the situation. Experts possess more content knowledge and they know what do with it (pedagogical and procedural knowledge). Content knowledge necessary for expertise development in the discipline is different from the pedagogical knowledge necessary to teach it (Hardré, 2005). Doctoral students' extensive content knowledge in their field may be a barrier to effectively teaching because as an 'expert' they have lost their ability to see the material from the (novice) undergraduate's point of view (Hardré, 2005). Despite possessing domain-specific information, TAs may be novices at instruction and e-learning and significant challenges can quickly arise if they are unaware or unskilled in online course design and facilitation. This novice-to-expert transition can be hastened by developmental instructional experiences of increasing difficulty (Hardré et al., 2008). While there may be many opportunities throughout the academic year (both mandatory and optional) to support and improve pedagogy, these are directed primarily to faculty. Training for TAs may occur at the beginning of an academic session but a specific focus on TAs' teaching online is rare. Because they are full-time graduate students, TAs may not be able to take advantage of these ad hoc opportunities that occur. Austin (2002) conducted a four-year longitudinal study with 79 graduate students. She reported that because TA hires reflect departmental needs for course coverage, developmentally organized and systematic PD is not the norm.

What TAs Need to be Successful Online Instructors

Faculty and graduate students bring divergent needs and contribute varying competencies to the e-learning environment. TAs and faculty are at different levels of development as instructors and therefore have PD needs unique to each position (Stanford Center for Teaching and Learning, 2007). TAs need both academic content knowledge specific to their discipline and also pedagogical content knowledge so that they can effectively deploy teaching strategies, explain concepts clearly and design examples so that students can integrate new knowledge (Ronkowski, 1998). "The myth that teaching depends only on domain knowledge, on subject matter expertise, still prevails in some departments and institutions" (Hardré, Ferguson, Bratton, Johnson, 2008, p. 14). TAs may not seek PD and/or teaching development resources out of concerns of appearing to their supervisors as lacking skills or being underprepared. They may also be discouraged by other TAs from attending PD sessions, dismissing these as a waste of time due to poor quality or a focus limited to technical 'how to' functions within the LMS.

Recent developments in e-learning and teaching which place emphasis on aspects of social engagement and learner control, challenge assumptions about the role and control of teachers. Extending beyond the traditional 'sage on the stage' methods, TAs need to know how to adopt a facilitator role and implement effective new strategies that can help students be successful in this evolving instructional medium (Benson & Brack, 2009). Palloff and Pratt (2002) posit that "promoting interactivity and the development of a sense of community within the student group to achieve successful learning outcomes" (p. 173) should be directly addressed. TAs cannot be expected to intuitively know how to design and deliver an effective online course or even how to best provide instructional support to the primary instructor. A mentoring relationship has been advocated (Palloff & Pratt, 2002; Nyquist & Wulff, 1996; Stanford Center for Teaching and Learning, 2007), creating a collaborative team through the pairing of experienced faculty and graduate students. Faculty can mentor TA's at each stage of their development from "senior learner" to "junior colleague" (Nyquist & Wulff, 1996). Another important area in which TAs may need online instructional guidance and direction is in time management. Graduate students have multiple responsibilities and maintaining balance between the need to be responsive to their students and their competing commitments can present a challenge. Mobile applications and devices such as tablet computers, smart phones, netbooks and ubiquitous Wi-Fi can potentially mean that the

TA is in the online "class" twenty-four hours a day, seven days a week. TAs need to learn how to establish good boundaries and time management strategies so that they are not inundated by the demands of their online course.

There are many learning objects (digital resources used to support learning, Wiley 2002) available that can be integrated into an online course to facilitate students' learning and TAs should be made aware of where to access them, evaluate their usefulness for their particular context and strategies to effectively integrate them into course activities. As was discussed previously, communication is a critical component of e-learning and successfully facilitating small and large groups requires careful planning and a keen understanding of how students learn through dialogue online. Managing discussions in a face-to-face class requires skill and energy. The text-based communication in online courses provides an accessible transcript of the students' postings that can be viewed in multiple formats (e.g. by sender, topic, date or theme) to facilitate the instructor's reading, organization and comprehension. Effective management of hundreds of messages is a skill that can prevent discussion forums from becoming overwhelming. Pelz (2004) offers examples of strategies that can enhance student participation levels and provide structure so that a TA monitoring a forum or with full teaching responsibility can promote cognitive and teaching presence. Discussion forums that are conducted well can be effective teaching tools in online courses. Additionally, quality discussions that foster critical thinking and deeper thinking (Biggs & Tang 2007) enhance student engagement and are less likely to veer off topic.

TAs should be grounded in an understanding of learning and theories (Batson, 2011) and consequently, PD efforts should include a review of basic learning theories and strategies for application of these theories in online courses. As adult learners themselves, TAs wish to understand the reasons for utilizing a particular strategy or implementing a certain approach. It is critical that TAs need to know the essential characteristics of the practice of online teaching (Goodyear, 2002). They need to understand learning theory to anchor instructional events and strategies that promote learning, retention and performance (Gagne & Medsker, 1996). Well-developed online courses are distinct from earlier distance-learning, *correspondence course* versions for several reasons, not least among these being that quality online courses emphasize and foster vibrant interaction between instructor and student as well as among students. This interaction is critically important for student satisfaction and retention (Lewis & Abdul-Hamid, 2006). Lewis & Abdul-Hamid (2006) present some of the most effective online teaching practices employed by exemplary faculty. In addition to domain specific content knowledge and pedagogy methods, TAs benefit from learning how to put the principles in action. The book *What the Best College Teachers Do* (Bain 2004), illustrates exemplary teaching practices and the metacognitive processes these instructors engaged in as they implemented their teaching practices. TAs who are scaffolded into their teaching role as "the guide on the side" do not have to unlearn strategies and practices that reflect the instructor-centered "stage on the (online) stage" model later on. Of course, there are limitations and restrictions on the amount of time that TAs can spend in face-to-face or online training and the amount of resources that can be devoted to provide such training. Given this reality, an efficient, targeted approach is recommended. The PD should go beyond the basic "tips & tricks" workshops frequently offered; however, but these can be a start. We would argue that there are many resources readily available online and TAs could benefit from strategies to locate and vet these materials in an efficient manner. TAs need to know about assessment of learning outcomes and methods that work well within the available LMS. As future faculty, reflective practice is also an important competency that TAs should possess (Schön, 1995). One of the challenges to engaging

in reflective practice is that TAs may be reluctant to candidly identify any areas of weakness and making reflective judgments known out of fear of losing their position. Taylor (2010) discusses what could be interpreted as the perceived risk of being a reflective practitioner and TAs may indeed interpret this as threatening behavior. As such, faculty supervisors and those responsible for professional development for TAs should be mindful to create safe spaces for TAs to ask questions, challenge assumptions and seek advice without worry about image management, reprisal or harsh judgment.

TAs need to know who they are teaching. Possibly members of Generation X, Y or a Millennial themselves, TAs cannot presume that they will share a cohort with their students. Whether they are in their 20's or have an AARP® card, graduate teaching assistants should have current and accurate information on the demographics and diversity of the students they are teaching.

TA Professional Development: Best Practices

In this section, the discussion is based on the assumption that online is not simply a teaching *approach* that can be considered in the same way as teaching strategies used in face-to-face settings in higher education. The 'tips & tricks' approach is minimally effective because this sort of PD tends not to situate online learning within the larger pedagogical and epistemological context with its own unique contributions to the scholarship of teaching and learning (Benson & Brack, 2009).

Professional development for graduate teaching assistants has been taking place for decades yet there remain very few reported studies with empirical research on the effectiveness or outcomes. An early article by Carroll (1980) identified studies that investigated the effects on TA knowledge, attitudes, and observed teaching behavior. Extending Carroll's investigation, Abbott, Wulff and Szego (1989) reviewed studies of various types of TA training between 1980 and 1989. Both papers indicate that empirical research on TA training remained deficient. "By the mid-1980's, several research universities had begun to initiate programs that addressed the training of graduate students to teach on campus and as future faculty" (p. 328). Border & von Hoene (2010) added that these training sessions took the form of workshops, seminars, and courses on teaching both in centralized programs and in individual college departments. The topics typically included a focus on pedagogy, assessment, basic course and syllabus planning. Developing these core competencies and nurturing the TAs teaching identity is essential and therefore should be approached in an intentional and consistent manner.

Training to teach online should be available for all TA's since it is likely that a large proportion of TAs will be involved in online or blended teaching during their doctoral years and in their future role as a faculty member. At the most basic level, the PD could consist of an orientation to the LMS and the related course tools (e.g., synchronous chats, discussions, grade book).

Hardré, Ferguson, Bratton & Johnson (2008) advocate for online professional development to "reach geographically distributed TAs and address their needs for flexible scheduling with remote access to fit their time and lifestyle constraints" (p. 20). Their research investigated the feasibility of a publicly available online professional development program for TAs. The researchers conducted an extensive review and analysis of the literature on teaching expertise and its critical components and developed an assessment of TAs' perceptions and preferences regarding online PD for teaching (p. 17). Their study included a representative sample of 60 TAs from a research university. Seventeen (28%) of the respondents reported that they use an online site for PD and to support their teaching endeavors. However, the TAs in the sample were not asked specifically about teaching online. Hardré (2005) asserts that utilizing Instructional Design principles (e.g., ADDIE model) can help TAs function at a higher level.

Instructional Design (ID) is an appropriate professional development tool-of-choice for TAs because it is applicable across domains and disciplines. An understanding of Instructional Design models can benefit a TA even if she/he is not involved in the development of the online course or has primary teaching responsibility for a course designed by someone else. ID models extend beyond course creation and involve both implementation and evaluation of the course materials and procedures (Gustafson & Maribe Branch, 2002). As such, including Instructional Design models is a strategy that can guide TAs' educational planning and management. Zhu, et al. (2010) investigated what programmatic changes can be made to enhance TAs instructional design training but did not explicitly address TAs teaching online. Overall, TA training research refers to instructional technology but online teaching is not specifically dealt with in the literature (Borden & von Hoene, 2010).

Meaningful and effective professional development can yield long-term benefits. Faculty who have experience with online teaching have a more favorable view and are more satisfied with it (Bolinger & Wolisik, 2009) and positive exposure as a graduate TA can be a good way to foster interest in online teaching. Given that faculty satisfaction is one of the Five Pillars of Quality for online learning cited by the Sloan Consortium (2002) the more positive experience a TA has prior to becoming a faculty member the better. Bolinger & Wolisik go on to state that faculty satisfaction relates to faculty motivation thus supporting the case that resistance and reluctance to e-learning may be reduced by guided experiences structured within professional development.

Teaching online courses has now become part of many faculty members' regular teaching load and consequently, the demand for well-qualified TAs will continue to increase. There is an expectation that all faculty and TAs gain experience and competence in teaching effectively online. In a study conducted by Hogan and McKnight (2007), online instructors in university settings experienced average emotional burnout levels, high levels of depersonalization, and low levels of personal accomplishment. These results should be of concern to university administrators because the success of online programs rests on the commitment of the faculty (and future faculty) and their willingness to continue the development and delivery of online courses (Betts, 1998). Since positive student outcomes are highly correlated with faculty satisfaction as suggested by Hartman et al. (2000), administrators will need to pay close attention to levels of faculty satisfaction. The investment in PD to enhance and support TAs' online teaching will pay dividends in the sustainability of quality online instruction henceforward. These training programs should model and teach best practices for online learning. The best practices as recommended by Boettcher & Conrad (2010) suggest that online instructors:

1. Demonstrate a high level of consistent instructional presence. Being in the course daily and communicating regularly helps students know that you are 'there.' However, TAs need not be overwhelmed by hundreds of student e-mail messages and discussion posts. For example, through application of instructional design practices (e.g., announcements, weekly updates) TAs can reinforce their presence in the course while supporting students' autonomy and peer interaction.
2. Create a supportive online course community. Closely aligned with instructor presence, this practice involves creating multiple opportunities for students to become acquainted and have learner-to-learner dialogues. Learner-to-resource and faculty-to-learner dialogues should not dominate.
3. Develop and explicitly communicate their expectations for how much time students should spend each week working in the course and frequency/method of communicating with students. This will help avoid

students' presumptions about when will be accessible to respond to them. Students may grossly over or underestimate the amount of time needed to successfully accomplish the learning objectives.

4. Use individual, small group and large group assignments. A variety of experiences will resonate with students' different learning preferences and should align with learning objective for a particular lesson module.
5. Use synchronous and asynchronous activities. Some departments require synchronous video conferencing or chat sessions as a component of all of their online courses. Even as an optional exercise, a TA could offer synchronous assignments or provide synchronous office hours or help sessions for students who prefer this format.
6. Request student feedback early in the course. Utilizing an informal early feedback (IEF) survey or prompts can provide valuable information about how the course is going to that point. Unlike the end-of-semester course evaluation, allows time for modifications if warranted.
7. Develop discussion questions that encourage reflection, dialogue, questions and multiple responses. In online discussions, students have more time to read, reflect and generate a thoughtful response. Consequently, discussion questions and prompts should encourage critical thinking, application of concepts and exploration of ideas.
8. Utilize digital content and online learning objects. Wiley (2002) defined learning objects as digital resources that support learning. These can be digital course materials such as podcasts, e-textbooks, embedded audio files, and online supplemental resources.
9. Combine core concept learning with customized and personalized learning. Identify the performance goals and learning outcomes. Develop learning activities with options that support students' goals and increase in

complexity so that students are challenged and their learning accomplish the outcomes.

10. Plan a closing activity near the end of the course. Just as an online course should have an initial welcoming activity, the instructional design should include a wrap-up module that could include students' reflection on their learning and summaries.

Evaluation of TA Professional Development

TA professional development should include a formative (process) and summative (outcome) evaluation. To facilitate the evaluation process, Benson & Brack (2009) suggest peer review of the materials, gathering participant feedback, and incorporating instructor/facilitator reflection. Ongoing PD should also incorporate performance assessment (Nyquist & Wulff, 1996). TAs want to know what are their supervisor's expectations and the extent to which they are meeting them. Additionally, departments and supervising faculty need information to provide support, guidance, and developmental feedback and to inform reappointment decisions. Data sources could include self-assessment, peer-assessment, supervisor observation, teaching portfolios of course artifacts related to the scholarship of teaching and learning (SOTL) (Davis & Kring, 2001). Course e-mail and discussion postings provide a high degree of access to the learner-instructor and learner-learner interactions within a course.

When evaluation of TA training programs has been reported, the findings indicated that TAs felt that the PD was often unproductive and mismatched to their instructional needs, described as disconnected, lacking in relevance (Zhu, Groscurth, Bergom & Hershock, 2010), level of teaching experience should be a consideration in designing PD strategies (Abbott, Wulff & Szego, 1989) and TAs have difficulty applying the information and skills in real teaching situations (Hardre, 2005). Evaluation information can be better utilized to plan and implement effective

TA professional development. Post-graduate school, longitudinal follow-up is generally not done because of the challenges associated with maintaining contact with TAs after they graduate and methodological challenges to assess online teaching effectiveness and its relationship to TA professional development. Boettcher (2004) addressed the cost of developing an online degree program. He noted, "If program planners use a working estimate of $10,000 per credit hour for a master's degree program, than a 30-credit master's degree program can require an investment of $300,000" (p. 5). Even the cost for a single online course can be significant underscoring the importance of professional development for all involved. Academic units expend a great deal of time and resources developing a research-based undergraduate curriculum and these units should be equally concerned about evaluating the effectiveness and efficacy of the professional development of the TAs charged with implementing that curriculum.

Recommendations

The following recommendations emerge from this chapter:

- Conduct a needs assessment to determine online TA training needs related to their content area, learning management system, instructional design models and level of teaching experience
- Professional development should mandatory, focused on personal and professional growth and ongoing throughout the TAs graduate program
- Supervising faculty and those responsible for PD should attentive and responsive to TAs reticence related to disclosing challenges she/he may be experiencing with an online course
- Evaluate process and outcomes of TA training including peer observation, faculty observation, video/digital recording,

reflective exercises such as developing a teaching philosophy statement, and developing a teaching portfolio

- Provide multiple options for PD including, online modules, small group meetings, face-to-face and web resources. Provide both formal and informal opportunities for TAs to exchange ideas, develop skills and solicit feedback
- Include mentoring and apprenticeship models and peer coaching from TAs with more online teaching experience
- Elevate the teaching role within doctoral programs and clarify the importance of online teaching, particularly in research universities
- Include instructional design elements into PD so that teaching assistants can apply ID models appropriately to create and facilitate engaging, interactive ELEs
- Consolidate and share resources across colleges, academic units and departments whenever possible to reduce duplication and maximize support

FUTURE RESEARCH DIRECTIONS

Building on the extant literature, future research should employ longitudinal methods to investigate the near-term and long-term outcomes of professional development for TAs who teach online. Research evaluating the efficacy of different approaches within and between institutions will be helpful.

As online teaching technology continues to evolve and anytime, anywhere learning becomes a standard student expectation, this research will be valuable so that institutions can be proactive rather than reactive in the practice and scholarship of teaching and learning online. Studies that involve assessment of the process and outcomes of TA professional development in various institutional and disciplinary contexts are also recommended.

CONCLUSION

Dramatic growth in online and blended courses means that future faculty will need specific competencies in teaching these courses to enter the job market and compete effectively for teaching positions. Increasingly, TAs will enter graduate programs with an expectation that they will teach online, both during graduate school and in their careers. It is essential that aspiring faculty invest in sustained professional development throughout their doctoral program (McDaniels, 2010) and the institutions make this investment in them as well. Academic content knowledge, pedagogical content knowledge and knowledge about how students learn specific to online environments are critical and necessary for TA professional development programs (Ronkowski, 1998).

The information presented in this chapter provides a glimpse of the fault lines around the issue of graduate teaching assistants when online education is not specifically addressed in ongoing professional development and some strategies that benefit TAs, faculty, academic units and students.

TA professional development is of critical importance for: Graduate students teaching in the near-term and in their faculty career, student learning outcomes, and the scholarship of teaching and learning. It is unwise to relegate online TA professional development to an after-thought status. The stakes are too high to move forward based on trial-and-error. Research has highlighted the best practices for online teaching as well as evidence on what improves student and instructor satisfaction, transfer, student self-efficacy, and transactional presence. The quality of undergraduate instruction by graduate teaching assistants (TAs) is a serious responsibility for which effective professional development opportunities have the potential to impact the educational outcomes of thousands of college and university courses nationwide.

REFERENCES

Abott, R., Wulff, D., & Szego, C. (1989). Review of research on TA training. In Nyquist, J. D., Abbott, R. D., & Wulff, D. H. (Eds.), *Teaching assistant training in the 1990s: New directions for teaching and learning* (pp. 111–123). San Francisco, CA: Jossey-Bass.

Allen, I. E., & Seaman, J. (2010). *Class differences: Online education in the United States, 2010.* Babson Survey Research Group.

Anderson, T. (2003). Modes of interaction in distance education: Recent developments and research questions. In Moore, M. (Ed.), *Handbook of distance education.* Mahwah, NJ: Lawrence Erlbaum.

Arbaugh, J. B. (2000). Virtual classrooms versus physical classrooms: An exploratory study of class discussion patterns and student learning in an asynchronous Internet-based MBA course. *Journal of Management Education, 24*(2), 207–227. doi:10.1177/105256290002400206

Arbaugh, J. B., & Benbunan-Fich, R. (2006). An investigation of epistemological and social dimensions of teaching in online learning environments. *Academy of Management Learning & Education, 5*(4), 435–447. doi:10.5465/AMLE.2006.23473204

Austin, A. E. (2002). Preparing the next generation of faculty: Graduate school as socialization for the academic career. *The Journal of Higher Education, 73*(1), 94–122. doi:10.1353/jhe.2002.0001

Bain, K. (2004). *What the best college teachers do.* Cambridge, MA: Harvard University Press.

Benson, R., & Brack, C. (2009). Developing the scholarship of teaching: What is the role of e-teaching and learning? *Teaching in Higher Education, 14*(1), 71–80. doi:10.1080/13562510802602590

Benson, R., & Samarawickrema, G. (2009). Addressing the context of e-learning: Using transactional distance theory to inform design. *Distance Education, 39*(1), 5–21. doi:10.1080/01587910902845972

Berge, Z. (2009). Changing instructor roles in virtual worlds. *Quarterly Review of Distance Education, 9*(4), 407–414.

Betts, K. S. (1998). An institutional overview: Factors influencing faculty participation in distance education in postsecondary education in the United States: An institutional study. *Online Journal of Distance Learning Administration, 1*(3). Retrieved from http://www.westga.edu/~distance/betts13.html

Boettcher, J. V., & Conrad, R. M. (2004). *Faculty guide for moving teaching and learning to the web.* Phoenix, AZ: League for Innovation in the Community College.

Boettcher, J. V., & Conrad, R. M. (2010). *Online teaching survival guide: Simple and practical pedagogical tips.* San Francisco, CA: Jossey-Bass.

Bolliger, D. U., & Wasilik, O. (2009). Factors influencing faculty satisfaction with online teaching and learning in higher education. *Distance Education, 30*(1), 103–116. doi:10.1080/01587910902845949

Border, L. B., & von Hoene, L. M. (2010). Graduate and professional student development programs. In Gillespie, K. J., & Robertson, D. L. (Eds.), *A guide to faculty development* (2nd ed.). San Francisco, CA: John Wiley & Sons, Inc.

Carroll, J. G. (1980). Effects of training programs for university teaching assistants: A review of empirical research. *The Journal of Higher Education, 51*(2), 167–182. doi:10.2307/1981372

Davis, S. F., & Kring, J. P. (2001). A model for training and evaluating graduate teaching assistants. *College Student Journal, 35*(1), 45–51.

Dennen, V., Darabi, A., & Smith, L. (2007). Instructor-learner interaction in online courses: The relative perceived importance of particular instructor actions on performance and satisfaction. *Distance Education, 28*(1), 65–79. doi:10.1080/01587910701305319

Dron, J. (2005). Designing the undesignable: Social software and control. *Journal of Educational Technology & Society, 10*(3), 60–71.

Ertmer, P. A. (1999). Addressing first- and second-order barriers to change: Strategies for technology integration. *Educational Technology Research and Development, 47*, 47–61. doi:10.1007/BF02299597

Fang, B. (2007). A performance-based development model for online faculty. *Performance Improvement, 46*(5), 17–24. doi:10.1002/pfi.129

Goodyear, P. (2002). Teaching online. In Hativa, N., & Goodyear, P. (Eds.), *Teacher thinking, beliefs and knowledge in higher education* (pp. 79–101). The Netherlands: Kluwer Academic Publishers. doi:10.1007/978-94-010-0593-7_5

Gorsky, P., & Caspi, A. (2005). Dialogue: A theoretical framework for distance education instructional systems. *British Journal of Educational Technology, 36*(2), 137–144. doi:10.1111/j.1467-8535.2005.00448.x

Gunawardena, C. N., & McIsaac, M. S. (2003). Distance education. In Jonassen, D. H. (Ed.), *Handbook of research on educational communications and technology* (2nd ed., pp. 113–142). Mahwah, NJ: Lawrence Erlbaum Associates, Inc.

Gustafson, K., & Maribe Branch, R. (2002). *Survey of instructional design models* (4th ed.). Washington, DC: Department of Education.

Hardré, P. L. (2005). Instructional design as a professional development tool-of-choice for graduate teaching assistance. *Innovative Higher Education, 30*(3), 163–175. doi:10.1007/s10755-005-6301-8

Hardré, P. L., Ferguson, C., Bratton, J., & Johnson, D. (2008). Online professional development for TAs: What they need, what they have, what they want. *Journal of Faculty Development, 22*(1), 11–23.

Hartman, J., Dziuban, C., & Moskal, P. (2000). Faculty satisfaction in ALNs: A dependent or independent variable? In J. Bourne (Ed.), *Online Education Volume 1: Learning Effectiveness and Faculty Satisfaction: Proceedings of the 1999 Sloan Summer Workshop on Asynchronous Learning Networks* (pp. 151-172). Needham, MA: Sloan Center for OnLine Education.

Hillman, D. C., Willis, D. J., & Gunawardena, C. N. (1994). Learner-interface interaction in distance education: An extension of contemporary models and strategies for practitioners. *American Journal of Distance Education, 8*(2), 30–42. doi:10.1080/08923649409526853

Hogan, R., & McKnight, M. (2007). Exploring burnout among university online instructors: An initial investigation. *The Internet and Higher Education, 10*, 117–124. doi:10.1016/j.iheduc.2007.03.001

Jacobs, R., & Osman-Gani, A. (1999). Status, impacts and implementation issues of structured on-the-job training: A study of Singapore-based companies. *Human Resource Development International, 2*(1), 17.

Kearsley, G. (2000). *Online education: Learning and teaching in cyberspace*. Belmont, CA: Wadsworth.

Keller, J. M. (2008). First principles of motivation to learn and e^3-learning. *Distance Education, 29*(2), 175–185. doi:10.1080/01587910802154970

Lewis, C., & Abdul-Hamid, H. (2006). Implementing effective online teaching practices: Voices of exemplary faculty. *Innovative Higher Education, 31*(2), 83–97. doi:10.1007/s10755-006-9010-z

Littlejohn, A. H. (2002). Improving continuing professional development in the use of ICT. *Journal of Computer Assisted Learning, 18*, 166–174. doi:10.1046/j.0266-4909.2001.00224.x

McDaniels, M. (2010). Doctoral student socialization for teaching roles. In Gardner, S., & Mendoza, P. (Eds.), *On becoming a scholar: Socialization and development in doctoral education* (pp. 29–44). Sterling, VA: Sylus Publishing.

Moore, M. (1989). Editorial: Three types of interaction. *American Journal of Distance Education, 3*, 1–6. doi:10.1080/08923648909526659

Moore, M. (1993). Theory of transactional distance. In Keegan, D. (Ed.), *Theoretical Principles of Distance Education* (pp. 22–38). London, UK: Routledge.

Nyquist, J. D., & Wulff, D. H. (1996). *Working effectively with graduate assistants.* Thousand Oaks, CA: Sage Publications.

Orr, R., Williams, M., & Pennington, K. (2009). Institutional efforts to support faculty in online teaching. *Innovative Higher Education, 34*, 257–268. doi:10.1007/s10755-009-9111-6

Page, M., Wilhelm, M., & Regens, N. (2011). Preparing graduate students for teaching: Expected and unexpected outcomes from participation in a GK-12 classroom fellowship. *Journal of College Science Teaching, 40*(5), 32–37.

Palloff, R., & Pratt, K. (2002). Beyond the looking glass: What faculty and students need to be successful online. In Rudestam, K., & Schoenholtz-Read, J. (Eds.), *Handbook of online learning: Innovations in higher education and corporate training* (pp. 171–184). Thousand Oaks, CA: Sage Publications.

Palmer, S. R., & Holt, D. M. (2009). Examining student satisfaction with wholly online learning. *Journal of Computer Assisted Learning, 25*, 101–113. doi:10.1111/j.1365-2729.2008.00294.x

Pelz, B. (2004). My three principles of effective online pedagogy. *Journal of Asynchronous Learning Networks, 8*(3), 33–46.

Ronkowski, S. A. (1998). The disciplinary/departmental context of TA training. In Marincovich, M., Prostko, J., & Stout, F. (Eds.), *The professional development of graduate teaching assistants.* Bolton, MA: Anker Publishing.

Schöen, D. (1995). The new scholarship requires a new epistemology. *Change, 27*(6), 26–34.

Selwyn, N. (2007). E-learning or she-learning? Exploring students' gendered perceptions of education technology. *British Journal of Educational Technology, 38*(4), 744–746. doi:10.1111/j.1467-8535.2006.00659.x

Sierra, J. (2010). Shared responsibility and student learning: Ensuring a favorable educational experience. *Journal of Marketing Education, 32*(1), 104–111. doi:10.1177/0273475309344802

Sloan Consortium. (2002). *The 5 pillars: Sloan-C quality framework.* Retrieved from http://sloan-consortium.org/5pillars

Stanford Center for Teaching & Learning (2007). *Speaking of Teaching Newsletters.*

Taylor, S. (2010). Negative judgments: Reflections on teaching reflective practice. *Organization Management Journal, 7*, 5–12. doi:10.1057/omj.2010.1

Van der Klink, M., & Streumer, J. N. (2002). Effectiveness of on-the-job training. *Journal of European Industrial Training, 26*, 196–199. doi:10.1108/03090590210422076

Vrasidas, C., & McIsaac, M. S. (1999). Factors influencing interaction in an online course. *American Journal of Distance Education, 13*(3), 22–36. doi:10.1080/08923649909527033

Wagner, E. D. (1994). In support of a functional definitions of interaction. *American Journal of Distance Education, 8*(2), 6–26. doi:10.1080/08923649409526852

Zhu, E., Groscurth, C., Bergom, I., & Hershock, C. (2010). Assessing and meeting TA's instructional technology training needs: Research and practice. *Journal of Faculty Development, 24*(3), 37–43.

Chapter 3
Multi–Modal Professional Development for Faculty

Sheri Anderson
University of North Carolina Wilmington, USA

Beth Oyarzun
University of North Carolina Wilmington, USA

ABSTRACT

This chapter describes a multi-modal faculty professional development program designed using the Analyze, Design, Development, Implement, and Evaluation process (ADDIE) and the Community of Learners model. The program includes a general training series, one-on-one trainings, on-demand training, as well as social events. The general training series is offered synchronously via face-to-face and webinar formats simultaneously. This training series is also offered asynchronously via training videos and slides that are published to a website. Additionally, the professional development program encourages faculty to support one another and share their experiences through social events and colloquiums. This multi-modal approach creates an adaptable and flexible environment that allows the professional development program to meet the needs of a diverse group of faculty.

INTRODUCTION

Online course offerings are growing at an exponential rate. According to the national center for educational statistics, in 2006, 89% of public 4-year universities offered distance education courses for credit hours (Parsad, Lewis, Tice, & National Center for Education Statistics., 2008). There is an increased need for higher education institutions to offer more professional development for faculty who teach online courses due to the increasing offerings of online courses. To date, universities and colleges employ a variety of methods to teach/train faculty on new technology and pedagogy from group technology training supported by an Information Technology department to creating Centers for Teaching Excellence on pedagogy (Blair & Madigan, 2000; Brown, Maeers, & Cooper, 2000). Too often these professional development programs provide one method of training faculty with separate technol-

DOI: 10.4018/978-1-4666-1963-0.ch003

ogy and pedagogy training. Often the teaching and learning styles between the trainer and faculty are misaligned or faculty expectations and the actual training content may be mismatched. As a result, this may lead to poor faculty experience with professional development (Lawlar, 2003). Utilizing multi-modality to design professional development for faculty applies several processes and models as well as integrates technology and pedagogy training. Multi-modality can eliminate known faculty barriers to integrating technology into their courses such as time constraints (Rutherford & Grama, 1995).

This chapter describes a multi-modal faculty professional development program designed using the Analyze, Design, Development, Implement, and Evaluation approach (ADDIE) combined with Community of Learning model. The program includes a general training series, one-on-one trainings, on demand training as well as social events. The Community of Learning model allows faculty to support one another through social events and colloquiums. This multi-modal approach creates an adaptable and flexible environment that allows the professional development program to meet the needs of a diverse group of faculty.

BACKGROUND

Faculty and Technology

Faculty members face shifting roles from being an instructor and lecturer to course developer and facilitator (Conrad, 2004). Online learning and instructional strategies are still in nascency. Faculty often resist to moving to this format for a variety of reasons. Rutherford and Grama (1995) have suggested faculty fear integrating technology due to following factors: time constraints, having to move backward to move forward, and not knowing where to begin. Tsounda (1992) states faculty are resistant to professional development due to a lack of technology skills. Also, training

workshops may not meet faculty's goals for development. Lawlar (2004) reported that faculty development workshops often had goals that did not align with faculty expectations. Additionally, timing of the workshops may not fit into faculty schedules. Lee and Busch (2005) found that faculty participation in distance education is related to their perception of training. Faculty members are more willing to participate in distance education instruction if they perceive the training offered is adequate and relevant to their instruction.

Universities offer many strategies and models for faculty development regarding technology and pedagogy, yet they only offer training in technology or pedagogy either face-to-face or online instead of a flexible approach that incorporates all. Many times there are "ideological constraints that maintain the separation of technology and pedagogy" (Blair & Madigan, 2000). One university's Teaching and Learning Center proposes a technology-pedagogy model that ensures that faculty will be able to integrate technology effectively for the initial planning stages of course development through implementation and assessment stages (Blair & Madigan, 2000). Another university utilizes the Community of Learners model for faculty development. This collaborative approach utilizes faculty discussing educational communication while learning technology skills (Brown, Maeers, & Cooper, 2000). Another university uses a Perceptual Control Theory (PCT) and ADDIE model (Georgina and Hosford, 2009). However, faculty indicate that combining technological and pedagogical training would be more effective for their instructional needs. In order to reach a diverse group across multiple departments, professional development programs must incorporate a variety of models and delivery modes.

Due to the pressures to technologize many faculty find themselves in a situation in which the *what's* and *how's* of technology are more important than the *why's* (Blair & Madigan, 2000). Integrating pedagogy into technology training in a flexible and adaptive model to reach the diverse needs of faculty is imperative for successful implementation of professional development, which in turn helps to reach higher education goals and standards.

ADDIE Process of Designing Instruction

ADDIE stands for Analyze, Design, Development, Implementation, and Evaluation and is based on systematic product development, which is a paradigm that refers to a family of models with a common underlying structure. Molenda (2008) states that ADDIE is a term used to describe a systematic approach. This process can be applied to the development of any micro or macro instructional development project. ADDIE is applied twice in this professional development setting. It is applied to the design and development of the professional development program for faculty by the instructional designers/trainers, and it is also modeled in order to encourage faculty to apply the process to their instructional development of online or web-enhanced courses.

Analysis

Analysis can also be considered the front-end analysis although analysis is often conducted through the ADDIE process. The analysis phase is the process of defining what is to be learned. During this phase a needs analysis is conducted. Collecting data about performance requirements, the context in which the task is to be completed, and about the people performing the task closes analysis phase of instructional design process (U.S. Army Field Artillery School, 1984).

Design

During the design phase the process of deciding what the content will be and how it will be delivered is addressed. During this process a blueprint for the learning materials is created (Seels & Glasgow,

1998). The instructional designer translates the instructional analysis results (needs) into learning outcomes. The learning outcomes are then used to develop assessment items or strategies. The final step in the design phase is establishing instructional strategies. In addition, instructional designers choose a delivery system before making decision about sequencing instruction, grouping students, and selecting specific learning activities (Dick, Carey, & Carey, 2005).

Development

The development phase includes the actual creation or authoring of the materials or product. Development of a product requires incorporating a variety of technology tools. In addition, as Seels and Ritchey (1994) explain *"development is the process of translating the design specifications into physical form"* (Seels & Ritchey, 1994, p. 35). Thus it is heavily driven by design and its underlying theories.

Implementation

Implementation addresses the interface between the learner and the instructional material or system. It consists of a wide range of activities and teaching strategies. The instructor engaged in the implementation phase is concerned with matching learners with specific activities and materials. During the implementation process, the learners are prepared for interacting with the selected materials and activities and are provided with guidance (Seels & Richey, 1994).

Evaluation

Seels and Richey (1994) define evaluation domain as *"process of determining the adequacy of instruction and learning"* (Seels & Richey, 1994, p. 54). The evaluation phase is guided by the systematic acquisition and assessment of information to provide useful feedback about products or learning processes. Most often, feedback is perceived as "useful" if it aids in decision-making. But the relationship between an evaluation and its impact may be very multifaceted. Despite this complexity, the major goal of evaluation should be to influence decision-making or policy formulation through the provision of empirically driven feedback.

There are many different types of evaluations depending on the object being evaluated and the purpose of the evaluation. For example, the object of evaluation may be a program, a project, or a product. In addition, the evaluation may focus on determining the merit, worth or value of a program (summative) or it may emphasize strengthening or improving a program or a product (formative). Thus, the most important basic distinction in evaluation types is that between *formative* and *summative* evaluation.

Evaluation process often begins with needs analysis, and clarification of goals and constraints. The instructor then collects data regarding the program, process, or product. This data can be collected using observations, surveys, questionnaires, or testing. Data is then analyzed and compared to the instructional goal to determine the overall effectiveness. This process is cyclic once revisions have been made.

MAIN FOCUS OF CHAPTER

Analysis

When conducting a needs analysis for a faculty professional development program, the instructional designers perform an analysis of training needs for faculty via survey prior to designing the program (see Appendix A for a sample). The electronic survey consists of technical and pedagogical topics as well as preferred delivery methods and times. The results of this needs analysis shape the design of the training series and the colloquiums offered. Often electronic surveys yield low results; therefore, faculty needs are not wholly represented.

To increase responses, the cover letter and survey are concise and a prize drawing incentive is included. During this professional development program the faculty members are also encouraged to complete a content and learner analysis prior to designing their online or web-enhanced course. The data collected from the needs analysis, formative, and summative evaluations helps the instructional designers and the faculty members determine the gap between the actual state of affairs and the desired learning outcomes of the instruction being designed.

Design

For the design of this professional development, the instructional designers translate the training needs analysis by designing a training series that meets the needs identified by faculty members in the analysis survey. Data collected in previous semesters are also incorporated into the design. Previous data indicated that faculty desired less "how-to" tool training and more training on pedagogical issues of incorporating tools into their teaching. This combined with the desired topics is what formulated the current training series. The learning outcomes of the training series are summarized in a checklist (Appendix B) that is provided to faculty at the beginning and end of the training series as a self-assessment.

The design of a professional development program is ever changing. For programs in their infancy, baseline data needs to be gathered. Conducting formative evaluations at certain points of the academic year shapes the program over time. Therefore various institutions will design programs differently based on technologies available and faculty input. Based on formative evaluation data, two of the key issues of attendance are scheduling and delivery method. The training is scheduled on a variety of days alternating mornings and afternoons to accommodate when faculty can attend. It is delivered simultaneously via face-to-face and webinar to address on-campus faculty, faculty at satellite campuses, and those teaching from a distance. A virtual classroom is used to deliver the webinar which allows the instructional designers to model appropriate synchronous pedagogy. This is also the tool that is available for faculty to incorporate into their online/web-enhanced courses thus they gain exposure to another tool available for their own classes.

The training is based on is Merrill's Instructional Transaction Theory. This includes presenting the goals, providing simulation, allowing for presentation and practice, and giving feedback followed up by hands-on demonstration, practice, and feedback (Reigeluth, 1999). The instructional strategies employed for the training include presenting best practices and tool training through text, visual aids, and hands-on activities. These instructional strategies were chosen to meet the needs of faculty locally and at a distance since the training is offered face-to-face and simultaneously as a webinar. The hands-on portions are intermittent and timed throughout the training after the presentation of a new concept or tool. Throughout the trainings, faculty members are encouraged to reflect on their course analysis, and address the needs in their individual course design based on course and program goals and objectives. Faculty members are also encouraged to conduct formative evaluations with colleagues or students while designing their materials.

General Training Series

The group-training category was designed to assist faculty in the analysis and design stages of creating a blueprint for their courses. The group trainings consist of a general overview of the tools and online teaching pedagogy for faculty and is designed to address the novice to the experienced. Generally, participants would like to gain further insight into best practices or exposure to new techniques and instructional strategies for course enhancement. The instructional designers also teach online

courses which assists with enhancing receptivity to the professional development (Beaudoin, 1990). An eight part training series that is offered twice each semester addresses a variety of pedagogical topics, tools, and techniques for online learning. The content of each training session is subject to change based on needs assessment and evaluation data. Currently, the series contains sessions with the following titles: Introduction Online/Web-Enhanced Instruction, Course Design Evaluation, Student Engagement I, Student Engagement II, Student Assessment I, Student Assessment II, Managing your Grade Center, and Incorporating Online Video Lectures into your Course. Formative and summative evaluation data is reviewed at the end of each training series. The material and training methods are then revised based on the feedback from the attendees.

The training series is offered in multiple formats to accommodate a variety of learning preferences established from the needs assessment and evaluation data. Synchronous or live trainings are offered face-to-face in a campus classroom and simultaneously broadcasted as a webinar; therefore, faculty members are able to attend from an alternate location. Training materials are delivered asynchronously via slides, training videos, and handouts that are published to a website. Faculty can refer to these materials for support after synchronous training or choose to receive the initial training in this format at their convenience. Customized departmental trainings can be requested at any time. These trainings address the specific needs of groups and may contain all or part of a variety of sessions from the series. The purpose of the general training series is to give instructors an overview of course design and development options. A short description of each training session is provided below.

Introduction to Online and Web Enhanced Instruction is designed for instructors who are new to the Learning Management System (LMS) and/or online or web-enhanced instruction. This training focuses on orienting the instructor to the layout of the LMS as well as how to customize the interface to suit the instructional needs. Instructors are exposed to terminology associated with online/web-enhanced courses as well as content organization, communication plans, and strategies to create an active social environment. These topics introduce the importance of the analysis and design phase of the ADDIE process. This is imperative to the course design due to the fact that if instructors do not integrate technology and pedagogy then they will have less than desired results (Knowlton, 2003). Live course examples are shown to the instructors during the training to give them a visual of the various options for setting up an online course. Instructors are also given access blank course shells to build content during the training.

Course Design Evaluation stresses the importance of the evaluation phase of the ADDIE process by reviewing an online course design rubric such as Blackboard's Exemplary Course Program (ECP) (Appendix B). Faculty or departments are encouraged to adopt one of these rubrics for peer evaluation. The objective of this session is for faculty to apply the main components of these rubrics to their course design. For example, when designing a syllabus for online instruction the instructor needs to include a communication plan such as instructor availability, response time, and mode of communication. Also, designing interaction between the instructor - student and student - student is imperative for a successful course (Miller & King, 2003). This training is offered early in the series to promote awareness of best practices prior to building their courses.

Student Engagement I deals with asynchronous whole class and/or small group interaction. Tool description, functions, and implementation strategies are discussed for the following tools: journals, discussions, blogs, wikis, voice tools, and email. Grading of each tool is also discussed as well as variety of rubrics that can be utilized. Instructors are urged to review their course goals/objectives to determine the best method for assessing learner

outcomes. Depending on the course and level, instructors are also guided on creating a social community in an online/web-enhanced course. Examples of various tools and student activity are shown to the faculty.

Student Engagement II focuses on synchronous interactive tools such as virtual classrooms, virtual worlds, and instant messengers. This session gives instructors a general overview of the tools, pedagogy, and a demonstration of synchronous engagement. Instructors are advised to determine the method of delivery for their course: face-to-face with online component, asynchronous fully online, synchronous fully online, blended asynchronous and synchronous. Instructors interested in incorporating virtual classrooms or worlds are advised to set up a one-on-one training for more in depth instruction on effective instructional strategies. For example, instructors should be prepared with all materials ahead of time or at the beginning of a live session, neutralize distractions, and during the session use virtual body language such as emoticons (Finklestein, 2006; Keegan, et. al., 2005). In the Course Design Evaluation session, instructors are encouraged to consider the communication strategies for the class in which this session provides an overview of additional communication tools, which can be incorporated. The synchronous tools can be integrated into the course for group work (student-student), office hours (instructor-student), or whole class lecture/discussion (instructor-student and student-student). These tools and strategies also assist in forming a social community within the classroom whether the class is web-enhanced or fully online (Crawford & Cook, 2008).

Student Assessment I and II reviews assessing student performances formally through tests, surveys, and assignments. The tools, pedagogy, and grading processes are reviewed topics include maintaining student academic integrity in an online situation. Practices such as test proctoring and utilizing anti-plagiarism tools are discussed as well as which tools should be used to assess course goals and objectives. Instructors are encouraged to integrate these concepts/strategies into their design plan. For example, if the instructor mandates the students locate and take tests with a proctor, they are strongly advised to inform the students of this practice in their syllabus at the beginning of the semester since often it takes time and money on the student's behalf to identify an appropriate proctor. Instructors are also informed on how to create and deploy exams/quizzes for students with special needs such as extended time. Best practices for assessing student-learning outcomes are also discussed such as incorporating a variety of methods to assess their students such as a variety of test item types such as multiple choice, short answer, and essay as well as incorporating appropriate assignments to match their goals and objectives (Miller & King, 2003).

Managing Students through the Grade Center was designed specifically for the LMS. All grading, grade overrides, and reports are generated through the grade center. Instructors can view the amount of time a student spends in the course, assignment submission times as well as the time taken to complete exams. Faculty members are informed to check student participation often via the reporting system (Miller & King, 2002). In an online asynchronous course since there is no physical presence; therefore, instructors can assess a student's performance through the various reports. This session ties into the implementation phase since the instructor utilizes this feature during a live course.

Incorporating Online Video into your Course reviews the current literature on incorporating e-lectures into a course topics include length of video and format. This session was created due to the high interest of faculty wanting to incorporate video lectures into their course but not knowing where to begin. Many difficulties included formatting and file size limitations. ADA compliance and other best practices such as including video scripts, closed captioning, and length of video are discussed as well as various software that can be utilized for creating video lectures and methods of deploying the videos (Hughes, 2009). Again, this session ties into the design of the course and whether instructors will utilize various media for delivery of their content.

Development

The training materials for the professional development program are produced during the development phase. These training materials include slides for live training and webinars, along with handouts and video tutorials for the website. The visual materials are developed using Mayer's Select, Organize, and Integrate method. This model requires highlighting the most important information for the user, structuring the text into outlines and headings, and integrating information into illustrations (Regieluth, 1999). Materials are developed prior to the beginning of the semester and edited between semesters based on formative evaluations. The training material development is a cyclic process due to technology upgrades. Being aware of upcoming changes is necessary. The instructional designers/trainers assist faculty with development of their course materials via training and/or one-on-one appointments that can be requested at any time during the process. Faculty members are urged to develop their materials with the same model. They are also encouraged to conduct formative evaluation of those materials with colleagues or students.

Implementation

During the implementation phase of the professional development program, faculty members are supported via group training, one-on-one assistance, on-demand video help, social gatherings, and colloquiums. The group training is a general overview of the system and tools, which allows the instructors to have guided assistance. During the group training, the instructional designers may also model troubleshooting skills if distance faculty members have technical difficulty during the training session. In order, to maintain time on task, there are typically an instructional designer and a graduate assistant delivering training.

One-on-one assistance is available for more advanced training or initial training for those faculty members with scheduling conflicts. One-on-one training includes hands-on assistance and may take place in the training room, faculty office, or via virtual classroom. For one-on-one trainings, instructors are encouraged to have course files available to work on their course at the time of training. The on-demand assistance is put in place for the emergency situation and can include attending virtual sessions or assisting with technical and pedagogical issues during instruction or testing. The on-demand training also includes shortened versions of the general training series in video format. The social gatherings and colloquiums are designed to allow faculty to share their course experiences with one another in formal and informal settings. These gatherings are held each month during the semester. The faculty member may choose to attend either the formal or informal setting depending on their availability and comfort level with the format.

One-on-One/On-Demand

One-On-One assistance is recommended to faculty members that have individualized needs during any stage of the ADDIE process. However, faculty members tend to utilize this service during the implementation stage of their online/web-enhanced course. The instructional design team manages the one-on-one appointments through a one-on-one calendar that tracks the frequency as well as training topics of these appointments. Most appointments are scheduled for one hour and can be conducted in the faculty's office . This data is also used to determine future training needs. This service is imperative to faculty support because they are able to work directly on their content at their convenience, which eliminates time constraints

and allows the faculty member to enhance their skills while working within their own curriculum materials. Hinson and LaPrairie (2005) suggest faculty working within their own curriculum can increases preparedness to teach online.

On-Demand Training is done on an as-needed basis. Faculty members can contact the instructional designers' office through a generic phone line or generic e-mail to receive emergency or on-demand assistance during business hours. This service is reserved for instances that need to be resolved immediately. For example, when an exam should be in progress but it has not been made visible within the learning management system. When the faculty calls or e-mails a help ticket is generated and the team resolves their issue immediately. The help ticket frequency and topic data is also tracked for reporting purposes and for future training ideas. The peak times for on-demand training are at the beginning of the semester and during mid-terms. The instructional designers are proactive and attempt to predict the common problems that will arise. Handouts and videos for common issues are created and deployed in the newsletter, on the website, and social media sites during these peak times.

Training materials are also published on a website that faculty can access at any time for assistance. These materials include training videos as well as printable handouts that are organized by topic. The training videos are a condensed version, less than fifteen minutes, of the live training. The asynchronous materials are available to meet the needs of those faculty members who are proficient with technology but need guidance with course design and development.

Social/Colloquium

In order to facilitate collegiality among faculty across various departments, socials and colloquiums are scheduled. The socials are held once a month in the evening at an informal cocktail setting. The cocktail setting enables the attendees to mingle with faculty in other departments. The location does not have Internet so participants feel more inclined to discuss pedagogy issues with the instructional designers as well as their colleagues. This setting also creates a community of learners/instructors and provides peer support. This service often benefits faculty during the implementation stage because they are able to discuss current issues with other faculty who may be in similar situations (Crawford & Cook, 2008).

The bi-monthly colloquiums are set as a roundtable discussion during business hours on a given topic. Guest speakers (faculty or students) are asked to present on these topics, which are determined through the faculty training needs assessment designed by the instructional designers/trainers. Past topics include copyright (fair use), ADA compliance, and creating online portfolios. Attendees are able to ask questions about how other faculty address issues. According to Taylor and McQuiggan (2008) faculty members benefit most from interactions with instructional designers and their experienced peers.

Evaluation

Formative evaluation is conducted throughout the academic year after each training series ends. Typically, formative evaluation is conducted throughout the development stage. Since technology changes rapidly, the instructional designers continually update the training as well as the materials. This is done formally through both qualitative and quantitative data gathered by an electronic survey. The one-on-one training is evaluated informally through conversations and with faculty. While updating the materials with the latest research, tools and more advanced features, the training format and delivery are revised based on the data collected.

The instructional designers have continually revised the general training series. The training began with a "follow along" concept in which the instructional designers would click the ap-

propriate link and the faculty would follow. Many "click-happy" instructors were not acquiring the pedagogy knowledge needed to teach because they were more focused on the technology itself. The training was then revised into a visual process using slides in which the instructional designers would show the faculty the tools visually via screen shots but did not have a hands-on section. Through formative evaluation, the instructors stated that hands-on time was very important; therefore, changes were made to the delivery where at certain points in the training, the instructional designers integrated timed hands-on section. The faculty members had the ability to "click" around yet it was still controlled and time on task was maintained.

Faculty members are also encouraged to have students complete voluntary formative evaluations of their course designs mid-semester and/or at the end of the semester to make decisions regarding improvement of the course content. Examples are provided to faculty by the instructional designers (Appendix D). This formative evaluation to improve course quality is optional for faculty and not monitored. Due to university accreditation processes, the instructional designer present at departmental meetings on the importance of course evaluation.

Summative evaluation is conducted at the end of the academic year to determine the services that will be provided or eliminated. The summative evaluation is based on the Kirkpatrick Model. The Kirkpatrick model is based on four levels: reaction, learning, performance, and impact. Reaction measures the instructor's perception of the training. Level two addresses the extent to which the instructors had a change in attitude, or increase of knowledge or skill. Behavior is measured in level three. This primarily addresses whether the instructor is now performing the new skill or knowledge. Level four addresses the overall effectiveness of the training (Kirkpatrick, 1994).

The instructional designers/trainers complete summative evaluations of the professional development program's content and delivery via electronic survey at the end of the training series. Faculty members are also urged to have their courses summatively evaluated by peers and students at the end of their courses to determine the course's value and worth. A peer review could be conducted by a colleague within their department or one of the instructional designer/ trainers utilizing a course design rubric such as Blackboard Exemplary Course Program (ECP) rubric (Appendix B). Student evaluation of the course design is an integral part of the Course Design Evaluation session and also a component of both the ECP rubrics. Such evaluation allows the students to feel they have an investment in the course design yet allows the instructor to make the necessary changes needed to the course.

FUTURE TRENDS

Currently the training series is optional for faculty. With the increase of online instruction, the need to set quality standards for course design and implementation is becoming more prevalent to school accrediting agencies. Therefore, more higher education institutions may see an increase in faculty becoming *certified* to design and implement distance education courses or setting policies to evaluate course design and implementation. Instructors that seek certification would require some professional development and possibly stipends during the semester they are designing and developing the course. Implementing these policy changes will require more budget dollars and administrative support. The instructional designers hope to use training evaluation and course achievement data to encourage these changes.

CONCLUSION

In conclusion, faculty will remain a diverse group with varied needs. While some faculty members are able to learn on their own through video tutorials, others may need multiple hands-on, one-one-one support. Higher education institutions need to re-consider professional development programs and be sure there are a variety of options for faculty to learn the pedagogy needed to design, develop, implement, and evaluate an online/web-enhanced course as well as integrate the tool training simultaneously. To increase the buy in faculty input on available options is imperative.

Professional development programs need to emphasize quality in course design so faculty will be able to meet the future standards enforced through accreditation agencies. Online or web-enhanced course design evaluation should become standard practice just as face-to-face peer observation and evaluation is standard. It will also be important to continually evaluate and revise course design rubrics to meet the ever changing technological advances.

Delivering professional development programs through various medias simultaneously is a relatively new practice. Measuring quality assurance of these types of professional development programs is an important topic for future research. Virtual training, especially synchronous delivery, is on the rise and participants expect equal quality as face-to-face training.

Peer support is an important aspect of professional development, particularly during the implementation phase of the design process. Peer support should be informally integrated into the professional development program, especially pertaining to delivering online/web-enhanced courses. Talking and listening to others that are in similar situations with comparable experiences increases the confidence of the "new" online instructor.

With the ever changing dynamic of technology and students, faculty will continually need support as well as training to deliver instruction on new technology platforms. Continually evaluating, revising, and updating the training program is paramount to continued success.

REFERENCES

Armstrong, G. (1996, May). One approach to motivating faculty to use multimedia. *T.H.E Journal, 23*, 69-71.

Beaudoin, M. (1990). The instructor's changing role in distance education. *American Journal of Distance Education, 4*(2), 21–29. doi:10.1080/08923649009526701

Blackburn, R. T., Boberg, A., O'Connell, C., & Pellino, G. (1980, June*). Project for faculty development program evaluation: Final report.* Ann Arbor, MI: University o Michigan, Center for the Study of Higher Education.

Blair, K., & Madigan, D. (2000). Involving faculty in faculty development: A recursive model. In D. Willis, et al. (Eds.), *Proceedings of Society for Information Technology & Teacher Education International Conference* (pp. 418-423). Chesapeake, VA: AACE.

Browne, N., Maeers, M., & Cooper, E. (2000). A faculty of education as a community of learners: Growing to meet the demands of instruction and technology. In Gillan, B., & McFerrin, K. (Eds.), *Faculty development. ERIC Document (ED444497).*

Conrad, D. (2004). University instructors' reflections on their first online teaching experiences. *Journal of Asynchronous Learning Networks, 8*(2), 31–44.

Crawford, C. M. (2002). *The design of a supportive faculty development model: The integration of technology within the university faculty's teacher candidate coursework.*

Crawford, C. M., & Cook, R. (2008). Creating and sustaining communities of learning within distance learning environments: Focusing upon making connections, creating communities of learning, and responsibilities. *International Journal of Learning, 15*(2), 179–193.

Dick, W., Carey, L., & Carey, J. (2005). *The systematic design of instruction* (6th ed.). New York, NY: Addison-Wesley Educational Publishers, Inc.

Finkelstein, J. (2006). *Learning in real time: Synchronous teaching and learning online.* San Francisco, CA: Jossey-Bass.

Horgan, B. (1998, August). Faculty, instruction and information technology. *The Technology Source.* Retrieved March 25, 2011 from http://ts.mivu.org/default.asp?show=article&id=75

Hughes, G. (2009). Using videos to bring lecture to the online classroom. *College Quarterly, 12*(1), Retrieved from http://www.collegequarterly.ca/2009-vol12-num01-winter/hughes.html

Keegan, D., Schwenke, E., Fritsch, H., Kenny, G., Kismihók, G., & Bíró, M. … Nix, J. (2005). *Virtual classrooms in educational provision: Synchronous elearning systems for European institutions.* Hagen, Germany: FernUniversitaet (ZIFF). Retrieved February 18, 2009 from: http://www.fernuni-hagen.de/ZIFF/synchronous.pdf.

Kirkpatrick, D. L. (1994). *Evaluating training programs: The four levels.* San Francisco, CA: Berrett-Koehler Publishers, Inc.

Knowlton, D. S. (2002). *Technology-enhanced courses versus traditional instruction: Empirical evidence, reflections from practice, and designing for maximum learning. The CyberPeer Newsletter.* Memphis, TN: Crichton Distance Education.

Lawler, P. A. (2003, Summer). Teachers as adult learners: A new perspective. In K. P. King & P. A. Lawler (Eds.), New directions for adult and continuing education (pp. 15–22). San Francisco, CA: Jossey-Bass. doi:10.1002/ace.95doi:10.1002/ace.95

Lee, J. A., & Busch, P. E. (2005). Factors related to instructors' willingness to participate in distance education. *The Journal of Educational Research, 99*(2), 109–115. doi:10.3200/JOER.99.2.109-115

Miller, T., & King, F. (2003). Distance education: pedagogy and best practices in the new millennium. *International Journal of Leadership in Education: Theory and Practice, 6*(3), 283–297. doi:10.1080/1360312032000118225

Molenda, M., & Boling, E. (2008). Creating. In Januszewski, A., & Molenda, M. (Eds.), *Educational technology: A definition with commentary* (pp. 81–139). New York, NY: Lawrence Erlbaum Associates.

Parsad, B., Lewis, L., Tice, P., & National Center for Education Statistics. (2008). *Distance education at degree-granting postsecondary institutions: 2006-07: First look.* Washington, DC: National Center for Education Statistics, Insitute of Education Sciences, U.S. Dept. of Education.

(1999). InReigeluth, C. M. (Ed.). Instructional-design theories and models: *Vol. 2. A new paradigm of instructional theory.* Hillsdale, NJ: Lawrence Erlbaum.

Reiser, R. A., & Dempsey, J. V. (Eds.). (2007). *Trends and issues in instructional design and technology.* Boston, MA: Pearson.

Rutherford, L., & Grana, S. (1995). Retrofitting academe: Adapting faculty attitudes and practices to technology. *Technical Horizons in Education Journal, 23*(2), 82–86.

Seels, B. B., & Glasgow, Z. (1998). *Making instructional design decisions* (2nd ed.). Upper Saddle River, NJ: Prentice-Hall, Inc.

Seels, B. B., & Richey, R. C. (1994). *Instructional technology: The definitions and domains of the field.* Washington, DC: Association for Educational Communications and Technology.

Taylor, A., & McQuiggan, C. (2008). Faculty development programming: If we build it, will they come? *EDUCAUSE Quarterly, 31*(3), 28–37.

Tsunoda, J. S. (1992, Fall). Expertise and values: How relevant is preservice training? *New Directions for Community Colleges, 79,* 11–20. doi:10.1002/cc.36819927904

U.S. Army Field Artillery School. (1984). *A system approach to training* (Course Student textbook; ST - 5K061FD92).

KEY TERMS AND DEFINITIONS

ADDIE: An acronym for analyze, design, develop, implement, and evaluate and is based on a systematic product development concept (Reiser & Dempsey, 2007).

Formative Evaluation: Conducted throughout the development stage in order to improve or refine the effectiveness of a program or training.

Instructional Designer: An expert in training and learning technologies who is responsible for all the methodological aspects of a training course.

Kirkpatrick Model: A model used to evaluate the effectiveness of training that identifies four levels of change that may take place as a result of training: Reaction, Learning, Behavior and Results.

Needs Assessment: A systematic study that incorporates data and opinions from varied sources in order to create, install, and evaluate educational products and services.

Systematic: (Systems approach and models for instruction): A logical, iterative process of identifying all the variables that can impact the quality of instruction, including its delivery, and then integrating information about each variable in the design, development, evaluation, and revision of the instruction (Dick, Carey & Carey 2005 p. 367).

Summative Evaluation: Judges a programs merit or worth one it has been implemented for the targeted learners.

APPENDIX A

1. Please rank your preferred delivery method for professional development. (1 is the most preferred)
   a. Face to face live training
   b. One-on-one training
   c. Online training
   d. "On-Demand" videos and handouts

2. If you have not yet attended the "Introduction to Web Enhanced/Online Instruction with Blackboard Learn" session, which delivery method would you prefer?
   a. Group
   b. One-on-one
   c. On-demand video
   d. N/A

3. Please choose the topics of interest you would like for OeL to offer as professional development sessions. (Choose all that apply.)
   a. Online Lectures
   b. Student Perspective of Online Courses
   c. Online Proctoring/Academic Integrity
   d. Revamping Syllabus for Online Class
   e. Online Design Decisions
   f. Respondus - (test creation software/Bb compatible)
   g. Plagiarism
   h. Live Virtual Class tips and tricks
   i. Virtual Office Hour Options
   j. Social Networking
   k. Team/Group Work Options for Online Students
   l. Copyright
   m. Electronic Portfolios
   n. Smart-boards
   o. Student Response Systems (Clickers)
   p. Design Decisions for Web-Enhanced Courses
   q. Digital Textbooks
   r. Use of Publisher Content
   s. Going Paperless - How to Web-Enhance your Course
   t. Applied Learning Online Activities
   u. Other, please specify

4. Please check whether you would utilize attend the following services or events. (yes/no)
   a. Course Design and Development
   b. Course Design Evaluation
   c. Evening Social
   d. Brown Bag lunch

5. Please enter any comments, concerns, topics, services, etc that you would like us to consider. (optional)

APPENDIX B

1. Introduction to Web Enhanced/Online Instruction with Blackboard Learn

Manage Files in Your Course

Skill

- Describe the different areas under Content Collection.

- Demonstrate the process of uploading a file from your computer to the Content Collection for a specific course and to All Course Content and when to use which one.

- Upload, download, and delete various types of files (.gif, .html, .jpg, .zip, .docx, .pdf., txt).

- Explain the use of the "Open in Web Folder" function.

Creating and Editing Course Content

Skill

- Understand how to change the Edit Mode views.

- Describe when to turn Edit Mode On or Off.

- Describe all the choices under Build Content.

- Edit using the Text Editor.

- Edit the HTML using the Toggle HTML Source Code function.

- Reposition items in the Course Menu and Main Content Area.

- Add Adaptive Release criteria for releasing content.

Adding items into Learning Modules

Skill

- Add, edit and delete Interactive Tools.

- Add, edit and delete Assessment Tools.

- Know when to use a Self and Peer Assessment and:

- Add, edit and delete questions and answers.

- Add a link to a tool.

- Create a Mash-up.

- Know when to use audio and video clips and:

- Add, edit and delete audio and video clips from content pages.

- Understand compatible file types for audio and video to be read via the web.

- List the plug-ins or helper applications that will be needed to view or hear the files.

APPENDIX C

2011 Blackboard Exemplary Course Program Rubric

The Blackboard Exemplary Course Program began in 2000 with the goal of identifying and disseminating best practices for designing engaging online courses and courses with online components.

Using the Blackboard Exemplary Course Program Rubric, instructors and course designers are able to evaluate how well their own course conforms to best practices for Course Design, Interaction and Collaboration, Assessment and Learner Support. Furthermore, they learn and better understand by internalizing the evaluation criteria, what makes an exemplary course?

The Blackboard Exemplary Course Program Rubric details a range of criteria to rate performance in each component of the course. The performance ratings are Exemplary, Accomplished, Promising, and Incomplete. Detailed feedback on expectations needed to meet to achieve a specific rating for each component in the course is provided. (refer to Figures 1, 2, 3, 4, 5, and 6).

Using the Blackboard Exemplary Course Program Rubric offers a number of advantages:

- The ECP Rubric allows course designers and instructors to become better judges of the quality of their own work. It provides detailed information about areas of strengths and areas of their course in need of improvement.
- The ECP Rubric allows assessment of online and hybrid/blended courses (those which have online and face-to-face components) to be more objective and consistent. An increased focus on student learning outcomes demands development of high quality courses whether they are fully online, or have online components.

- The ECP Rubric reduces the amount of time it takes to assess the quality and completeness of a course. This is especially helpful if you are using the rubric to assess the courses across a program of study or the work of multiple course developers.

For more information about the Blackboard Exemplary Course Program, best practices in course design, and examples of exemplary courses please visit http://www.blackboard.com/ecp.

Figure 1.

Course Design *(page 1 of 2)*
Course Design addresses elements of instructional design. For the purpose of this program, course design includes such elements as structure of the course, learning objectives, organization of content, and instructional strategies.

	Exemplary	Accomplished	Promising	Incomplete
Goals and Objectives	Goals and objectives are easily located within the course; are clearly written at the appropriate level and reflect desired outcomes; are written in measureable outcomes (students know what they are expected to be able to do), are made available in a variety of areas in the course (within the syllabus and each individual learning unit)	Goals and objectives are located within the course syllabus or the individual learning units; objectives are written to reflect desired learning outcomes, although not all are written as measureable outcomes; students have some understanding of what is expected of them;	Goals and objectives are not easily located within the course; are not clearly written in measurable learning outcomes; students may be unsure of what they are expected to be able to do; the level does not match the desired outcomes;	Goals and objectives are not easily located within the course; some are missing and others poorly written ; the level does not match the desired learning outcomes;	
Content Presentation	Content is made available or "chunked" in manageable segments (i.e., presented in distinct learning units or modules); navigation is intuitive; content flows in a logical progression; content is presented using a variety of appropriate mechanisms (content modules, single pages, links to external resources, RSS Feeds, print material); content is enhanced with visual and auditory elements; supplementary resources are made available (course CDs, textbooks, course manuals, etc.)	Content is made available or "chunked" in manageable segments (i.e., presented in distinct learning units or modules); navigation is somewhat intuitive, but some "exploring" is required to determine the flow of content; content is presented using a variety of mechanisms (content modules, single pages, links to external resources, RSS Feeds, print material); visual and/or auditory elements occasionally enhance the content; supplementary resources are made available (course CDs, textbooks, course manuals, etc.);	Some content segments are overly large (or possibly too small) for the specified objectives; navigation is only occasionally intuitive, thus the flow of content is sometimes not easily determined; the design does not avail of the content presentation tools (content modules, single pages, links); few or no visual and/or auditory elements are used to enhance the content; supplementary resources may be made available (course CDs, textbooks, course manuals, etc.)	Content is not "chunked" into manageable segments; navigation is not intuitive and the flow of content is unclear; the design does not avail of the content presentation tools (content modules, single pages, links); no visual or auditory elements are used to enhance the content; supplementary resources are not made available (course CDs, textbooks, course manuals, etc.)	

Course Design *(page 2 of 2)*

	Exemplary	Accomplished	Promising	Incomplete	
Learner Engage-ment	It is clear how the instructional strategies will enable students to reach course goals and objectives; course design includes guidance for learners to work with content in meaningful ways (e.g., pre-reading outlines, web-quests, devil's advocate challenges, etc.); higher order thinking (e.g., analysis, problem solving, or critical reflection) is expected of learners and explained with examples or models; individualized instruction, remedial activities, or resources for advanced learning activities are provided;	Instructional strategies are designed to help students to reach course goals and objectives, although this relationship may not be obvious to learners; guidance is provided, but could be improved with greater detail or depth; higher order thinking is required for some activities but is not well-explained or supported (e.g., by providing examples of "good answers"); differentiated instruction (such as remediation) may be available on a limited basis;	It is not clear how the instructional strategies will help learners achieve course course goals and objectives; guidance in using content materials may only be provided on a limited basis; higher order thinking is not required or encouraged; differentiated instructional opportunities are not provided, although there may be supplementary content resources available;;;	Instructional strategies do not provide students with skills needed to achieve course goals and objectives; content is provided but it is not clear what students are expected to do with it; higher order thinking is not expected from students; no supplementary resources or activities are provided for remediation or advanced study;	
Technology Use	Tools available within the CMS are used to facilitate learning by engaging students with course content; CMS tools are used to reduce the labor-intensity of learning (e.g., providing links to needed resources where they will be used in the course); technologies are used creatively in ways that transcend traditional, teacher-centered instruction; a wide variety of delivery media are incorporated into the course;	Tools available within the CMS could be utilized more (or more creatively) to engage learners with course content; CMS tools are made available to assist students, but could be organized or arranged for even greater usefulness; technologies within the course are used in many cases merely to replicate traditional face-to-face instruction; there is some variety in the tools used to deliver instruction;	Tools available within the CMS are not used to their full extent or not used when it would be appropriate to do so; only a few tools (of those available within the CMS) are used in a way that streamlines access to materials and activities for students; technologies within the CMS are used primarily by instructors and not students ("students as recipients of content" model); there is little variety in use of technologies within the CMS;	Technologies used within the CMS do not engage students with learning; tools that could reduce the labor-intensity of online instruction are not utilized; students are not expected to use technologies available within the CMS; only a few technologies available within the CMS are used;	

Figure 2.

Figure 3.

Interaction and Collaboration

Interaction and Collaboration can take many forms. The ECP criteria place emphasis on the type and amount of interaction and collaboration within an online environment.

Interaction denotes communication between and among learners and instructors, synchronously or asynchronously. Collaboration is a subset of interaction and refers specifically to those activities in which groups are working interdependently toward a shared result. This differs from group activities that can be completed by students working independently of one another and then combining the results, much as one would when assembling a jigsaw puzzle with parts of the puzzle worked out separately then assembled together. A learning community is defined here as the sense of belonging to a group, rather than each student perceiving himself/herself studying independently.

	Exemplary	Accomplished	Promising	Incomplete
Communication Strategies	There are plentiful opportunities for synchronous and/or asynchronous interaction, as appropriate; asynchronous communication strategies promote critical reflection or other higher order thinking aligned with learning objectives; synchronous communication activities benefit from real-time interactions and facilitate "rapid response" communication (i.e., students gain practice discussing course content extemporaneously without looking up basic, declarative information);	Several communication activities are included to reinforce the desired learning outcomes; asynchronous communications sometimes require reflection or other higher order thinking; synchronous interactions are meaningful but may not take full advantage of the real-time presence of instructor and/or peers;	Communication strategies are included, however, they may not consistently reinforce desired learning outcomes; asynchronous communications are focused primarily on lower levels of thinking (e.g., summarizing, describing, interpreting, etc.); synchronous interactions are used mostly for instructor explanation or clarification of content, or other instructor-focused activities;	Little to no attention has been devoted to communication strategies; interaction activies that are included do not invoke critical thinking, reinforce learning, or take advantage of the specific strengths of the communication tools used;
Development of Learning Community	Communication activities are designed to help build a sense of community among learners; student-to-student interactions are required as part of the course; students are encouraged to initiate communication with the instructor; collaboration activities (if included) reinforce course content and learning outcomes, while building workplace-useful skills such as teamwork, cooperation, negotiation, and consensus-building;	Communication activities may help learners build a sense of community, but do not appear to be designed with this in mind; some student-to-student interaction is built into the course; students interact with the instructor, although primarily as a result of instructor-initiated contact; collaboration activities (if included) support some team-building skills, but may not purposefully integrate these elements;	Effort has been devoted to fostering a sense of community in the course, but only minimally. More focus is needed on designing activities and a course climate that foster student-to-student interactions as well as student-to-instructor interactions.	Little to no attention has been devoted to building a sense of community in this course.
Interaction Logistics	Guidelines explaining required levels of participation (i.e., quantity of interactions) are provided; expectations regarding the quality of communications (e.g., what constitutes a "good" answer) are clearly defined; a rubric or equivalent grading document is included to explain how participation will be evaluated; the instructor actively participates in communications activities, including providing feedback to students; the instructor uses communication tools to provide course updates, reminders, special announcements, etc.;	Expectations of student participation in communication activities are given, but would benefit from more detail; expectations regarding the quality of communications are included, but may be sketchy and lack detail or illustrative examples; minimal information may be provided regarding grading criteria for communications activities; the instructor is occasionally involved in communication activities; the instructor sometimes takes advantage of CMS tools to post announcements, reminders, etc.;	Instructor expectations of student interactions are not made clear; little information is provided regarding what constitutes a "good" response or posting; students are not given a clear set of criteria for how communications activities will be graded; the instructor appears to be largely absent from communications activities; few announcements, reminders, or other updates are provided;	Few or no guidelines are provided to students regarding the desired quantity or quality of communications/interactions within the course; the instructor does not participate in communications activities with students;

Assessment

Assessment focuses on instructional activities designed to measure progress towards learning outcomes, provide feedback to students and instructor, and/or enable grade assignment. This section addresses the quality and type of student assessments within the course.

	Exemplary	Accomplished	Promising	Incomplete
Expectations	Assessments match the goals & objectives; learners are directed to the appropriate objective(s) for each assessment; rubrics or descriptive criteria for desired outcomes are provided (models of "good work" may be shown, for example); instructions are written clearly and with sufficient detail to ensure understanding;	Assessments match the goals & objectives; rubrics or descriptive criteria for desired outcomes are included for some assessment activities; instructions are written clearly, with some detail included;	Students are assessed on the topics described in the course goals and objectives; there may be some explanation of how assessments will be scored/graded; instructions lack detail that would help students understand how to complete the activities;	Assessments bear little resemblance to goals & objectives; expectations or grading criteria are not provided; instructions are limited or absent;
Assessment Design	Assessments appear to measure the performance they claim to measure (e.g., activities are explained using appropriate reading level and vocabulary); higher order thinking is required (e.g., analysis, problem-solving, etc.); assessments are designed to mimic authentic environments to facilitate transfer; assessment activites occur frequently throughout the duration of the course; multiple types of assessments are used (research paper, objective test, discussions, etc.)	Assessment activities have "face validity" (i.e., they appear to match the curriculum); some activities involve higher order thinking; assessment activities may focus on tasks similar to real-world application of skills; multiple assessments are included; at least three different types of assessments are used;	It is not clear whether the assessment activities actually measure the desired skill; the vast majority of assessments require only low-level thinking (memorization, for example); assessment activities typically do not include tasks that are relevant beyond the scope of this course; multiple assessments are included; two types of assessments are included, at a minimum;	Assessment activities appear to lack validity due to bias, lack of clarity in questions or tasks, or because students are evaluated on performance unrelated to the stated objectives; no higher-order thinking skills are required to complete assessment activities; there is little or no evidence of authenticity built into assessments; assessments are too few and far apart for the course content;
Self-assessment	Many opportunities for self-assessment are provided; self-assessments provide constructive, meaningful feedback;	Some self-assessment activities are included; self-assessments provide feedback to learners;	There may be self-assessment activities, but they are limited in scope and do not offer useful feedback;	A few self-assessments may be included, but they offer little more feedback than flash cards;

Figure 4.

Figure 5.

Learner Support *(page 1 of 2)*

Learner Support addresses the support resources made available to students taking the course. Such resources may be accessible within or external to the course environment. Specifically, learner support resources address a variety of student services including, but not limited to the following.

	Exemplary	Accomplished	Promising	Incomplete
Orientation to Course and CMS	Clearly labeled tutorial materials that explain how to navigate the CMS and the specific course are included; tutorials are found easily (few clicks) whether internal or external to the course, with easy return to other areas of the course; tutorial materials support multiple learning modalities: audio, visual, and text based;	Clearly labeled tutorial materials that explain how to navigate the CMS and the specific course are included; tutorials may not be easily accessed, or require the learner to leave course site without an easy return; tutorial materials support multiple learning modalities: audio, visual, and text based;	Tutorial materials that explain how to navigate the CMS and/or the specific course may be evident, but not easily found; materials do not support multiple learning modalities and are text-based only;	Tutorial materials explaining how to navigate the CMS or the specific course may be included but are difficult to find, lack detail, are not well organized, or are incomplete; tutorial materials that are included do not support multiple learning modalities;
Supportive Software (Plug-ins)	Clear explanations of optional and/or required software including any additional costs (in addition to the CMS) are provided within the course; software required to use course materials is listed with links to where it can be captured and installed; links are located within the course where learners will use the software (i.e., near the materials requiring its use);	Clear explanations of optional and/or required software (in addition to the CMS) are provided within the course; software required to use course materials is listed but links to where it can be captured and installed are not found near where it will be used;	Software (in addition to the CMS) required to use course materials is mentioned, but not explained; links to where it can be captured and installed are provided, although they may not be conveniently located;	The need for additional software required to use course materials may be mentioned; links to software may be missing or incomplete;
Instructor Role and Information	Contact information for the instructor is easy to find and includes multiple forms of communication (for example, e-mail, phone, chat, etc.); expected response time for e-mail replies is included; instructor's role within the course is explained (for example, whether he/she will respond to "tech support" type questions); the instructor's methods of collecting and returning work are clearly explained;	Contact information for the instructor is included but may not be easy to find; contact information includes more than one type of communication tool; expected response time for e-mail replies may be included; instructor's role within the course not clearly spelled out to students; the instructor's methods of collecting and returning work are clearly explained;	Contact information for the instructor is provided but not easy to find; contact information includes only one way to reach the instructor; no information concerning response time for e-mail replies is not included; little or no information is given regarding the instructor's role in the course; the instructor's methods of collecting and returning work are evident but not clearly explained;	Contact information for the instructor is sketchy, at best; no information concerning response time for e-mail replies is included; information regarding the instructor's role in the course is not included; Instructor's methods of collecting and returning work are confusing or non-existent;

Figure 6.

Learner Support (page 2 of 2)

	Exemplary	Accomplished	Promising	Incomplete
Course/ Institutional Policies and Support	Links to institutional policies, materials, and forms relevant for learner success (for example, plagiarism policies) are clearly labeled and easy to find; links allow easy navigation from the course to the information and back; course/instructor policies regarding decorum, behavior, and netiquette are easy to find and written clearly to avoid confusion; links to institutional services such as the library, writing center, or financial aid office are clearly labeled and easy to find;	Links to institutional policies, materials, and forms relevant for learner success (for example, plagiarism policies) are included but may require searching to find; links allow easy navigation from the course to the information and back; course/instructor policies regarding decorum, behavior, and netiquette are included and are written clearly to avoid confusion; links to institutional services such as the library, writing center, or financial aid office may be included but require searching to find;	Links to some institutional policies, materials, and forms relevant for learner success (for example, plagiarism policies) are included but are difficult to find; course/instructor policies regarding decorum, behavior, and netiquette are included but are not clearly written or would benefit from more detail; a few links to institutional services such as the library, writing center, or financial aid office may be included but require searching to find;	Links to some institutional policies, materials, and forms relevant for learner success (for example, plagiarism policies) are not included; some course/instructor policies regarding decorum, behavior, and netiquette may be included but are not clearly written or would benefit from more detail; links to institutional services such as the library, writing center, or financial aid office are not included;
Technical Accessibility Issues	Course materials use standard formats to ensure accessibility; if specific software is required to which some learners may not have access, alternative file types are provided; large files are identified to help learners consider download times; alternative (smaller) files are provided where appropriate; video are streamed whenever possible; graphics are optimized for web delivery and display without needing extensive scrolling;	Course materials use standard formats to ensure accessibility; if specific software is required to which some learners may not have access, alternative file types are sometimes provided; large files are not identified as such; alternative (smaller) files are not provided; video files are streamed in some cases; graphics are not be optimized for web delivery but display without extensive scrolling;	Course materials use standard formats to ensure accessibility; if specific software is required to which some learners may not have access, alternative file types are not provided; large files are not identified as such and alternative (smaller) files are not provided; video files are not streamed; graphics are not optimized for web delivery and may require extensive scrolling;	Course materials sometimes use standard formats to ensure accessibility; if specific software is required to access course materials, no mention of this is included and alternative file types are not provided; large files are not identified as such and alternative (smaller) files are not provided; video files are not streamed; graphic files are not optimized for web delivery and require extensive scrolling;
Accomm- odations for Disabilities	Supportive mechanisms allow learners with disabilities to participate fully in the online community; the design and delivery of content integrate alternative resources (transcripts, for example) or enable assistive processes (voice recognition, for example) for those needing accommodation; links to institutional policies, contacts, and procedures for supporting learners with disabilities are included and easy to find; design factors such as color, text size manipulation, audio and video controls, and alt tags reflect universal accessibility considerations;	Supportive mechanisms allow learners with disabilities to participate in the online community for most activities; the design and delivery of content integrate some alternative resources or enable assistive processes for those needing accommodation; links to institutional policies, contacts, and procedures to support learners with disabilities are included but may not be easy to find; design factors such as color, text size manipulation, audio and video controls, and alt tags have been considered in some cases;	Supportive mechanisms allow some learners with disabilities to participate fully in the online community; the design and delivery of content do not include alternative resources nor enable assistive processes for those needing accommodation; links to institutional policies, contacts, and procedures to support learners with disabilities are not evident; design factors such as color, text size manipulation, audio and video controls, and alt tags have not been considered;	Supportive mechanisms allow some learners with disabilities to participate in the online community for some activities; the design and delivery of content do not apply alternative resources nor enable assistive processes for those needing accommodations; links to institutional policies, contacts, and procedures to support learners with disabilities are not evident; design factors such as color, text size manipulation, audio and video controls, and alt tags have not been considered;
Feedback	Learners have the opportunity to give feedback to the instructor regarding course design *and* course content both during course delivery *and* after course completion; feedback mechanisms allow students to participate anonymously in course evaluation;	Learners have the opportunity to give feedback to the instructor regarding course design and/or course content, but only after course completion; feedback mechanisms allow students to participate anonymously in course evaluation;	Learners have the opportunity to give feedback to the instructor regarding course design or course content, but only after course completion; feedback mechanisms do not guarantee privacy to the student;	Learners do not have the opportunity to give feedback to the instructor regarding course design or course content; feedback mechanisms do not guarantee privacy to the student;

APPENDIX D

1. Please discuss the effectiveness of the instructor.

2. What would you like to see the instructor do differently?

3. What would you like to see changed in the course (regarding course design)?

4. Discuss the virtual classroom environment and any changes you would like to see.

5. Do the office hours and other points of contact (email, phone) meet your needs? If not, please provide suggestions on how these points of contact could improve.

Chapter 4
The Networked Learning Framework:
A Model for Networked Professional Learning Utilizing Social Networking Sites

Nathaniel Ostashewski
Athabasca University, Canada

Doug Reid
Wayfinder Education Group, Canada

ABSTRACT

This chapter describes the Networked Learning Framework (NLF), a networked learning model utilized in the development of a networked teacher professional development (nTPD) program. The NLF is a model which combines the use of social media tools found in common social networking sites with guided online activities to deliver innovative and engaging learning opportunities. One implementation of the NLF, the nTPD Courselet, delivered in a social networking site for Alberta teachers, is described in detail. Teachers report that the sharing of resources, reflective blogs, and collegial discussions are the most valuable outcomes of nTPD Courselets. Design principals and factors for designers of faculty PD developers to follow when using the Networked Learning Framework, as well as descriptions of two other NLF implementations, are presented in the chapter. Further research to identify effective supports for social networking novices and ways to build online facilitator capacity are needed.

SOCIAL MEDIA AND EDUCATION

There is little doubt that digital media continues to transform how people create, share and collaborate in our ever increasingly globalized world. Technology is recognized as the primary method people use to stay in contact, collaborate with others, and increasingly to be in control of their own learning (Johnson, Smith, Levine, & Haywood, 2010). Social media technologies are becoming pervasive in work environments and digital media literacy comes to the fore as a key skill in almost every profession (New Media Consortium, 2010). As our societies transition from the Information

DOI: 10.4018/978-1-4666-1963-0.ch004

Age to the Social Media Age, education is one area that stuggles to make sense of that transition.

Educators are facing many challenges as social media technology becomes more prevalent. One pressing challenge for education is to identify and share ways in which social media technologies can be implemented into educational environments. Outside of the classroom, new media technologies underscore every part of student life as tools for social networking, online collaboration, and media sharing are all rapidly maturing and becoming accessible online (Hovorka & Rees, 2009). As with any transition in education practices, teacher professional development and training is key in bringing about changes that make a difference for students.

A second challenge that education systems are facing is increasing learner demands for on-line learning opportunities. Online enrollments continue to rise (Allen & Seaman, 2010) in both K-12 and post-secondary education and these levels still show few signs of leveling off. Despite recent questions about the quality of online learning, academic leaders report that online learning is of comparable or better quality remain than face-to-face learning (Allen & Seaman, 2010). Three quarters of the public school districts in the United States offer online or blended courses and it is anticipated that these online enrollments numbers will continue to grow (Allen & Seaman, 2008) for some time yet. Several reasons exist for the rising enrollments. For example, online learning opportunities allow students in rural areas or small school districts to provide learners with course choices that could not otherwise be offered (Picciano & Seaman, 2008). Flexibility is another example of a reason that online learning is becoming more and more sought. Despite this demand, administrators report that fewer than 30 percent of educators (Allen & Seaman, 2009) accept the value of online education. As enroll-ments increase, the need for educators who can provide quality online experiences for students will continue to be an issue.

Educators in the emerging Social Media Age are charged with the task of creating learning activities that include social media, although few have any formal training in digital technolo-gies and social media (Whitehouse, Reynolds, & Caperton, 2009). This challenge to educators is compounded by the fact that social media technologies are emerging more quickly than they can be integrated into course material and textbooks. Even newly graduated teachers are sorely behind in their knowledge of this types of media technologies in which they are expected to be skilled practitioners. A national study of K-12 teachers found that online teachers felt that their teacher education did not prepare them adequately for teaching online (Archambault, 2011). One solution suggested was that teachers themselves need to take online courses as part of their teacher preparation.

Teacher professional development (TPD) that focuses on the integration of these new technolo-gies into teaching practice is critical. At the same time the access to timely, ongoing, and relevant TPD opportunities to meet these kinds of needs in an effective way continues to be a challenge for administrators and educational planners. Par-ticularly so when one-day seminars and lectures have been recognized as a rather ineffective way of providing technology TPD. Today's teachers must be adaptive experts and lifelong learners, continually seeking and developing knowledge and skills, rather than working to acquire a core set of skills to be used for an entire career (White-house, Reynolds, & Caperton, 2009). Online teacher professional development (oTPD) has been identified as one type of TPD that is capable of fulfilling these needs in this emerging Social Media Age (Dede, Ketelhut, Whitehouse, Breit, & McCloskey, 2009; Herrington, Herrington, Hoban, & Reid, 2009; Vrasidas & Glass, 2004), particularly where the access to high quality oTPD activities has been identified as critically important (Borko, 2004).

One way to measure the success of TPD is to determine how effective the learning opportunities are for teachers. The characteristics of teacher professional development that makes an impact on teaching practice is a key concern for education administrators and planners. Desimone (2009) reports that there is recent research consensus on the critical characteristics of effective TPD. These features include content focus, active learning, coherence, duration, and collective participation. Of these features, content focus and how students learn that content was considered the most influential for teacher professional development success. The oTPD implementation described in this chapter encompasses all these essential features.

With respect to teacher professional development activities, online digital media capabilities affect the nature and methods of teaching and learning that can take place. The term "Learning 2.0 web" has been used by Whitehouse, Reynolds & Caperton (2009) to describe these newest technologies that require a demand-pull rather than supply-push teaching and learning approach. They argue further that the Learning 2.0 web may also provide unique opportunities for meeting education's online learning challenges and needs. It is in this mileau of online social media and technologies that the potential of networked learning can and is being realized, both informally and with guidance and design, in more formal course spaces. One implementation that utilizes the Learning 2.0 web is the nTPD Courselet that has been designed using a learning design model called the Networked Learning Framework (NLF).

COURSELETS

The information reported in this chapter is part of an ongoing design-based program of research centered on the development, design, and evaluation of "Courselets,"; a delivery model for online teacher professional development using content-focused instructional packages. Courselets involve about 10-15 hours of teacher interaction time delivered in a website (Ostashewski, 2010; Ostashewski & Reid, 2010a). The courselet structure has the potential to provide learning opportunities that are both inexpensive and scaleable when delivered in an online social networking site.

The online learning experiences designed into Courselets are valuable to teachers in two ways; firstly providing an opportunity to use new communication technology tools to learn online, and secondly to have the access to specialized TPD at a distance. Using online forums, blogs, video, and other social media embedded in the oTPD delivery provides numerous opportunities for teacher-centered online learning experiences. Delivered within a social networking site, Ostashewski and Reid (2010b) have described this specific type of oTPD as networked teacher professional development (nTPD). One of the goals of this chapter is to describe and identify the components of nTPD and provide design principals that can be utilized by other oTPD developers and planners. The use of a social networking site, characterized as a Mashup of Web 2.0 tools, to deliver nTPD activities has advantages over other types of online delivery platforms.

Networked Teacher Professional Development (nTPD)

There are three main advantages of utilizing an online social networking framework as the delivery platform for nTPD activities. First, the online platform supports and encourages teachers to learn collaboratively, while allowing them to retain personal control over time, space, presence, activity level, identity, and relationships (Anderson, 2006). Traditionally the demands on teachers' time and lack of selection for personally relevant TPD activities results in one-time, PD workshop sessions which have been well documented to have little transition to classroom practice (Borko, 2004). However, the delivery of PD through online social networking allows teachers to control their access and participation in practice-relevant activities.

The second advantage of nTPD is that it promotes the development of teacher relationship networks which teachers can access to support their classroom teaching practices beyond the more formal nTPD activities. Profiles, "friending", private member messaging, and chat features of social networking sites allow for convenient searching and communicating between site members. Members of social networks can unobtrusively learn about other member's interests and shared resources prior to engaging in conversations with them. Additional motivation for teachers to continue using the tools on the site come from this sharing of online resources and access to communication tools found on the online site.

And thirdly, the delivery of nTPD via a social networking site provides teachers with firsthand experiential learning about online technologies using tools such as blogs, forums, hyperlinks, video and file sharing. The opportunity to actively engage with online tools for the purpose of creating engaging in practice-centered learning provides teachers with an invaluable experience of how online technologies might be used in their own classrooms.

Emerging research is beginning to show that nTPD activities provide teachers with new ways of learning with other teachers. Results of recent research (Ostashewski & Reid, 2010b; Whitehouse, 2010) provides evidence that identifies that the a variety of learning can occur in nTPD activities. These activities include:

1. Teachers become learners with their students.
2. Teachers learn virtually by discussing their practice with other teachers online.
3. Teachers learn by stealth (browsing class wikis).
4. Teachers are exposed to virtual mentoring.

These kinds of learning activities stem from the networked nature of the activities and may in fact provide a unique solution for teacher professional learning.

Networked Learning Framework (NLF)

The Courselets and other learning situations have all been prepared based on a networked learning design model called the Networked Learning Framework (NLF). The NLF utilizes social networking tools and processes to support teacher learning and practice. As well it is an instructional design model for learning designed for delivery within social networking sites and is the basis for the design framework of the nTPD Courselet. Other learning design implementations of the NLF are also presented in this chapter to describe additional contexts where this type of learning design could be utilized.

In summary, the primary objective of this chapter is to fully detail and describe an evidenced-based model of networked teacher professional development which can be utilized when developing online teacher professional development. This type of TPD is specifically teacher profession-centered learning within an online learning community that shares common curricular interests and needs. The foci of the discussion has three key components, including describing how the nTPD model utilizes online technologies such as blogs, discussion forums, and file-sharing. A second focus is on the sharing and discussion around profession-centered resources. The third focus is the utilization of social media and social networking to allow teacher-learners to "network" with other educators in ways they choose or wish to pursue.

Background to the Development of The Networked Learning Framework

The term online teacher professional development can be ascribed to a variety of oTPD implementations (Sinha, Rosson, Carroll, & Du, 2010) including the nTPD Courselet. Sinha et al (2010) identify that there exists a need to differentiate between oTPD communities, oTPD resource sites, and oTPD course delivery sites. The purpose and affordances of an oTPD learning environment has a direct impact of the potential connections teachers can make with each other before, during, and after a formal learning oTPD event occurs. This led to our definition of nTPD as a sub-type of oTPD. We define networked teacher professional development as a group of activities delivered in an online social networking environment that supports and encourages teachers to learn together, both formally and informally, while allowing them to retain control over their time, space, presence, activity level, identity, and relationships (Ostashewski & Reid, 2010b). In sum, there are three characteristics of networked teacher professional development that are key to the overall concept:

1. nTPD allows teachers a technology facilitated opportunity to develop a network of relationships which they can access to support their classroom teaching practices beyond the more formal oTPD activities.
2. nTPD provides teachers with firsthand experiential learning about online social media tools such as blogs, forums, video and file sharing that affords teachers an authentic experience of how online tools can be used in their own classrooms.
3. nTPD allows teachers to participate in professional learning that is just-in-time, accessible, and that is potentially self-guided.

This process of defining nTPD ties it to the description of the Networked Learning Framework used to develop and create the learning activities of the nTPD Courselet.

The nTPD Courselet was developed for teacher professional development for a collaborative online environment called www.2Learn2Gether.ca (Ostashewski, 2010). This online environment was developed as a location for teachers around the province of Alberta, Canada to collaborate using social networking. It provided members with

tools commonly found in social networking sites like Facebook. Collaboration on this site involved user-created groups, discussion forums, personal and group blogs, event calendars, and the sharing of a variety of format of files all on one website. The development of nTPD, which is a specially structured form of oTPD, was one major intiative in the growth of this community of educators that evolved over time. Revisions to individual Courselets and the whole Courselet design process were based on a pilot study (Ostashewski & Reid, 2010a) and led to the development of a learner management system within the social networking site. Continuing evaluations and research around Courselet implementation resulted in the further revisions resulting in the current nTPD model. The resultant nTPD model described in this chapter is intended for a fully online, continuous intake delivery of a module of study focussed on a topic-specific curricular practice within a social networking site.

As a result of research during the development of the nTPD Courselet model, a networked learning instructional design model, the Networked Learning Framework (NLF) was developed. The NLF is informed by research into online learning, distance education, media in education, and social networking fields. The NLF will be presented in detail throughout this chapter describing the theoretical background of the Networked Learning Framework, the nTPD Courselet design principals, and details of other NLF implementations that are relevant to professional development or learning.

The Network Learning Framework (NLF) is a instructional design model which takes advantage of social networking site affordances in the design of formal learning activities. Presently many formal online learning activities for learners have been developed in formal learning systems, such as WebCT or Moodle. However the NLF attempts to leverage the member connections inherent in a social networking site. Figure 1 presents a diagram of the Networked Learning Framework.

Figure 1. Networked learning framework

The organizational structure of the NLF is represented by a series of concentric rings representing the most important part of the learning process – learner interactions with the learning environment. In the NLF these interactions can be:

- With other learners or information within the group,
- With other learners or information within the social networking site, or
- With other learners or information available within the collective.

In the case of the NLF, all interactions between the learner are controlled by the learner. However the path through interactions with resources or others may be identified by the facilitator, other learners, or even the learning resources.

At the center of the NLF model is the learner. While working through the program of studies designed using the NLF, the learner participates in a series of activities correlating to internalized learner conceptualizations. The NLF activities – Engage, Explore, Discuss, Create – are intended to engage the learner and to result in new information being assimilated or created as a result of the learning experiences. The internalized learner conceptualizations represented in the NLF are sequential in presentation to the learner and take the learner from perception, to deliberation, to conception, and finally action with regards to the content of the program of learning. In this way, the actual activities learners participate during the program of studies are designed to lead them through the series of learner conceptualizations that build a cohesive understanding of the subject.

The concentric rings of the NLF represent learner access to the global network of data. As already mentioned, the learner is at the center of the NLF and belongs to the "group" of learners participating together for the explicit purpose of learning a particular subject. Learners interest in exploring the subject drives their joining and further participation in the group. The group is the vitual space in which the learning activities – engage, explore, discuss, create – take place during the learning process.

The social networking site is the next larger structure in which the group resides. The learner belongs to a membership of individuals who can further support the learning as the social networking site is a large network of connected members who have many tools by which they can communicate and share information. Learners can access members of the site to support the learning occurring within the members of the group. An example of this would be a learner following tags regarding the subject of learning to an expert, or perhaps following another social networking site member who has posted blogs or resource links about the subject.

The outside ring of the NLF is the Collective. The Collective is composed of all globally available digital information from information websites, to online databases, to search engines and global social networking sites. Much of the information available in the Collective is freely available, however subscribed materials could also be a part of the collective "information" available for the learner to access. An example of an interaction of the learner and the Collective would be the learner "searching" for information on a search engine such as Google or Yahoo, and following suggested links to resources that support the subject being explored. A second example would be the learner accessing other networked data that leads to yet other kinds of online collections (i.e. museums, online repositories, etc...) where information relevant to the subject being learned is found by the learner.

Four learning activities engage learners in the learning process over the course of the learning program. The first activity is to ENGAGE the learner with the current research and information relating to the subject of study. Having learners explore the context of the subject allows them to situate their own initial understandings and concepts regarding the subject. This is accomplished by having the learner examine subject materials and engage in reflections and discussions with other group members.

The second activity strives to provide for the learner to EXPLORE the subject in greater detail. Connections and learner interactions with resources that can be found in the Collective are discovered and shared during Explore phase of activities of the NLF. This identification of resources is potentially a collaboration among learners and facilitators leading to the next phase of the model.

The third NLF learning activity, DISCUSS, focusses on learner discourse with other people regarding the subject and practices in that field. Learner understanding and knowledge of the subject is refined in this phase of activities. Key in this activity is the learner reflecting and negotiating meaning of the content with other learners.

The fourth learning activity is the CREATE activity where the learner is tasked with developing a new artifact related to the subject of the learning. This artifact is shared with other learners in the group. The sharing of the artifacts is intended to both motivate learners and allow for other people to examine and discuss these artifacts further.

As with any type of learning program, there is a variety of lengths of programs of learning from several weeks to several months. This allows for the potential to have learners work through several cycles of learning in the NFL model. In shorter programs of study (i.e. six to eigth weeks) developed using the NLF model, the learning activities – Engage, Explore, Discuss, Create – may only cycle once on a particular subject. Other longer learning programs (i.e. four months or longer) may have learners cycle through numerous iterations of the phases of learning activities exploring a series of related subjects.

Several unique characteristics of the NLF instructional design model make it very useful for the development of programs of study which are profession-centered or long-term learning types of study. The first, and perhaps most interesting of these characteristics is that it allows for the persistance of the "group" learning space over time, providing learners for access to the group space for as long as they wish. Resources, conversations, artifacts and relationships are then able to persist over time. This allows for the option for members to continue to participate in the group without having a mandated learning outcome and activities prepared by designers or facilitators. This gives members the control of the group and people can participate as much or as little as they would like for as long as they want.

The second key characteristic of the NLF involves a inherent component of social networking sites called the "personal profile" tool. Personal profiles are one way in which these sites foster members "finding" commonality amongst each other and forming relationships on their own. In fact, that is the basis for the "social" part of a social networking site. A third characteristic of the NLF is the "group" forming capability of the social networking structure. This group creation capability of the social networking website is key and becomes the primary online learning space presented to learners. The formal learning occurs in this group space and is the common virtual "place" where learners take part in the online activities.

A final key unique characteristic of the NLF is that it can be used to design implementations which incorporate a system of continuous enrollment and completion, a capability demanding considerable administration in most learning management systems.

Theoretical Underpinings of the Networked Learning Framework

The Networked Learning Framework has a basis in the current literature regarding learning and professional development. The NLF evolved and is informed by previous research in distance education including the Practical Inquiry Model (Garrison, Anderson & Archer, 2001), the Networks concept (Dron and Anderson, 2009) and the Web-based Problem-based Learning (PBL) model (Malopinsky, Kirkley, and Stein, & Duffy, 2000).

The theoretical basis from which the NLF originates is a constructivist pedagogy acknowledging the situated, reflective, and social nature of learning. Constructivist and constructionist approaches contextualize the activities in the Networked Learning Framework. In this model, constructionism is viewed as the instructional approach which has the potential to support meaningful active learning artifacts to meet the needs of networked connectionist (Papert, 1992) distance education.

Numerous definitions of constructionism are found in the literature, but one of the simplest is the following: "constructionism boils down to demanding that everything be understood by being constructed" (Papert & Harel, 1991, p. 2). Hands-on learning, learning by doing, and learning through constructive play or gaming are other descriptions of the application of constructionism and provide insight into the application of this learning theory. Constructionism shares the constructivist connotation of learning as building knowledge structures irrespective of the circumstances of the learning. It then adds the idea that this happens especially felicitously in a context where the learner is consciously engaged in constructing a public entity, whether it is a sand castle on the beach or a theory of the universe (Papert & Harel, 1991, p. 1). According to constructionism theory, tools, digital media, artifact construction, and reflective discourse on the artifact are the basis of new knowledge construction.

Similarly, the Social Media web provides a framework where learners are equipped with a constantly expanding array of online digital tools allowing them to construct and share their digital artifacts instantly with others around the world, a feat that Papert and others probably considered impossible 30 years ago. The following four tenets of constructionism as a learning theory have been identified by Bers, Ponte, Juelich, Viera, & Schenker (2002) provide a context for the NLF approach:

1. Learning occurs by designing meaningful projects and sharing them in a community,
2. Manipulation of objects helps concrete thinking about abstract phenomena,
3. Powerful ideas come from different realms of knowledge,
4. And self-reflective practice and discourse with others is crucial.

The Networked Learning Framework Design

The NLF is an instructional design model for developers of networked, professional or connectivist learning implementations. As a constructionist implementation the activities are intended to be delivered in a manner that engages learners in "doing" and "creating" as the significant driver for learning. As discussed earlier, the four cornerstone activities of the Networked Learning Framework are as follows:

1. ENGAGE with research and practices: new understandings come from learner interactions with content, environment, and other learners.
2. EXPLORE resources and strategies: cognitive conflict is a learning stimulus for determining what is learned.
3. DISCUSS ideas and potentials: knowledge evolves through continued reflection and social negotiation.
4. CREATE implementations and share practices: networks provide opportunities for learners to explore, contribute, and validate new knowledge.

As well, developers should recognize that a primary driver of the learning in an NLF implementation is the CREATE event that results in the production of an authentic artifact, generated as a result of the learning. Both "learning how to learn" and "constructing artifacts" are crucial to making the event activities of the NLF relevant, situated, and socially constructed. As such developers should be concerned that this Create event should result in a valuable artifact for the learner and the group of learners as a whole. In our experience, learners both appreciate and are futher motivated to create artifacts if there is a value of the final product to themselves or others. One example is where learners studying the subject of social media create an example of the use of particular type of social media to share with other members of the learning group. Another example is where a group of educators "creates" and shares a series of lesson plans or resources that is valuable to the whole group of learners.

In order to be successfully used in the design of a learning program, the NLF requires three critical design factors to be incorporated in the delivery: a social network, a facilitator, and social media tool useage. The first design factor of the Networked Learning Framework is the online environment in which it occurs which is a mashup of Web 2.0 technologies that forms the basis of a social net-

working site. Examples of such Mashups are Ning, Facebook, and Elgg implementations. Inherent in these systems is the ability of members to create groups. In the case of the NLF the purpose of creating the groups is to create the virtual space where learners come together to participate in a particular learning program. This group creation capability of the social networking site is precisely with what Dron and Anderson (2007, p.7) identify when stating that social networking sites may "spawn groups that are created to meet emergent needs usually associated with explicit leadership and a focused task."

A second design factor of the Networked Learning Framework is the role of the facilitator. As with online course moderation, the role of an online facilitator is significantly different than someone who simply answers learner questions. This role requires someone familiar with the processes of online facilitation and social media tools. Tasks the facilitator conducts include managing group membership, pointing to or developing supporting media, providing helpdesk comments, promoting discussions, and providing guidelines for activity progress. The facilitator also needs other e-moderation skills in order to lead reflective and supportive online discourse, such as knowing when and how groups need motivational support to keep activities from stagnating. Our research in online tutor competencies (Reid, 2002) guides our description of the role of the facilitator in the Networked Learning Framework. Categories of competencies (Reid, 2003) we have identified as crucial for facilitators are:

1. Content expertise: analysis of student questions, having students do relevant educational tasks, enriching students interactions with the content through finding & providing appropriate content resources.
2. Course management: offering, managing and administrating the online educational experience.

3. Evaluation: evaluation of the entire online educational offering, providing assessment for students as well as evaluating the course and planning changes, modifications or corrections to improve the entire online educational experience.
4. Process facilitation: understanding of online process, personal characteristics and online communication skills.
5. Technical knowledge: technical skills and comfort with the use of technology.

An *educational tour guide* is one analogy that provides another way of looking at this factor in the Networked Learning Framework. An example of how the role of the facilitator is important in the NLF is that a facilitator would avoid one-to-one communications with learners and guide online discourse toward group learning opportunities. Without an experienced and conscientious online tour guide, the learning activities of a Networked Learning Framework program may quickly become meaningless and disjointed resulting in little or no value to the learning experience.

Since the facilitator is such a key design factor of the NLF, it behooves us to speak about how we believe this educational tour guide role can be nurtured. One way is to mentor and support existing online educators who would already be familiar with online teaching methods. As part of an NLF design, many of the media supports and guiding message posts can be developed prior to being delivered to the learners buy a design team that is very familiar with social media tools. We have observed that the facilitator role engages in a significant amount of administrative tasks at the start of a learning event, and as the event unfolds over time, the task switch to more supportive and motivational type tasks. Mentoring or co-facilitating the NLF activities are methods that we have found can result in capable online educational facilitators of the kind needed for this type of implementation.

The third design factor of the NLF are the social media tools available in the social networking site, and specifically how the tools can be utilized in designing activities around the four cornerstone events (Engage, Explore, Discuss, Create). These social media tools come in various shapes and forms, often being plug-in type applications. The networking toolset provides for what Anderson (2009) describes as the "affordances of self-paced learning technologies." These social networking toolsets include some or all of the following social media tools listed in no particular order:

- Member profiles
- Search functions: site, members, tags
- Member "friending" and messaging capabilities
- Group management functions
- Blogs
- Discussion forums
- File sharing
- Tagging
- Live chat
- Microblogging
- Wiki pages
- Social bookmarking
- Video/Image hosting and display
- Calendars

Delivery of the NLF cornerstone activities includes the use of a variety of these tools over the course of the learning event. Activity instructions are managed and presented to learners in wiki pages. Blogs are used for personal reflection activities and discussion forums for threaded conversations between learners. Tagging, social bookmarking, and file sharing are used for pointing and sharing resources between learners. Video presentation (either internal or external) is used for providing helpdesk support, activity introductions or support, and promoting facilitiator-learner socialization. These are some of the ways in which the social networking tools have been utilized in delivery of the NLF learning events we have developed and refined over the past several implementations. We next turn our attention to a description of the nTPD Courselet implementation of the Networked Learning Framework.

The nTPD Technology Courselet

As previously discussed, the Networked Learning Framework is the instructional design model which guides the development of activities for an nTPD Courselet implementation. However, the NLF is intended as a general professional learning or networked learning design model, not one specific to teacher professional development. Therefore a second source of data informs the nTPD Technology Courselet model, which is current body of research literature on effective TPD.

A distinct set of characteristics of effective teacher professional development has been identified in the literature (Desimone, 2009; Schwille et al., 2007). Schwille et al., (2007) identify two key dimensions of effective TPD: core features and core structures. The core features are a focus on content, active learning, and coherence. The core structures are duration, form, and participation. Desimone (2009) affirmed that recent research reflects a consensus about some of the characteristics critical to effective TPD that increases student achievement: content focus, active learning, coherence, duration, and collective participation. With these effective TPD characteristics in mind, the development of a successful nTPD Courselet required that these characteristics were present in the nTPD implementation.

Building from these TPD design principles, and taking into consideration the lessons learned from ongoing TPD delivered in the 2Learn2Gether.ca social networking site, an nTPD Courselet model evolved. A series of seven design principles have been developed based on theoretical, pedagogical, and practical considerations of nTPD delivery. These seven design principles are presented below with a description of the corresponding nTPD Courselet learning activities that were designed for teachers to participate in during the Courselet. These principles intersect with the organizational structures of the NLF: the group, the social networking site, and the collective. The design principles are:

1. Design learning relevant to teacher professional practice.
   a. Ensure that the resources and the learning experiences are relevant to the learner.
   b. Situate learning in current teaching challenges.
   c. Design the learning activities so that they lead to an outcome that can be applied in teacher professional practice.
2. Provide for easy teacher access designing for flexibility and ongoing support
   a. Provide short focused Courselets addressing specific technology issues.
   b. Design activities to allow for flexibility and teacher choice in activities
3. Provide theoretically and pedagogically sound activities
   a. Provide a rich array of resources to support the learners' individual needs.
   b. Support the teacher in linking conceptual understanding and practical application.
   c. Provide activities that engage teachers with the content area using technology tools.
4. Provide support for learners with varied experience levels
   a. Provide a scaffolded educational environment that supports learning and reflection for a variety of learners.
   b. Scaffold teacher opportunities for inquiry, engagement, and reflection.
   c. Make available pre-Courselet materials (in a variety of formats) to support tool use for new social networking site users.

5. Provide authentic opportunities for networked learning skill development
   a. Provide external resources as primary content.
   b. Design activities to utilize blog and forum contributions.
   c. Provide online lesson plan tools.
6. Support sharing and discourse between learners
   a. Design activities that focus on reflective practice.
   b. Design activities that lead to meaningful learner discourse.
   c. Provide opportunities for teacher collaboration
7. Support learning connections to the broader networked community
   a. Utilize information sources external to the group
   b. Identify and share other potential sources of content information

When developing an nTPD offering and making use of these design principles as the basis for development, our research indicates that teachers will be provided with meaningful, "worth-it" PD that is quite different from other types of TPD. As Whitehouse (2010) states and we concur, the networked learning environment blurs the meaning of "present" as teachers work across time and location bringing new experiences of learning from social networking sites. This is therefore the potential that our nTPD research continues to strive for - to create opportunities for new teacher learning experiences online.

Delivery

While the design principles of the nTPD Courselet have been described, it is likely helpful to educators to clearly understand which social media technologies were used in our nTPD implementations as the model was honed. The nTPD Courselet

structure provided the following elements for teacher participants at the start of the Courselet:

- **Courselet Overview:** A short description of the Courselet goals and outcomes of participation.
- **Courselet Activity Guide:** Presented links and participant expectations for each week of Courselet activities. Instructions and links to external articles and websites, as well as internal Courselet videos were described in each of the weekly activity guides.
- **Group Blogs:** With it's threaded comments tools are used by participants to track their own professional growth and challenges during the nTPD activities.
- **Personal Blogs:** Used in some Courselets to allow participants to make private posts or public within the social networking site, but not constricted to the group space.
- **Discussion Forum:** Used to initiate discussions to support the TPD activities that the facilitator moderated.
- **Embedded Videos:** Included instructional segments on tools found within the Courselet, such as "how to post a blog" as well as external content exemplars found presented from YouTube.
- **Event Calendar**: Listing dates or suggested start times for activities within the Courselet.
- **External Social Bookmarking Site**: External site used to provide a collection of links around the specific topic being explored in the Courselet.
- **File Sharing Folder**: The file-sharing capability allows documents, such as additional "how to" guides, to be readily available for teacher participants. As well as the file-sharing capability made it possible for participants to upload images that demonstrated completed activities and share documents such as lesson plans.

- **List of Courselet Participants**: Provides easy access to profiles of Courselet participants to all participants

Evaluations of nTPD Courselet Delivery

Design-based research (DBR) has been used in the research and development of the nTPD Courselet. Design-based research can be differentiated from predictive research as the goal of DBR is to develop, evaluate, implement, and disseminate a solution to a complex educational problem (Herrington, McKenney, Reeves, & Oliver, 2007). It blends empirical educational research with theory-driven design of educational environments and is an important research methodology for detailing when, why, and how innovative educational solutions work in practice (Design-based Research Collective, 2003). Reeves (2006) argues that it is the resulting innovations of this type of research process that will help educators to understand the relationships among theory, designed innovation, and practice.

One relevant feature of design-based research is the iterative cycle of develop-design-deliver-evaluate to that allows researchers to refine an implementation. With regards to the nTPD Courselet, this was initialized with the pilot study (DBR iteration 1) of an oTPD Courselet on Interactive Whiteboards in the Classroom. The second iteration explored and evaluated several other oTPD technology Courselets (DBR iteration 2). The second DBR iteration resulted in a development of a scalable internal Learning Management System (LMS) being built within the social networking site. The third development DBR cycle (DBR iteration 3), built on the previous iterations and incorporated networked learning instructional designs (Ostashewski & Reid, 2010b) and is presented in this chapter as the nTPD Courselet model.

Our research findings indicate that a successful nTPD Courselet is characterized by the following features:

1. Providing a narrowly focused topic of curriculum implementation: Interactive Whiteboards (IWB) in the classroom (Iteration 1), refined to be IWB in the Secondary Classroom (Iteration 2), resulting in nTPD Courselet - IWB in Secondary Biology Subjects (Iteration 3).

2. Support materials need to be provided in multiple formats (PDF, text, video).

3. Learning materials and activities should be scaffolded to provide for a variety of participant experience levels (provide basic and extension activities)

4. Online delivery structure must allow for flexibility (asynchronous access) to accommodate the needs of busy teachers.

5. Teacher PD activities must be designed to be relevant and authentic.

6. Design opportunities for teacher collaboration and discussions to foster and encourage teacher discourse.

7. Ensure the product of the Courselet is relevant and can be shared.

8. Provide pre-Courselet activities for participants prior to the specific TPD courselet activities such as ones that support participant understandings of the benefits of networked learning activities. Have participants spend time engaging with other sections of the social networking site practicing their use of the tools available.

9. Design for continuous enrollment and completion of activities where participants control their progress through the activities over time, allowing them to participate when they have the time and need.

In summary, participant feedback currently indicate that the value of both the discussions and the blog postings revolved around the *sharing of resources* and *teaching strategies* using these resources. The social networking site tool experiences have been also reported by teachers as valuable contributing to the overall value to teachers of this type of nTPD. These key findings are consistent with the literature (Borko, 2004; Desimone, 2009; Herrington, Herrington, Hoban, & Reid, 2009) on oTPD and similar social networked TPD activities occuring online. However, as we have reported previously, the nTPD Courselet is a new type of teacher professional development particularly because of the networked nature of the implementation. Teachers are able to return to the group over time, continue to share resources with the other Courselet participants, and continue to use the social networking site toolset to support their profession-centered learning as they wish. These are the particular factors that we feel distinguishes networked learning from other types of online learning – the persistance of the group, the learner control, and the connected nature of the interactions between the learners.

FUTURE TRENDS

There is little doubt that online learning for all ages of learners, K-12 and adult learners engaged in active employment, will continue to expand over the near future. As reported by numerous studies identified in this chapter, online learning is a viable learning option, and in many cases provides accessibility and quality that is not found locally in face-to-face learning programs. Therefore it is important that research into design and delivery of online learning for all kinds of learning programs be explored using the tools available. With the explosion of Web 2.0 and social media tools, there is an ever increasing array of tools to utilize to connect learners and engage them in "Worth-it" learning activities. We feel that the Networked Learning Framework is a step in the right direction, regardless of the social networking environment employed.

Contemporary pedagogies, social networked learning environments, connectivist goals, and freely available access to the collective knowledge of the globe are the kinds of key factors we identify as important for learning online into the future. Several obstacles remain in place going forward for delivery of effective and valuable online learning using socail networking sites as the delivery framework. Some of the more obvious challenges are user familiarity with online tools, personal motivation for learning, ability to access and use collective resources. Other challenges are the privacy policies of formal learning institutions, finding qualified online facilitators, developing institution social network websites are examples of some. However, we feel that over time there will be more and more educators who develop the skills to be excellent facilitators of the kind of learning design implemented by using the NLF. MOOCs, Massive Open Online Courses, are being explored by leaders in the field like George Siemens and Stephen Downes, and we suspect that over time connectivist approaches may become more familiar to educators and learners alike. To this end we continue to develop and assist others in implementing the NLF as this type of learning also has the advantage of already capable of another key trend we see continuing and that is mobile learning.

Two iterations of the NLF are of interest for additional discussion in this chapter. One is a course provided to graduate students in a university based ELGG implementation of a social networking site, and the second is a complete program of study for teachers of dance by a not-for-profit organization.

Athabasca University, one of the leaders of distance education research and delivery, have been developing an ELGG social networking site. The educational research arm of the university embarked on this development in an attempt to provide their students, both undergraduate and graduate level, with an alternative way in which to communicate with each other. The Athabasca University Landing site allows all their students to participate using their student IDs as the login, and makes available dozens of social media tools to the student. Twitter feeds, wiki pages, image uploading, video embedding capacities, profiling, friending, tags, and search functions abound in the site for students to customize and control. Current iterations of the site include providing members with the ability to present any or all of the information they post open to the public (Google search engines), open to groups that the learner belongs to, or public. This includes the development of several profile tabs that allows students to even display different profiles to the public or to the membership of the AU Landing.

In 2010, the authors were given the opportunity to develop a three month course in the landing entitled "Social Media Tools and Supporting Your Professional Learning". This course continues to reside in the AU Landing, and is open for any student to join now and in the future. Designed using the Networked Learning Framework, the course engaged students in explorations of social media tools and provided activities for discourse and exploration of social media tools. The course was co-facilitated, and students reported that the activity introduction videos which were provided weekly were an important motivativator for their learning. Student participants also indicated that the format and delivery allowed for scaffolded learning opportunities, experiential learning, and most importantly, connecting with other students in the distance university which were not in the same program. As a whole, the course remains as a repository for students to access now and in the future. Although not designed as a continuous intake and completion course, nor as a course resulting in a graded mark, the successes of the

learners indicates that this kind of structure meets the needs of professional learning for adults utilizing the collective, the network, and the group for delivery of a small program of learning.

A second implementation of the Networked Learning Framework that the authors are involved with is a complete program of study for teachers of Ukrainian Folkdance by a not-for-profit organization. The Alberta Ukrainian Dance Association (AUDA) embarked on a needs analysis of their membership, particularly looking for a way to support their dance community through dance teacher education. The challenges in providing professional development activities for this community of teachers is that they are very busy teaching in the evenings and weekends, involved in taking their students to festivals throughout the year, and are spread across a large area – Alberta and connected to a community across the world. Past AUDA teacher support practices included bringing teachers together to deliver face-to-face weekend seminars. While useful for executing dance choreography and lexicon with teacher, the other components of teaching were rarely if ever presented because of time constraints. AUDA identified the online environment as being one "place" that could support instructors over time and space and embarked on the development of a program of studies for delivery in the online environment. After exploring other needs, an online community of dance teachers, the Canadian Ukrainian Dance Academy, was chosen and developed as a private online social network for the AUDA community. Currently the community is in its infancy, however over 10 of 26 continuous enrollment modules have been developed for this community of dance teaching practicioners. Challenges yet exist in the delivery of this program over time, however expressions of interest to participate from Ukrainian dance teachers in several provinces of Canada, and countries such as Brazil and Australia are being explored by AUDA.

CONCLUSION

With the explosion of social networks like Facebook, Ning, LinkedIn, and other customizable software packages, the potential for networked professional learning in a formalized manner will continue to grow. Therefore the need for the Networked Learning Framework which supports the development of this type of educational offering as will continue as well. Online faculty PD programs are one type of learning situation that will continue to expand as accessibility and mobile access issues continue to decrease over the next few years. For smaller organizations or institutions that are not able or wanting to develop their own social networking site, the opportunities of Facebook groups or Ning groups will provide virtual spaces for online professional development that is inexpensive to deliver online. Certainly there are challenges that need innovative solutions before networked professional development will be widely accessible, however with proper design and prepared facilitators the value to organizations may be significant. The NLF has been designed to work in these spaces and has already found a great deal of success across iterations. We feel that the scalability of networked learning, persistence of the resources and learning place over time, the ability to provide continuous enrollment, and the connections that this kind of learning program can provide make it a viable option to consider for any professional learning program.

REFERENCES

Allen, E., & Seaman, J. (2008). *Staying the course: Online education in the United States, 2008.* Newburyport, MA: The Sloan Consortium.

Allen, E., & Seaman, J. (2009). *Learning on demand: Online education in the United States, 2009.* Newburyport, MA: The Sloan Consortium.

Allen, E., & Seaman, J. (2010). *Class differences: Online education in the United States, 2010.* Newburyport, MA: The Sloan Consortium.

Anderson, T. (2006). Higher education evolution: Individual freedom afforded by educational social software. In Beaudoin, M. (Ed.), *Perspectives on the future of higher education in the digital age* (pp. 77–90). New York, NY: Nova Science.

Archambault, L. (2011). The practitioner's perspective on teacher education: Preparing for the K-12 online classroom. *Journal of Technology and Teacher Education, 19*(1), 73–91.

Bers, M. U., Ponte, I., Juelich, K., Viera, A., & Schenker, J. (2002). Teachers as designers: Integrating robotics in early childhood education. *Information Technology in Childhood Education Annual,* (1): 123–145.

Borko, H. (2004). Professional development and teacher learning - Mapping the terrain. *Educational Researcher, 33*(8), 3–15. doi:10.3102/0013189X033008003

Dede, C., Ketelhut, D., Whitehouse, P., Breit, L., & McCloskey, E. (2009). A research agenda for online teacher professional development. *Journal of Teacher Education, 60*(1), 8–19. doi:10.1177/0022487108327554

Design-based Research Collective. (2003). Design-based research: An emerging paradigm for educational inquiry. *Educational Researcher, 32*(1), 5–8. doi:10.3102/0013189X032001005

Desimone, L. (2009). Improving impact studies of teachers' professional development: Toward better conceptualizations and measures. *Educational Researcher, 38*(3), 181–199. doi:10.3102/0013189X08331140

Dron, J., & Anderson, T. (2009). How the crowd can teach. In Hatzipanagos, S., & Wartburton, S. (Eds.), *Handbook of research on social software and developing community ontologies* (pp. 1–17). Hershey, PA: Information Science Reference. doi:10.4018/978-1-60566-208-4.ch001

Garrison, D. R., Anderson, T., & Archer, W. (2001). Critical thinking, cognitive presence, and computer conferencing in distance education. *American Journal of Distance Education, 15*(1), 7–23. doi:10.1080/08923640109527071

Herrington, A., Herrington, J., Hoban, G., & Reid, D. (2009). Transfer of online professional learning to teachers' classroom practice. *Journal of Interactive Learning Research, 20*(2), 189–213.

Herrington, J., McKenney, S., Reeves, T., & Oliver, R. (2007). Design-based research and doctoral students: Guidelines for preparing a dissertation proposal. In C. Montgomerie & J. Seale (Eds.), *Proceedings of World Conference on Educational Multimedia, Hypermedia and Telecommunications 2007* (pp. 4089-4097). Chesapeake, VA: AACE.

Hovorka, D., & Rees, M. (2009). Active collaboration learning environments - The class of web 2.0. In *Proceeding of the 20th Australasian Conference on Information Systems Active Collaboration Learning Environments*. Melbourne, Australia: ACIS

Johnson, L., Smith, R., Levine, A., & Haywood, K. (2010). *The 2010 horizon report: K-12 edition*. Austin, TX: The New Media Consortium.

Malopinsky, L., Kirkley, J. R., Stein, R., & Duffy, T. (2000). An instructional design model for online problem based learning (PBL) environments: The learning to teach with technology studio. In *Proceedings of the Association for Educational Communications and Technology*. Denver, CO: AECT.

New Media Consortium and EDUCAUSE. (2010). *The 2010 horizon report*.

Ostashewski, N. (2010) Online technology teacher professional development courselets: Design and development. In D. Gibson & B. Dodge (Eds.), *Proceedings of Society for Information Technology & Teacher Education International Conference 2010* (pp. 2329-2334). Chesapeake, VA: AACE.

Ostashewski, N., & Reid, D. (2010a) Online teacher professional development: Redesign and delivery of a technological pedagogical courselet within a social networking site. In *Proceedings of World Conference on Educational Media, Hypermedia and Telecommunications 2010* (pp. 1111-1116). Chesapeake, VA: AACE.

Ostashewski, N., & Reid, D. (2010b). Networked teacher professional development: Applying the networked learning framework to online teacher professional development. In *Proceedings EDGE 2010 e-Learning: The Horizon and Beyond Conference*. St. John, NL.

Papert, S. (1992). *The children's machine*. New York, NY: Basic Books.

Papert, S., & Harel, I. (1991). Situating constructionism. In Harel, I., & Papert, S. (Eds.), *Constructionism* (pp. 1–11). Norwood, NJ: Ablex Publishing Corporation.

Picciano, A., & Seaman, J. (2008). *K–12 online learning: A 2008 follow-up of the survey of the U.S. school district administrators*. Newburyport, MA: The Sloan Consortium.

Reid, D. (2002). A classification schema of online tutor competencies. *Conference Proceedings, International Conference for Computers in Education 2002*. Auckland, New Zealand.

Reid, D. (2003). "Was she smiling when she typed that?": An exploratory study into online tutor competencies and the factors which affect those competencies. *Conference Proceedings, AS-CILITE 2003* (pp. 684-690). Adelaide, Australia.

Schwille, J., Dembélé, M., & Schubert, J. (2007). *Global perspectives on teacher learning- Improving policy and practice. Fundamentals of Educational Planning, 84*. Paris, France: UNESCO.

Sinha, H., Rosson, M. B., Carroll, J., & Du, H. (2010). Toward a professional development community for teachers. In D. Gibson & B. Dodge (Eds.), *Proceedings of Society for Information Technology & Teacher Education International Conference 2010* (pp. 2390-2397). Chesapeake, VA: AACE.

Vrasidas, C., & Glass, G. V. (Eds.). (2004). *Online professional development for teachers*. Greenwich, CT: Information Age Publishing.

Whitehouse, P. (2010). Networked teacher professional development: The case of Globaloria. *Journal of Interactive Learning Research, 21*(4).

Whitehouse, P., Reynolds, R., & Caperton, I. (2009). Globaloria pilot year one: New directions for 21st century Teacher professional development. In I. Gibson et al. (Eds.), *Proceedings of Society for Information Technology & Teacher Education International Conference 2009* (pp. 1590-1597). Chesapeake, VA: AACE.

KEY TERMS AND DEFINITIONS

Constructionism: A pedagogical approach that describes learning as being an activity that is accomplished through the construction of artifacts, and discouse about those artifact with other learners. Hands-on learning, learning by doing, and learning through constructive play or gaming are other ways to describe the constructionist pedagogy.

Courselet: Online mini-courses of about 10 - 20 hours of teacher interaction time delivered for the purpose of teacher professional development within a social networking framework.

Networked Learning Framework: An instructional design model that utilizing the delivery structure of a social networking site to deliver constructionist activities that engage learners with content and other learners.

Online Teacher Professional Development: Online teacher professional learning activities with the goal of increasing the knowledge and skills of teachers with the understood goal of improving student learning.

Networked Teacher Professional Development: Online teacher professional development delivered in an online social networking environment that supports and encourages teachers to learn together, both formally and informally, while allowing them to retain control over their time, space, presence, activity level, identity, and relationships.

Online Facilitator: An instructor or facilitator of education programs or courses delivered in a fully online delivery format.

Social Media Tools: Web 2.0 tools that have the ability to share information with others easily utilizing online technologies. Examples are blogs, microblogs, discussion forums, etc.

Social Networking Site: Online networked tools that support and encourage individuals to communicate while retaining individual control over their time, space, presence, activity, identity and relationships. Examples are Facebook, Ning, Elgg, and LinkedIn.

Teacher Professional Development: An ongoing process that includes regular opportunities and planned experiences intended to promote growth and development in the professional practice of teachers.

Chapter 5
Two Quadrants for the Development of Virtual Environments to Support Collaboration between Teachers

Ken Stevens
Memorial University of Newfoundland, Canada

ABSTRACT

The purpose of this chapter is to outline how pre-service teacher education can be adapted to the emergence of virtual educational structures and processes that complement traditional classes. The chapter is based on research conducted in rural schools in the Canadian province of Newfoundland and Labrador that links in-service and pre-service teachers to provide insights for the latter into real-life, networked classrooms, particularly those located in communities located beyond major centres of population, to which most students were likely to be appointed. Face-to-face groups of pre-service teachers were able to include virtual practicing teachers in their discussions. The significance of this study will be judged by the extent to which professional discourse between pre-service and in-service teachers reflects the virtual challenge of intranets to the physical isolation of traditional schools.

INTRODUCTION

The rapid growth and educational application of the Internet has led to a challenge to traditional ways of teaching and learning at a distance (Ben-Jacob et al, 2000) that were based on paper and the postal system. E-Learning is Internet-based and does not require the degree of central control that distance educators have traditionally employed within dedicated institutions. The growth of e-learning in schools has led to pedagogical considerations and to the development of new ways of managing knowledge that enable these institutions to assume extended roles in the regions they serve.

DOI: 10.4018/978-1-4666-1963-0.ch005

The province of Newfoundland and Labrador has a population of approximately 500,000 people, of whom less than 30,000 live in Labrador. In Newfoundland, the island portion of the province, almost all of the population lives in coastal settlements, including the capital, St John's. Approximately two thirds of schools in the province are located in rural communities. The decline of traditional rural education in Newfoundland and Labrador coincided with a national initiative to prepare people across the country for the Information Age (Information Highway Advisory Council, 1997; Ertl and Plante, 2004) that provided impetus for the classroom application of emerging technologies. In rural Newfoundland and Labrador the introduction of the Internet and internet-based technologies has had a transforming effect on the capacity of small schools to deliver programs (Brown, et.al. 2000, Healey and Stevens, 2002; Stevens, 2001, 2002b; 1999a). In other developed countries with substantial rural populations to be educated there have also been major changes in the configuration of small schools in isolated communities. In New Zealand (Stevens, 2000; 1999b), Finland (Tella, 1995), Iceland (Stevens, 2002a), Russia (Stevens et al, 1999) and the USA (Dorniden, 2005; Glick, 2005; Schrum, 2005) a variety of communication technologies have been engaged to promote educational opportunities for students and more efficient ways of organizing and managing knowledge in collaborative electronic structures that have implications for regional economies.

In the last decade two e-learning developments have changed the nature of education in rural Newfoundland and Labrador: (i) the introduction of the opportunity to study online from schools located in remote communities and (ii) the possibility of enrolment in Advanced Placement (AP) courses from rural schools. Both developments have implications for the professional education of teachers.

BACKGROUND

The Development of Collaborative Structures to Support Rural Canadian Schools

The search for appropriate new educational structures for the delivery of education to students in rural Newfoundland and Labrador has led to the development of school district intranets, within which virtual classes have been organized. In the process of developing e-teaching within school district intranets, several challenges have had to be met. The electronic linking of eight sites within the former Vista school district to collaborate in the teaching of AP Biology, Chemistry, Mathematics and Physics created a series of open classes in rural Newfoundland that became known as the Vista School District Intranet. The creation of the Vista School District Intranet was an attempt to use information and communication technologies to provide geographically-isolated students with extended educational and, indirectly, vocational opportunities. The development of the intranet within a single school district involved the introduction of an open teaching and learning structure to a closed one. Accordingly, adjustments had to be made in each participating site so that administratively and academically, AP classes could be taught. The Vista school district initiative challenged the notion that senior students in small schools have to leave home to complete their education at larger schools in urban areas. By participating in open classes in real (synchronous) time, combined with a measure of independent (asynchronous) learning, senior students were able to interact with one another through audio, video and electronic whiteboards.

In eight schools within the rural Vista school district of Newfoundland and Labrador, 55 students were enrolled in AP Biology, Chemistry, Mathematics and Physics courses. While AP courses are a well-established feature of senior secondary education in the United States and Canada, it was unusual for students to be able to enrol for instruction at this level in small schools in remote communities. The advanced nature of these courses requires highly qualified and experienced teachers who are often difficult to attract and retain in small schools in rural communities. Furthermore, small rural schools, because of their size, have few students who are able to undertake instruction at this level. This initiative was significant for rural Canadian education in that it was, as far as can be ascertained, the first time courses at this level were delivered to students who would otherwise not have had access to them because of the size and location of their schools. By introducing AP subjects to small schools in a remote region of Canada, a step was taken toward inclusion of rural people in the emerging knowledge economy. Several graduates of this program were subsequently able to enrol in science and engineering faculties at the local university with a small part of their post-secondary program already completed. Perhaps, more importantly, they entered universities with the knowledge that they could successfully compete academically with students anywhere in North America.

From Closed to Open Teaching and Learning Environments

The major change for students in the first intranet in Newfoundland and Labrador was the opportunity to study advanced science subjects and mathematics as members of open classes from their small, remote communities. Students in the Vista school district intranet were frequently subject to scrutiny by their peers as they responded to one another through chat-rooms, audio and video as well as with their AP on-line teacher. The intranet provided students with access to multiple sites simultaneously, as well as the opportunity to work independently of a teacher for part of the day. The need to prepare for classes before going on-line

became increasingly apparent to both teachers and students if the open, synchronous, science classes were to succeed.

The advent of the intranet had implications for students who began to interact with teachers and their peers in a variety of new ways. Many students experienced difficulty expressing themselves and, in particular, asking questions in open electronic classes when they did not know their peers from other small communities. The organization of social occasions for students learning science in open classes in the Intranet helped overcome these problems. As students became more comfortable with one another, inhibitions such as asking questions on-line were overcome. The e-teachers had little to guide their practice in teaching at this level for the first time. Each of the four AP science subjects was taught in a different way. For example, the physics and mathematics teachers had little need for video in their interactions with students, but access to electronic whiteboards was critical so that the development of equations and calculations could be managed interactively. For the e-teacher of chemistry experimental work posed a problem because of the dispersed locations of the students. Videos of experiments that were to be conducted in person, at designated sites and pre-arranged times, were found to be useful in preparing students for the laboratory component of the AP course.

In an evaluation of the Advanced Placement experiment rural students commented:

I have been introduced to one of the best teachers I have ever had

The highly-esteemed teacher would not have been encountered by this student had it not been for the AP online development. This comment illustrates the possibility of providing rural students with expertise from other than local sources.

The experience of working at post-secondary school level through Advanced Placement courses was not, until this development, available to students in small, rural high schools. The intellectual challenge for university-bound students was considered to be useful. One student advised:

If you are planning on doing post-secondary education, do one of these (AP) courses;

Another student reported at the end of the school year:

This course has exceeded all my expectations - I believe I have passed.

In the process of developing e-teaching and e-learning within intranets in rural Newfoundland and Labrador, teachers, learners and administrators had to adapt to a new, electronic educational structure. In the open teaching and learning environment of an intranet, participating institutions academically and administratively interfaced for that part of the school day during which classes were taught. This was, for teachers and administrators, a different educational structure from the traditional and, by comparison, closed educational environment of the autonomous school with its own teachers and its own students.

There was potential conflict between the local school as an autonomous educational institution serving a designated area and schools that became, in effect, sites within electronic teaching and learning networks that, in effect, began to serve a region. Principals and teachers appointed to the closed, autonomous learning environments of traditional schools frequently discovered that the administration of knowledge required the development of open structures within which they were increasingly expected to collaborate with their peers located on a range of distant sites. Many discovered that the positions to which they were appointed in traditional (closed) schools became, in effect, locations within new (open) electronic schools.

The need for increased technical support for the new, open structure became increasingly urgent for teachers and students who were using information and communication technologies to teach and learn across dispersed sites. Both had to be provided with expert advice and instruction in the use of new applications. A problem that emerged was difficulty in securing and maintaining instructional design expertise in the preparation and upgrading of courses, although this issue is common in the development of on line courses at high school level. An essential aspect of the development of open electronic classes was the coordination of both hardware and software between schools. Without synchronized technology, schools cannot fully participate in electronic networks. However, the purchase of appropriate hardware and software was initially a matter of confusion for many Principals, teachers and school boards who had to seek expert advice and support. Many rural schools with open electronic classes realized that the successful administration of a network required shared local technical support. Unless adequate technical support systems could be established, electronic networked classes could, potentially, be curtailed by teachers who argued, with justification, that there was insufficient technical support for their investment in e-learning. While there were doubts by some teachers and administrators about the adequacy and robustness of the technology that was available, the solutions that were sought and the infrastructure that was implemented were at the regional rather than local school district level.

The changes that took place in the closed learning spaces of traditional rural schools in Newfoundland and Labrador with the introduction of an intranet and AP instruction online led to a ministerial inquiry into the implications of these developments for the future of rural education in the province. The provincial government, after a ministerial inquiry (Government of Newfoundland and Labrador, 2000) expanded the linking of schools through the creation of the Centre for Distance Learning and Innovation (CDLI) within the Newfoundland and Labrador Department of Education. CDLI (http://www.cdli.ca/) develops and administers online learning that complements traditional classes in schools throughout the province. Since its inception it has considerably extended e-learning throughout Newfoundland and Labrador.

Quadrant One: Face to Face and Virtual Teaching

The development of the first school district intranet in Newfoundland and Labrador involved a combination of technological, pedagogical, organizational and conceptual change (Stevens, 2007). In rural Newfoundland and Labrador this combination supported the creation of a rural school district intranet of four interconnected quadrants (refer to Table 1).

*T*echnologically, the development of the school district intranet was difficult. In many parts of the province the telecommunications infrastructure was barely adequate to link schools within such a structure. Minimum specifications were adopted for computer hardware and network connectivity. All schools involved in the project had DirecPC satellite dishes installed to provide a high speed down-link. In most rural communities in this part of Canada, digital telecommunications infrastructures do not enable schools to have a high speed up-link to the internet. Appropriate software had to be identified and evaluated for both the development of the resources and the delivery of instruction within the Intranet. Front Page 98 was selected as the software package. Additional software was used for the development of images, animated gifs and other dimensions of course development. These included Snagit32, Gif Construction Set, Real Video, and similar packages. Many software packages were evaluated and finally WebCT was selected. This pack-

Table 1. Four interconnected quadrants

Technological	Pedagogical
Organization	Conceptual

age enabled the instructor to track student progress; it contained online testing and evaluation, private E-mail, a calendar feature, public bulletin board for use by, instructor and student, a link to lessons and chat rooms for communication between teacher and student. For real - time instruction, Meeting Point and Microsoft NetMeeting were selected. This combination of software enabled a teacher to present real-time interactive instruction to multiple sites. An orientation session was provided for students prior to the implementation of this project. Students had to learn how to communicate with each other and with their instructor using these new technologies before classes could begin.

Pedagogically the integration of schools in a single district meant teaching in ways that were different from traditional classroom practices. Instead of providing instruction exclusively within their own classrooms, teachers had to consider teaching collaboratively from one site to another in what became shared teaching and learning space. The challenge of teaching between rather than exclusively in schools focused attention on what Van Manen (2002) terms "the pedagogical task of teaching." For some teachers this was difficult to accept when a colleague on another site had the role of teaching AP students on line in his or her school, from another school in the district intranet. For those teachers who taught the initial AP subjects of Chemistry, Mathematics, Physics and Biology within the new collaborative structure (the school district intranet) there was little pedagogy to guide them other than, for one of the teachers, previous experience as a distance education instructor. Issues arose in the delivery of classes between schools (or sites) involving the balance of synchronous and asynchronous instruction, motivation, control, student lack of confidence based on inexperience in learning other than by formal classroom instruction and assessment. One of the first challenges for students was how to interact online, with peers they had not met. In some cases this led to awkwardness and embarrassment that threatened to impede learning. Teachers had to adjust to talking less during lessons and to prepare questions very carefully so that all students could participate. The development of judicious questioning by teachers helped students learn from one another as they all considered how to respond.

Organizationally, the integration of schools in a district intranet involved institutional collaboration beginning with the coordination of senior class timetables so that students located on multiple sites could be taught together online. Unlike earlier initiatives in New Zealand (Stevens and Moffatt, 2003), where self-governing schools do not have assistance and direction from school boards, Newfoundland and Labrador schools were organized in school districts in each of which there was a board office that provided administrative, curriculum and technological support. The first rural district digital network was organized by the board office, including the selection of online teachers together with technical and organizational support. During the first year of operation the issue of schools coordinating their timetables for senior classes was not fully resolved so that some classes had to be repeated. It became apparent during the initial year that students needed on site as well as on line support if they were to succeed. This was not understood before the intranet was established as the participating students were considered by everyone – teachers, parents and themselves to be "independent learners." In almost all cases AP students in each of the four initial science subjects reported that they needed help to stay "on task" to succeed. In subsequent years some teachers were appointed as "mediating" teachers (M-teachers)

whose job, in addition to teaching traditional classes on site, was to mentor and assist where necessary and liaise with the e-teacher teaching from another site (Barbour and Mulcahy, 2005).

Conceptually, the development of a school district intranet involved a different way of thinking about teaching, learning and the organization of schools. The first conceptual change for teachers was that rather than being appointed to teach their own classes, in their own classrooms, in the schools to which they were appointed, a selected few were asked to teach other teacher's students, located in other classrooms beyond their own school and community, on-line. A second conceptual change that the first school district intranet initiated was the introduction of learning at a distance in traditional classrooms. In the first intranet in Newfoundland and Labrador some teachers were introduced to the notion of teaching both in a traditional classroom and on line, through the internet. This was an important step in the integration of virtual and actual teaching. Students were also introduced to the notion of learning both on site and on line during a school day. These were significant steps in the integration of on-site and on-line education or the merging of actual and virtual classes (Stevens, 2005; Stevens and Stewart, 2005). A third conceptual change was that schools that were small in terms of the number of students attending in person, on site, and the number of teachers who were appointed to them, could become relatively large schools in terms of the range of subjects they could offer with the addition of online instruction. Finally, there was a conceptual change in the realization by students, parents and teachers that school location was not necessarily a barrier to accessing areas of the curriculum that had not traditionally been provided on site in traditional classrooms. Advanced Placement subjects, taught in large urban schools throughout North America, could be made available to senior students in small and geographically-isolated schools.

Each of the four parts of the matrix was shaped though collaboration between each of the other parts. The organization of the intranet depended on the connectivity provided by internet-based technologies, assisted by the installation of satellite dishes in Newfoundland and Labrador schools. The technological dimension depended on the organizational skills of administrators in the school district office collaborating with on-site administrators and teachers. Several times during the first year of operation there were technological problems that were solved collaboratively by administrators and teachers working alongside technicians. Technological changes introduced by the internet and its application to school district organization to facilitate the administrative and academic linking of classrooms in small and dispersed schools, encouraged teachers to consider new, collaborative ways of teaching in open learning environments. The introduction of the first school district intranet in Newfoundland and Labrador challenged the exclusivity of traditional classrooms in which a defined number of students were taught, in person, by a single teacher.

Three Developments in Teaching and Learning in Networked Classes

Three stages can be identified in the development of teaching and learning in networked virtual environments that have application for the provision of education in sparsely-populated regions such as the Canadian province of Newfoundland and Labrador and, possibly, for other remote regions of the world in which students are educated beyond major centres of population.

One: The Development of Awareness of Collaborative Teaching and Learning Structures

With continuing out-migration most small schools in Newfoundland and Labrador are decreasing in size and during the last decade many have

closed and local students have had to travel to larger centres to continue their education. The structural changes that have taken place in the province since the inception of the first intranet, within which initial AP courses were developed and taught, has advanced to become a system that provides online instruction to almost all schools in Newfoundland and Labrador. Today CDLI develops and administers online learning that complements traditional classes in schools throughout the province. Awareness of what was taking place in the delivery of education in the province has had to be developed by pre-service as well as practicing teachers who have traditionally been prepared to teach in autonomous, or closed, teaching and learning environments known as classrooms. While many members of the profession will continue to provide instruction in traditional closed environments, an increasing number will teach in open, collaborative, internet-based learning spaces.

Two: The Development of Awareness of Collaborative Teaching and Learning Processes

Students have been prepared to teach in Newfoundland and Labrador schools in which they could expect to have their own classrooms and their own students on a single site. It is likely that many teachers will not now teach exclusively in classrooms but in the spaces between schools, such as intranets, as classes are academically and administratively integrated for at least part of the school day. Teachers in rural Newfoundland and Labrador will, to an increasing extent, teach on site as well as online, in virtual as well as in actual classes. This change requires a different way of thinking about teaching and the organization of learning. Future teachers in the province's high schools will require skills that their predecessors of a decade ago did not need. In Memorial University of Newfoundland's secondary teacher program in the Faculty of Education students have been introduced to the concept of learning circles within which they can collaborate by sharing ideas and experiences about their initial observation visits to local schools and, in particular, their semester-long internships. Not all students return from the intern experience to the university aware of the changes that are taking place in the delivery of education in the province, particularly if they spent their time in urban schools. However, it was accepted that learning circles provided a collaborative process that complemented the structural changes that have been introduced in the organization of schools over the last decade in Newfoundland and Labrador. To be professionally prepared for the reality of new, virtual educational structures and processes in Newfoundland and Labrador, it was necessary to introduce pre-service teachers to institutional as well as professional collaboration. The contradiction of teaching in closed learning spaces (or traditional classrooms) located in collaborative networks of schools, challenges students to re-examine the changed nature of education in the province. Pre-service teachers were asked to consider research on the use of computers in education (Lowther et.al., 2003; Mathiasen, 2004) and their potential for collaborative teaching as well as shared learning between dispersed sites (Cavanaugh, 2001; Collis, 1996; Ertl and Plante, 2004; Hawkes, and Halverson, 2002). A first step was to organize students into learning circles within which they could share recent classroom experiences from their internships and from which they often discovered common problems. Students were placed in learning circles that were heterogeneous in that they comprised many different curriculum teaching areas. Mathematics, language, social science, visual art, science and physical education teachers were encouraged to discuss common issues in teaching and learning within learning circles. A second step was to encourage students to project themselves from their university learning circles into the near future when they are appointed to schools across Newfoundland and Labrador (most of which are located in rural communities) or in other Canadian provinces, with a view to continuing to work collaboratively across disciplines by sharing common educational problems. The purpose was to encourage the development of awareness in pre-service teachers that members of their profession have traditionally been isolated from one another in their classroom spaces but that this is not always appropriate in an internet-based network of schools. Students may be physically-isolated from other teachers within intranets spanning schools in rural communities, but they do not need to be professionally-isolated in ways they organize teaching and learning if collaboration is fostered.

Three: Cybercells for the Integration of Virtual and Actual Structures and Processes

A challenge for teacher educators engaging new members of the profession has often been linking the practice of teaching and learning in schools to educational theory. In learning circles students were asked to bring to their discussions appropriate reading from academic journals and books that complemented discussions about their recent teaching practice as interns. They were asked to consider how the academic literature could support (or refute) ideas that were under discussion, drawn from recent classroom experience. Learning circles, schools, intranets and the provincial educational system are all social structures within which students had to work. They were encouraged to consider the sociological implications of these structures and, in particular, classroom issues they encountered. Pre-service students were encouraged to locate their recent practical experiences as interns in schools within an appropriate theoretical perspective. Discourse about shared experience between students and between teachers facilitated the creation of new realities as participants discovered common perceptions, experiences and problems. The development of shared realities through cybercells challenged teacher and student isolation in a way that is similar to how intranets have challenged the physical isolation of rural schools in Newfoundland and Labrador over the last decade. In a cybercell teachers who collaborated on an actual site (or school) could share their discussions with virtual colleagues from other sites located within their internet-based network and beyond. Cybercells enabled shared realities to be created both on-site, for example, in a particular school, as well as virtually, by enabling participants at a distance to engage in discourse with those in a given, physical location.

Quadrant Two: Implications for the Professional Education of Teachers

Changes in rural education in Newfoundland and Labrador can be further considered within another four interconnected quadrants. The creation of school district intranets and the advent of e-learning led to the development of collaborative structures and processes, adaptation of and innovative ways of using new technologies in schools, and, ultimately, the preservation of the distinct cultural identity of rural communities in Newfoundland and Labrador (see Table 2).

Collaboration has been critical to the success of e-learning in rural schools in Newfoundland and Labrador. As rural schools changed from closed, autonomous institutions to become administratively and pedagogically open to other sites (schools) within intranets, collaborative teaching and learning was facilitated. Collaborative teaching and learning are not dependant on school size or location; neither are they dependent on school district intranets. The lesson for the global community from collaborative teaching and learning in Newfoundland and Labrador has been the creation of structures and processes to support this.

The creation of school district intranets was based on organizational and managerial *innovation* that led to the development of virtual educational structures to support traditional schools. Innova-

Table 2. Changes in rural education

Collaboration	Innovation
Adaptation	Cultural Identity

tion that led to the creation of new educational structures and processes in Newfoundland and Labrador was grounded in the demise of the fishing industry and rural outmigration. The organizational and managerial response has been the development of extended learning opportunities for young people and, indirectly, for their families and communities.

Educational changes that have taken place in rural Newfoundland and Labrador have been based on the *adaptation* of existing structures and processes within which teaching and learning have been extended through the integration of traditional and virtual classrooms. In adapting traditional small rural schools to internet-based structures and processes, capacity building has taken place. Many small Newfoundland and Labrador schools have become, in effect, sites within extended teaching and learning environments.

Through collaboration, innovation and adaptation in Newfoundland and Labrador, sustainable rural schools have been created and an important aspect of the *cultural identity* of the province has been preserved. It could be argued that the Centre for Distance Learning and Innovation supports the cultural identity of the province and sustains rural communities through the creation of extended learning opportunities.

Implications of E-Learning in Rural Schools for the Professional Education of Teachers

The Canadian study, outlined above, has three implications for educators, particularly those who are charged with providing instruction for students whose homes are located in small communities distant from major centres of population. The first implication is that collaborative pedagogy can be adapted to meet the reality of schools in internet-linked structures. In addition to preparing teachers for traditional closed, autonomous classrooms, e-teaching and e-learning can extend classrooms in terms of space, time, organization and capacity. Second, the introduction of virtual, collaborative teaching and learning presences in traditional school environments challenges the notion of geographical isolation as an educational policy consideration. Third, the advent of cybercells and the creation of integrated virtual and actual learning communities have policy, pedagogical and organizational implications for enhancing access to both teaching and learning opportunities. Finally, the introduction of cybercells and, through them, collaborative educational communities, may facilitate new understandings of teaching and learning.

The problems that have faced rural Newfoundland and Labrador over the last decade and the community response to them are of interest to educators and policy makers beyond the province. The above quadrants show how schools and, indirectly through them, rural communities can be sustained.

There are several lessons from Newfoundland and Labrador for the global community in the building of sustainable rural schools based on e-learning. First: Small schools can become large schools. Schools that are small in terms of the number of students who attend, in person, on a daily basis, can become large educational institutions in the way they electronically access and disseminate teaching and learning. In Newfoundland and Labrador this has been achieved by the first two cells in the above quadrants: acceptance of new technologies and using them in collaborative ways. A lesson for the rest of the world from this province is that school size and location are no longer important in educational

terms. Second: The Importance of collaboration in teaching to complement new collaborative structures is highlighted by recent developments in this part of Canada.

Third: Virtual and actual teaching and learning can be integrated. In Newfoundland and Labrador steps have been taken to integrate traditional and virtual teaching and learning within intranets and, more recently, through the Centre for Distance Learning and Innovation. Today many young people attend small schools in their rural communities in this province while also being taught by e-teachers employed by CDLI. In Newfoundland and Labrador virtual teaching and learning integration can be considered within the second cells of the above two quadrants: pedagogical changes (e.g., e-learning) combined with an innovative approach to the delivery of education such as the steps taken a decade ago in academically and administratively linking small schools within intranets.

Finally, teaching and learning in traditional small schools can be complemented through the introduction of new structures and processes. The third cells of the above quadrants – organization and adaptation were applied in the development of the Vista School District Intranet. This structure introduced revolutionary change in the way education was delivered in the province. The intranet was organized around building increased teaching capacity in small schools through application of the first two lessons – accepting and adapting new technologies and making space for virtual teaching and learning in traditional classrooms. While

FUTURE TRENDS

Teachers have traditionally been prepared for what have been, in effect, closed, autonomous classrooms in schools. It is now necessary to consider the implications of networked, virtual environments that complement traditional schools. Collaborative approaches to teaching, including learning circles and cybercells, have been found to complement the advent of networked virtual environments. Students preparing to become teachers in rural Canada, will, to an increasing extent, be expected to contribute instruction to open, networked, virtual learning environments from the schools to which they are appointed (Furey & Stevens, 2008). The integration of virtual and actual (face to face) learning spaces provides opportunities to develop collaborative teaching and learning.

CONCLUSION

The Newfoundland and Labrador model of rural e-learning has much to offer the global rural community because it is simple and is built on the idea of enhancing capacity in existing schools. The model demonstrates that size and location need not be significant in educational terms as long as appropriate structures and processes are developed to encourage sharing and collaboration.

The development of new structures and processes that have transformed access to educational and, indirectly, vocational opportunities in small and isolated communities in this province could become a template to be modified and introduced in other parts of the world.

REFERENCES

Barbour, M., & Mulcahy, D. (2004). The role of mediating teachers in Newfoundland's new model of distance education. *The Morning Watch, 32*(1).

Ben-Jacob, M. G., Levin, D. S., & Ben-Jacob, T. K. (2000). The learning environment of the 21st Century. *Educational Technology Review, 13*, 8–12.

Brown, J., Sheppard, D., & Stevens, K. (2000). *Effective schooling in a tele-learning environment.* St. John's, NL, Centre for Tele-Learning and Rural Education, Faculty of Education, Memorial University of Newfoundland.

Cavanaugh, C. (2001). The effectiveness of interactive distance education technologies in K-12 learning: A meta-analysis. *International Journal of Educational Telecommunications, 7*(1), 73–88.

Collis, B. (1996). *Telelearning in a digital world - The future of distance learning.* London, UK: Thompson Computer Press.

Dorniden, A. (2005). K-12 schools and online learning. In Howard, C., Boettcher, J. V., Justice, L., Schenk, K., Rogers, P. L., & Berg, G. A. (Eds.), *Encyclopedia of distance learning* (pp. 1182–1188). Hershey, PA: IGI Global. doi:10.4018/978-1-59140-555-9.ch176

Ertl, H., & Plante, J. (2004). *Connectivity and learning in Canada's schools.* Ottawa, Canada: Government of Canada.

Furey, D., & Stevens, K. (2008). New systemic roles facilitating the integration of face-to-face and virtual learning. *Online Journal of Distance Learning Administration, 11*(4).

Glick, D. B. (2005). K-12 online learning policy. In Howard, C., Boettcher, J. V., Justice, L., Schenk, K., Rogers, P. L., & Berg, G. A. (Eds.), *Encyclopedia of distance learning* (pp. 1175–1181). Hershey, PA: IGI Global. doi:10.4018/978-1-59140-555-9.ch175

Government of Newfoundland and Labrador. (2000). *Supporting learning: Report on the ministerial panel on educational delivery in the classroom.* St John's, Canada: Department of Education.

Hawkes, M., & Halverson, P. (2002). Technology facilitation in the rural school: An analysis of options. *Journal of Research in Rural Education, 17*(3), 162–170.

Healey, D., & Stevens, K. (2002). Student access to information technology and perceptions of future opportunities in two small Labrador communities. *Canadian Journal of Learning and Technology, 28*(1), 7–18.

Information Highway Advisory Council. (1997). *Preparing Canada for a digital world*. Ottawa, Canada: Author.

Lowther, D., Ross, S., & Morrison, G. (2003). When each has one: The influences on teaching strategies and student achievement of using laptops in the classroom. *Educational Technology Research and Development, 51*(3), 23–44. doi:10.1007/BF02504551

Mathiasen, H. (2004). Expectations of technology: When the intensive application of IT in teaching becomes a possibility. *Journal of Research on Technology in Education, 36*(3), 273–294.

Schrum, L. (2005). E-learning and K-12. In Howard, C., Boettcher, J. V., Justice, L., Schenk, K., Rogers, P. L., & Berg, G. A. (Eds.), *Encyclopedia of distance learning* (pp. 737–742). Hershey, PA: IGI Global. doi:10.4018/978-1-59140-555-9.ch107

Stevens, K., Sandalov, A., Sukhareva, N., Barry, M., & Piper, T. (1999). The development of open models for teaching physics to schools in dispersed locations in Russia and Canada. In Grementieri, V., Szucs, A., & Trukhin, V. I. (Eds.), *Information and communication technologies and human resources development: New opportunities for European co-operation* (pp. 148–154). Budapest, Hungary: European Distance Education Network.

Stevens, K. J. (1999a). A new model for teaching in rural communities – The electronic organisation of classes as intranets. *Prism – Journal of The Newfoundland and Labrador Teachers'. Association, 6*(1), 23–26.

Stevens, K. J. (1999b). Telecommunications technologies, telelearning and the development of virtual classes for rural New Zealanders. *Open Praxis, 1*, 12–14.

Stevens, K. J. (2000). Télé-enseignement et éducation en milieu rural en Nouvelle Zélande et à Terre Neuve. *Géocarrefour - Revue de Geographie de Lyon - Espaces Ruraux et Technologies de L'Information, 75*(1), 87 – 92.

Stevens, K. J. (2001). The development of digital intranets for the enhancement of education in rural communities. *Journal of Interactive Instruction Development, 13*(3), 19–24.

Stevens, K. J. (2002a). Minnkandi heimur -Rafrænt net smárra skóla- Óvænt tengsl Íslenska menntanetsins við Nýja Sjáland og Kanada, (Making the world smaller -The electronic networking of small schools–Some unseen connections of the Icelandic Educational Network in New Zealand and Canada). [Icelandic translation by Karl Erlendsson]. *Skólavarðan, 2*(2), 22–24.

Stevens, K. J. (2002b). The expansion of educational opportunities in rural communities using web-based resources. In Santana Torrellas, G. A., & Uskov, V. (Eds.), *Computers and advanced technology in education* (pp. 221–225). Anaheim, CA: ACTA Press.

Stevens, K. J. (2005). The integration of virtual and actual classes in sparsely populated regions. In Kinshuk, G. Sampson, & P. Isaias (Eds.), *Cognition and exploratory learning in the digital age* (pp. 517-520). Lisbon, Portugal: IADIS Press.

Stevens, K. J. (2007). A matrix for e-collaboration in rural Canadian schools. In Kock, N. (Ed.), *Encyclopedia of e-collaboration* (pp. 444–449). Hershey, PA: IGI Global. doi:10.4018/978-1-59904-000-4.ch068

Stevens, K. J., & Moffatt, C. (2003). From distance education to telelearning - The organization of open classes at local, regional and national levels. In Bradley, J. (Ed.), *The open classroom – Distance learning in and out of schools* (pp. 171–180). Sterling, VA: Kogan.

Stevens, K. J., & Stewart, D. (2005). *Cybercells – Learning in actual and virtual groups*. Melbourne, Australia: Thomson-Dunmore Press.

Tella, S. (1995). *Virtual school in a networking learning environment*. Helsinki: University of Helsinki, Department of Teacher Education.

van Manen, M. (2002). The pedagogical task of teaching. *Teaching and Teacher Education, 18*(2), 135–138. doi:10.1016/S0742-051X(01)00058-0

KEY TERMS AND DEFINITIONS

Asynchronous: In delayed time

Intranet: Schools that are academically and administratively linked through the internet for collaborative teaching and learning.

Open Classses: Classes that are academically and administratively integrated to facilitate e-collaboration

Pedagogy: Teaching; The work of the teacher

Rural Schools: Country or non-urban schools.

Synchronous-: In real time

Virtual: A computer-based, online community through which people interact with one another

Chapter 6
A Model for Online Instructor Training, Support, and Professional Development

Vassiliki I. Zygouris-Coe
University of Central Florida, USA

ABSTRACT

Online learning is a popular learning option for millions of students in US colleges and universities. Online facilitation plays an important role in student learning. With a growing number of courses offered online, there are many challenges associated with the quality of online instruction. This chapter presents information on a large-scale online project for preK-12 educators. The author presents detailed information on a model for training, support, professional development, and monitoring of online instructors. The author also discusses implications for further development and monitoring of online instructors' knowledge, skills, and dispositions that promote successful online experiences and learning for students.

INTRODUCTION

In this chapter, the author will describe and discuss a model for online faculty recruitment, training, support, retention, and professional development. The purpose of this chapter is to present the successes and challenges associated with a situated large-scale online professional development project for preK-12 educators in the US. The author will provide detailed information about the context, content, implementation, sup-

port systems, and online facilitation monitoring processes associated with this online project. The author will also share data and examples related to the online instructor training, support, professional development, and quality assurance processes that contributed to the success of this project. The professional development, mentoring, and support of online faculty play a key role in the quality of online facilitation and student learning. Selection, certification training, mentoring, support, and monitoring of online facilitation are necessary, complex, and multi-layered processes.

DOI: 10.4018/978-1-4666-1963-0.ch006

BACKGROUND

As advances in technology influence and become a major part of our everyday lives, interest continues to grow in the use of the Internet to provide professional development for teachers. The flexibility that online learning provides has made it a strong catalyst for improving teacher content knowledge and pedagogy. That is, overcoming problems with gaining access and a lack of face-to-face interaction are easily surmounted by the need for educators to find time in their busy and demanding schedules to obtain the professional training needed to keep up to date in their field. Furthermore, providing teachers with access to high-quality professional development via a long distance medium not only reduces monetary costs but it also has potential for providing valuable just-in-time learning for teachers.

Online professional development can expand educators' experiences to include content-rich learning opportunities in an interactive virtual environment that is personalized to the subject area and grade level that they teach. This is especially true for teachers in rural areas who may otherwise be challenged to find high-quality professional development that fits their specific needs (ACME, 2002). The preparation of online faculty, to teach and help students learn online, is a core factor for student and program success. The professional development, mentoring, and support of online faculty will determine both the quality of online instruction and student learning in online learning environments. Selection, certification training, mentoring, support, and monitoring of online facilitation are complex and multi-layered processes.

Students' satisfaction of online facilitators/ instructors was found to contribute significantly to their satisfaction of online courses (Finaly-Neumann, 1994; Williams & Ceci, 1997). Promptness, approachability, communication skills, content knowledge, and encouragement of facilitators were considerably related to student satisfaction of online courses (Bolliger, 2004). The first three were also found to be a key factor in predicting participants' overall satisfaction of online facilitators to a great extent (Wang, Huh, & Zygouris-Coe, 2007). Northrup (2002) found that timely feedback was a key factor in supporting online learning.

Competencies in the aforementioned factors are what online facilitators should have in order to effectively facilitate asynchronous discussions so that their participants can maximize their potentials with satisfaction with their learning experience. Despite emphasis on the importance of facilitator skills in asynchronous discussions, there is a lack of research identifying applicable indicators for measuring quality of facilitator asynchronous discussions.

According to Anderson and Moore (2008, p. ix), distance education is "the most significant development in education in the past quarter century." The rapid growth of online distance education courses requires university faculty to face new challenges and different decisions in the areas of course management and design, delivery, student communication, creation and maintenance of a positive and engaging learning environment, assessment, and use of new technologies. Online teaching and learning place unique demands both on instructor and students. The most successful online course experiences for students and instructors depend on the preparation and expertise of a well-prepared online instructor (Jones, 2006). Such expertise is not developed overnight. It requires a model for faculty recruitment, training, support, and professional development and many resources.

According to Levy (2003), faculty members are faced with a number of new situations when teaching an online learning class as opposed to a traditional class. Some of these include the following: the administration or management of online courses; the course design; course content development, delivery method for the content (e.g., text, graphics, audio/video, etc.); the various communication methods that the students will use such as email, discussion boards, and synchronous and asynchronous chats; ways to facilitate and stimulate student involvement; appropriate student assessments for online learning; and, a working knowledge of all the technologies being implemented in the online course. Online teaching and learning warrants an orchestration of technological, content, and pedagogical knowledge. In addition, online instructors need to learn about andragogy (adult learning) in an online medium.

With such a growing number of courses offered online, many challenges exist in online facilitation or instruction—how do we help online faculty develop and deliver quality online instruction? What systems of support need to exist in order for online faculty to develop their online instruction knowledge, skills, and dispositions? What monetary, design, and infrastructural challenges exist with online learning, teaching and preparation of online faculty? What will happen when training for online faculty alone is not sufficient to produce desired student outcomes and sustainability of learning over time? How will online instructors facilitate student learning in an online learning environment? How will instructors motivate students to learn in the online learning environment? What is the role of online faculty mentoring, resources, and ongoing professional development in their learning and success? Meeting the professional development needs of online instructors is a moving target as our knowledge and experiences in this discipline continue to grow (Taylor & McQuigann, 2008). It is important that we invest heavily on the training, support, and professional development of the "glue that holds the online learning together", the online instructor, and that we continue our research efforts in order to monitor the changes and trends in the field of online teaching and learning.

The Case for Online Professional Development

Students in the twenty-first century will need highly qualified teachers to help them meet the demands of a highly competitive global society. While it is well documented that professional development (PD) is a key factor in producing and maintaining high-quality administrators, teachers, and staff (Kleiman, 2004; SEDTA, 2005), it is also becoming well recognized that PD is empowered when it is delivered in a sustained and consistent manner. The State Educational Technology Association's "Class of 2020 Action Plan" calls for action steps to "make ongoing, sustainable professional development available to all teachers (SEDTA, 2008, p. 6). The US Department of Education recognizes that PD is most effective when it is sustained, intensive, and collaborative (Kleiman, 2004). Thus, it is important that educators receive comprehensive, interactive, relevant, and current professional development. The Southern Regional Education Board (SREB) advises school and state leaders to promote online professional development for teachers, school administrators, and other faculty (SREB, 2004).

Research has shown that teacher quality is strongly correlated with students' academic achievement (Darling-Hammond, 2000; Jordan, Mendro, & Weerasinghe, 1997; Nye, Konstantopoulos, & Hedges, 2004; Rice, 2003; Rivken, Hanushek, & Kain, 2005; Wright, Horn, & Sanders, 1997). One of the strategies for improving teacher quality focuses on improving the quality of inservice teachers through PD. In an effort to increase access, provide alternative PD options, meet the PD needs of many teachers, increase convenience and improve cost-efficiency, there has been a growing interest in online delivery of professional development (OPD) (Dede, 2006; Kleiman, 2004; Galley, 2002; Ginsberg, Gray, & Levin, 2004).

In this chapter the author will describe a model she developed and implemented for the development, management, and support of a statewide online professional development project for K-12 educators in reading. This project supported the content needs of 44,344 educators in the state of Florida for eight years. This chapter will also examine success factors, challenges, and barriers for online instructors, will highlight major themes prevalent in the literature related to "quality control or assurance" in online instruction, and will provide practical strategies for instructors and online course developers to design and deliver effective online instruction. Recommendations will be made on how to prepare instructors for quality online instruction and student learning.

MAIN FOCUS OF THE CHAPTER

The Florida Online Reading Professional Development (FOR-PD) Project: A Situated Perspective

The *No Child Left Behind Act* (NCLB) of 2001 brought about groundbreaking educational reform, including a strong focus on effective personnel and quality instruction in every classroom. In response to national and state policy, Florida Online Reading Professional Development Professional Development (FOR-PD), Florida's first large-scale statewide online professional development PD project, has been a major vehicle professional development for meeting the needs of Florida educators since 2003. The project was developed at the University of Central Florida, College of Education by Dr. Vicky Zygouris-Coe (2002-2010) and Dr. Donna Baumbach (2002-2004). FOR-PD offered a free 14-week online course designated to enable preK-12 educators to keep abreast with emerging standards, current scientifically based research, best instructional practices, and the ever-changing literacy needs of an increasingly

diverse group of students. Completion of FOR-PD resulted in 60 professional development points; the course was equivalent to a three- credit hour graduate course. Since the official launch of the course in 2003, the project provided services to over 44,344 educators, to all 67 Florida's school districts, seven state universities, and six community college Educator Preparation Institutes (EPIs).

FOR-PD was developed originally as a vehicle for preK-12 Florida educators to meet Competency 2 of Florida's Add-On Reading Endorsement: Foundations of Research-Based Practices. This endorsement was Florida's effort to help especially teachers in secondary grades, and those specifically teaching reading or English Language Arts, expand their knowledge about reading development, research, and instruction. This goal paralleled the state's goal for every student in Florida reading at grade level by 2014. Florida teachers needed FOR-PD or its equivalent in order for them to be considered highly qualified according to the No Child Left Behind (NCLB) Public Act of 2001.

Because of a wide range of participant demographics, the fact that FOR-PD was a statewide project that supported the Florida Department of Education literacy initiatives, the urgent need for its participants to learn about reading research and instruction, and the large number of enrolled participants each semester, it was critical for the project to have course facilitators who maintained higher quality of their services—the project's goal was to maximize positive participant experiences with the project and learning. Facilitators of FOR-PD courses (also called sections) were certified through the project's online training and certification program and were expected to become an effective liaison between the project and participants; their main role was to facilitate participants' learning. The project also provided professional development courses for the facilitators and developed a unique quality assurance check (QAC) process for monitoring progress

Figure 1. Graphic representation of the FOR-PD project's model for online instructor training, support, and professional development

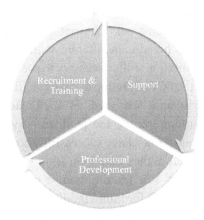

and quality of online facilitation. Figure 1 presents a visual representation of FOR-PD's model for selecting, retaining, and supporting quality online facilitators. The author will expand upon each component of this model in the following sections of this chapter.

Online Facilitator Recruitment, Training, and Certification

The Facilitator Specialist

As part of the FOR-PD model, the Facilitator Specialist was in charge of the facilitator division. This staff was highly qualified in e-learning and instructional technology. As part of her core responsibilities, the facilitator specialist was the liaison between the project and all online facilitators. She received, reviewed, and evaluated all facilitator applications, entered data in the Facilitator database, updated the facilitator training course and facilitator manual, collaborated with the Principal Investigator in developing professional development for facilitators, monitored facilitator performance, provided additional support in means of email, phone, synchronous and asynchronous communications, and handled facilitator-related matters.

Facilitator Recruitment and Application Process

FOR-PD recruited potential online facilitators through an online application process. In addition, collaborating school districts, universities, and community colleges assigned potential facilitators to receive online training and certification from their respective agencies and institutions. FOR-PD graduates who showed exceptional performance in the course, displayed leadership potential, and had suitable educational experiences, were recommended by their course facilitator and later solicited by FOR-PD to consider applying for facilitator training. Aside from recommendations, performance, relevant experiences, and characteristics, the FOR-PD Facilitator Specialist also interviewed and carefully screened all applicants. Over the years and as a result of shifts in participant demographics, FOR-PD solicited facilitator applicants who had specific certifications or upper grade level teaching experiences. A careful monitoring of facilitator progress and performance occurred on a semester basis. Immediately when an individual applied to become a facilitator, his or her information were entered into the database. The database, in addition to being a record-keeping tool, helped the Facilitator Specialist to manage facilitator demographics and other data. As part FOR-PD model, goals, and participant characteristics and needs, content expertise was a major requirement. The project provided selected applicants with a seven-week online facilitator training and certification course as well as much mentoring, support, and professional development in online facilitation, e-learning, and andragogy. The following were key selection criteria for facilitator applicants:

- Successful completion of the FOR-PD course (80% and above completion rate)
- A minimum of three years teaching experience (required)
- Advanced knowledge of research-based reading strategies and technology

- Ability to provide explicit instruction in the following elements of reading as they apply to appropriate grades: phonemic awareness, phonics, fluency, vocabulary, and comprehension
- Ability to systematically use effective reading strategies that have been tested and have a record of success
- Identified by school or district as a reading/literacy leader
- Any of the following:
  ○ Master's Degree in reading or other related areas
  ○ Bachelor's Degree plus completion of the Reading Endorsement
  ○ Hold a position as a Reading Coach or Curriculum Coach

Facilitator Demographics

Over time, FOR-PD trained and certified over 350 facilitators. The project's goal was to attract and retain effective online facilitators. Project enrollment determined how many online sections of the course were offered per semester. In addition, the FOR-PD team utilized data from participant completion rates, participant feedback about the quality of facilitation, as well as participation in professional development and adherence to the project's policies and goals as determining factors for assigning facilitators to courses per semester. FOR-PD facilitators represented 45 out of 67 school districts. About two-thirds of FOR-PD facilitators designated themselves as *other educational professional*; about 20% taught at the middle- or high-school level and the other 20% taught at the elementary level. Almost all (98%) have taught at the K-12 level and 95% were female; 80% of active facilitators taught one FOR-PD course per semester. In addition, facilitators were from five state universities: University of Central Florida, University of Florida, University of West Florida, Florida Gulf Coast University, and Florida International University.

Facilitator Training and Certification Course

The Facilitator Training and Certification Course (FTCC), a seven-week long online course, was designed to prepare facilitators with the basic online facilitation skills necessary to successfully facilitate the FOR-PD course. It was facilitated by a successful and "seasoned" FOR-PD facilitator and was monitored by the facilitator specialist. All facilitators must have successfully completed FOR-PD before they could enroll in FTCC. For the most part, this training course provided an exemplary model for future facilitators to follow.

As part of FTCC the facilitators were required to review all of the content of the FOR-PD course. This was important as the course changed over time. The *content* of FTCC provided exemplary communication and problem-solving strategies, and a thorough overview in usage of the various tools available in the course. The course was reviewed and updated on a semester basis; updates included new technology, policies, content and other changes to the FOR-PD course, facilitator issues, updates to the facilitator manual and other project policies, more practice with using certain Learning Management System (LMS) tools and features, modeling of teaching presence, assessments, and ways to help all FOR-PD participants learn and succeed.

The FTCC course covered the following topics, skills, and dispositions necessary for successful online facilitation:

- Basics of online staff development
- Facilitator's role in online learning
- Online facilitation best practices
- Social, teaching, and cognitive presence online
- Working in the LMS environment
- Working with adult learners online
- Practical work with FOR-PD course content

In addition, the project conducted an evaluation of the FTCC course on an ongoing basis. Feedback from trainees assisted the project team to plan and make future improvements to the course in an effort to best prepare online facilitators to meet the technology, content, and learning needs of educators in the FOR-PD course. Discussions on the effectiveness of the FTCC course continued with facilitators on an ongoing basis. It was important to the FOR-PD team to receive ongoing feedback on the impact of the training on online facilitators' ability to deal effectively with their daily roles and responsibilities, difficulties they experienced with technology, and also with addressing the content questions of their course participants.

The overall goal of the FTCC course was to ensure that each online facilitator understood the importance of his or her role for teacher success. Survey results indicated that the majority (75%) of online facilitators indicated that the course facilitator was the most important factor that would contribute to student success within the course; 16% indicated course structure was the most important factor, nine percent cited the content, and no one felt assessment would contribute to the success of students. Below are sample comments from facilitators about the FTCC course:

I feel that we need more experience with the grade book part of the course. I am still unclear about how to go about entering grades.

I would like to have had more hands-on practice with the grade book. Great class wonderful facilitator and a true learning experience. Thank you.

I would like to learn more about how to encourage more learner-learner interactions.

The FTCC facilitator was very helpful and answered questions and concerns immediately. In addition she began this learning community with a terrific model of introduction and set a tone of

easiness for all involved. I applaud her attention to detail and community building.

This was a great course. I feel as if it fully prepared me to take on the role of facilitator.

The FOR-PD project also tapped into participant feedback about the role of the online facilitator in the online learning experience. The majority of the respondents indicated they enjoyed collaboration and communication:

I thought the discussion with the facilitator and other participants about the course and the tools for facilitating the course were the most useful.

Sharing of ideas and frustrations with facilitator and classmates.

I liked the discussions between the participants and the facilitator. It was a risk-free environment and I feel as if I learned so much from the discussions I had with others.

Other respondents commented on the specific facilitators:

The most useful part of this course was the wonderful support and caring by Wendy, the course facilitator. She made all of us into a community of learners!

Having an understanding facilitator made all the difference! Her e-mails were so supportive and I hope that I will be able to communicate with FOR-PD participants as well as she did with us.

Nancy!! She is an incredible facilitator. She responds immediately; she provides detailed feedback; maintains a positive and professional environment while adding humor to the discussions; she also encourages interaction among the students taking the course.

Facilitator training is imperative for online facilitator preparation; facilitators need training in e-learning, andragogy (the study of adult learning), technology, content, and also in communication, monitoring, and assessment of student learning in an online environment.

Online Facilitator Support

The FOR-PD project invested heavily in supporting online facilitators and building their facilitation skills over time. This investment of resources and capital resulted in a comprehensive model of facilitator support, in the development of a qualified cadre of online facilitators who produced high completion rates and participant satisfaction, and in a positive online facilitator community. Much of the project's success is attributed to these types of support (beyond the FTCC) for online facilitators. Training and certification for online facilitation is fundamental, but support beyond training will help to strengthen online facilitators' knowledge and skills and will also contribute to the overall success of any online professional development project. In the following section, the author will describe the main means of support for FOR-PD's online facilitators.

Facilitator Specialist

The FOR-PD Facilitator Specialist was a core means of support for the project's online facilitators. She functioned not only as a liaison between the project and facilitators, but she also acted as the community builder for all facilitators. She worked with all facilitators, reviewed facilitator applications, addressed facilitator issues (e.g., online facilitation, compensation, etc.), shared participant issues that involved facilitators, wrote the monthly facilitator e-newsletter, collaborated with the FOR-PD team on aspects of the FTCC course and FOR-PD course, held focus groups, updated the facilitator database, collaborated with the Principal Investigator in the development of

facilitator professional development, and played a key role for the project and its facilitators. Her knowledge of instructional technology and e-learning helped her to become a role model for facilitators. The Facilitator Specialist communicated on an ongoing basis with facilitators via synchronous and asynchronous communications, Skype, AIM, ichat, Voki, animation, email, discussion forums, phone, and face-to-face meetings (via annual focus groups). The expertise and availability of the Facilitator Specialist contributed to the selection and retention of quality online facilitators.

Facilitator Manual

One of the most important documents available to facilitators, the Facilitator Manual, outlined specific tasks facilitators must complete before their section of the FOR-PD course began—the manual became their guiding document about roles, responsibilities, policies, communication and assessment means, and the "how-to" of online facilitation. The Facilitator Manual offered detailed explanations for before, during, and after-course tasks. The manual also described the various support mechanisms available to facilitators and outlined the responsibilities of key stakeholders including participants, school districts, and the FOR-PD office. Conditions of employment were carefully explained and tutorials for synchronous and asynchronous chat, discussion boards, email tools, and grade book tools were provided. The manual's appendix offered sample messages for a variety of purposes including welcoming participants to the course, helping those with login trouble, notices to those who were lagging behind, and sample messages for communicating with participants.

Performance Support Tools

FOR-PD course facilitators had access to a variety of performance support tools to help them in their role as course facilitator. Specifically requested by course facilitators, printable rubrics streamlined assignment grading for busy facilitators who preferred to use a paper-based method of grading course assignments. The grade book template offered examples and tips for storing grades electronically. Developed at the request of course facilitators, model postings provided examples for facilitators to share with participants as needed and in a way controlled by the facilitators. The model postings also helped facilitators calibrate their own grading standards. The end-of-course checklist served as a convenient reminder to facilitators about the specific tasks that must be carried out to assure proper in-service credit for participants and prompt payment to course facilitators.

Electronic e-Newsletter for Facilitators

Entitled *FOR-PD Facilitation Fundamentals* (FFF), the monthly facilitator e-newsletter helped to keep course facilitators informed of the latest online facilitation research and tips featured a core aspect of online facilitation with research and more resources for further reading and learning. The purpose of the FFF e-newsletter was to a) be an informational source for facilitators; b) serve as a communication vehicle between the FOR-PD office and the facilitators; and, c) provide information intended to strengthen facilitation skills.

FFF presented project and policy (national, state, and local) updates about literacy and preK-12 issues, highlighted FOR-PD facilitation updates, addressed issues and feedback from participants and facilitators, shared updates and reminders about technology help desk data and calendar. In addition, FFF addressed quality assistance checks, and information about upcoming virtual facilitation meetings, guest speakers, as well as information about online resources and technology tools.

The e-newsletter also served as a source of professional development for facilitators. The Facilitator Specialist provided facilitators with professional development in order to ensure they had the necessary skills, knowledge, and abilities to successfully facilitate a FOR-PD course. The FFF focused on building an online community between facilitators with opportunities provided for online discussion postings based on topics presented in the newsletter about practical ways to improve teaching and learning. In the "Facilitator Resource of the Month" section of the newsletter, we focused on building a sense of community by explicitly including resources about online communities (e.g., articles for facilitators to read about building online communities) and implicitly, by informing facilitators of the bi-monthly discussion topics for the month and instructing them to post their thoughts in the "For Facilitator Only" discussion area.

Facilitator Forum

Housed on the FOR-PD course server, the Facilitator Forum was a series of discussion boards offering 24/7 access for facilitators to interact with each other, to share information and ideas about the FOR-PD course, to ask for help from others, and to share successes. Specific discussion areas included a place to meet fellow facilitators, to ask for and offer help, hints, and advice, to make suggestions for an upcoming FFF, and to share success stories. The Facilitator Coffeehouse discussion board enabled facilitators to interact with each other on matters unrelated to the FOR-PD course, but likely to be of general interest. Finally, there was a discussion area specifically for facilitators to discuss issues related to each of the 14 FOR-PD lessons.

Monthly Technology-Related and Online Facilitation-Related Chats

Monthly facilitator synchronous chats served to keep facilitators in touch with each other about technology-related issues, LMS issues, and the

FOR-PD office. Synchronous chats were conducted using ADOBE CONNECT. As part of the technology chats, the facilitator specialist, a technology support staff and other expert facilitators discussed their successes or challenges with certain technology tools, shared new uses of technology, and planed for future tools. E-learning national and local guest experts participated and shared much information on online facilitation topics (e.g., discussions, communication and interactions with participants, online collaborations, the mechanics of online facilitation, online community, time management, etc.). These chats became an important means of support for online facilitators—they helped them to learn more about technology usage, the LMS and other course and technology tools. Online facilitation helped to build both their self-efficacy to facilitate online and the FOR-PD facilitator community.

Technology Help Desk

The FOR-PD project instituted a weekday and weekend technology support help desk for facilitators and participants. This proved to be a very important means of facilitator support. Facilitators' concerns or online facilitation challenges were addressed by technology experts. In turn, facilitators would also mentor their students about certain uses of technology and LMS tools. Common areas of concern included disruption of technology, grading, inactive links, posting assignments, pop-up blocking issues, use of specific tools, participant registration and login issues, etc. Expert staff were available via a toll-free phone number, instant messenger, email, or chat for technical issues during standard day office hours, evening (4-10 PM), and on Saturday (3-6 PM). This type of support helped to reduce facilitator anxiety about technology-related usage and challenges and helped to develop their technology and online facilitation knowledge and skills.

Facilitator Mentors

A team of seven expert online FOR-PD facilitators was selected by the FOR-PD team to serve as an additional level of support, as mentors, for online facilitators and the Facilitator Specialist. Criteria for selection of facilitator mentors included the following: an excellent record of student completion rates, a supportive and motivating personality style, good knowledge of technology, experiences in mentoring adult educators, and a propensity for learning more about technology, online facilitation, and content. These seasoned online facilitators also provided valuable feedback for updates to the facilitator division of the project and the FOR-PD course. As a team, along with the Facilitator Specialist, the Principal Investigator, and the project's Technology and Reading Specialists, they co-constructed sample rubrics, examples to assignments, plans for "remediating" online facilitators who were not performing at a desired level, and became an important level of support for the project.

Reading Specialist

The Reading Specialist played another key role in the FOR-PD project. Although her responsibilities were predominantly in the area of course participants (i.e., preK-12 educators), course content and literacy resources, she provided support in the area of course content to the Facilitator Specialist, the facilitator mentors, and the online facilitators. Her feedback about participant issues and content-related questions assisted facilitators with how they could address participant needs. The Reading Specialist and the Principal Investigator collaborated in developing tips, examples, sample messages to participants, suggestions about how to respond to participants' content questions, and feedback to course assignments. Content support was equally important to participant success.

Facilitators (and participants) benefited from her expertise, assistance, and sharing of resources. The Reading Specialist held monthly content-related synchronous meetings and invited facilitators to attend and learn more about the course content. In addition, she shared valuable information with facilitators about how participants were understanding or misunderstanding content, assignments, and what they could do to better facilitate the course content and maintain a positive online learning community.

Virtual Book Clubs

FOR-PD facilitators participated in various virtual book clubs over time. This type of support aimed to build facilitator knowledge about literacy and online facilitation and community among facilitators. Decisions about which book to select were based on feedback from facilitators about areas they needed to build their knowledge on and also on data from participant and facilitator progress.

The "Coffee House" and "Book Sharing" discussion boards provided a way for facilitators to discuss personal topics, such as books they were reading and personal interests they had about the topics. Book Reviews conducted by the Facilitator Specialist, Reading Specialist, and the Principal Investigator were also taken into consideration. Book Reviews also provided opportunities for facilitators to reflect on their facilitation skills and how they were utilizing the book's topics in their courses. Books focused on professional development, online facilitation, literacy, and teacher learning.

Resources

FOR-PD developed and maintained a comprehensive repository of online facilitation and technology resources. These resources were updated on an ongoing basis using data from facilitators, facilitator mentors, participants, FOR-PD staff, and others. They were used as a means of fa-

cilitator support and professional development. Facilitators shared resources, shared feedback from use of resources, experimented with use of new technology tools, wrote "how-to" for usage of tools for other facilitators, and contributed national and other related resources on an ongoing basis. Online facilitation knowledge and expertise is a fluid, ongoing process; data from project evaluation showed that facilitators appreciated the many resources FOR-PD selected, provided, modeled, and reflected upon on an ongoing basis. Lastly, the Technology Specialist, the Quality Assurance Check Specialist, and other FOR-PD staff, also provided other types of support to facilitators.

Quality Assurance Checks

In order to maintain the high quality of education required of professional development and teacher preparation, online programs need to be held accountable for the quality of the programs offered. The need for quality assurance in professional development and online programs is evidenced by the myriad of frameworks developed by agencies, such as the five pillars from the Sloan-C Consortium (Lorenzo & Moore, 2002), the *Distance Education: Guidelines for Good Practice* developed by the American Federation of Teachers (AFT, 2000), and the *Accreditation and Assuring Quality in Distance Learning* from Council for Higher Education Accreditation (CHEA, 2002). However, all of these general benchmarks for quality do not explain how online programs should develop and maintain programs for quality assurance. Although quality assurance should theoretically be a fundamental part of web-based activities, it is a relatively new "hot topic" and thus not much valid research has been conducted in this area. Various online programs have standard ways of assuring quality online facilitation; for example, qualifications and training of instructors and end of course evaluation surveys. However, what current research in this area *is* available both confirms the advantages of quality assurance and attests to the importance integrating a quality assurance regimen into online programs.

One of the most recurrent findings suggest that monitoring of online facilitation is essential to the establishment of adequate support systems in order to promote the collaboration between participants and facilitators. Facilitator-participant communication is vital and should be established in the early stages of the course. This connection between the parties boosts the confidence and motivation of the participants while apprising the facilitators of any issues with the course. More specifically, communication in the form of facilitator feedback to participants has also been identified as a crucial component that monitoring of facilitation (or what is also referred to as "quality assurance checks (QAC)") aim(s) to regulate. Feedback must be timely in order to be useful, and so "quality checks on processing time should be standard" (Clarke, Butler, Schmidt-Hansen, & Somerville, 2004). Effective communication can also foster a sense of online community where participants and facilitators can expand their understanding of the potential offered by a web-based program. Although good communication between facilitators and participants has been emphasized, there is research to suggest that inter-peer support is just as essential (Clarke et al., 2004). Participants should be encouraged to socialize with one another and support each other during the course. Seeing to good relations between participants is the responsibility of the facilitators and can be monitored through the QAC.

Lastly, research suggests that employing a general quality assurance approach can significantly enhance web-based learning (Fresen, 2005). Taking into consideration the human elements inherent in QAC and the infrastructure in which QAC will be used can help in designing an effective quality assurance approach that will satisfy the needs of both facilitators and participants. Overall, a balance with educational innovation and professional development on one side and accountability on the other must be established if truly enhanced online learning is to occur. FOR-PD provides online facilitators with a multi-layered system of support. For example, a seven-week facilitator training course, asynchronous discussions with facilitator specialist, monthly online synchronous and asynchronous meetings, a monthly facilitator e-newsletter, a facilitator specialist, a full-time day and part-time evening and weekend help desk support, semester-long professional development, and numerous other resources. Because of the high accountability associated with FOR-PD, the project could not "afford" ineffective facilitation. The project's Principal Investigator developed an additional and more specific system of assessing our facilitators' practices. The type of facilitation a FOR-PD facilitator provided to fellow-educators in the course "either made or broke" the course. Participant success, experiences with online learning, and development of knowledge is highly affected by the course facilitator's presence, absence, support, and overall facilitation. In an effort to achieve this goal, FOR-PD developed and implemented a series of Quality Assurance Checks (QAC) for both participants and facilitators. The goal of QAC was to monitor and track participant and facilitator progress and allow for individualized assistance for both audiences. In other words, QAC were developed in an effort to maximize both the participants' and facilitators' online experiences. Additionally, QAC provided support across a number of composites for both the facilitators and the participants. Quality Assurance Checks were advantageous in many ways for facilitators and participants. The QAC helped to promote and therefore strengthen communication between the facilitators, participants, and the FOR-PD staff. The increased communication and support helped to boost motivation among participants and facilitators and fostered effective exchange of ideas. Facilitators gained the opportunity to receive a personal evaluation, including quality feedback on their performance, communication guidance, and reminders about upcoming responsibilities. Participants reaped the benefits of QAC as well, including information about resources and available support and an incentive to continue with the course. QAC also helped to promote a sense of online community, which lead to an improved understanding of the content and tools, an increased awareness of course expectations, and overall improved facilitator and participant performance.

Systematic FOR-PD QAC began in August 2004 and continued through August 2010. During Fall 2004, the QAC were completed sporadically by existing staff members. Because of the perceived benefit of QAC, beginning in January 2005, a new system of participant and facilitator QAC was implemented for enhanced analysis of participant and facilitator performance. Due to the increased work volume associated with QAC, a staff member was assigned as a Quality Assurance Specialist. This new job role allowed for increased interaction and monitoring of FOR-PD participants and facilitators with an ultimate goal of enhancing FOR-PD's ability to help participants and facilitators succeed in the online learning experience. An analysis of participant and facilitator QAC revealed that many participants who had fallen behind in the course had non-functioning email addresses, others were behind in progress, while others were non-responsive to project or facilitator communications. Simple factors such as non-functioning emails impact all—e.g., facilitators may have been unsuccessful or unable to communicate critical course information to those participants. In addition, many of the participants who had fallen behind reported they were extremely busy and had come to the realization that they would be unable to dedicate a sufficient amount of time to the FOR-PD course. These participants, though unable to complete the course at that time, often expressed a desire to complete the course at some future date. Few participants reported technical problems, and the majority were satisfied with the interaction and assistance provided by FOR-PD facilitators. The facilitator QAC sought to verify that facilitators were engaging in course activities, such as the discussion board, and grading in a timely fashion.

Emails were sent to facilitators who appeared to need encouragement in participation and/or completion of grading. The results of the facilitator QAC were quite positive. Facilitators expressed appreciation for feedback on their facilitation style, and many subsequently increased their communication with the FOR-PD office regarding participants and other issues.

Soon after the QAC model was formed, participant and facilitator QAC began to follow a specific timeline per semester. What follows is a brief description of how they worked. During the second and third weeks of the 14-week course, both a participant and a facilitator QAC were completed. The participant QAC tracked five critical components for each individual course section: 1) the number of participants enrolled; 2) the number of participants who had dropped the course and notified the FOR-PD office of the drop; 3) the number of participants who were two to five lessons behind; 4) the number of participants who had logged in but had not started the course; and 5) the number of participants who were up-to-date on course assignments. Participants who were two to five lessons behind at both QAC were considered capable of catching up and received additional support from the course facilitator. Participants who were further behind were considered "too far behind" to successfully complete and benefit from the course. As a result of the first participant QAC, two groups of participants were then identified: 1) those who had not logged on at all and those who had logged on but had not started the course were considered one group; and 2) those participants who had fallen behind. Once the two groups were identified, a standard email was sent to the participants notifying them of their status within the course and encouraging them to either get started, or continue the course. Furthermore, in these emails, participants were directed to numerous resources offered by FOR-PD, including the Help Desk. They were also reminded to contact their course facilitators, as they were very willing to help. To ensure that facilitators were aware of participant needs, facilitators were copied on emails sent to participants. FOR-PD made great effort to assist participants in any way possible.

The first facilitator QAC was also undertaken during the second and third weeks of the course. The facilitator QAC tracked five critical components for each course facilitator: 1) posting of a course schedule; 2) posting of a Welcome Message; 3) posting of a "Meet Me Here" (an introductory, community-building discussion; 4) responses to participant discussions; and 5) up-to-date grading. As a result of the first facilitator QAC, facilitators were made aware of participant enrollment and participation. Facilitators were encouraged to continue contacting and supporting participants who were lagging behind, and the Quality Assurance Specialist made herself and other staff, i.e. the Help Desk staff, available to assist. Any concerns with facilitator performance were carefully expressed directly to each facilitator. A second facilitator QAC was conducted during weeks six and seven of the FOR-PD course. This QAC tracked two critical components: 1) responses to participant postings; and 2) up-to-date grading. Facilitators were encouraged to continue their interaction with participants and were provided with guidance and support as needed. During weeks nine and ten of the FOR-PD course, a second and final participant QAC was conducted. The same five critical components from the first QAC were again documented: 1) the number of participants enrolled; 2) the number of participants who had dropped the course and notified the FOR-PD office of the drop; 3) the number of participants who were two to five lessons behind; 4) the number of participants who had logged in but had not started the course; and 5) the number of participants who were up-to-date on course assignments. As a result of this second QAC, two groups of participants were identified: those who were between two to five lessons behind and those who were more than five lessons behind. Again, participants who are two to five lessons behind were considered capable of completing the course in a timely manner and

sent an encouraging email. Those participants who were more than five lessons behind were not contacted, as they were considered too far behind to complete the course in a timely and educationally sound manner. Again, facilitators were included as recipients of the e-mails sent to those participants who were two to five lessons behind. A third and final facilitator QAC was completed during weeks eleven and twelve of the course. This QAC tracked the same two critical components as the second QAC: responses to participant postings and up-to-date grading. Facilitators were encouraged to continue their interaction with participants and were provided with guidance and support as needed. Facilitators were reminded of course closing procedures and completion dates. Again, FOR-PD offered any assistance needed. In addition to the QAC model, a survey component was added to gauge the effectiveness of the QAC in helping to increase interaction in the FOR-PD course among both participants and facilitators. This survey was sent to the facilitator of each course section after the first QAC. Since some facilitators worked in more than one section, it is possible that some facilitators received more than one survey so it became important that facilitators completed surveys for each course they facilitated in order to capture the impact of the QAC on all course sections. The Quality Assurance Check Survey contained seven questions using a five-point Likert scale, three multiple-choice questions, and an open-ended question. The Likert statements encouraged facilitators to reflect on the QAC's stimulation of a) understanding of participant needs; b) reemphasizing facilitator roles and expectations; c) encouraging frequent interactions with participants both in the discussion area and in other areas of the course; d) building an online learning community; and e) providing general facilitation methods. The multiple choice questions sought to elicit information on the number of participants who increased activity as a result of the QAC, the consistency of facilitator and

FOR-PD course records, and the overall value of the QAC. Lastly, facilitators were asked to verbally document their plans to increase participant interactivity in the course. All QAC were designed and implemented in a positive manner; they were not intended to chastise participants or facilitators; they were reminders and invitations for support and communication—the motives and intentions of the QAC model were understood by both participants and facilitators. Facilitators welcomed the additional data, specialized student progress reports, and added resources to maximize participant success. Not all participants responded to the QAC emails—some participants ignored them but overall, the majority of participants responded and were open about the reasons that contributed to their delayed progress or absence from the course.

The QAC were instituted as a monitoring system for the project as well as an additional support mechanism for both participants and facilitators. Although the QAC were proven to be beneficial in a multitude of areas, there were still some issues that were elicited through the QAC. For example, the pace of the course (completing too fast or too slow) was a source of contention. Participants often lagged behind as a result of personal issues and constraints. The QAC identified and supported these participants in their efforts to complete the course. One facilitator noted, "It is those personal touches that have kept the majority of my participants moving through the course." Also, QAC were utilized when deciphering which facilitators would be assigned to a course the following semester. Basically, if a facilitator had not met the facilitator requirements (i.e., quality facilitation criteria, professional development participation, communication with project, completion rates) on more than one occasion there was a chance he or she would not be given a course the following semester. The QAC helped to keep facilitators apprised of what was expected. One facilitator wrote to FOR-PD staff to say, "Thank you for the quality checks--it

helps to get some feedback from 'cyberspace'--something concrete! I have tried to respond to all participants in the first few lessons… in order to have them participate in discussions … it is indeed a learning process! Thanks for your feedback--I will make adjustments as needed!" The results of these checks were also used to continually improve the FOR-PD and the FTCC courses. Components of the courses that needed to be improved often became apparent in the QAC process. For example, the QAC resulted directly in the implementation of new resources available to participants and facilitators: Facilitator Expectations Document, Participant Expectations Document, FOR-PD Facilitator Monthly E-Newsletter's focus on what is being seen and suggestions to correct the problems, and the Literacy Newsletter's Focus on participants. In addition, other issues that had transpired from the QAC included the quality of facilitator communications and discussions with participants and the use of facilitator feedback and resources. It was imperative that the themes that emerged from the QAC resulted in proper intervention implementation. Therefore, the QAC data helped protect the FOR-PD project, facilitators, participants, and ensured a positive interactive learning experience for all involved. While there is no way to determine a cause and effect relationship between QAC and FOR-PD completion rates, there appeared to be somewhat of a correlation. Additionally, data indicated that the course facilitator played a key role in student completion rates.

The QAC process benefited the project and its audiences in many ways (see Table 1). They resulted in increased communication between FOR-PD office and facilitators, increased communication between facilitators and participants, increased completion rates, increased awareness of course expectations, improved sense of online community, improved facilitator and participant performance, improved understanding of the content and tools, and improved participation and exchange of ideas. QAC also directly benefited

Table 1. Impact of QAC data

QAC Support for Facilitators and Participants		
Facilitators	**Participants**	
• Positive feedback and encouragement • Personal evaluation • Concise overall data on each section • Help in communicating with participants • Reminders about important facilitator information	• Reminder of critical course information • Motivation to complete the course • Provided information on support systems for participants	
Results of the Quality Assurance Checks		
Facilitators	**Participants**	**FOR-PD Project**
• Increased communication with FOR-PD office • Increased communication with students • Increased participation in discussion • Increased completion rates • Streamlined expectations for FOR-PD facilitators • Created an outlet for comments, questions, and tips • Insured the dissemination of correct information to facilitators	• Increased communication/personal connection with FOR-PD office • Increased communication with facilitator • Increased success (completion and understanding) in course • Created an outlet for comments and questions about facilitator and course • Increased awareness of student support (ex: help desk) • Insured the dissemination of correct information to facilitators	• Directed information to appropriate staff member • Increased question turnaround time • Compiled "big picture" issues • Identified course problems • More accurate "dropped student" data • QAC database and information became accessible to all staff • Increased office awareness of facilitator and student activity/concerns • Easier/more effective monitoring of facilitators and students

facilitators and participants. Facilitators were given specific, timely feedback, personal evaluations, help and support in communicating with participants, and email reminders of important information. A facilitator commented, "I really am trying to do some things better than before and it is so nice that it has been noticed. Thanks for the encouragement!" Participants benefited by the QAC through being reminded of critical course information and support systems available. Participants also gained motivation to complete the course through the gentle reminder emails sent by both FOR-PD staff and facilitators. Another facilitator said, "I really appreciate the quality assurance checks and FOR-PD's viewpoint on how the course is progressing." The QAC helped support facilitators and participants in building an online community by ensuring that facilitators are meeting expectations and increasing communication between facilitators and participants and facilitators and FOR-PD staff.

The call for high-quality online programs demands accountability and quality assurance in learning. FOR-PD developed and implemented a situated QAC model to answer this demand. QAC required resources in the form of time and money, but the QAC were an invaluable community builder between the project and facilitators. QAC can assist online projects to make data-driven decisions concerning facilitator and participant performance. In this context, QAC were proven to increase participant completion, communication with facilitators and FOR-PD staff, and the course itself, which in turn impacted student performance, perceptions and attitudes, and learning in the FOR-PD course. The FOR-PD QAC model allowed the Principal Investigator of the project to reflect on the course and make necessary changes to promote more participant completion and community building.

Online Facilitator Professional Development

Quality professional development plays a crucial role in increasing teacher knowledge and student achievement—it is a must for teacher growth. Providing professional development for facilitators was a very important aspect of the FOR-PD developers and staff. FOR-PD strived to provide various elements to increase, promote, and encourage professional development among the facilitators. The Principal Investigator believed that all FOR-PD professional development plans must be data-and standards-driven. As a result, the FOR-PD team was very strategic in studying facilitator and participant needs; they planned for professional development that would maximize both facilitator and participant success. Over the years, FOR-PD provided different types of ongoing professional development for its online facilitators. As described in earlier sections of this chapter, the Facilitator Specialist, the facilitator mentors, the FFF (Monthly E-Newsletter), the discussion forums, monthly synchronous and asynchronous technology, online facilitation, and literacy meetings, annual focus groups, and ongoing communications also functioned as means of ongoing professional development for facilitators.

In addition, FOR-PD developed four online professional development courses for facilitators. These courses were designed to provide in-depth training on critical elements of online facilitation. The aforementioned courses were updated on a semester basis to reflect current research, practice, and examples from FOR-PD best practices online facilitation. Lastly, FOR-PD executed a system of differentiated professional development for novice, expert, and struggling online facilitators. Participation in different forms of professional development was a mandatory condition for continued employment as a FOR-PD facilitator. The facilitator professional development e-courses were facilitated by a facilitator mentor; each course was four-weeks long. These courses will be described in detail in the following section.

Teaching Presence and Building of Online Community

Teaching presence is defined as the design, facilitation, and direction of cognitive and social processes for the purpose of realizing personally meaningful and educational worthwhile learning outcomes (Anderson, Rourke, & Archer, 2001). Our goal was to develop tools that were efficient, reliable, and practical in the task of helping teachers to both understand and improve their online teaching. We examined messages for their contribution to three critical functions of the online (and classroom) teacher--designing and administrating learning activities, establishing and maintaining an active learning community, and providing direct instruction. Our tools allowed teachers to assess their own postings and served as valued feedback for reflection and improvement of the teaching function. Secondly, the tools could be used for research to test hypothesis or diagnose problems in online teaching.

As part of the course, facilitators learned more about what makes an effective online learning environment. They also discussed examples from their personal online facilitation about how they demonstrated teaching presence in their online course, and how they cultivated a sense of a professional online learning community. In addition, the course focused on a theoretical model for teaching presence and its importance for student learning and success in an online environment. Facilitators studied best practices about online teaching presence and were given opportunities to implement them in their courses and then reflect on their plans.

Other course topics included how to recognize teaching presence, how to encourage student-facilitator interactions, student-student collaborations and interactions, and how to facilitate active student learning. More topics addressed the importance of providing participants with timely and relevant feedback and the role of facilitator-participant communication in online learning. Facilitators learned more about how to focus and direct discussions, how to manage one's time and provide summaries to student discussions, how to present their knowledge about content or technology, how to respond to technical issues, how to establish netiquette, and diverse ways adults learn in an online medium. Facilitators discussed and reflected on their teaching presence, the importance of establishing trust and building strong social connections, on ways they facilitated discourse in their online course, the presence or absence of direct instruction, and aspects of instructional design and course organization that facilitated or impeded teaching presence. Lastly, online facilitators discussed implications of high levels of online teaching presence or student learning and success, for instructional design, community-building, and e-learning.

Facilitating Content

Interactions between learner and content are vital for online learning. In the context of a 14-week online professional development course, such interactions become even more important. For students to engage with online content, the online course materials must be well designed, relevant and motivating. In addition, the online course material should also be aligned with the course learning objectives and outcomes and should be matched to course activities and assessment tasks (Biggs, 2003). This course focused on teaching facilitators how to help participants navigate the course material, meaningfully engage with it, and how to direct their attention and learning to pertinent content in the FOR-PD course that would help shape their knowledge of reading research and instruction, affect their instructional practices, and promote learning and success in the course and beyond.

Facilitators learned from theory and research on the topic and also from one another. They received best practice examples from facilitator mentors and other colleagues and were also given an opportunity to reflect on their own instruction. In addition, they were asked to develop and share their own ways of facilitating course content. Busy adult educators can benefit from a knowledgeable facilitator's comments and direction about how to "navigate", interact, and learn from content in

an online course. Facilitators learned that it is not sufficient to just share the objectives of a learning module or topic; instead, adult learners will interact more with content if their facilitator provided some relevant and stimulating examples about how they might benefit from the topic at hand. Facilitators learned about effective questioning skills, how to make students think about issues and relate them to their own classroom practice, how to model effective online discussions and providing evidence for their assertions, ask students to come up with their own questions about the topic, share observations, offer feedback to another student in class, have students work in groups and critique each other's work. Overall, facilitators learned about how to facilitate content online, how to stimulate engagement and discussions with content, and how to direct and promote learning in an online environment.

Managing Time

One of the most important skills that any online facilitator or learner will need is how to manage one's time. In the context of the FOR-PD experience, time management was significant for both facilitator and participant success. In this course, facilitators learned more about how to manage their time and how to offer tips and suggestions to their participants about managing their time learning online. An online facilitator "wears" multiple hats; he or she is an instructor, a motivator, a manager, a cheerleader, a counselor, or a mentor. These roles and responsibilities become difficult to harness when one is teaching an online course of 20-25 adults and is working with adults who have varied content and technology knowledge.

This course focused on providing facilitators with more tips and tools about how to manage their time facilitating online. They learned from various resources but also from one another; facilitator mentors and others shared their personal "tried and true" tips with time management.

Facilitators also exited the course with a revised and personalized time management plan. Major areas of focus included: how to share pertinent information with participant in a timely fashion, how to answer content and technology questions, how to facilitate student-student interactions, how much feedback to provide for course assignments, how to engage them in learning, how to maintain effective and timely communication with the entire class, and the never ending battle of being in a "search and rescue" mission with those students who are either not showing up for the course, are lagging behind, or are not responding to any facilitator communications.

In addition, facilitators learned about how to create templates for grading assignments, use FOR-PD rubrics, sample assignments, and other existing means of facilitator support, how and when to communicate with the Facilitator Specialist about students who lagged behind or were no longer participating in the course, how to utilize QAC data, how to communicate expectations and timelines with participants, and how to use tips for stimulating discussions and engaging students in the course.

Personalizing Online Learning

The absence of a face-to-face component creates a need for personalization in online courses. In order for students to become part of an online learning community, they need to feel the presence and personality of the facilitator and other students. This course focused on providing facilitators with more models on how they could personalize their courses. Facilitator mentors and other facilitators shared "tips and tricks" from their own courses that resulted in a great list of ideas about how to personalize an online course. Facilitators learned more ways to present an introductory email, audio and video tools to communicate with students and send messages in the place of email, learning more about each other, using images, and sharing more

about their style, hobbies, books they were reading, favorite recipes, etc. Many facilitators shared how they used family and pet photos to create a welcoming online community, while others created a pet gallery, a travel log, and shared lots of information about themselves. They also learned about shared leadership (i.e., students facilitating discussions), how to stimulate more sharing from students in the class, and how to create a safe and welcoming learning environment. Facilitators also learned about various ways to write the introductory course letter and how important it is for students to have all pertinent information for course login, expectations, calendar, and requirements. They learned about more ways to make students feel welcome and excited about the course, how to use technology for office hours, and how to grade or review assignments using screen recording software, video and animation. Overall, this course provided them with much information on technology and multimedia usage for personalizing online learning.

In addition to these four online facilitator professional development courses, facilitators were invited to select topics of their own choice and means of other professional development to learn more about online facilitation. Several facilitators chose free online resources, watched videos, participated in webinars, and then reported to the facilitator community about what they learned. This also helped to expand the FOR-PD repository of resources for ongoing facilitator professional development. Facilitators enjoyed learning more about online facilitation and provided FOR-PD with much feedback about the impact of these courses on their instruction.

Solutions and Recommendations

Meeting the professional needs of 43,344 preK-12 educators via an online medium over a period of eight years is a significant feat--one that has had tremendous impact on reading instruction in the state of Florida. The FOR-PD project paved the way for other online professional development projects and met multiple statewide literacy initiatives' needs. Such accomplishments did not occur void of vision, support, literacy and technology expertise, and numerous challenges associated with all aspects of project development, implementation, management, and growth. One of the major factors for the success of this large-scale online project is attributed to the comprehensive and strategic development of a facilitator training, support, professional development, and retention model.

Retaining skilled online facilitators is an important success factor for online programs. Although online facilitation responsibilities were many and compensation was low, FOR-PD managed to retain 90% of its certified online facilitators; the 10% of facilitators who did not remain did so for personal reasons only. Creating and maintaining a positive professional learning community for online facilitators and equipping them with relevant training and ongoing support are important elements for facilitator, participant, and project success. Facilitators contributed to an 89.9% completion rate of an admission-free, 14-week-long, comprehensive online professional development in reading.

On the other hand, there are several challenges that still remain with online facilitators. Learning to facilitate adult learning online is an ongoing challenge; it is important to best educate online facilitators about andragogy and how learning takes place in a virtual environment. Improving the communication skills of online facilitators is another ongoing challenge. Facilitator expectations and styles vary and many do not realize how certain messages transfer via an online medium. Much professional development is necessary in these areas. Lastly, helping facilitators deal with frustrations related to motivating students to become engaged and learn becomes a main means of support and facilitator retention.

FUTURE RESEARCH DIRECTIONS

The role of the facilitator in online learning is expanding. Online facilitation carries implications for facilitator training, support, and course design. This chapter presented a situated model for online professional development with a focus on the training, support, professional development, and monitoring of online facilitators. Online facilitation is a multi-faceted process that involves much knowledge about andragogy, content, technology, and online learning. Wallace (2003) stated that, "The work of online teaching, especially as it relates to interacting about subject matter, is not well described or researched" (p. 272). The role of the online facilitator in student learning is paramount; there is a need for more research that explores the role of the online facilitator in student learning and how the role is developed, supported, carried out, and monitored.

According to Bonk, Wisher, and Lee (2004) online instructors' role is not to just support student-student interaction but they also need to know how to direct student learning, develop and maintain a positive learning community, and help students in constructing new knowledge. The online facilitator is also described as instrumental in synthesizing knowledge and guiding students toward deeper learning (Collison, Elbaum, Haavind, & Tinker, 2000). Facilitators need support and ongoing professional development in many areas of online facilitation. They also can benefit from mentoring, tools, and resources that would help them to provide quality online facilitation.

The monitoring of online facilitation is essential in order to pinpoint the areas of support facilitators and participants need. Further research should examine the changing skills and processes of online facilitation that parallel technological growth, the role of the facilitator in rise blended learning, and ways to monitor, assess, and evaluate the quality of online facilitation and its impact on student learning.

CONCLUSION

Online facilitation requires knowledge about online learning, technology, content, and andragogy. Online facilitators need a comprehensive system of support and a strong learning community for them to learn, succeed, and continue to facilitate. Investing in facilitators' sustainability of knowledge and skills will bring about positive results on participant and project success. The role of the facilitator is key to participant success. Professional development helps facilitators to learn more about their role, the factors that facilitate participant success in an online environment, and the importance of creating a safe environment for adults to communicate, collaborate, and learn together. Facilitators need to have a balance between technology and content knowledge. Ongoing professional development is a must for sustaining facilitator knowledge and skills and promoting student success in an online environment.

REFERENCES

Advisory Committee on Mathematics in Education (ACME). (2002). *Continuing professional development of teachers of mathematics: Advisory committee on mathematics in education.* Retrieved from http://tinyurl.com/3u9pcmm

American Federation of Teachers (AFT). (2000). *Distance education: Guidelines for good practice.* Washington, DC: American Federation of Teachers. Retrieved from http://www.aft.org/pubs-reports/higher_ed/distance.pdf

Anderson, T., Rourke, L., Garrison, R. D., & Archer, W. (2001). Assessing teaching presence in a computer conferencing context. *Journal of Asynchronous Learning Networks, 5*(2), 1–17.

Anderson, W. G., & Moore, M. G. (2003). *Handbook of distance education.* Mahwah, NJ: Lawrence Erlbaum.

Biggs, J. (2003). *Teaching for quality learning at university.* Berkshire, UK: Open University Press & McGraw-Hill.

Bolliger, D. U. (2004). Key factors for determining student satisfaction in online courses. *International Journal on E-Learning, 3*(1), 61.

Bonk, C., Wisher, R. A., & Lee, J. Y. (2004). Moderating learner-centered e-learning: Problems and solutions, benefits and implications. In Roberts, T. S. (Ed.), *Online collaborative learning: Theory and practice* (pp. 54–85). Hershey, PA: Information Science Publishing.

Clarke, M., Butler, C., Schmidt-Hansen, P., & Somerville, M. (2004). Quality assurance for distance learning: A case study at Brunel University. *British Journal of Educational Technology, 35*(1), 5–11. doi:10.1111/j.1467-8535.2004.00363.x

Collison, G., Elbaum, B., Haavind, S., & Tinker, R. (2000). *Facilitating on-line learning: Effective strategies for moderators.* Madison, WI: Atwood.

Council for Higher Education Accreditation (CHEA). (2002). *Accreditation and assuring quality in distance learning. CHEA Monograph Series 2002, Number 1.* Washington, DC: Author.

Darling-Hammond, L. (2000). Teacher quality and student achievement: A review of state policy evidence. *Education Policy Analysis Archives, 8*(1), 1–44.

Dede, C. (Ed.). (2006). *Online professional development for teachers: Emerging models and methods.* Cambridge, MA: Harvard Education Press.

Finaly-Neumann, E. (1994). Course work characteristics and students' satisfaction with instructions. *Journal of Instructional Psychology, 21*(2), 14–19.

Fresen, J. (2005). *Quality assurance practice in online (web-supported) learning in higher education: An exploratory study.* Unpublished Master's thesis, University of Pretoria, Pretoria, South Africa, Africa.

Galley, M. (2002). E-training offers options. *Education Week, 21*(35), 41–44.

Ginsburg, A., Gray, T., & Levin, D. (2004). *Online professional development for mathematics teachers: A strategic analysis.* Washington, DC: National Center for Technology Innovation, American Institutes for Research.

Jones, S. (2006). Evaluation of instructor knowledge on structuring and facilitating effective online discourse. *The Journal of Educators Online, 3*(2). Retrieved from http://www.thejeo.com/Volume3Number2/JonesFinal.pdf

Jordan, H. R., Mendro, R., & Weerasinghe, D. (1997). *Teacher effects on longitudinal student achievement: A preliminary report on research on teacher effectiveness.* Paper presented at the National Evaluation Institute, Indianapolis, IN.

Keller, B. (2005, July 27). Teachers flocking to online sources to advance and acquire knowledge. *Education Week, 24*, 22–24.

Kleiman, G. M. (2004). *Meeting the need for high quality teachers: E-learning solutions.* A paper presented at the U.S. Department of Education Secretary's No Child Left Behind Leadership Summit (July 12–13). Retrieved from http://www.ed.gov/about/offices/list/os/technology/ plan/2004/site/documents/Kleiman-MeetingtheNeed.pdf

Levy, S. (2003). Six factors to consider when planning online distance learning programs in higher education. *Online Journal of Distance Learning Administration, 6*(1). Retrieved from http://www.westga.edu/~distance/ojdla/spring61/levy61.htm

Lorenzo, G., & Moore, J. C. (2002). *The Sloan Consortium report to the nation: Five pillars of quality online education.* The Alfred P. Sloan Foundation.

Northrup, P. T. (2002). Online learners' preferences for interaction. *Quarterly Review of Distance Education, 3*(2), 219–226.

Nye, B., Konstantopoulos, S., & Hedges, L. V. (2004). How large are teacher effects? *Educational Evaluation and Policy Analysis, 26*, 237–257. doi:10.3102/01623737026003237

Rice, J. K. (2003). *Teacher quality: Understanding the effectiveness of teacher attributes.* The Economic Policy institute.

Rivkin, S. G., Hanushek, E. A., & Kain, J. F. (2005). Teachers' schools, and academic achievement. *Econometrica: Journal of the Econometric Society, 73*(2), 417–458. doi:10.1111/j.1468-0262.2005.00584.x

Southern Regional Education Board. (2004). *Standards for online professional development: Guidelines for planning and evaluating online professional development courses and programs.* Atlanta, GA: Author.

State Educational Technology Directors Association. (2005). Making the case for online professional development. *National Leadership Institute's toolkit 2005: Professional development* (pp. 11-19). Retrieved from ttp://tinyurl.com/md8g99

State Educational Technology Directors Association. (2008). *Class of 2020: Action plan for education.* Retrieved from http://tinyurl.com/69lndb

Taylor, A., & McQuiggan, C. (2008). A faculty development survey analyzed what faculty want and need to be successful teaching online. *EDUCAUSE Quarterly*, *31*(3). Retrieved from http://www.educause.edu/EDUCAUSE+Quarterly/EDUCAUSEQuarterlyMagazineVolum/FacultyDevelopmentProgrammingI/163099

Wallace, R. (2003). Online learning in higher education: A review of research on interactions among teachers and students. *Education Communication and Information*, *3*(2), 241–280. doi:10.1080/14636310303143

Wang, P., Huh, J., & Zygouris-Coe, V. (2007). Key factors affecting participant satisfaction of course facilitators in a large-scale online professional development context. *Proceedings of the 13th Sloan-C International Conference on Online Learning*. Orlando, FL: The Sloan Consortium.

Williams, W. M., & Ceci, S. J. (1997). "How am I doing?" Problems with student ratings of instructors and courses. *Change*, *29*, 12–23. doi:10.1080/00091389709602331

Wright, S. P., Horn, S. P., & Sanders, W. L. (1997). Teacher and classroom context effects on student achievement: Implications for teacher evaluation. *Journal of Personnel Evaluation in Education*, *11*, 57–67. doi:10.1023/A:1007999204543

ADDITIONAL READING

Allen, M. W. (2007). *Designing successful e-learning: Forget what you know about instructional design and do something interesting*. San Francisco, CA: Pfeiffer.

Anderson, T. A. (Ed.). (2008). *The theory and practice of online learning* (2nd ed.). Edmonton, Canada: AU Press, Athabasca University.

Aragon, S. R. (2003) (Ed.). *New directions for adult and continuing education, no. 100*. New York, NY: Jossey-Bass.

Bingham, T., & Conner, M. (2010). *The new social learning: A guide to transforming organizations through social learning*. Alexandria, VA: ASTD Press.

Bonk, C. J. (2009). *The world is open: How web technology is revolutionizing education*. San Francisco, CA: Jossey-Bass.

Bonk, C. J., & Graham, C. R. (Eds.). (2006). *Handbook of blended learning: Global perspectives, local designs*. San Francisco, CA: Pfeiffer Publishing.

Clark, R. C., & Mayer, R. E. (2008). *e-Learning and the science of instruction*. San Francisco, CA: Jossey-Bass.

Collison, G., Erlbaum, B., Haavind, S., & Tinker, R. (2000). *Facilitating online learning: Effective strategies for moderators*. Madison, WI: Atwood Publishing.

Comeaux, P. (Ed.). (2005). *Assessing online learning*. Bolton, MA: Anker.

Davidson-Shivers, G. V., & Rasmussen, K. L. (2006). *Web-based learning: Design, implementation, and evaluation*. Upper Saddle River, NJ: Merrill-Prentice Hall.

Dawley, L. (2007). *The tools for successful online teaching*. Hershey, PA: IGI Global. doi:10.4018/978-1-59140-956-4

Dede, C. (2006). *Online professional development for teachers: Emerging models and methods*. Cambridge, MA: Harvard Education Press.

Friedman, T. L. (2005). *The world is flat: A brief history of the twenty-first century*. New York, NY: Farrar, Straus, and Giroux.

Garrison, D. R., & Anderson, T. (2003). *E-Learning in the 21st century: A framework for research and practice*. London, UK: Routledge. doi:10.4324/9780203166093

Horton, W., & American Society for Training and Development. (2001). *Evaluating e-learning*. Alexandria, VA: American Society for Training & Development.

Hunter, D. (2009). *The ART of facilitation: The essentials for leading great meetings and creating group synergy* (rev. ed.). San Francisco, CA: Jossey-Bass.

Lehman, R. M., & Conceicao, S. C. O. (2010). *Creating a sense of presence in online teaching: How to be "there" for distance learners*. San Francisco, CA: Jossey-Bass.

Lindberg, J. O., & Olofsson, A. D. (2010). *Online learning communities and teacher professional development: Methods for improved education delivery*. Hersey, PA: IGI Global.

Marquardt, M. J., Kearsley, G., & American Society for Training and Development. (1999). *Technology-based learning: Maximizing human performance and corporate success*. Boca Raton, FL: St. Lucie Press.

Moore, M. (Ed.). (2007). *Handbook of distance education* (2nd ed.). Mahwah, NJ: Lawrence Erlbaum.

Palloff, R. M., & Pratt, K. (2005). *Collaborating online: Learning together in community*. San Francisco, CA: Jossey-Bass.

Palloff, R. M., & Pratt, K. (2009). *Building online learning communities: Effective strategies for the virtual classroom*. San Francisco, CA: Wiley.

Palloff, R. M., & Pratt, K. (2011). *The excellent online instructor: Strategies for professional development*. Wiley.

Ragusa, A. T. (Ed.). (2010). *Interaction in communication technologies and virtual learning environments: Human factors*. Hershey, PA: IGI Global. doi:10.4018/978-1-60566-874-1

Salmon, G. (2011). *E-moderating: The key to teaching and learning online* (3rd ed.). London, UK: Routledge.

Stavredes, T. (2011). *Effective online teaching: Foundations and strategies for student success*. San Francisco, CA: Wiley.

Van Dam, N. (2004). *The e-learning field book: Implementation lessons and case studies from companies that are making e-learning work*. New York, NY: McGraw-Hill.

KEY TERMS AND DEFINITIONS

Formative Evaluation: Evaluation that is typically conducted by an external evaluator during the development or improvement of a program or product, or staff, and it is conducted over time for in-house staff of the program with the intent to improve processes and outcomes.

Online Facilitation: The process of "managing", directing, and assisting learners and the learning process through an online medium.

Online Facilitator: A trained educator who assists a group of learners in an online course understand and meet their online learning objectives through assistance, guidance, supervision, and feedback.

Online Learning: All forms of electronically supported learning and teaching. The delivery of a training or education program by electronic means. Online earning involves the use of a computer or other electronic devices and means to provide training, educational or learning material.

Online Professional Development: A comprehensive, sustained, and intensive approach to improving educators' (and others') knowledge, skills, instruction, and overall professional growth that is delivered through an online medium.

Online Professional Learning Community: A group of people who share common interests and are actively engaged in learning from one another in an online environment.

Quality Assurance: A system of monitoring and evaluation various aspects of a project or services to maximize the probability that minimum standards of quality are being implemented by the production process.

Social Presence: Refers to the ability of participants in a learning community to project themselves socially and emotionally as 'real' people, through communication.

Summative Evaluation: Evaluation that is usually conducted at the end of a program or product's term and provides information on a project's, or product's ability to do what it was designed to so.

Chapter 7
Professional Development in a Virtual World

Richard B. Speaker Jr.
University of New Orleans, USA

Greg Levitt
University of Nevada, Las Vegas, USA

Steven Grubaugh
University of Nevada- Las Vegas, USA

ABSTRACT

The virtual world Second Life (SL) can be part of professional development deployment and mentoring using online learning. This chapter provides a portrait of professional development and teaching in SL. While SL requires a more extensive learning curve than might be expected, the virtual campus becomes a functioning instructional site for all disciplines, supplementing personal and text-based asynchronous learning in various other platforms with synchronous voice and text, enhancing the interactions in virtual professional development settings. In addition to regular face-to-face professional development meetings, the virtual campus allows faculty and staff to meet for professional development, mentoring, discussion groups, committees, and virtual academic conferences. Key ideas for operating educational sites in SL include training prospective faculty, staff, and instructors, mentoring, dealing with appropriate presentations of self as avatar, tracking activities and behaviors in SL, choosing modes of communication, and moving from lecture to discussion to immersive learning in media rich constructed spaces.

INTRODUCTION

Distance education (DE) is complicated and has profound implications for the nature and quality of educational experiences for participants and the universities or schools that they attend;

yet faculty development in distance education is often limited and idiosyncratic. Universities and schools have bought learning management systems (e.g., BlackBoard) and various databases for communications and workflow (e.g., Sharepoint, Webstar, GoogleDocs) while others have focused on personnel and an open source LMS

DOI: 10.4018/978-1-4666-1963-0.ch007

(e.g., Moodle). This paper reports on the use of Second Life (SL), as part of an overall hybrid deployment of DE with professional development, using autobiographical, archival, survey, and interview methods to provide a portrait of one implementation of instruction in a virtual world. The project started in 2006 and received funding from 2008 to 2011 from the Louisiana Board of Regents SELECT fund.

Faculty development has a tradition of formality. The faculty members meet and receive a lecture and then go their way. This results in virtually no implementation of the new ideas presented in the session, even with the best intentions and acceptance of ideas from the presentation. The flaw is the one-shot presentation without follow-up support. The use of technologies for instructional development fits this sort of framework, especially in the days of uncertainty surrounding the implementation of various online and distance education schemes. Online virtual worlds provide opportunities for presence and support for innovation that goes beyond tech-support, but certainly includes it. Park (2011) provides a framework for ubiquitous learning using various mobile devices that is based on the embeddedness of computing devices in various environments and connectedness of communication devices. He proposes the importance of using high levels of interactivity with distance learning that is compatible with synchronous platforms. A constructivist, hands-on, mentored, curricular model for faculty development (Bereiter, 1994; Glasersfeld, 1996; Joseph, Bravmann, Windschitl, Mikel, & Green, 2000; Keengwe, Kidd, & Kyei-Blankson, 2009; Kincheloe, 2005; Phillips, 1995; Pinar, 1994; 1998; 2004; Steffe, & Thompson, 2000) can replace the traditional model, using mentoring, collaboration and virtual words to achieve technology integration.

Generally, published research has yet to investigate synchronous support functions adequately. Supporting the notion of online instructor presence, Sheridan and Kelly (2010) found that the most important factors of that presence related to timeliness of feedback, clarifying requirements, and response to student needs. Although they did not investigate use of any synchronous platform, Sheridan and Kelly denigrate synchronous contacts and face-to-face online communication. Rodriguez and Anicete (2010) found a need for live online support from the instructor during the periods of online activities in the hybrid course, suggesting a need for synchronous involvement in faculty development training. McAnuff-Gumbs (2011) used asynchronous discussions to train coaches in best practices in literacy coaching. However, her participants indicated that the best practices could be difficult to carry out, and she did not follow up with their implementation although she found a mismatch between the presented environmental situations and those of the participants. Hu, Caron, Deters, Moret, and Swaggerty (2011) found that higher-education instructors benefited from establishing collaboration through an online learning community. Douglas-Faraci (2010) considered both synchronous and asynchronous issues in delivery of online professional development, suggesting that the potency of the learning comes from the use of various multimedia: audio, video, animation, graphics and text that activate various participant learning styles or preferences. She also noted that administrators and staff developers need to embrace both synchronous and asynchronous online development tools to further standards-based instruction using e-learning. Chiero and Beare (2010) demonstrate the feasibility of online development of teachers, with considerable advantage in their performance on various measures, and consider that their online population might be different from the campus-based population because of self-selection for the online course of study.

Yet we know that students and faculty engage in technological support. Darby and Speaker (2009) found students used cell phone more than any other technology to maintain contact and communicate orally and with text. Face-to-face

(FTF) instruction has seen an explosion of multimedia technology (Dermody & Speaker, 2003; Gremain-Mccarthy, Haggery, Buxton, & Speaker, 2003; Grubaugh, Levitt, Speaker, & Rector, 2010; Speaker, Johnson, & Graveline, 2009; Speaker, Johnson, Scaramella & Cashner, 2008; Speaker, 2007; Speaker, Dermody, Knighten, Suzuki, Wan, & Parigi, 2001). Various online platforms that are mostly text based (Blackboard and MOODLE), some that incorporate video (Wimba, Adobe Connect), and some that provide immersive virtual worlds (Second Life) can augment these FTF technologies.

We concentrate on the features of the virtual world of Second Life because it provides a window into the possibilities of immersion into learning with synchronous and asynchronous activity, and commitment and support for faculty development (Speaker, Graveline, Johnson, Darby, & Heath, 2010). Indeed, all teacher/faculty development can apply Downes (2009) ARRFF Model for mesh-networked learning (Aggregate, Remix, Repurpose, Feed Forward) and Speaker's collection-selection repertoire (Speaker, Laskowitz, Thompson, Speaker, Chauvin, Darby, & Willis, 2005) by having participants engage in active collection of ideas, information and strategies, finding ways to use them during support, and committing to their online classrooms, with a theoretical orientation to critical and constructivist practices (Bereiter, 1994; Glasersfeld, 1996; Kincheloe, 2005; Phillips, 1995; Steffe, & Thompson, 2000).

SECOND LIFE BACKGROUND

Second Life (SL) is an on-line, three-dimensional, virtual world where users develop personal avatars that represent them in the world. Through the avatar, the user can interact using voice or text in the virtual world and participate in various learning activities while immersed in the simulated spaces, called SIMs. While SL requires a more extensive learning curve than might be expected, the virtual

campus has become an functioning instructional site for eight semesters with courses in five disciplines (Biology, Business, Education, English, and Spanish), supplementing text-based asynchronous learning in various learning management systems with synchronous voice and text-based activity, greatly enhancing the interactions in DE settings according to instructors. In addition to regular class meetings, the virtual campus allows faculty, staff, and students to meet for discussion groups, office hours, committees, and virtual academic conferences.

The current virtual campus, called the Louisiana Regents Estate, consists of eight islands in SL with one additional island appended to the site. Originally this site consisted of one island, the New Orleans Island, then five islands constructed in 2007 (http://virtualcampus.uno.edu/), and the current cluster of nine islands. The current capacity of the nine islands is 450 avatars simultaneously, so a 24-hour per day operation could accommodate over 10,000 students and instructors per day. The professional development related to Second Life and various other online platforms used in this case study (Blackboard, Moodle) includes a range of activities: information sessions, face-to-face workshops, online conferences, online committee meetings, online workshops, and personal mentoring. Seven faculty members and one staff member are involved in mentoring others to use Second Life and to run the complex of islands.

The participants in SL include educators and researchers from over 400 universities, businesses, gamers, software designers, and, unfortunately, pornographers. Controls in SL allow the filtering of the type of information using three categories: general, mature, and adult. Each participant in SL is represented by an on-line, three-dimensional avatar, a "self" which the individual can modify infinitely to meet personal interests and activities in SL. Each individual can dress the avatar, using clothing provided by SL or make or buy other clothing. Avatars can move, fly, teleport, text, talk, IM, build, shop, and engage in a multitude of other virtual activities. While the avatars in SL were initially cartoonish, they have gradually evolved into more complex representations that can be almost photorealistic for those who want a more complete mapping of self into the virtual world.

Virtual worlds offer a wide range of options, but each requires the participant to learn some aspects of their software in order to browse the particular virtual world. SL has various orientation islands to help with learning. It requires high-speed Internet connections and fast computers with high-end video/graphics cards (PC or Mac). SL is free but members can also subscribe for additional privileges.

Second Life has a vibrant educational community. The regions where avatars engage in activities include islands, estates (collections of several islands), and a mainland. Many universities and professional societies have developed islands or larger regions (estates). More than 400 universities are currently participating with islands or estates, and some have developed elaborate simulations (SIM) of their real world (RW) and various processes. Other estates are built or maintained by groups of enthusiasts who may or may not be affiliated with a university; for instance, the Roma SIM simulates the Roman Empire in about the second century CE, and has a group dedicated to improving the accuracy of the using historical texts and current archaeological work.

The University of New Orleans developed an island (UNO Island) in 2006, and through Louisiana SELECT funds has collaborated with Southern University New Orleans (SUNO), Tulane, and Southeastern to build an estate of five contiguous islands. A second round of funding in 2009 from Louisiana SELECT allowed expansion that included University of Louisiana Monroe, Loyola University New Orleans, and Delgado Community College to add islands to the estate. On the islands, managers from each university construct buildings that can be used for a variety of purposes. The initial build of the UNO Island had one large building, which contained an informational area, two classrooms, a conference room, various offices, and student lounge areas. Other smaller buildings, a lighthouse and landscaping were constructed, and later an instructor built a castle for meetings of various groups. The current UNO Island has five buildings for various purposes, including classrooms, offices, lounges, informational areas, and a sandbox located 600 m. in the sky for participants to practice building, and a variety of other floating platforms in the sky devoted to art and biological sciences.

Virtual worlds are hastening change in how instruction and instructional communications occur. In the virtual world, users inject a sense of "presence" lacking in 2-dimensional Internet communication by creating an avatar that can interact with other users—see them, talk to them, and share an electronic virtual universe; these users form communities, build economies, and establish businesses. At university sites, credit courses are offered in virtual classrooms, attracting students from the world using Second Life and other platforms; as of this writing, Second Life has over 14 million "residents," or individual avatars.

Second Life: Teaching and Learning

Key ideas in the operation of SL as an educational site include: providing learning opportunities and spaces in SL; learner presentation of self; asynchronous, synchronous and immersive learning; and media-rich interaction space for participants. Various forms of discussion and immersion are possible in SL settings; some settings offer full courses implemented in SL while others have hybrid courses that use SL supported with other media in a metaphoric cloud of multimedia computing. There are many issues that need to be addressed by individuals and institutions offering instruction in SL or other metaverse environments. They are discussed below from autobiographical perspectives of instructors in SL. The specific courses taught on UNO's virtual campus in SL have provided students with a range of opportunities for learning. By semester they have been:

Fall, 2007

- GEOG 1002 World Regional Geography

Spring, 2008

- EDCI 6793 Graduate Special Topics in Curriculum and Instruction
- EDAD 6991 Special Topics in Educational Administration
- ENGL 2238 Introduction to Fiction 1
- MANG 3401 Introduction.to Management & Organizational Behavior

Fall, 2008

- EDCI 4400/G Foundations of Literacy Development
- ENGL 2239 Introduction to Fiction 2
- MANG 3401 Introduction.to Management & Organizational Behavior

Spring, 2009

- EDCI 4400/G Foundations of Literacy Development
- ENGL 2238 Introduction to Fiction 1
- MANG 3401 Introduction.to Management & Organizational Behavior

Fall, 2009

- EDCI 4400/G Foundations of Literacy Development
- ENGL 2238 Introduction to Fiction 1
- Spanish 1001 Basic Spanish I

Spring, 2010

- EDCI 4400/G Foundations of Literacy Development
- Spanish 1001 Basic Spanish I
- Spanish 1002 Basic Spanish II

Summer, 2010

- BIOS 1053 Contemporary Biology
- Spanish 1001 Basic Spanish I

Fall, 2010

- EDCI 4400/G Foundations of Literacy Development
- Spanish 1001 Basic Spanish I

These are full courses taught in SL with support using Blackboard and e-mail. Some instructors also use a variety of other resources from the computing cloud including digital books, Facebook, voice-over the Internet protocols like Skype, blogs, wikis, and simulations. Other instructors bring classes into SL for shorter periods of time.

Learning Opportunities and Spaces in SL

Formal learning spaces need to be developed for students in SL. The current estate of nine islands includes a range of neo-classical buildings for information, offices, conferences, and classes, landscaped exteriors where groups can meet, four sandboxes for experimental work, and a central shared arena. In classroom areas, instructors can post PowerPoint presentations, stream video, present lectures, discuss course materials and content, answer questions, and support student learning with activities and research, ranging from visiting other SIMs and libraries to building their own structures to house performances or processes for learning. Several groups operate on the UNO Island that are related to managing the estate and activities on the island, communicating with participants who have visited the islands, topical interests, and establishing specific courses in the virtual world. Some of the spaces available are very traditional lecture halls where instructors tend to use PowerPoint on white boards and hold various text and oral discussions. Other spaces have been build for specific groups; for instance the Japan Studies group has a teahouse as its meeting place, and the Spanish Conversation group meets in a pavilion in front of a replica of Picasso's Guernica. Both of these groups also take virtual field trips to SIMs that present various historic periods and language learning spaces immersed in aspects of culture.

Faculty Learner Presentation of Self

Faculty Learner presentation of self allows tremendous flexibility for the learner. Each individual has almost limitless abilities to construct his/her avatar with the ability to edit body parts and clothes along a wide range of dimensions. Avatars can change shape and many features, then they can add clothing, bling, fur, different bodies (including non-human), wings, devices, vehicles, weapons, animations, gestures. For instance, although the basic avatar is devoid of genitalia, editing the body allows changes in gender, shape, skin, hair and eyes along such dimensions as height, body thickness, body fat, head size, head stretch, head shape, head length, face shear, forehead angle, brow size, upper cheek puffiness, lower cheek puffiness, cheek bone position, eye size, eye opening, eye spacing, direction of outer eye corner, direction of inner eye corner, eye depth, upper eyelid fold, eye bags, eyelash length, eye pop, ear size, ear angle, earlobe, ear tips, nose size, nose width, etc. In addition, individuals can purchase photographic quality features or even use their own photographs to create their avatars.

But nothing requires an individual to have an avatar that resembles their real world (RW) appearance; indeed, most avatars are tall, slender to muscular, and symmetrical, but whatever choices the individual makes for her/his avatar's appearance, the avatar becomes part of the autobiographical presence of that individual in SL. Although avatars can be kept entirely anonymous, some participants find it useful or necessary to give up that anonymity when participating in educational settings in SL; a primary example of this is when someone is teaching a course to students in SL – the instructor's avatar can hardly remain anonymous. To allow for this, some participants possess multiple avatars for various purposes, some public, others private. Instructors, also, must have a list of avatars and the name of the student whom they represent to assess performance in classes and give grades. Students need to be able to identify their instructors in SL and RW so the concept of anonymity has its limitations. Finally, many handicaps become irrelevant as individuals and groups participate in the metaverse, constructing their own realities through interactions in the virtual world.

Asynchronous, Synchronous, and Immersive Learning

Asynchronous, synchronous and immersive learning can be developed in SL environments. SL offers a range of options for developing curriculum and instruction on islands in the virtual world. While the construction of an island provides the basic space for teaching and learning, modifying it for functionality and aesthetics helps the new participant be at ease in a new world. Instructors can take advantage of this by designing both stand alone asynchronous learning objects and using synchronous features of the metaverse environment to produce learning events. The synchronous events can simulate traditional lectures and discussions using voice chat or combinations of voice and text chat. Participants can set up social networking structures with friends and groups and participate in various conference calls and IM each other with ease while on-line simultaneously. If the message is sent when an avatar is offline, it is stored for later.

Groups allow the posting and storage of IMs and proposals for two weeks while notecards can be stored indefinitely in the avatar's inventory. Of course, if an instructor lectures, students can pass private text messages to each other or even the instructor at any time, and lectures or discussions that are mostly text-based can be saved on notecards for future reference. In addition, new features allow for broadcast and recording of voice and video of events in SL, but these features require large amounts of storage to archive. Some instructors have developed complete animations and holodecks in their SIMs to provide learners with another immersive experience related to content learning. In some cases the participants in the SIM develop performances that are in themselves learning events; examples would include performance of plays in language, costumes and theater buildings designed to specifications from a historical period, or enacting a religious ritual based on Roman history, texts, and archaeology in a reconstruction of a Roman setting. Among the hundreds of SIMs already available to participants are New Orleans; Rome; Kumamoto, Japan; Solomon's Temple in Jerusalem; the Temple of Amun in Luxor, Egypt; and the process of spermatogenesis in the testes. And for those instructors who wish to use an instructional platform in SL, SLOODLE is available as the SL implementation of MOODLE.

One instructor is currently building activities for genetics using simulated rabbits and horses that students will raise. In his classes, students will be able to follow generations of their own animals and map inherited traits of rapidly reproducing, simulated species over a semester.

Media-Rich Interaction Spaces

The major goal often becomes developing a media-rich interaction space for participants, enhancing learning with comfortable spaces and images relating to the learning. Indeed, often the learners contribute to the development of this space. Developers and participants collect images, textures, photographs, texts, and videos related to the topic and build clothes, animations, tools, gestures, scripts, or special avatars to perform in immersive environments that represent their best knowledge about the setting or situation. The initial stage in the planning of such immersive media-rich interaction space for participants involves geoforming an island and a plan for the buildings of structures using architectural plans that are appropriate for the learning situation. These should include spaces that seem familiar to novice participants: maps, walkways, paths, landscaping, signs, and buildings with lobbies, rooms, classrooms, stairs, offices, classrooms, laboratories, conference rooms, libraries and furniture. These culturally familiar settings provide comfort and recognition for new participants before they encounter floating spaces designated for various functions like buildings and art displays. Some universities choose to provide recognizable features of campus buildings to further enhance their brand name in the metaverse, and some instructors build their own buildings and furnish them with personalized trappings (built by themselves or bought from vendors in SL): paintings, prints, statues, artifacts, rugs, drapes, musical instruments, music feeds, books, bookcases, chairs, tables, sofas, desks, computers, televisions, mobiles, lamps, stained glass, plants, and textures and color schemes to fit their individual tastes. Participants to explore and manipulate voice, text, video, sound (environmental, musical), textures, simulation, and social interaction.

A variety of issues are posed by the nature of SL as a learning and teaching platform. Some of these are the same as in any on-line environment while others are peculiar to SL. Identification of the learner and assessment security are issues in any educational institution, more so with on-line and distance education than with traditional educational institutional settings. Second Life begins to change the curriculum, learning, and even the participants' epistemologies. In SL's media-rich interaction space for participants, the teacher and the student participate in construction of knowing and learning through simulations, experiences and discourses, and 'objects' can carry information about themselves and other related 'texts' ('text' in this sense is multimedia and carries the possibility of non-print and hypertextual media that may link elsewhere in SL and the web). We will discuss four issues related to the SL learning and teaching platform: i) The epistemological shift for a metaverse, ii) The learning curve for "newbies", iii) The stability of the platform, and iv) Competition from full video-rendering platforms.

The Epistemological Shift for a Metaverse

The creation of a metaverse is an amazing technological feat. For an avatar to appear to be moving in three dimensional space on the computer screen requires that the computer redraw the graphics around the avatar for each movement, forward, backward, side-to-side, up, down, fly, teleport, and to present frames that show the animations of these movements in an acceptable way to the viewer behind the avatar. That viewer, outside the computer, must learn to recognize virtual objects and to negotiate with them in a mosaic of visual space that includes many menus and pop-up information panels. Information is not scarce in the metaverse, rather it is dense, and the user must learn to filter what is useful in a particular situation. Every virtual object in the metaverse has a menu that gives information about it and can

potentially link to other information and locations in the metaverse or on the Internet. This leads to a layered epistemology (Cary & Mutua, 2010) where the entities on the screen become real to the user and actions of the avatars have real consequence in the virtual world.

New information and formats can overwhelm the novice, especially with the new visual matrix and its data streams. Indeed, everything is new at first and fear can become a barrier to acting. Despite the relative safety, the environment can intimidate anyone who is uncomfortable in a highly technological setting. Furthermore, considerable uncertainty dawns on the user because not everything you see is experienced the same way by other avatars. Several problems with learning the new online environment may be learner factors: the learner may not have any gaming interests or skills relevant to using the new environment, especially technology skills; the learner may not have the time for immersion in a new learning environment like SL; the learner may not be comfortable without nonverbal cuing systems (gestures, facial expressions); and the learner may not be aware of nor understand the ubiquitous information present in the metaverse. For example, currently avatars don't have facial expressions, and all gestures need to be carefully planned because some require special animations in the avatar's inventory. Although an avatar interacts with another as if that avatar were a person with the attributes of the avatar, the range of avatars is increasingly complex including human forms (normal or unusual size, colors, and shapes, and some may be extreme), animal forms (cats, dogs, raccoons, dragons, mythical beasts) and even inanimate forms (blobs, robots). Multiple individuals can share an avatar while some individuals may have multiple avatars.

Objects and perceptions depend on the settings of the computer and choices made by the user. Each avatar can choose the time of day from sunrise, noon, sunset, midnight without regard to other avatars' settings in the metaverse. Many menus allow the avatar to copy virtual objects and their associated information and links into an inventory that the avatar carries around. Some objects can interpenetrate others while some are invisible and yet can influence avatars or other objects within a certain range. Wind is ubiquitous in Second Life, so some objects move with it. Some objects perform various actions using programming scripts that can make interaction strange or fun. Flying and teleporting are necessary for rapid movement from one location to another. Some users participate in options for shopping, selling, and building on their own virtual land.

The Learning Curve for "Newbies"

Like every new technology, SL has a learning curve. New skills are needed to deal with the 3-D environment and such actions as movement (walking, running, flying and teleporting), the fixed menus at the top and bottom of the SL browser and other menus everywhere. Understanding the visual matrix and its data streams takes some time and the newbie runs some danger of overload from information in unfamiliar locations.

Learning to use objects and processes in SL requires an exploration mindset, and perhaps a particular personality that enjoys discovery and interacting with others. Newbies often arrive in a tutorial location; although these have gotten better, they still have some issues. For instance, sometimes avatars 'pile' into the tutorial locations and seem too intimate. Newbies must read and click on various locations in the visual matrix to learn to move and interact with their unfamiliar environment. Sometimes the main urge is to get away for these newly formed, awkward, intrusive individuals who are impinging on personal space in the metaverse. They initially are very impolite by real world standards and develop politeness only with practice in the new environment. Newbies also complain about running into walls, buildings and other objects, but fortunately in SL, there is no pain.

As with other new technologies, access has three components before learning can occur: technological access to SL and avatar construction; skill with the media and social aspects of SL; and time to construct messages from objects, other avatars and activities in SL. Many participants seem to have forgotten the learning curves for previous innovations like BlackBoard or are unready to invest the time in learning a metaverse like SL. Or they may remember their initial learning of other innovations too painfully.

Appropriate behavior must be redefined for higher education participants in SL. Both griefing (SL graffiti) and pornography are present in SL, although minimal if the avatar and region settings control for this. Advertisement and businesses can be distracting and offensive in the avatar's face. Participants in these settings may need to edit their group participation lists in their profiles and their avatars made to be less provocative in their learning settings.

Instructors need awareness of the advantages and activities possible in a virtual world. They need the time to learn the virtual environment and support in learning new instructional ideas. To help spread awareness of SL and to develop these skills, we conduct workshops several times each semester that focus on learning different aspects of SL. All of these workshops have a hands-on component where participants interact in SL. We have found that one to one and a half hour doses of SL have gradually helped more faculty members handle aspects of the virtual world, but they are not enough to gain proficiency. Topics of these workshops have included avatar creation and basic movement, using the various menus in SL, communicating in SL, and teleporting. These workshops have occurred in real life in computer labs on campus, but we are now planning more workshops in SL after the success of our first SL Conference.

The Stability of the Platform

Any new platform presents technological challenges to those using it. SL is completely dependent on high-speed Internet connections from the Linden Labs server banks to the individual user. When any component goes down, the performance of SL degrades or can even cease. The number of users of SL is steadily increasing (58,000 – 70,000 simultaneous users is common). At peak usage times, the lag time for actions and communications within SL can slow significantly, and crashes can occur, throwing users off line. Since SL is a media-rich, on-line environment, bandwidth is an issue for all users. Each computer user will have slightly different settings, so getting the SL settings right takes time and tinkering so that buildings and avatars resolve in a reasonable amount of time. Over the two years that we have been operating in SL, the number of disruptions have gradually decreased and the new versions of the SL viewer/browser appear less frequently; for example, in Spring, 2008, there were 4 new browser versions while in Fall, 2008, there was only one.

Understanding Second Life Implementation for Faculty and Students

To provide a portrait of our use of SL for teaching and learning, instructors and students were surveyed and interviewed. Here we summarize some of our findings from these interviews and provide a case study of one mentoring situation. Participants in courses and activities in SL tended to have a strong technology background and to self-identify as technologists or at least "early adopters". For example, consider items A and B, below, which are typical autobiographical sketches of participants:

- **Item A:** Having grown up in a technological era, I feel pretty comfortable incorporating different forms of technology in my personal life, education, and career. It's hard to say when I was first introduced to the use of technology being so young myself. I've had the opportunity to work with computers, cell phones, DVD cameras, digital cameras, and other technologically advanced equipment my entire life and plan to continue the use of it, especially in the classroom My most recent adventure ('04-present) in technology has been through the internet networking world of Facebook. Through Facebook, I've been able to create a profile with pictures, interests, websites, contact information, friends, work and education information, and so much more. I'm able to network through different organizations, schools, workplaces, and friends. I can keep in closer contact with people all over the world and even upload parts of my life to give others insight.

- **Item B:** I am a technologist. I believe that one of the essential human traits is to use whatever technology is available and to seek out new technologies to solve problems. The computer with its increasing multimedia proclivities and connection to the World-Wide-Web has become essential to my daily activities; communicating, reading, writing, editing, listening, speaking, visually representing, sensing, thinking, and teaching all involve computer technologies. Web pages are a natural part of any current curriculum planning, and I use on-line platforms to help organize my activities. Obviously this was not always so.

The participants were often already aware of SL or of similar virtual worlds and included faculty who had been involved in setting up computer labs on various campuses and schools as early as 1980. Several ran computer networks for large educational entities like school districts. Two of the participants brought with them a long history of funded projects related to technology (more than $3 million in such projects from local, state and federal funding agencies). One participant has a history of higher education administration from departmental to college to central levels.

Multiple surveys were conducted. Most surveys involved small sample and population sizes, but the results provided at least a first glimpse into the way that Second Life is viewed by users and how virtual worlds can be used by educators. Students were asked about their involvement with Second Life. At the beginning of the semester, most of the students had only limited experiences in Second Life, although some indicated that they have some skill but still have lots to learn. In surveying a group of 17 graduate students in a course in Second Life at their third week, 71 per cent indicated they were on their way to becoming skilled but were not there yet, despite having an instructor who viewed them has having many "newbie" issues related to movement and searching. They indicated that they have been using SL more frequently over the past few weeks (57 per cent), but only two indicated that they had more regular involvement. The graduate students were sophisticated users of technology. All indicated that they kept cell phones with them for emergencies, while 67 per cent kept radio, television and laptops with them. One-third kept an mp3 player or a digital still camera with them and one kept a flash drive.

With regard to Second Life, specifically, respondents indicated that they had more knowledge than that of a typical newcomer ("newbie"), but still had much to learn. This finding confirms the relative sophistication of users, even though at the time of the survey they could not claim extensive knowledge of the platform. Respondents displayed high levels of confidence with simpler SL tasks like logging in and registering, but they were not confident with more complex tasks like terraforming, or offering teleports. Their confidence seems closely related to the tasks that they have used in SL rather than more general knowledge of perform-

ing functions in virtual worlds. Indeed this pattern of using only the minimal capabilities of SL may produce a functionalist view of the SL platform as a place to talk about topics related to learning in a particular course and not allow the student time to see the larger possibilities for social and cultural exchange in SL. An anecdotal example is the student sent on a field trip to a Russian-oriented SIM who was amazed that participants were speaking Russian there--suddenly SL was a vehicle for exploring new worlds.

Respondents have had a variety of problems with Second Life. Freezing and lag are common problems, as are microphone issues. These can be persistent without a relatively new computer, USB headset, and fast Internet connection. Using voice chat seems to present a wide range of problems at least partially because of the various settings that have to be adjusted. In addition, some uses of microphones in other applications seem to need to be reset manually every time for use in SL. On occasion, the SL browser freezes, and the user must quit the browser, restart the computer, and log in again. The frequency and severity of problems seem to have decreased over the last year with the introduction of new browser versions. However, students generally favored learning to use SL as a platform, the problems notwithstanding.

Respondents offered very complimentary assessments of the value of SL to the educational process, the technical glitches aside. Respondents in this graduate-level education course, for example, commented that (referring to SL):

It gives me a different view of how online learning can be in the future.

It gives me a better understanding of gamers and their obsession with certain scenarios. It beats the tar out of staring at a Blackboard assignment list with no instructor feedback. I can actually find my instructor and ask him questions in real time, if need be. The SIMS are wonderful and better than books. For instance, visiting Stonehenge or

Rome would be cost prohibitive. The mosaics at the Alpin Meadow Monestary [sic] are wonderful and as good as I've seen in Italy!

Second Life is an enhanced version of on-line learning. I [would] much rather [take an] on-line course taught in Second Life. The personal interaction with the instructor and other students is a big factor. I felt that I was participating in the latest technology. I definitely have a different view of on-line courses and what they can be like.

Another respondent remarked (paraphrased): SL added a real sense of interacting with other people, far beyond email and discussion boards alone. Respondents stressed the importance of "presence" in the learning environment—i.e., being near one another even if only in electronic space. It is the possibility of "presence" that elevates 3-D Web above more typical methods of online learning.

Interviews with faculty participants covered a range of experiences with technology and teaching in SL. Items C and D show the involvement of one faculty member in on-line teaching/learning and entry into SL teaching.

- **Item C:** The post-Katrina mini-semester in 2005, forced me to confront various issues with on-line learning and teaching, especially in Bb. I wrote and posted volumes of text for students to use and used discussion boards to build discussions of readings and concepts related to the course. Students who kept up with their readings and these discussions did well in these courses, but many fell behind or struggled to keep up, especially as they dealt with all the problems of dealing with insurance companies, the Road Home processes, and rebuilding. Nevertheless, I found some success in these on-line teaching endeavors and gradually added to my repertoire of activi-

ties, sources, and files to use in Bb courses. Almost every semester since then I have taught one or more on-line courses.

- **Item D:** In the Spring of 2008, I taught my first Second Life course, a graduate seminar on on-line platforms in teaching and learning, mostly for education students. This had two major goals: developing students' comfort and experiences in using SL as a learning platform, and having them study and test some of their ideas from research about using technology in their teaching and learning. I was unhappy with the limitations of BlackBoard (Bb) from the start. It seems a sterile, unfriendly environment for teaching and learning. I found that UNO did not support the use of chats and other synchronous features of Bb from the start. I worked around this by posting PowerPoints with or without sound and some videos as documents for students to use, but I often found that they had difficulty downloading large files and running them when they had downloaded them. At first, on-line resources seemed rather impoverished, but I found that Questia (www.questia.com) was a repository of thousands of texts including some of the most important ones in literacy and curriculum that had been published over the years, and some were under one year old. Despite my attempts to get students engaged and keep them engaged in on-line courses, I find that they often have difficulty keeping up with the demands of reading and writing and self-direction in these courses. I see that this may stem from the demands of the course in an on-line format (many of which I have imposed), their unfamiliarity with on-line courses and the course management systems (like Bb, Moodle, or ICT), their unfamiliarity with the local environment and navigation in the course, their lack of time to fully engage in a course (taking an overload with several on-line courses is not a good idea), and the demands of their daily lives (jobs, family, life).

In technology and teaching, interviewees listed a wide range of activities for professional self-development:

- **Item E:** I have used various group structures on-line: Yahoo, MSN, Webcrossing, Google groups, Google docs, Second Life and some other virtual worlds, BlackBoard, moodle, hybrid structures, Facebook.
- **Item F:** In SL, I sought out groups that had interesting topics of discussion and were fairly active to experience the ways they operated so I could develop my own style in SL teaching. These groups included Philosophy House, Thothica, Second Philosophy, and various Roma Groups. Because of my activity in philosophy discussion groups in SL, I was invited to participate in the Oxford University pilot test of combining SL and Moodle to teach and learn philosophy. I'm currently participating as a learner in this on-line experience, which focuses on various philosophical topics related to epistemology, ontology, and metaphysics.

In addition, several pointed out SL groups like SLED and ISTE that provide discussion opportunities about using SL for activities with students:

- **Item G:** This course was a case of the blind leading the blind. I set up a group in SL for the course participants. My syllabus included a lengthy bibliography of books related to technology in education all available through Questia (www.questia.com). I held a session to tutor students in SL in the Mac Lab in the ED Building;

four of 17 students attended. I spent time getting the students to use various aspects of Second Life. The first night in SL, I focused on getting to know how to do things in SL, getting set up for voice, getting their avatar names associated with their real names (I used an excel spreadsheet to keep track of this) and searching. After a while, I sent the participants on a scavenger hunt to locate and bring back various objects from around SL. For the two students who had experience in SL, this was too easy, but, for most, it was a challenge to start learning and using a new platform for learning. I rezzed a white board with information about the course, and I sent notecards to the participants in the group.

This instructor reported having some difficulty with whiteboards, voice, student access, SL crashes during class meetings, freezes for students, and new versions of the SL viewer/browser that appeared regularly. Yet, the same instructor had no problems with building or communicating with students using hybrid methods including face-to-face meetings, e-mail, BlackBoard, and later Skype video.

Of course, New Orleans and the Gulf South were severely affected by Hurricanes Gustav and Ike in late August and early September of 2008.

- **Item H:** The university closed for about a week for Hurricane Gustav and then for a day for Ike. These closings were right at the start of the semester and raised students and faculty stress even if we weren't suffering from post-traumatic stress from Katrina and Rita. During my evacuation, I stayed in hotels with fast Internet connections and of course, had my laptop. I was pleased to see students and some faculty used SL as a means of communication when everything else went down for a few days. There weren't any class meetings, but there were signs posted with information and I talked with several students (none of my own) and two professors.

One interviewee summarized learning about teaching in SL with the following statements:

- **Item I:** Things I learned:
  - Take time the first class session to focus on using Second Life; delay the content until the second meeting.
  - Set up a group in SL for the class, and use it to deliver something to the students at every meeting such as notes, agenda, special locations, assignments, and transcripts of previous sessions.
  - Use a variety of environments in SL for different functions, either within one SIM or across several; although lecture can work easily in SL, text and voice discussions, using images and figures, and immersing the learners in activities work, too, and engage the learners in different ways.
  - Decide before the start of class whether you want students to use voice; if so, require headsets with microphones; if not, be prepared for typing madly.
  - Build a document that you can view during SL meetings with the names of students and their avatars; I use an excel file.
  - Send the UNO SL/VW policies to all students. Have them read and sign the document.
  - For the first class meeting, have several assistant avatars to help with newbies.
  - Use hybrid formats to support student learning: I suggest using BlackBoard, Questia, and Skype to build commu-

nicative redundancy, but I'm experimenting with Moodle and Sloodle.
  - Everything takes longer than you expect! (I keep relearning this every time I'm in danger of forgetting it.)

Grading in on-line courses is always an issue. Testing is difficult to monitor. Some instructors chose alternate assessment processes:

- **Item J:** I have stopped giving tests for my course that I teach in SL and BlackBoard. Instead, I have 10-12 competencies that students must demonstrate throughout the course. Some of these are broadly phrased like "read widely on the course topics" and "conduct a project" which becomes operationalized in SL as "hand me cards about your reading each week" before we hold our discussions of the material and "develop or build a presentation for your project", but I'm still experimenting with these ideas and trying to figure out more immersive ways of involving students in SL. I also keep notes when doing my final checklists of student work that the student in SL had kept up with the readings and the other competencies far better than students had in my BlackBoard only course.

In general, faculty members who have taught in SL reported success in getting students involved and noted only a few technical problems during their teaching. They seemed more satisfied with the use of SL than with BlackBoard as the sole on-line platform. They investigated the building of various hybrid course structures with SL, Skype, Moodle, Sloodle, OpenSIM, face-to-face meetings, and social networking sites like Facebook. Some have given students options of building projects in SL sandboxes to complete requirements for courses; others have brought students in-world for specific activities; and some have done the bulk of their courses' instruction in SL.

Administration of the islands in the estate requires skill in SL and with budget operations. Various oversight groups and even maintenance groups are needed. Someone has to watch for griefers (SL graffiti "artists"), regulate building (and "rezzing" of objects), supervise and support instructors and discussion groups, maintain schedules, and the accumulation of junk in the virtual environment. The experience with the first U.N.O. Island is instructive:

- **Item K:** Soon after I joined Second Life on 1/8/2007, I found that my university had an island. I think that I read about it in the newspaper and in the Chronicle of Higher Education. I sent e-mail to various people on campus and found that Merrill Johnson had started an oversight committee. I was invited to join the committee because he was seeking members from different colleges, and I was the first faculty member of the College of Education and Human Development to express an interest. This committee met approximately monthly and was composed mostly of members from liberal arts and staffed with a few faculty members from business administration. We met mostly in SL and had parties with music as the buildings on the virtual campus took shape. We circulated a policy for conduct in virtual classes and adopted it. The Provost had funded the construction of the first island and the committee participants terraformed the island and built initial buildings for the initial course offerings.
- Gradually the virtual land became a bit cluttered, but by then the grant had been funded, and we were faced with a variety of issues, including establishing accounting procedures to manage funds in SL and in the real world, establishing the consortium of universities and their operating processes, designing and building five islands,

contracting for virtual buildings, furnishing these buildings to make them functional and familiar, and conducting the processes for the grant. Of course, this took longer than we expected; the opening that we had planned for April or May of 2008 didn't occur until September (of course, two hurricanes did intervene). We established an administrative avatar for the entire estate to hold ownership of the estate, the buildings, the plants, and the virtual objects that were part of the project and to keep track of in world purchases that would be used for facilitating instruction, meetings and making the virtual world seem somewhat familiar. We still have trouble getting participants to actually put SL meetings into their calendars and close their office doors, but I'm at fault with this, too. We also had each member of the university consortium with an island build an administrative avatar with responsibilities for a single island. This hasn't always worked well, but gradually more active members of our SL community are stepping up to help control the island administration.
- Having an SL technically savvy student worker is very important to maintaining the estate and finding new tools to use. Eventually we need a group of techie students who participate actively in the maintenance of our SL estate. We've had minimal griefing (Sl graffiti), but that may be because we keep the estate fairly closed and have required group membership for access rather than a completely open SIM. We've started a newsletter for SL and participated in recruiting students in SL. We've held an opening ceremony and our first conference in SL. We're getting a sophisticated holodeck, and we've created a technician-avatar that student workers can share. We've built an interface that will rez our new students and faculty right on our

islands rather than going through the standard orientation procedures and orientation island. Stay tuned. We'll be trying more.

Suddenly we are running a virtual university, but for the most part without staff or special expertise beyond our own interests in technology. We have basic policies set for the real world university, but they have to be reconfigured to apply to our pixilated campus.

Operational Issues

Key ideas for operating an educational site in SL include training prospective instructors and students, dealing with appropriate presentations of self as avatar, tracking activities and behaviors in SL, choosing modes of communication for various purposes, and moving from lecture to discussion to immersive learning in media rich constructed spaces.

The pitfalls that must be considered include the nature of the epistemological shift for engaging in learning in SL, the learning curve for "newbies", technological issues with the SL browser and connections, the performance stability of the platform, and lessons learned from various instructors. Some learners and instructors object to using an avatar, but the possibilities of self-representation are developing rapidly, so soon a photorealistic avatar based on a photograph will be readily available for those who want to maintain their real life version in SL.

CASE STUDY: DR. SPEAKER MENTORS DR. GRUBAUGH IN SECOND LIFE

Introduction

I recently had the privilege of being mentored online by a faculty member, Dr. Richard Speaker, at the University of New Orleans, who had extensive experience in teaching with and through Second Life. This mentoring experience addressed several needs that I, Dr. Steven Grubaugh, had and could not solve on my own campus at the University of Nevada, Las Vegas.

What follows is an introduction to the problem, the solution through face-to-face, but blended with mostly virtual mentoring with avatars in Second Life (SL), advanced training online, followed by the successful transfer of my learning to teaching my college students. Additionally, I was able to execute advanced lessons in SL resulting in lessons as good as they would have been in my face-to-face classroom. The resulting positive student attitudes and instruction with the avatars was effective and motivational for everyone.

The Problem

As a college professor, I know that many college students have taken online courses and are familiar with online learning conventions and protocols such as reading materials, responding to guiding questions and activities, and writing responses and papers of various sorts. However most online "conversations" have been text-based where students read, write and respond to learn.

My problem was that I wanted to communicate with my students in real-time to supplement and enhance our asynchronous classroom experiences on Web Campus (Blackboard). I wanted synchronous voice and text-based communication because I was convinced it would greatly enhance our interactions as we took our class online. I also wanted students to be able to present PowerPoints and work in groups in real-time oral discussions online to meet needs that I had for my instructional purposes.

I knew of a fellow faculty member in my field who had done extensive work, teaching in SL and had even helped design and build the UNO virtual campus funded by a technology grant from the state of Louisiana. One-day while I was complaining about not being able to achieve my vision of teaching class using the technology on my campus, he suggested that I try teaching in SL as a possible solution to my instructional communication problems.

I was hesitant at first; intimidated by the prospect of using avatars to teach my students and handling all the complicated issues involved in having students use the technology themselves seemed like a lot of trouble. I wasn't even sure I wanted to use avatars since I've always found them a little creepy. Even though I was reluctant, Richard assured me that I could meet all my instructional goals in the online part of my hybridized class sessions by being able to hold real-time discussions and conduct complicated group work as well as instruct in the traditional asynchronous method.

What I Wanted to Do

Together, Richard and I assessed what I was doing in my courses and what I wanted to do. Like many university faculty, I teach through face-to-face as well as online instruction. One of the courses that I had hybridized is a face-to-face content area literacy course with mathematics, science, English, social studies, foreign language, and art education students. The course is blended by including four to five weeks of online instruction with the remainder consisting of face-to-face instruction. I like to hybridize my face-to-face courses to capitalize on the writing/responding strengths many of my students bring to class online.

My further challenge was to launch an innovation where students build avatars online and use them to work in a Team-Based Learning (TBL) structure (Michaelsen, 2009). This allows students to communicate vocally with each other through the avatars online, and operate in a socio-technological team-based philosophy of learning, using online resources and their avatars as motivational devices to leverage TBL learning outcomes. With the avatars, I wanted to take my

content area reading class into virtual worlds, like inside science experiments, to historical sites, into the solar system and galaxy, and into virtual museums for the art students. I knew all this was possible in SL. I was also interested in motivating my class by having them enter a game like scenario, design new bodies and personas for their avatars, yet be able to speak and interact with each other online. Consequently, Richard and I were able to see the need for me to change and together we set goals and made a plan for my faculty development.

The Solution through Faculty Mentoring: Learning by Doing in Second Life

Richard and I began the faculty development face-to-face. Since I was meeting him over the 2010 Thanksgiving holiday, he began mentoring me face-to-face. He loaded the SL browser onto my computer and began by guiding me to make a few simple choices on what I wanted my avatar to look like including the avatar's age (I chose 22 years old), height, body type, etc. Additionally, I chose what clothes to wear (jeans and a t-shirt just like I wore 30 years ago) and other minor tweaks to the character.

The following week, we continued with the development by "doing" online. He provided me with the coordinates of the UNO SL virtual campus, and we went there for a tour. Under Richard's guidance, I quickly learned the avatar controls to walk and steer my avatar around (left, right, forward and backward arrows) and visit the various classroom buildings and other facilities on the campus. So we had a very good face-to-face orientation with the software and the technology and the movement of the character while some of the other avatar and SL basics were achieved later online.

The subsequent meeting between us one week later was an online meet up where we both materialized at a set time and place on the virtual campus with our avatars. It was really cool to see both avatars materialize on the screen much in the same way that Capt. Kirk and Mr. Spock materialized as they beamed down on to other planets.

Learning to Fly

In December 2011, we began a more in-depth training session. We reviewed some of the basics again such as better walking and steering where I had to keep pace with Richard. We then ran our avatars to a few of the buildings to explore them as possible classroom sites for my classes. Finally Richard taught me to use the fly function. Selecting fly allowed each avatar to rise into the air a few feet and fly around the virtual campus using the same forward and backward controls we did when we were walking and running. As we flew around, Richard showed me a much broader vista of the full virtual campus. We even flew to inviting sights on an island, such as a lecture hall, an art gallery and a teahouse, where I thought my students and I would like to hold our classes once the spring semester began. Once our classroom site was selected, Richard showed me around the classroom and how to sit my avatar down and have him turnaround to face class as a student would.

Richard and I met again several times in SL prior to the beginning of my spring classes for more basic training. The functions of these meetings were to practice walking, talking, gesturing and handling all of the various avatar functions and idiosyncrasies of the site, and to generally become more familiar with the SL environment so that I could, in turn, be a very good guide to my students in SL.

In one of our last sessions in Second Life prior to me going live in my first class in SL, Richard took me on a shopping trip to dress my avatar. He was able to mentor his Nevada protégé as we went to men's stores to pick out hipper clothes, shoes, and accessories, as well as some avatar body features

like a goatee and glasses just to look a little more like an avatar professor. Richard reminded me that even online, a professor never gets a second chance to make a good first impression.

Advanced Training

Also, prior to my first class in Second Life, Richard and I did some more advanced preparation for instruction in Second Life. For instance, one of the more difficult tasks for me was to learn to upload PowerPoints onto the presentation screens in SL so that I could present PowerPoints and other material to students in the classroom while talking about them orally. This was a complex problem for me but Richard was very patient, and I was able to finally master the presentation skills that I would need to present PowerPoints in Second Life.

Finally, Richard provided me with guidelines and ethical standards for using avatars in the classroom, as well as a basic set of instructions for students on how to get online in SL, build their avatar and locate the UNO virtual campus. This instruction was crucial for me because I didn't think some of my students would be able to handle the technology or be able to join the Second Life class. Richard's guidelines helped to relieve my anxiety about losing students right from the beginning of the SL experience because I was very worried about some of them not being able to use the technology to join our class online in avatar form.

Mentoring during the Orientation of my Classes

Having hybridized my classes, I began spring semester with two weeks of face-to-face classes to prepare my students for the tasks ahead including orienting students to SL and revealing our challenge to meet online as avatars. I decided to orient my students using a blended learning model, the same way Richard had taught me, so I held an in-class SL introductory session, then a follow up session for those students who were still not comfortable with the technology or the Second Life protocols.

One little glitch was that as I began my initial orientation in front of the full class, I signed in to SL on an unfamiliar computer and as I began to materialize, I realized, in horror, that my avatar was naked. Fortunately, Richard had come to class in avatar form to help with the orientation, and he helped me figure out how to put my clothes back on my avatar. After this brief, but humiliating moment, I was able to overcome my embarrassment and proceed.

Richard and I were both able to help orient students to SL, and Richard became a guide and support person for helping students handle the technology related issues and skills they needed to operate in the virtual world with their avatars. He did much individual troubleshooting with students, which allowed me to concentrate my energy to do a pretty good job with the SL orientation.

Ongoing Mentor as Real Time Coach, Troubleshooter, and Guest Lecturer

For the fourth week of class, my students and I went live online from our own individual computers in SL. I was amazed that we all showed up in avatar form in the predestined coordinates on the UNO virtual campus. Richard's avatar continued to do quite a bit of coaching to help us smooth out problems we encountered. Richard also helped us with our attitudes about using such an unusual technology for class, and as we finished the orientation sessions, class members felt they had smoothed out many problems and were ready, willing and able to meet as a class in SL.

Richard's avatar joined us again for subsequent lessons in SL and worked quietly to solve some additional last minute problems some students were having. This allowed me to successfully teach my lessons and interact with class. Although

I had a little stage fright, my lessons went quite well. During one class, Richard was able to take over my instructor role and give a 30-minute guest lecture followed by class discussion. Thanks to Richard's mentorship, I was well on my way to a very good teaching experience using Second Life to conduct my college classes. Near the end of the semester, I was able to teleport one additional outside science expert in avatar form to my class. I was happy to realize that through SL, I could bring in experts from anywhere in the world as well as teleport my class to many interesting and exciting places for instructional purposes.

The Development of Advanced Techniques

Having the basics down, and with continued coaching from Richard, I was able to effectively execute some very advanced team-based strategies with my class in SL. This is where the true challenges of my SL skills were put to the test. As my students and I became more proficient in our SL classroom, I had my students use avatars online to work and learn in a team-based learning (TBL) environment.

Team-based learning is a complex series of classroom events that requires individual work by students, students working in teams of 4-6 members, and to have students return to the whole class for discussion after they have worked in their teams. The use of the avatars enabled students to vocally communicate with each other online and function in a socio-digital team-based philosophy of learning using their avatars as motivation to leverage learning outcomes.

To begin, I assigned students to heterogeneous content area team-based learning groups. The students, represented by their avatars, were able to apply the principles and strategies of team-based learning including the use of the Readiness Assurance Process test (individually and in teams) online, complete their follow-up reading and mini research assignments, and have their avatars question the instructor's avatar to clarify concepts under study. Students worked in avatar groups to facilitate online spoken discussions as well as to employ written text in SL and Web Campus also. Avatar teams were given credit for both Second Life and in-class application activities and longer-term team projects. Teams developed PowerPoints on digital screens in Second Life to present findings to the whole class through their avatars.

Some of the advantages I found using team-based learning online in SL included:

- Teaching and learning as avatars embraces an innovative way to teach with technology.
- The ability to hybridize class and retain synchronous online vocal communication for lessons and every aspect of TBL.
- Fun, engaging and motivational for most students: choosing and styling their own avatar, and walking, running, flying and teleporting around campus.
- Avatars can collaborate, analyze, organize, calculate, and audit just like real people in real situations.
- Avatars were able to successfully complete a complex TBL session on a complex social topic. Further, avatars were able to change sex, body style and clothing for a gender switching activity to closely simulate the objectives of a lesson on Critical Literacy.
- Students seem to really care about the treatment of their avatars.
- Cloaked in the anonymity of the avatar, some students found new strengths, such as participating more and making more authentic responses.
- Guest speakers can join class anytime from anywhere.
- Students enjoy a beautiful and mystical campus environment and classroom.
- Students find it cheaper, safer and greener to meet in a virtual world.

The disadvantages included:

- Time-consuming initial technology set up and training for students and very challenging for some who are not skilled with technology.
- The necessity to purchase a headset ($15-20) for better and clearer communication through avatars through the SL site.
- Some students experienced technology barriers and were not able to fully participate.
- Some students disliked using avatars.
- Large class discussion was awkward because human interactions, like reading facial expression, are lost. Turn taking is awkward.
- A few students tried to "game" the system by parking their avatars in the classroom for attendance purposes.
- Needed a code of conduct for potential avatar misbehavior.

Assessment of my Faculty Development

Considering the challenges, and online engagement experiences to enhance effective teaching and learning in the SL learning environment, I was very pleased with the results that I achieved. My SL mentor helped me hybridize my classroom, conduct SL orientations for me and my students on getting the technology to work, moving and working in avatar form and persona, presenting lessons in SL through lecture and using Power-Points, having students make effective presentations, work in small groups communicating with each other as avatars, and working in larger groups communicating with each other as avatars.

I found that even though some students had a fear of using this new technology and some found it difficult to use, the rewards were great. By the end of the semester, almost everyone in class was able to overcome resistance to using SL as a teaching and learning medium and express positive attitudes. Some students who complained about being inept with technology ended up very capable in SL, moving, speaking and participating fully. Students were also able to feel a personal connection to other class members through their avatars since we all knew each other from our first weeks in class face-to-face before we began meeting in SL. As a result, we quickly learned to interact with each others' avatars since we could recognize each other's voices. Amazingly we, as avatars, were able to pick up the dynamics of our face-to-face class almost as if we were meeting in person.

Also, the students and I learned to present in class using the technology, even though some students found it more comfortable to download their PowerPoints and documents the old fashioned way onto WebCampus, then use the SL and Web Campus screens side-by-side during our time online. We all found SL very effective for meeting and working in groups and teaching and learning in whole class situations. Perhaps most importantly, we had lots of fun and coalesced as an effective working group both in our face-to-face group and as avatars online. Additionally, graduate students did not have to drive to campus to meet a 4-6:45 Thursday night class for a few of our sessions.

Using a Blended Teaching and Learning Model to Develop Skills and Confidence

As substantiated in the recent meta analysis of evidence-based practices in online learning (U.S. Office of Planning, Evaluation and Policy Development (OPEPD), 2010), the training model described herein becomes an exemplar of a blended learning environment that clearly improves training interactivity and reveals significant advantages over face-to-face learning toward solving the problem of differences in technical skill levels.

We found it very advantageous to have participants in Second Life professional development learn to use the program in a blended learning environment and we avoided most of the beginner, or newbie problems mentioned earlier in the chapter. Evidence-based studies suggest that blended learning is most effective (OPEPD, 2010), and this is certainly true for professional development in SL because the mentor or supervisor can take the first one or two face-to-face sessions to help the learner(s) with important prerequisite computer-related setup tasks including installing the software, setting up and signing into the account, installing and establishing optimal audio connection through the headset, selecting and outfitting the avatar and establishing an initial location to meet. Confidence building is an essential aspect of using both the computer and the Second Life program for students who are unsure of any aspect of this process prior to engaging in professional development. Peer tutoring with the help of peers who are technologically competent can also serve the same function in an initial face-to-face session with blended learning. Anyone intending to use Second Life must recognize that the setup requirements are slightly different for Mac and PC users, and different even for different models and ages of computers, so it is preferable to have a person, or peers who are familiar with both systems available, or preferably, some minor Second Life technical support available for individual users through campus or organizational IT support.

Once the initial face-to-face meeting(s) allows participants to properly set up their computer and the technical settings are established and working properly, professional development learners can be quickly oriented to the Second Life program and be up and running with their avatars within the first hour or two in Second Life thus meeting the goal of having all participants independent with the program from that point on. Following that, full online professional development can take place online or, in blended learning, and/or back face-to-face for further or advanced training when necessary. This is the exact model used in this chapter's case study where his Second Life mentor, Dr. Speaker, trained Dr. Grubaugh in this way. Furthermore, once trained, trainees can apply this same blended learning model with students or trainees of their own as Dr. Grubaugh subsequently did as he trained his students for blended online learning in Second Life and the physical classroom.

Conclusion of the Case Study

Thanks to the faculty development of one professor from his friend and colleague, the SL technological challenges were overcome and the goal of hybridizing the face-to-face classes by going online in SL for a third of the semester was achieved. With such a strong face-to-face orientation, students gained confidence with the technological SL prerequisites and subsequently were motivated and excited to use the medium of Second Life as an alternative classroom and learning context. Dr. Speaker and I continue to meet in SL with our avatars and explore SL for teaching and learning in future classes. As is the great theme for most learning in faculty development settings, I learned SL by doing SL, a typical constructivist process (Cherakov, Brunner, Smart, & Lu, 2009; Glasersfeld, 1996; Joseph, Bravmann, Windschitl, Mikel, & Green, 2000; Keengwe, Kidd, & Kyei-Blankson, 2009; Kincheloe, 2005; Steffe, & Thompson, 2000).

FUTURE TRENDS

We consider the projections of this technology over the next five years and the costs. Commitment to using virtual worlds provides a wide range of possibilities for teaching, learning, and professional development.

The future is now! Avatars and their worlds are already remarkably developed (Cherakov, Brunner, Smart, & Lu, 2009). Given the pace of current technological development, Second Life and other virtual worlds will be many times more remark- able five years from now because the potential for avatar use and expansion in faculty development is unlimited. Improvements in technology will bring better access and much faster processing of virtual worlds so simulations become even more like our real world. Avatars will be ever more realistic and eventually could be exact replicas of faculty members. Academic virtual worlds will be explored through faculty immersion, for instance, by science faculty visiting the planet mars or by a cadre of history professors making decisions in a WWII battle simulation. Three-D renderings will make these immersive learning environments almost like being at a real place and time. Importantly, funding will be available for these kinds of faculty development experiences because both time and money will be saved with greatly improved training and resulting mentoring and teaching effectiveness.

Faculty, in seminars, will be able to learn more authentically because using avatars will allow them to change shape, roles, sex, race, religion, culture, or any other diversity category, even species, to experience life in that altered role. For cultural sensitivity training, faculty could embody a totally neutral avatar, allowing them to interact with others in a diversity neutral setting – no gender, class, racial, religious or cultural identifiers. Or, training could be designed to have faculty embody avatars anonymously to learn from behind a mask, for instance, if a faculty member was embarrassed about remediating an area of academic weakness or needed counseling anonymously, they could do so online in the privacy of their avatar persona. This would provide faculty with the freedom to learn or receive help without reservations in a critical, constructivist curricular model (Bereiter, 1994; Cherakov, Brunner, Smart, & Lu, 2009; Glasersfeld, 1996; Joseph, Bravmann, Windschitl, Mikel, & Green, 2000; Keengwe, Kidd, & Kyei-Blankson, 2009; Kincheloe, 2005; Phillips, 1995; Pinar, 1994; 1998; 2004; Steffe, & Thompson, 2000).

In our view, faculty training for using virtual worlds in their own classes will accelerate. Professors will be able to have students solve problems, for instance, making calculations to stress-test a concrete bridge support, then forwarding the calculations to a proxy bridge in Second Life to determine the bridge's capacity to stand up to simulated traffic weights and forces.

With the Katrina-Rita Disaster of 2005, the University of New Orleans was faced with an unprecedented challenge. Unlike other schools in the area, the University did not officially close for a semester; but to survive, university faculty had to adopt a variety of Internet-based solutions to replace traditional face-to-face settings. Some of this was unsuccessful because the personal mentoring infrastructure exemplified in our case study was not available. Although UNO had already established BlackBoard (Bb) sites for every course, few instructors made use of on-line communication in Bb before Katrina; indeed, few departments had non-UNO e-mail lists for faculty, staff and students. UNO opened a mini-semester in October of 2005, using Bb and remote locations. Since then, UNO has added a variety of technological options to its emergency response capabilities, including reliance on its SL campus as a destination of first resort. The virtual campus was put to use in the fall of 2008 when Hurricane Gustav led to the evacuation of much of New Orleans and the closure of University campuses. Future training for disasters and other simulated learning will be more common in virtual worlds. Or, a faculty representative could be trained as an Emergency Management Specialist on campus, then get highly realistic real-time disaster problems to solve in Second Life simulations representational of their own campus.

Avatars are new, fun and interesting and it is true that the more we use avatars and their simulated worlds, the more we will see the potential for their use in faculty development and mentoring situations. We are only at the beginning stages of using avatars and virtual worlds for faculty development but the future will bring

spin-offs and whole new possibilities, here-to-fore not considered. Research in all of these areas is highly probable.

Current Costs

The cost of building and maintaining an entire island in SL is generally minimal. They depend on how complicated a build that the university wants to have and whether branding requires that some of the spaces on the virtual campus be developed to simulate real world campuses. The basic building of the island costs $700.00 to $1000.00, and there was an annual fee of $1770.00 until 2011 (but this has recently been raised to $3540.00). These costs give 24-hour use of an island that can be decorated with buildings and landscaped in any way. Many companies offer building on such islands at costs ranging from $2500.00 to $50,000.00 depending on the complexity of the buildings. If additional programming is needed, various contractors will submit bids. Our island builds cost $5000.00 per island. There is now an option to run a private island behind your university or business firewall and completely control access to it, but that costs about $50,0000.00 and requires in-house operators competent to handle all the software issues.

Owning an island allows control of access and participation. It can be completely accessible to the public, or it can have access restrictions based on membership in particular groups. Permission to build can be restricted to individuals or specific groups. Up to 100 avatars can be on the island at any one time, but lag occurs when 50 avatars are simultaneously on an island. This allows classes or meetings to be scheduled in the same way as in regular classrooms on real campuses; we have designated a specific course section for those courses meeting in SL. Faster Internet connections in the future should improve these capabilities dramatically.

CONCLUSION

While conclusions are very preliminary, they are instructive. Faculty development, mentoring, courses and meetings work in SL, but newbies need preparation to a greater extent than we expected. Support groups are important for faculty and students. If SL follows patterns of other technologies, there will be a gradual growth in interest, but a critical mass of student and faculty interest has not yet been reached. Faculty members and staff talk to various student, faculty, and administrative groups about participating in SL. Some members of the academic community continue to resist the cartoonish nature of avatars and see SL as a "game," rather than a potential learning environment. Some administrators are afraid to risk putting sections of classes in an environment that requires high-speed Internet access and fast computers with sophisticated graphics cards, even though these technologies are becoming increasingly mainstream. The development of faculty in the synchronous technological environment of SL needs initial hands-on and then mentoring in the online setting. From our experiences, we concur with the numerous studies of online learning (OPEPD, 2010), and recommend blended learning for one or two face-to-face meetings to achieve effective setup and orientation to SL.

There are several key benefits for using SL in conjunction with other course/learner management systems like BlackBoard and Moodle. SL provides key synchronous features that are absent from other platforms. SL virtual campuses are cheap! The current annual cost for an island is about $3500 per year and the Louisiana Regents Estate is being maintained with three faculty/staff members working on the project part–time, one or two additional faculty members from the other colleges/universities, and one student worker. SL provides instructors, students, administrators, and other participants with a presence in which they can use voice communications with relative ease in immersive settings that provide complex and often stunning visual fields. In the event that a participant does not have a microphone, text chat is fully integrated into the virtual world and can be used while listening to others as they talk asking questions and making comments (although it is slower than voice chat). There are various features to make voice and text private and to record it as needed.

Many universities are including an SL presence as part of their distance education strategies and website designs. These virtual settings can be customized for any purpose and changed to reflect the nature of the meeting or class and the aesthetics of the participants. These settings are available 24-hours per day for classes and group meetings on servers that are remote from the state of Louisiana. Thus, they function during emergencies such as hurricanes and can be accessed from most public libraries or universities or even hotel rooms for evacuated student-faculty communication. In addition to conducting classes in SL, current uses for virtual spaces include faculty development and mentoring services, office hours for individual conferences, committee meetings, special interest groups, and both instant and delayed messaging. Since SL has vibrant social networking functions, faculty, faculty mentors and other participants can find and support various groups and peers with similar interests, even if they participate at different universities.

REFERENCES

Bereiter, C. (1994). Constructivism, sociocultvralism, and Popper's world 3. *Educational Researcher*, *23*, 21–23.

Cary, L. J., & Mutua, K. (2010). Postcolonial narratives: Discourse and epistemological spaces. *Journal of Curriculum Studies*, *26*(2), 62–77.

Cherakov, L., Brunner, R., Smart, R., & Lu, C. (2009). *Virtual spaces: Enabling immersive collaborative enterprise, Part 1: Introduction to the opportunities and technologies.* IBM: DeveloperWorks. Retrieved September 18, 2011, from http://www.ibm.com/developerworks/webservices/library/ws-virtualspaces/

Chiero, R., & Beare, P. (2010). An evaluation of online versus campus-based teacher preparation programs. *Journal of Online Learning and Teaching, 6*(4), 780–790.

Darby, D., & Speaker, R. (2009, October). *Underprepared African American college students' perceptions of the impact of technology in a developmental reading course.* Paper presented at the Annual Meeting of e-Learning Association for the Advancement of Computing in Education, Vancouver, Canada.

Dermody, M., & Speaker, R. B. Jr. (2003). Multimedia literacy in the urban classroom and the reading methods course. *Journal of Reading Education, 28*(1), 24–31.

Douglas-Faraci, D. (2010). A correlational study of six professional development domains in e-learning teacher professional development. *Journal of Online Learning and Teaching, 6*(4), 754–766.

Downes, S. (2009). *Beyond management: The personal learning environment.* Keynote address presented at the ED MEDIA Conference. Honolulu. Retrieved June 1, 2011, from http://www.downes.ca/presentation/225

Germain-McCarthy, Y., Haggerty, D., Buxton, C., & Speaker, R. B., Jr. (2003). Crafting the technological solutions in high school science and mathematics teaching and learning: Matthew effects and the digital divide (pp. 1041-1048). In C. P. Canstantinou, & Z. C. Zacharai (Eds.), *Computer Based Learning in Sciences: Conference Proceedings 2003 Volume 1 New Technologies and their Applications in Education.* Nicosia, Cyprus: University of Cyprus.

Glasersfeld, E. V. (1996). *Radical constructivism: A way of knowing and learning.* London, UK: Falmer Press.

Grubaugh, S., Levitt, G., Speaker, R., & Rector, P. (2010). Supporting, motivating and engaging all learner in online learning: Literacy and critical thinking in virtual school content area courses. *Proceedings of NSSA Conference.*

Hu, R., Caron, T., Deters, F., Moret, L., & Swaggerty, E. A. (2011). Teacher educators teaching and learning together: A collaborative self-study of support within an online literacy learning community. *Journal of Online Learning and Teaching, 7*(1), 57–67.

Joseph, P. B., Bravmann, S. L., Windschitl, M. A., Mikel, E. R., & Green, N. S. (2000). *Cultures of curriculum.* Mahwah, NJ: Lawrence Erlbaum Associates.

Keengwe, J., Kidd, T., & Kyei-Blankson, L. (2009). Faculty and technology: Implications for faculty training and technology leadership. *Journal of Science Education and Technology, 18*(1), 23–28. doi:10.1007/s10956-008-9126-2

Kieff, J., & Speaker, R. B., Jr. (2003). Teaching sciences and mathematics concepts in the early grades: K-3 teachers engaging developmentally appropriate practice which incorporated technologies (pp. 1049-1054). In C. P. Canstantinou, & Z. C. Zacharai (Eds.), *Computer Based Learning in Sciences: Conference Proceedings 2003 Volume 1 New Technologies and their Applications in Education.* Nicosia, Cyprus: University of Cyprus.

Kincheloe, J. L. (2005). *Critical constructivism primer.* New York, NY: Peter Lang.

McAnuff-Gumbs, M. (2011). "Virtually There": Making online training 'real' for Caribbean literacy coaches – What government can do. *Journal of Online Learning and Teaching, 7*(1), 134–146.

Means, B., Toyama, T., Murphie, R., Bakia, M., & Jones, K. (2010). *Evaluation of evidence-based practices in online learning: A meta-analysis and review of online learning studies.* Research Report, U.S. Office of Planning, Evaluation and Policy Development (OPEPD). Retrieved from the www.ed.gov/about/offices/list/opepd/ppss/reports.html

Michaelsen, M. S. (2009). *Team-based learning: Small group learning's next big step. New Directions for Teaching and Learning, 116.* Hoboken, NJ: Jossey-Bass.

Park, Y. (2011). A pedagogical framework for mobile learning: Categorizing education applications of mobile technologies into four types. *International Review of Research in Open and Distance Learning, 12*(2).

Phillips, D. C. (1995). The good, the bad, and the ugly: The many faces of constructivism. *Educational Researcher, 24*(7), 5–12.

Pinar, W. F. (1994). *Autobiography, politics, and sexuality: Essays in curriculum theory, 1972-1992.* New York, NY: Peter Lang.

Pinar, W. F. (1998). Understanding curriculum as gender text: Notes on reproduction, resistance, and male-male relations (pp. 221-243). In W. F. Pinar (Ed.), *Queer theory in education.* Mahwah, NJ: Erlbaum Associates. Retrieved June 1, 2011 from www.questia.com

Pinar, W. F. (2004). *What is curriculum theory?* Mahwah, NJ: Lawrence Erlbaum.

Rodriguez, M. A., & Anicete, R. C. R. (2010). Students' views of a mixed hybrid ecology course. *Journal of Online Learning and Teaching, 6*(4), 791–798.

Sheridan, K., & Kelly, M. (2010). The indicators of instructor presence that are important to students in online courses. *Journal of Online Learning and Teaching, 6*(4), 767–779.

Speaker, R., Graveline, L., Johnson, M., Darby, D., & Heath, P. (2010, May). *Shaping distance education in a virtual world: A case of a university developing its virtual campus within a state-wide network.* Paper presented at the Annual Meeting of the Athens Educational Research Conference, Athens, Greece.

Speaker, R., Johnson, M., & Graveline, L. (2009). Toward understanding student and faculty perceptions of teaching, learning and disaster resilience in Second Life. In C. Fulford & G. Siemens (Eds.), *Proceedings of ED-MEDIA 2009: World Conference on Educational Multimedia, Hypermedia and Telecommunications* (pp. 585-590) Chesapeake, VA: Association for the Advancement of Computing in Education. (CD version; Abstract volume: p. 101 Retrieved from http://www.aace.org/conf/edmedia/sessions/index.cfm/fuseaction/PaperDetails?CFID=10556463&CFTOKEN=72042024&presentation_id=38776

Speaker, R., Johnson, M., Scaramella, L., & Cashner, R. (2008). Technology failures and successes with Hurricane Katrina: Voices from the University of New Orleans tell stories of the disaster and rebuilding. In J. Luca & E. Weippi (Eds.), *Proceedings of ED-MEDIA 2008: World Conference on Educational Multimedia, Hypermedia and Telecommunications* (pp.857- 862). Chesapeake, VA: Association for the Advancement of Computing in Education.

Speaker, R. B. Jr. (2007). Technologies for teaching science and mathematics in the K-12 schools: Review, observations and directions for practice in the southern United States. In Hirschbuhl, J. J., & Kelley, J. (Eds.), *Computers in education* (12th ed., pp. 123–128). Dubuque, IA: McGrawHill.

Speaker, R. B. Jr, & Barnitz, J. G. (1999). Electronic and linguistic connections in one 21st-century classroom. Column on linguistic perspectives in literacy education. *The Reading Teacher, 53,* 874–877.

Speaker, R. B., Jr., Dermody, M., Knighten, B., Suzuki, T., Wan, C., & Parigi, A. (2001). Student/faculty relationships, methods courses and K-12 classrooms: Examples of integration of technology in teacher education. In C. Spirou (Ed.), *Proceedings of the 2nd International Conference on Technology in Teaching and Learning in Higher Education* (307-313). Athens, Greece: National and Kapodistrian University of Athens.

Speaker, R. B. Jr, Laskowitz, R., Thompson, C., Speaker, P., Chauvin, B., Darby, D., & Willis, E. (2005). Collections, critical selections and the teaching repertoire: Examples from autobiographical memoirs and multimedia teaching units. In Griffin, R. E., Chandler, S. B., & Cowden, B. D. (Eds.), *Visual literacy and development: An African experience* (pp. 187–196). Loretto, PA: International Visual Literacy Association.

Steffe, L. P., & Thompson, P. W. (Eds.). (2000). *Radical constructivism in action: Building on the pioneering work of Ernst Von Glasersfeld.* London, UK: Routledge Falmer.

Wang, L., & Speaker, R. B., Jr. (2002). Investigating education faculty perspectives of their experiences technology project: Issues and problems related to technology integration (pp. 2011-2016). In P. Baker, & S. Rebelsky (Eds.), *Proceedings of ED-MEDIA 2002: World Conference on Educational Multimedia, Hypermedia & Telecommunications.* Norfolk, VA: Association for the Advancement of Computing in Education.

KEY TERMS AND DEFINITIONS

ARRFF: The ARRFF (Aggregate, Remix, Repurpose, Feed Forward) Model (Downes, 2009) for mesh-networked learning provides a theoretical framework for active engagement in online learning

Asynchronous: Not happening in real time -- the texts often posted in discussion boards of platforms like Blackboard and Moodle are asynchronous in that they are more permanent parts of the learning from text in these platforms

Avatar: The online representation of self that each individual creates to become active in a virtual world

Immersion: Learning that places a learner into a world situation or simulation that provides significant and realistic stimulation of the senses during the learning activity -- Immersive education puts the student into as real a situation for study as possible such as in a simulated emergency room or a reconstruction of the city of Rome in 200 CE.

Second Life (SL): The virtual world used in this project. For full information visit: http://secondlife.com/

Synchronous: Happening in real time -- the texting, voice, and animation of a virtual world provide synchronous interactions of the avatars in the virtual world

Team-Based Learning (TBL): A student-centered teaching strategy in which heterogeneous groups of students work to achieve a common academic goal.

Virtual World: An online space composed of specialized webpages that requires a special browser or viewer to simulate a three-dimensional world on the computer screen

Chapter 8
Using Virtual World Technology as a Faculty Development Tool in Higher Education

Linda W. Wood
The Art Institute of Atlanta, USA

ABSTRACT

Higher education institutions are constantly challenged with the task of educating a technology savvy generation of students. Colleges must be able and ready to meet the needs of these digital-age students. What are the perceptions of college faculty of using virtual world technology as a teaching tool in the classroom? The purpose of this chapter is to explore how virtual world environments can be used as a faculty development tool in order to encourage the use of virtual worlds as a teaching tool in the classroom. This chapter references research from a mixed methods study exploring college faculty perceptions of the adoption of virtual world technology into the classroom, which in turn, provides insight to the willingness of higher education faculty to adopt this type of technology. In addition, the final section of the chapter includes a suggested guide on how to create a virtual world faculty development workshop based in Linden Lab's Second Life.

INTRODUCTION

Using different instructional delivery methods allow the learner to absorb instructional content in a way that fits the individual learner. Today's college students have been immersed in digital technology as long as they can remember. However, perhaps many higher education faculty are still not speaking the same digital language as their students. On the other hand, the issue may be that the pedagogical and epistemological beliefs of faculty who are not as technologically savvy as the students in their classrooms, affect the teaching methods used in the higher education classroom today. Faculty perceptions and beliefs can impact whether or not an instructional technology is used in the classroom. Creating faculty development workshops in using and implementing virtual world technology in the classroom is one way to educate faculty on incorporating different teaching techniques to engage students about the subject taught.

DOI: 10.4018/978-1-4666-1963-0.ch008

BACKGROUND

Virtual learning environments offer opportunities for faculty to engage students in learning in an immersive way, simulating reality: "Delivering course material via a virtual environment is beneficial to today's students because it offers the interactivity, real-time interaction and social presence that students of all ages have come to accept in our gaming rich community." (Hodge, Tabrizi, Farwell, & Wuensch, 2007, p.105) Multi-User Virtual Environments (MUVEs), such as Linden Lab's *Second Life*, allow users to create their own character (avatar) and explore different simulated environments. Additionally, educators who have used *Second Life* in the classroom feel the students are more interactive and expressive in *Second Life* than they are compared to traditional online platforms (Appel, 2006).

While some of the literature does not specifically address the use of virtual world technology, it may be reasonable to presuppose that the same concerns that faculty have in regards to adopting new technology in general, could apply to virtual world technology. Immersion in the learning environment appears to have a positive affect on learning outcomes. Duncan (2005) states: "The greater the immersion of self in the learning process, the higher the intrinsic rewards derived from the experience." (p.891) Kluge and Riley (2008) support the theory that colleges will need to consider adopting immersive methods of teaching in order to perhaps engage today's college students. Furthermore, the authors point out that, "digital technologies not only change what students should learn, but what students can learn" (Kluge & Riley, 2008, p.128). Coffman and Klinger (2007) agree with Duncan (2005) and Kluge and Riley (2008) in that students tend to be more engaged in learning, when virtual world technology is used, since virtual world technology supports constructivist learning. Thus, it appears that using interactive technology (such as virtual world technology) as

a teaching method is potentially a viable option to engage students in learning in an immersive way.

On the other hand, faculty perceive that there are barriers and challenges to adopting new technologies in general, which can possibly reflect on the potential to adopt virtual world technology as a teaching tool. Ertmer (2005), suggests that if faculty perceive there are barriers to an adoption of an innovation (such as virtual world technology) or have had a negative past experience with a technology innovation, then potentially that negative experience could possibly transfer to another technology innovation in the future. In addition, accessibility issues can be problematic when adopting emerging technologies in the college classroom. Unreliable and slow Internet connection, are cited as challenges in using virtual environments (Duncan, 2005; Kluge & Riley, 2008). Additional challenges include creating classes in virtual environments, which require knowledge and skills that many faculty in today's higher education institutions do not possess, thus supporting the theory that the learning curve for faculty might be a high one (Kluge & Riley, 2008). Liability issues, such as students possibly being subjected to undesirable behavior by other participants in the virtual world, cost issues, and learning management issues, are all perceived challenges for faculty in using virtual world technology, such as *Second Life*, in their classes (Kluge & Riley, 2008).

Reigle and Matejka (2005) suggest that some educators feel that virtual worlds, such as Second Life, is not conducive to convey academic content and that perhaps virtual worlds "have no connection to the real world" (p.6). Beggs (2000) performed a study with 348 university faculty on their "use of technology, factors influencing their use of technology, and perceived barriers to the use of technology in the classroom." (p.4) The results of Beggs' (2000) study showed that faculty perceive six challenges that potentially hinder the adoption of new technology in the classroom: a lack of time; accessible equipment;

training; personal interest; relevance to subject taught; and accessible faculty development opportunities. Ertmer (2005) also feels that time is a factor in hindering faculty adoption of new technologies. By the time that faculty learn the new technology, the new technology may be replaced by an even newer and more relevant technology (Ertmer, 2005). Furthermore, Rogers' (2000) study showed that faculty do not feel that they have the support or the commitment from the institution in providing professional development for learning new technologies.

Whether or not faculty actually have the support or commitment from their college in providing professional development for learning new technologies (such as virtual world technologies), the colleges must address the perception that faculty are not supported. Faculty development is essential in order for the faculty to learn about new technologies or innovations to diffuse into their teaching (Adams, 2002). Providing faculty development opportunities for learning how to use and implement virtual world technology into their classes, can perhaps not only address the perception of the lack of support, but also provide the tools needed to implement the technology in the classroom.

Faculty Perceptions of Using Virtual World Technology in the Classroom

Faculty perceptions about a technology can influence whether or not a technology is adopted in the classroom. When addressing the use of virtual world technology in the classroom, some faculty may not have enough knowledge about virtual world technology to have formed a belief about using the technology, but perhaps might have a perception instead. Faculty perception, beliefs, and knowledge constructs are interwoven and intertwined. Pajares (1992) points out that self-efficacy affects the way people perceive themselves, which can translate into beliefs, perceptions, and behavior. In addition, Pajares (1992) suggests that

teacher's perceptions and beliefs can possibly be influenced by experiences the teachers had when they were students. It is argued that perceptions can possibly lead to beliefs (Armstrong, 1993; Vision, 2008). Beliefs tend to be more firmly held, since they are possibly based from a combination of experience and knowledge (Pajares, 1992), whereas perceptions can be more fleeting: "To perceive is, cognitively, just to think, to entertain propositions" (Smith, 2001, p.287). Beliefs can influence perceptions (Pajares, 1992; Vision, 2008). Pajares (1992) states: "There is the self-fulfilling prophecy – beliefs influence perceptions that influence behaviors that are consistent with, and that reinforce, the original beliefs." (p.317)

Affordances of using virtual world technology in the classroom include the effect this technology potentially has on student learning outcomes. Some faculty perceive that students can perhaps become more engaged in the subject matter when learners can construct their own learning within a virtual environment (Kluge & Riley, 2008). The social aspects of virtual world technology are an additional affordance of using the technology in the classroom. With so many college students using social networking applications, students have become accustomed to instant access and instant response (Willard, 2006). There is a perception that the social aspect of virtual world technology is an accepted way of interacting with people, much like face-to-face interaction. In the virtual world environment, participants can create their own character (avatar) as well as construct their own environment within the virtual world. Virtual world participants view the virtual environment as three-dimensional spaces that "become places, which, to a large degree, are culturally imagined and the practice of participants, their actions, conversations, movements, and exchanges, can define the world and continually infuse with new meanings." (Thomas & Brown, 2009, p.3)

Hodge, Tabizi, Farwell, and Wuensch (2007), claim that using virtual environments as a teaching tool in the classroom benefit students by offering interactive learning environments. Mullen, Beilke, and Brooks (2007), promote the theory that virtual world environments immerse learning through interactive learning environments. Coffman and Klinger (2007), state that *Second Life* can be used to engage students in discovery learning (a type of learning where students discover as they learn). In addition, Coffman and Klinger (2007) advocate the need for educators to consider implementing virtual world technology in the classroom, if the technology meets the instructional needs of the class. Incorporating the use of virtual world technology as a teaching method in the classroom can perhaps further enhance the chances of engaging our digital-savvy students, demonstrating a potential affordance to faculty. Therefore, it is reasonable to ascertain that if faculty perceive a positive student learning outcome from incorporating an innovation as an instructional tool in the classroom (such as virtual world technology), faculty may see the innovation as an affordance.

A mixed methods research study was conducted with 309-college faculty from 21 different design colleges across North America on their perceptions of using virtual world technology in the higher education classroom (Wood, 2010). The aforementioned research study took place over a period of one year. A link to the online survey (the *Faculty Perception Towards Virtual World Technology Survey*) was emailed out to 2,273 faculty in 43 colleges across North America by the Deans or Faculty Development Directors of the respective colleges. Faculty from 21 of the 43 colleges responded to the survey. Three hundred thirty faculty out of 2,273 actually participated in the online survey for a response rate of 14.52%. However, 21 respondents of the 330 did not complete the survey (309 completed the survey), resulting in a completion response rate of 13.6%. At a 95% confidence level, the corresponding confidence interval was ± 2.63% with a range for the true population proportion falling into the range from 91.01% to 96.27% (Wood, 2010). The online survey used in this research study consisted of

50 quantitative-type data questions administered through an online survey collector. At the end of the 50-question survey, the respondents had the option to volunteer to be interviewed about their perceptions regarding the use of virtual world technology in the higher education classroom. The participants had the option of submitting their email address for a potential post-interview survey.

Out of the 309 faculty who completed the online *Faculty Perception Towards Virtual World Technology Survey*, 151 participants agreed to a possible semi-structured interview. A random purposeful sample was used to select the interview participants from those who volunteered their email address. According to Onwuegbuzie and Leech (2007), random purposeful sampling involves the researcher choosing, "cases at random from the sampling frame consisting of a purposefully selected sample. That is, the researcher first obtains a list of individuals of interest for a study." (p.113) After the survey data were analyzed, the 151 potential interviewees were narrowed down by random purposeful selection using distinguishing factors in order to provide a wide range of faculty opinions.

Twelve faculty members were interviewed for the semi-structured phone interviews. Three specific questions were asked in the semi-structured interviews concerning: (1) their perception about using virtual world technology (such as *Second Life*) as a teaching tool in the classroom; (2) their perception of the affordances of using virtual world technology in the higher education classroom; and (3) their perception of the challenges of using virtual world technology in the higher education classroom (Wood, 2010).

The results of the *Faculty Perception Towards Virtual World Technology Survey* and the follow-up interviews indicated that there was an overall perception that virtual world technology offers affordances in the classroom but that the faculty surveyed perceive that they did not know how to incorporate virtual world technology into their courses. The faculty participating in the survey and interviews felt that faculty development opportunities should be available in order for faculty to have the confidence necessary to use this type of technology in the classroom. In addition, the results of the survey indicated that faculty perceived that they could not depend on access to the hardware or essential software (such as *Second Life* or other virtual environment software) in order to use virtual world technology as a tool in their courses (Wood, 2010).

Creating a Virtual Worlds Technology Faculty Development Workshop

In order for faculty to have the confidence necessary to use virtual world technology in the classroom, faculty development opportunities need to be offered. Faculty development workshops on how to incorporate virtual world technology into the classroom can potentially be delivered either face-to-face, online through a web conferencing application, or through a virtual world software application, such as *Second Life*. This section includes a suggested guide on how to create a virtual world faculty development workshop, based on a pilot study conducted over a period of one year (Wood, 2010). Wood (2010) conducted a pilot study, consisting of a series of faculty development workshops, based in the virtual environment, *Second Life*, in several design colleges in four different cities located throughout the United States.

Follow-up case studies could be conducted with faculty members who chose to incorporate virtual world technologies into their classroom as a direct result of participating in a virtual worlds workshop. These case studies could potentially ascertain whether virtual world technology is an effective tool for instructional delivery and possibly assist in determining whether any perceived affordances of virtual world technology outweigh any perceived barriers to adoption of the technology.

Purpose

The purpose of a Virtual Worlds Faculty Workshop is to expose higher education faculty to a Multi-User Virtual Environment (MUVE) as a potential teaching tool in the classroom by taking the learner through activities or tasks within the virtual worlds environment. In the following faculty development workshop, Linden Lab's *Second Life* (http://secondlife.com/) is used as the virtual worlds environment. However, it is important to note that other virtual worlds environment software exists that perhaps will achieve similar results. As stated previously, a Virtual Worlds Faculty Workshop can potentially be delivered either face-to-face, online through a web conferencing application, or through the virtual world software application being used in the workshop. The suggested length of a Virtual Worlds Faculty Workshop is between four and six hours, depending on the activities and tasks assigned. In order to conduct a Virtual Worlds Faculty Workshop, the facilitator and the participants should have access to a computer that has a high-speed Internet connection as well as the appropriate virtual world software (in this case Linden Lab's *Second Life*) installed prior to conducting or participating in the workshop. In addition, the facilitator conducting the workshop should create a Workshop Wiki as a resource for the participants in the workshop.

Suggested instructional objectives of a Virtual World Faculty Workshop might include the following:

- Learners will demonstrate how to create an avatar and navigate in the virtual world environment
- Learners will demonstrate how to use a virtual world environment as an instructional tool
- Learners will employ the use of a virtual world environment in an instructional setting

By completing the tasks and activities in a Virtual Worlds Faculty Workshop, the learners explore the virtual environment by task completion, build knowledge about the environment, and transfer that knowledge to perhaps eventually utilize the MUVE in their own classroom as a teaching tool. By incorporating a MUVE, such as *Second Life*, into the classroom (whether in an online class or a face-to-face class), the faculty member adds interactive and collaborative activities to the classroom environment, thus increasing the opportunity to actively engage students in the learning.

Suggested Instructional Plan

The activities and tasks the learners will perform in a MUVE include:

- Demonstrating the ability to navigate in the MUVE
- Demonstrating that they can teleport to different places within the MUVE
- Demonstrating that they can set Landmarks in the MUVE
- Demonstrating that they can take Snapshots in the MUVE
- Explaining the uses and benefits of using a MUVE as a teaching tool in the classroom

The facilitator of the Virtual World Faculty Development Workshop should consider the following when using this suggested instructional plan including the:

- Creation of teams of learners to promote collaborative learning for the activities and tasks assigned
- Creating a Workshop Wiki so that the learners can share learning experiences from the MUVE activities and tasks

Suggested Teaching Guide

This suggested teaching guide is intended to teach higher education faculty how to use and incorporate learning activities base in a virtual worlds environment in their own classroom. By participating in a faculty development workshop based in a MUVE, the participating faculty can utilize what they learn in this workshop and apply those same concepts to their own classroom.

The facilitator for a Virtual World Faculty Development Workshop should be aware that faculty participants (the learners in this case) need to be prepared prior to participating in the workshop. For example, the facilitator needs to:

1. Check if the learners know how to use a computer and how to access the Internet
2. Ascertain if the learners have past experience using a MUVE
3. Provide an overview of the learning objectives of the Virtual World Faculty Development Workshop
4. Provide an overview of the tasks and activities planned
5. Show examples of the outcomes of the tasks and activities
6. Show a video about using a MUVE, such as *Second Life*, as an educational tool (For example: Show a video from YouTube that demonstrates how *Second Life* can be used as an instructional tool in the classroom)
7. Conduct a discussion about using interactive, collaborative techniques as teaching tools in the classroom (to assist in determining the potential advantages and disadvantages of using this type of technology in the classroom)

Furthermore, activities should be planned in advance to prepare the faculty for the learning tasks involved in a Virtual World Faculty Development Workshop. These activities should include:

1. An overview of the assigned tasks
2. Assignment of learners into groups or teams consisting of even numbers for task completion
3. Overview of each group's or team's responsibilities in completing tasks
4. Explanation of assessment criteria for the tasks
5. Explanation of peer evaluations to be performed after the tasks are completed
6. Take the learners through the first activity step-by-step in creating an avatar within the MUVE

The following activity – *Scavenger Hunt* – is recommended:

1. Give an overview of the Scavenger Hunt, explaining the rationale.

The goal of the Scavenger Hunt is to familiarize the learner with the MUVE by exploring different aspects within the virtual environment. The learner is sent to different locations within the MUVE by teleporting to those sites. The learner searches for a location within the MUVE, teleports to that location, explores the location, and takes a Snapshot of his or her avatar at that location to provide evidence of the visit. In order to complete the tasks successfully, the learner will need to spend time in the MUVE, becoming familiar with the workings of the environment. In doing so, the learner will perhaps eventually be able to incorporate the MUVE into the classroom as an online activity.

2. Explain and demonstrate how to create a Friends List within the MUVE.
3. Explain and demonstrate how to teleport within the MUVE.
4. Explain the definition of a Landmark and demonstrate how to make a Landmark in the MUVE.

5. Show an example of a Snapshot in the MUVE. Explain and demonstrate how to take a Snapshot within the MUVE.
6. Explain and demonstrate how to save a Snapshot to the computer.
7. Show the learner's the Workshop's Wiki and demonstrate how to post a Snapshot on the Wiki.
8. Demonstrate how to post a comment on the Wiki for the Snapshots posted.

Directions for the Scavenger Hunt

For this Scavenger Hunt, the learner will find places within the MUVE, such as historical place, museums, and educational sites. Before proceeding with the Scavenger Hunt, the learner must be able to understand how to teleport, set a Landmark, and take a Snapshot within the MUVE.

1. At each location, the learner will be required to take a Snapshot of the place with his or her avatar in the Snapshot in order to demonstrate that the learner has completed the activity.
2. The learner will save the Snapshot to his or her computer.
3. At the completion of the Scavenger Hunt, the learner will post his or her Snapshots to the Workshop Wiki that the facilitator has created for the workshop.
4. The learner will post a summary of his or her Scavenger Hunt experience and describe a favorite place visited.

The Scavenger Hunt Tasks

The facilitator will assign specific locations within the MUVE (an example would be: "Search for The Globe Theatre") for the learners to search, discover, and document with the Snapshots. It is important to note that locations within the MUVES change frequently and prior to each workshop, the facilitator should verify that the links to the assigned locations are working properly.

At the required locations, the facilitator can assign specific tasks for that particular location. For example, the facilitator can require that the learners watch a video that is imbedded within the MUVE location and write a critique about the video.

Another suggested activity related to the Scavenger Hunt, would include having each student explore an additional location (or two) within the MUVE on their own during the workshop, Landmark the location, and teleport the rest of the class to that location (to demonstrate that the learner can actually teleport others to the location by creating a Friends List and inviting another "Friend" to join them in their new location). Thus, demonstrating that the learner can find locations within the MUVE on their own and teleport others to that location for a virtual field trip.

The facilitator will request that the learners save their Snapshots to a folder on their computer as they locate the required sites to eventually post on the Workshop Wiki. In addition, the facilitator can require that the learners document their experiences at the different locations by journaling their experiences and posting it to the Workshop Wiki.

An additional activity is the use of a WebQuest to discover the benefits of the uses of a MUVE as a teaching tool. The purpose of a Web Quest activity is to assist higher education faculty in identifying the uses and benefits of incorporating a MUVE, such as *Second Life*, into the classroom. In this activity, the learners will create assignments for the activities completed in *Second Life*. A WebQuest "is considered to be an effective way to organize chaotic Internet resources and help learners gain new knowledge through a guided learning environment" (Patterson & Pipkin, 2001, cited in Zheng, Stucky, McAlack, Menchana, & Stoddart, 2005, p. 41).

The WebQuest Activity

This is a collaborative activity. Divide the workshop participants into groups consisting of even

numbers to complete the tasks. Complete the activities as a group and post the results as directed for each WebQuest.

Task 1: Benefits and Uses of Using *Second Life* (or a MUVE) in the Higher Education Classroom

1. Each group will research different web resources in order to identify the benefits and uses of *Second Life* (or a MUVE) in the classroom.
2. Research online videos (such as YouTube videos) to view videos on how to use *Second Life* as an educational tool in the classroom. As an example, search for "*Second Life* for Educators" in the YouTube search box and view related videos. Document your findings and save the URLs.
3. Compile a list of different web resources, including articles and videos (making sure to cite the URLs). Capture screenshots of videos (citing the URL) and save to a file on the computer.
4. Document the findings of the group, using the specific examples found in the WebQuest. Synthesize the information and create a scrapbook, illustrating the benefits of using *Second Life* in the higher education classroom. Save the scrapbook as a PDF file.
5. After the scrapbook is completed, post the PDF to the Workshop Wiki.

Task 2: Creating Assignments in *Second Life* (or a MUVE)

1. The groups will research different web resources to learn how to create assignments based on activities in *Second Life*.
2. Research online videos (such as YouTube videos) to view videos on how to create classroom assignments in *Second Life*. As an example, search for "*Second Life* Class Assignments" in the YouTube search box and view related videos. Document your findings and save the URLs.

3. After completing the web research on creating class assignments in Second Life, the groups will synthesize the information (using citations), and document.
4. Each group will create a set of four postcards. The postcards can be created in a word processing software application or a desktop publishing application. Each postcard should measure 4" x 6" in size, and will be double-sided. The groups can research how to make postcards on the web.
5. On the front of the postcard, a Snapshot in Second Life, related to the assignment for the card, should be placed, illustrating an assignment in Second Life. The written assignment should be placed on the backside of the postcard. The postcards can be set up to be side-by-side instead of front and back.
6. Save the postcards as a PDF file.
7. After the postcards are completed, the groups post the PDF files to the Workshop Wiki.

Plans for Assessment and Evaluation of a Virtual Worlds Faculty Workshop

The learning outcomes from a faculty development workshop should be evaluated and assessed. The learning outcomes from the workshop can be assessed through the completion of the Scavenger Hunt and the WebQuest tasks. Surveys should be administered to the participating faculty in order to evaluate the effectiveness of the workshop. A formative survey should be administered at the beginning of the workshop, prior to the first activity, to provide the facilitator with a baseline. Questions in the formative survey could cover issues such as: prior use of social computing applications; courses taught; how many years teaching in higher education; have they taught online classes previously; and their general perception about using virtual world technology as a teaching tool prior to taking the workshop.

A summative survey should be administered at the end of the workshop in order to assess the strengths and weaknesses of the content of the workshop, as well as the general perception about the use of virtual world technology in the classroom after having completed the workshop. Questions in the summative survey could cover issues such as: how they felt about using the MUVE; how they felt about navigating in the MUVE and completing the workshop tasks; what advantages they perceive in using a MUVE in the classroom; what challenges they perceive in using a MUVE in the classroom; if they felt they needed more instruction on using a MUVE in the classroom; and if they anticipated using virtual world technology in their classroom in the future. The outcomes of the two evaluations (the formative and summative surveys) could potentially be compared to each other and an assessment based on those outcomes can be used for improvements to future Virtual Worlds Faculty Workshops.

FUTURE RESEARCH DIRECTIONS

Future research could focus on specific areas of opportunities revealed in the responses to the formative and summative surveys from a Virtual Worlds Faculty Workshop in order to assess whether the learning outcomes of the workshop are being met. If a facilitator conducts a series of Virtual Worlds Faculty Workshops, the summative surveys of the series of workshops could be compared in order to determine improvements for future workshops. In addition, future research on integrating virtual world technology into the higher education classroom could possibly include follow-up case studies on faculty who chose to incorporate virtual world technology into their classroom as a direct result of participating in a Virtual Worlds Faculty Workshop. As previously stated, these follow-up case studies could potentially ascertain whether virtual world technology is an effective tool for instructional delivery and possibly assist in determining whether any perceived affordances of virtual world technology outweigh any perceived barriers to adoption of the technology for faculty.

CONCLUSION

Today's students thrive on instant interaction, instant satisfaction, and instant reward (Hodge, et al., 2007). "Today's students are innovative, investigative, thrive on multi-tasking and multi-processing information, and are highly exploratory and independent" (Leung, 2002, as cited in Pursel & Bailey, 2007, p. 5). These students prefer graphic interfaces to the written word and grew up immersed in a technology world, where everything can be accessed instantly (Hodge, et al., 2007). However, Moser (2007) states: "Many faculty lack the necessary technical and pedagogical competencies to successfully integrate educational technology into their teaching" (p. 69). In order to address the needs of our digital students (or digital minds), higher education faculty perhaps need to change the way they think in order to engage students in the learning (Jones, Harmon, & O'Grady-Jones, 2005).

Jacobsen (1997) feels that faculty development opportunities perhaps would assist in faculty adoption of new technologies: "The main reasons that mainstream faculty hesitate to adopt [new technologies] are the lack of effective training and support" (p. 24). Providing faculty development opportunities can increase self-efficacy in faculty (Jacobsen, 1997), which possibly in turn can affect faculty perceptions and beliefs about using technology. Christensen (2002) emphasizes proper faculty development in the use of technology in the classroom as an important element to successful integration of the technology: "the instructor who has learned to integrate technology into existing curricula may teach differently than the instructor who has received no such training" (p. 413).

College faculty perceive that there are affordances to using virtual world technology in the classroom and see it as a useful teaching tool (Wood, 2010). They realize that their students are a video-gaming generation. However, college faculty also perceive the lack of training in virtual world technologies as a challenge to adopting the technology in the classroom (Wood, 2010). In order for faculty to feel comfortable using new instructional technologies, faculty development opportunities must be offered. By offering faculty development workshops in virtual world technology, faculty are presented the opportunity to learn how to incorporate virtual world environments as a teaching tool in order to perhaps enhance the learning experience for the students and potentially engage the students in the learning.

REFERENCES

Adams, N. B. (2002). Educational computing concerns of postsecondary faculty. *Journal of Research on Technology*, *34*(3), 285–303.

Appel, J. (2006). *Second Life develops education following: Virtual world being used by some educators and youth groups for teaching*. Retrieved from http://www.eschoolnews.com/news/top-news/index.cfm?i=42030&CFID=8638975&CFTOKEN=21337481

Armstrong, D. M. (1993). *A materialist theory of the mind*. New York, NY: Routledge.

Beggs, T. A. (2000). *Influences and barriers to the adoption of instructional technology*. Retrieved from http://frank.mtsu.edu/~itconf/proceed00/beggs/beggs.htm

Christensen, R. (2002). Effects of technology integration education on the attitudes of teachers and students. *Journal of Research on Technology in Education*, *34*(4), 411–434.

Coffman, T., & Klinger, M. B. (2007). Utilizing virtual worlds in education: The implications for practice. *International Journal of Sciences*, 2(1), 29–33.

Duncan, H. (2005). On-line education for practicing professionals: A case study. *Canadian Journal of Education / Revue Canadienne de L'éducation*, 28(4), 874-896. Retrieved from http://www.jstor.org

Gibson, J. J. (1977). The theory of affordances. In Shaw, R., & Bransford, J. (Eds.), *Perceiving, acting and knowing*. Hillsdale, NJ: Erlbaum.

Hodge, E. M., Tabrizi, M. H. N., Farwell, M. A., & Wuensch, K. L. (2007). Virtual reality classrooms strategies for creating a social presence. *International Journal of Sciences*, 2(1), 105–109.

Jacobsen, M. (1997). Bridging the gap between early adopters' and mainstream faculty's use of instructional technology. *Information Analysis*. Retrieved from http://eric.ed.gov/ERICDocs/data/ericdocs2sql/content_storage_01/0000019b/80/16/ed/23.pdf

Jones, M. G., Harmon, S. W., & O'Grady-Jones, M. K. (2005). Developing the digital mind: Challenges and solutions in teaching and learning. *Teacher Education Journal of South Carolina*, 2004-2005, 17–24.

Kluge, S., & Riley, L. (2008). Teaching in virtual worlds: Opportunities and challenges. *Issues in Informing Science and Information Technology*, 5, 127–135.

Moser, P. K. (1986). Perception and belief: A regress problem. *Philosophy of Science*, 53(1), 120–126. doi:10.1086/289297

Mullen, L., Beilke, J., & Brooks, N. (2007). Redefining field experiences: Virtual environments in teacher education. *International Journal of Social Sciences*, 2(1), 22–28.

Norman, D. A. (1988). *The design of everyday things*. New York, NY: Basic Books.

Onwuegbuzie, A. J., & Leech, N. L. (2007). A call for qualitative power analyses. *Quality & Quantity*, 41, 105–121. doi:10.1007/s11135-005-1098-1

Pajares, M. F. (1992). Teachers' beliefs and educational research: Cleaning up a messy construct. *Review of Educational Research*, 62(3), 307–332.

Pursel, B. K., & Bailey, K. D. (2007). *Establishing virtual learning worlds: The impact of virtual worlds and online gaming on education and training*. Retrieved from http://citeseerx.ist.psu.edu/viewdoc/download?doi=10.1.1.121.1959&rep=rep1&type=pdf

Rogers, P. L. (2000). Barriers to adopting emerging technologies in education. *Journal of Educational Computing Research*, 22(4), 455–472. doi:10.2190/4UJE-B6VW-A30N-MCE5

Smith, A. D. (2001, March). Perception and belief. *Philosophy and Phenomenological Research*, 62(2), 283–309. doi:10.1111/j.1933-1592.2001.tb00057.x

Thomas, D., & Brown, J. S. (2009, January). Why virtual worlds can matter. *International Journal of Media and Learning*, 1(1).

Vision, G. (2009). Fixing perceptual belief. *The Philosophical Quarterly*, 59(235), 292–314. doi:10.1111/j.1467-9213.2008.566.x

Willard, N. E. (2006). *A briefing for educators: Online social networking communities and youth risk*. Retrieved from http://www.csriu.org/cyberbully/docs/youthriskonlinealert.pdf

Wood, L. W. (2010). *Faculty perceptions about virtual world technology: Affordances and barriers to adoption*. Unpublished Doctoral dissertation, Middle-Secondary Education and Instructional Technology Dissertations, Georgia State University, Atlanta. Retrieved from http://digitalarchive.gsu.edu/msit_diss/70

Zheng, R., Stucky, B., McAlack, M., Menchana, M., & Stoddart, S. (2005). WebQuest learning as perceived by higher education learners. *Tech-Trends: Linking Research & Practice to Improve Learning, 49*(4), 41-49. Retrieved from http://www.eric.ed.gov

KEY TERMS AND DEFINITIONS

Affordance: Based on the Affordance Theory by James Gibson (Gibson, 1977) and adopted as "perceived affordance" by Donald Norman (Norman, 1988). An action performed based on the intended function of an object or innovation. For example, when one sees a doorknob, one perceives that the doorknob will open the door (Norman, 1988).

Avatar: A computer-animated graphic character or identity that represents a user, and is manipulated by the user on a computer.

Beliefs: Based on values held by an individual; a tenet; a conviction of a phenomenon. "Beliefs are basically unchanging," are not "open to evaluation and critical examination," and are strong "predictors of behaviors" (Pajares, 1992, p. 311).

Mixed Methods Research: Involves combining qualitative data and quantitative data into a merged dataset in order to determine research findings.

Multi-User Virtual Environments (MUVEs): Software-based applications that simulate an environment using real-time interaction between participants within the computer environment through a 3-D graphic representation of the real world.

Perception: To observe or become aware of your surroundings; to "form beliefs about objects and events" (Musto & Konolige, 1993, p. 90); to form a concept about an object, event, or process (Armstrong, 1993); "requires a particular belief" about an object (Moser, 1986, p. 121).

Virtual World Technology: Includes software-based applications that simulate an environment. The virtual world environment is considered a 3-D graphical representation of the real world.

Chapter 9

Assessment Processes for Online Professional Development

Lesley Farmer
California State University Long Beach, USA

ABSTRACT

Professional development (PD) assessment is an ongoing, integral activity in order to improve results at individual, training, program, and institutional levels. Principles of assessment are outlined, and the general processes of assessment design, delivery, and analysis are explained. Technology greatly expands the possible data that can be collected for assessment purposes. Emphasis is placed on online environments, noting the issues that are unique to that environment.

INTRODUCTION

Assessment serves as a core activity in professional development (PD) at individual, training, program, and institutional levels. The intent is participant, instructor, and program improvement. First, educational goals and objectives need to be identified; who makes those decisions? Locating or developing a valid and reliable assessment instrument (or set of tools) requires answering

a number of questions: what is assessed, who is assessed, who does the assessing, when and how frequently is the assessment done, how is it done, how are the data analyzed, who analyzes the data, how are the findings acted upon, who acts upon them, what accountability is present? These decisions may be made and perhaps acted upon by the PD enterprise.

In an online environment, participants and instructors can interact more often, and preserve their thinking processes more easily. Work can be posted and shared quickly and efficiently. Conver-

DOI: 10.4018/978-1-4666-1963-0.ch009

sations about PD topics can continue without few space and time constraints. As a result, assessment can be more effective.

BACKGROUND ON ASSESSMENT

Principles of Assessment

Assessing professional development programs and their support mechanisms takes time and effort: from deciding what to assess through choosing an appropriate instrument, gathering the data, and analyzing the results. Any slip along the way can lessen its effect and benefits, so the process needs to be planned and implemented carefully.

To this end, the American Association of Higher Education (AAHE) Assessment Forum (2003) identified nine principles to guide assessment of participant learning. These principles apply well to assessing professional development in general and to online environments in particular.

1. Use educational values as your touchstone. Measure what you value. In online PD, values are determined all the stakeholders, particularly the PD provider, the participants, and the workplace.

2. Assessing adult learning as a complex set of skills, knowledge, and dispositions gained over time. As such, use a variety of assessment methods from different points of view and time. In online PD, assessment normally begins long before the training session occurs. Input is derived from the target audience, the workplace, and professional organizations. However, online PD needs to also assess the learners at the beginning of a training session in order to ascertain current needs and resources, which impacts the content and method of delivery. For example, media-rich resources might need to be omitted if participants cannot access a high-speed network; additionally, the PD

provider might need to remediate participants who lack some prerequisite skills.

3. Have clear, specific educational goals. Assessment should lead to improvement, so all stakeholders should agree on precisely what needs to be examined – and why. Just as the needs assessment should involve all stakeholders, so too should assessment decisions. However, participants in online PD may well come from different backgrounds, and decide to engage in online PD for different reasons so that consensus on assessment goals might be difficult to achieve. Nevertheless, the educational goals should be clearly stipulated up front, and are often the basis for the audience to decide whether or not to participate in the online PD.

4. Consider both processes and products. How an adult learner solves a problem reflects both internal mental schemas as well as instructional approaches and content. In online environments, assessment needs to address technical expertise of both the instructor as well as the participants. In addition, achievement may be constrained by the technology itself, particularly on the side of the participant.

5. Assess on an ongoing basis. Baselines, benchmarks, and culminating experiences need to be assessed so timely interventions can be incorporated to optimize learning. There should be a spirit of continuous improvement. Online PD has the potential for immediate feedback and ongoing monitoring. The instructional design and the online platform greatly impact the capacity for ongoing and interactive assessment. Furthermore, the instructor's own practice impacts how assessment is implemented.

6. Foster broad involvement. Each stakeholder brings a unique perspective that can impact others' efforts. Active participation by the entire learning community also optimizes communication and systematic coordination.

Online PD has the potential for continuous interaction and community building, depending on how it is structured and supported. Dynamically-built online PD that is based on a community of practice is most likely to involve stakeholders actively. Pre-packaged online PD has to involve the stakeholders at the instructional design stage in order to frontload the training session such that it can incorporate the perspectives of the participants without changing the pre-determined content.

7. Focus on the use of assessment. Do not assess just for the sake of the process but in order to take justified action on issues that people truly care about. One-shot online PD precludes program improvement, so a series of online PD opportunities should be considered from the start. PD participants should be informed about assessment processes so they can feel that their perspectives will make a difference in future PD planning and implementation.

8. Consider assessment as an integral part of the larger picture to improve the learning community and organization. Assessment should not be a separate entity or sidebar entity, but a main ingredient for decision-making. Online PD is a common form of in-service improvement efforts for the workplace and professional organizations. As such, the learning should transfer to those work sites, and impact the functionality of those entities. Too often, the impact of online PD is not assessed in terms of organizational effectiveness.

9. Consider assessment as an accountability issue. Educational institutions are accountable to their participants and to the community at large. Assessment keeps education "honest" in the eyes of the public. Online PD providers are specifically held responsible for their efforts and results. Especially if the workplace or professional organization pays for these services, it will want to measure its return on investment (ROI). Because online PD is often done on a voluntary basis, that is, the audience chooses whether or not to participate, the rate of returning participants to future online PD sessions is one indication of success and provides a natural consequence for PD provider responsibility.

On the practical side, here are major questions to ask when determining the most effective assessment process, with implications for online PD.

- Why assess? To gather baseline information, to diagnose strengths and weaknesses, to evaluate, to facilitate planning, to redirect efforts, to change content or instruction, to allocate resources, to motivate, to reward or punish (e.g., hiring, graduation), to maintain accreditation or licensure (Mowl, 1996). Online PD ultimately aims to improve practice, which can also positively impact associated organizations such as the workplace or professional association.

- What is being assessed? Needs (of participants, instructors, community, etc.), learning environment and support (including technology), content, instruction, outcomes. The ultimate major assessment target is participant performance. Online PD itself is a major target of assessment, particularly since it is usually based on perceived needs, more than other forms of education. The context of the PD must then also be part of the assessment target: needs, pre-existing conditions, environment, and stakeholders.

- Who is being assessed? Participants, instructors, administrators, technicians, other institutional staff members, employers, community at large; the entire population or a sample (representative or targeted). Online PD ultimately assesses the person who is participating in the PD. However, that participant also serves as the basis for assessing the PD itself (curriculum, design, instructor, delivery) as well as the context: organization and the profession at large.

- Who is assessing—and analyzing data results? Learners, instructors, administrators, other institutional staff members, employers, workplace clientele, community at large, outside consultants. With online PD, the participants usually play a major role in assessment. Usually the PD provider analyzes the data, although the PD instructor may also examine the data if intending to do another PD session.
- When does assessment occur? Before, during, or after instruction/input; at the end of a semester or year; upon exiting a program or school; upon being hired, time of day or week. Online PD should start with a needs assessment as a basis for designing the curriculum. In instructional design, assessment should be done at every benchmark. Not only should assessment occur throughout the PD, but follow-up assessment even a month or year later provides useful information about its impact as well as the basis for further PD.
- Where does assessment occur? In classrooms, at home, at work, online. Although most online PD assessment occurs online, pre- and post-PD assessment could occur anywhere: at professional meetings, during a phone call, or at an alternative PD venue.
- How is assessment conducted? By survey, observation, work analysis, test, rubric, interview, focus group, self-assessment, systems analysis. Online PD can incorporate all types of assessment, but tends to focus on performance and satisfaction surveys. Informally, ongoing assessment is done whenever participants are engaged via observation and analyzing their responses,

and even unengagement provides valuable data that should be acted upon.

Defining the Process

Several terms are used in the assessment world, which should be defined so all parties have a common understanding as they embark on online PD (Maloy, et al., 2011).

- **Standard:** A statement indicating what participants should know and do; curriculum standards state what should occur in the learning environment.
- **Outcome:** The desired and measurable goal, specifying what the relevant organization wants constituents to accomplish.
- **Descriptor:** Concrete description of an outcome (e.g., uses technology responsibly, legally, and ethically).
- **Indicator:** Specific criteria that demonstrate that one has met a standard or satisfied an outcome (e.g., recommends appropriate physical therapy interventions).
- **Rubric:** A scoring guide with differentiated rating descriptions. Usually rubrics entail a number of indicators or criteria.
- **Benchmark:** Learning performance standards at pre-determined points in time such as the end of the year, or key points in a project such as a first draft of a report. Benchmarks enable all parties to reflect on their performance or progress formatively so that they can redirect their efforts to optimally meet the ultimate standard. Wikis (that is, quick webpage editors) exemplify an effective technological way to maintain an accurate record of revisions.

Before online PD assessment can occur, the stakeholders have to define the domain of learning. They may choose to adopt existing definitions drawn up by national educational entities, by professional organizations, or by local education.

They may build on existing content or curriculum standards. The discussion about terminology, indicators, and benchmarks can be time-consuming and sometimes frustrating, but it is imperative to gain consensus from the start in order to assess participants effectively.

Sometimes it is easier to list the tasks that indicate professional competence (Ingalls, 1972). The characteristics of those tasks can then be deconstructed into their component aspects. What variables can be identified, such as creating chemical solutions or ascertaining a client's perspective? What skills make a difference in the quality of the final product? What distinguishes unacceptable, acceptable, and target performance? At that point, those variables can be operationalized; that is, transformed into concrete, measurable requirements.

Online PD activities must then be designed to address those variables, instructing participants on how to meet the requirement and giving them opportunities to demonstrate their competence. By this point, the assessment measures need to be identified and incorporated into the instructional design process. The organizational enterprise should be involved in coordinating those PD activities so that they occur across the professional domains and articulate between levels. For online PD, technical experts need to be consulted to make sure that assessments are feasible technically. In that way, participants can apply these competencies in numerous content areas with different contexts and formats, resulting in deeper knowledge.

Systems Thinking about Online Assessment

As noted above, online PD assessment should not be limited to participant performance. It is equally important to assess the organizational conditions for enabling participants to become more proficient. Thus, in determining tasks, the actual design and implementation of PD activities need to be deconstructed into their composite elements to determine which actions lead to positive conditions for gaining competency. Does collaboration between the instructor and workplace personnel, for instance, impact performance? Does the presence of a rich collection of current and relevant online resources correlate with content knowledge? In short, the entire enterprise's processes and products need to be examined in light of PD impact. An effective approach to assessment is a systems approach where each input and output factor is identified. Assessment should occur at every level: individual participant and PD designer/instructor, the PD session or course, a PD curriculum/program, and the organization providing the PD (Roblyer & Doering, 2009).

An effective approach to assessment is a systems approach where each input and output factor is identified (Laird, 1985). The following critical questions can guide PD designers as they assess their environment and review relevant research literature relative to online PD initiatives.

Input

- What competencies and dispositions do PD designers bring to the online learning environment? Are they credentialed in their area? Are they new to the field, or do they bring valuable experience from other settings – or other fields? Do they have expertise in teaching in online environments?
- What curriculum are PD designers following? How closely does online practice align to academic content frameworks or professional standards? Does the curriculum reflect the latest trends in the workplace as well as reflect andragogical (adult education) practice? How the curriculum incorporate and advance technological skills?
- What resources are used to deliver the curriculum? Who determines which learning systems and program resources to use? Are

high-quality electronic resources readily available and accessible, including to users with special needs? Do PD designers develop their own learning aids; do they have the technical skills in order to produce and use them?

- What instructional strategies are used? What kinds of PD activities are used to provide participants with opportunities to learn, practice and demonstrate professional competence? How does the online environment facilitate content knowledge and application? Do strategies include explicit technical instruction—or resources to help participants use the requisite technology?

- How is time allocated: within an online module or chat session, in terms of course and participant pacing, relative to PD and opportunities for technical help?

- What governance and enterprise structures are in place to facilitate andragogy: PD opportunities, databases or repositories to share best practice, telecommunications to facilitate collaboration, funding for PD participation?

- What background, experiences, skills and dispositions do participants bring to the online PD environment? At what point are participants in their career, which might impact the curriculum choices? PD designers should assess participants' technological skills as they engage in PD in order to optimize learning experiences. What pre-requisite technical skills are lacking? Without addressing those prior skills, PD designers and participants will be frustrated in their work.

- How do workplace and community members interface with participants and the rest of the PD enterprise? What resources, including online, do they provide? What competing priorities do they reflect?

Output

- Does participant work reflect content knowledge and application as well as technological competency? PD designers should routinely examine current student products in order to assess the impact of their efforts.

- How do students perform on assessments? Do they "test" consistently, or does their performance depend on content matter or technological circumstances? Whenever possible, assessment data should be disaggregated by demographic data, instructor, and technological factors.

- What PD grades are participants receiving? How consistent is grading between instructors, especially those teaching the same content? Is there a connection between grades and technological incorporation?

- What PD are participants taking? What is the basis for PD enrollment? What PD do participants drop? Does the online environment impact PD choice?

- What happens to participants when they finish PD? On what basis do they leave? Surveying participants after they exit (both after a PD session or series) provides valuable insights into their sense of being prepared for future efforts.

- Other output measures provide indirect data about performance: time spent online, computer "down" time, employer conferences, instructor turn-over rate.

The Role of Technology in Assessment

With the incorporation of technology, the assessment process can increase its effectiveness significantly for several reasons, as detailed by the Committee on the Foundations of Assessment, et al. (2001).

- **Speed:** Data can be collected and analyzed quickly.
- **Record-Keeping:** Online and video interviewing and other electronic communications are instantly archived; digitized data can be exported for efficient analysis.
- **Synchronicity and Asynchronicity:** Communication can be conducted and transmitted at times that are convenient for both assessor and assessee.
- **Variety of Dissemination Options:** Assessment instruments can be broadcast for wide-range access and also directed to individual, targeted audiences.
- **Public and Private Options:** Data can be collected in a public venue or kept private to insure participant confidentiality.
- **Standardized and Individualized Assessments:** Assessments can be systemized so that data can be easily merged and compared; just as easily, instruments can be customized to gather very specialized information.
- **Statistical Features:** Data analysis software programs such as SPSS and SAS facilitate a broad range of sophisticated processes that can be conducted in hours instead of days. Even standard spreadsheet programs provide quick formula calculations and graphic representations.
- **Equitable Access and Participation:** Assessment processes optimize participation through electronic language translation services, flexibility of response methods and timing, choice of communication formats (text, sound, image, motion), accommodations for populations with special needs.
- **Increased Writing and Reflective Practice:** Technology increases opportunities and means to express facts and perspectives, and facilitates metacognitive

processes; participants can transcend reactive activity and become more engaged and productive.

Online PD delivery has significantly advanced professional development contemporary assessment, and can incorporate several assessment methods. Here is an example of technologies used within a college of education to assess participants, courses, programs, and the college itself. This kind of grid may be applicable to other types of PD providers. Table 1 shows how the author's educational institution incorporates and coordinates technology to assess effectiveness of online teaching and learning on several levels.

DETERMINING THE ASSESSMENT INSTRUMENT

As PD tasks, variables, and learning activities are defined, the assessment instrument should also be considered so that all aspects of instructional design and learning are aligned and leveraged for maximum effect: outcome, teaching and learning assumptions, content transmission, along with assessment (Maki, 2002). PD entities should develop a set of inter-connected assessment tools across the curriculum and stakeholders, articulated with workplace environments. These tools, then, support the entire entity's mission and are used to provide baseline data about PD, diagnose gaps in and obstacles to participant achievement, as well as measure progress and ultimate success. Several factors need to be considered when determining which assessment instrument to use, regardless of its format. Some typical online assessment instruments described, noting their strengths and weaknesses

Too often educators assess what is easy rather than what is important. The designated assessment instrument must measure the most significant

Table 1. College of education technology for assessment

Technology Tool	Features	Use for Assessment
http://my.csulb.edu	Course enrollment/grades; individual advisement information	Individual participant progress, course management/grades
University enrollment services database	Participant demographics; degree statistics	Degree statistics and demographics
College/department/program website	Documents/files/forms, links to resources	Number of hits, surveys, template for eportfolio
Graduate Office database	Demographics, program progress	Program process, candidate information
Credential Center database	Demographics, program progress	Program process, candidate information
TaskStream	State content standards, templates,	Eportfolio, participant work
Course management system	Documents/files/forms, email, discussion forum, surveys, quizzes, grading program, use statistics, MyContent	Grades, use statistics, participant work, narrative analysis, eportfolio
College intranet	Links to assessment tools	Forms for assessment

content learning variables accurately and reliably time after time. It is probably more effective to measure a few really important knowledge-base and application variables well than to assess many simple, low-level skills.

Typically, the level of assessment aligns with the level of learning (Biggs, 2003). For instance, a multiple choice test can measure use of a driver's manual. A concept map can measure knowledge of terms and their interrelationships. A questionnaire can measure simple perceptions about health care. Authentic assessment can work for a range of competencies, from locating a local auto supply store to conducting a sophisticated research project to address a local social issue problem.

The assessment not only measures participants' performance but it can be used to validate the variable itself. For example, if students know how to outline, does that lead to better reports? If not, then the true contributing variable must be found. As with online PD activities, determining and designing assessments should be an institutional or at least programmatic effort in order to leverage measurements so that adult learners do not need to be tested constantly and so interventions can impact adult learning in several courses simultaneously.

Representative Assessment Instruments

Some typical online assessment instruments follow, noting their strengths and weaknesses for PD (Palloff & Pratt, 2008).

- **Individual Interview:** Provides open-ended, interactive, in-depth data. This method may be done synchronously through online chat or web conferencing, both of which usually provide a transcript of the interaction. Labor-intensive and time-consuming, the data are only as accurate as the questions being asked and individual being interviewed so this approach requires training; language and technical barriers may exist as well. The audience for the online PD varies greatly, depending on the origin and goal of the PD, so that the objective of the interview needs to be carefully delineated as it impacts the data collected and how it is analyzed.
- **Focus Group:** Provides open-ended, interactive, in-depth data and group dynamics. Online chat and web conferencing offer real-time interaction, although it is pos-

sible to utilize threaded discussion over a set time period. Data may be skewed or missing because of group norming; this approach requires training; language and technical barriers may exist as well. Focus groups are usually best implemented at the instructional design stage, and participants should be chosen based on their fit with the projected audience of the PD.

- **Content Analysis:** Provides unobtrusive data that can be repurposed. Confidentiality may limit access or application; data may need to be contextualized. Content analysis can be done to reveal practitioners' PD needs, as well as during online PD to make instructional adjustments, or after a PD to measure learning or transfer of new knowledge to the workplace.

- **Authentic Assessment:** Asking for the behavior that the learner is expected to exhibit if the intended learning outcome is met. Usually a realistic task is called for that closely approximates the real world application of the identified competency. Because the simulation task is complex and often "fuzzy" (ill-defined) – to measure complex behavior, authentic assessment requires careful delineation of critical criteria, close observation, and holistic grading. An example of an authentic assessment is critiquing learner-produced anti-smoking advertisements. Authentic assessment may assume a different form in an online environment; for instance, simulations can record each decision point if so programmed. Another way to use authentic assessment is to measure the degree of learning transferred to the workplace.

- **Performance-Based Assessment:** Direct observation of learner behavior that usually involves creating products. Learners' actions thus reflect their knowledge and skills within a real-world context. Usually de-

scriptive rubrics are used to assess the relative quality of the learner's performance. Again, an online environment differs from a face-to-face situation; video recording a performance is one way to capture some of the nuances of a performance, although camera angle limits the assessor's perspective. This approach is also applicable to workplace transfer of learning.

The most common commercial assessment tools are standardized tests. High-quality ones have been validated with many populations, and provide longitudinal reliability. Government licensure and accreditation processes frequently rely on these tests because they provide cross-site comparisons. They may be norm-referenced (i.e., test results are compared) or criterion-referenced (i.e., results are compared to the correct answer), the latter usually being preferred. In those areas where experts can agree on measurable criteria, representative prompts, and correct answers, then those tests offer a way to assess many learners efficiently. However, for high-level career-specific competencies, such agreements are difficult to achieve. Standardized tests are most appropriate for assessing declarative knowledge such as the use of basic tools or the application of straightforward processes. Most of these tests are stand-alone products that are not explicitly aligned with curriculum; nor do PD designers normally have access to the tests themselves or the results (Association for Assessment in Counseling, 2003).

Some factors need to be considered when determining which assessment instrument to use in online PD, regardless of its format (Palloff & Pratt, 2008):

- **Cost:** For the instrument itself, recording forms, labor involved in development, administration, data entry and analysis
- **Time:** For development, administration, coding, analysis

- **Availability:** Of instrument, of associated technology, human resources for development, administration and analysis
- **Skills:** For development, administration, data collection training, data entry and coding, analysis
- **Legalities:** Of confidentiality and privacy, use of instrument, parental permission
- **Culture:** Attitudes towards the instrument, language issues, fear of high stakes or repercussions.

Courseware

Courseware represents a number of online course "packaging" products that enable PD providers to integrate email, listserv, organized access to documents, quizzes or surveys, class management, and productivity functions without needing to know markup languages. Each of these features constitutes a technology that can facilitate assessment, but the entire package is an effective way to address assessment issues as a whole and note how different features can link with one another relative to the objective and methodology of the assessment.

Courseware provides an especially effective assessment method for examining PD course delivery and participant performance (Jamieson, Chapelle, & Preiss, 2004). Particularly when participant work is submitted via courseware, the archival features of this course packaging facilitates rich data analysis. Not only can the instructor critique participant work, but when that same work is submitted to a peer audience (i.e., all the participants in the PD), participants can analyze each others' work. In the process, the fact that the work is being made relatively public often results in raising the bar for product development. It should be noted that outside experts can also be called upon to assess participant work, and provide useful feedback. In a traditional class, such practices would be harder to execute; technology can collapse space and time.

A powerful practice involves the use of group pages. Participants can be assigned to a group in order to share ideas and products; no one except the instructor can see their communication so they experience a safe area for peer assistance. In some cases, one collaborative product is developed by the entire group. However, individual work can also be generated and subjected to peer review before submitting it formally to the rest of the class or to the instructor. The process of development can be analyzed as well as the quality of peer review by the instructor; in either case, subject knowledge as well as analytical ability can be assessed.

Along with substantive papers or reports, participant responses to readings and controversial prompts can be communicated in threaded discussions, which also enable participants to respond to each other's comments and add to the knowledge base. Both instructor and participants are assessing what others know – and don't know, and providing feedback based on the prior commentary. Such an approach resembles the group page process, but differs in that the entire class is usually involved and the product is not a polished effort. PD instructors can also encourage participants to pose questions or issues for discussion, which fosters a community of practice as well as provides another data point: analyzing what issues interest or concern participants.

Synchronous and asynchronous chat lends itself well to interviews, which can be archived in a technological environment. The former measures participants' ability to ask appropriate questions and respond appropriately within the context of the flow of the conversation. In some cases, participants may come prepared with questions, which attitude also becomes quickly apparent in the discussion. Asynchronous chat helps level the playing field because some participants cannot type as quickly, express as easily in English, or have high speed Internet connections. Thus, two different learning environments are being assessed, hopefully taking advantage of the differences to measure different skills. For example, such differences underscore the variability of interview techniques.

One particularly fruitful activity that lends itself to assessment of both participant achievement and course delivery is reflective journaling, which is associated with narrative inquiry (Monaghan & Columbaro, 2009). The premise is that participants contextualize coursework in terms of their professional and personal lives in order to make sense of their learning and apply it meaningfully. In terms of assessment, the choices that participants make in linking course to personal situations bespeak participants' understanding of course concepts. Even the choices that participants make in terms of identifying related practices reveal the depth and appropriateness of their understanding. Further details about the use of online narrative inquiry are discussed in the case study later in the chapter.

Exemplars and rubrics can also aid in assessment practice. Technology facilitates both learning/assessment aids because these items can be posted immediately, including on the basis of existing participant submissions. Having these concrete benchmarks also helps participants self-assess their work as they develop it as well as give peers an objective upon which to remark on the work of their colleagues without getting into personal biases.

Although surveys and quizzes are not used extensively by most instructors (because they can be very laborious to develop, and might not be very secure) these tools can act as diagnostic tools to help participants identify their own areas for growth as well as help instructors modify their course to address needed areas of learning. In general, surveys are used to generate data about the group as a whole; quizzes test individual knowledge. Thoughtfully constructed quizzes provide immediate feedback to the participants so they can access other resources in order to learn the required information. As with traditional surveys and quizzes, instructors can use the results to determine whether to provide more instruction

or more opportunities for participant practice and application of PD concepts.

Some online PD is provided through educational institutions, with grade options. Besides the obvious advantage of online gradebooks that allow each participant to look up their own grades – and compare their work with others in terms of descriptive statistics rather than individual grades –upon demand, courseware usually has statistical features that allow the instructor to find out how often and when participants are accessing the site, and which parts of the site are being accessed. Usually, the instructor can identify individual behaviors as well as overall actions. While there is often no correlation between the number of connections and a participant's grade (if for no other reason than the program usually does not measure the length of time that the participant is connected – or the amount of active engagement that is occurring, rather like having the TV or radio turned on in the background), if a participant is not accessing the site at all or minimally, such inactivity can act as a signal for the instructor to contact the participant to find out if any connectivity problems are occurring – and address them.

Instructors can also export data collected in online environments to other data analysis tools, such as SPSS, MiniTab or Nudist. The first two are useful for generating meaningful statistics, and the latter facilitates content analysis. Some of the applications of such tools include:

- Grades/achievement across time
- Correlations between achievement and demographics, number of courses taken, instructor, prior experience, job placement, etc.
- Patterns in use of professional terms, decision-making processes, citations, etc.

Interestingly, even when courseware-using PD instructors use traditional participant products as their basis for assessment rather than online products, over time as they become more comfortable with courseware, instructors tend to assess their own instruction and course delivery more explicitly. In general, they first ask what can be done using courseware. Then they determine whether they can use the particular courseware features. Ultimately, though, they decide what courseware features optimize participant learning and design their courses accordingly. Moreover, courseware-using PD instructors tend to adopt a community of practice model that facilitates the collaborative building of knowledge (Farmer, 2003). In any case, assessment becomes a conscious activity that improves both PD as well as participant performance.

DEVELOPING ASSESSMENT TOOLS

Developing assessment tools "from scratch" can be time-consuming and unproductive. Since the main considerations are validity (measuring the intended competence) and reliability (obtaining consistent results), evaluating the assessment instrument itself is key. If a credible entity has already designed and validated an assessment tool that measures a desired outcome with the same kind of population, then one should seriously consider using it if it is feasible to so do (i.e., affordable and doable).

Nevertheless, sometimes an assessment instrument needs to be developed "from whole cloth" because the objectives are site-specific or the target audience has unique needs. Authentic performance assessments are a good example of occasions where customized instruments are needed to be developed in order to capture localized or specific standards (Perlman, 2003). Fortunately, technology has facilitated this task. The PD designer can now repurpose documents as assessment instruments more easily and can disseminate them more efficiently. Files can also be imported into spreadsheet and statistical software programs without rekeying.

One obvious way to find out if someone is competent is to ask him or her to create a product that reflects the specific competency. Traditionally, written critiques have been used to demonstrate that a student has understood the source, and research papers have been used to demonstrate that a student can conduct research independently. Ideally, the products should demonstrate conceptual and procedural knowledge applied to real world contexts. With the advent of digital technology, the repertoire of products has grown exponentially. Most of these can be posted online or linked to an online source.

- **Text:** Report, white paper, essay, white paper, bibliography, biography, article, brochure, press release, resume, instructions, poem, dramatization
- **Visuals:** Illustration, storyboard, timeline, cartoon, photojournal, concept map
- **Video:** Commercial, documentary, interview, drama
- **Audio:** Podcast, soundscape documentary
- **Multimedia:** Web page, multimedia presentation, computer-aided design, spreadsheet, database, simulation, e-story.

In assessing these products, both the end results and the supporting processes should be considered (Perlman, 2003). Rubrics serve as a customizable tool for assessing the different elements either holistically to get a general picture or analytically to examine each factor – during the production as a means to make adjustments as well as at the end. In each case assessment lists of grids provide qualitative and quantitative descriptors for each identified key criterion. Typically, PD designers build on sample work, identifying the key features that distinguish high-quality products from mediocre ones. The rubric is then constructed by specifying the assessment indicators, each criterion measuring one unique aspect. The rubric should be pilot-tested with additional work samples and refined. As much as possible, participants can learn how to use rubrics to guide their efforts by calibrating their assessments using exemplar samples. Building on their own experiences, participants can develop their own rubrics. The following websites on rubric creation offer a good start: http://rubistar.4teachers.org and http://www.teach-nology.com/web_tools/rubrics/

MAKING USE OF THE DATA

Does assessment in online PD make a difference? It can if the process is well done and acted upon It is not enough to collect data. The results need to be analyzed and acted upon. Ultimately, the point person in control of the assessment should also be the person who directs the data analysis. However, several steps need to be accomplished along the way (Committee on the Foundations of Assessment, 2001).

Data Analysis

Once the data are collected, they have to be organized and presented in a way that can be analyzed. Depending on how online queries are developed, the responses can be exported into spreadsheet or statistical programs. Charting the data facilitates understanding. Missing and bogus data also have to be addressed; should an incomplete questionnaire be eliminated or should blatantly dishonest responses be ignored?

Open-ended questions are more problematic. Interviews should be recorded and then transcribed; typically, it takes six to eight hours to transcribe one hour's worth of recording manually; fortunately, online chat automatically provides a transcript. Responses need to be coded to generate patterns. The data analyzer should read over the responses to get an overall sense of the data as well as start to pick up reoccurring phrases or themes; jotting down notes while examining the responses helps generate useful categories. A second closer reading can verify and refine the initial categories.

At this point, a grid may be generated, cross-referencing the content with demographics; do males search the Internet differently from females, for instance (they do). Subsequent readings can pick up nuances. While software programs such as Nudist and Atlas/ti can help in this process if items are already in digital form, it should be remembered that these programs work based on word-frequency and word-proximity algorithms so may be somewhat arbitrary in their associations; they are best used as a starting point.

Once the data have been organized, then statistics may be applied. Often the population is small enough that only descriptive statistics may be used: frequency, range, means, median, mode, and variance. These figures can still give the audience an idea of the scope of the findings, and start to see if two sets of findings reflect similar or different populations. Inferential statistics usually make or *infer* generalizations about significantly large populations based on sampling; typically, analysis tries to find correlations between two variables, such as number of books read and reading comprehension ability. The most important statistical consideration is the characteristic of the derived numbers; misaligning a statistical method with number property causes misleading conclusions. The chief "offender" is ascribing mathematical equations to emotions (e.g., one person is 2.5 times as satisfied as another person). Data may also be distinguished as discrete (whole numbers such as the number of students) or continuous (analogue such as length). Most numbers in assessment are discrete ordinal or interval kinds

As much as possible, data should be disaggregated by demographics such as sex, age, ethnicity, and socio-economic background in order to help identify at-risk groups; if possible, data can also be disaggregated by preferred learning style or preferred subject matter. For example, females tend to prefer collaborative work so interventions should be custom-designed to motivate and help that group.

Acting on Findings

By analyzing the data derived from assessments, an assessment team can make recommendations to address the emergent issues. For instance, if bibliographies cite web pages inaccurately, then more emphasis on that source can be made via guide sheets. If industry standards are seldom mentioned in design briefs, then either they need to be mentioned explicitly in instruction or made more visible on web sites; follow-up assessment can determine the basis for low usage. Both process-based and product-based interventions should be considered. In identifying an effective solution, the entire system should be examined since any of the entities might impact the outcome.

Assessment findings, analysis, and recommendations should be communicated with all stakeholders and those being assessed in order to show that their interest and participation made a difference. These groups can also provide input to refine recommendations. The communiqué should include the background need, the results, and intended recommendations. Technology can facilitate broadcasting and repurposing of information. The ultimate uses of assessment, though, are participant competency and organizational improvement.

Action Research

One way to optimize assessment is to systematize it to conduct action research (Cook & Farmer, 2011). Action research refers to a process of studying one's own practice in order to improve it. As such, it involves planning, acting, and reflecting. It differs from every day practice because it is explicitly grounded in a systematic and research-based methodology, including assessment. A careful examination of existing research studies centred on a well-identified problem precedes data collection. Factors affecting the problem's outcome are carefully identified and aligned with reliable and valid assessment instruments.

In terms of online PD, first the PD designer needs to describe the current situation. For example, the PD objectives might be training staff to promote literacy and reading within a library. It is important to incorporate information from all stakeholders, including library non-users. Only then can PD designers analyze the data, and determine the basis of the problem. Relevant research can be used to guide the analysis and make valid conclusions.

Once the gap between the current situation and the intended outcome is determined, PD designers can review the research literature to discover how other libraries and associated entities addressed the problem. What methods did they use? What material and human resources were needed? What data were collected – and how and when?

Based on the research literature review and analysis of the local situation, PD designers can plan and implement PD that will improve reading and literacy promotion. Throughout the process, PD designers should document and assess their efforts to optimize its impact.

CASE STUDY: USING JOURNALING AS AN ASSESSMENT TOOL

In an effort to study assessment as an element in online PD, the researcher of this investigation (who is also this chapter author) incorporated narrative inquiry into her foundations of information (LI 500) and library media management (LI 550) courses. For developing a thick dataset of course-centric impact, this kind of critical autographical representation was an effective assessment approach. Specifically, participants in LI 500 were required to write weekly online wiki self-reflections about information within the context of the course. Participants could draw upon coursework, career efforts, and personal experience. LI 550 participants posted online entries about three course-related critical incidents that they experienced that semester. In both courses, participants responded to their peers' reflections online through threaded discussions. As a final project, LI 500 participants had to analyze a peer's entire semester of online entries to identify information patterns over time.

The instructor developed content analysis matrices of these online archived narratives as a basis for to: 1) identify possible reasons for differences among participant performances; and 2) review course content and delivery. LI 500 journals were analyzed in terms of timing, source of inspiration, and insights/outcomes. LI 550 critical events were analyzed in terms of conflict/problem, source of support, and resolution. Captured demographic data included: employment status, number of years working in a school or other type of library, presence of other library staff, years of classroom teaching experience, library media courses taken.

Theoretical Context

Reflective journaling provides a means for participants to critically analyze their life experiences, framing theory contextually. When participants share these reflections, they can then compare both their experiences and their conclusions in order to draw valid inferences across contexts and generate knowledge (Boud, 2001). This exercise has been recommended specifically for library science preparation and more generally for professional development (Yontz & McCook, 2003; Schon, 1983). Technology optimizes this process because participants can access, analyze, and respond to peers' entries at their convenience. In terms of research methodology, drawing from experience to deepen understanding of the theoretical may be linked to naturalistic inquiry: research that captures authentic experiences in natural settings (Lane, 2002). Additionally, reflective journals facilitate communities of practice as peers relate to one another through their shared experiences (Monaghan & Columbaro, 2009).

On the instructional design level, the online PD designer can use participant narratives to determine how well the PD meets their needs. Do the entries align with course content? Are participants able to apply their coursework to real life problem-solving? When a disconnect occurs, the instructor can use that information to modify the PD content to address participant issues – or to make sure that other PD will address the issue. In those cases where the content has been delivered, the instructor can follow up with questions to ferret out reasons for participant difficulties in those areas. In some cases, the issue is a matter of control where the work situation is beyond the participant's influence; even that kind of information is useful to both participant and instructor and can be folded into the PD discussion.

Two representative practices are: writing an online weekly journal relating the course and personal life, and identifying critical events that relate to the course. In both cases, participants have control in choosing the connections to make and drawing appropriate conclusions. They are, in effect, self-assessing their own learning. Simultaneously, the instructor is assessing the participants' depth of understanding and their decision-making processes, both in terms of identifying issues to share as well as describing their own responses and actions. The instructor can also analyze participants' progress over the duration of a semester or longer. To add another dimension, instructors can have participants critique each other's journal entries.

Findings

LI 500 Findings

Over time, participants tended to become more theoretical and action-oriented with respect to information. They tended to grow from a consumer-based, emotional response to information, relating it to personal experience, to a more objective and abstract construct with a greater impetus for proactive change. Participants responded significantly to issues of ethics, and became more committed to engagement in information flow as a result of such awareness. It appears that introducing this topic later into the semester was an appropriate strategy since participants had already gained a better perspective about the creation and dissemination of information by that time. Participants who made these generalizations and strategic plans tended to earn higher grades, probably because they were able to synthesize and apply theory more effectively; the sophistication of their insights were reflected in their assignments.

LI 550 Findings

Participant choice of topic depended on current employment activities, current course activities, and response or "resonance" with other participants' submissions. A semester was not long enough to discern significant growth in means of solving management problems, although participants did mention the use of policies that they had learned about during the course. Gender and ethnicity did not seem to affect the choice or discussion of the critical event. Major management issues were: 1) human relationships, 2) resources, 3) administration, and 4) technology. In general, there was no significant correlation in terms of the types of issues identified and the amount of library experience. In general, critical events focused on outside elements that affected library service rather than library service that impacted other constituencies; the participants were usually in a *reactive* stance. Source for help in solving the problem were ranked as follows: 1) administrators, 2) fellow teachers, 3) self, 4) policy, 5) library media specialist. In identifying what they learned from the incidents, participants ranked concepts as follows: 1) effective communication, 2) principal support, 3) collaboration. In essence, reflective journaling acted as a means for participants to: 1) self-assess their areas of strength and weakness; 2) assess peer situations and problem-solving approaches; 3) assess content areas that needed addressing. On the part of the instructors, journals

helped them to: 1) assess participants' areas of concern; 2) assess how participants solved critical issues; 3) assess the degree to which course content deal with participant-identified critical events.

Implications

Both case studies are limited to a very small population. However, the critical autobiographical narrative inquiry research method was a useful course delivery method and assessment vehicle. It proved to be an effective way to garner thick, authentic, descriptive datasets of information to analyze. It also facilitated a sense of a community of practice, extending interactivity beyond formal class time. Posting identified issues of importance to participants, and provided a means to share concerns and effective problem-solving techniques. Participants had control of the content and presentation so they could assume more responsibility for independent learning, and the instructor used the data to provide a reality-based means to improve course content. The use of journaling and content analysis of journal entries can be extended to other courses and other populations to draw more general conclusions.

FUTURE TRENDS

Particularly with the advent of interactive Web 2.0, online assessment incorporates peer review and commentary. With open dissemination of learners' work to authentic audiences, the motivation level and the bar of excellence are raised.

Wikis (based on the Hawaiian term "wiki wiki," which means "fast") are web pages that can be generated without markup language knowledge. Wikis can be used to address academic and professional skills, knowledge, and dispositions: knowledge synthesis and generation, written and media communication skills, collaboration, technical skills, and organizational skills. The ease of page generation enables individuals to concentrate on meaningful content rather than on technical issues. Some of the activities that can be assessed using wikis follow (Knobel & Lankshear, 2009).

- **Knowledge Management:** Participant research is organized under one wiki by incorporating frames and tags.
- **Group Projects:** Each participant is responsible for one aspect of a project (e.g., a community portal containing different types of information such as education page, local agencies, health groups, upcoming events, homework help, etc.).
- **Point of View Study:** A topic such as free trade agreements can be investigated from different points of view, each learner assuming the role of a different stakeholder
- **Planning (learning activities, units, and grants):** Participants can collaboratively develop project units and grant applications.
- **Case Studies:** Participants can share their perspectives on a case study, or develop one collaboratively.

Online PD instructors may sometimes feel overwhelmed by the number and length of wiki entries when assessing them. Peer review can ameliorate the situation, and participants can be placed in groups with a student monitor in charge of keeping order (and erasing off-task comments). The wiki's tracking feature helps the instructor see who has contributed and what content they added.

Technology has enabled assessors to use interactive software programs that measure learners' information competency through performance (Issenberg & Scalese, 2008). These programs set up scenarios with decision-points that the user acts upon. At the least, the program facilitates documentation of the performance through graphic organizers or dialog box. Many programs branch to different tasks or assessments based on the user's decisions, thus tracking the mental processing.

Upper-end programs export the user's decision points into a database file for later assessment.

WebQuests exemplify this interactive assessment quality. Basically, structured online resource-based learning activities, WebQuests usually frame an essential question as a compelling scenario leading to an authentic task to be achieved in small collaborative groups. Each person assumes a role, and investigates pre-determined relevant resources in order to generate a group solution. Each step is recorded, later to be assessed using a rubric. Bernie Dodge developed WebQuests; his website explains how to create one's own WebQuest (http://www.webquest.org).

Increasingly, PD designers are exploring the use of virtual learning environments as a means to assess learner competency. A closed virtual universe is created in which artifacts reside. Scenarios are posed for the participants to engage in, and their steps are recorded as a means of assessing information competency. One such prototype was developed by Newell (2004). The advantage of such a simulated environment is that learners can participate independently at their own convenience, thus freeing the PD designer to provide just-in-time specific interventions. The data collected should also be analyzed; if these virtual environments can diagnose learning gaps, and provide guidance for that specific subtask, then assessment can be use formatively in an efficient and individualized manner.

Video has re-emerged as a viable online assessment tool (Cuper & Gong, 2010). Video has been used for decades to accurately capture an event such as a presentation or skit. The persons being video recorded can examine their own behaviors, noting delivery as well as content. They can also control the tape in order to replay a critical scene or pause to spot some specific detail. Video recording can occur in *situ*, offering an opportunity for evaluators and peers to observe critically in an asynchronous fashion. With the advent of digital video and built-in computer video editors (e.g., iMovie and MovieMaker), participants can edit their own videos relatively easily in order to identify key learning moments and comment on their decision-making process. Likewise, assessors can select video clips that exemplify high-quality–or low-quality–performances. In either case, learners and assessors can insert video clips pivotal points into authoring programs and online environments for group discussion and discernment. It should be noted that video recording and editing require equipment and time, so that participants and assessors may wonder what is being evaluated: the performance itself, selection and organization of information, or technical skill: separate assessment tools should be considered for each of these processes.

Portfolios have become a popular way to assess competencies over time (Cambridge, Cambridge, & Yancey, 2009). Basically a collection of sample work, a portfolio addresses the problem of single assessments. Instead, multiple efforts can reflect a complex set of competencies. While it is possible to collect *every* piece of evidence (sometimes done as learning records), one of the values of portfolios is selection, which is a key information competence. Portfolios also require organization, another important information skill. Thus, portfolio form and function meld well to show competency. Furthermore, portfolios can assume a variety of formats: print, audio-visual, and digital. The latter, though, offers the greatest flexibility in data storage and retrieval because learners can repurpose and link evidence to the relevant standards or outcomes. As with other online PD assessment tools, e-portfolios need to be carefully designed and include answers to such questions as – what is the purpose of the portfolio; what kind of evidence is expected; what learning activities will be provided so learners can create artifacts demonstrating competency; how selective should the evidence be; what is the time frame for the work to be collected; what reflective components are needed; what organization is required; to what extent will organization impact assessment results; how will the portfolio be as-

sessed; and what actions will occur as a result of the assessment?

Because e-portfolios usually represent substantial effort over time, coordination of the stakeholders and the learning environment is needed from the start. Participants should be informed of the outcome, e-portfolio requirements, and assessment methods early on so they can begin to collect and think about their work as well as learn the technology required to assemble the e-portfolio. Likewise, by collecting e-portfolio data and disaggregating it by standard and demographics, the online PD instructor and the enterprise as a whole can identify possible learning gaps across the PD population, and create targeted interventions can be developed and assessed in order to optimize PD programmatically.

CONCLUSION

In summary, online PD assessment serves several purposes.

- It provides timely feedback for participants and instructors to change content or behavior.
- It places greater emphasis on timely, formative assessment and ongoing participant improvement.
- It facilitates just-in-time course adjustments and interventions in participant effort.
- It provides a greater sense of a community of practice.
- It optimizes data-driven program improvement interventions.

Nevertheless, for such assessments to be effective, it needs to be continuous and aligned, from the level of the individual learner to the PD provider and supportive organization as a whole. Likewise, assessment needs to be used throughout the PD instructional design process, from the beginning needs assessment to final evaluation of the PD and its impact on the workplace as the online PD learning is transferred to professional practice. At each point, online assessment can be used to make informed decisions: about curriculum, resources, technology, packaging of content, learning activities, delivery modes, and implementation. A variety of online assessment instruments are now available, so choosing the most effective online assessment instrument to measure the identified objective is critical. Furthermore, the data from the assessment needs to be appropriately analyzed and used to improve the results of the online PD.

REFERENCES

American Association of Higher Education. Assessment Forum. (2003). *9 principles of good practice for assessing participant learning.* Brevard, NC: Policy Center on the First Year of College. Retrieved from http://www.brevard.edu/fyc/relatedlinks/aahe.htm

Association for Assessment in Counseling. (2003). *Responsibilities of users of standardized tests* (3rd ed.). Alexandria, VA: Association for Assessment in Counseling.

Biggs, J. (2003). *Teaching for quality learning at university* (2nd ed.). Buckingham, UK: Open University Press/Society for Research into Higher Education.

Boud, D. (2001). Using journal writing to enhance reflective practice. In English, L., & Gillen, M. (Eds.), *Promoting journal writing in adult education* (pp. 9–18). San Francisco, CA: Jossey-Bass. doi:10.1002/ace.16

Cambridge, D., Cambridge, B., & Yancey, K. (2009). *Electronic portfolios 2.0: Emergent research on implementation and impact.* Sterling, VA: Stylus Publishing.

Cook, D., & Farmer, L. (2011). *Using qualitative methods in action research.* Chicago, IL: American Library Association.

Cuper, P., & Gong, Y. (2010). Video analysis as a reflective tool. In Yamamoto, J., Penny, C., Leight, J., & Winterton, S. (Eds.), *Technology leadership in teacher education* (pp. 67–82). Hershey, PA: IGI Global. doi:10.4018/978-1-61520-899-9.ch005

Farmer, L. (2003). Facilitating faculty incorporation of information literacy skills into the curriculum through the use of online instruction. *RSR. Reference Services Review, 31*(4), 307–312. doi:10.1108/00907320310515220

Ingalls, J. (1972). *A trainer's guide to andragogy* (rev. ed.). Waltham, MA: Data Education.

Issenberg, S., & Scalese, R. (2008). Simulation in health care education. *Perspectives in Biology and Medicine, 51*(1), 31–46. doi:10.1353/pbm.2008.0004

Jamieson, J., Chapelle, C., & Preiss, S. (2004). Putting principles into practice. *ReCALL, 16*(2), 396–415. doi:10.1017/S0958344004001028

Knobel, M., & Lankshear, C. (2009). Wikis, digital literacies, and professional growth. *Journal of Adolescent & Adult Literacy, 52*(7), 631–634. doi:10.1598/JAAL.52.7.8

Laird, D. (1985). *Approaches to training and development.* Reading, MA: Addison-Wesley.

Lane, D. (2002). *Theory and research methods.* Lexington, KY: University of Kentucky.

Maki, P. (2002). Developing an assessment plan to learn about student learning. *The Journal of Academic Leadership, 28*(1), 8–13.

Maloy, R., Verock-O'Loughlin, R., Edwards, S., & Woolf, B. (2011). *Transforming learning with new technologies.* Boston, MA: Pearson.

Monaghan, C. H., & Columbaro, N. L. (2009). Communities of practice and students' professional development. *International Journal of Teaching and Learning in Higher Education, 20*(3), 413–424.

Mowl, G. (1996). *Innovative assessment.* Newcastle, UK: University of Northumbria. Retrieved fdrom http://www.city.londonmet.ac.uk/deliberations/assessment/mowl_fr.html

Newell, T. (2004). Thinking beyond the disjunctive opposition of information literacy assessment in theory and practice. *School Library Media Research, 7.*

Palloff, R., & Pratt, K. (2008). *Assessing the online learner: Resources and strategies for faculty.* San Francisco, CA: Jossey-Bass.

Pellegrino, J., Chudowsky, N., & Glaser, R. (Eds.). (2001). *Knowing what students know: The science and design of educational assessment. Committee on the Foundations of Assessment, Board on Testing and Assessment, Center for Education, Division on Behavioral and Social Sciences and Education, National Research Council Washington.* DC: National Academic Press.

Perlman, C. (2003). Performance assessment. In Nettles, A., & Nettles, M. (Eds.), *Measuring up: Assessment issues for teachers, counselors, and administrators.* Boston, MA: Kluwer Academic.

Roblyer, M., & Doering, A. (2009). *Integrating educational technology into teaching.* Boston, MA: Allyn & Bacon.

Schon, D. (1983). *The reflective practitioner.* London, UK: Temple Smith.

Yontz, E., & de la Pena McCook, K. (2003). Service-learning and LIS education. *Journal of Education for Library and Information Science, 44,* 55–68. doi:10.2307/40323942

KEY TERMS AND DEFINITIONS

Action Research: Situationally-based research that seeks to improve a concrete issue; the researcher is an active participant in the situation.

Andragogy: The art and science of helping adults learn.

Courseware: An online application that allows course elements (e.g., content, communication, assessment) to be packaged together.

Curriculum: Content that learners need to be able to understand and apply.

Demographics: Statistics about human populations.

Feedback: Information about a person or system given to the source of that action.

Indicator: A specific, concrete behavior or disposition that demonstrates that a person has met a standard.

Instructional Design: A systematic analysis of training/PD needs and the development of aligned instruction.

Learning Environment: The conditions, resources, facilities, physical and virtual space in which one learns.

Narrative Inquiry: An approach to understanding behavior through large collections of self-generated anecdotal material.

Needs Assessment: The process of determining the needs of a targeted population.

Portfolio: An organized compilation of artifacts that gives evidence of one's performance.

Stakeholder: A significant constituent who has the potential to be impacted by, or can influence, an effort; an invested party.

Threaded Discussion: Online discussion that follows a topic.

Virtual World: Computer-based simulated environment where participants interact via avatars.

Section 2
Understanding E–Learning and Best Practices in Teaching and Learning in Online Environments

Chapter 10
Definition and History of Online Professional Development

Carol A. Brown
East Carolina University, USA

Renée E. Weiss Neal
East Carolina University, USA

ABSTRACT

There exists a consensus on the importance of teacher professional development. This chapter provides a knowledge base for environments, describes the benefits, best practices, and sources for quality online professional development. The attributes associated with online professional development can be examined within the framework of web conferencing, web cast, and online teaching and learning. An annotated bibliography and extensive glossary related to online professional development are included in this chapter.

INTRODUCTION

Professional development (PD) is an important source of growth for practitioners as well as faculty working in academia. Even though a valued activity, most people are less than enthusiastic about scheduling the time needed for workshops, seminars, and other venues for learning the practical aspects and skills in their profession. Less than desirable experiences with the one-shot workshop, time constraints both professionally and person-

ally, economic changes leading to shortfalls related to salaries, resources, and opportunity for travel have led to an increasing interest in online education. For practitioners and faculty in education, opportunities for online professional development are becoming attractive alternatives to traditional methods for professional growth. The purpose of this chapter is to provide a knowledge base for environments, tools, benefits, current best practices, and sources for quality online professional development (OnLPD).

DOI: 10.4018/978-1-4666-1963-0.ch010

The National Staff Development Council remains a strong advocate for teachers by grounding the organization's research in professional development. Much of what they do is based on the definition of the term *professional development*--"a comprehensive, sustained, and intensive approach to improving teachers' and principals' effectiveness in raising student achievement (NSDC, 2011)." Teaching as a function of university and college faculty can adopt a similar definition. The comprehensive, sustained, and intensive approach to improving faculty effectiveness could be described as teaching practices grounded in research, focused productivity as a scholar, and thoughtful service to the academy or community. Teaching and research understandably require support through professional development (PD) activities. One does not usually associate activities in professional *service* with professional development, however we make the choice to grow professionally through these service oriented tasks. Teaching springs forth from our life-long pursuit of learning. Inquiry is the driving force behind our learning. Whether concepts, principles, or skills, inquiry leads to learning, and ultimately, is translated into our knowledge base. As academics, we like to think of knowledge as entirely delivered to the student, yet as we entered 20th century classrooms it was discovered that learning is generated within the learner (Dewey, 1916, 1991). Transformation was needed to move students from the receiver of information to problem solvers capable of generating solutions and new ideas; thus began the age of constructivism with the learner as the central focus of instruction. Teacher-centered lectures, while useful for presentation of base knowledge, were often being replaced with small group dialog and Socratic questioning (Davis, 2007). Learning becomes deeper, more durable as students personalize concepts. Through small group discussion, there are connections between concepts and authentic life experiences (Innes, 2007). Traditionally, the instructional use of small groups was designed as face to face interaction in the classroom; however, group dialog has become a common instructional method used within the design of online instruction (Courtney & King, 2009).

Research has shown that fostering teachers' ability to use student-centered approaches has been associated with use of online professional development (Vrasidas & Zembylas, 2004). Teachers have been able to maintain a sustained community of practice while engaged in constructivist learning experiences. This is important because professional development for teachers goes beyond skills-based training sessions. Developing as a professional is a formative process in which we engage in learning, self-assessment, reflection, and communication with others. Whether in a lab setting or online, a systematic process must be employed for change in teaching practices to occur. The process follows known strategies within the field of educational technology beginning with needs and task analysis, learner analysis, and follow-through with use of appropriate strategies, resources, and evaluation (Molenda, 2011). Online Professional Development (OnLPD) is effective when designed to include opportunities for collaborative dialog, applied problem solving, and sustained support through team teaching and peer mentoring (Treacy, 2002). In addition, teachers must be able to adapt to new modes of communication. Both the presenter and participant are experiencing a wide range of possibilities using online environments (Pillai, 2009). All of these lead to change in how educators grow in the profession. New modes of teaching and learning will require intentional commitment to professional development.

In an article archived in the online version of *Education Week*, Price (1993) describes changes in how children learn demanded extensive professional development for teachers.

...In recent years a consensus has emerged that students will need certain higher-order competencies, such as creative thinking and problem-solving, in

order to function in the 21st century. Cultivating those competencies will require mastery by educators of new modes of teaching and learning. .... In order for reform to reach beyond the motivated few teachers and their fortunate pupils to the majority of teachers and their students, there's simply no avoiding a major investment in retooling the teacher corps. (p. 1).

More recently, Michelle Davis (2009) reports in *Education Week* the importance for busy teachers to be able to gain new knowledge and skills under flexible conditions. According to Dede (cited in Whitehouse, Breit, McClosky, Ketlhut, & Dede, 2006) easy access to resources and experts, not available locally, is appealing for many teachers. The flexibility of anytime, anywhere learning is always a strong motivator for teachers to participate in online courses (FIT&L, 2002). Convenience and flexibility have been strong motivators, but the hidden benefits lie in teachers' engagement in virtual learning communities, reflection in their own practices as a student-centered teacher, and growing expertise in use of inquiry based methods for the classroom. Online environments foster the use of multiple databases, education portals, and Internet experts at universities and government agencies (Illinois Online Network, 2010).

A Change in Paradigm

At the end of the first decade of the new century, the academy began an intentional investigation in the pervasive use of digital information, social networks, and instruction delivered through the Internet. For example, EDUCAUSE Center for Applied Research (Caruso & Salaway, 2007) reports an 80% increase in laptop ownerships for college students. These 21st century students report a high level of confidence in their use of Internet related tools. They expect their professors to use technology and to use these tools with expertise. Tallent-Runnels, Thomas, Lan, and Cooper (2006) conducted a review of the literature in online

teaching and suggest, not only skilled use of the technology, but also emphasize the importance of learner-centered design for online classes. Thus, the most recent research in online teaching suggests a move from text-based assignments, along with innocuous discussion forums, to more dynamic, interactive, multimodal delivery for the highly social learner of the current decade. Faculty should not be marginalized as "content experts" while others design the instructional methods and pedagogy for their courses (Wright, 2005). Thus professional development in support of online teaching is critical for those of us who are transitioning from what had been the traditional methods for teaching and learning to the newer virtual environments. With growing use of the Internet in daily life activities, learners take on the role of "knowledge workers" (Purdue, 2003). Incentive for continuing professional development has become more intrinsic with expectations for higher quality in work performance. Course design that includes dialogic exchange, reflection, and self assessment of the learning process has become an expectation of those enrolled in an online class. Thus, faculty must keep pace with changes through their own commitment as *knowledge workers*. One method for acquiring new knowledge is through careful selection of online faculty development opportunities.-

The Three W's

Professional development in Education faces both enabling and inhibiting factors. Caffarella and Zinn (1997) combine factors identified in K12 schools and apply these to professional development in a university setting. People and interpersonal relationships may enable faculty to engage in PD when there is collegiality and a climate of fairness within the unit. Even though faculty typically do not like to consider home and family as impacting professional productivity, these are a reality and are important considerations. Illness, death, and divorce will affect focus on professional growth.

Table 1. Comparison of formats for online web meetings and delivery of professional development

Format	Characteristics	Comparison
Web Conference Meeting	Same as F2F meeting; preplanned with agenda; few in number to many in attendance; may include presentations; collaboration and team building is valued. Technology is based on use of VoIP tools; analog media is converted to digital media to permit real-time voice communication. Special downloads are needed to provide interactive functions during the conference. Permits polling, access to screen whiteboard, and two way communication.	Highly interactive in which participants can share desktops and applications; chats are possible; VoIP functions may be used in which participants communicate using Internet *telephony*. Typically these meetings are not archived but could be upon request. Software is sophisticated; High-speed Internet connection, microphone and webcam are required for participants. Cost by vendors is determined by actual number of registered participants.
Webinar	Presenter invites participants to register in advance; agenda is provided; presentation includes voice; presenter usually not visible; interaction with participants is limited and usually follows presentation by webinar host and presenters. Most webinars have designated facilitator. Common format includes: introductions, advance organizers with overview of content, length of time, tips for use of the tools, presentations with slides, and Q&A. Archival is a plus for both presenter and participant.	Less interactive and collaborative than web meetings. Participants often struggle with use of tools within the conferencing software. Requires download of special applications to participate in the session. Access to microphone and webcam are beneficial to participants. Presenter may use webcam. Slides, whiteboard and/or web browsing are often included in the presentation. Presenter has option for polling the audience. Archival is a plus for both presenter and participant.
Webcast	A pre-recorded presentation is pushed to the audience using calendars, email, or websites. The session is similar to educational television or radio. The technology is based on linear streaming of audio/video content.	Little or no collaboration; typically content is more accessible and requires fewer application downloads. No need for mics or webcams for the participants. Focused and information rich sessions provide professional development for geographically dispersed audience. Participants have the option for re-visiting the presentation. Cost by vendor is based on pre-determined set amount.

Institutional structure is a second factor to consider. Plans to grow professionally are the personal decision of the faculty member but these should reflect the overall mission of the institution. Harmony between scholarship, teaching, and service and how these reflect the goals of your unit will impact professional growth. Personal, intellectual, and psychosocial characteristics are no less important when planning online professional development. These decisions are foundational leading to next decisions for learning environments. For OnLPD, this means web conferencing tools.

Most OnLPD venues can be placed in one of three categories— web (conference) meeting, webinar, and webcast. When looking for OnLPD opportunities, it is helpful to understand the differences and advantages for each category. Those planning professional development would consider the design for each format based on 1)

audience, 2) timing with relation to information to be presented, 3) emphasis (and need) for collaboration, and 4) potential accessibility by participants. Costs for the various forms of web communication varies by type of conference, tools employed (audio, video, software functions), length of seminar, and number of registered participants (T&D, 2008). See Table 1 with comparison of formats.

Web Conferencing

Web conferences are meetings conducted online and are similar to a conference call. Participants can interact in every way as if in a live meeting with the exception of human touch (Heinrich, 2006). While hand-shaking and personal touch are obviously not included, lack of personal contact is offset as cost advantages associated with web meetings increase yearly (Communications

News, 2004; iLinc Communications, Inc. 2011). Web conferencing software provides synchronous video and audio communication along with capability for users to share desktop applications (Cisco Systems, 2010). Access to tools and improvements in infrastructure have contributed to increasing use of professional meetings across geographic lines. Web conferencing is one solution to real time communication and has capacity for both team building and presentation. In a report by market analysts Mayrhofer, Back, and Hubschmid (2004) web conferencing leads to cost reduction for commercial and educational collaboration—reduced travel costs, instructor costs, reduction in time away from workplace, and options for reuse of materials. One important benefit often overlooked is reduction in costs related to venue. After the initial costs for purchase of web conferencing software, there are few costs associated with classrooms, desks, labs, and other equipment. Web conferencing used for collaboration usually consists of a smaller number of participants.

There are increased uses in application sharing, document sharing, and presentation of materials through interactive whiteboards. When used for presentation, web conferencing can be used to present educational materials to a much larger audience; as many as 2,500 have been known to participate (Mayrhofer et al., 2004). Interactivity is higher with collaborative meetings and becomes correspondingly lower when used for presentation purposes.

Webinar

Webinar is short for Web-*based sem*inar, a presentation, lecture, workshop or seminar that is transmitted over the Web. A key feature of a Webinar is its interactive elements – the ability to give, receive and discuss information as opposed to Webcast, in which the data transmission is one way and does not allow interaction between the presenter and the audience. From PC Magazine- (WEB-based semINAR) a workshop or lecture delivered over

the Web. Webinars may be one-way (similar to Webcast) or there may be interaction between the audience and the presenters. Software used for *web conferencing* could be used for *webinars*. The difference is in purposes for the session.

The number of participants can be large or small for either; however, interaction between facilitator and participants is less using the webinar design. Interaction between participants is limited to posts to a chat window. Video and audio exchanges are not typically included. For a smaller number of participants, the most common form of communication is audio exchange using microphone or text chat. For larger webinars, communication between participants and presenters would be chat text. In Figure 1 see the design of a typical interface using conferencing software for webinars. The roster of participants is visible on the left side of the screen. Chats in progress are displayed in the center of the screen, and slides displayed by the facilitator and presenters are shown on the right hand window of the screen. This type of conferencing software was used with the 4th Annual International Symposium sponsored by Merlot. *MERLOT* is a free and open resource designed primarily for faculty and students of higher education. This and similar webinars can be accessed at http://www.merlot.org/merlot/index.htm.

Webcast

Webcast requires use of the Internet to broadcast live or delayed audio and/or video transmissions. It is much like traditional television and radio broadcasts. For example, a university may offer on-line courses in which the instructor webcasts a pre-recorded or live lecture. In another example, an enterprise may webcast a press conference in lieu of, or in addition to, a conference call. Users typically must have the appropriate multimedia application in order to view a webcast. Within webcasting environments, *s*treaming means to send live audio or video to the user from a website. It is the Internet counterpart to traditional radio and TV

Figure 1. Emerging technologies for online learning, an interactive webinar sponsored by Merlot

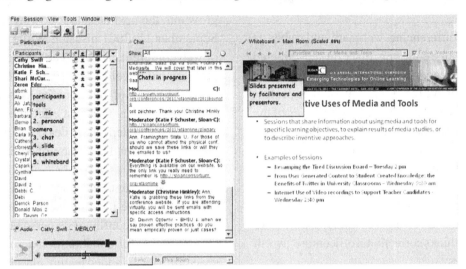

broadcasting. Essentially, a webcast is composed of streaming audio and/or video distributed over the Internet. It is asynchronous in design but has the advantage of reaching a large geographically diverse group of participants.

Webcasts have been used to augment the traditional classroom lecture. Students have the opportunity to review complex demonstrations and the option for viewing after the original class was scheduled. Lewis and Abdul-Hamid (2006) studied the effect of webcasts on student performance and attendance in college classes across several different disciplines. Implications from the study suggest that video podcasts used to present content increases availability of time that can be used to schedule hands-on projects with the students. Students used the podcasts to view lectures when absent from class, to prepare for exams, and to reduce anxiety in the course. In another example, the Medical University of South Carolina provided webcasts of surgical procedures. Medical students were surveyed on satisfaction with the design and delivery of the webcasts. Reviews by students suggest only a mediocre response to usefulness of the webcasts (Bacro, 2007). In another case, Yang and Liu (2004) received favorable feedback from teachers

in online professional development workshops, however, technology at the time of that study showed some barriers to access. Video streaming was not smooth and teachers reported frustration with trying to view the 8 to 10 minutes podcasts included in the workshop materials. As this chapter is being written, increased bandwidth and improved delivery methods promote expectations for better and more efficient uses of webcasts in professional development. Methods for increased bandwidth, compression, and improvements in encoders increase access for most home Internet connections. The vendor Zeroonezero.com provides an interesting showcase of streaming videos matched a wide variety of professions. See online http://www.zeroonezero.com/video/index.html. Access from home, school, or college classrooms is possible with the ever increasing speed and efficiency of the webcast technology.

Benefits for OnLPD

The following discussion spotlights some major advantages and benefits in use of web conferencing tools for professional development and for the purpose of collaborative meetings in education.

Personal and Professional Growth

Use of web conferencing, webinars, and webcasts reflects the value educators place on self-directed learning and accountability by professionals. By taking responsibility for one's own career, professional growth is placed back into the hands of the teacher, scholar, or other working adult. Kathy Black-Dennis (2009) has reported a favorable response from professionals in an environment not often associated with professional development—correctional officers. She compares PD with the personal care of an individual. In her editorial she thinks correctional officers are "worth it". She states:

It's a chance to enhance our knowledge or to reinvent ourselves. People change; we become different people with different needs, interests and perspectives. This is especially true today as we stay in the work force longer. (p.6)

Somewhat related to concerns for personal satisfaction and growth of staff and employees is the realization of a workforce employed longer and past the traditional retirement age of 52 to 62 years. Meeting the needs of an aging workforce is an important consideration for planning online PD. (Sauer, 2007)

Working Longer with Less

Limited resources will lead to cost effective methods for delivery of PD, The advantage for online is being documented and provides resources that may not be available during time of economic shortfall. Professionals are working longer and are often faced with reduced access to resources (Mandel, Hamm, Matlack, Farrell, & Palmer, 2011). Strategies for reducing cost while providing resources for professional growth has prompted the use of online meeting tools. After the attacks on the World Trade Center, Wainhouse (2002) reported a noticeable increase in web conference meetings. The use of online meetings continues to grow into the next decade following the crisis of September 11, 2001 disaster. While not all uses of web conferencing would be for the purpose of professional development, it is presumed planners are aware of the benefits associated with web conferencing as a cost effective method for delivery of content and ideas. For example, a well known advantage in use of audio and video communication is the ability to archive presentations so participants and students have the option for revisiting the meeting, or catching-up if the meeting was in conflict with personal schedules. Opportunities for collaboration across time and space are a value-added feature of web conferencing. Efficiency gains in terms of time and costs are a major benefit (Frost & Sullivan, 2001).

Ecological Advantages

In addition to cost savings in time and resources, online meetings are the new *green* when providing professional development experiences for faculty, staff, and other professionals in the workplace. In a report by Cisco, (2011) gas emissions from jet fuel will increase 60% by the year 2025. This gives members of the Academy opportunity to set the example in use of online venues to protect and sustain environmental resources. In addition to saving resources through less travel, time needed to bring people together is significantly reduced. In a demonstration project conducted at the 2009 U.N. Climate Change Conference (Cisco, 2011), delegates conducted simultaneous dialog with participants from six continents. These individuals, in turn, immediately communicated with news reporters in their home countries. The results showed efficient, productive meetings without ever boarding an aircraft.

As indicated, much of the literature in online education consistently reports advantages and benefits for OnLPD, there being a number of common attributes across learning environments and methods for teaching.

Best Practices for OnLPD

Professional development to prepare faculty to teach online, or for those designing a course previously taught in the classroom, has been lacking consistency and quality in design. Methods for presenting PD include: instructor-led workshops (frantic in-between semester sessions), synchronous webcasts, video-conferenced demonstrations, multi-day boot camps, asynchronous, self-paced courses, and robust websites (containing both print-based instruction with screenshots and streaming videos with audio tutorials). Faculty receive weekly 'technology tips' distributed by email and quarterly hands-on 'project day' seminars (Beith, 2006; Marek, 2009; Santovec, 2004; Simmons, Jones, & Silver, 2004; Tarr & McDaniel, 2005). While the methods for presenting PD can be varied, the core of PD is systematic design. When designing online PD, it is important to consider the teaching process by selecting a preferred model and following it with consistency. For example, TPACK (Technology Pedagogy Content Knowledge) has been reported as a simple, but effective model for planning a technology-enhanced lesson (Mishra & Koehler, 2006). Used primarily in K12 educational environments, TPACK framework seamlessly brings together teaching methods with subject matter using technology tools effectively. This methodology has been reported as successfully applied to the design and development of online PD (Archambault & Crippen, 2009). Begin with the *content* for the PD module. Teaching strategies and *pedagogical* decisions are driven by *content*. The use of *technology* is the last decision and must uphold and enhance both content and pedagogy. In the following paragraph is an example using the TPACK model.

Example of TPACK

The teacher or instructor is teaching a unit on perspective-taking using primary source documents.

He plans to retrieve a list of online primary sources and provide a sample lesson in which high school students can think deductively to determine point of view. Knowing the content requires historical thinking, a list of websites with diaries, journals, and other historical documents provide the ideal technology based resources for the lesson. Content is history, pedagogy is reading to compare and contrast documents for perspective-taking, and technology is use of digital primary source documents. Students will report on their perspectives using small groups in the online discussion forums. Perspective-taking leads to rich dialog within small groups (adapted from Facing History and Ourselves, 2011).

Most faculty agree with the importance of collaborative group learning. Students learn through interaction with the instructor and by interaction with each other (Hogarth, Day, & Dawson, 2004). Modeling small group processes is an effective method for bringing about change and adopting the best practices needed for online teaching. Suppose the online course content is in the area of information literacy for school librarians. Content can consist of many digital resources that are useful for teaching research skills for K12 children. In order to ensure content is understood and applicable to the school setting, pedagogical decisions might include decisions on choosing various research models appropriate for K12 students and how to best ensure librarians can apply these to their work setting. The designer might select a streaming video with a live action school media center and students engaged in use of small group processes. Or, the designer might prepare lists of links leading to well known research models grounded in research for school libraries. The course participants might review links and prepare projects based activities for their own students to be reported, reviewed, and evaluated by peers in the online course. At this point the designer could make the decision for the use of technology through online display of slides or videos with K12 student work-samples.

The TPACK model is useful for planning synergy across content, teaching strategies (pedagogy), and technology (tools to enhance learning).

Other important attributes should also be readily identified in the planning of online professional development.

- **Strategies for Fostering Interaction**: These include questioning strategies; how to redirect students in online discussions; and ensuring all students are engaged (Garrison & Cleveland-Innes, 2005).
- **Planning Appropriate Feedback**: Research in online teaching report the importance for clear and consistent feedback to students (Yang & Liu, 2004). Various models have been suggested. Instructors and facilitators may provide summarized narratives at the end of an assignment, quick feedback in email, Q&A forums on the conferencing software, and video or audio podcasts with desktop demonstrations are also useful.
- **Selection and Evaluation of Outside Resources to Facilitate Learning**: Course assignments can make best use of outside resources through integrated digital resources. Instructional strategies might include Internet searches grounded in theory related to a topic, compilation of resources for ePortfolios or fieldwork investigations followed by student presentations (Segrave & Holt, 2003).
- **Strategies for Maintaining Enthusiasm**: Maintaining enthusiasm for teaching online is a major challenge for faculty. Personal contact with students in advance of the meeting dates is one method for keeping students connected. Assuming a personal identity is also an effective method for maintaining enthusiasm for both instructor and students (Eunjoo & Suhong, 2009).

Many educators teach as they were taught, rather than considering the advantages and disadvantages of alternative approaches (Hartman, 2001). Teaching online is no different. In relation to this, in the following section tools and strategies commonly used within online environments are considered. Marek (2009) conducted an exhaustive review of the literature to identify how faculty learns to teach online and specifically the support they receive during their professional development experiences. Among the many features discovered with regard to effective teaching online was the importance of multimodal delivery of courses. One method for assuring a move from flat text based courses is the use of web conferencing environments. She stated:

A significant concern with online courses is that the current delivery mechanisms seem to flatten the traditional multi-sensory learning environment. How do we learn to add back those critical multidimensional elements into the learning environment? One way is to take advantage of web conferencing systems. With web-based synchronous learning environments, professors and students can begin to recapture the human touch we miss in the frequently-silent online course structure. (p.277)

Selecting the Tools for Teaching

When planning online instruction, pedagogical considerations are primary in the planning process. Implementing decisions related to pedagogy, selection of tools and learning environment is an important next step. Interactive synchronous environments are characterized by real-time, back and forth communication. For example, conversations on a cell phone are synchronous where the first speaker communicates his or her thoughts while the receiver immediately begins the decoding of the message or interrupts it. It is an open and free dialog but online synchronous communication doesn't usually enjoy the same freedom. Even with two-way exchange of words, the dialog is limited by click and wait for the message to travel electronically. Texting, chats, and instant message might be considered synchronous but the freedom to interrupt or enhance the other person's words is limited. An exception to this is through interactive web conferencing software. When the facilitator and participants are connected with webcam and microphone, communication is possible through a natural exchange of words. Typically the conference administrator can be seen and heard but the microphone button must be pressed for the two-way synchronous communication. The facilitator has control over access through the conferencing software.

For large numbers of participants, use of polling features can be built into the software. The facilitator can pose a question or ask for responses to an idea while participants may respond by clicking "buttons" used for the polling functions. The yes or no response is visible by all participants and listed in the order of each person's response making it possible for the facilitator is respond to participants in logical order of their response. Very often the facilitator will present content using slides displayed in a large window on the conference site. The polling device shown in Figure 2 is from the Berkman Center at Harvard Law School.

This and similar devices are described at http://cyber.law.harvard.edu/teaching/ilaw/2011/How_To_Participate_at_iLaw Participants have the option for posting questions and comments on a smaller chat window displayed one side of the slides window. The conference host may monitor the chat questions and compile these for the presenter who can then respond to questions following the main presentation (Mitra, 2005). In some ways, this is more advantageous than a face-to-face presentation session. The presenter is uninterrupted while slides are clearly visible by all participants. The order of questions is sequentially listed, thus a sense of fairness and equity is built into the learning environment.

Disadvantages include challenges in use of the technical functions included in the software, access to adequate bandwidth, and resistance by some of the participants in use of multitasking skills (Bross, Beck, Leffler, 2011).

Best Practices for Synchronous and Asynchronous

Interactive Web 2.0 has made online communication highly motivating. A variety of communication tools will motivate both the course instructor as well as students. Selection of tools that fit the needs of participants is an important first step for planning delivery of web conference, webinar, or webcast. It is important to consider the content and purpose of the communication for these will impact the selection of communication tools.

In his work on teaching effectiveness, Bain (2004) defined several characteristics of highly effective teachers in a college classroom. Oral communication was reported as an important attribute for effective teaching. An articulate and knowledgeable speaker is more likely to keep students engaged and motivated. It is likely that these principles may also apply to both synchronous web conference and the one-way asynchronous web seminar. A well-organized presentation for online professional development accomplishes two objectives. Firstly, it is an exemplar for effective online teaching because through advance script preparation and rehearsals to assess the quality of voice and level of sound, the participants are more likely to make the time investment needed to complete the module (Hofmann, 2004). A second advantage is participants' time becomes a priority and faculty under various constraints and pressures will value efficiency in presentations and more likely to remain motivated and engaged. In the traditional classroom, questioning strategies should be designed to promote critical and creative thinking by which participants are able to make best use of dialog with the course instructor. It is well documented (Koopman, 2010; McNamara

Figure 2. Real time polling system (Image used by permission, The Berkman Center)

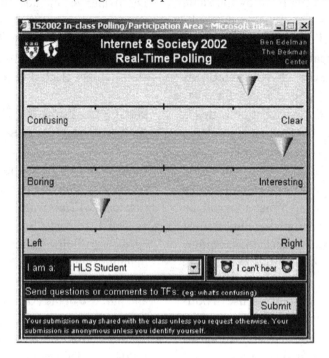

& Brown, 2009) that online instruction permits reflection prior to responding to classroom discussion questions. Many students have reported this as liberating and are more comfortable with responding to questions and posting personal perspectives. Questioning strategies can be employed through the use of several tools. Discussion forums and the interweaving of thoughts through the use of *threads* have been consistently used for online classes. Chat sessions may be more difficult for ensuring students engage in deep and durable learning, however immediate feedback is an important advantage in use of chat. The course facilitator (instructor) should examine advantages for both chat and use of discussion threads for exchanging ideas in a class discussion (Cook, 2007).

Course instructors can periodically check for understanding by using web conferencing software that includes polling devices. These can be used to poll participants understanding and interest level during a webinar. Similar to the polling devices used with commercial web conferencing software, the Real Time Polling System (RTPS)

used by the Berkman Center for Internet & Society (2011, online) at Harvard University helps the instructor or facilitator track students during a webinar. Students may respond to prompts "clear", "confusing", "interesting", "boring", etc. (See Figure 2). Since response is immediate and quick, the presenter can self-assess pace and content for the presentation.

The RTPS would not be used to promote deep thinking and reflection. Instead, the designer would require collaborative responses outside class, or threaded posts to a discussion forum. Other strategies might follow the iterative *Delphi* method. Participants would receive an individual question on which to give their opinion about the probability, frequency, and intensity of possible events or phenomenon within the course of study. The course facilitator receives all responses and sends summaries to participants for a second or third round of responses. Each participant's response remains anonymous through out each cycle of questioning. When consensus is reached the course facilitator presents to the class. According to Gordon and Pease (2006), this promotes a form of reflective thinking resulting in durable, deep, and collaborative learning experiences for participants.

The Online Instructor's Toolbox

Online professional development provides unique opportunities to include multimodal learning experiences using video, audio, animation, and hyper linking to outside resources. Traphagan, Kucsera, & Kishi (2006, p. 21) conclude, "... webcasts and enhanced podcasts should improve student learning in comparison to text-heavy textbooks, notes taken from class lectures, or from other learning resources, such as PowerPoint. Based on the work of Mayer (2001) and Moreno (2006) the design of instructional media often includes images used to clarify ideas and processes. The unique advantage in use of webinars, webcasts, and podcasts is the capability to simultaneously present audio, pictorial information (both still images and video), and text. Many of the web conferencing tools make it possible for presentations to include video clips. Online delivery has archival capabilities which can support the limited time available for most faculty. Online courses are able to ensure students have a broad understanding of concepts through the use of podcasts, readings, and learning objects (Lewis & Abdul-Hamid, 2006). Learning becomes deep when problem solving activities associated with resources are linked to the course. Critical and creative thinking activities are enhanced through simulations and virtual worlds that are supremely suited for online learning environments.

In addition to a variety of techniques using media, creative use of communication tools lead to critical thinking and collaborative dialog. According to Lewis and Abdul-Hamid (2006), there are several factors that influence the effectiveness of an online course: 1) fostering interaction, 2) providing feedback, 3) facilitating learning, 4) maintaining enthusiasm, and 5) organization. If these are applied to professional development

modules, participants might expect interaction within a live web conference to include guided discussion with appropriate re-direction by the facilitator. For a webinar, the presenters still can pose deep thinking questions and offer several alternative solutions or situations to support the deeper thinking.

Feedback is important to ensure participants continue to honor the time commitment needed to remain in the webinar. In addition, feedback is a vital scaffolding tool and needed to ensure participants are processing new information and accurately applying concepts and skill to their own teaching. An effective OnLPD is designed to help the learner process new information through reading, listening, and viewing. In addition, online learning has the advantage for re-reading or reviewing instructional resources that are aligned with the workshop topic. All of these facilitate learning.

To summarize, the presenter should demonstrate enthusiasm for the topic presented. Content may not always warrant exuberance, however a clear and consistent commitment to the level of importance for the content will lead to a better learning experience. Organization for most OnLPD follows a specific order—introductions, presentation of agenda with time allotments for each item, presentation of content, question and answer sessions, closing commentary with bibliography. Organization helps participants anticipate attention levels and a standard form of organization provides cues for reviewing webinars at a later time.

Methods for Assessment

The National Staff Development Council recommends several key elements for quality in the design of professional development for teachers. These elements for success can be applied to online as well as traditional forms of staff development. In a report by the National Staff Development Council and the National Institute for Community Innovations (NSDC.org, 2001, p. iv), staff development for teachers can be designed and delivered online to:

- Provide more just-in-time professional learning;
- Create job-embedded learning opportunities;
- Ensure content-rich learning opportunities;
- Expand personalized professional development;
- Increase access to professional learning experiences; and
- Potentially reduce the costs of professional development programs.

Design of the professional development, whether online or traditional face to face, must be research-based and instructional strategies appropriate for both the participants and content (Morrison, Ross & Kemp, 2004). It will be important to identify certain enabling factors that will lead to professional growth. Caffarella and Zinn (1999) identified enabling and impeding factors associated with the design of professional development experiences. It is important to plan the PD event to include opportunities for participants to demand excellence in their own work rather than simply "getting by." Participants should recognize and internalize the value for professional development and how it leads to becoming active teachers, scholars, and life long learners. PD should lead to self-confidence in one's respective field of study because professionals need to feel like their work makes a difference in the lives of their students and other educators. PD should help alleviate feelings of discouragement or frustration in their roles as educators and faculty members. It should spawn intrinsic motivation to pursue a line of inquiry and PD should lend itself to presenting the big picture in the life of the university and community.

For institutions of higher education, the Sloan Consortium has provided a list of benchmarks for evaluating online courses, degrees, and programs of study. Criteria evolved out of the work reported through the Institute or Higher Education Policy (2000). The *Quality Scorecard* provides criteria for assessing institutional support in the area of policy and planning, copyright, and value added to online courses. Other areas for assessment include technology support, guidelines for course development and instructional design, strategies for teaching and learning, support for student social engagement, and methods for course evaluation (Sloan-C, online).

SOURCES FOR QUALITY ONLINE PD

By Top Tier Universities

Using the search engines within the universities listed in Table 2, two categories for professional development were identified. The keywords *faculty development* returned links to online modules devoted to faculty development, and in some instances, staff development for university employees. Institutions varied with numbers of modules and quality of offerings. A second search using keywords *continuing professional development modules online* returned many more sources for adult learners. Continuing Professional Development (CPD) was offered in traditional face to face with fewer than anticipated online options. Furthermore, schools varied by costs ranging from free to a range of several thousand dollars with the costly modules being business and management. The Apple™ iTunes store partners with universities (iTunes Teaching in Higher Education, www.teacherinhighered.com) to provide free podcasts for professional development for university faculty.

By Professional Organization

Professional development is available through a variety of online portals, universities, and government websites. Using criteria included the best practices described in this chapter, a bibliography of resources are listed below.

Table 2. Top Tier Universities listed in 2011 issue of U.S. News and World Report

Top Tier Universities-as listed in U.S. News & World Report	Faculty and staff development offered through HR or outsourced.	Online Modules for continuing education tuition based or complimentary
Harvard	Catalog of Webinars through the Harvard School of Innovations	Online instruction modules through School of Law e.g. Cyber crime
Princeton	Webinars and online tutorials	Interactive Modules offered through ippx Princeton Online provides modules for Continuing Professional Development (CPD)
Columbia University of New York City	Online courses for Learning and Development	CPD offered through the School of Public Health
Massachusetts Institute of Technology (MIT)	Faculty Development themed to *Diversity*	MIT's Lincoln Laboratory offers series of CPD online modules
University of Chicago	Catalog listed with links to professional development topics	Graham school of General Studies limited online modules; Great Lectures series through podcasts https://grahamschool.uchicago.edu/
Yale	Partners with professional organizations for faculty development	Career Development Opportunities provides webcasts
California Institute of Technology		Complimentary webinars for economic development—monthly schedule Webinars through Industrial Relations Center
University of Pennsylvania	Webinars offered in personal and professional development	
Duke		Professional Development outsourced to PRIM & AHEC http://ceuq.com/ *Area Health Education Center* (AHEC). 28 separate modules with slides and audio narration.
Brown	Webinars offered through Learn.Eduventures	Online tutorials for using the library.
Cornell	Center for Teaching Excellence Blogs	Online tutorials for using the library. http://www.ecornell.com/ CPD certificates
Rice	Faculty Development Blogs	
Vanderbilt	Online Modules with Readings Center for Teaching	CPD outsourced to various professional organizations.
Notre Dame	Open Courseware Professional Development in use of OpenCourse software	Online endorsements and certificate programs
Emory	One of several universities offering wide variety of podcasts through iTunes. Topics of interest for faculty, students and CEU participants.	

1. Lifelong Learning with iTunes-U (http://www.apple.com/education/itunes-u/)

iTunes-U is a distribution system for over 350,000 free lectures, films, and other media resources. It is through iTunes-u that major universities' iTunes accounts can be accessed. A quick search method uses Google with keywords iTunes-u followed by the name of the university. The iTunes-u directory includes lectures as podcasts, video clips, audio books, and other multimedia for students. Resources can be accessed and displayed through Blackboard™ as this appears to be an efficient method for storing and categorizing a rich library of instructional materials. It also provides access to countless educational materials free or with a reasonable fee structure.

2.   Center for Excellence in Education (http:// www.iaf-cee.org/faculty-development.php)

The center is a nonprofit organization providing online, comprehensive faculty development program for career colleges and universities. Faculty associated with the center are prepared to facilitate professional development sessions using the National Standards for Quality Online Teaching adopted by the North American Council for Online Learning (NACOL). The NACOL is formed to provide online professional development for K12 educators.

3.   Carnegie Foundation for the Advancement of Teaching (http://www.carnegiefoundation. org)

The Carnegie Foundation is an independent policy and research center. The Carnegie Foundation seeks to revitalize more productive research and development in education by providing access to webinars, online discussion forums, slide presentations, and blogs with options for posting comments. Added value to Carnegie webinars is design that includes follow-up Q&A and ongoing dialog related to the question/problem presented with the webinar. A typical webinar sponsored by Carnegie would include the scheduled webinar session, access to slides for participants to download, webinar recording for access at later time, and additional materials that provide a strong research base for the sessions. A rich selection of articles, video, and supporting documents ensure the professional development provided by Carnegie will lead to continued scholarship and enhanced teaching for the participants.

4.   EDUCAUSE (http://www.educause.edu)

EDUCAUSE is a nonprofit association whose mission is to advance higher education by promoting the intelligent use of information technology. EDUCAUSE programs include professional development activities, applied research, strategic policy advocacy, teaching and learning initiatives, online information services, print and electronic publications, special interest collaborative communities, and awards for leadership and innovation. Tabs on the Educause.edu website include Major Initiatives, Resources, Professional Development, and Community. Links to professional development provide resources related to regional, topical, and national conferences. Descriptions of webinars include abstracts, cost, and descriptive information on technical requirements for online courses.

5.   E-Learning for Educators (http://www2. ed.gov/teachers/how/tools/initiative/e-learning.pdf)

E-learning for Educators is a Teacher to Teacher initiative developed through the U.S. Department of Education and the No Child Left Behind legislation. It is a program designed to provide professional development through online courses presented by teachers in various regions throughout the U.S. The NSCD has partnered with eLearning for Educators by providing assistance in the implementation of standards for online professional development.

6.   EdTech Leaders (http://edtechleaders.org)

EdTech is a project of the nonprofit Education Development Center (EDC), Inc. EDC designs, delivers and evaluates innovative programs offering solutions to problems in education, health, economic disparity. Original funding for EdTech Leaders was provided by AT&T. Seed money was used to develop a program that would spawn other groups who were prepared to design and develop their own online PD programs. A key characteristic of this organization is the preparation of teachers and other educational leaders as effective facilitators and presenters. Their facilitators model effective strategies and techniques for teaching online, and course participants are able to experience the online environment as learners, gaining critical preparation for teaching online. As a final product, participants collaborate with their colleagues to create their own plan to offer online workshops for local teachers and/or administrators. (Kleiman & Treacy in Dede, p. 32)

7. Multimedia Educational Resource for Learning and Online Teaching (Merlot) (www.merlot.org)

Merlot is a community who share resources used for online teaching and learning. Membership is numbered at 58,000+ with representatives from higher education faculty, k12 teachers, and students. The Merlot collection includes 18 different categories of materials—animation, assessment tools, assignments, case studies, special collections, development tools, drill and practice objects, learning objects repository, online course resources, journal articles, access to online textbooks, presentations, quizzes, simulations, social networking tools, tutorials, and workshop materials. One key advantage in use of Merlot is access to materials that are peer reviewed before being added to the collection. The user can be assured of quality of materials based on evaluation of faculty and other educators. Unlike most search engines in which a keyword will return hundreds of thousands of hits, Merlot will return fewer hits with higher quality selection of articles, podcasts, lesson plans, and other formats related to the term being searched. For example, results from a search using the keywords online professional development yields 66 items from the Merlot collection. Ten of the items were peer reviewed

with comments posted by the reviewer for each item. Criteria for the review include an overview of the item, learning goals associated with the item, target audience, prerequisite knowledge or skills needed to use the item, type (genre) of the material, recommended uses, and technical requirements. If a particular item is added to personal folders of community members, this also appears in the review. Merlot follows the policy of Creative Commons, thus materials receive appropriate recognition by designers and authors but also permit the shared use of materials for noncommercial purposes. Merlot is nonprofit organization supported in large by California State University at Fullerton. Other supporters are Cornell, Lane Community College, Montana State University-Billings, Niagara County Community College, and Northern Michigan University.

8. Sloan-C (http://sloanconsortium.org)

Sloan-C is a consortium of individuals, institutions, and organizations committed to quality online education. In addition to journals and newsletters, the organization provides professional development through workshops, certificate programs, and webinars. Resources for summative and formative assessment are available through a comprehensive portal leading to information in online programs, degrees, and conferences. Recognition for outstanding online programs contributes to quality control in OnLPD. Recognition is give through several awards:

- Excellence in Institution-Wide Online Education
- Excellence in Online Teaching
- Excellence in Faculty Development for Online Teaching
- Outstanding Achievement in Online Education by an Individual
- Outstanding Online Program

Focus for each award is centered on innovation, effective instructional design methods, impact on teaching faculty, and scalability of online programs. Following the review of the literature, Sloan-C appears to be one of the most comprehensive sources for faculty OnLPD. Workshops are typically two weeks in length and include synchronous sessions, multimedia presentations, and access to additional online resources. Webinars provide 60 to 90 minute topical overviews. The cost for Sloan-C members is $99 per workshop. One year Institutional membership provides workshops at a reduce cost. The purpose for the workshops is to provide pedagogical grounding for teaching online, opportunity to enhance online skills as both teacher and learner, and experiences in an online environment.

In summary, online professional development provides a learning environment that is apropos for teachers and university faculty living in the new century. Teaching methods can be adapted for highly diverse audiences. Pedagogy can be planned to foster critical creative thinking that is collaborative in design, and inquiry methods have unlimited access to resources. Although access to electronic conferencing is widely available, there are many regions of the globe that lack equitable access. With the growing interest in these tools and resources, online professional development might eventually become effective and widely available to all educators in all environments.

REFERENCES

Archambault, L., & Crippen, K. (2009). Examining TPACK among K-12 online distance educators in the United States. *Contemporary Issues in Technology & Teacher Education, 9*(1). Retrieved from http://www.citejournal.org/vol9/iss1/general/article2.cfm

Bacro, T. R. (2007). Integration of Webcast lectures in a traditional gross anatomy course. *The FASEB Journal, 21*(5), 591–596.

Bain, K. (2004). *What the best college teachers do*. Cambridge, MA: Harvard University Press.

Beith, L. (2006). *Hybrid faculty learning communities as a professional development strategy*. Paper presented at the "22nd Conference on Distance Teaching and Learning". Madison, Wisconsin. Retrieved from http://www.uwex.edu/disted/conference/Resource_library/proceedings/06_4229.pdf

Berkman Center for Internet & Society. (2011). *Berkman Center meeting technology tools*. Retrieved from http://cyber.law.harvard.edu/

Bross, V., Beck, M., & Leffler, J. J. (2011). Like a haven in the shifting economic sands: Making the most of web conferencing tools. *The Serials Librarian, 6*(1-4), 203–205. doi:10.1080/0361526X.2011.556035

Caffarella, R. S., & Zinn, L. F. (1999). Professional development for faculty: A conceptual framework of barriers and supports. *Innovative Higher Education, 23*(4), 241–254. doi:10.1023/A:1022978806131

Caruso, J. B., & Salaway, G. (2008, October). *The ECAR study of undergraduate students and information technology: Roadmap*. Boulder, CO: EDUCAUSE Center for Applied Research. Retrieved from http://net.educause.edu/ir/library/pdf/ers0706/rs/ERS0706w.pdf

Cisco Systems, Inc. (2010). *Cisco video collaboration guide*. Distributed by Tandberg.com. Retrieved from http://www.tandberg.com/collateral/video_conferencing_guide.pdf

Cisco Systems, Inc. (2011). *Go green with Cisco Telepresence*. Retrieved from http://www.cisco.com/en/US/solutions/ns669/networking_solutions_products_genericcontent_green_solution.html

Communications News. (2004). Web meeting saves firm 1.9 M. *Communications News, 41*(9), 44–45.

comprehensive market survey. Working reports of the Learning Center. Institute of Information Management of the University of St. Gallen, Switzerland. ISSN: 1424-8557.

Cook, D. A. (2007). Web-based learning: Pros, cons and controversies. *Clinical Medicine, 7*(1), 37–42.

Courtney, A. M., & King, F. B. (2009). Online dialog: A tool to support preservice teacher candidates' understanding of literacy teaching and practice. *Contemporary Issues in Technology & Teacher Education, 9*(3). Retrieved from http://www.citejournal.org/vol9/iss3/languagearts/article1.cfm

Davis, J. (2007). Dialog, monologue, and soliloquy in the large lecture class. *International Journal of Teaching and Learning in Higher Education, 19*(2), 178–182.

Davis, M. (2009). Creating value with online teacher training. *Education Week*. Retrieved from http://www.edweek.org/tsb/articles/2009/03/16/02onlinepd.h02.html

Dede, C. (2006). *Online professional development for teachers*. Cambridge, MA: Harvard Education Press.

Dennis, K. B. (2009, April). Taking responsibility for your own career. *Corrections Today, 71*(2), 6.

Dewey, J. (1916). *Democracy in education*. Macmillian Publishing. Retrieved from http://www.ilt.columbia.edu/publications/digitext.html

Dewey, J. (1991). *How we think*. Amherst, NY: Prometheus Books.

Eunjoo, O., & Suhong, P. (2009). How are universities involved in blended instruction? *Journal of Educational Technology & Society, 12*(3), 327–342.

Facing History and Ourselves. (2011). *Café conversations*. Retrieved from http://www.facinghistory.org/resources/strategies/caf%C3%A9-conversations

Frost & Sullivan. (2001). *The European web conferencing market* (pp. 3989-74). New York, NY: Frost & Sullivan. FIT&L. (2002). Some best practices in online teaching and learning. *Online: RIT Online Learning*. Retrieved from http://www.edpath.com/images/RITWorkshop.pdf

Garrison, R., & Cleveland-Innes, M. (2005). Facilitating cognitive presence in online learning: Interaction is not enough. *American Journal of Distance Education, 19*(3), 133–148. doi:10.1207/s15389286ajde1903_2

Gordon, T. J., & Pease, A. (2006). RT Delphi: An efficient, "round-less", almost real time Delphi method. *Journal of Technological Forecasting and Social Change, 73*(4), 321–333. doi:10.1016/j.techfore.2005.09.005

Hartman, H. (2001). Teaching metacognitively. In H. J. (Ed.), *Metacognition in learning and instruction: Theory, research, and practice*. Dordrecht, The Netherlands: Kluwer Academic Publishers. Retrieved from ttp://condor.admin.ccny.cuny.edu/~hhartman/tchmtlyhjh.html

Heinrich, T. (2006). Web conferencing 101. *OfficePro, 66*(1), 24.

Hofmann, J. (2004). *The synchronous trainer's survival guide: Facilitating successful live and online courses, meetings, and events*. San Francisco, CA: Pfeiffer.

Hogarth, K., Day, I., & Dawson, D. (2004). Online professional development in support of online teaching: Some issues for practice. *International Journal of Instructional Technology & Distance Learning, 1*(9). Retrieved from http://www.itdl.org/Journal/Sep_04/article05.htm

iLinc Communications, Inc. (2011). *State of Arizona relies on web and video conferencing to cut costs and CO² emissions.* Retrieved from http://www.ilinc.com/pdf/case-studies/ilinc-state-of-arizona-case-study.pdf

Illinois Online Network. (2010). *Instructional strategies for online courses.* Retrieved from http://www.ion.uillinois.edu/resources/tutorials/pedagogy/instructionalstrategies.asp

Innes, R. B. (2007). Dialogic communication in collaborative problem solving groups. *International Journal for the Scholarship of Teaching and Learning, 1*(1), 1–17. Retrieved from http://academics.georgiasouthern.edu/ijsotl/2007_v1n1.htm

Institute for Higher Education Policy. (2000). *Quality on the line: Benchmarks for success in Internet-based distance education.* A report prepared for The Institute for Higher Education Policy, Washington, DC.

Kleiman, G. M., & Treacy, B. (2006). EdTech leaders online: Building organizational capacity to provide effective online professional development. In C. Dede (Ed.), *Online professional development for teachers: Emerging models and methods* (pp, 31-47). Cambridge, MA: Harvard Educational Press.

Koopman, B. (2011). From Socrates to wikis: Using online forums to deepen discussions. *Phi Delta Kappan, 92*(4), 24–27.

Lewis, C., & Abdule-Hamid, H. (2006). Implementing effective online teaching practices: Voices of exemplary faculty. *Innovative Higher Education, 31*(2), 83–95. doi:10.1007/s10755-006-9010-z

Mandel, M., Hamm, S., Matlack, C., Farrell, C., & Palmer, A. (2005). The real reasons you're working so hard and what you can do about it. *Bloomberg Businessweek.* Retrieved from http://www.businessweek.com/magazine/content/05_40/b3953601.htm

Marek, K. (2009). Learning to teach online: Creating a culture of support for faculty. *Journal of Education for Library and Information Science, 50*(4), 275–291.

Mayer, R. E. (2001). *Multi-media learning.* Cambridge, MA: Cambridge University Press.

Mayrhofer, D., Back, A., & Hubschmid, R. (2004). *Web-conferencing software tools: A*

McNamara, J., & Brown, C. (2009). Assessment of online discussion in work-integrated learning. *Campus-Wide Information Systems, 26*(5), 413–423. doi:10.1108/10650740911004822

Mishra, P., & Koehler, M. (2006). Technological pedagogical content knowledge: A framework for teacher knowledge. *Teachers College Record, 108*(6), 1017–1054. doi:10.1111/j.1467-9620.2006.00684.x

Mitra, A. (2005, June). Weaving a new web. *Parks and Recreation.* Retrieved from http://www.nrpa.org/content/default.aspx?documentId=2298

Molenda, M. (2011). Historical perspectives. In Spector, M., Merrill, D., Van Merrienboer, J., & Driscoll, M. (Eds.), *A handbook of research for educational communications and technology* (3rd ed., pp. 12–14). Bloomington, IN: Association for Educational Communications and Technology.

Moreno, R. (2006). Does the modality principle hold for different media? A test of the method-affects learning hypothesis. *Journal of Computer Assisted Learning, 22,* 149–158. doi:10.1111/j.1365-2729.2006.00170.x

Morrison, G. R., Ross, S. M., & Kemp, J. E. (2004). *Designing effective instruction* (4th ed.). New York, NY: John Wiley & Sons, Inc.

National Staff Development Council. (2001). *E-Learning for educators: NSDC-NICI. Implementing standards for staff development. NSDC, 1128 Nottingham Road* (p. 49230). MI: Grosse Pointe Park.

Pillai, P. (2009). *Creating an online community of teachers and the librarian for*

Price, H. B. (May 12, 1993). Teacher professional development: It's about time. *Education Week.* Retrieved from http://www.edweek.org/ew/articles/1993/05/12/33price.h12.html

Professional Development through Social Networking Tools. Paper presentation at the International Conference on Academic Libraries (ICAL), October 5, 2009, Vice Regal Lodge, University of Delhi, Delhi India.

Purdue, K. (2003). Web-based continuing professional education: Uses, motivations, and deterrents to participation. In Moore, M. G., & Anderson, W. G. (Eds.), *Handbook of distance education* (pp. 615–630). Mahwah, NJ: Lawrence Erlbaum Associates Inc.

Santovec, M. (2004). Training the people who train the teachers. *Distance Education Report, 8*(20), 3–6.

Sauer, J. (2007). *Employment planning for an aging workforce.* A report for Knowledge Management AARP. Retrieved from http://assets.aarp.org/rgcenter/econ/ca_employer.pdf

Segrave, S., & Holt, D. (2003). Contemporary learning environments: Designing e-Learning for education in the professions. *Distance Education, 24*(1), 7. doi:10.1080/01587910303044

Simmons, S., Jones, W. Jr., & Silver, S. (2004). Making the transition from face-to-face to cyberspace. *TechTrends: Linking Research & Practice to Improve Learning, 48*(5), 50–85.

Sloan-C. (n.d.). *A quality scorecard for administration of online education programs.* Retrieved from http://sloanconsortium.org/quality_scoreboard_online_program

Tallent-Runnels, M. K., Thomas, J. A., Lan, W. Y., Cooper, S., Ahern, T. C., & Shaw, S. M. (2006). Teaching courses online: A review of the research. *Review of Educational Research, 76*(1), 93–135. doi:10.3102/00346543076001093

Tarr, T., & McDaniel, R. (2005). IUPUI 'Jump Start' program for new faculty. *Distance Education Report, 9*(2), 8.

T&D. (2008). What does it cost to host web conferences and webcasts? *T&D, 62*(9), 88.

Traphagan, T., Kucsera, J. V., & Kishi, K. (2010). Impact of class lecture webcasting on attendance and learning. *Educational Technology Research and Development, 5*(1), 19–37. doi:10.1007/s11423-009-9128-7

Treacy, B., Kleiman, G., & Treacy, K. P. (2002). Successful online professional development. *Learning and Leading with Technology, 30*(1), 42–47.

U.S. News & World Report. (2011). *US News rankings.* Retrieved from http://www.usnews.com/rankings

Vrasidas, C., & Zembylas, M. (2004). Online professional development: lessons from the field. *Education + Training, 46*(6/7), 326–334. doi:10.1108/00400910410555231

Wainhouse. (2002). *Survey results: Usage trends of collaboration technology by business travelers.* Wainhouse Research.

Whitehouse, P., Breit, L. A., McCloskey, E. M., Ketelhut, D. J., & Dede, C. (2006). An overview of current findings from empirical research online teacher professional development. In Dede, C. (Ed.), *Online professional development for teachers: Emerging models and methods* (pp. 17–20). Cambridge, MA: Harvard Educational Press.

Wright, A. (2005). *From ivory tower to academic sweatshop.* Retrieved from http://dir.salon.com/tech/feature/2005/01/26/distance_learning/index.html

Yang, S. C., & Liu, S. F. (2004). Case study of online workshop for the professional development of teachers. *Computers in Human Behavior, 20,* 733–761. doi:10.1016/j.chb.2004.02.005

KEY TERMS AND DEFINITIONS

Camera: Typically referred to as a *webcam*, the video camera can be used to feed images directly to a computer and a computer network. A USB connection is used to attach the webcam directly to the computer.

Codec: The codec converts the video and audio into a digital signal and compresses it before sending it out over the network. At the other end, the codec decompresses the signal and feeds the picture to a monitor and the sound to a loudspeaker.

Electronic Slide Presentation and Whiteboard: Most web conferencing software includes functions for screen-sharing and (facilitator) leader-synchronized web browsing.

Immersive Telepresence: The blending of multiple images together to create a single seamless panorama view. In the immersive teleconference paradigm: one frame of the teleconference is a panorama that is constructed from a compound-image sensing device. These frames are rendered on a projection surface that surrounds the user, creating an immersive feeling of presence and participation in the teleconference.

Internet Protocol (IP Network): Basic Internet protocol for delivery data packets over a communications network. Unlike ISDN, only maintenance and technical costs are needed for IP delivered web conferences.

Integrated Services Digital Network (ISDN): A network commonly used to transfer both digital data and analog audio over the same line. For teleconferencing, both local and long distance phone charges apply.

Microphone: Used for *voice chat* during webinars and web conferences. A headset microphone combination is often recommended for use during web conferences. Like the camera, it is connected to the computer through the USB port. Audio messages are fed directly to the computer and the computer network.

Polling: After a webinar is scheduled, surveys can be designed to gather information from registered participants. Responses can also be solicited during the live webinar or conference. As participants select yes-not responses within the conferencing software, the tallies will display within the conference window.

Scheduling Applications: Many webinar software applications include functions for enrolling attendees through an online scheduler. After scheduling, email contact can be pushed to the participants with reminders of the date and time of the webinar. Surveys can also be administered using the contact information collected through the scheduling application. Calendar of events can also be displayed for future planning by participants.

Telephony: The term is used to encompass all components related to analog or digital voice communication. The term is usually used with web conferencing software to refer to any form of voice communication.

VoIP Video Over Internet Protocol: The technology that permits analog sound signals be converted to digital signals for use by a computer system. VoIP makes it possible to place telephone calls over the Internet. One popular vendor that provides VoIP is Skype™.

Web Conferencing Software: An exhaustive list of vendors supplying web conference software can be viewed through Wikipedia.org. Available online (http://en.wikipedia.org/wiki/Comparison_of_web_conferencing_software)

Web Conferencing: Refers to a service that allows conferencing events to be shared with remote locations. Most vendors also provide either a recorded copy of an event or a means for a subscriber to record an event. The service allows information to be shared simultaneously, across geographically dispersed locations in nearly real-time.

Chapter 11
Professional Development for Online Educators:
Problems, Predictions, and Best Practices

Angela Velez-Solic
Indiana University Northwest, USA

Jennifer Banas
Northeastern Illinois University, USA

ABSTRACT

A professional development program for online faculty members can be difficult to create, implement, and sustain. Its components will vary depending on the location of the online faculty, the institutional budget, and who is administering the program. A professional development program is essential if institutions wish to keep instructors up-to-date on technological advances and pedagogical shifts as online classrooms change. Today's online faculty members are inundated with "information overload" due to the internet and because information is increasing exponentially, which results in pressure to "keep up" (Sherer, Shea, & Kristensen, 2003). Because of this pressure and the proliferation of learning tools, institutions need to help faculty filter and use the information available to them. This chapter will focus on essential components of professional development programs, issues and potential solutions, examples from successful programs, and future trends in online professional development.

BACKGROUND

Research shows online faculty members need adequate preparation to teach online (Muirhead & Betz, 2002; Velez, 2010). Once the faculty member is trained and has taught his or her first course, what can be done to ensure that the faculty member remains adequately informed about new technologies, techniques, and ideas in distance learning? If institutions want their online learning programs to grow, they must depend on the engagement of their faculty members to provide students with quality instruction, as they are the primary source of success for any online learning

DOI: 10.4018/978-1-4666-1963-0.ch011

initiatives (Tabata & Johnsrud, 2008). Research shows that even though someone is a good teacher in a classroom, that person might struggle in the online learning environment if they are unfamiliar with technology-enhanced learning tools and environments (Howell, Williams, Lindsay, & Laws, 2004). Technology is only one area upon which faculty members' success is contingent in the online environment.

Online faculty members need support from their institutions on a continual basis (Shapiro, 2006). Unfortunately, scant literature exists on online faculty development programs (Taylor & McQuiggan, 2008) and guidelines for developing them. Having a robust faculty development program as well as a group of skilled faculty members are aspects of a quality online learning program (US Department of Education, 2006; North Central Association of Colleges and Schools, Higher Learning Commission, 2007).

Despite the lack of literature on established faculty development programs for online instructors, some best practices are mentioned, as well as reasons why institutions should make continual development a priority on their campus. Unfortunately, opportunities for university-sponsored professional development for online instructors seem to be limited (Bennett, Priest & Macpherson, 1999). What is known is that a permanent, always-accessible development program should be created that is rich in material, but also rich with collaboration and communication for the instructors (Serdiukov, Niederhauser & Reynolds, 2000). A campus has a unique opportunity to promote a *community of practice* for its online faculty through collegial sharing (McQuiggan, 2007). This chapter will share evidence that online faculty need and want professional development (McKenzie, Mims, Bennett, and Waugh, 2000; Velez, 2010), discuss examples of successful professional development programs, and provide guidance to those who wish to implement a sustainable, scalable professional development for online faculty.

Technology and Constant Change

Professional development opportunities for online faculty might cover various subject areas such as student issues, testing integrity, instructor involvement, assessment, and other pedagogical concerns; however, the one area of professional development that is needed most for faculty members who teach online is technology. Technology has profoundly affected everyone's lives and has changed the culture of education, the university, and learning environments where information is created and delivered (Appana, 2008; McFarlane, 2011). The main reason why technology should be part of any professional development program is its swiftly changing nature. Not only is technology changing teaching, it is changing the nature of research-and the way we communicate inside and outside the "classroom" (Schneckenberg, 2009).

The rapid rate of technological change does not impact traditional, face-to-face instructors as greatly as it does online instructors because their students are using some form of technology to learn and access information every hour of every day. Technology has drastically changed the landscape of learning and the expectations placed upon faculty members (Schuster & Finkelstein, 2006). Online instructors are significantly affected, as they are deep within the trenches of the technological world, teaching in the cloud versus a classroom.

Learning *basic* technologies to teach online should occur during initial preparation (Velez, 2010), but teaching with more advanced technology tools requires practice (Weaver, Robbie, & Borland, 2008). The faculty members who are technologically savvy typically practice and try new technologies. These faculty members might have some advantages over those who have been resistant or who refuse to utilize it. For example, using technology can empower faculty members and increase their self-confidence levels (Tabata & Johnsrud, 2008). Increasing self-confidence can lead to more comfort and exploration as tools become available. Additional benefits include the reputation faculty members might get from their peers and others at their institutions for being an "innovator" (Tabata & Johnsrud) and the personal pleasure in delivering learning to students in new, exciting, and creative ways.

The technologies that affect their teaching change rapidly; a technology that is new today might be replaced by a better technology in a month or less (Ansah, Neill, & Newton, 2011). Therefore, online instructors must become experts at adapting and incorporating new technologies as they become available. Depending on the institution, this could be relatively continuous (Williams, 2000). When the web was in its 1.0 phase, having faculty members who served as content experts as well as skilled technologists worked well; however, new and interactive technologies require greater specialization and expertise for faculty and a greater need for support staff and instructional experts (Orr, Williams, & Pennington, 2009).

One of the technologies for which faculty members could receive training is the university's learning management system (LMS). The LMS serves as a "virtual learning environment", where teaching and learning via distance is completed (Dillenbourg, Schneider, & Synteta, 2002). LMS's change rapidly and more appear in cyberspace to improve the quality of learning experiences for students (McFarlane, 2011). Faculty members who teach online should be well-skilled with the institution's chosen LMS (Velez, 2010), and if the faculty member only received basic training in the tool, then more training should be provided when the instructor is ready to learn additional features that could benefit students and instructional practices (Craig, 2007).

Faculty members have been shown to use additional technologies to deliver learning content, but the focus has not been on innovative uses of technologies (Trenton, 2006). Some institutions have made attempts to introduce technologies gradually in order to train faculty to look at technologies critically and analytically (Trenton).

Some additional technologies include new tools such as synchronous communication tools, free programs that enhance learning, or required programs like plagiarism detection or test integrity software. Even if an institution does not plan on changing learning management systems or purchasing new programs, online faculty members should have opportunities to learn what is new and how to make their online classrooms more dynamic. Web 2.0 technologies like wikis, blogs, virtual worlds, social networking, and other forms of interactions do require faculty to have greater technological skill to use them appropriately (Orr, Williams, & Pennington, 2009).

The rapidly evolving landscape of learning technologies requires a set of faculty members who are competent in learning technologies and knowing in which circumstances the technologies should be applied, how they should be applied, and why they should be applied to any given learning context (Schneckenberg, 2009). Tabata and Johnsrud (2008) found that faculty members who have busy lives trying to teach, research, and serve, are more likely to view technology favorably if they understand how it benefits their teaching. After all, faculty members are hired because they are experts in their fields; they are not trained how to teach and usually teach how they've been taught or how they like to learn (Meyer, 2003). Fortunately, online education is challenging the traditional modes of teaching and giving attention to different ways to achieving learning outcomes, including the use of technology.

Individuals, institutions, and companies are offering free tools every day that could make an online classroom more visual, more interactive, and make an online instructor's job easier. Without a proper professional development program to share these tools with instructors, and without a means to train instructors how to use them, these tools might never be utilized, or if they are utilized, they might not be used effectively (Valentine, 2002). A very important question was posed by Barbules and Callister (2000), "Which technologies have educational potential for which students, for which subject matters, and for which purposes?" It is not acceptable to merely introduce faculty members to learning technologies; they need to understand how to correlate the tool with the desired student outcomes and collect performance data (Meyer, 2003).

Paloff & Pratt (2000) proposed that technology is not what teaches the students, the instructor teaches the students. Therefore, while it is important and imperative to prepare instructors to teach with technology, time should be spent on making sure that the instruction given is effective (Valentine, 2002). The very best online instruction is delivered by faculty members who are informed, creative, and critically evaluative (Greenberg, 1998). Orr, Williams and Pennington's (2009) study found that while faculty members who teach online do appreciate technology support, there is a distinct need for pedagogical assistance as well, especially the need for support staff who are instructional experts. Having instructional experts on hand is one part of the complicated but important process of developing and managing a professional development program.

Creating and Managing a Professional Development Program

Institutions should show commitment to faculty growth and development, which might include leadership development, teaching skills, and mentoring (Villar Angulo & De La Rosa, 2006), as well as significant time spent on learning technologies. That commitment should result in training that is continuous and ongoing (Eaton, 2002). The training, though, should be applicable to the individual teaching contexts of the faculty members who are participating so that what is learned can be immediately applied (Schneckenberg, 2009). Training could take place at a departmental level, or even a course-level. Instructors who teach math courses could take part in a workshop that teaches them how to find videos or audio files

to help explain difficult math concepts as well as how to upload them into the LMS. If general workshops are offered, the facilitator should be aware of the applicability of the content to the various contexts of the attendees and ensure that instructors understand how the content is appropriate for their work.

Successfully managing a distance education program requires a number of people who are invested in its growth and development. It involves administrative duties as well as direct faculty support and training. Williams (2003) discovered 13 roles necessary to facilitate this management and support for those who teach online: administrative manager, instructor/facilitator, instructional designer, Technology Expert, Site Facilitator/ Proctor, Support Staff, Librarian, Technician, Evaluation Specialist, Graphic Designer, Trainer, Media Publisher/Editor, and Leader/Change Agent (p. 1). That information might seem staggering for institutions that lack people who can fill these roles, and lack the funding to provide them. However, many times one person can serve the campus in more than one of the roles above. Ideally, the campus might have someone already on staff that has the ability to design and facilitate a professional development program.

Institutions can learn lessons from others that have created professional development programs in the past. For example, six institutions from the Midwest to the Southwest of the United States collaborated on a project to provide professional development to a group of instructional designers. The logistical lessons that they shared were: (a) start early and plan well in advance of delivering your professional development program; (b) communicate well, with those who are working on the project as well as with the participants; (c) start small, especially if an institution is trying inter-institutionally collaborate on a project; (d) find opportunities to improve by seeking formative and evaluative feedback; and (e) go beyond what is promised to the participants (Santovec, 2004, p. 6). Institutions can learn from this and seek opportunities to collaborate with others in their area or abroad. Administrators or directors could join organizations such as the USDLA (United States Distance Learning Association) to meet other institutions that have similar goals and perhaps share professional development resources.

At Empire State College, part of the State University of New York (SUNY), their professional development program has gone through four distinct stages, shedding light on best practices for institutions that are just beginning to offer programs to support their online educators. Although Empire State's distance education efforts are over thirty years old, their current direction is still the same, which is to be a solution for working adults who want to get an education (Stover, 2005). What was distinguishable about their faculty development program in its onset was that in the early 1990's, they started a peer mentoring program for faculty. They maintain that focus now, even though their program has manifested into a new, modern program reflective of the current nature of online education.

Empire State has found success in their professional development program because they broke down the process into steps. First, they laid plans for their online program and made sure that their online courses were offered and availability of online courses was increasing. After the program was sustainable, they focused on mentoring (Stover, 2004). An instructional designer mentored faculty members while a course was being developed, and a formal mentoring program was created in 1998 called the Mentoring Institute (Stover) that offered workshops on teaching and learning for faculty.

The third tier in Empire State College's development was the specialization phase (Stover, 2004), which was indicated by the increased experience of faculty with online learning and technology. The faculty who were already experienced were no longer interested in learning the basics about online teaching or technology, so Empire State responded by providing advanced training opportunities, a technology help desk, as well as an experienced faculty coach (Stover).

Stage four of Empire's program is a focus on direct support for online instruction and pedagogy by offering seminars for faculty on issues that relate to teaching online, facilitated group discussions, "shadowing" opportunities to visit experienced faculty members' online courses, and funding for opportunities that are not offered on campus (Stover, 2004). One area in which Empire State's faculty want more attention is new technology tools, which might be the fifth part of their program if it has not yet been developed.

If an institution has a director or coordinator of online learning, this coordinator/director might be in charge of leading the effort towards creating a development program for its online instructors. Because online faculty members spend a great deal of time on the computer and do not have as much face-to-face time, they might be willing to share the duties of creating this program-whether it is face to face, online, or hybrid. Bringing faculty members together, even if it is only virtually, not only eases the administrative burden of program creation, but also creates a sense of community and collegiality between the instructors (Floyd, 2003).

The instructors are the major stakeholders in this initiative; therefore, it seems natural that they need to be an integral part in creating it. One suggestion for creating and managing the program is to have the instructors teach their own workshops (virtual or face to face) in areas they know well. Some instructors might know lesson-authoring programs like Lectora; others might be familiar with creating learning objects; and one might be skilled in efficient paper grading. If the instructors offer their own workshops, then the university may not need to spend money bringing in outside speakers, or have to pay conference and travel fees. Mainka (2007) insists that an institution's staff should be first on its administrator's priority list as the faculty is an asset, not a cost. It should devote resources, time, and financial support to professional development as well as encouraging best practices in online pedagogy. Additional best practices are shared in the following section.

Best Practices

Professional development programs should be focused on teaching, not just technology (Bennett et al., 1999). Also, faculty members do want to have training in "best practices" of teaching online (Kosak, Manning, Dobson, Rogerson, Cotnam, Colaric & McFadden, 2004). For faculty members, the idea of what is "best" and how to apply it can be unclear and intimidating (Lewis & Abdul-Hamid, 2006). Therefore, a professional development program should not only highlight what online instructors need to know, but also how to apply that knowledge to their classes effectively.

One area of concern for online faculty is the lack of visual cues and physical interactions with students (Levy, 2003). Instructors need to be prepared for this shift, which might, at first, seem unnatural to them. This means that they need to have training in ways to interact with the students virtually, and a good understanding of communication techniques for the online environment (SREB, 2009). One of those techniques is verbal immediacy, which includes the use of humor, referring to students by their names, providing written encouragement, sharing personal examples and information, and encouraging students to contact the instructor (Hutchins, 2003).

A way to increase interaction between course participants and create a culture of rapport is by developing an online *e-learning community*, where the students and the instructor are involved in creating, sharing, and reflecting (Shrivastava, 1999). This interaction is typically the center of the online course environment, and those who are exemplary online faculty ensure that interaction is rich, dynamic, interesting, and engaging (Lewis & Abdul-Hamid, 2006). Participation and interaction should never be optional for students or for faculty.

Those who teach faculty members in training or workshops need to be aware that faculty members are adult learners and effective principals of adult learning need to be considered when planning and delivering a professional development program (King, 2002). The three areas that are fundamental to adult learning theory are: experiential learning, personal reflection, and the social nature of learning (Marienau & Reed, 2008). To respect the roles of the adult learners, Lawler & King's (2001) principles of adult learning should be used while planning professional development (McQuiggan, 2007). The principles are: (a) creating a climate of respect, (b) encouraging active participation, (c) building on experience, (d) employing collaborative inquiry, (e) learning for action, and (f) empowering learners (Lawler & King, 2001). Those who offer the professional development should make an effort to respect the faculty members, encourage their regular participation, as well as encourage sharing and collaboration.

If the adult learning framework is accepted as a model for professional development, the first principal is respecting the faculty members. If programs are facilitated, then the facilitator should be sensitive to the needs of the faculty members and make sure to communicate with respect at all times. It is important to show value to what the faculty member's share, and give attention to their issues, concerns, and feelings.

Encouraging faculty members to play an active role in their professional development is also an integral part of adult learning theory. If instructors are encouraged to speak (or to write, if that is the case), share their stories, concerns, and experiences, they are actively engaging in the learning environment. In addition, they might leave the experience with more knowledge than if they are lectured about the subject. If they are learning about technology, having them "play" and practice the tools also engages them in active learning.

One of the richest ways to increase learning is to reflect upon past experiences. As educators, faculty members have experience from which they can pull examples and situations for current learning. Their experiences should be shared so that new learning can build upon past learning, which is a key to learning for any student, regardless of age. In this regard, professional development can be designed with specific prompts that can ask faculty members about past teaching or learning experiences. They can be asked to use those experiences to frame discussion question answers, share in reflective activities, or offer assistance to a faculty peer who can gain knowledge from another persons' experiences. Nicolle and Lou (2008) found that discussing technology, issues, and potential failures with peers in an informal environment was more helpful than formal training sessions. Because of that, institutions should consider fostering these informal interactions, perhaps with "brown bag" meetings that are face-to-face and/or online.

Faculty members might be used to working individually or in departmental silos, but room does not exist in a quality professional development program for that. Caffarella and Zinn (1999) share that faculty are used to staying current in their disciplines, incorporating technology, and developing their teaching on their own. While this is the traditional notion of personal and professional development, faculty members do typically enjoy working with their peers (Sherer, Shea, & Kristensen, 2003). Consequently, faculty members should be encouraged to work collaboratively to design lessons, practice using technology tools, respond to student scenarios, and participate in discussion activities. Learning from each other is better than learning from the facilitator alone.

If a faculty member is choosing to participate in professional development, then that faculty member has chosen to learn something new, or build upon knowledge he/she might already have. The new knowledge provided through strategically planned and delivered professional development should seek to empower the faculty members, to give them a renewed sense of purpose and to get them excited about applying their new skills or approaches. In addition, they should be provided with opportunities to share their current frustrations and concerns (McQuiggan, 2007) and,

through collaborative inquiry and participation, they are empowered to deal with the problems they might be facing.

Some instructors might be new to online instruction and may not know what is needed in terms of professional development, or how to find it (Serdiukov, Niederhauser & Reynolds, 2000). In order to serve the needs of the faculty, a permanent program should be developed, including a location full of resources (such as a portal or website) that allows for collaboration and communication between instructors (Serdiukov et al.). This program should offer continuous support for the faculty members, which is essential in terms of offering a quality program (Parscal & Riemer, 2010). Examples of support include, but are not limited to having a reliable department or contact for questions, concerns, and issues, providing regular opportunities to learn more, as well as create and maintain a virtual professional development portal.

Instructors might be willing to make adjustments to how they teach or design courses if they are offered consistent support and opportunities to learn (Hinson & LaPrairie, 2005). However, institutions need to be careful to not "force" professional development on its faculty (Kinuthia, 2005). What they also need to consider is that faculty members will have different levels of skills and it might be beneficial to offer several different types of opportunities such as a basic level and a more advanced level (Trentin, 2006). This is especially important for training and workshops in technology. Trentin (2006) developed a taxonomy that illustrates the levels of adoptions related to information and communication technologies. This taxonomy is helpful because it exemplifies the basic level of adoption, "informative use" through the upper level of use, which is "networked learning". The taxonomy is shown below in Table 1.

While Trentin (2006) developed this taxonomy to describe levels of information and communication technologies, each level does not necessarily preclude the other and technology use and

Table 1. Trentin's taxonomy

Level	Description
Informative Use	Basic level. Instructors use technology to share dates, and basic course information
Distributive Use	Instructors share learning materials like documents, presentations, lectures, articles, and
Interactive Use	exams. Items might be from face to face course placed in a Learning Management System.
Blended Solutions	Focus is on interpersonal communication, such as teacher to student (electronic feedback),
Content-Driven Learning	synchronous activities like live classroom experiences, and asynchronous situations like
Networked Learning	group discussion forums and virtual collaboration
	Instructors use both face to face classroom experiences seamlessly with online interaction
	Instructors design courses for the online environment without loading material meant for
	face to face learning experiences. The content is created the students in mind and various
	learning needs as well.
	Instructors design the course as described above, but also integrate student self-study and
	group collaboration as the main mode of learning in the course

integration might be found across the different levels. What institutions can learn from this, however, is where their instructors might be on the taxonomy, and be able to develop effective, need-based professional development to bring the instructors to their next levels and deliver it in such a way that models the behaviors and processes they want them to emulate.

The professional development activities should be delivered in different formats such as online workshops, online courses, and face-to-face workshops, depending on what the faculty members want (Kinuthia, 2005). According to the Southern Regional Education Board's Educational Technology Cooperative (2009), there is no single answer to the question of, "What is the best way to provide professional development for online educators?" They suggest using many strategies like "real-time" and "anytime" opportunities for training so that every instructor has a deep understanding of online teaching strategies like: (a) models of effective online teaching, communication, and role-playing opportunities to apply strategies, (b) how to handle difficult student issues, (c) using case studies and scenarios to differentiate instruction, (d) how to use or provide faculty-faculty mentoring, (e) reviewing current research and best practices, (f) hands-on training with the LMS and other technology tools (p. 2). Before starting or enhancing a faculty development program, the faculty members should be surveyed or interviewed in order to meet their specific needs. Doing so will also increase the likelihood that faculty will participate since they will see that their needs are being considered.

Another way for professional development to developed that ensures the likelihood for faculty acceptance is by institutionalizing professional development, in other words, making it part of the institution's culture (Blanton & Stylianou, 2009). Institutions need to make deliberate efforts to promote a culture of learning and that is not something that can happen quickly; rather, it is born after opportunities to learn are created and then sustained by as many parts of the institution as possible (Frankman, 2004). What seems to be more typical at campuses is that individuals seek opportunities for professional development, but it is difficult to gather a larger group that represents most, if not all, disciplines on a campus (Blanton & Stylianou). A challenge for institutions is mobilizing larger groups of faculty in sustained professional development. Perhaps creating a community of practice is an answer.

Ideally, a community of practice should be developed at the institution focused on online teaching and learning. The activities in this community of practice should follow Lawler and King's (2001) adult learning principles in order to respect the learning needs of the instructors who participate. Faculty members who are active in this professional development community might be willing to make adjustments in their teaching or in their course curriculum if they are offered continual and practical professional development opportunities (Hinson & LaPrairie, 2005). One way to potentially offer "continual" development opportunities might be through the creation of virtual communities of practice. The process of creating communities of practice and faculty learning communities will be discussed next.

Communities of Practice and Faculty Learning Communities

Faculty members in higher education are in the industry of creating, disseminating, and facilitating knowledge and because of that, they should be part of a community that is actively engaged in collaboration about how to filter and use the information they are constantly given (Brown & Gray, 1995). A community of practice for an institution's online educators might be the answer.

Etienne Wenger and Jean Lave developed the idea of communities of practice in 1998 and suggested that when people gather to learn and refine what they do within a certain community, or group, they are in a community of practice (Fenwick, 2008). An integral part to communities of practice is the social nature of the process and how their interactions with different groups on a daily basis (Smith, 2003). Three key aspects mold the community of practice model: *joint enterprise*, *mutual engagement*, and *a shared repertoire of communal resources*. Joint enterprise is a group of common activities and goals for the group; mutual engagement describes the process of the group members becoming an entity that is sustained through activities and common goals; finally, the shared repertoire of communal resources provide the group with their own habits, styles, and means of communication that develop over time (Lave & Wenger, 1991).

Once faculty members teach online at an institution, they might already find themselves on the outskirts of the institution's community of practice for those who teach online and/or hybrid courses. Because faculty members teach in different departments and have different levels of responsibilities due to their rank, they may not know each other; in that case, an infrastructure needs to be designed so that instructors are brought in to the community of practice so that relationships can be built to sustain it (Schwen & Hara, 2003). Creating and sustaining a virtual community of practice is essential for institutions providing online learning opportunities because participation in the community might positively affect the instructors' performance in class (Lesser & Storck, 2001).

An institution's community of practice for online educators provides an outlet and a means to handle any issues that the campus might have for online learning and delivery; the members share their knowledge and experiences, helping each other grow and learn as professionals without having the direct involvement of an administrative plan, or a formal workshop series. Telling stories about experiences empowers the faculty member who is sharing, helps shape their change in identity, and shapes the culture of the community of practice (Blanton & Styliano, 2009).

The communities can assist in the momentum of the university's strategic plan through the individual and collective activities of the participating faculty members of the community (Lesser & Storck, 2001). The very social nature of the community experience is powerful and can lead to change in faculty attitude, performance, and behavior, which can affect the institution's effectiveness, and, for some, profitability (Smith, 2003). One part of this change is the existence of "old timers" in the community and the "newcomers"; the people who have been integral to the community, the old timers, share their stories and experiences with the new members and assist them, "hook" them, essentially, into the community and its culture (Blanton & Styliano, 2009). This interaction is critical to institutional change, and crucial to growing and sustaining the community of practice.

Creating and delivering appropriate faculty preparation for online teaching, and providing formal and informal, direct and indirect faculty development opportunities enrich the community of practice as those who are participants interact as a whole, and perhaps in smaller groups within the larger whole, called *faculty learning communities* (Cox, 2004). Faculty learning communities, called FLCs, are groups of 8 to 12 faculty members from various disciplines who participate in active discussions on a specific issue related to students, curriculum, or some other issue involving teaching or learning (Cox, 2002). Evidence shows that FLCs positively affect faculty interest in teaching and learning, and provide ongoing support to faculty members (Miami University of Ohio), which is essential in sustaining any online learning initiative.

Online teaching is in a constant state of flux as technologies change, student demographics change, and curricula change. These changes require that faculty have the ability to adapt and respond appropriately; having a community of practice and FLCs in place can assist faculty through these fluctuations (Davis & Niederhauser, 2005). FLCs are powerful as they are the result of a group of dedicated individuals who volunteer their time, effort, and knowledge towards a common goal of supporting each other through change so that progress can be made (Shulman, Cox, & Richlin, 2004). FLCs take time to develop, and do require the commitment of dedicated and passionate faculty members.

Institutions hire faculty members because they are experts in their discipline, not because they are excellent teachers. By participating in a community of practice and/or a faculty learning community, faculty members are actively involved in a *teaching*-focused community that has the potential to shift the faculty members' identities from expert and scholar to teacher and scholar (Blanton & Styliano, 2009). This is significant because most faculty members do not start teaching with any formal training in pedagogy or adult learning theory, which is the basis of FLCs.

It is important for institutions to realize that FLCs and communities of practice are based on adult learning theory; they are pragmatic, and they work (Cross, 1998). They may not work when an institution has issues dealing with change prior to developing a community of practice and FLCs. If that is the case, then these efforts may not work as well (Shulman et al., 2004). That does not mean that creating and developing them is a waste of time, however. They can still be key components of faculty support and professional development.

FLCs can enhance both scholarship and the scholarship of teaching and learning, which are vital to the life of higher education institutions (Richlin & Cox, 2004). The FLCs have two categories: *topic-based* and *cohort-based* (Cox, 2002). The topic-based FLCs focus on a specific need, issue, or opportunity in teaching or learning (Cox, 2002). The faculty members who are actively involved in the topic-based FLCs might come from varying disciplines as well as have different ranks in the institution (Cox). Some examples of topic-based FLCs are: Using Technology to Enhance Teaching and Learning, and Teaching Writing-Enriched Courses. In these smaller groups, faculty members investigate, discuss, and evaluate processes, technologies, approaches, and results of their experiences. Both of these and about 100 other FLCs are found at Miami University of Ohio (Cox).

Cohort-based FLCs are slightly different as the group of faculty members who are participating have a shared experience like their status (new, mid-career, or senior faculty members), or another similarity that they share. As a cohort, they meet and work on different topics that relate to their cohort (Cox, 2002). If properly sustained and supported, these cohort-based FLCs can have a positive impact of the climate of the institution, as evidenced by Miami University of Ohio. Two examples of their cohort-based FLCs are: Senior

Faculty for Teaching Excellence, and Department Chairs Enhancing Leadership and Productive Change (Cox). These FLCs have had the power to initiate and sustain change while also pulling faculty into the culture of reflection and transformation.

From a management perspective, a leader needs to be in place that oversees the FLCs. That leader (a) coordinates funding, (b) provides technology support, (c) educates the faculty members and administrators about the FLCs, (d) identifies faculty members with common interests who would make a good FLC, (e) helps faculty members and FLCs find resources relevant to their groups, and (f) forms partnerships with other campus departments (Sherer, 2005). In addition, each FLC should be led by an experienced faculty member (Cox, 2004) as this leadership is integral to the success of the FLCs (Ingram, 2005). Choosing faculty leaders is one of the most important steps in the FLC process. One idea is to have faculty members self-nominate to lead a FLC.

Most of the literature discusses face-to-face FLCs, but a few authors discuss managing virtual FLCs (Ingram, 2005; Sherer, 2005). Using the computer and internet as a medium to communicate can enhance FLCs because they are provided with the means to meet wherever they are at any given time (Sherer). An example of successful, virtual FLCs is at Kent State University where they have been successful with their virtual FLCs focused on technology, adult learning, educational psychology, online learning, and others (Ingram). The virtual FLCs combine some face-to-face interaction with virtual meetings and interaction on their Learning Management System. In the LMS, participants focus on helping their online students learn and methods to encourage student learning. They share their experiences and resources online, so that their words are recorded and able to be viewed by others who might join the FLC at a later date, or for those who are interested (Ingram). Their learning and interactions can be shared easily with others who desire the information.

The ability of the group to affect campus climate, individual change, and collective transformation is dependent upon the strength of the group. Henri and Pudelko (2003) found that the stronger a group's social bond, focus, and intentions, the stronger the group is as a community of practice. The indication is that for FLCs, the director should ensure that the FLCs have a strong membership of individuals dedicated to a distinct focus and purpose. They should also have consistent opportunities to interact with each other.

Members of virtual FLCs can utilize the experience for personal and professional development. As a group they can engage in professional development opportunities like taking a short course or workshop in an area of interest. They can download trial versions of software programs and learn the program together, sharing their creations with each other. In addition, they can serve the institution as experts in their particular areas of expertise. These groups have an overwhelming opportunity to have endless professional development opportunities for the members and reach a wider audience for the scholarship of teaching and learning (Sherer, 2005). While FLCs are a great idea and addition to a campus climate, the initial focus of any professional development program should be the basics of teaching online, or the core competencies that are needed to teach in a virtual classroom, which will be discussed next.

Competencies of Online Educators

One model of professional development is the competency-based model. For this discussion, competency for online instructors is defined as "one who effectively and efficiently accomplishes a task [instructs] in a given context [digital distance education] using appropriate knowledge, skills, attitudes, and abilities that have adjusted and developed with time and needs" (Varvel, 2007). What remains to be defined is "knowledge", "skills", "attitudes" and "abilities" as they relate to online educators. Once those words have been operationalized, professional development opportunities can include learning and practice in these competencies. It is important to note, however, that competencies might vary depending on the institution's expectations of faculty members, and the type of institution. Those who teach in K-12 settings might have different competencies than those who teach in higher education. Regardless of the institution, a competency document should be written to mold the professional development plan (Varvel).

Institutions might review their state resources for core competencies for online educators. States such as Illinois have the Illinois Online Network (ION) that provides rubrics and documentation of competencies in many areas of online teaching and learning. Further, the National Educational Technology Standards for Teachers can be explored to find competencies, and other states have regional education commissions like the Southern Regional Education Board (SREB). It is challenging to find a single set of competencies for any online learning situation as competencies are similar across published literature. Therefore, research can inform institutions while their own competency document is designed.

Some competencies can be defined as student-focused. For example, Dede (2004) discussed how higher education institutions can meet the needs of Neomillennial students and learning styles by focusing on investing in technology and professional development. He asserted that the new and emerging students want "mediated immersion" in "distributed learning communities" that include (a) being fluent in various media and simulations, (b) individual and community-based learning that involves diverse, but contextualized experiences that are shared, (c) balancing experiential learning, guided mentoring, and collaborative reflection, (d) the ability to express oneself through non-linear modes of communicating, and (f) collaboratively-designed learning experiences that can be personalized (p. 1).

Because of these potential emerging needs, instructors need to be prepared for difficult shifts and perhaps experience some of these mediated immersed environments while also learning how to: (a) develop personalized learning experiences (b) design collaborative learning experiences and opportunities to share knowledge, (c) use case-based simulations and presentations, and (d) move beyond the test and design collaborative forms of assessment and peer-based assessment (Dede, 2004). Asking faculty members to change the way they teach can be challenging, but a faculty development program that is designed to assist faculty in making adjustments, which includes examples and resources, can make change less intimidating.

Many of the online teachers' competencies start with instructional design. Campuses may not have funding to hire and sustain a campus instructional designer; therefore, the design of the courses rests with the faculty members. This is not necessarily negative. Faculty members who design their classes need to have time to do so (Appana, 2008; Dykman & Davis, 2008). One suggestion by Dykman and Davis is to provide a consistent look and feel to the courses that are offered at an institution, as students might have increased stress if different courses have different navigations and information locations. Therefore, time should be spent ensuring that faculty members understand the basics of consistent course design.

Faculty members also need to be skilled in promoting a sense of community within their courses as community is integral to student learning, retention, and satisfaction (Exter, Korkmaz, Harlin, & Bichelmeyer, 2009). Faculty members can support the development of community by offering opportunities for social networking as well as the ability to meet synchronously during the term (Exter et al.). Other ways to meet this competency is to provide welcome messages to students as the class beings to set a positive tone (Renes & Strange, 2010) as well as offer a place for students to share personal information like interests, hobbies, and family as well as professional information.

Another important area is immediacy. Faculty members who teach online need to learn how to support their students, and that requires time and commitment. Faculty members need to be prepared that students will need help when the class begins and that requires them to answer emails quickly and provide a means of contact that is reliable (Dykman & Davis, 2008). Students also need effective and timely feedback that is chal-lenging as well as supportive (Dykman & Davis), which requires faculty to plan ahead of time and be cognizant of their tone when they respond to students electronically.

Lewis and Abdul-Hamid's (2006) study effectively condensed competencies of online instructors into five categories that are summarized in Table 2.

Those in faculty development can explore this table and discover learning opportunities through each of the descriptions. For example, a workshop or self-paced learning module can be created on

Table 2. Competencies of exemplary online faculty

Competency	Description
Fostering Interaction Providing Feedback	Interaction between instructor and student and student to student. Meaningful, collaborative interaction with course content; requiring students to offer substantive contributions each week. Designing thought provoking, interesting questions to promote interaction and variation in answers from students. Sharing the value of group work and assigning group projects Individualized feedback should be provided on all student work. Grading policies should be made clear on all student work, such as rubrics and grading matrixes. All feedback should be encouraging, regardless of students' performance levels. Develop "banks" of comments and replies that are typical to ease the time burden of feedback. Use voice tools, if available, to give feedback differently than typing.
Facilitating Learning Maintaining Enthusiasm and Organization	Promote active learning that is interactive and reflective. Start lessons with reminders about the learning objectives and wrap up lessons with a reflection on what should have been learned that lesson. Have an opportunity for students to post responses and comments about difficult course content to get help from each other and the instructor. Have students post about what they learned during a lesson and post their own reflective, through-provoking questions, and personal experiences related to the learning. Make sure that course content is current and relevant. Consider using virtual guest speakers. Use small group activities. Add video clips and other digital resources to support and enhance learning. Faculty members need to show energy and enthusiasm as well as be visible in the course. The course needs to be well planned in advance. Send reminder announcements or emails about weekly course goals and activities. Constantly assess activities and course layout. Seek feedback from the students during and after the course.

how to show energy and enthusiasm in the online environment. During a workshop, faculty members can collaborate on ways to seek formative feedback during a course and what to do if the data show that something is not working effectively. As shown by Lewis and Abdul-Hamid's (2006) study, exemplary online faculty are rich with knowledge and wisdom about best practices and competencies that take an online instructor from 'competent' to 'exceptional'.

Sample Development Programs

Allen and Seaman (2009) discovered that staff development for online learning is greatly limited. There are some professional development programs that can serve as examples, such as a few that are mentioned in this section of the chapter. The problem is that most of them are not virtual. For campuses with faculty members all over the world, this is a challenge. However, programs such as those discussed below could provide insight into strategies that could be translated into a virtual environment.

One professional development program is located at Kapi'olani Community College in Honolulu, Hawaii. The institution took their professional development program online in the hopes that the faculty members throughout their seven-campus system could make connections with one another (Hiser, 2008). While this program was not created for online instructors, it is possible to follow their lead, as their program created an interactive experience with a real sense of community for the faculty (Hiser). Another example is in Australia, where faculty members at three universities in the same Australian state share professional development opportunities to learn about technology for the online classroom, copyright laws, instructional design, and other issues (Weaver, Robbie, & Borland, 2008).

The University of Central Florida has an extremely comprehensive professional development program that consists of three tiers and it is delivered through their Center for Distributed Learning. The program starts with a basic eight-hour course, then a 35-hour course for those who wish to teach online, but not design a course, and then an 80-hour course for those who wish to design and then teach an online course (McCarthy & Samors, 2009). In addition to that program, they offer extensive faculty trainings in all areas of online learning and technology throughout the year in mixed mode formats.

Kent State offers a different strategy. Their virtual professional development consists of virtual Faculty Learning Communities, which is a group of faculty members who get together to meet about technology, adult learning, online teaching, and other areas (Ingram, 2005). They met virtually in their learning management system, and sometimes meet face to face (Ingram). The members of these communities share their experiences in the classroom, using technology, and their research in the virtual environment, which is preserved to be passed on to other instructors as needed.

Sherer (2005) suggested that faculty who are members of a virtual FLC like those at Kent State might be able to use the virtual environment to: (a) take an online course together related to what they want to learn, (b) download trial versions of software programs and discuss them, (c) participate in chat rooms or listservs with outside faculty members from other institutions, (d) collaborate to create or to contribute to an online newsletter, and/or (e) serve as an expert group for other colleagues interested in their areas of focus. In addition, virtual communities have intrinsic benefits like the ability to create more opportunities for faculty development, to respond quickly to faculty members who are in need, and to reach a wider audience in the scholarship of teaching and learning (Sherer).

One urban university sought to increase the technology skills of their faculty members by designing a program called the "Technology Fellows Program" in order to encourage and support the faculty members who might be technological leaders on their campus (Axley, 2008). Faculty members could apply to participate in the program, that rewarded them with a laptop, a stipend, and yearlong, personalized technology assistance (Axley). The program's goals were: (a) to develop an interdisciplinary community of practice who would become campus leaders in technology for instruction, (b) increase collaboration between faculty members to enhance teaching and learning, (c) to increase and sustain students' levels of technology fluency (Axley). The program had many face-to-face meetings and workshops, all focused on learning new, innovative technologies and culminated in each fellow designing a technology project for their particular department.

This process could be mirrored even if face-to-face meetings were not included, especially due to the availability of virtual meeting spaces. Institutions can design a similar fellowship program aimed at similar goals and deliver the program virtually. Experts from the fields of the fellows could hold virtual discussions for the fellows, and those discussions can be recorded so others in their departments could benefit. The LMS could be used for collaboration between the fellows and to continue developing their community of practice.

In another example, six institutions collaborated in a project to provide professional development to a community of instructional designers; while these people are not faculty members, lessons can be learned through their innovative approach to providing professional development. The six schools involved were: The University of Florida, Texas A&M, Texas Tech, University of Idaho, University of Missouri-St. Louis, and Iowa State (Santovec, 2004). Together, these institutions collaborated thru a multi-stage process that is described below.

The first step in their process was discovering what the training needs were for the group of people involved. After they surveyed the group, they found that training in asynchronous learning design, design for adult learners, best practices in

distance education, and organizing a course into acceptable units (Santovec). What that knowledge of their population, a team designed learning modules to deliver within their LMS that fit those areas of need. Each of the units that were covered contained a combination of synchronous and asynchronous activities that included some video, multimedia presentations with audio, chats and/or threaded discussions. At the end of each unit, participants completed activities that applied the knowledge they learned to a given context (Santovec).

After evaluating the experience, the group discovered preferences of the adult professionals who stated that they would rather experience less reading requirements and more activities, increased opportunities to collaborate with each other, and the availability of self-paced learning (Santovec). In addition, the team learned the following lessons about providing professional development to adults: (a) know your audience. They suggested that those who deliver the professional development should become familiar with those who will be learning from it, (b) show the relationship between learning objectives and assignments/activities, (c) encourage interaction between those who are participating, (d) be aware of the length of the course/workshop and understand that the longer a program is, the higher the attrition rate. They suggested that self-paced learning modules might work well for adult learners, and (e) understand each participant's motivation and goals for the program (Sandovec, 2004, p. 3).

The lessons learned from their experiences are excellent suggestions for those creating, maintaining, or redesigning a professional development program. The faculty members who seek development should be well known by those facilitating it. Best practices in instructional design should be followed when designing the course or learning module, which includes many opportunities for interaction and reflection. Finally, the length of the program needs to be flexible to serve the needs and constraints of the faculty members who are involved.

The final example of a program is another collaboration between nearly 75 institutions in the state of Ohio and beyond. The development of the Ohio Learning Network's (OLN) statewide faculty learning community program was created based on the question, "How could a state agency best work with campuses across the state on faculty development efforts that would result in pedagogically robust and technologically advanced programs, courses, modules and learning objects…?" (Hansen, Kalish, Hall, Gynn, Holly & Madigan, 2004). The answer to their question was the development of faculty learning communities.

A benefit to the OLN was that it already had a wealth of people invested in faculty learning communities thanks to the pioneering of FLCs at Miami University of Ohio. However, they wished to develop more communities and decided to accept members from outside of the state of Ohio if they were interested. Funding was available through grants, and people were recruited through an application process. The OLN hoped that each community, that would have eight to twelve members, would be made up of faculty, librarians, instructional designers, students, teachers, and members of the community (Hansen et al., 2004). Those who wanted to apply would have a project in mind that their FLC would work on during a specific period of time. After the groups were chosen, twenty-three institutions were involved. To get them started, OLN offered five themed learning institutes that assisted the FLCs. Those themes were: Collaborating, Improving Our Teaching, Preparing Future Teachers, Building and Assessing Sharable Content, and Supporting Student Learning (Hansen et al., p. 75).

What the OLN planners discovered that could help other institutions that might attempt something similar is that it is imperative that institutions show commitment to faculty growth and development as well as make sure each FLC has specific goals that align with the goals of the institution (Hansen et al.). They also offered that having a facilitator of each FLC, as a leader of

the group, was particularly crucial, even if that person has never been in a FLC before. They found that the campuses were much stronger due to their FLCs and the knowledge gained through their collaborative inquiry, and active learning.

Problems and Potential Solutions

A few issues that affect an institution's ability to create a sustainable professional development for its online faculty are the disconnect sometimes seen between university administrators and distance learning leaders, lack of faculty buy-in for professional development, finding faculty leaders, faculty distance from campus, and technology. Institutional administrators might view professional development programs as an additional cost when their budgets are already strained. Husmann and Miller (2001) discovered that administrators of distance learning programs realize that their largest investment should be in their faculty as the quality of the programs is distinctly related to the level of faculty performance. The financial discussion can be problematic, especially if the professional development program is not obviously cost effective.

Institutions might not realize that their own faculty members might have the knowledge and skills to deliver workshops for their peers. This direct participation not only decreases cost, but also increases faculty buy-in and support of a new program. Professional development not only helps individual faculty members, but also benefits the institution because its faculty is more skilled, adaptable, and motivated (Milligan, 1999). It is possible for the director of online learning to seek the faculty members who teach online and request their support for a faculty-drive and faculty-delivered program.

Another issue is the distance between the instructors and the institution. This might not be problematic for institutions that have faculty on campus who just happen to teach online; however, many campuses hire online faculty from different states, and even different countries. In this situation, providing virtual professional development opportunities is the answer. After all, professional development is successful when it is continuous and provided in the environment where the faculty members work, which is online (SREB, 2009). Even if instructors are in different locations, they can be asked to deliver workshops through a synchronous tool; this will keep them involved, connected, and appreciated.

In terms of developing a community of practice, it can be very challenging to gather a collective group of faculty members to initiate the process, who feel strongly about the scholarship of teaching and the necessity of reflection and change (Saroyen, et al., 2004). It is absolutely necessary to the success of an institution's community of practice that fully involved members are dedicated to its cause and to bringing in new faculty members (Blanton & Stylianou, 2006). In order to solve this issue, someone on campus who has a positive rapport with the faculty should make efforts to recruit participants for the community of practice or the FLC. If professional development opportunities are offered regularly, and certain faculty members tend to participate often, perhaps those faculty members should be recruited. Care should be taken to include faculty members who are dedicated to teaching excellence and sharing what they know with others.

Besides finding faculty leaders, institutions need to ensure that faculty members have adequate resources to teach online and integrate technology into their courses (Axley, 2008). If instructors have outdated computers, and lack modern software that students might need to learn, then their efforts to teach online and integrate innovative technologies might be affected. If budgets are strained, it would be beneficial to develop a plan to replace equipment where it is needed most. In addition, faculty or staff can apply for grants to assist in updating hardware and software, or find creative solutions to the issue.

The last area is both a potential problem as well as a future trend. Technology is accelerating so quickly that it is difficult for technologists to keep up; therefore, faculty and institutions face a dilemma about how to handle a "moving target" that is technology (McLoughlin, Chen Wang, & Beasley, 2008). After all, students are learning material, even technologies that will be outdated before they graduate. New technologies develop, and some institutions have been so slow to adopt that they are resistant and behind 'the times' (Barone, 2001). The problem is that integrating technology requires training and support, which is a professional development issue. If faculty are resisting, and the institution is already behind, implementing change can be daunting as faculty can see using additional technology as adding more work for them (McLoughlin et al.).

This problem might never be solved, especially if technology keeps moving quicker as the years pass. New faculty who are hired might bring with them comfort and interest in technology as well as skill since they might have been raised with computers, smart phones, and other forms of technology that they use regularly. Having a younger faculty population will eventually ease the frustration as they will not resist technology, but rather embrace it. Until then, however, faculty developers should introduce technology strategically, and make sure that faculty members fit the right technology with their teaching styles so that they will be more likely to experiment (Finley & Hartman, 2004). This will take knowing who the faculty members are as well as how they teach, and it will take support from a department on a consistent basis.

FUTURE TRENDS

One of the most significant trends that can affect professional development for online faculty is the changing demographics of the students. Students who attend college are, for the most part, technologically savvy and prefer to be "tuned in" to technology and use it fairly constantly (Oblinger, Barone, & Hawkins, 2001). They want to learn by doing, do not prefer to learn passively, and are more comfortable typing than writing (Oblinger et al.). Students are demanding learning that fits into their lifestyles, and because of that, online learning is going to grow substantially. That means that professional development needs to stay aware of trends, and serve the needs of students because the trend is that students will "shop around" to find a program that fits their needs, and traditional institutions can lose students if they do not respond (Bates, 2000).

Unfortunately, the economy is likely to affect professional development programs across the world, and while budgets might be cut, institutions will need to find creative ways to respond while maintaining an effective program for their faculty members. One way of responding is to use the institution's faculty as a key resource. As mentioned previously, institutions can seek their faculty members and have their talents highlighted in workshops and presentations on campus or online. This is a cost-effective solution that can benefit the campus immensely. Not only is the faculty member sharing his or her skills, but also the process of faculty-delivered professional development could help or sustain a community of practice. This could be a trend, as the economy remains fragile and uncertain.

A study of nearly six hundred faculty and administrators by Kim and Bonk (2006) revealed some predictions about the future of online education, and several of those predictions affect professional development. The respondents predicted that the use of learning management systems will increase significantly in the next 5 to 10 years as will the use of streaming video, and online testing (Kim & Bonk). In terms of content delivery, they predicted that reusable learning objects and wireless technologies will have the most drastic impact for online learning.

What was found to have the most effect on faculty adoption and success in online learning was monetary support; what rated second was pedagogical competency (Kim & Bonk), which is an area that was discussed significantly in this chapter.

The top five trends for the skills needed in the future to teach online effectively were predicted to be, in order of rating are: (a) course developer, (b) learning facilitator, (c) subject-matter expert, (d) instructor, and (e) student counselor/advisor (Kim & Bonk, 2006). In terms of pedagogical skills and approaches, the participants in Kim and Bonk's study responded that collaborative learning, problem-based learning (PBL), and case-based learning would be the most preferred methods for instructing in the next 10 years. The indications for professional development point towards increasing faculty skills as course developers, facilitators of student learning (versus deliverers of learning). Furthermore, increasing their comfort with and knowledge of collaborative learning strategies, PBL, and case-based learning will be necessary.

CONCLUSION

Further research needs to be explored in terms of what makes professional development programs sustainable, especially in difficult economic times. In addition, more research is needed to determine how to best provide for those who mix online and face to face teaching for the same campus. Since hybrid, or blended, instruction has been shown to be the most effective means of delivering learning (United States Department of Education, 2009), efforts should be made to provide specific professional development to this type of teaching.

Overall, since having a "one size fits all" program is unlikely, institutions must work within their means, within their demographics, and within their knowledge base to create a sustainable program that is proactive, supportive, and dynamic.

The focus should be on what the students need and want, as the shift has occurred and students have the attitude of consumers versus passive takers of knowledge (Howell, Williams & Lindsay, 2003). To meet the needs to students and the fiscal demands of states and institutions, developing and sustaining communities of practices and faculty learning communities is suggested. Further, where and if possible, collaborations among institutions can ease the burden, increase participation, and develop strong inter-institutional relationships. Above all, the best investment higher institutions of learning could make for overall optimum productivity is their faculty.

REFERENCES

Allen, I. E., & Seaman, J. (2007). *Online nation: Five years of growth in online learning.* Needham, MA: Sloan Consortium.

Ansah, A. O., Neill, P., & Newton, J. (2011, Spring). Who's on first in distance education? *Online Journal of Distance Learning Administration, 4*(1).

Appana, S. (2008). A review of benefits and limitations of online learning in the context of the student, the instructor, and the tenured faculty. *International Journal on E-Learning, 7*(1), 5–22.

Axley, L. (2008). The integration of technology into nursing curricula: Supporting faculty via the technology fellowship program. *Online Journal of Issues in Nursing, 13*(3).

Barbules, N., & Callister, T. (2000). Universities in transition: The promise and the challenge of new technologies. *Teachers College Record, 102*(2), 271–293. doi:10.1111/0161-4681.00056

Bates, T. (2000). *Distance education in dual mode higher education institutions: Challenges and changes.* Retrieved from http://bates.cstudies.ubc.ca/papers/challengesandchanges.html

Bennett, S., Priest, A., & Macpherson, C. (1999). Learning about online learning: An approach to staff development for university teachers. *Australian Journal of Educational Technology, 15,* 207–221.

Blanton, M. L., & Stylianou, D. A. (2009). Interpreting a community of practice perspective in discipline-specific professional development in higher education. *Innovative Higher Education, 34,* 79–92. doi:10.1007/s10755-008-9094-8

Bower, B. (2001). Distance education: Facing the faculty challenge. *Online Journal of Distance Learning Administration, 4*(11). Retrieved from http://www.westga.edu/~distance/ojdla/summer42/bower42.html

Cox, M. D. (2002). Achieving teaching and learning excellence through faculty learning communities. *Toward the Best in the Academy, 14*(4), 1-3.

Cox, M. D. (2004). Introduction to faculty learning communities. *New Directions for Teaching and Learning, 97,* 5–23. doi:10.1002/tl.129

Craig, E. M. (2007). Changing paradigms: Managed learning environments and Web 2.0. *Campus-Wide Information Systems, 24*(3), 152–161. doi:10.1108/10650740710762185

Cross, K. P. (1998). Why learning communities? Why now? *About Campus, 3*(3), 4–11.

Davis, N. E., & Niederhauser, D. S. (2005). Sociocultural analysis of two cases of distance learning in secondary education. *Education and Information Technologies, 10,* 249–262. doi:10.1007/s10639-005-3006-7

Dede, C. (2005). Planning for neomillennial learning styles. *EDUCAUSE Quarterly, 28*(1). Retrieved from http://net.educause.edu/ir/library/pdf/eqm0511.pdf

Dillenbourg, P., Schneider, D. K., & Synteta, P. (2002). Virtual learning environments. In A. Dimitracopoulou (Ed.), *Proceedings of the 3rd Hellenic Conference "Information & Communication Technologies in Education* (pp. 3-18). Kastaniotis Editions, Greece.

Dykman, C. A., & Davis, C. K. (2008). Online education forum: Part two-teaching online versus teaching conventionally. *Journal of Information Systems, 19*(3), 281–289.

Ehrmann, S. C. (2010, September/October). Taking the long view: Ten recommendations about time, money, technology, and learning. *Change,* (n.d), 16–22. doi:10.1080/00091383.2010.503175

Exter, M. E., Korkmaz, N., Harlin, N. M., & Bichelmeyer, B. A. (2009). Sense of community within a fully online program. *The Quarterly Review of Distance Education, 10*(2), 177–194.

Fenwick, T. (2008). Workplace learning: Emerging trends and new perspectives. *New Directions for Adult and Continuing Education, 119,* 17–26. doi:10.1002/ace.302

Finley, L., & Hartman, D. (2004). Institutional change and resistance: Teacher preparatory faculty and technology integration. *Journal of Technology and Teacher Education, 12,* 319–337.

Frankman, M. (2004). The developers' apprentices. In Saroyan, A., & Amundsen, C. (Eds.), *Rethinking teaching in higher education* (pp. 153–167). Sterling, VA: Stylus.

Glowa, E. (2009, March). *Guidelines for professional development of online teachers.* Southern Regional Education Board. Retrieved from http://publications.sreb.org/2009/09T01_Guide_profdev_online_teach.pdf

Greenberg, G. (1998). Distance education technologies: Best practices for K-12 settings. *IEEE Technology and Society Magazine,* (Winter): 36–40. doi:10.1109/44.735862

Hansen, S., Kalish, A., Hall, W. E., Gynn, C. M., Holly, M. L., & Madigan, D. (2004, Spring). Developing a statewide faculty learning community program. *New Directions for Teaching and Learning,* (n.d), 97.

Henri, F., & Pudelko, B. (2003). Understanding and analyzing activity and learning in virtual communities. *Journal of Computer Assisted Learning, 19,* 472–487. doi:10.1046/j.0266-4909.2003.00051.x

Howell, S. L., Williams, P. B., & Lindsay, N. K. (2003, Fall). Thirty-two trends affecting distance education: An informed foundation for strategic planning. *Online Journal of Distance Learning Administration, 6*(3).

Hutchins, H. (2003, Fall). Instructional immediacy and the seven principles: Strategies for facilitating online courses. *Online Journal of Distance Learning Administration, 6*(3). Retrieved from http://www.westga.edu/~distance/ojdla/fall63/hutchins63.html

Ingram, A. (2005). Kent State offers learning communities for online instructors. *Distance Education Report, 9*(13), 8.

Kim, K., & Bonk, C. (2006). The future of online teaching and learning in higher education: The survey says. *EDUCAUSE Quarterly, 29*(4), 22–30.

King, K. P. (2002). Educational technology professional development as transformative learning opportunities. *Computers & Education, 39,* 283–297. doi:10.1016/S0360-1315(02)00073-8

Kosak, L., Manning, D., Dobson, E., Rogerson, L., Cotnam, S., Colaric, S., & McFadden, C. (2004, Spring). Prepared to teach online? Perspectives of faculty in the University of North Carolina System. *Online Journal of Distance Learning Administration, 7*(3). Retrieved from http://www.westga.edu/~distance/ojdla/fall73/kosak73.html

Lave, J., & Wenger, E. (1991). *Situated learning: Legitimate peripheral participation.* Cambridge, UK: University of Cambridge Press.

Lawler, P., & King, K. (2001, March). *Refocusing faculty development: The view from an adult learning perspective.* Paper presented at the Pennsylvania Adult and Continuing Education Research Conference, Indiana, PA.

Lawler, P. A. (2003, Summer). Teachers as adult learners: A new perspective. In K. P. King & P. A. Lawler (Eds.), New directions for adult and continuing education (pp. 15–22). San Francisco, CA: Jossey-Bass. doi:10.1002/ace.95doi:10.1002/ace.95

Lesser, E. L., & Storck, J. (2001). Communities of practice and organizational performance. *IBM Systems Journal, 40*(4). Retrieved from http://www.research.ibm.com/journal/sj/404/lesser.html doi:10.1147/sj.404.0831

Levy, S. (2003). Six factors to consider when planning online distance learning programs in higher education. *Online Journal of Distance Learning Administration, 6*(1). Retrieved from http://www.westga.edu/~distance/ojdla/spring61/levy61.htm

Lewis, C. C., & Abdul-Hamid, H. (2006). Implementing effective online teaching practices: Voices of exemplary faculty. *Innovative Higher Education, 31*(2), 83–98. doi:10.1007/s10755-006-9010-z

Marienau, C., & Reed, C. (2008). Educator as designer: Balancing multiple teaching perspectives in the design of community based learning for adults. *New Directions for Adult and Continuing Education, 118,* 61–74. doi:10.1002/ace.296

McCarthy, S., & Samors, R. (2009). *Online learning as a strategic asset, Vol. 1: A resource for campus leaders.* Washington, DC: Association of Public and Land-Grant Universities. Retrieved from http://www.aplu.org/NetCommunity/Document.Doc?id=1877

McFarlane, D. A. (2011, Spring). The leadership roles of distance learning administrators (DLAs) in increasing educational value and quality perceptions. *Online Journal of Distance Learning Administration, 4*(1).

McLoughlin, J. A., & Wang, L.-C. C. (2008). Transforming the college through technology: A change of culture. *Innovative Higher Education, 33,* 99–109. doi:10.1007/s10755-008-9065-0

McQuiggan, C. (2007). The role of faculty development in online teaching's potential to question teaching beliefs and assumptions. *Online Journal of Distance Learning Administration, 5*(3). Retrieved from http://www.westga.edu/~distance/ojdla/fall103/mcquiggan103.htm

Meyer, K. A. (2003). The web's impact on student learning. *T.H.E. Journal, 30*(10), 14.

Nicolle, P. S., & Lou, Y. (2008). Technology adoption into teaching and learning by mainstream university faculty: A mixed methodology study revealing the "how, when, why, and why not.". *The Journal of Educational Research, 39*(3), 235–265.

North Central Association of Colleges and Schools, Higher Learning Commission. (2007). *Best practices for electronically offered degree and certificate programs.* Retrieved from http://www.ncahlc.org/download/Best_Pract_DEd.pdf

Oblinger, D., Barone, C. A., & Hawkins, B. L. (2001). *Distributed education and its challenges: An overview.* American Council on Education (ACE). Retrieved from http://www.acenet.edu/bookstore/pdf/distributed-learning/distributed-learning-01.pdf

Orr, R., Williams, M. R., & Pennington, K. (2009). Institutional efforts to support faculty in online teaching. *Innovative Higher Education, 34*, 257–268. doi:10.1007/s10755-009-9111-6

Padavano, D., & Gould, M. (2004, December). Best practices for faculty who teach online. *DEOSNews, 13*(9). Retrieved from http://www.ed.psu.edu/acsde/deos/deosnews/deosnews13_9.pdf

Parscal, T., & Riemer, D. (2010, Summer). Assuring quality in large-scale online course development. *Online Journal of Distance Learning Administration, 13*(2).

Renes, S. L., & Strange, A. T. (2011). Using technology to enhance higher education. *Innovative Higher Education, 36*, 203–213. doi:10.1007/s10755-010-9167-3

Richlin, L., & Cox, M. D. (2004). Developing scholarly teaching and the scholarship of teaching and learning through faculty learning communities. *New Directions for Teaching and Learning, 97*, 127–135. doi:10.1002/tl.139

Santovec, M. L. (2004, October 15). Training the people who train the teachers. *Distance Education Report,* (pp. 3-6). Retrieved from http://www.magnapubs.com/newsletter/issue/444/

Saroyen, A., Amundsen, C., McAlpine, L., Weston, C., Winer, L., & Gandell, T. (2004). Assumptions underlying workshop activities. In Saroyen, A., & Amundsen, C. (Eds.), *Rethinking teaching in higher education* (pp. 15–29). Sterling, VA: Stylus.

Schneckenberg, D. (2009). Understanding the real barriers to technology-enhanced innovation in higher education. *Educational Research, 51*(4), 411–424. doi:10.1080/00131880903354741

Schwen, T. M., & Hara, N. (2003). Community of practice: A metaphor for online design? *The Information Society, 19*, 257–270. doi:10.1080/01972240309462

Serdiukov, P., Niederhauser, D., & Reynolds, R. (2000, February). *Teachers' distance professional development and support model.* Paper presented at the Society for Information Technology & Teacher Education International in San Diego, CA. (ERIC Document Reproduction Service No. ED444497)

Sherer, P. (2005). Web-based technology improves faculty development. *Academic Leader, 21*(1), 2–8.

Shrivastava, P. (1999, December). Management classes as online learning communities. *Journal of Management Education, 23*, 691–702. doi:10.1177/105256299902300607

Shulman, G. M., Cox, M. D., & Richlin, L. (2004). Institutional considerations in developing a faculty learning community program. *New Directions for Teaching and Learning, 97*, 41–49. doi:10.1002/tl.131

Smith, M. K. (2003). Communities of practice. *The Encyclopedia of Informal Education.* Retrieved from http://www.infed.org/biblio/communities_of_practice.htm

Stover, C. (2005, April 15). The four stages of faculty development at Empire State. *Distance Education Report,* 3-6. Retrieved from http://www.magnapubs.com/newsletter/issue/498/

Tabata, L. N., & Johnsrud, L. K. (2008). The impact of faculty attitudes toward technology, distance education, and innovation. *Research in Higher Education, 49,* 625–646. doi:10.1007/s11162-008-9094-7

Trenton, G. (2006). The Xanadu project: Training faculty in the use of information and communication technology for university teaching. *Journal of Computer Assisted Learning, 22,* 182–196. doi:10.1111/j.1365-2729.2006.00168.x

US Department of Education. Office of Post-secondary Education. (2006). *Evidence of quality in distance education programs drawn from interviews with the accreditation community.* Retrieved from http://www.ysu.edu/accreditation/Resources/Accreditation-Evidence-of-Quality-in-DE-Programs.pdf

US Department of Education. Office of Planning, Evaluation, and Policy Development Policy and Program Studies Service. (2010). *Evaluation of evidence-based practices in online learning: A meta-analysis and review of online learning studies.* Retrieved from http://www.ed.gov/about/offices/list/opepd/ppss/reports.html#edtech

Valentine, D. (2002, Fall). Distance learning: Promises, problems, and possibilities. *Online Journal of Distance Learning Administration, 5*(3).

Varvel, V. (2007, Spring). Master online teaching competencies. *Online Journal of Distance Learning Administration, 10*(1). Retrieved from http://www.westga.edu/~distance/ojdla/spring101/varvel101.htm

Velez, A. M. (2010). Creating and sustaining virtual communities of practice by operationalizing constructs of preparation, collegiality, and professional development. *UMI ProQuest Dissertations & Theses.* (UMI No: 3409364)

Wang, H. (2009). Best practices: Preparing faculty for online teaching. In I. Gibson, et al. (Eds.), *Proceedings of Society for Information Technology & Teacher Education International Conference 2009* (pp. 1339-1343). Chesapeake, VA: AACE.

Weaver, D., Robbie, D., & Borland, R. (2008). The practitioner's model: Designing a professional development program for online teaching. *International Journal on E-Learning, 7,* 759–774.

Wolf, P. (2006). Best practices in the training of faculty to teach online. *Journal of Computing in Higher Education, 17*(2), 47–78. doi:10.1007/BF03032698

KEY TERMS AND DEFINITIONS

Communities of Practice: Communities of Practice are formed when individuals who have a shared interest or concern gather as a group and collaborate about the shared interest.

E-Learning Community: People who interact entirely online, through an online class, or other online community, can form an e-learning community. Within the community the participants share experiences, develop relationships, and could collaborate on projects.

Experiential Learning: Experiential learning is a mode of learning discussed by David Kolb and other educational theorists. This mode of learning is indicated by direct experience, or learning by doing.

Faculty Learning Communities: Faculty learning communities are groups of faculty members from various disciplines who meet and work on issues or projects for a specific period of time at an educational institution.

Chapter 12
Teaching in the Digital Age:
Preparation for the Successful Teaching of an Online Course in Teacher Education

Kate Thornton
Victoria University of Wellington, New Zealand

Brenda Service
Victoria University of Wellington, New Zealand

Louise Starkey
Victoria University of Wellington, New Zealand

ABSTRACT

The shift to teaching online is not straightforward, and faculty new to online teaching needed to be adequately prepared and supported to ensure quality courses and successful student learning outcomes. This chapter outlines both the theoretical and practical influences that informed the teaching of a successful online course. These elements are reflected on and analysed in order to provide recommendations for future professional learning programmes. These recommendations include encouraging faculty members to reflect on their beliefs and values, helping motivate them to make the necessary changes to their teaching practice, ensuring that they are informed about digital age learning theory, and providing ongoing support for both the pedagogical and practical aspects of online teaching.

INTRODUCTION

The turbulence created by trying to link pedagogy, technology and learner needs in online teaching in higher education has been described as a 'perfect storm' (Kim & Bonk, 2006). Given that most faculty have significant face-to-face teaching responsibilities, publishing expectations and supervision responsibilities, what will motivate them to invest time and energy in the professional learning needed to develop effective online teaching? Some faculty may consider the time, difficulty, and trauma to be too high a personal cost and be resistant to significant change. Others

DOI: 10.4018/978-1-4666-1963-0.ch012

may relish the challenges involved in shifting their teaching practice to better suit the online environment and teaching in a digital age. This chapter will present the influences both theoretical and practical that informed the design and teaching of an online initial teacher education course in a New Zealand tertiary setting. These influences include: the lecturers' beliefs and values around effective teaching practices; feedback from students in the initial teacher education programme; two of the authors' doctoral studies, in teaching and learning for the digital age, and the use of blended action learning to support professional development; and involvement in a Faculty Digital Technology Working Party. The three authors will share how they developed their online course so that content was not 'delivered', rather the learning activities were underpinned with pedagogical approaches aligned with learning theory relevant in a digital age. Although the faculty involved in this teaching did not take part in any formal professional development process, their experiences can be used to inform future professional learning experiences for faculty teaching online.

The objectives of this chapter are to:

- Present a model of learning in the digital age and provide examples of each aspect
- Present the experiences of faculty involved in a teaching successful online course
- Analyse the factors supporting this effective teaching experience
- Identify elements of effective professional learning experiences for faculty teaching online

The chapter will begin by setting the context and describing the relevant online course. This will be followed by a review of the literature that informed the way the course was taught. A pedagogical model for the digital age underpinned by connectivism which incorporates critical and creative thinking, collaborative learning, making connections, and the development of conceptual understanding will be outlined and linked to aspects of this course. The lecturers' preparation and their online teaching experience will be described and student feedback on the teaching and the learning will be incorporated. How the professional learning from this development process has been shared across the university setting to influence how faculty teach in other online courses will also be described. The chapter will conclude with implications for future research and practice.

BACKGROUND

The course that is focus of this chapter is the final course in a one year online graduate diploma of teaching programme in a New Zealand university. There were 138 students in the course, entitled The Teacher in Context, and all were training to be early childhood, primary or secondary teachers. The objectives for this course included: demonstrating an understanding of the impact that contextual factors have on teaching and learning; critically reflecting upon their identities as teachers and understand the impact this has on their practice; and demonstrating an understanding of the ethical, professional, moral aspects of teachers' work and the legal requirements with which teachers work. Although the course had been available on campus the previous year, 2010 was the first year it has been offered online. Feedback from the students in previous courses in the programme had not been positive and therefore the Associate Dean of primary and secondary education, set up a Digital Technology Working Party to address student concerns and to help ensure the online learning environment for this final course was underpinned with digital age learning theory. Involvement in this working party and reflection on their values and beliefs around effective teaching and learning encouraged the two lecturers responsible for teaching the course (Thornton & Service) to carefully consider how their online teaching could reflect these values and beliefs.

Beliefs around Teaching and Learning for the Digital Age Underpinning the Course Design

Both constructivist and connectivist learning theory informed the design and teaching of this course. Educationalists have recently been examining and debating learning theory that may provide an appropriate framework for the digital age (Starkey, 2011; Brown, 2006; Mishra & Koehler, 2008;). Constructivist theory advocates for the construction rather than the transmission of knowledge, and is informed by the belief that learning is an active process that involves engagement in meaningful tasks and includes consideration of multiple perspectives (Orland-Barack, 2005). However, pedagogical models developed before the digital age may not reflect universal access to existing and emerging ideas and the ability to interact and develop knowledge collaboratively through digital media.

Societies change over time through events, innovations and evolving ideologies. Technological revolutions have profoundly changed society in the past. The introduction of digital technologies and related infrastructure could signify the commencement of an era similar to that experienced during the industrial revolution. Pedagogical beliefs during the industrial age were underpinned by a positivist epistemology. The belief that some greater force designed the universe meant that the researcher's mission was to discover the 'truth'. This truth was what learners learnt through formal education so that they could understand society and the world in which they live. The written word was an ideal way of recording the truth and books were an important educational resource.

The importance of books for learning within a positivist epistemology is reflected in the writing of John Dewey (1920) who believed it was important for everyone in a democratic society to be able to understand symbols and text. He was a proponent of universal access to schooling so that the next generation could learn what the previous generation knew. Dewey believed that the purpose of school was to ensure that society did not regress to '*barbarism*', the next generation could not learn through an apprentice/mentoring model (he noted this was what 'savages' used), but needed to master the 'symbols of knowledge' (reading, writing and arithmetic). He advocated for everyone in society to gain this knowledge through education. The importance of the book as being the place where knowledge or the truth is learnt in the industrial age influenced the perspective of effective pedagogical approaches. Effective pedagogy included the transmission of the content through sequential learning activities that scaffolded the learners enabling them to understand prescribed skills and knowledge. Examinations were an effective way of testing whether the learners had attained the prescribed learning objectives.

The industrial age provides a comparison for consideration of effective pedagogy in the digital age. The digital age began with the development of digital technologies and supporting infrastructure. Like the industrial age, there have been a series of related innovations which appear to be significantly altering how communities, nations and societies function and interact. The changes and innovations are likely to continue to occur over decades and the way that teaching and learning occurs and perspectives of effective pedagogy will evolve.

In the digital age information is widely available and people are able to instantly communicate globally. Knowledge is not perceived as being restricted to books, academics, and religious leaders. Varying perspectives are recognized about what is 'known' and knowledge can be critiqued, debated and developed across societies. The ability to communicate instantly to share documents, simulations, models, and ideas with a collaborative group, audience, or peer enables the development of knowledge through these global connections. The speed of knowledge development is such that by the time a book is published, aspects may have been superseded or revised within the cyber communities of learners or researchers. The epistemological beliefs about knowledge and learning in the digital age will contrast with those in the industrial age because of instant access to information and global communication networks.

Connectivism aims to provide a theory which considers how people, organisations and technology can collaboratively construct knowledge. The theory builds on ideas that have emerged since the introduction of widespread interaction and access to information through the internet and is underpinned by complexity theory. Siemens developed 'connectivism' as a learning theory for the digital age. Siemens (2004) describes connectivism as:

The integration of principles explored by chaos, network, and complexity and self-organization theories. Learning is a process that occurs within nebulous environments of shifting core elements – not entirely under the control of the individual. Learning (defined as actionable knowledge) can reside outside of ourselves (within an organization or a database), is focused on connecting specialized information sets, and the connections that enable us to learn more are more important than our current state of knowing. (paragraph 21)

A learning theory for the digital age should consider learning as a continual process within a complex environment rather than an event. A central idea in the learning theory of connectivism is the continual expansion of knowledge as new and novel connections open new interpretations and understandings to create new knowledge. Effective pedagogies in the digital age will be influenced by epistemological beliefs such as those underpinning connectivist and constructivist learning theories and include the opportunity for learners to be in control of the learning process.

Weistra (2000) describes the content dimension of online e-learning as either being offered by the instructor in a structured manner or presented in a way that could be explored by the learner. Analysis of the programme in the graduate diploma found

that the content in previous online courses had been highly structured. This method was more consistent with an acquisition- orientated model than with a contribution-orientated one as described by de Boer and Collis (2002). Acquisition orientated courses are those constructed to transmit knowledge. Contribution orientated courses are those in which learners contribute to the learning materials with others, the learners and the instructor co-construct the learning, learners learn from realistic materials, and the instructor designs activities and provides feedback and monitoring.

Acquisition orientated courses appear to be common in the E-learning environment. de Boer and Collis (2002) cite a study carried out by Mioduser and Nachmias in which 500 educational websites were examined. It was found that most involved acquisition processes, that there was little evidence of higher learning skills, and that only 3% supported any sort of collaborative learning. Feedback was also scarce with automatic feedback measured at 16.3% and human feedback 5.5%. A study by Bonk (2002) in a tertiary environment found that 'online activities such as online simulations, data analyses, laboratories, performances, and critical and creative thinking were ranked as highly important by more than 40 percent of the respondents. However, actual use ranged from 23 percent to 45 percent.' (p.16). The most sought after online instructional activities by the participants in his study were those meant to foster student critical and creative thinking.

The student preference for critical and creative thinking aligns with ideas about effective pedagogies in a digital age learning environment. Learners need the capacity to analyse and critique the diverse range of information available to consider the value of that information to their learning progress. In the industrial age the content of what was learnt was considered the truth, therefore critical thinking involved considering whether something was true of false (such as hypothesis testing). Evaluating information remains important in the digital age where the learner will consider the perspectives being presented, origins of ideas, clarity, and accuracy of information. Effective digital age learners also self-critique their learning progress through the application of metacognitive strategies and use critical thinking to explore the boundaries of concepts and skills (Starkey, 2011).

Creative thought is a second aspect underpinning effective pedagogy in the digital age. Learners connect ideas and explore possibilities to create and share knowledge within a society where knowledge creation occurs through connections and there is open access to participate (Starkey, 2011). Within a learning programme students not only master concepts and skills but also mesh together different ideas to create knowledge and consider what they have learnt within different contexts.

Effective pedagogy in the digital age will incorporate collaboration and learning through connections. Knowledge creation occurs through connections between ideas and skills, people, experiences, and technology (Seimens, 2004). Digital age learners share knowledge they create through networks. This collaboration and the sharing of critical feedback on ideas informs the learners' learning progress. Students not only collaborate with their peers but also make connections with experts, resources, or people with similar study interests beyond the learning environment.

Effective pedagogy in the digital age will include mastery of concepts and skills relevant to the learning programme. Understanding of the key concepts, beliefs and methods that inform a body of knowledge gives digital age students the building blocks for knowledge creation. Students construct understanding based on their prior understanding and the information they interact with through processes underpinned within constructivist learning theory. A programme in the digital age does not limit learning to prescribed concepts and skills, but has open ended aims which encourage course designers and students to develop knowledge and explore the possibilities within the context of their learning. Teaching in the digital age is about the learner's critique and creation of knowledge rather than transmission or delivery of knowledge (Starkey, 2010).

Effective pedagogies in the digital age differ from those in the industrial age as the availability and beliefs about the creation of knowledge have altered due to technological and social innovations. Table 1 compares some of these ideas in the industrial age with the digital age.

Table 1. Comparison of ideas underpinning pedagogies in the industrial and digital ages

	Industrial age	Digital age
Epistemological beliefs about knowledge	Positivism; Knowledge develops as scholars discover the truth. This is shared or learnt through presentations or books.	Connectivism; Knowledge develops or evolves through connections. What is thought to be known is revised and developed.
Critical thinking	Used to evaluate the truth or find the right answer (e.g. hypothesis testing).	Used to evaluate and explore possibilities. Critique learning progress, ideas, and skills.
Creative thought	To create representations of what is known.	Connecting of ideas, concepts, perspectives, and skills to develop new possibilities.
Collaboration and connections	Individual connecting their knowledge and experiences with concepts and skills being learnt.	Collaboration within and beyond the learning environment through connections which may be digitally enabled.
Mastery of concepts and skills	Mastery of concepts and skills of what is 'known'.	Mastery of skills and concepts key to the learning programme, exploring different perspectives and boundaries of these, and possibly developing them further.

Learning theory for the digital age would therefore consider how knowledge has been developing since the introduction of widespread interaction and access to information through the internet. Connectivism is a theory aiming to provide a basis for examining how multiple aspects of knowledge creation interact and evolve (Siemens, 2004). A central idea in the learning theory of connectivism is the continual expansion of knowledge as new and novel connections open new interpretations and understandings to create new knowledge. Knowledge creation thus becomes a continual process within a complex environment rather than an event. Connectivist learning theory considers how people, organizations (such as universities) and technology make connections through which knowledge is constructed. Constructivist learning theory provides a means to understand how individuals develop their personal knowledge base.

A focus on learning in a digital age necessitates a change in approach from faculty involved in teaching in both campus- based and online courses. So how can faculty be supported to prepare for this different way of teaching and learning? The following section of the chapter will present the experiences of the two lecturers involved in this course. It will also link this experience to relevant literature that helps makes sense of the experience.

The Faculty Experience

Teachers are the key influence on and designers of a learning experience, therefore their beliefs and practices are critical in the process of educational change. Senge et al. (2000) emphasise the importance of a teacher's personal mental models to their practice, and outline how changes to mental models might occur. While not much is known about the ways and to what extent teachers really change or develop their beliefs research literature suggests that teachers can change with the influence of credible colleagues and if they can see that the change will help them achieve their

valued goals (Beijaard & De Vries, 1997). Teachers typically invest heavily in their work with the goal of helping students to achieve success (Schmidt & Datnow, 2005). In the context of educational change in the digital age, significant change in learning processes and outcomes for the learners is most likely to occur when teachers align their teaching practice with digital age learning theories which are embedded within their mental models.

Teachers, like students, bring to any learning situation a range of prior knowledge and experiences that influences how they respond to new information. Their schemata are persistent and resistant to change and therefore play a key role in how information is assimilated and accommodated. Teachers therefore make sense of any innovation through the lens of their existing cognitive structures (Timperley, 2008; Spillane, Reiser & Reimer, 2002). Most teachers develop their cognitive structures throughout their careers (Beijaard & De Vreis, 1997). These ideas are a blend of personal beliefs, dispositions, practical knowledge and educational theories mediated by interpretation of their experiences (Assaf, 2008; Briscoe, 1991; von Glaserfeld, 1989; Schmidt & Datnow, 2005). This blend forms an 'encyclopaedia of personal knowledge' (Duffee & Aikenhead, 1992). It is these ideas or personal pedagogy which need to be understood if change is to take place (Cuban, 1995; Spillane et al., 2002). It has been suggested that teachers do not like change particularly if considering ideas radically different from those that they hold (Hyslop-Margison & Strobel, 2008).

The challenge for the faculty involved in the course this chapter is based on was to consider how their constructivist beliefs and practices could be transferred to their online teaching. This involved creating a new vision of themselves as online teachers consistent with that of their face-to-face teaching, and projecting themselves into that image (Briscoe, 1991). The lecturers in this instance felt a discrepancy between current practices in the online environment as evidenced by critical feedback from the students who would be in their course on their current experiences of online teaching. This student feedback was disturbing and had an emotional impact on the lecturers. This part of the learning process felt at times like being battered by a storm. Good teaching is charged with positive emotion (Hargreaves, 2005). Good teachers aren't just well oiled machines. The lecturers were passionate about ideas, learning and their relationships with students. The feedback therefore did not fit with their image of themselves as teachers. While images of teaching constructed from years of experience as students and as teachers, cannot be changed on words alone (Briscoe, 1991), the emotional response to the feedback was a motivating force and made them open to change.

The situation facing the lecturers was filtered through their personal knowledge and their beliefs about teaching and learning beliefs (Duffee & Aikenhead, 1992), their personal professional needs and their moral purpose all of which constructed their vision of themselves as teachers. It is this vision which orientates their practice by providing frames that enables teacher to conceptualise their actions (Nespor, 1984). The feedback from the students led to the lecturers examining their beliefs and thoughts about what they did and why they did it. Reflecting on their face-to-face beliefs and practice and consulting the literature, they recognised that they was framed within a constructivist pedagogical paradigm (Kim 2001; Richardson 2007). Practices evident in the lecturers' face-to-face teaching fitted with the four general categories of indicators representing constructivist practices identified by Partlow and Gibbs (2003). This review of 25 research articles found the following categories: tasks that require higher order thinking; project based learning tasks; collaborative and cooperative small group work; and infrequent use of direct instruction activities. These categories fit well with the digital learning approaches described above and their incorpora-

tion into the course will be described in a later section of the chapter.

The inconsistency between current and ideal practice motivated these faculty members to seek ways to improve their practice. The need for a discrepancy to trigger shifts in practice is discussed by Armenakis, Bernerth, Pitts and Walker (2007) who identified the following five key precursors as the foundation of change models that would indicate a readiness for change.

- **Discrepancy:** A belief that change is needed. For teachers this would involve recognition that current practice is not achieving the desired outcomes.
- **Efficacy:** Teachers believe they are capable of including the changes in their practice
- **Leadership Support:** A confidence that the change is supported by key personnel
- **Appropriateness:** A belief that the implemented changes will work towards eliminating the discrepancy
- **Valence:** Teachers will personally feel the benefits of the change.

The discrepancy precursor has been discussed above; however, the other four precursors were also relevant in this context and will be discussed in the following section. For the lecturers in this study to believe in their own efficacy they knew they would need considerable technical support. Fortunately, as will be discussed below, this was readily available. Leadership support was also evident with the associate dean providing a forum for discussion and exploration, and the resources needed. Guskey (1995), researching change in educational sectors, maintains that teachers are motivated to make changes to their practice if they have evidence that the new practices are beneficial to student learning. His model of change requires teachers to make changes in their practice followed by an evaluation of the impact on student learning. If teachers perceive the changed practice to benefit their students, this will bring about change in their beliefs, which will eventually support embedded change in instructional practice. Carlisle and Baden-Fuller (2004) appear to support Guskey's model. Their study of change in the oil industry found that when employees realised that the required changes benefited the aspects of their work that they valued, they subsequently re-evaluated their response to change. In the situation being discussed the feedback from the students did provide evidence that the changes had benefitted their learning. At the stage of planning the changes valence was aspirational, however the course evaluations, some of which will be presented in a later section of the chapter provided proof of valence for the lecturers.

Leadership support was provided through the establishment of a Digital Technology Working Party which began about 2 months before the course was due to start. This group was made up of the three authors of the chapter as well as two lecturers experienced in online delivery, and publishing centre staff who were helping set up the online learning platform. As previously mentioned the working party was set up because of student feedback from the online cohort, who felt that the graduate diploma of teaching programme was too transmission based and not as interactive as a digital age programme within education should be. It was hoped that by ensuring that the final course was taught effectively and reflected learning in the digital age that the students would be more positive about their online learning experience.

Weekly meetings of the working party, which continued in the semester in which the course was taught, were held to discuss various aspects of online teaching. A new version of Blackboard, 9.2, was being used which offered some new ways of presenting material and the potential uses of this were discussed. Online course material from other faculties within the university was also looked at as part of the working party to see if it would be useful in the teaching of this course. Most of the

strategies used by other courses, such as sending out DVDs with pre-recorded lectures, were rejected because they were based on a transmission learning model and did not fit with the connectivist and constructivist theory that underpinned the lecturers' work. Drafts of the course material were brought to each meeting and discussed. This working party was a very useful part of the preparation for online teaching as over the course of the 2 months, gradual but significant shifts were made in the way the lecturers conceptualised and prepared the course materials. The expertise and differing perspectives of various group members helped to clarify ideas and to motivate faculty members to make the course design innovative and pedagogically sound.

The faculty members' previous experiences and the strong collaborative relationship were also important influences on how they approached the design and teaching of this course. Although author A had not taught a totally online course before, her doctoral research was in the area of blended action learning to support leadership development (Thornton, 2009). Her role in this study combined both research and facilitation as she facilitated a leadership development programme as part of her research. A large focus of this research study was the role of the blended action learning facilitator, a position that included two important and complementary aspects, providing a structure and process that enabled learning and acting as a trusted inquisitor. The enabling learning aspect of the blended action learning facilitator role involved designing and facilitating a structured learning process, motivating and encouraging participants, offering technical support and providing resources. This enabling role provided the platform for meaningful leadership learning to occur and it was the trusted inquisitor role that inspired that process. The main purpose of the trusted inquisitor role was supporting and challenging participants in their leadership learning, twin principles in encouraging honest self-disclosure according to Pedler and Abbott (2008). This role involved a number of complementary facets including building trust, building relationships between participants, providing support, offering leadership expertise, questioning and coaching and role-modelling (Thornton & Yoong, 2011). The role taken in this study influenced Thornton's approach to teaching online as she realised the importance of establishing relationships with students, ensuring they had opportunities to related their learning to their experiences, and encouraging collaboration between students.

Service was also new to online teaching. In her teaching she sought strategies to promote the students creative and critical thinking and collaborative practice. She was therefore enthusiastic about investigating online practice that would fit with her beliefs about teaching and learning. The two lecturers had worked together as critical friends to develop their face-to-face practice in several previous courses including the campus based version of 'The Teacher in Context'. This process involved observing each other practice and together analysing and reflecting on its effectiveness. They had therefore developed a trusting professional relationship. Student feedback on their campus based courses was positive and the learning outcomes for students were impressive. It was challenging for them to realise that the online students did not believe their learning needs were being met, hence their willingness to explore new ways of teaching.

Although there was some temptation to try to replicate the course content and format of the course material that had been taught on campus the previous year because of time constraints, the incongruence between this way of teaching and digital learning theory approaches meant that considerable changes had to be made to the material. Instead of lecture and tutorial material, the course content was organised into weekly

learning modules. These modules consisted of a range of visual and oral presentations of key course concepts. Their use and the student reaction to them will be explained in the following section of this chapter.

The Course Design and Student Experience

The course management software Blackboard, version 9.2, was used as the learning platform for this course. A variety of teaching approaches were employed throughout the four weeks the course ran. These different approaches and the reaction of the students to them will be discussed in this section. The student feedback comes from an anonymous online survey completed by students at the end of the course and also from unsolicited forum posting and emails, the inclusion of which the relevant students have consented to.

The course consisted of four learning modules, one to be completed each week of the course. These modules included a variety of different tools that allowed students to develop critical and creative thought, learn collaboratively, make connections within and beyond the learning environment, and to develop conceptual understanding. The first learning module began with introductions from both lecturers explaining their background and explaining the course objectives and format. This was followed by the presentation of an interactive diagram of the course framework. Students were able to click on each area to find an explanation and links to the weekly learning modules. Interacting with this diagram helped students understand the key concepts and skills, how they were connected and where in the course they would be covered. Other material in this and subsequent modules was presented in a variety of ways including recorded multimedia presentations, streaming of guest lectures that had been presented to the campus students, written material, and integrated course readings. Students were also expected to post weekly blogs. The learning module format was appreciated by students as the following comment illustrates:

There was a good balance between written, interactive and visual material in each module which made engaging with the material informative and interesting, and easy to understand.

Having the lecture material specially recorded for the online environment was valued by the students. Comments included that this approach made them feel connected as the following comments show:

Enjoyed the video presentations - put a 'human face' to the 'teachers'; felt more inclusive and added variety to how material was presented.

The material was presented in a great way; I liked how your presentations were not just recordings of a lecture, but personally to us.

The use of the learning module format allowed the integration of the different teaching approaches. While the campus students had an electronic reading list they could access, and attended lectures, tutorial and studio times (scheduled times where they would meet to work on a task without the support of a lecturer or tutor), online students had all these aspects integrated within learning modules. For example when learning about professional identity in the first week of the course, students listened to a recorded presentation, read several relevant articles, completed an interactive values activity, and completed several blog entries, all within one learning module. Students were encouraged to develop critical thought by reflecting on the material presented, linking it to their previous knowledge and answering reflective questions. Creative thought was encouraged by challenging students to explore future trends in teaching and learning and consider how their

role may change in the future. This integration of approaches was appreciated by the students who commented that it allowed them to personalise their learning.

The streamed lectures/mediasite presentations with powerpoints were really helpful. You could pause when you needed to read something or complete a blog, skip ahead if you wanted to - it allowed for learning at one's own pace.

I appreciated that each learning section was concise, and was all there. You did not have to travel between resources, as everything was listed chronologically. This allowed for a great flow of learning.

Different approaches were used in subsequent weeks with some guest presentations given to the campus students recorded and streamed to the online students. The lecturers ensured that extra microphones were available so that the questions and responses from students in the lecture theatre could be heard by the online students. In the case of one presenter, a Youth Law advocate whose session was recorded and streamed, an online forum to which he had access was set up so that students unable to talk to him in person could ask questions and interact. This forum, although optional, was very popular with over 50 posts and helped the students establish connections with experts from the wider community and broaden their perspectives.

I loved the streamed presentations. Helped me feel as if I was part of the lecture rather than working in isolation. I enjoyed hearing all the lecturers' comments and also the students' questions.

Seeing the interaction with the on campus group during these lectures is great, because often the questions you have in your head as you do the lecture online are the ones the on campus students are asking during the lecture!

Overall the variety of approaches, which contrasted with previous courses which were mostly either all streamed or all written documents, was appreciated by the students.

Greatly appreciate the use of a variety of media; it helps maintain interest... All extremely well planned and presented; easy to follow and clear guidelines and instruction.

Perfect mix in this course. I give it 9.5 out of 10.

Great to see a paper actually tailored to online students - all approaches were useful and helped to maintain interest during the process.

Collaborative learning can be a challenge in an online learning environment and the lecturers worked hard to ensure students has multiple opportunities to work together and learn from each other. The students were organized into blog groups based on peer mentoring groups that all students has been allocated to at the beginning of the year. This meant that, with a few exceptions where students had transferred from the campus based course to online, the students were working with others whom they knew and had previously interacted with. The size of these groups ranged from four to eight students which meant that they did not have to read so many other blog postings and that their reflections were more private.

The blog set-up was much easier than the discussion boards we had in other courses, and it was great to be in a group of just 7 or 8 so that we weren't overwhelmed with hundreds of comments to read.

Blogs - I found this was good as it allowed me to edit and add my thoughts throughout the week. I enjoyed the fact that you could add comments to other people's reflections and locate feedback from peers.

Table 2 shows how each of the underpinning ideas about pedagogy in the digital age relate to aims for students, what digital tools could be used, and provides examples from the Teacher in Context course to illustrate how each of approach was used in the course design and teaching.

The preparation of the online course challenged both lecturers to reflect on the effectiveness of teaching in the equivalent on campus course. As a result of the experience of preparing the course to be taught online both lecturers reviewed their lecture material and believed that their face-to-face teaching was more effective because of this experience.

In the case being discussed, the positive feedback to the lecturers after the course provided evidence that the new practices were beneficial to the students. In addition, the student comments confirmed that the way the course was designed and taught fitted with their beliefs about teaching and learning, and that their online teaching was a fit with their image of themselves as teachers.

Dissemination of Learning

Due to the positive feedback from students regarding the teaching of this course, the three authors of this chapter made presentations at both faculty and university level on this experience. A presentation at a university wide seminar on teaching and learning was entitled 'Engaging learners: a pedagogical approach to the use of digital technologies'. This seminar also presented the pedagogical model and examples, and faculty teaching in other disciplines seemed interested in this model and approach. In the faculty level presentation the pedagogical model presented in Table 2 was used as a basis for discussion and various aspects of the course were used to illustrate each of the pedagogical approaches.

It was hoped that this experience would encourage and motivate other faculty members to significantly change the way their online courses were taught. However while training in the new

Table 2. Planning teaching based on ideas about learning in the digital age

Pedagogical approach:	Aim is for students to:	Examples of digital Tools:	Examples from The Teacher in Context
Develop critical thought	Reflect: students consider their previous knowledge and emerging knowledge Consider metacognitive approaches Compare, contrast, evaluate, analyse	Critique of readings (e-reserve), peers, self, resources etc. through a blog, test tools, discussion board or social networking site (guided to be critical),	Why is teaching a profession? Critical thought developed through reflection, probing questions, peer and group discussion.
Develop creative thought	Mash or combine ideas Consider different perspectives Develop, build, representation	Wiki, multimedia presentations developed by students, developing models and representations.	Teaching for the future Exploring trends in teaching and learning and considering how they might teach in a digital, demographically different society.
Collaborative or cooperative learning	Peer critique Share and develop ideas collaboratively Collaborate, discuss,	Blogs, wiki, social networking sites, skype, cellphone, discussion boards, videoconferencing, ICTs.	Puzzles of practice. Putting students into small groups (based on PDM groups) who then work collaboratively through blogs.
Making connections within or beyond the learning environment	Link with experts/peers Synthesise, Connections between student's existing knowledge and pedagogical concepts in the course.	Wiki, ICTs, videolinks (skype, videoconferencing), social networking sites,	Youth law- guest speaker in mediasite presentation and with discussion board question and answer.
Developing conceptual understanding/ mastery	Understand key concepts and skills identified in the learning objectives of the course. Explain, demonstrate, explore,	Web, test tools, Flash diagrams, guided activities, mediasite presentations, readings,	Framework for the course, variety of ways of scaffolding and presenting concepts. Integration of concepts and learning activities in the modules. Regular and timely feedback to students

learning can be offered, engaging the will of those who are expected to implement the change is challenging (McLaughlin, 1987). Kwakman (cited in Van Eekelen, Vermunt & Boshuizen, 2006) took an inventory of the degree of participation in several professional learning activities and found that many teachers do not use opportunities to learn at work. It appears that certain conditions are necessary to support this type of learning. In their syntheses of professional learning that made a difference to teacher practice and subsequently to student learning, Timperley et al., (2007) identified effective contexts including: extended time to learn, external expertise, challenging of prevailing discourses challenged, opportunities to practice in a professional community of practice, coherence with educational policies, and effective leadership (p. xi). While extended time to learn is always a

challenge, in the university external expertise was made available to all lecturers. The team involved with the paper under discussion provided the nucleus of a professional learning community in which lecturers could develop their practice and in which prevailing discourses could be challenged through peer and student feedback.

It remains to be seen whether the professional learning opportunities provided do lead to a change in practice in other faculty members in the context described in this chapter. Despite teachers having access to professional learning there remains a large gap between educational knowledge of effective teaching and learning and actual practice which, in the opinion of some researchers, is the result of teacher resistance to change (Guskey, 1995; Hargreaves, 1997). It could also be because these teachers are not motivated to make the changes because of the lack of discrepancy and efficacy. It is therefore crucial that faculty who do take part in the professional learning to have opportunities to reflect on their values and beliefs, to be made aware of digital age learning theory and to be able to see that the changes made result in benefits to students learning.

Best Practices for Supporting Online Faculty

This section of the chapter analyses the effective elements of the preparation and support provided to faculty for the successful teaching of this new online course. These elements include both personal experiences and motivation, and pedagogical and faculty support.

As previously discussed, support for online faculty will only be beneficial if there is a willingness to learn and to make shifts in thinking and practice. Motivation is the key, with both lecturers involved in teaching this course being enthusiastic and willing to put the time into transforming the course content to fit the online environment. Their critical friend relationship meant that they felt comfortable to take risks and to challenge each other to try new teaching strategies that better suited the online environment. The pedagogical and faculty support was also very important; the digital working party involved participation in a community of learners where ideas could be put forward and discussed. This involves both pedagogical and technical discussions. Support from general staff for some of the technical and interactive components meant that these tasks were shared and that academic staff could focus on the pedagogical rather than technical issues and approaches.

Drawing from this experience we suggest that rather than training programmes, faculty members need opportunities to work in collaborative and supportive partnerships or groups that will encourage them to reflect on and modify their teaching practices. The model of pedagogical approaches

for the digital age described earlier could be a useful framework for encouraging faculty to reflect on their teaching practices. Faculty members also need opportunities to reflect on their values and beliefs around online teaching and learning and how these can be reflected in their courses.

Mentoring relationships with more experienced in online teachers may be a beneficial way of supporting faculty new to online teaching. Mentoring is an enabling process that can encourage transformative learning on the part of the mentee (Brockbank & McGill, 2006). It usually involves modelling and supporting (D'Abate, Eddy & Tannenbaum, 2011). A supportive mentoring relationship would also encourage reflection and allow for faculty to become confident in their online teaching at their own pace. Part of the role of the mentor would be to encourage the faculty new to online teaching to reflect on their beliefs and practices and how these may fit with digital age learning theory.

FUTURE TRENDS

Online teaching and learning is becoming more common, however, are faculty teaching online aware of approaches to teaching that reflect a digital age and are they supported to modify their teaching practices accordingly? Designing and teaching an online course that encourages critical and creative thinking, and supports collaborative learning, making connections, and the development of conceptual understanding will help ensure that students have meaningful learning experiences. Faculty involved in online teaching could find the model of digital age learning theory presented in this chapter a useful framework for reflection on their teaching practice. Once defined, pedagogical approaches, clear aims for students' learning, and examples of digital tools could be showcased to the wider faculty.

The experience outlined in this chapter signals several areas in which further research would be valuable. These include research into how digital age learning theory is incorporated into online courses and whether faculty find this is a useful framework for both designing and teaching; how the prevailing discourses of lecturers can be challenged; and what support will encourage faculty to the implement effective online practice.

CONCLUSION

This chapter has presented the experiences of faculty teaching in a successful online course. These experiences have been linked to constructivist and connectivist learning theory and to pedagogical approaches to digital age learning. Successful online teaching is not a matter of chance and faculty need to be supported to make the necessary shifts in their thinking and practice to ensure student engagement and learning. Enabling students to experience digital age pedagogy involves providing opportunities for critical and creative thinking, collaborations and connections and mastery of concepts and skills. It can be concluded that professional learning that supports faculty to teach online effectively needs to consider and a range of factors and approaches. These include: how to encourage faculty members to reflection on their beliefs and values and to motivate them to make the necessary changes to their teaching practice, how to ensure teaching approaches reflect theory around learning in the digital age, and provides support for both the pedagogical and practical aspects of online teaching.

REFERENCES

Armenakis, A., Bernerth, J., Pitts, J., & Walker, H. (2007). Organizational change recipients' beliefs scale: Development of an assessment instrument. *The Journal of Applied Behavioral Science*, *43*(4), 481–505. doi:10.1177/0021886307303654

Assaf, L. (2008). Professional identity of a reading teacher: Responding to high stakes testing. *Teachers and Teaching:Theory and Practice*, *14*(3), 239–252. doi:10.1080/13540600802006137

Beijaard, D., & De Vries, Y. (1997). Building expertise: a process perspective on the development or change of teachers' beliefs. *European Journal of Teacher Education*, *20*(3), 243–255. doi:10.1080/0261976970200304

Bonk, C. (2002). *Online training in an online world.* Bloomington, IN: CourseShare.com.

Briscoe, C. (1991). The dynamic interactions among beliefs, role metaphors, and teaching practices: A case study of teacher change. *Science Education*, *75*(2), 185–199. doi:10.1002/sce.3730750204

Brockbank, A., & McGill, I. (2006). *Facilitating reflective learning through mentoring and coaching* (pp. 63–92). London, UK: Kogan Page.

Brown, T. (2006). Beyond constructivism: Navigationism in the knowledge era. *Horizon*, *14*(3), 108–120. doi:10.1108/10748120610690681

Carlisle, Y., & Baden-Fuller, C. (2004). Reapplying beliefs: An analysis of change in the oil industry. *Organization Studies*, *25*(6), 987–1019. doi:10.1177/0170840604045093

Cuban, L. (1995). The hidden variable: How organizations influence teacher responses to secondary science curriculum reform. *Reforming Science Education*, *34*(1), 4–11.

D'Abate, E., Eddy, R., & Tannenbaum, S. (2011). What's in a name? A literature-based approach to understanding mentoring, coaching, and other constructs that describe developmental interactions. *Human Resource Development Review*, *2*(4), 360–384. doi:10.1177/1534484303255033

de Boer, W., & Collis, B. (2002). A changing pedagogy in e-learning: From acquisition to contribution. *Journal of Computing in Higher Education*, *13*(2), 87–101. doi:10.1007/BF02940967

Duffee, L., & Aikenhead, G. (1992). Curriculum change, student evaluation, and teacher practical knowledge. *Science Teacher Education, 76*(5), 493–506.

Guskey, T. (1995). *Results-orientated professional development: In search of an optimal mix of effective practice.* NCREL Literature Review. Retrieved from http://www.ncrel.org/sdrs/areas/rpl_esys/pdlitrev.htm

Hargreaves, A. (1997). *Rethinking educational change: going deeper and wider in the quest for success.* Alexandria, VA: Association for Supervision and Curriculum Development.

Hargreaves, A. (2005). Educational change takes ages: Life, career and generational factors in teachers' emotional responses to educational change. *Teaching and Teacher Education, 21*(8), 967–983. doi:10.1016/j.tate.2005.06.007

Hyslop-Margison, E., & Strobel, J. (2008). Constructivism and education: Misunderstandings and pedagogical implications. *Teacher Educator, 43*(1), 72–86. doi:10.1080/08878730701728945

Kim, B. (2001). Social constructivism. In M. Orey (Ed.), *Emerging perspectives on learning, teaching, and technology.* Retrieved from http://projects.coe.uga.edu/epltt/

Kim, K., & Bonk, C. (2006). The future of online teaching and learning in higher education. *EDUCASE Quarterly, 29*(4). Retrieved from http://www.educause.edu/EDUCAUSE+Quarterly/EDUCAUSEQuarterlyMagazineVolum/TheFutureofOnlineTeachingandLe/157426

Mishra, P., & Koehler, M. (2008). *Introducing technological pedagogical content knowledge.* Paper presented at the AERA Annual Meeting, March 2008, New York.

Nespor, J. (1987). The role of beliefs in the practice of teaching. *Journal of Curriculum Studies, 19*(4), 317–328. doi:10.1080/0022027870190403

Orland-Barak, L. (2005). Cracks in the iceberg: Sufacing the tensions of constructivist pedagogy in the context of mentoring. *Teachers and Teachers: Theory and Practice, 11*(3), 293–313.

Partlow, K., & Gibbs, W. (2003). Indicators of constructivist practices in internet-based courses. *Journal of Computing in Higher Education, 14*(2), 68–97. doi:10.1007/BF02940939

Pedler, M., & Abbott, C. (2008). Am I doing it right? Facilitating action learning for service improvement. *Leadership in Health Services, 21*(3), 185–199. doi:10.1108/17511870810893010

Richardson, M. (2007). Constructivism in education: An overview of contributions to the literature and to the JPACTe annotated bibliography. *JPACTe, 2*(1), 1–16.

Richardson, V. (1990). Significant and worthwhile change in teaching practice. *American Educational Research Association, 19*(7), 10–18.

Rowlands, I., Nicholas, D., Huntington, P., Gunter, B., Withey, R., Dobrowolski, T., et al. (2008). *Information behaviour of the researcher of the future.* Retrieved from http://www.jisc.ac.uk/whatwedo/programmes/resourcediscovery/googlegen.aspx

Schmidt, M., & Datnow, A. (2005). Teachers' sense-making about comprehensive school reform: The influence of emotions. *Teaching and Teacher Education, 21*(8), 949–965. doi:10.1016/j.tate.2005.06.006

Senge, P., Cambron-McCabe, N., Lucas, T., Smith, B., Dutton, J., & Kleiner, A. (2000). *Schools that learn. A fifth discipline fieldbook for educators, parents, and everyone who cares about education.* New York, NY: Doubleday/Currency.

Siemens, G. (2004). *Connectivism: A learning theory for the digital age.* Retrieved from http://www.elearnspace.org/Articles/connectivism.htm

Spillane, J., Reiser, B., & Reimer, T. (2002). Policy implementation and cognition: Reframing and refocusing implementation research. *Review of Educational Research, 72*(3), 387–431. doi:10.3102/00346543072003387

Starkey, L. (2010). Teachers' pedagogical reasoning and action in the digital age. *Teachers and Teaching, 16*(2), 233–244. doi:10.1080/13540600903478433

Starkey, L. (2011). Evaluating learning in the 21st century: A digital age learning matrix. *Technology, Pedagogy and Education, 20*(1), 19–39. doi:10.1080/1475939X.2011.554021

Thornton, K. (2009). *Blended action learning: Supporting leadership learning in the New Zealand early childhood education sector.* Unpublished PhD thesis, Victoria University of Wellington, Wellington.

Thornton, K., & Yoong, P. (2011). The role of the blended action learning facilitator: An enabler of learning and a trusted inquisitor. *Action Learning Research and Practice, 8*(12), 129–146. doi:10.1080/14767333.2011.581021

Timperley, H., Wilson, A., Barrar, H., & Fung, I. (2007). *Professional learning and development: Best evidence synthesis iteration (BES).* Wellington, New Zealand: Ministry of Education.

von Glasersfeld, E. (1989). Cognition, construction of knowledge, and teaching. *Synthese, 80*(1), 121–140. doi:10.1007/BF00869951

Waugh, R., & Punch, K. (1987). Teacher receptivity to system wide change in the implementation stage. *Review of Educational Research, 57*(3), 237–254.

Weistra, H. (2000). *E-Learning, waar zijn we mee bezig? (E-learning, what are we doing?).* Keynote at the Best Practices E-Learning Conference, Nijrnegen, November 2000. Retrieved from http://www.sbo.nl/

KEY TERMS AND DEFINITIONS

Blended Action Learning: Working on issues or problems with the support of a group, involving both face-to-face and online interactions.

Change Models: Models that explain how change can be implemented.

Connectivism: A theory providing a basis for examining the interaction and evolution of knowledge creation.

Constructivism: A theory suggests that learners construct knowledge through interaction between their experiences and their ideas.

Critical Friends: Trusted people who provide support and challenge in supporting learning at work

Digital Age Learning Theory: A theory that explains how learning might occur in the digital age. Such theories are underpinned by epistemological beliefs congruent with participating in a society in which digital devices are ubiquitous and have a range of functions that enhance people's ability or opportunities to communicate, access and process information, interact, plan, and learn.

Pedagogical Approaches: Ways in which teachers design and implement learning experiences.

Chapter 13
Motivation of the E-Learner:
Theories, Practices, and Perceptions

Lex McDonald
Victoria University of Wellington, New Zealand

Allie McDonald
University of Canterbury, New Zealand

ABSTRACT

The study of motivation in E-learning is an emerging field but there is a paucity of data about what learners and facilitators believe are the important factors involving and sustaining the interest of the learner. It is emphasised that more prominence needs to be given to the key players' perspectives in balancing what is known about E-learning motivation. In this literature review, consideration is given to how E-learning evolved and impacted upon learners. Theoretical approaches to understanding learning and motivation are discussed and the importance of instructional design as a motivating factor identified. Research concerning the motivational matrix of the E-learner, facilitator, and educational environment is then detailed to provide a context for understanding E-learner motivation. Following this, phenomenologically-oriented research related to learner and facilitator perspectives on what motivates the E-learner is discussed and links to the social cognitive theory are acknowledged. Implications and an exploratory model of E-learners' motivation are detailed followed by recommendations for future research.

INTRODUCTION

With the rapid growth of the World Wide Web and technology over the past 20 years, there have been immense changes in learning, communication and accessing of information (Bonk, 2002). Moreover, Keller and Suzuki (2004) suggest

technology offers many innovative features to make instruction more appealing and hence the issue of motivation in E-learning has become a central focus. However, although there has been considerable research concerning the benefits and limitations of E-learning (e.g., Kruse, 2004) and instructional design (ID), relatively little has been written about why the motivational issues of those

DOI: 10.4018/978-1-4666-1963-0.ch013

involved in these programs are an important consideration (Kim, 2009). As Cocea and Weibelzahl (2006) note, although ID is important for motivation, knowledge about the processes of learner motivation can help with tailoring the content and interventions. Therefore, it is the purpose of this review to examine E-learner motivational issues and then, in more specific terms, identify if the learners' and facilitators' perspectives about the processes that engage the learner are consistent with this literature.

E-learning is a relatively new term and is associated with notions of computer-based learning, but it is much wider than this. Kaplan-Leiserson (2003) defines it as "a wide set of applications and processes, such as Web-based learning, computer-based learning, virtual classrooms, and digital collaboration." (para 85). E-learning enables education to reach a diverse and geographically dispersed student base in a cost-efficient manner and it can be on demand, at any time, and at virtually any place (Clark & Mayer, 2011). It is a mode of learning adopted by many institutions but more research is needed to examine the circumstances of its operation (Herrington, Reeves & Oliver, 2010; Kim, 2009).

As indicated, this review is about motivation and the E-learner, and following a consideration of the background and contextual research the perspectives of the learners and facilitators are examined. Learner and communication variables were considered important by both learners and facilitators and task variables were also given prominence by the learners. Relating these findings to the social cognitive theory (SCT) provides an important context to understand the research. Various sources of information were accessed and specialist librarians and others having E-learning knowledge became valuable sources. All the data relating to perceptions were then considered in relation to the development of an exploratory integrated model of how motivational issues are perceived by the learners and facilitators.

The Context and Methodology

It is accepted that E-learning has assumed a particular significance in facilitating the knowledge economy (Clarke, 2007) and, accordingly, this has generated investigations into its qualities as an instructional mode. Importantly however, it is necessary to consider E-learning within the context of general education theories and acknowledge that there is a growing awareness of E-learning and motivation issues which adds to E-learning theory (Keller, 2008). However, it is also essential to note that E-learning is also linked to theories related to computer mediated communication (Thurlow, Lengel & Tomic, 2004) and hence concepts of communities, complex multi-way interactions, and synchronous and asynchronous communications need to be incorporated within the explanations. Given this, it is understood that although research into E-learning is relatively new, there is considerable literature on what motivates learners – but little on what motivates learners to engage with E-learning (Kim, 2009). However, some exploratory studies are emerging such as the research undertaken by Kim (2009) and Ke and Xie (2009) who have examined participants' perceptions of their motivation to engage with E-learning. In this survey of the literature, both positive and negative motivational factors were considered as having impact on the student but only qualitative data were considered but reference made to some quantitative studies. What is also required is a context for understanding and interpreting such studies.

Relevant literature was located by accessing scholarly articles via electronic databases. Descriptors, 'E-learning' and 'motivation' (or synonyms), yielded many results; however, overall there were relatively few reports linking the two key descriptors and even fewer relating to the reported perspectives of the learner and facilitator. Essentially, the review examined three categories of research information: motivation in E-learning, material relating to E-learner motivation, and the perceptions of learners' motivation from the perspective of learner or facilitator.

The literature concerning learner and facilitator perceptions centred upon phenomenologically-oriented studies. Phenomenological research is concerned with the studying of experience from the perspective of the individual subject and as such, it was a powerful tool in gaining insight into subjects' experience, motivation and actions (Lester, 1999). While data gathered are more likely to be a true representation of participants' experiences and personal perspectives, phenomenological reporting also has some limitations. Some consider phenomenological research to have validity problems because the gathered data are messy, difficult to generalise, and biased and, as well, researcher involvement with the participants and data interpretation raises issues of unreliability (Lester, 1999). Overall, however, perhaps a most important consideration relates to 'truth' – the data obtained from phenomenological studies are not necessarily 'truth' in an objective sense. Nevertheless, herein also lies a strength – it is subjective 'truth', and it is that which matters to the individual. Hence, phenomenological research has some limitations but it can provide rich meaningful data from the most significant sources – the actors themselves. Although there have been relatively few studies of the E-learners' motivation from the key players' perspectives, it is an important standpoint to consider as the subjective experiences of learners is an important influence on behaviour (Wong, 2006). Relating such findings to existing knowledge is needed.

In this review, background and theoretical issues, ID and E-learning motivation issues will be outlined and then learner and facilitator perspectives about learner motivation will be considered. Studies and commentaries that have utilised a phenomnenologically-oriented approach will be the emphasis of the review for the learners' and facilitators' perceptions.

MOTIVATION AND E-LEARNING

This literature review is centred on motivation and E-learning with particular reference to the perceptions of the learner and facilitator. It is acknowledged that learning does not occur without motivation (Ormrod, 2008) and therefore motivation has a particularly important role to play in determining how successful E-learning is attained.

The traditional conception of learning involves a teacher face-to-face with a learner, but since the development of distance education, teachers and learners have been able to communicate across vast distances (Ala-Mutka, Gaspar, Kismihok, Suurna & Vehovar, 2010). It had very humble beginnings however. For example, in Great Britain in the 1840s shorthand courses were able to be learnt via lessons delivered in the post (Aranda, 2007) and, indeed, distance education like this persisted well into the latter part of the 20th Century (Graziadei, 1993). Meister (2002) noted this was later supplemented by radio, TV and other mass media utilisation. Eventually it evolved into E-learning as the use of personal computers became available but the materials were still delivered to the learner. Soon after this, alongside the postal method, learners were supplied with prepared curriculum materials via the use of a personal computer. With the advent of the internet, the personal computer was used not only as a means of communication but as a means to access information and curriculum content. Indeed, the internet has promoted the personal computer to become one of the most important learning tools of the 21st century (Bonk, 2002). So, eventually in the 1990s with the internet becoming more popular and accessible, the use of the postal service was no longer required as the computer became not only the means to access course content but also a means to communicate with facilitators and other course members. Nowadays, there is an expanse of strategies available to facilitate personal and professional learning, such as email, webpages, Wiki Spaces, blogs, Skype, Youtube (etc).

As distance education moved through these phases, the developments were associated with significant shifts in learning theory and technology (Taylor, 1999). The current generation of e-learners can utilise a range of technologies making their learning opportunities qualitatively different than the earlier correspondence modes. Synchronous and asynchronous communication with student-teacher, student-student and collaborative group work are now options for the learner and facilitator. Kaufman (1989) and McConnell (2000) noted that these developments in technology have been motivating because they have resulted in more learner and less facilitator control, increased learning opportunities via dialogue, group effort, and the opportunity for growth of higher-level thinking skills beyond comprehension (Kaufman, 1989; McConnell, 2000). Clark and Mayer (2011) discussed how the new developments have created opportunities, providing the instructional methods fit the mode and there is an acknowledgement of the learning processes (e.g., motivation of the learner). They identified the unique instructional approaches as tailoring content with instructional methods (e.g., practice with automatic tailored feedback), learning engagement (e.g., using approaches that obtain behavioural and psychological engagement), using appropriate multimedia (e.g., forums to facilitate interaction) and simulations to accelerate expertise development (e.g., a simulated classroom to develop management expertise). But apart from these instructional differences, Clark and Mayer noted a range of other unique characteristics. For example, e-learning creates a virtual classroom in the learner's choice of location, learners' technology skills are important for success, the facilitation skills of the instructor assume importance, and the institution regards it as a business that can enhance profits providing learning objectives are met.

Motivation is one of the most discussed and enduring topics in learning and most educators would agree that motivation is an important, if not the most important, influence upon learning, including E-learning (Cole, Field & Harris, 2004; Ryan, 2001). It is often defined as an individual's drive or energy to engage and remain involved in activities; it determines the amount of effort which an individual is willing to direct towards an activity (Snowman, et al., 2009). Therefore, motivation is particularly important for e-learners' interest and enjoyment in the learning event and it is responsible for effort that an individual mobilises to achieve goals and engage in activities. Accordingly, motivational theories are often the justification for developing the circumstances that influence the conditions for successful learning (Snowman, et al., 2009). However, motivation is one of the most complex contributing elements to learning and no one theory is capable of explaining individuals' varying levels or orientations. Indeed, orientation of motivation is determined by many factors such as age, race, religion, gender, beliefs, values, interests and needs. Nevertheless, differing theories are capable of shedding light on why an individual is motivated by something, whereas another is not. Understandably, with the expansion of E-learning there has been a renewed interest in motivation, its applicability, and how it impacts upon this mode of learning (Kim, 2009).

Undoubtedly the two most important theoretical perspectives that have contributed to E-learning are the behavioural and cognitive approaches. Behavioural theories of motivation are premised upon incentive theory which specifies that a person's actions always have ramifications and if these consequences are positively received, the person is likely to engage in the behaviour again, whereas if negatively perceived, the individual is less likely to act in this manner again (Snowman et al., 2009). Motivation of this type is usually associated with extrinsic factors (e.g., a certificate) whilst the cognitive approach is centred on intrinsic motivation (e.g., sense of achievement), but there is the need to recognise that both assume an important position in motivation and learning (Hynds & McDonald, 2010).

Recently there have been considerable advances in understanding motivation from the cognitive perspective which evolved significantly from the information processing model and this has had considerable implications for E-learning. A number of approaches have influenced thinking. The expectancy-value theory (Fishbein & Ajzen, 1975), attribution theory (Weiner, 1992) and self-worth theory (Covington, 2000) have emphasised the role of success or the belief to succeed. Social cognitive theory (SCT), which is an approach that has increasingly assumed importance in relation to E-learning (Cocea & Weibelzahl, 2006), is founded upon the interaction of environmental, behavioural and personal (cognitive, affective and biological) factors (Bandura, 1986). It postulates that factors that motivate individuals include viewing of others' experiences (observational learning) and one's self-belief and self-regulation to succeed at a task. Other cognitive motivational theories centre on goal setting. The goal setting theory (Locke & Latham, 2002) emphasises achievable goals. Ames's (1992) goal orientation approach distinguished between mastery (intrinsic interest) and performance (ability orientation) goals. A further group of theories include the environment as a key factor. The self-determination theory of Deci and Ryan (2002) identifies an internal locus of causality or external locus of a social psychological perspective (Weiner, 2005) and indicates the importance of socio-cultural environmental influences (e.g., social affiliation and recognition) in the learning environment.

These behavioural and cognitive theories can provide insight into the motivation of the E-learner. However, the awareness of the growth of E-learning and its context has led to researchers and commentators considering its specific relationship and connections to learning theory (Keller & Suzuki, 2004), and one area of particular interest is motivation and E-learning (Kim, 2009). To date, however, there is only a limited literature on the topic and according to Boyle (2004), these centers around three key interactive considerations: ID, the learner, and the facilitator.

Instructional Design and Motivation

ID focuses on the way E-learning content is delivered (Ke & Xie, 2009) and until recently, it has been interpreted as the predominant means of motivating E-learners (Cocea & Weibelzahl, 2006). For example, two well-known motivational ID theory models, ARCS (attention, relevance, confidence and satisfaction) (Keller & Suzuki, 2004) and the ADDIE (analysis, development, design, implementation and evaluation) (Dick & Carey, 1996) specify the importance of analysing the needs of the learner, the desired goals and the intervention. Mödritscher, Spiel & Garcia-Barrios (2006) stated that simple technology-focussed approaches do not guarantee successful teaching, and accordingly ID design assumes importance in ensuring the quality of content and delivery. Therefore, a shift to pedagogy-based initiatives can be detected within the field of E-learning and most attention has been directed toward behavioural, cognitive, social constructivist and critical pedagogies.

Behavioral theory instruction is based upon an objective value-free reality and can be used to benefit planning for E-learning as succinct and structured lessons (e.g., drill, practice, assessments, feedback) and help learners quickly acquire new factual information, skills and concepts (Atkins, 1993). The behavioural theory stipulates that the environment activates learning but learning itself remains an internal process. Obviously the instructivist approach has a place in E-learning, particularly for self-directed independent learners (Edleson, 1997) and the uniform presentation of knowledge is also, at times, important (Winn & Synder, 1996) but practice has revealed that this may be insufficient to motivate the learner.

Cognitive theory also has a considerable contribution to make to E-learning ID. Its foundation was based upon the idea that learners receive and process new information and then transfer that into long-term memory (Clarke, 2007). E-learning course designers consider the manner in which content is presented to meet differing learning styles, individuals' motivation and meta-cognitive processes that facilitate the processing of the information. A range of cognitive approaches has evolved for ID use and although well regarded and able to make E-learning ultimately more user friendly, there are some limitations. What is appropriate for one individual, may not be for another; therefore the designing of E-learning can be time consuming and costly. Furthermore, along with the behavioural approach, a major limitation is the emphasis upon teacher directed learning (Herie, 2005).

Social-constructivist pedagogy moves from the behavioural and cognitive teacher-centred approaches to a student-centred approach. This theory was developed long before the advent of the internet or E-learning but it is now well used in online communication (Salmon, 2004). It is based upon two key ideas: learning is an active constructive process and secondly, it is a process of facilitating and supporting learning rather than transmitting it (Duffy & Cunningham, 1997). Emphasis is upon approaches such as reciprocal teaching, problem-based learning, learner query, and the different ways of knowing. The supporters of this approach suggest E-learning best occurs with the use of media such as Skype, chat and online collaborations in the arenas of wiki space, Blackboard, forums, (etc).

Critical pedagogies are unlike the other approaches in that there is an emphasis upon embedded power within the educational process (Foley, 2001). It highlights the dysfunctional maintenance of a dominant group's power base in society (including education) and urges a rethink of learner and facilitator roles and the importance of honouring students' background, experience and ideas. The value of this approach lies in its attention to teaching practices and beliefs and the opportunities that need to be afforded to learners. It has impacted upon E-learning in particular because it has highlighted the learner's voice and emphasised the role that distance education can play in reaching groups of people not previously engaged (Herie, 2005).

THE MOTIVATIONAL MATRIX: E-LEARNER, FACILITATOR, AND EDUCATIONAL ENVIRONMENT

ID theories embody ideas about what motivates E-learners and consequently considerable research has been conducted on motivational features that, amongst other aspects, inform course design and address the high rates of learner drop-out (Kim, 2009). Kember (1989) proposed a wider conceptual model for E-learner motivation which demonstrated a complex relationship between family, context and background, personal motivation, ability, depth of commitment to completion, previous educational experiences and achievement and institutional support. Boyles (cited in Dagger & Wade, 2004), building upon Kember's study, identified three themes relating to E-learner motivation:

1. Learner characteristics including background, maturity, personal circumstances and previous experience;
2. Environmental aspects such as the technical, physical environment and the virtual social/ organisational environment; and
3. Academic aspects including course design and the facilitators' experience and support.

Within these areas, some research has addressed issues relating to the motivation of E-learners, and Dearnley (2003) emphasised that background, including knowledge, skills and attitudes, is particularly important. Not only is it important for individuals to be oriented and psychologically prepared for online instruction but also an adequate background of skills prior to commencing E-learning is necessary (Carr, 2000). It was noted that students who have insufficient ICT skills are more likely to withdraw or have difficulty completing course requirements and less likely to be motivated. Correspondingly, those who also have poor writing skills were found to lack motivation, as E-learning is embedded primarily in a text-based environment (Smith & Rupp,

2004). Furthermore, personal characteristics are also significant in determining individuals' success with E-learning. Kearsley (2000) identified that autonomy and freedom entice many to engage; however, it was considered correspondingly important that the learners displayed initiative and self-discipline. Those who were identified as intrinsically motivated were likely to successfully complete courses, and engage in E-learning again (Rivera & Rice, 2002). Those found to have had positive experiences with online instruction previously were more likely to be intrinsically motivated and successful, and additionally they were found to be more likely to consider E-learning as a method of gaining qualifications in the future (Kim, 2009). Personal circumstances such as living arrangements, work and family commitments also seem to impact upon motivation. Yum, Kember and Siaw (2001) commented that E-learners would find it difficult to juggle their studies with other commitments, and would often cite such reasons for attrition.

Environmental parameters, for example the technical aspects, have also proven to impact upon learners' motivation. This refers to the software and hardware used to access the online course, the physical environment, where the learner actually engages in the study and the social/organisational construct of the course, such as whether tasks are completed in a group or individually (Zaharias, 2009). Macguire (2001) noted that motivation can be impacted upon if there is inadequate software or hardware and may result in disengagement. Gaining access is also considered an issue and, as Kearsley (2000) outlined, E-learning is designed to be accessed 24 hours a day, 7 days a week, but Rumble (2000) pointed out, remote areas often have limited bandwidth or intermittent functioning internet access. Bose (2003) also suggests that in universities, access is often a major issue for high-speed bandwidth often becomes a problem beyond the campus confines. Furthermore, the environment in which E-learners study is of significance – poor lighting, noise level and distractions may prevent learners from engaging in

courses and prevent achievement of learning goals (Maguire, 2001). Indeed, Kim (2009) indicated that if students are not able to locate a space to work uninterrupted they are less likely to succeed in online courses, are likely to take longer to complete tasks, are less likely to report enjoyment, and enrol in subsequent online courses. Another factor considered important in the environment is the virtual dimensions (Mechlenbacher, 2000) and this too can impact significantly upon the learner's motivation. Ke and Xie (2009) found courses with collaborative elements such as discussion tasks and pairs or group activities were more likely to have higher rates of success. Courses that did not require students to communicate with other students or lecturers on a regular basis encouraged feelings of isolation and loneliness in learners, which decreased the levels of motivation.

Academic/instructional variables, which include the course design and the facilitator, have also been found to have a significant impact upon E-learner motivation. For example, poorly designed online courses are de-motivating for many students. Ivergard and Hunt (2005) analysed courses and found that they were often difficult to navigate, lacked guidance, stressed students, and fostered a sense of resentment that often led to student withdrawal from programs. A range of other instructional variables has also been related to learners' motivation including learner control, level of interaction and applicability of content to the workplace (Keller & Suzuki, 2004). Not surprisingly, Kim (2009) identified inclusion of interactivity in online courses as the most widely reported motivational variable determining success in such courses.

According to De Cicco (2002), the facilitator has a most significant role in motivating the E-learner because not only are the usual teaching skills required but also a set of additional specialised roles that impact upon learner motivation. Hootstein (2002) believes these to be on-line instructor, social director, program manager, and technical assistant. Dringus (2003) outlined the importance of the facilitator qualities and the impact on the instructional environment – although E-learning may appear simple to implement (e.g., lack of student face-to-face contact), facilitators often find online courses overwhelming if there is no previous experience. Students may post questions, contribute to forums or send emails at any time and this on-going learning and teaching demand may be difficult for a novice facilitator to manage (Newton, 2003). Additionally, online courses are more time consuming for facilitators as student queries must be responded to individually and in writing. Therefore, without adequate experience, support and systems, facilitators will often provide a sub-standard service and as a result, students' motivation can be affected (Kathawala, Abdou & Elmulti, 2003).

Establishing facilitative conditions and gaining learner success does not necessarily imply motivation, however. ID approaches have been used to facilitate success and have provided some data about how individuals are motivated, but these designs are a task-oriented attempt to motivate the learner (Cocea & Weibelzahl, 2006). Furthermore, del Soldato and du Boulay (1995) have suggested that domain-based planning (e.g., moving from one successful step to the next) in e-learning may be insufficient to maintain motivation and have developed a planner to highlight the importance of integrating the learner's effort, confidence and independence with the domain planner. But Cocea and Weibelzahl (2006) go further and state that assessing motivation via a learner's interactions within the system is also insufficient because the learner has not been involved in this motivation assessment. They note the importance of the centrality of the E-learner and highlight the value of SCT in identifying self-efficacy (learner's belief about capacity to perform) and self-regulation (learner control) as key motivational concepts. Not only is it a well-established motivational theory linking behaviour, personal factors and environment but it has many practical implications. For example, two of its key concepts, self-efficacy and self-regulation, can provide insight into how

domain learning and ID can best be adapted to motivate the learner. Indeed, according to Cocea and Weibelzahl, SCT fits well with the e-learning trends of personalisation (e.g., empowerment of learner), adaptivity (e.g., making content suitable to learner's performance level), affective tutoring (e.g., assessing learner feedback) and collaborative learning (e.g., individuals working together to produce a solution) as the learner responses are promoted by the interaction of the individual, the environment, and already learned behaviours.

The issues outlined above have provided a format for interpreting motivational issues for E-learners. However, as Niles (1995) points out, there is a need to understand more clearly learner and facilitator perceptions of motivational issues in E-learning for they are the key stakeholders. Their perceptions provide a valuable insight and can significantly contribute to the overall understanding of E-learning motivational issues.

Learners' and Facilitators' Perceptions of E-learner Motivational Factors

Although there is growing research on motivational issues for E-learners, in terms of the affective, cognitive, behavioural, and social components (Liaw, Huang & Chen, 2007) there is relatively little research on the actual perceptions of the learners or research that focuses on the perceptions of the learners. Some quantitative studies (e.g., Elango, Gudep & Selvam, 2008; Liaw, et al., 2007; McCullough & Aimard, 2006) have approached the issue but emphasis has been upon facilitator and learner preferences for the qualities of E-learning programs and E-learner usage characteristics and not motivational issues *per se*. This is especially the case for research concerning the views of the learner. However, from surveying the existing learner perception literature, a set of key motivators were identified. These motivators are:

- Flexibility and perceived convenience;
- A sense of control;
- Interactivity;
- Communication with facilitator and peers; and
- Authenticity and relevance of tasks.

Flexibility and convenience refer to the extent to which E-learning may fit around learners' other commitments such as careers, family, etc. Kim (2009) found E-learners reported high levels of motivation due to the flexibility and convenience offered by this mode of learning. As noted by Liaw et al. (2007), being able to control the pace and place of the learning was a key motivator to learners – many E-learners, for example, were employed full-time and unable to attend regular classes (Gonzalez, Gasco & Llopis, 2005; Thomas, 2001). However, although online courses offer some advantages in terms of the delivery flexibility and learning, they can be problematic for other learners. For example, in contrast to the students who found flexibility beneficial, Kim outlined that some students reported it as un-motivating as it was easier for the students to justify non-completion of tasks. According to Rovai, Ponton, Wighting & Baker, (2007), this difference in experiences could be explained by intrinsic and extrinsic motivational needs – those who are motivated by a less controlling environment tend to be more intrinsically motivated.

In the E-learning context, learner control refers to the ability of the student to manage the pace, sequence and time of access to learner resources (Alessi & Trollip, 2001), and a number of studies (e.g., Schnackenberg & Sullivan, 2000) have outlined the importance of E-learner control in relation to reported motivational levels. Studies by Grolnick and Ryan (1987) and Miserandino (1996) support this finding and have demonstrated a negative effect that controlling environments can have on learner motivation, attitudes and results. Furthermore, Huang and Liaw (2007) outline learner reports of having a sense of control as a

strong motivator to engage at a deeper level and remain in E-learning courses, despite experiencing difficulty. For example, students rated 'learner controlled' aspects such as video tutorials, in a study conducted by Schroff, Vogel, Coombes and Lee (2007) as being highly motivating and enjoyable. According to Benbunan-Fich and Hiltz (2003), E-learners reported they became more motivated in online course curricula that consisted of activities that were relevant and then could over-look sections that did not apply to them. Indeed, as Kim (2009) noted, E-learners who were most motivated by aspects of control, reported only enrolling in online courses, as the level of control desired was not achievable via a traditional classroom.

Interactivity in online instruction is also identified as an important theme determining the motivation of E-learners. Not dissimilar to control, interactivity in E-learning may be defined as tasks that are embedded within the content which require the learner to complete applied and reflective activities (Zhu, Valcke & Schellens, 2010). E-learning students reported that in a number of studies, interactive elements assisted engagement with content and offered a chance to practise skills. Learners reported interactive activities helped keep them engaged, gave them a feeling of being proactive and helped to increase motivation as learners felt they were engaging in a reciprocal conversation (Schackenberg & Sullivan, 2000). Tung and Deng (2006) confirmed this and outlined that interactive programs allowed E-learners to perceive a sense of social presence from the computer which increased levels of motivation. Kim (2009) found students reported interactivity as one of the most interesting features of online course and cited lack of it as a reason for attrition.

Another motivational factor identified as important was the form of interaction. For example, Chen, Lin and Kinshuk (2008) found that the level of communication and interaction among classmates had significant influence on motivation. Aspden and Helm (2004) received reports from E-learners that the use of Blackboard helped induce and sustain motivation as communicating with other learners reduced feelings of isolation and anxiety. It seemed that the inclusion of discussion and collaborative tasks provided additional opportunity to reflect, share and confirm ideas (Bernard & Lundgren-Caryol, 2001). However, not only are levels of motivation affected by communication components, but also the way in which students perceive the course itself. Aragon (2003) found students reported E-learning courses as being of 'quality' if they provided varied resources to engage with the course facilitator and other students, such as Blackboard, email lists, forums and discussion tasks. Kim (2009) reported contradictory findings in that a lack of communication with other students was cited as a reason for attrition by one student, whilst others reported communication was not required so it was not likely to impact upon motivation.

Communication from course facilitators is equally important for E-learners' levels of motivation. For example, it was identified by Elango et al. (2008) and Liaw et al. (2007) that facilitator leading and support were particularly important to learners. But Morgan (2003) reported that it was the *clarity* of facilitator contact that was critical and those who received clear course instructions and advice prior to the course reported feeling motivated because they knew what was expected. The personal dimension was also important. Kim and Keller (2008) conducted research into the effects of facilitator contact with students during courses and found that students who received personalised emails from facilitators were more likely to report high levels of motivation. Interestingly, Kim (2009) found those in a workplace setting had less need for a course facilitator than those within a tertiary or home setting. Kim postulated that those within a workplace were able to discuss matters with colleagues.

Considerable commentary exists in the general literature about the importance of relevance in determining motivation (e.g., Wlodkowski, 2008). Authenticity and relevance of tasks in the context of E-learning refers to the extent to which the online content is similar in nature to real-life situations and to what degree it is of significance to the learner. This was another feature considered important in understanding learner motivation in E-learning. Adler, Milne and Stablein (2001) and Horton (2000) proposed that E-learning students value tasks more highly if considered relevant and genuine in nature, and Liaw et al. (2007) noted the importance of multimedia presentations in achieving this for learners. Stephenson (2003) also stated that students reported a key motivating factor as the authenticity of tasks – in this study students had identified the main reason for their involvement in E-learning initially was to learn new skills for their jobs, personal development and for future careers. If they deemed the activities an unconvincing simulation of the 'real-world', they felt it was time wasted. Commenting upon transfer of learning, Kim (2009) found students reported high levels of interest and motivation when the course activities involved tasks that required them to apply what they had learned in an authentic situation that would be required once they had completed training.

This literature concerning learners' perceptions of motivational issues in the E-learning environment, although limited, has produced a number of relevant themes that need considering when planning programs. Flexibility and convenience, learner control, interactivity, authenticity and communication features afforded in an E-learning environment are features that, when optimally arranged, can impact positively on an E-learner. These qualities are important because they provide the learners' viewpoint and although self-report is used in many of the research reports, it is an important perspective to consider in planning.

As indicated, literature on E-learners' perceptions regarding motivational issues is limited but it is even more so for facilitators' perceptions of motivational issues for E-learners. Considerable literature regarding the issues facilitators believe E-learners encounter is available and motivation is frequently noted as an important variable. However, there is a paucity of information outlining the specific motivational issues facilitators perceive important for the learner. From this limited literature the following motivators were identified:

• Communication between the stakeholders;
• ICT skills and e-course experience of learners;
• Learners' personal factors.

A similar finding to that of the learners is that facilitators perceive communication as a key issue affecting E-learners' motivation (McCullough & Aimard, 2006). Studies reveal facilitators believe E-learners experience a sense of detachment from other learners and facilitators if there is no opportunity to engage face-to-face. Interaction is then considered important and not surprisingly, facilitators perceive E-learners who regularly contribute to discussion boards and forums as more motivated and likely to engage in the future (Packham, Jones, Thomas & Miller, 2006). Conversely, facilitators perceive those who do not engage in communication as more likely to withdraw from the program (Anderson & Kanuka, 1997).

The level of skill which E-learners possess with the technology required to participate in online instruction is also considered by facilitators to be a key factor in determining the motivation. Berge and Collins (2000) found facilitators perceived students who had advanced computer skills as confident and highly motivated while those with beginner computer skills were more likely to experience difficulty throughout online courses and more likely to demonstrate a lack of motivation. Contrastingly, however, some facilitators noted that E-learners with few computer skills were determined to overcome their inexperience and were more motivated than other learners

(Palloff & Pratt, 1999). Additionally, individuals' prior experience with E-learning was suggested by Salmon (2004) to impact upon facilitators' perceptions of E-learners' motivational issues. Facilitators perceived that if learners had been successful in E-learning courses previously, they would be highly motivated. They also reported that motivation of learners could be affected if a student had previously withdrawn or found E-learning unsatisfying. If a learner had not engaged in E-learning previously, facilitators believed that the motivation could fluctuate depending on the level of anxiety (Salmon, 2004).

Personal factors, events occurring within the learners' lives outside of the online course, were perceived by facilitators to also have a significant impact upon learner motivation. For example, the ability to manage time appropriately was considered an important factor impacting upon E-learners' motivation as they observed many of them struggle to manage their career, family and study commitments (Packham, Jones, Miller & Thomas, 2004). It was believed by facilitators that those learners who struggle with this balance and do not achieve a resolution will often not complete courses. However, it was noted that students who are capable of managing the demands of both worlds were likely to be more motivated and less likely to view the learning as a burden.

This brief outline of facilitators' viewpoints about E-learners' motivation indicates that an emergent perspective is evident but limited in scope. There are indications that facilitators' concerns are primarily centred on the learner's ability to communicate, the learner's level of computer skills' and their students' previous experience with online instructions. As well as self-report, facilitator input is important as they are at the 'chalk-face' and it is likely that as more research is undertaken, it will add to the understanding of how best to motivate E-learners.

It is evident from the literature that the perceived motivational issues for E-learners are wide ranging and indicate complexity. These factors are perceived by the key actors to impact upon E-learners' levels of motivation and hence provide a valuable source of information for planning and sustained involvement of the learners. What is important is that contingencies are in place to plan for the varying levels of motivation of E-learners.

In relation to the SCT (Bandura, 1994), which stresses the interrelationship between the environment, behaviours and personal factors, these findings have significance. One of the key elements identified by the learners and facilitators was self-regulation (e.g., deciding the where and when; controlling of personal life issues; ICT skills development). Furthermore feedback (communication) impacts upon the self-regulatory aspect on an individual to monitor future behaviour and hence influence self-efficacy. The communication and interaction with the facilitator and other learners provides an opportunity for modelling to occur and the potential for social persuasion by these others. The learners emphasised authenticity, relevance and interactivity all of which are key features of another important SCT dimension – facilitating reproduction, which is concerned with putting newly acquired knowledge into practice. Importantly, the interactivity also provides opportunities for the individual to consolidate emotional coping and to apply the knowledge reliably and accurately which increases the self-efficacy. Hence, the learners' and the facilitators' perspectives provide further evidence of the validity of the SCT for interpreting motivational issues.

IMPLICATIONS OF THE PERCEPTIONS AND PROPOSED EXPLANATORY MODEL

The literature examining learners' and facilitators' perspectives have essentially confirmed a number of key findings from wider research endeavours.

Nevertheless, the key players perspectives remain important to consider as they represent two unique set of factors deemed significant for E-learning – according to the learners and facilitators it is these particular factors that need to be prioritised to achieve learner motivation. Furthermore, there is significance in the differences identified by the key players – communication is highlighted by both but learners believe it is control and convenience factors driving the learner where as the facilitators stress the importance of skills and personal factors as important learning issues. The learners also stressed the motivational quality of task variables. These motivational perspective differences could have implications for engagement, planning, programming and assessment. Understanding each other's perspective would provide greater clarity about how best to ensure e-learning occurs.

At a more general level of analysis this discussion has identified a number of themes about E-learners' motivation from which eight principles can be determined. These specify that:

1. E-learning courses should be flexible to suit the needs of learners; however, there should be some set timelines to ensure learners remain motivated and on task.

2. Significant amounts of content, which can be controlled by the learner and thereby ensure more relevance, should be detailed.

3. Courses need to include considerable amounts of interactive activities that allow learners to practise skills and reflect on learning.

4. Forums and other interactive dimensions for course-related social learning opportunities need to be a component part of the course. The facilitator should contribute to guide and encourage discussion with reflection.

5. Activities should closely reflect what the learner will be expected to perform 'on the job'.

6. Course facilitators should identify those who have previously and successfully completed E-learning programs and those who have limited computer skills. Early contact, particularly with those students at risk, would be advantageous.

7. Facilitators should make contact with all students prior to commencement of the course and outline expectations so that the there is a readiness for the course.

8. Learner and facilitator sharing of perspectives about what factors are likely to sustain interest in the learning can provide valuable information that can impact upon program planning, attainment and retention in the program.

As indicated above, this review of the literature has highlighted a number of important issues relating to E-learning and motivation, and in particular the perspectives of the learners and the facilitators have been examined to provide a 'voice' to the findings. In the model (Figure 1), detailed below, an attempt has been made to capture the key ideas of this relationship. It provides the beginnings of a theoretical explanation for understanding learner and facilitator perceptions concerning E-learning as well as indicating future research areas. The model captures the essence of the literature relating to the perceptions of the learner and facilitator with regard to learner motivation in an E-learning context. The outer circle represents the potential set of forces that impact upon the thinking and behaviour of the learner. Such influences were identified in the general literature pertaining to motivation and in E-learning. Examples of such influences were detailed only briefly in the discussion. In the inner circle, the perceptions of the learner and facilitator are indicated and have arisen from a collapsing of the issues identified.

Figure 1. An exploratory model of e-learning motivation based upon learner and facilitator perceptions

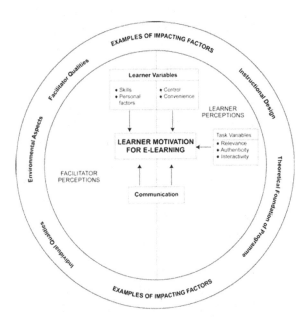

There were two key areas identified by the learners and facilitators that were similar: learner variables (skills and personal issues identified by facilitators and control and convenience issues identified by learners) and the importance of communication activities.

Learners identified a number of task variables (e.g., relevance, authenticity, technical interaction) to be significant as well. It is postulated that learner variables, communication and task considerations interact with each other but this needs to be confirmed by research.

MOVING FORWARD

This review of the literature and the development of the exploratory model have indicated that there are a number of research opportunities outstanding. The following details a range of these potential research issues needing investigation:

1. As indicated in this review, there is a need to undertake further phenomenologically-oriented studies to examine in depth the motivational issues in E-learning. For example, what are the perceptions of facilitators about their motivations for engaging in E-learning?

2. To date, most studies in the area have been qualitative and therefore there is a need to undertake a range of quantitative and mixed studies that explore causality and inter-relationships. For example, what is the relative strength of the dispositional qualities of the facilitator? What is the relative strength of the learner's personal variables impacting upon motivation?

3. Studies that examine the varying conditions/contexts of E-learning and how these impact upon motivation would be useful. For example, are there differences in the motivational processes for recreational, personal and academic E-learning programs? What are the motivational processes involved in blended and m-learning (mobile learning)? What role do different models of collaborative learning play in motivating learners? What motivational factors are at play when E-learning is voluntary vs. compulsory requirement for course completion?

4. There is a need to consider more intensively the *learning* in E-learning and the facilitator's role and skills in motivating learners. Research studies investigating various ID in different contexts and the impact this has on motivation would be valuable.

This literature review has investigated motivational issues of E-learning with a particular emphasis upon the perspectives of the learner and the facilitator regarding learner motivation. Perception data provide opportunities to investigate an issue from the inside, and this is its value – the subjective nature of the reports is valuable because humans are subjective and influenced by their beliefs, experiences and values. Individuals operate on the basis of their perceptions and attitudes. The value of this review is that it can promote theoretical development and form a foundation for initiating future research endeavours. Furthermore, although there is limited phenomenological research to date, a number of important themes have been identified which could serve to inform future practice in E-learning design and implementation.

REFERENCES

Adler, R., Milne, M., & Stablein, R. (2001). Situated motivation: An empirical test in an accounting class. *Canadian Journal of Administrative Sciences*, *18*(2), 101–115. doi:10.1111/j.1936-4490.2001.tb00248.x

Ala-Mutka, K., Gaspar, P., Kismihok, G., Suurna, M., & Vehovar, V. (2010). Status and developments of e-learning in the EU 10 member states: The cases of Estonia, Hungary and Slovenia. *European Journal of Education*, *45*(3), 494–513.

Alessi, S., & Trollip, S. (2001). *Multimedia for learning: Methods and development*. Boston, MA: Allyn & Bacon.

Ames, C. (1992). Classrooms: Goals, structures, and student motivation. *Journal of Educational Psychology*, *84*, 261–271. doi:10.1037/0022-0663.84.3.261

Anderson, T., & Kanuka, H. (1997). *Evaluating the workplace center on-line forum: Knowledge construction and learning communities*. Unpublished Research Report. Office of Learning Technologies, Human Resources, Canada.

Aragon, S. (2003). Creating social presence in online environments. In Aragon, S. R. (Ed.), *New directions for adult and continuing education, 85*. San Francisco, CA: Jossey-Bass.

Aranda, N. (2007). *A brief history of e-learning and distance education.* Retrieved September 16, 2010, from http://ezinearticles.com/?A-

Aspden, L., & Helm, P. (2004). Making the connection in a blended learning environment. *Educational Media International – Special Issue. Distributed Learning Environments, 41*(3), 66–84.

Atkins, M. (1993). Theories of learning and multimedia applications: An overview. *Research Papers in Education, 8*(2), 251–271. doi:10.1080/0267152930080207

Bandura, A. (1986). *Social foundations of thought and action: A social cognitive theory.* Englewood Cliffs, NJ: Prentice Hall.

Bandura, A. (1994). Self-efficacy. In Ramachaudran, V. S. (Ed.), *Encyclopedia of human behavior* (*Vol. 4*, pp. 71–81). New York, NY: Academic Press.

Benbunan-Fich, R., & Hitz, S. (2003). Mediators of the effectiveness of online courses. *IEEE Transactions on Professional Communication, 46*(4), 298–302. doi:10.1109/TPC.2003.819639

Berge, Z., & Collins, M. (2000). Perceptions of e-moderators about their roles and functions in moderating electronic mailing lists. *Distance Education: An International Journal, 21*(1), 81–100. doi:10.1080/0158791000210106

Bernard, R., & Lundgren-Caryol, K. (2001). Computer conferencing: An environment for collaborative project-based learning in distance education. *Educational Research and Evaluation, 7*(2-3), 241–261. doi:10.1076/edre.7.2.241.3866

Bonk, C. (2002, January). *Online training in an online world.* Retrieved from http://www.jonesknowledge.com/corporate/index.php

Bose, K. (2003). An e-learning experience: A written analysis based on my experience with primary school teachers in an e-learning pilot project. *International Review of Research in Open and Distance Learning, 4*(2), 77–98.

Boyle, A. (2004). The eLearning place: Progress report on a complete system for learning and assessment. In M. Ashby (Ed.), *8ᵗʰ International CAA Conference* (pp. 71–77). Loughborough, UK: University of Loughborough.

Brief-History-of-E-learning-and-Distance-Education&id=496460

Carr, S. (2000). As distance education comes of age, the challenge is keeping the students. *The Chronicle of Higher Education, 23*, 12–15.

Chen, N., & Lin, K., & Kinshuk. (2008). Analysing users' satisfaction with e-learning using a negative critical incidents approach. *Innovations in Education and Teaching International, 45*(2), 115–126. doi:10.1080/14703290801950286

Clark, R. C., & Mayer, R. E. (2011). *E-learning and the science of instruction: Proven guidelines for consumers and designers of multimedia learning* (3rd ed.). San Francisco, CA: John Wiley & Sons. doi:10.1002/9781118255971

Clarke, A. (2007). The future of e-learning. *Adults Learning, 18*(7), 14–15.

Cocea, M., & Weibelzahl, S. (2006, Dec). Motivation – Included or excluded from e-learning? In D. Kinshuk, J. Sampson, P. Spector (Eds.), Cognition and exploratory learning in digital age (pp. 435-437). *Proceedings of the International Conference of Cognition and Exploratory Learning in Digital Age*, Barcelona, Spain

Cole, M., Field, H., & Harris, S. (2004). Student learning motivation and interactive effects on students' reactions to a management class. *Academy Education, 3*(1), 64–85. doi:10.5465/AMLE.2004.12436819

Covington, M. V. (2000). Goal theory, motivation, and school achievement: An integrative review. *Annual Review of Psychology, 51,* 171–200. doi:10.1146/annurev.psych.51.1.171

Dagger, D., & Wade, V. (2004). *Evaluation of adaptive course construction toolkit.* Retrieved from http://wwwis.win.tue.nl/~acristea/AAAEH05/papers/6-a3eh_daggerd IOS_ format_v1.1.pdf

De Cicco, E. (2002). *The role of the facilitator within online discussion groups: A case study.* Global Summit Conference, Adelaide. Retrieved from http://www.educationau.edu.au/globalsummit/papers/ecicco.htm

Dearnley, C. (2003). Student support in open and distance learning: Sustaining the process. *International Review of Research in Open and Distance Learning, 4*(1), 12–34.

Deci, E., & Ryan, R. (2002). Self-determination research: Reflections and future directions. In Deci, E., & Ryan, R. (Eds.), *Handbook of self-determination research* (pp. 431–441). Rochester, NY: University of Rochester Press.

del Soldato, T., & Du Boulay, B. (1995). Implementation of motivational tactics in tutoring systems. *Journal of Artificial Intelligence in Education, 6*(4), 337–378.

Dick, W., & Carey, L. (1996). *The systematic design of instruction* (4th ed.). New York, NY: Harper Collins.

Dringus, L. (2003). From both sides now: On being an online learner and online instructor. *E-Learn Magazine, Association of Computing Machinery.* Retrieved from www.elearnmag.org/subpage/sub_page.cfm?section=3&list_item=1&page=1

Duffy, T., & Cunningham, D. (1997). Constructivism: Implications for the design and delivery of instruction. In Jonassen, D. (Ed.), *Handbook of research for educational communications and technology* (pp. 170–198). New York, NY: Simon & Shuster Macmillan.

Edelson, P. (1997). *Technology and the adult classroom of the future: New possibilities for teachers and learners.* Twenty-Second International Conference on Improving University Teaching and Learning, Rio de Janeiro, Brazil. (ERIC Document Reproduction Service No. 411469. Centre).

Elango, R., Gudep, V., & Selvam, M. (2008). Quality of e-learning: An analysis based on e-learners' perception of e-learning. *The Electronic Journal of E-learning, 6*(1), 31–44. Retrieved from http://www.ejel.org

Fishbein, M., & Ajzen, I. (1975). *Belief, attitude, intention, and behavior: An introduction to theory and research.* Reading, MA: Addison-Wesley.

Foley, G. (2001). Radical adult education and learning. *International Journal of Lifelong Education, 20*(1/2), 71–88. doi:10.1080/02601370010008264

Gonzalez, R., Gasco, J., & Llopis, J. (2005). Information systems outsourcing reasons in the largest Spanish firms. *International Journal of Information Management, 25*(2), 117–136. doi:10.1016/j.ijinfomgt.2004.10.002

Graziadei, W. (1993). Virtual instructional classroom environment in science (VICES). *Research, Education, Service & Teaching (REST).* Retrieved from http://www.cni.org/projects/netteach/1993/prop01.html

Grolnick, W., & Ryan, R. (1987). Autonomy-support in education: Creating the facilitating environment. In N. Hastings & J. Schwieso (Eds.), *New directions in educational psychology, Volume 2: Behavior and motivation in the classroom* (pp. 213–231). London, UK: Falmer Press.

Herie, M. (2005). Theoretical perspectives in online pedagogy. *Journal of Technology in Human Services, 23*(1-2), 29–52. doi:10.1300/J017v23n01_03

Herrington, J., Reeves, T., & Oliver, R. (2010). *A guide to authentic e-learning.* New York, NY: Routledge.

Hootstein, E. (2002, October 21). Wearing four pairs of shoes: The roles of e-learning facilitators, learning circuits. *ASTD Online Magazine.* Retrieved from http://pre2005.flexiblelearning.net.au/guides/facilitation.html

Horton, K. (2000). *E-learning tools and techonologies.* Indianapolis, IN: Wiley.

Huang, H., & Liaw, S. (2007). Exploring learners' self-efficacy, autonomy, and motivation toward E-learning. *Perceptual and Motor Skills, 105*(2), 581–586. doi:10.2466/pms.105.2.581-586

Hynds, A., & McDonald, L. (2010). Motivating teachers to improve learning for culturally diverse students in New Zealand: Promoting Māori and Pacific Islands student achievement. *Professional Development in Education, 36*(3), 525–540. doi:10.1080/19415250903319275

Ivergard, T., & Hunt, B. (2005). Towards a learning networked organization: Human capital, compatibility and usability in e-learning systems. *Applied Ergonomics, 36*(2), 157–167. doi:10.1016/j.apergo.2004.09.006

Kathawala, Y., Abdou, K., & Elmulti, D. (2003). The global MBA: A comparative assessment for its future. *Journal of European Industrial Training, 26*(1), 14–23. doi:10.1108/03090590210415867

Kaufman, D. (1989). Third generation course design in distance education. In Sweet, R. (Ed.), *Post-secondary distance education in Canada* (pp. 61–78). Athabasca, Canada: Athabasca University.

Ke, F., & Xie, K. (2009). Towards deep learning for adult students in online courses. *The Internet and Higher Education, 12*(3-4), 136–145. doi:10.1016/j.iheduc.2009.08.001

Kearsley, G. (2000). *Online education: Learning and teaching in cyberspace.* Stamford, CT: Wadsworth. Retrieved from http://home.sprynet.com/~gkearsley/chapts.htm

Keller, J. (2008). First principles of motivation to learn and e-learning. *Distance Education, 29*(2), 175–185. doi:10.1080/01587910802154970

Keller, J., & Suzuki, K. (2004). Learner motivation and e-learning design: A multinationally validated process. *Journal of Educational Media, 29*(3), 229–239. doi:10.1080/1358165042000283084

Kember, D. (1989). A longitudinal-process model of drop-out from distance education. *The Journal of Higher Education, 60*(3), 278–301. doi:10.2307/1982251

Kim, C., & Keller, J. (2008). Effects of motivational and volitional email messages (MVEM) with personal messages on undergraduate students' motivation, study habits and achievement. *British Journal of Educational Technology, 39*(1), 36–51.

Kim, K. (2009). Motivational challenges of adult learners in self directed e-learning. *Journal of Interactive Learning Research, 20*(3), 317–335.

Kruse, K. (2004). *The benefits and drawbacks of e-learning.* Retrieved from http://www.E-learningguru.com/articles/art1_3.htm

Lester, A. (1999). *An introduction to phenomenological research.* Stan Lester Developments: Education and training systems. Retrieved from http://www.sld.demon.co.uk/resmethy.pdf

Liaw, S., Huang, H., & Chen, G. (2007). Surveying instructor and learner attitudes toward e-learning. *Computers & Education, 49*(4), 1066–1080. doi:10.1016/j.compedu.2006.01.001

Locke, E., & Latham, G. (2002). Building a practically useful theory of goal setting and task motivation: A 35-year odyssey. *The American Psychologist, 57*(9), 705–717. doi:10.1037/0003-066X.57.9.705

Maguire, M. (2001). Methods to support human-centred design. *International Journal of Human-Computer Studies, 5,* 587–634. doi:10.1006/ijhc.2001.0503

McConnell, D. (2000). *Implementing computer supported cooperative learning*. London, UK: Kogan Page.

McCullough, C., & Aimard, V. (2006). *E-learning in Europe: How do trainers, teachers and learners rate e-learning?* European Centre for the Development of Vocational Training. Retrieved from http://www.cedefop.europa.eu/etv/Upload/Exchange_views/Surveys/Report_survey_Teachers_and_Learners_and_E-learning_final.pdf

Mechlenbacher, B. (2000). Internationality as one of the many neglected dimensions. *ACM Journal of Computer Documentation, 24*(1), 25–30. doi:doi:10.1145/330409.330413

Meister, J. (2002). *Pillars of e-learning success*. New York, NY: Corporate University Exchange.

Miserandino, M. (1996). Children who do well in school: Individual differences in perceived competence and autonomy in above-average children. *Journal of Educational Psychology, 88*(2), 203–214. doi:10.1037/0022-0663.88.2.203

Mödritscher, F., Spiel, S., & García-Barrios, V. (2006). Assessment in e-learning environments: A comparison of three methods. In *Proceedings of Society for Information Technology and Teacher Education* (pp. 108–113). Chesapeake, VA: AACE.

Morgan, G. (2003). *Faculty use of course management systems*, Educause Centre for Applied Research. Retrieved from http://net.educause.edu/ir/library/pdf/EKF/ekf0302.pdf

Newton, R. (2003). Staff attitudes to the development and delivery of e-learning. *New Library World, 104*(1193), 412–425. doi:10.1108/03074800310504357

Niles, F. (1995). Cultural differences in learning motivation and learning strategy: A comparison of overseas and Australian students at an Australian university. *International*International. *Journal of Intercultural Relations, 19*(3), 369–385. doi:10.1016/0147-1767(94)00025-S

Ormrod, J. (2008). *Educational psychology: Developing learners*. Upper Saddle River, NJ: Pearson.

Packham, G., Jones, P., Thomas, B. & Miller, B. (2004). E-learning and retention: Key factors influencing student withdrawal. *Education + Training, 46*(6/7), 335-342.

Packham, G., Jones, P., Thomas, B., & Miller, C. (2006). Student and tutor perspectives of on-line moderation. *Education + Training, 48*(4), 241–251. doi:10.1108/00400910610671915

Palloff, R., & Pratt, K. (1999). *Building learning communities in cyberspace*. San Francisco, CA: Jossey-Bass.

Rivera, J., & Rice, M. (2002). A comparison of students outcomes & satisfaction between traditional and web based course offerings. *Online Journal of Distance Learning Administration, 5*(3), 222–239.

Rovai, A., Ponton, M., Wighting, M., & Baker, J. (2007). A comparative analysis of student motivation in traditional classroom and e-learning courses. *International Journal on E-Learning, 6*(3), 413–432.

Rumble, G. (2000). The globalisation of open and flexible learning: Considerations for planners and managers. *Online Journal of Distance Learning Administration*, *3*(3), 1–15. doi:10.1080/026805100115425

Ryan, S. (2001). Is online learning right for you? *American Agent & Broker*, *73*(6), 54–58.

Salmon, G. (2004). *E-moderating: The key to teaching and learning online*. London, UK: Routledge Falmer.

Schnackenberg, H. L., & Sullivan, H. J. (2000). Learner control over full and lean computer-based instruction under differing ability levels. *Educational Technology Research and Development*, *48*(2), 19–35. doi:10.1007/BF02313399

Shroff, R., Vogel, D., Coombes, J., & Lee, F. (2007). Student e-learning intrinsic motivation: A qualitative analysis. *Communications of the Association for Information Systems*, *19*(12), 241–260.

Smith, A., & Rupp, W. (2004). Managerial implications of computer based online/face-to-face business education: A case study. *Online Information Review*, *28*(2), 100–109. doi:10.1108/14684520410531682

Snowman, J., Biehler, R., Dobozy, E., Scevak, J., Bryer, F., & Bartlett, B. (2009). *Psychology applied to teaching*. Milton, Australia: John Wiley.

Stephenson, J. (2003). *A review of research and practice in e-learning in the work-place and proposals for its effective use*. Paper presented at the American Educational Research Association, Chicago, USA.

Taylor, J. C. (1999, June). *Distance education: The fifth generation*. Paper presented at the 19th ICDE World Conference on Open Learning and Distance Education, Vienna.

Thomas, K. Q. (2001). Local colleges providing online learning programs. *Rochester Business Journal*, *16*(43), 28.

Thurlow, C., Lengel, L., & Tomic, A. (2004). *Computer mediated communication: Social interaction and the internet*. London, UK: Sage.

Tung, F., & Deng, Y. (2006). Designing social presence in e-learning environments: Testing the effect of interactivity on children. *Interactive Learning Environments*, *14*(3), 251–264. doi:10.1080/10494820600924750

Weiner, B. (1992). *Human motivation: Metaphors, theories, and research*. Newbury Park, CA: Sage.

Weiner, B. (2005). Motivation from an attribution perspective and the social psychology of perceived competence. In Elliot, A. J., & Dweck, C. S. (Eds.), *Handbook of competence and motivation* (pp. 73–84). New York, NY: Guilford Press.

Winn, W., & Synder, D. (1996). Cognitive perspectives in psychology. In Jonassen, D. (Ed.), *Handbook of research on educational communications and technology* (pp. 112–142). New York, NY: Simon & Schuster.

Wlodkowski, R. (2008). *Enhancing adult motivation to learn: A comprehensive guide for teaching all adults*. San Francisco, CA: Jossey-Bass.

Wong, Y. (2006). Strength-centered therapy: A social constructionist, virtues-based psychotherapy. *Psychotherapy (Chicago, Ill.)*, *4*(2), 133–146. doi:10.1037/0033-3204.43.2.133

Yum, J., Kember, D., & Siaw, I. (2001). Study examines coping methods in part time students. *The Newsletter of the National Resource Center for the First Year Experience and Students in Transition*, *14*(1), 4–5.

Zaharias, P. (2009). Usability in the context of E-learning: A framework augmenting 'traditional' usability constructs with instructional design and motivation to learn. *International Journal of Technology and Human Interaction, 5*(4), 37–59. doi:10.4018/jthi.2009062503

Zhu, C., Valcke, M., & Schellens, T. (2010). A cross-cultural study of teacher perspectives on teacher roles and adoption of online collaborative learning in higher education. *European Journal of Teacher Education, 33*(2), 147–165. doi:10.1080/02619761003631849

KEY TERMS AND DEFINITIONS

Behavioral Theory: This theory specifies that an individual's behaviour is determined by interaction with the environment. Positive reinforcers (often erroneously termed rewards) and punishers define whether behaviours are likely to occur or not.

Cognitive Theory: This range of theories attempts to explain human behaviour by understanding an individual's thought processes which direct behaviour.

Critical Theory: This theory is concerned with power interests between groups and individuals within society, those who gain and those who lose. A central concern is how the privileged groups maintain authority.

E-learning: A wide set of applications and processes, such as Web-based learning, computer-based learning, virtual classrooms, and digital collaboration

Instructional Design: This identifies an instructional process that determines the needs of the learners, the goals of instruction and the instructional intervention

Motivation: A force that energises individuals to engage in behaviours

Phenomenology: A method of inquiry based on the idea that reality is perceived in the individual's consciousness (and not by researcher's observation, measurement, etc)

Social Cognitive Theory: This theory specifies that human functioning is determined by the interaction of personal factors, behaviour and environmental influences.

Social Constructivist Theory: A theory emphasising the communal (peer) construction of new knowledge.

Student-Centered Learning: Student-centered learning is focused on the student's needs, abilities, interests, learning styles and knowledge with the teacher as a facilitator (not transmitter) of learning.

Teacher-Centered Learning: Teacher-centered learning is focussed on the teacher being in a central role as the instructor in the classroom. The teacher takes responsibility for the transmission of knowledge and skills to the learners.

Chapter 14
Adult Learning Influence on Faculty Learning Cycle:
Individual and Shared Reflections While Learning to Teach Online Lead to Pedagogical Transformations

Karen Skibba
University of Wisconsin-Whitewater, USA

ABSTRACT

The purpose of this chapter is to share results of a qualitative research study that investigated how faculty members learn to teach adult learners using online course delivery. In this study, experienced faculty members needed to learn anew and rethink pedagogical strategies when designing and teaching online delivery formats. Faculty members who are learning to teach are also adult learners who learn through experience. Research themes emerged from interviews regarding how instructors learned to teach adult learners online: (a) adapted to market demand, (b) anchored by adult learning strategies, (c) experimented in online laboratory, (d) evolved from trial and error to collaboration, and (e) rethought pedagogical possibilities. Understanding how faculty members learn to teach adult students online offers great potential to identify the challenges that faculty members face and how they meet these challenges to improve teaching practice. Implications for online professional development practices are discussed.

DOI: 10.4018/978-1-4666-1963-0.ch014

INTRODUCTION

Faculty demands in higher education are changing dramatically because of the growing adult student population. To increase access to that population, many colleges are offering online courses and programs. The U.S. Department of Education's National Center for Education Statistics (2002) reported that nontraditional students (56%) are more likely than traditional students (21%) to participate in distance education. The 2010 Sloan Survey of Online Learning of more than 2,500 colleges and universities nationwide found that approximately 5.6 million students were enrolled in at least one online course in fall 2009 (Allen & Seaman, 2010). Online enrollment rose by almost one million students from a year earlier, representing a 21% increase over the previous year (Allen & Seaman, 2010).

To meet the demands of students who need more flexibility, especially adult learners, more instructors are being required to teach online courses. Allen, Seaman, and Garrett (2007) found that core faculty members teach online courses (64.7%) about as frequently as they teach face-to-face courses (61.6%). Yet many instructors do not receive training in the fundamentals of teaching or how to teach online (King & Lawler, 2003; Knapper, 1995).

This chapter reveals how faculty members learn to teach online through experience and provides practical guidelines for helping faculty members to learn how to meet the needs of adults, as well as other students. This information will benefit instructors who seek to master online design and teaching skills, as well as faculty developers, instructional designers, and administrators who assist faculty members in this process.

BACKGROUND

As of fall 2009, 42% (8.6 million) of the 20.4 million students enrolled in degree-granting postsecondary institutions (academic, career and technical, and continuing professional education) were 25 years of age or over, and 61% (5.2 million) of those students were female and 39% (3.4 million) were male. According the National Center for Education Statistics (2010, Table 119), enrollment of students age 25 and over rose 43% from 2000 to 2009, while enrollment of students under the age of 25 rose only 27%. Nontraditional students, especially women, who are not able to fit courses into their schedules due to work and family commitments, are not able to complete a degree (Brown, J. A., 2004; Kasworm, Polson, & Fishback, 2002; Kramarae, 2003). Belanger (1996) noted, "The question is no longer whether adult learning is needed, and how important it is. The issue today is how to respond to this increasing and diversified demand, how to manage this explosion" (p. 21). The top reason cited by institutions for moving to online courses and programs is improved student access to education (63% said that this was *very important* and 30% chose *important*). Two thirds of institutions cited growth in continuing and/or professional education as an objective for their online offerings, chiefly due to the appeal of online instruction for nontraditional students (Allen & Seaman, 2007).

The instructor's ability to provide positive learning experiences is a major factor in adult student retention and degree completion (Donaldson, Flannery, & Ross-Gordon, 1993; Flint, 2005; Kasworm & Blowers, 1994; Lau, 2003; Mancuso, 2001; Pearson, 2005; Ross-Gordon, 1991, 2003). Factors that have been found to have positive influence on student retention when teaching via online formats include (a) enhancing students' comfort level with technology; (b) developing sensitive online instructors who know how to generate trust, collaboration, and credibility; and (c) creating a safe environment for students to communicate (Hiltz & Shea, 2005). In addition, students are often not prepared to learn online and faculty members may know little about how to assist students to be successful (Rodriquez & Nash, 2004; Schrum & Hong, 2002). Hiltz and Shea (2005) explained, "Interaction with the teacher is the most significant contributor to perceived learning" (p. 155). This interaction includes being flexible, respectful, and caring of adults' special circumstances, as well as the ability to provide quality, meaningful instruction that includes utilizing interactive learning strategies to develop a community of learners and foster critical thinking and communication skills (Clarke & Gabert, 2004; Graham & Gisi, 2000; Kasworm & Blowers, 1994; Kerka, 1988; King & Lawler, 2003; Lau, 2003). Students who did not have adequate access to their instructors reported that they learned less and were less satisfied with their courses. Because the instructor's teaching skills are central to increasing student satisfaction and retention, it is important to understand how faculty learn to teach online and what skills are required to meet students' needs that lead to academic success, especially for adult learners.

Research has found that, in addition to meeting student needs, instructors face many challenges when learning to teach online. Many studies have shown that designing and teaching online courses is time intensive and requires that faculty members completely redesign face-to-face courses to include more learner-centered and interactive activities, use facilitative practices to give students more control over their learning, utilize new types of student assessments and feedback, allow management of online interaction to provide opportunities for student discourse and critical reflection, use new technologies such as course management systems, create social presence online, and motivate students to participate (Anderson, Rourke, Garrison, & Archer, 2001; Arabacz, Pirani, & Fawcett, 2003; Biro, 2004;

Bonk, Kirkley, Hara, & Dennen, 2000; Bower, 2001; Conceição-Runlee, 2001; Dziuban, Hartman, Moskal, Sorg, & Truman, 2003; Dziuban, Shea, & Arbaugh, 2005; Lawler, King, & Wilhite, 2004; Seaman, 2009).

Many faculty members are unsure about how to use technology effectively, which is necessary to teach online (Bates & Poole, 2003; CDW-G, 2008; Guerrero, 2010). According to King and Lawler (2003), "Rapid changes in technology lead to the need for more frequent training of educators in their use and application of new advances in their instruction" (p. 8). This is especially intriguing because many higher education institutions do not require training for online instruction. In institutions that offer training, results of a national survey of 10,700 faculty from 69 universities found that instructors perceived that their campus training and support structures for online teaching were below average (Seaman, 2009). Research studies have shown that some faculty members do not have time to attend training or do not see the value of these initiatives (King & Lawler, 2003). Therefore, many instructors in higher education still learn how to teach only through experience (Austin & Wulff, 2004; Chism, Lees, & Evenbeck, 2002). While experience can be a good teacher, if it is not guided by educational theory, instructors may simply teach how they were taught, which may not be based on best pedagogical practices. Faculty members are taught to be experts in their own disciples and are usually not taught how to teach unless they are in a field that requires that skill (Knapper, 1995).

How Faculty Learn to Teach

The most common learning theories that are utilized to explain how faculty members learn to teach are experiential learning, situated learning, and reflective practice. According to Fenwick (2003), the most dominant perspective of experiential learning is the constructivist view, in which true learning occurs only when a learner actively participates in an experience and then links what is learned from that experience to prior knowledge (Dewey, 1938, 1954, 1997; Jarvis, 1995; Knowles, 1970, 1980; Kolb, 1984; Lindemann, 1926). Kolb (1984) added to the theory of experiential learning, explaining that it is "a holistic integrative perspective on learning that combines experience, perception, cognition and behavior" (p. 21). Participants' understanding of an experience is based on their own perspectives and observational skills.

Jarvis (1987) elaborated on Kohl's model by arguing that "learning is not just a psychological process that happens in splendid isolation from the world which the learner lives, but it is intimately related to the world and affected by it" (p. 11). This is the focus of the situative perspective of experiential learning (Boud & Walker, 1991; Brown, J. S., Collins, & Duguid, 1989; Greeno, 1997; Lave & Wenger, 1991; Usher, Bryant, & Johnston, 1997; Wenger, 1998). This perspective holds that learning is embedded in the situation in which a person participates with others instead of taking place in the mind of the person who reflects on this knowledge and constructs his/her own meaning. Communities of practitioners are bound by socially constructed beliefs that are important in understanding how they act (Geertz, 1983). Lave and Wenger (1991) used the term '*legitimate peripheral participation*' to describe the process of how newcomers to the community grasp skills and knowledge that are needed to move toward full participation in the sociocultural practice of a community. In their view, senior faculty who are already full community participants provide access to "arenas of mature practice" (p. 110) and become mentors to guide newcomers on how to become part of the community. They also pointed out that beginning learners start from the periphery and progress to the center, where they in turn become leaders and continue the process of guiding newcomers to be part of the community.

Schön (1983, 1987) encouraged professionals to use reflective practice as an important method for professional development. According to Merriam, Caffarella, and Baumgartner (2007), "Reflective practice allows one to make judgments in complex and murky situations—judgment based on experience and prior knowledge" (p. 172). Merriam et al. explained that, theoretically, reflective practice should result in useful and thoughtful solutions to problems, which may not happen depending on the educator's beliefs about this practice. Wellington and Austin (1996) argued that beliefs and values affect practitioners' orientations to reflective practice. "When practitioners become aware of their own preferences and prejudices across models, they can begin to reflect upon a wider range of questions and develop a wider range of responses" (p. 314). Based on the work of Argyris and Schön (1978), Osterman and Kottkamp (2004) situated reflective practice within the framework of theories-in-use (actions) and espoused theories (beliefs). Using this framework, the authors viewed the reflective practice cycle as a method to help practitioners to become aware of their espoused theories and what they actually do so they can reflect and act on the discrepancies. For example, a teacher may want to use more learner-centered approaches but may not have time or knowledge and may instead rely on lecturing or giving quizzes, which are teacher-centered methods.

Faculty Learning Cycle Framework

Chism (2004) drew on reflective practice (Schön, 1983, 1987), action research (Carr & Kemmis, 1986), and experiential learning (Dewey, 1938, 1954, 1997; Kolb, 1984) theories to develop a conceptual framework that can be used to understand how faculty members develop in teaching, especially when using instructional technologies. This framework depicts how faculty members learn to teach through experience by planning a course of action, acting on their plans, observing

Figure 1. Faculty learning cycle (Chism, 2004, p.40; Reprinted with permission.)

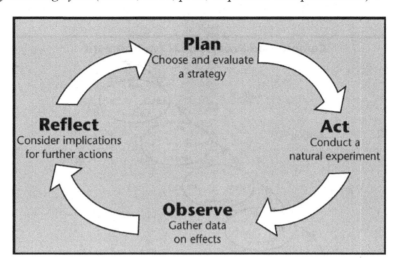

what happened, reflecting on the results, and starting the process again (Figure 1). Chism (2004) explained that these cycles can be thought of as spirals that occur frequently during peak times of development and become less frequent during routine practice. According to Chism, these cycles continue "fairly automatically as faculty develop and refine their teaching routines, but can be transformative when a problematic situation is recognized" (p. 40). This includes learning how to incorporate technology into learning.

Faculty members act on potential solutions and experiment with new teaching approaches within the context of the campus and the faculty member's disciplinary group, as shown in Figure 2. Values and assumptions about teaching are communicated through administrator and peer pronouncements, organizational structures, and campus and department policies and practices. According to Chism (2004), the context in which the faculty member teaches can either nurture or hinder individual growth. Therefore, these are important considerations when understanding how faculty members learn to teach.

The faculty learning cycles proposed by Chism (2004)—plan plan, act, observe, and reflect—are based on the steps of action research. Action re-

search is often used in education for teachers to enhance student learning, improve teaching practices, provide insight into problems involving many educators (Creswell, 2005), or solve specific problems within a community, organization, or program (Patton, 2001). According to Moon (2004), the action research cycle is "closely associated with experiential learning, but demonstrates a different sequence of activities that includes reflection" (p. 36). The sequence of cycles suggests a process by which practitioners might realize that their practice is in need of change and then plan, execute, and evaluate the change. Jaworski (1993) applied this cycle of action research to classroom teaching: A classroom event triggers a process of reflection about an event. There is then a critical analysis of the event, a subsequent reflection to observe the change, and the cycle repeats. The two frameworks proposed by Chism (2004) simplify the learning theories of how instructors learn to teach utilizing technology, including experiential learning, reflective practice, and action research. These frameworks combine and simplify many of the individual and organizational dimensions in the aforementioned learning theories of how faculty members learn to teach using instructional technologies.

Figure 2. Faculty learning in the context of the campus and profession (Chism, 2004, p. 40; Reprinted with permission.)

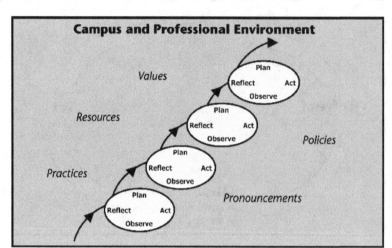

Purpose of the Study and Research Method

The research reported in this chapter is based on selected findings and further analysis of a dissertation study on how faculty members learn to teach adult learners in a blended program (Skibba, 2011). Blended programs include a mix of credit courses offered for a degree through any combination of fully online, hybrid (partially online, also referred to as blended), and face-to-face (Hartman, Otte, & Niemiec, 2006). This chapter focuses on higher education instructors' individual reflections on how they learned to teach adult students online. Ten research participants converted face-to-face courses to online formats. Five participants taught in an undergraduate degree program and five taught in a graduate degree program. Both programs focused on teaching adult learners over the age of 25. To guide this inquiry, the following questions were investigated:

- How do faculty members perceive they learn to teach adult students online?
- How do faculty members adapt or not adapt their instruction to teach adults online?

- What led faculty members to make or not make modifications?
- How do faculty members perceive that teaching adults online influences their overall teaching practices?

The research study employed a basic qualitative interpretive approach to understand how instructors learn to teach adults online, what meaning they attribute to how their teaching practices are influenced, and how they construct their experiences teaching online by describing their experiences (Merriam, 2002). In-depth interviews were the main data collection method. In addition to interviews, data collection included a gatekeeper questionnaire, a faculty background questionnaire with reflective questions, and a teacher learning audit. The data were analyzed using the constant comparative method (Patton, 2001), in which inductive category coding was combined with simultaneous comparison of all units of meaning obtained and categorized into a coding scheme and grouped into themes (Glaser & Strauss, 1967; Maykut & Morehouse, 1994).

Methods used in this study to assure quality and trustworthiness were triangulation, pilot tests, member checking, and peer review of data.

Triangulation occurred by looking for relevant themes and convergence of information in all sources gathered. Member checking took place by the researcher summarizing and clarifying information with the research participants during and after the interviews (Lincoln & Guba, 1985). Data were peer reviewed by another graduate student in the field of faculty development to ensure that the topics and themes described the data and addressed the research questions.

FINDINGS AND DISCUSSION

The research questions guiding this study were focused on understanding how faculty members learn to teach adult students online. The research participants learned how to teach adults online through interrelated interactions among five themes that emerged from the research data: (a) Adapted to Market Demand, (b) Anchored by Adult Learning Strategies, (c) Experimented in Online Laboratory, (d) Evolved from Trial and Error to Support, and (e) Rethought Pedagogical Possibilities. Each theme followed a pattern of a faculty learning cycle that included four phases: planning, acting, observing, and reflection (Chism, 2004). The faculty members learned to teach by reflecting individually and with colleagues on each cycle, based on observation of their experiences and actions.

Results of the study showed that how faculty members learn to teach is a personal process involving reflection on individual beliefs, assumptions, motivations, and challenges. All of these factors must be negotiated to determine what is possible to achieve online within the limited time, resources, and support available. While the faculty members in this study were excited about the possibilities of teaching online, they were also concerned about whether they would have time, would be supported by the institution, and would know how to use online technology properly to enhance learning. The faculty members in this study made it clear that, while experience was their most significant teacher when learning how to teach online, they wanted and needed more help, and they wanted this help even if they did not specifically ask for it.

Faculty Online Learning Process

This study focused on the research participants' individual reflections on how they learned to teach online and how they learned to convert face-to-face courses to online courses. The themes identified in this study are depicted in Figure 3. To synthesize this analysis, Figure 3 depicts the five themes that emerged from the data and shows how they are interconnected to answer how instructors learn to teach adults online. These themes can occur at any time while a faculty member is learning how to teach online.

The theme shown at the top of Figure 3, *Adapted to Market Demand,* provided the context as to why faculty members needed to convert traditional courses to online. The bottom of Figure 3 features the second theme in this study: *Anchored by Adult Learning Strategies.* This theme is the anchor of the Faculty Online Learning Process because this study focused on how faculty members learn to teach *adult learners* online. The research participants described their experiences using the lens of adult learners as they explained their experiences regarding how they learned to teach. Therefore, as described in detail in the analysis section, all five themes were anchored and influenced by the instructors' perceptions of the needs of adult learners when learning online.

The other three themes in this study are also depicted in Figure 3: *Experimented in Online Laboratory, Evolved from Trial and Error to Collaboration, and Rethought Pedagogical Possibilities.* The middle of Figure 3 shows that all of the themes centered on the experience of faculty members. The Faculty Learning Cycle, which provides a useful framework (plan, act, observe,

Figure 3. Faculty online learning process; (Adapted from Skibba, 2011, p. 173.)

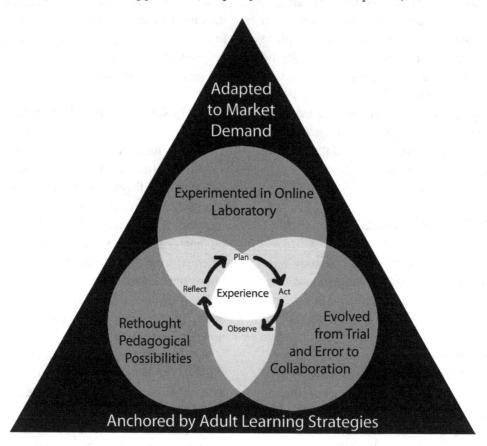

and reflect) to analyze how faculty members learn to teach, was selected to analyze the findings of the themes in this study. These learning cycles are ongoing and may go back and forth among planning, acting, observing, and reflecting phases while faculty members try new methods of teaching online. Figure 3 shows how these cycles focus on faculty experiences within each theme. These cycles are shown circling around the word "experience" because instructors are continually examining and refining their teaching by planning, acting, observing, and reflecting on their teaching (Chism et al., 2002). Reflective practice (Schön, 1983, 1987), action research (Carr & Kemmis, 1986), and experiential learning (Dewey, 1938, 1954, 1997; Kolb, 1984) theories explain how people learn through experience by planning a course of action, acting on their plans, observ-

ing what happened, reflecting on the results, and starting the process again. Chism (2004) modified these cycles to develop a framework for faculty development as explained in the literature review and summarized in Table 1.

Chism (2004) explained, "When moments of exploration occur, faculty mentally try out different solutions, selecting the ones that they judge most likely to be effective in the context they face" (p. 42). Then instructors act on potential solutions and experiment with new teaching approaches. This study found that these cycles take place as faculty members learn to teach adults online. The cycles of plan, act, observe, and reflect were found in varying degrees within the five themes. Faculty members are always at various points in cycles of learning while teaching online. Following is an analysis and discussion of the five themes and supporting literature.

Table 1. Faculty learning cycles and cycles of change

Cycles or moments of change	Faculty learning cycles	Cycles of change applied to teaching
Plan	Choose and evaluate a strategy	Selecting a new teaching practice
Act	Conduct a natural experiment	Experimenting with the teaching practice
Observe	Gather data on effects	Collecting information on what kind of learning the practice produced
Reflect	Consider implications of practice for further actions	Reflecting on desirability of the change, as well as whether the practice should be continued, modified, or discarded under a specific set of conditions

Note. Table combines summaries of two frameworks to synthesize action research studies that describe four cycles of change: plan, act, observe, and reflect. The third column is modified from "Faculty Development for Teaching Innovation," by Chism, Lees, and Evenbeck (2002), which the authors used to describe four cycles or "moments" of change planning, acting, observing, and reflection. The second column shows how Chism later simplified the wording (Chism, 2004).

Adapted to Market Demand

This theme, like all of the themes, focuses on faculty members' experiences in teaching adult learners online. Faculty members' development is embedded in the situation in which a person participates (Boud & Walker, 1991; Brown, J. S., et al., 1989; Greeno, 1997; Lave & Wenger, 1991; Usher et al., 1997; Wenger, 1998). Therefore, it is important to consider both individual development and the context in which development takes place to understand how faculty members learn to teach (Chism, 2004). According to Chism, "The power of this learning is that it arises from a felt need" (p. 40). The research participants realized that, to avoid becoming obsolete, they had to plan and teach online courses that adult learners wanted and needed to fit into their lives. As one participant said, adult students were "voting with their feet" when they registered for online courses. Chism (2004) noted that external pressures can stimulate reflection, such as the pressures that participants encountered to meet market demand. This study found that the instructors observed and reflected on the market demand and realized that they had to change or adapt course delivery formats to meet the needs of adult learners.

The market demand and need for flexibility in course participation by adult learners forced the instructors to adapt by learning how to teach online more quickly than they may have been prepared to teach online. Several participants were "dragged kicking and screaming into teaching online" because they had to abandon the face-to-face courses that they preferred to teach. A benchmarking survey by the Association of Public and Land-Grant Universities Sloan National Commission on Online Learning (Seaman, 2009) found that the majority (80%) of faculty members with no online teaching or development experience "believed that the learning outcomes for online courses were 'inferior' or 'somewhat inferior' to those for face-to-face instruction" (p. 29). Before they could adapt to teaching online, several of the research participants had to grapple with their belief that face-to-face was the best way to teach. Several explained that they were concerned that they would lose personal communication and sharing of content that they had experienced when teaching face-to-face courses. They were also concerned that taking away face-to-face options would force students to take online courses that they might not want or were not prepared to take. One instructor said, "I think live is probably on its way out. And the challenge is that some students will do a lot better in a live format. I think we will leave some people behind. For some people, it's really a disaster."

When reflecting on plans to eliminate face-to-face courses, the research participants shared concerns that not all instructors would be effective in teaching online courses. One participant summed up what many said: "I believe that there are styles of instruction as much as there are styles of learning, and some people have a wider aperture and can handle it and other people are much more narrow in their strengths." The research participants were concerned that administrators or instructors do not have an understanding of the special skills and time required to learn both the technology and pedagogy of teaching online courses. Participants expressed concern that faculty who are not trained well to teach in these formats could "mess up" the learning experience for students. This concern is supported by reports in the literature that the instructor's ability to provide quality learning experiences and facilitate learning is a critical factor in retention of adult learners in online courses (Donaldson et al., 1993; Flint, 2005; Kasworm & Blowers, 1994; Lau, 2003; Pearson, 2005; Ross-Gordon, 1991, 2003).

This theme confirms that it is important to understand both the market and individual factors that influence how faculty members adapt to learn to teach online. These factors influence both what course delivery format instructors learn to teach, either voluntarily or as required by their university, and how open they are to learn new ways of teaching online. Being required to teach online forced the research participants to reflect on the situation and to resolve their concerns about not teaching face-to-face. They realized that they had to offer online courses to meet the market demands of adult learners and plan new ways to teach to be effective.

Anchored by Adult Learning Strategies

Experience in teaching *adult learners* significantly influenced how the research participants made the transition from teaching face-to-face to teaching online. Through experience, the research participants realized that many of the learning strategies and methods that they utilized to teach and meet the needs and expectations of adult learners were similar and provided a useful "pedagogical anchor" for teaching online.

Since most adult learners tend to take online courses because of their busy schedules and life circumstances, it was important for the research participants to develop strategies to increase success in an online environment by providing flexible due dates, clear guidelines, organized course structure, and frequent and personal communication so students would not feel isolated and would know what was expected of them. One research participant explained that, while adult learners enroll in online courses for convenience and flexibility, they also think that online learning will be easier. He noted that, because of this misconception, the first semester is "like throwing cold water on people" to help them realize that "online learning is *not* easy and it's not easier than doing it live." The research participants were especially concerned about the time required to help adult students who are not ready for online learning, since "it takes self discipline" and the commitment and ability to work independently because it is easy for the student to "put an online course on the back burner if your life is very busy." The research participants noted the necessity to make critical modifications in online courses because more self-directed learning is required (Swail, 2002).

One research participant explained that adult learners' fear of learning and lack of "confidence in their skills and ability" are compounded when they are pushed into taking online courses, since fear of using technology is added. "If all of a sudden they then have to work online, basically we have to handhold them through that process... because they are not ready and they don't understand how to do it." These research findings are supported by a benchmarking survey by the Association of Public and Land-Grant Universities

Sloan National Commission on Online Learning (Seaman, 2009) that found that one of the barriers to teaching online was that students needed more discipline. The authors of the study raised the same concern that research participants in this study voiced: "Online courses typically attract students who might otherwise have not been able to attend traditional on-campus instruction, either because of work, family, or other obligations" (p. 13). Therefore, when teaching adult online learners, the research participants had to learn similar strategies and make modifications to help students to be successful online, including building confidence in the students' use of technology (Lowry & Bush, 2009).

The research participants found, as was noted in the literature, that adults do not learn from experience on their own; they need to reflect and make meaning of their own experiences to develop and grow (Merriam et al., 2007). The research participants utilized online discussion forums to facilitate individual and group reflection and to build on adult learners' experiences. The findings of this study are congruent with the adult learning literature that explains that skillful instructors of adults should allow opportunities for open discussion; tailor instruction to student needs; set a climate for learning by being accessible, respectful, and caring; and provide quality and meaningful instruction (Kasworm & Blowers, 1994; Kerka, 1988; Mancuso, 2001). In addition, this study and the online learning literature verified that learner-centered strategies are often preferred by students in adult learning and in online learning activities (Hiltz & Shea, 2005; McCombs & Vakili, 2005).

Anchored by their experience in teaching adult learners, the research participants utilized what they observed and learned from teaching adult learners to plan and implement strategies that worked well online. Strategies included experience-based, reflective, personalized, and learner-centered teaching and developing courses with flexible due dates, clear guidelines, and

organized course structures with content that is relevant and personal to the learners. Since many of the needs of adult and online learners are similar, the research participants reflected on how they could apply adult learning strategies to online courses. These research findings are consistent with a literature analysis conducted by Cercone (2008) that compared adult learner characteristics and theories and the implications for online learning design. The research participants learned how to teach adult learners online as they went through the Faculty Learning Cycles: They planned learner-centered strategies, acted on student expectations, observed the need for student preparation, and reflected on how incorporating adult learning strategies helped in the transition to online course delivery. Therefore, understanding adult students' expectations and needs helped the research participants to more easily transition into teaching online.

Experimented in Online Laboratory

The research participants spent more time experimenting with designing and teaching online courses than they did face-to-face courses. One research participant summarized that learning to teach online is "always a work in progress." Several research studies have reported that faculty members who learned to teach online continued to make revisions as they continued to learn how to improve their courses (Biro, 2004; Conceição, 2006). The strategies that the research participants learned in converting face-to-face formats to online formats aligned with the framework proposed by Berge (1995), which described the managerial, pedagogical, social, and technological roles that online instructors assume when they teach online.

The *managerial role* includes all aspects of coordinating a course, including scheduling interaction, setting due dates, and managing assignments, discussions, assessments, student roles, and workload (Berge, 1995). The research participants in this study experimented with ways to manage the work required in online courses. All participants expressed the importance of planning online courses in a more "upfront" approach than they would in face-to-face courses. They explained that a face-to-face course could be developed just before and during class. One instructor noted that teaching face to face "was more like a quick analysis of the situation and options and plugging things in." She added, "This process wasn't as random as trial-and-error, nor was it the result of a lot of reflection—I didn't have time for that!" While they did plan face-to-face courses in advance, the research participants also made many changes prior to or during class meetings. The participants described face-to-face instruction as similar to what Schön (1983) explained as reflection-in-action, when changes are made while actions or events are in progress. This "on-the-spot experimentation" is triggered when a situation is not working well (Schön, 1987, p. 28). This quick analysis and adjustment is possible when teaching in person. As one research participant explained:

If you're an organic teacher, you figure you kind of do a little lecture, do a little seeing what the people are thinking about and discussing, and the plan, oh, there's a plan, but what the hell, because you're going to meet them next week.

Instructors who typically do not plan courses in advance are likely to face difficulties with online instruction. That is because, in contrast to face-to-face courses, the research participants explained that online courses should be planned completely in advance before opening them to students. While some changes are made while online courses are in progress, it is more difficult to make major changes. Online learning "has to be excruciatingly well organized;" otherwise, "students get lost." Most of the research participants had learned how to utilize the course management system to organize grades, discussions, and content. The outline of an online course must be set in advance to keep on track and so students know what is expected. The participants observed that course creation is "brutally time consuming." The research literature confirmed faculty concerns about the time-consuming aspect of designing online courses. For example, a benchmarking survey of 10,700 faculty members from 69 colleges showed that respondents overwhelmingly agreed that more effort is required to develop and teach an online course than is required for a face-to-face course (Seaman, 2009).

The *pedagogical role* includes both design and delivery of instructional learning activities (Berge, 1995). The research participants experimented with a variety of ways to present content online. Several research participants noted the importance of being more facilitative of learning and engaging students with the online content so they can learn it on their own through practice. The majority of the research participants found that it was important to provide collaborative learning experiences so students could learn and reflect on content by sharing experiences and ideas. This finding is supported by a summary of teaching and learning trends presented by the ERIC Clearinghouse on Higher Education, which reported that collaborative and cooperative learning were discussed most as techniques for engaging students in knowledge construction (Kezar, 2000). The research participants learned multiple ways to convert teaching methods used in a traditional classroom to the online environment. Examples of their instructional adaptations included typing lectures to post online, incorporating audio or video to present lectures or content, and providing a variety of online resources as "multiple means of presentation, engagement, and motivation."

The *technological role* refers to instructors utilizing technology to organize course content and to assist students with technology issues (Berge, 1995). While most of the research participants relied on the university's course management system or their own website to deliver content online, they noted that they were exploring use of other social technologies to enhance student learning and add interest and relevance to their courses. They expressed concern about being "fluid" with technology for the sake of the students. Several said that they had "struggled" with learning new technologies and were "constrained" by what they could do and the time required to learn new technologies. Bates and Poole (2003) and Parisot (1997) found that barriers to using technology included the significant amount of time required to learn how to use it effectively. Learning and staying current with technologies increased stress and workload for research participants because they did not have the "luxury to play around with something new and try something different and see how this might work." One participant described the stress of learning new technologies: "Every time you learn something new, there's something else new coming along. And that's a frustrating feeling because you never feel like you're at a point of stasis where you can say, 'Okay, this is good enough.'" Taylor and McQuiggan (2008) found that faculty members' top interest (55.9%) related to online faculty development was to learn how to choose appropriate technologies to enhance their online courses.

The *social role* involves communication between the instructor and students and among students in the course to create a friendly and nurturing environment to support a community of learners (Berge, 1995). The research participants learned new ways to build "camaraderie" and "cohesiveness" that naturally takes place in the classroom so that it also takes place online. Many research participants reflected on the importance of creating a "community of learners," which is a well-known challenge in online education (Brufee, 1999; Harasim, Hiltz, Teles, & Turroff, 1995). To create this community, participants shared their experiences of establishing "social presence," also known as a feeling of connection and community (Short, Williams, & Christie, 1976). One participant reported that, when she was about to teach her first online course, she almost made a

"fatal mistake" by believing that online community building was not necessary because the students already knew each other from taking other courses together. She discovered, "You don't really have learning unless you have trust built within a community in an online environment." The participants experimented with ways to build community online and learned to do so by using humor, forming groups, demonstrating care for students, sharing personal and professional information pertinent to the topic, using various media such as videos to show the instructor's personality and make the learning a "human" and personal experience, and providing frequent feedback.

Consequences of lack of feedback reported by the research participants were reduced learning, student isolation, lack of participation, being "lost online," and "the course will just die." Many participants reflected on the importance of "being present" in a course by responding often to students; however, they struggled to find time to be responsive. Discussion forums are often used to build community in online courses and to increase feedback (Swan & Shea, 2005). The research participants explained that they had to experiment a great deal on how to craft and organize discussion questions that would build knowledge and to explain expectations and encourage student participation. The research participants shared that it was difficult to learn how to "move an intellectual rather than experienced-based discussion forward." They noted that it was difficult to keep discussions on track without "killing" the instructor. The ability to facilitate effective online discussions is cited in the research literature as the most important yet most difficult skill for online instructors (Anderson et al., 2001). Strategies that research participants used to reduce workload in discussions included forming groups and having a spokesperson report summaries of the group in the discussion forum.

Teaching online created the need for the research participants to experiment with a variety of online design and teaching strategies. The steps or cycles that the research participants undertook in developing and teaching courses and observing results were critical in their planning and reflection process when they modified a course. Faculty members are always in various cycles of modifying and teaching courses, which is how they learn to teach. The more the research participants struggled with the managerial, pedagogical, social, and technological roles of teaching online, the more they learned how to teach in new ways that enhanced all of their courses, regardless of format.

Evolved from Trial and Error to Collaboration

The research participants were experienced instructors of adults; however, they found themselves learning anew when they were required to teach online. Several authors have mentioned that experienced teachers feel like beginners again in the online environment (Gallant, 2000; King, 2002a; Lawler et al., 2004). Learning new course formats put the participants in the role of an adult learner, much like the students whom they teach. Daley (2001) clarified, "In professional practice, the context shapes how professionals look at new information, influencing not only what information professionals seek to learn but also what information they try to incorporate into their professional practice" (p. 38). The research participants in this study learned how to teach from being immersed in teaching adult learners.

Similar to findings in the literature, the research participants were not taught how to teach online courses and did not have a clear plan on how to improve their teaching practice (Austin & Wulff, 2004; Chism et al., 2002). Most faculty members, including the research participants, were trained to be experts in their discipline and did not usually receive training on how to teach the subjects in which they had become experts (Golde & Dore, 2004). The research participants described this lack of training as learning through "trial and error," "by the seat of the pants," and

through "intuition." One instructor summarized, "We were never trained to do this kind of work." The research participants agreed that they became better at teaching through experience, but several noted that they did not recommend the trial-and-error approach "because it takes time and you make mistakes and the students suffer from your mistakes."

However, when the research participants needed to teach online, they realized that they had to learn new ways to teach. Overall, the research participants said that they had learned some useful ideas and pedagogical strategies and technologies from workshops, adult education courses, books and literature, research, professional organizations, and conferences. They recommended that faculty members seek such resources for ideas and to continue to learn. However, these methods were not rated as significant to their learning as first-hand experience and sharing ideas with other instructors. Similar findings were reported from a survey ($N = 117$) by Kyei-Blankson (2009) that investigated resources available to instructors who taught or planned to teach online. When asked about the usefulness of the resources available to them at their university, 68% said that peers and other colleagues were *useful/very useful* resources and 72% rated departmental instructional technology consultants as *useful/very useful*. On the other hand, only 43% and 33%, respectively, rated books and professional development courses offered online as *useful/very useful*.

Most of this study's research participants reported that they could handle learning new technology on their own, despite the challenge and time required. They said that their universities provided adequate and sometimes an "overload" of training on course management system but they also wanted to learn about other innovative technologies. They were frustrated that their university's professional development departments focused on how to use the technology but not on pedagogy. No matter how much experience they had teaching online, they wanted to learn new technology and pedagogical skills to continue to improve. As one research participant expressed, "I've gone as far as I can go without really understanding what sort of state-of-the-art online pedagogy is." However, the research participants pointed out that many faculty members are not eager to be taught about pedagogy "because we all tend to think we know what we're doing." A national survey by the Sloan Consortium found that the majority of universities (81%) offered some type of formal or informal training for teaching online, including internally run courses (65%) and informal mentoring (59%; Allen & Seaman, 2010). However, as confirmed by this study, faculty members do not always take advantage of these services. The participants in this study had the opportunity to attend faculty development initiatives provided by their universities but attended few due to lack of time or interest. Most preferred to learn on their own since their expectations had not been met regarding learning both technology and pedagogy best practices.

The research participants described how they learned to teach online by experimenting with various approaches and then reflecting after the course was completed on how well students had responded to course activities. Many participants noted that student course evaluations provided important feedback to help them teach, design, and organize courses. The instructors explained that student course evaluations helped them to "figure out what has to be in the course, and what you can let go of to replace with something else." However, the most significant way in which faculty members learned to teach these formats was from mentors or colleagues who had shared best practices and by observing their courses and "sharing what was successful or not" and why. Instructors in this study had colleagues who had taught online for a long time and they mentored other instructors with online courses. Everett Rogers (1962, 1995) would characterize these instructors as "early adopters": people who embrace new technology before most other

people do and usually have a high degree of opinion leadership. This was also true for this study, since later adopters of online continually referred to early adopters when explaining how they had learned to teach online. Taylor and McQuiggan (2008) found that the most preferred learning mode (55.9%) for professional development to teach online was with a mentor or colleague.

In addition to learning from reflecting individually on experience, the research participants said that they learned the most from reflecting on feedback from other faculty members. The research participants had spent time with colleagues sharing ideas, advice, and pedagogical strategies, especially when learning how to teach online. Most of this sharing took place informally "around the coffee pot," during lunch, or in the copy room. This finding was supported by Kyei-Blankson (2009), who found very similar interactions among faculty members that took place spontaneously and informally. Chism (2004) stated, "Although many think of reflection as a solitary activity, it is enhanced in a social environment where probes, affirmation, and additional insights can be brought to the task" (p. 41). The current study found that reflection, both individually and with colleagues, was critical to build on the instructors' own and others' experiences and knowledge to continue to improve and learn effective teaching strategies.

Rethought Pedagogical Possibilities

This theme describes how the research participants rethought pedagogical assumptions that helped them to discover ways to improve all course delivery formats and student learning. Lowes (2008) found that actually teaching the course led teachers to re-examine fundamental differences between online and face-to-face classroom cultures. Lowes explained that teachers who move to online teaching "leave the familiarity of the face-to-face classroom for the uncharted terrain of the online environment" (para. 2). This reexamination helps faculty members to learn how to develop additional effective teaching practices. In this theme, reflection is integral to each cycle of the Faculty Learning Cycle (Chism, 2004), as participants shared how they challenged and changed their assumptions about what constitutes good teaching and learning after experiencing teaching online.

After they had observed what is possible with online learning, the research participants' perspectives evolved from skepticism to acceptance to appreciation of online instruction. As confirmed in the research, instructors who had not taught online were skeptical or assumed that online education was not as good as face-to-face instruction; however, once they had taught online, they realized that learning outcomes in an online course were "as good as or better than face-to-face instruction" (Seaman, 2009, p. 29). What changed assumptions that online instruction was "terrible" or "impersonal" was observing what actually took place online. For example, the research participants observed that effective learning communities could be developed through online discussions that provided opportunities for reflection and collaboration. In fact, many participants also observed that the work that students did online "was of higher quality" than work done in face-to-face courses because there was more time for students to reflect and students could not "hide" online, so they had to participate in required discussions and collaborate to learn content. Other best practices learned while teaching online included providing unlimited online resources, incorporating more collaborative and interactive activities, improving course organization, rethinking assessment, allowing time for in-depth analysis, and utilizing a variety of technologies. This finding is supported by King (2002b), who found that learning and using technology offered opportunities to reflect on practice and rethink and evaluate teaching and learning.

Even though these research participants were experienced adult educators who had used participatory learning methods, teaching online made them "rethink" and modify how they structured and taught, not just online courses but also face-to-face courses. One participant explained that teaching in different course delivery formats "shakes up the way you approach a classroom" and had forced her to question her assumptions of how students learned. Lowes (2008) referred to these teachers as "trans-classroom" teachers because they moved between the two environments while transferring strategies, practices, and ideas. The research participants noted that, by teaching online, they learned how to incorporate "learner-centered" approaches to learning by accepting "a wider range of interpretations" of assignments, giving some control of learning to students and providing more opportunities for students to collaborate. As one research participant explained, "Teachers teach best when they effectively set the stage for learning, not when they are *telling* students what they know." Similar to adult learning theories, learner-centered instruction requires that faculty members give students some control over their own learning processes (Weimer, 2002). Lowes (2008) investigated how virtual high school teachers had changed their practice as they migrated from teaching between online and face-to-face courses. Lowes suggested that the "teacher's migratory journey to and from the online classroom can transform that teacher's face-to-face classroom practice in subtle and important ways" (para. 19). This can be accomplished by incorporating more learner-centered teaching practices and improving both face-to-face and online environments by requiring independent and group work, providing opportunities for reflection, and giving more timely feedback.

Expressing the feelings of all of the research participants, one instructor noted that the most important and unexpected benefit derived from teaching online was that the learning process was a catalyst to improve pedagogy in other course delivery formats: "Having the online element made me rethink pedagogy and so that has made my teaching develop and evolve in a new way."

One participant said that she had become "so accustomed to teaching fully online" that she was not sure what to do when she had students "live in front of me." One participant, who still had reservations about teaching online, said that he was more open to the idea that learning can take place online even if it is learning and teaching in a different way. Another said, "Online education can be just as rich and powerful and transformative as live education—and sometimes more so. I believe that we are just beginning to learn how to do this effectively and efficiently." By teaching online and observing its effect on teaching and learning, instructors gained teaching strategies that enhanced overall teaching practices regardless of course formats.

FUTURE TRENDS

This study added more voices to faculty development, online learning, and adult education literature and research. For example, instructors perceived that it was easier to move to online teaching because they were already skillful instructors of adults. Therefore, it may be helpful to inform faculty about adult learning strategies, characteristics, and research theories so they can utilize this knowledge to be successful online. Also, the findings of this study confirm a benchmarking survey by the Association of Public and Land-Grant Universities Sloan National Commission on Online Learning (Seaman, 2009) that identified barriers to teaching online, including lack of student preparation and increased workload of teaching and developing course content. This study added to the literature that found that barriers or disorienting dilemmas, such as being required to learn how to teach online to adapt to changing students needs, encouraged faculty members to reflect on and learn new ways to teach and improve overall teaching practices (King, 2000, 2002b; Lowes, 2008).

Recommendations for Faculty Development

This study supports the professional development literature that treats faculty members as adult learners and applies adult learning principles when teaching them how to teach online (King & Lawler, 2003; Lawler, 2003; Lawler & King, 2000). As it is for the students whom they teach, it is important for faculty members to take responsibility for their learning, immediately apply what they learn, and use self-assessment and reflection. Like most adult learners, instructors bring a wealth of experience that can be shared in a learning environment. In a faculty development program, instructors should be encouraged to share their teaching experiences, including what went well and what did not, so they can learn from each other. Based on this research study, it is important to ask: Are adult learning strategies being utilized to help faculty to learn to teach online? Are colleges providing opportunities for both new and experienced instructors to teach online and reflect on and learn from their teaching experiences? Are they given opportunities to share what they have learned so this knowledge from experienced instructors is not lost?

It is important to help instructors to learn not only how to use the technology but also how to apply the pedagogy of adult learning principles to online learning. The research participants were able to more easily adapt from face-to-face to online course design and teaching by applying adult learning strategies, including learner-centered, collaborative, and experiential approaches that are effective in online learning. The "sage on the stage" mentality does not work in the online environment. However, some instructors are not always open to changing their teaching methods. It is easy to fall into patterns of routine practice that keep instructors from trying new design and teaching strategies because it is time consuming and challenging to redesign courses. Instructors may also feel that the way they are teaching is working well enough, so why change? They are often afraid to try something new that may fail or negatively influence student ratings. Instructors may not seek new ways to teach until they make a personal commitment to improve their teaching or need to change because they are required to teach new course delivery formats to meet market demands. Thus, instructors should be encouraged and supported to periodically break out of the mold of teaching only one course delivery format and experiment with new technologies. By teaching online, instructors can re-examine classroom cultures and strategies that can lead to developing additional effective teaching practices. It should be noted that teaching and experimenting with online courses do not automatically make instructors better teachers or course designers. This development can happen when instructors critically reflect on their practice and make changes based on observation and evaluation of student learning.

To help instructors begin to transform their perspectives of teaching online, faculty development professionals should consider providing development opportunities beyond traditional workshops that only create awareness of new technologies (Cranton, 1996; Cranton & King, 2003; King, 2001, 2003). Instead, as Cranton and King (2003) explained, meaningful faculty development should go beyond learning new technology and should provide opportunities to reflect on and critically evaluate educators' "values, beliefs, and assumptions about teaching and their ways of seeing the world" (p. 33). This can be accomplished by getting faculty members actively involved in the learning process; providing opportunities for self-direction, self-assessment, reflection; and providing opportunities to apply immediately what has been learned. King (2001) suggested a "spiral model" for faculty development in which faculty members can "construct knowledge, explore uncharted territory, and reflect on their teaching practice" (p. 127). Chism (2004) explained that faculty developers can help faculty members reflect on the best way to incorporate technology into teaching by providing resources

and support, helping faculty members to gather data, and offering personal encouragement from peers and instructional designers.

To provide assistance for instructors who are learning to teach online, Chism (2004) noted that faculty developers should take into account where faculty members are in the Faculty Learning Cycles of plan, act, observe, and reflect. Chism pointed out that it is important to work with faculty advisory groups, learning centers, and learning technology centers to develop ways to "build on the faculty learning cycle in delivering services" to faculty members who are learning to teach online (p. 44). During the *planning* phase, professional development professionals can provide information to help faculty members to evaluate ideas on how to use technology and online activities and strategies effectively for teaching and learning. While workshops have been rated as not consistently useful in helping faculty members to learn how to teach, they can be useful in the planning cycle to introduce ideas and technologies for later experimentation. In addition, one-on-one discussions with instructional designers can help instructors to determine what methods could be introduced in courses to improve practice, which resources are available to gain this knowledge, what additional training is available, which conferences would be worthwhile to attend, and whether it would be possible to conduct course-related research.

During the *act* phase particularly but also through several phases of the learning cycle, faculty members would benefit from personal support, including help from mentors, support groups, or instructional designers. When commenting about mentors and instructional designers, Chism (2004) suggested, "Rather than being highly proficient technologically, however, these people need to be knowledgeable about teaching and learning and capable of understanding disciplinary approaches to teaching and learning" (p. 44). Providing assistance during the act phase is important; otherwise, faculty members may become frustrated and abandon experiments on using new technologies or trying new teaching techniques. During the *observation* phase of the learning cycle, faculty members evaluate the effectiveness of their experimentation based on what takes place online and the effect on student learning. At this point, faculty developers can provide feedback on assessments being utilized and suggest informal evaluation methods, such as midcourse evaluations or observation of in-class or online activities. Faculty developers can help instructors to develop or interpret results of formal methods, including student evaluations, tests, and assignments. Faculty developers can also assist instructors in gathering data to help improve teaching and student learning, including research on the scholarship of teaching and learning.

After using these observational methods, during the *reflective* phase of the cycle, faculty developers can help instructors to realize how more learner-centered strategies and technologies, including online activities, can be used to enhance student learning. Reflection is an integral way for faculty members to learn to teach, whether through self-directed methods such as learning through experience or through formal training (Brookfield, 1995; Cranton, 1996; King, 2003; Osterman & Kottkamp, 2004). According to Chism et al. (2002), "Instead of relying primarily on 'tips' and workshops that model effective techniques, those involved in the work of faculty development have come to operate on the principle that cultivating intentionality in teaching is at the heart of their work" (p. 34). Therefore, methods that promote reflective practice to promote "intentional practice" have been found to be effective. Such methods include asking reflective questions during training, facilitating discussions, seeking and reflecting on student feedback, utilizing teaching portfolios and self-reflective journals, and conducting research on their own teaching and course student learning. However, this self-reflection is more transformative if it is shared with and guided by mentors, colleagues, or faculty development

professionals. These reflective methods can help faculty to identify their teaching beliefs and assumptions and find ways to improve their teaching practice in all course delivery formats.

Faculty learning communities can be utilized during each phase of the faculty learning cycle and throughout the faculty member's career to improve teaching practice. According to Cox (2004), a faculty learning community is a cross-disciplinary faculty-and-staff group (recommended size 8 to 12 members) "who engage in an active, collaborative, yearlong program with a curriculum about enhancing teaching and learning and with frequent seminars and activities that provide learning, development, the scholarship of teaching, and community building" (p. 8). Chism et al. (2002) explained that using reflective practice methods has helped faculty development to "become more in harmony with the learner-centered education being promoted for students" (p. 34). This includes emphasizing the social aspect of learning for faculty members; therefore, "faculty development is no longer being envisioned as an individual and private activity" (p. 36). This was confirmed in this research study as instructors wanted to learn from each other and from other experts. One method that is growing in popularity is to enroll faculty in an online course, either a course in their discipline or a course on how to design and teach online courses. Experiencing an online course as a student along with other faculty members to reflect on the experience together is an effective way for instructors to learn firsthand how to design and teach online courses.

Experiential Learning Faculty Development Model

Following the faculty learning community model and many of the learning strategies that were found in this research study to be effective, the University of Wisconsin (UW)-Whitewater developed a 10-week faculty development series (UW-Whitewater Learning Technology Center,

2012). This series is conducted over the summer with five days of face-to-face sessions and eight fully online modules. The online portion of the series uses an experiential learning model in which participants design and develop their own online or hybrid course while participating in course activities and technologies as students would, including participating in collaborative discussions and online reflective and interactive activities through the university's course management system. Instructional designers guide the faculty participants through a course design process that shares pedagogical best practices, including audience and course analysis, developing learning goals, creating interactive activities, building learning communities, creating course organization, and developing formative and summative assessments. Experienced online instructors share lessons learned during in-person sessions and consultations with instructional designers are offered to assist the participants with their own course design. One faculty participant explained:

It is a valuable systematic approach to pedagogy that alerts us to the unique nature of the online learning environment—thus waking us from any dream that we can just continue doing what we already do and have it be vital for our students... Much of what we learned has pedagogical value well beyond the online environment.

In an end-of-workshop series survey 91% ($N = 34$) of the participants said that the online units of the summer workshop series were useful and would help them to design online or hybrid courses. They also shared that "this course is not only about online teaching but also about teaching in general" and "has helped a great deal as a catalyst for thought." Many agreed that training for instructors teaching online should be "mandatory," even though it is not required at UW-Whitewater.

Teaching online is not an intuitive process and one certainly can't just translate F2F [face-to-face]

materials into an online format and think things are going to go well. If the college is invested in excellence in online teaching, then classes like this one should be required.

The UW-Whitewater faculty workshop series participants strongly agreed that "working together collaboratively" with other faculty as part of an online course while participating as an online student was an "eye-opening" experience and the peer collaboration made the "process more approachable." The participants said that it was "validating not only to hear other peoples' opinions and suggestions, but also to watch as others sometimes struggle with the same issues." Another said, "The challenge to my assumptions has been painful but very worthwhile." The online course faculty participants said that the experience of being an online student had a "tremendous" impact on how they design and teach online courses in the future. "It gave me a model of how to do it and how to do it well but it also gave me an experience of walking in the shoes of one of my students." Lessons learned included the importance of keeping up with deadlines, building community, planning clear course organization, and aligning course goals with learning activities and assessments.

The findings of this research study and the literature shared in this chapter confirm that no matter how much experience instructors had with teaching, they still wanted to learn new pedagogical and technological approaches to improve teaching and learning. Engaging the teachers of adults in active dialogue will create goodwill and a cooperative environment during workshops, online training programs, and other faculty development initiatives. Adult students, including instructors, learn by reflecting on experience individually and with peers. Providing opportunities, either formally or informally, for instructors to share best practices and seek new ways to teach can reinvigorate practice, lead to pedagogical transformations, and enhance student learning.

FUTURE RESEARCH DIRECTIONS

This research study updated existing literature on how faculty members learn to teach adult learners. As more adult learners continue to reenter education and take more online courses, more research in this area will broaden understanding of this growing population, how this group has evolved, and how faculty members can meet their needs and help adults to learn online. While this study focused on how faculty members learned to teach adult learners, it would also be useful to understand how faculty members learn to teach other types of learners online, including undergraduate traditional-age students and students from diverse cultures and ethnicities. Would there be a steeper learning curve if faculty members were not familiar with adult learning strategies that are similar to online learning? Or would the learning curve be the same? Would other challenges and opportunities emerge depending on the type of students whom faculty members teach while learning to teach online?

This study involved experienced instructors who had learned to teach face-to-face courses many years ago; some had also learned to teach online a long time ago. It would help to compare experienced and inexperienced instructors as they learn to teach online. Future studies could research how institutional structures can support or hinder growth in online teaching and course development. This could include how various factors influence how faculty members learn to teach, such as appraisal and reward systems, tenure, organizational climate, and faculty training and development opportunities. Specifically, it would be worthwhile to compare instructors who have participated in a formal faculty development program with those who have not done so to understand how this influences how faculty members learn how to develop and teach online courses and what they learn that may impact teaching practice and student learning.

CONCLUSION

Faculty members face many challenges as they experiment with learning how to teach online, including: meeting market demands, learning new technology, discovering what works best when teaching various course delivery formats, identifying what learning strategies are most effective with adult learners, how to manage the workload of teaching online, overcoming the fear of not being a good instructor, and assuming what is an effective way to teach and what is not. This research study found that experienced faculty members needed to learn anew and to rethink pedagogical strategies when converting face-to-face courses to the online environment. Faculty members who are learning to teach are also adult learners who learn through experience and by conducting experiments (King & Lawler, 2003; Lawler, 2003; Lawler & King, 2000). These teaching experiments include observing the effect of student learning followed by reflection on whether this strategy should be used again (Chism, 2004). Teaching online provides a laboratory to experiment with many pedagogical possibilities to teach, design courses and learning activities, and meet the needs of adult learners.

This study showed that it is important to understand all experiments or factors involved in learning how to teach. The factors, or research themes, that influenced how the participants learned to teach adult learners online were: (a) Adapted to Market Demand, (b) Anchored by Adult Learning Strategies, (c) Experimented in Online Laboratory, (e) Evolved from Trial and Error to Collaboration, and (e) Rethought Pedagogical Possibilities. Each theme provides insight into why and how faculty members learn through experience. However, these themes also provide evidence that experience is not enough to learn how to teach adults online. Each theme followed a common pattern in the Faculty Learning Cycles of planning, acting, observing, and reflecting. The faculty members learned to teach by reflecting on each cycle based on observation of what takes place from their experiences and actions. In the "Adapted to Market Demand" theme, faculty members realized that they needed to change the way they taught to adapt to the changing needs of adult learners who were registering for more online courses. To make this transition, the research participants, who were experienced instructors of adults, utilized adult learning strategies such as collaborative and constructivist learning as an anchor to build on strategies that worked well in online formats. The research participants experimented with these methods to see what worked well and made appropriate modifications. Since they had not been trained to teach, the research participants had learned through trial and error, experimenting with a range of methods of teaching. Most sought help and collaborated with colleagues to learn methods for teaching online. Then the instructors acted on their plans and used more up-front planning than they had in face-to-face courses to develop online learning activities and strategies. The research participants observed what happened and reflected, finding that teaching online challenged their teaching assumptions, encouraged them to rethink pedagogy, and provided new strategies to use when teaching all course delivery formats.

According to Merriam and Caffarella (1999), learning is not an end product; instead, it is a process that "focuses on what happens when the learning takes place" (p. 250). This study confirmed that faculty members learned through each stage of investigating how to utilize technology effectively to teach online and then applied this knowledge to all course delivery formats. A message for faculty development professionals is that it is important to listen to instructors' stories of how they learned to teach and what they learned from experience. The faculty members in this study made it clear that, while experience had been their most significant teacher when learning how to teach online, they wanted and needed more help, even if they did not specifically ask for it. Helping instructors to learn to teach online is

also helping them to fulfill their ongoing role as adult learners, with a goal of improving teaching practice, and ultimately, student learning.

REFERENCES

Allen, I. E., & Seaman, J. (2006). *Making the grade: Online education in the United States, 2006.* Needham, MA: The Sloan Consortium.

Allen, I. E., & Seaman, J. (2007). *Online nation: Five years of growth in online learning.* Needham, MA: The Sloan Consortium.

Allen, I. E., & Seaman, J. (2010). *Learning on demand: Online education in the United States, 2009.* Needham, MA: Babson Survey Research Group, The Sloan Consortium.

Allen, I. E., Seaman, J., & Garrett, R. (2007). *Blending in: The extent of promise of blended education in the United States.* Needham, MA: Sloan Consortium.

Anderson, T., Rourke, L., Garrison, D. R., & Archer, W. (2001). Assessing teaching presence in a computer conferencing context. *Journal of Asynchronous Learning Networks, 5*(2), 1–17.

Arabacz, P., Pirani, J., & Fawcett, P. (2003). *Supporting e-learning in higher education.* Boulder, CO: Educause Center for Applied Research.

Argyris, C., & Schön, D. (1978). *Organizational learning: A theory of action perspective.* San Francisco, CA: Jossey-Bass.

Austin, A. E., & Wulff, D. H. (2004). The challenge to prepare the next generation of faculty. In Wulff, D. H., & Austin, A. E. (Eds.), *Paths to the professorate: Strategies for enriching the preparation of future faculty* (pp. 3–16). San Francisco, CA: Jossey-Bass.

Bates, A. W., & Poole, G. (2003). *Effective teaching with technology: Foundations for success.* San Francisco, CA: Jossey-Bass.

Belanger, P. (1996). Trends in adult education policy. *Adult Education and Development, 47,* 19–29.

Berge, Z. L. (1995). Facilitating computer conferencing: Recommendations from the field. *Educational Technology, 35*(1), 22–30.

Biro, S. C. (2004). *How to support faculty as they prepare to teach online.* Paper presented at the Joint International Conference for the 45th Adult Education Research Conference (AERC) and the 23rd National Conference of the Canadian Association for the Study of Adult Education, University of Victoria, Canada.

Bonk, C. J., Kirkley, J., Hara, N., & Dennen, V. (2000, April). *Advances in pedagogy: Finding the instructor in post-secondary online learning.* Paper presented at the American Educational Research Association, New Orleans, LA.

Boud, D., & Walker, D. (1991). *Experience and learning: Reflection at work.* Geelong, Australia: Deakin University Press.

Bower, B. L. (2001). Distance education: Facing the faculty challenge. *Online Journal of Distance Learning Administration, 4*(2).

Bright, B. (1993). What is reflective practice? *Curriculum, 16,* 69–81.

Brookfield, S. D. (1995). *Becoming a critically reflective teacher.* San Francisco, CA: Jossey-Bass.

Brown, J. A. (2004). Marketing and retention strategies for adult degree programs. *New Directions for Adult and Continuing Education, 103*(Fall), 51–60. doi:10.1002/ace.148

Brown, J. S., Collins, A., & Duguid, P. (1989). Situated cognition and the culture of learning. *Educational Researcher, 18*(11), 32–42.

Brufee, K. A. (1999). *Collaborative learning: Higher education, interdependence, and the authority of knowledge* (2nd ed.). Baltimore, MA: John Hopkins University Press.

Carr, W., & Kemmis, S. (1986). *Becoming critical: Education, knowledge, and action research.* London, UK: Falmer Press.

CDW-G. (2008). *The 21st-century campus: Are we there yet? Challenges and opportunities for campus technology.* Retrieved from http://newsroom.cdwg.com/features/feature-10-13-08.html

Cercone, K. (2008). Characteristics of adult learners with implications for online learning design. *AACE Journal, 16*(2), 137–159.

Chism, N. V. N. (2004). Using a framework to engage faculty in instructional technologies. *EDUCAUSE Quarterly, 2,* 39–45.

Chism, N. V. N., Lees, N. D., & Evenbeck, S. (2002). Faculty development for teaching innovation. *Liberal Education, 88*(3), 34–38.

Clarke, L. E., & Gabert, T. E. (2004). Faculty issues related to adult degree programs. In Pappas, J., & Jerman, J. (Eds.), *Developing and delivering adult degree programs* (Vol. 103, pp. 31–40). San Francisco, CA: Jossey-Bass. doi:10.1002/ace.146

Conceição, S. (2006). Faculty lived experiences in the online environment. *Adult Education Quarterly, 57*(1), 26–45. doi:10.1177/1059601106292247

Conceição-Runlee, S. (2001). *Faculty lived experiences in the online environment.* Doctoral dissertation, University of Wisconsin-Madison, Madison, WI.

Cox, M. D. (2004). Introduction to faculty learning communities. In Cox, M. D., & Richlin, L. (Eds.), *New directions for teaching and learning* (Vol. 97, pp. 5–23). New York, NY: Wiley.

Cranton, P. (1996). *Professional development as perspective transformation.* San Francisco, CA: Jossey-Bass.

Cranton, P., & King, K. (2003). Transformative learning as a professional development goal. In King, K., & Lawler, P. (Eds.), *New directions for adult and continuing education: New perspectives on designing and implementing professional development of teachers of adults* (*Vol. 98*, pp. 31–37). San Francisco, CA: Jossey-Bass. doi:10.1002/ace.97

Creswell, J. (2005). *Educational research: Planning, conducting, and evaluating quantitative and qualitative research* (2nd ed.). Upper Saddle River, NJ: Pearson.

Daley, B. (2001). Learning and professional practice: A study of four professions. *Adult Education Quarterly, 52*(1), 39–54.

Dewey, J. (1938). *Experience and education.* New York, NY: Macmillan.

Dewey, J. (1954). *Experience and education* (18th ed.). New York, NY: Macmillan.

Dewey, J. (1997). *Experience and education.* New York, NY: Simon & Schuster.

Donaldson, J. F., Flannery, D. D., & Ross-Gordon, J. M. (1993). A triangulated study comparing adult college students' perceptions of effective teaching with those of traditional students. *Continuing Higher Education Review, 57*(3), 147–165.

Dziuban, C. D., Hartman, J., Moskal, P., Sorg, S., & Truman, B. (2003). Three ALN modalities: An institutional perspective. In Bourne, J., & Moore, J. C. (Eds.), *Elements of quality online education: Into the mainstream* (pp. 127–148). Needham, MA: Sloan Center for Online Education.

Dziuban, C. D., Shea, P., & Arbaugh, J. (2005). Faculty roles and satisfaction in asynchronous learning networks. In Hiltz, S. R., & Goldman, R. (Eds.), *Learning together online: Research on asynchronous learning networks* (pp. 169–190). Mahwah, NJ: Erlbaum.

Fenwick, T. J. (2003). *Learning through experience: Troubling orthodoxies and intersecting questions.* Malabar, FL: Krieger.

Flint, T. A. (2005). *How well are we serving our adult learners? Investigating the impact of institutions on success and retention.* Chicago, IL: Council for Adult and Experiential Learning (CAEL).

Fulton, C., & Licklider, B. L. (1998). Supporting faculty development in an era of change. *To Improve the Academy, 19,* 51-66.

Gallant, G. (2000). Professional development for Web-based teaching: Overcoming innocence and resistance. In Burge, E. J. (Ed.), *New directions for adult and continuing education* (pp. 69–78). San Francisco, CA: Jossey-Bass. doi:10.1002/ace.8807

Geertz, C. (1983). *Local knowledge.* New York, NY: Basic Books.

Glaser, B. G., & Strauss, A. L. (1967). *The discovery of grounded theory.* Chicago, IL: Aldine.

Golde, C. M., & Dore, T. M. (2004). The survey of doctoral education and career preparation: The importance of disciplinary contexts. In Wulff, D. H., & Austin, A. E. (Eds.), *Paths to the professorate: Strategies for enriching the preparation of future faculty* (pp. 19–45). San Francisco, CA: Jossey-Bass.

Graham, S. W., & Gisi, S. L. (2000). Adult undergraduate students: What role does college involvement play? *NASPA Journal, 38*(1), 99–121.

Greeno, J. G. (1997). On claims that answer the wrong questions. *Educational Researcher, 26*(1), 5.

Guerrero, S. (2010). The role of teacher thinking in technology-based reform: A multiple case study. *Journal of the Research Center for Educational Technology, 6*(2), 18.

Harasim, L., Hiltz, S. R., Teles, L., & Turroff, M. (1995). *Learning networks: A field guide to teaching and learning online.* Cambridge, MA: MIT Press.

Hartman, J., Otte, G., & Niemiec, M. (2006). *Blended learning institutional strategies for success.* Paper presented at the 12th Sloan-C International Conference on Asynchronous Learning Networks, Orlando, FL.

Hiltz, S. R., & Shea, P. (2005). The student in the online classroom. In Hiltz, S. R., & Goldman, R. (Eds.), *Learning together online* (pp. 145–168). Mahwah, NJ: Erlbaum.

Jarvis, P. (1987). *Adult learning in the social context.* London, UK: Croom Helm.

Jarvis, P. (1995). *Adult and continuing education: Theory and practice* (2nd ed.). New York, NY: Routledge.

Jaworski, B. (1993). Professional development of teachers: The potential of critical reflection. *British Journal of Inservice Education, 19,* 37–42. doi:10.1080/0305763930190307

Johnstone, J. W. C., & Rivera, R. J. (1965). *Volunteers for learning: A study of the educational pursuits of American adults.* Chicago, IL: Aldine.

Kasworm, C. E., & Blowers, S. S. (1994). *Adult undergraduate students: Patterns of learning involvement (Final research report to U.S. Department of Education).* Knoxville, TN: University of Tennessee, College of Education.

Kasworm, C. E., Polson, C. J., & Fishback, S. J. (2002). *Responding to adult learners in higher education.* Malabar, FL: Krieger.

Kerka, S. (1988). *Strategies for retaining adult students: The educationally disadvantaged.* Columbus, OH: ERIC Clearinghouse on Adult Career and Vocational Education.

Kezar, A. J. (2000). *Teaching and learning: ERIC trends, 1999-2000.* Washington, DC: George Washington University Graduate School of Education and Human Development.

King, K. (2000, June). *Educational technology that transforms: Educators' transformational learning experiences in professional development.* Paper presented at the Adult Education Research Conference, Vancouver, Canada.

King, K. (2001). The tail of the comet: Helping faculty focus on their pathway of discovery in learning and using technology. *Journal of Faculty Development, 18*(4), 123–129.

King, K. (2002a). Identifying success in online teacher education and professional development. *The Internet and Higher Education, 5,* 231–246. doi:10.1016/S1096-7516(02)00104-5

King, K. (2002b). Technology catalyzing change in how faculty teach and learn. *Journal of Continuing Higher Education, 50*(2), 26–37.

King, K. (2003). Learning the new technologies: Strategies for success. *New Directions for Adult and Continuing Education, 98,* 49–56. doi:10.1002/ace.99

King, K., & Lawler, P. (2003). Trends and issues in the professional development of teachers of adults. In King, K., & Lawler, P. (Eds.), *New directions for adult and continuing education: New perspectives on designing and implementing professional development of teachers of adults* (*Vol. 98,* pp. 5–13). San Francisco, CA: Jossey-Bass. doi:10.1002/ace.94

Knapper, C. K. (1995). Understanding student learning: Implications for instructional practice. In Wright, W. A. (Eds.), *Teaching improve practices: Successful strategies for higher education* (pp. 58–75). Boston, MA: Anker.

Knowles, M. S. (1970). *The modern practice of adult education: Andragogy vs. pedagogy.* New York, NY: Cambridge Books.

Knowles, M. S. (1980). *The modern practice of adult education: From pedagogy to andragogy.* Chicago, IL: Association Press/Follet.

Kolb, D. A. (1984). *Experiential learning: Experience as the source of learning and development.* Englewood Cliffs, NJ: Prentice-Hall.

Kramarae, C. (2003). Gender equity online, when there is no door to knock on. In Moore, M. G., & Anderson, W. G. (Eds.), *Handbook of distance education* (pp. 261–272). Mahwah, NJ: Erlbaum.

Kyei-Blankson, L. (2009). *Learning to teach and teaching online: Faculty-faculty interactions in online environments.* Paper presented at the Society for Information Technology & Teacher Education International Conference, Chesapeake, VA.

Lau, L. K. (2003). Institutional factors affecting student retention. *Education, 124*(1), 126–136.

Lave, J., & Wenger, E. (1991). *Situated learning: Legitimate peripheral participation.* New York, NY: Cambridge Press.

Lawler, P. (2003). Teachers as adult learners: A new perspective. In King, K. P., & Lawler, P. A. (Eds.), *New directions for adult and continuing education* (pp. 15–22). San Francisco, CA: Jossey-Bass. doi:10.1002/ace.95

Lawler, P., & King, K. (2000, April). *Refocusing faculty development.* Paper presented at the Adult Education Research Conference (AERC), Vancouver, British Columbia, Canada.

Lawler, P., King, K., & Wilhite, S. C. (2004). *Living and learning with technology: Faculty as reflective practitioners in the online classroom.* Paper presented at the Joint International Conference of the 45th Adult Education Research Conference (AERC) and the 23rd National Conference of the Canadian Association for the Study of Adult Education, University of Victoria, Canada.

Lincoln, Y., & Guba, E. (1985). *Naturalistic inquiry.* New York, NY: Sage.

Lindemann, E. (1926). *The meaning of adult education.* New York, NY: New Republic.

Lowes, S. (2008). Online teaching and classroom change: The trans-classroom teacher in the age of the Internet. *Innovate: Journal of Online Education, 4*(3). Retrieved from http://www.innovateonline.info/

Lowry, P., & Bush, R. (2009). *Technologies and delivery methods.* Paper presented at the International Conference on e-Learning, Academic Conferences.

Mancuso, S. (2001). Adult-centered practices: Benchmarking study in higher education. *Innovative Higher Education, 25*(3), 165. doi:10.1023/A:1007647531576

Maykut, P., & Morehouse, R. (1994). *Beginning qualitative research.* Philadelphia, PA: Falmer.

McCombs, B., & Vakili, D. (2005). A learner-centered framework for e-learning. *Teachers College Record, 107*, 1582–1600. doi:10.1111/j.1467-9620.2005.00534.x

Merriam, S. B. (2002). *Qualitative research in practice: Examples for discussion and analysis* (1st ed.). San Francisco, CA: Jossey-Bass.

Merriam, S. B., & Caffarella, R. S. (1999). *Learning in adulthood: A comprehensive guide* (2nd ed.). San Francisco, CA: Jossey-Bass.

Merriam, S. B., Caffarella, R. S., & Baumgartner, L. M. (2007). *Learning in adulthood: A comprehensive guide* (3rd ed.). San Francisco, CA: Jossey-Bass.

Millis, B. J. (1994). Faculty development in the 1990s: What it is and why we can't wait. *Journal of Counseling and Development, 72*, 454–464. doi:10.1002/j.1556-6676.1994.tb00974.x

Moon, J. A. (2004). *Reflection in learning & professional development: Theory & practice.* New York, NY: Routledge Falmer.

National Center for Education Statistics. (2002). *Nontraditional undergraduates (NCES 2002-012)*. Washington, DC: U.S. Government Printing Office.

National Center for Education Statistics. (2010). *Digest of educational statistics*. Retrieved from http://nces.ed.gov/pubsearch/pubsinfo. asp?pubid=2011015

Osterman, K. F., & Kottkamp, R. B. (2004). *Reflective practice for educators: Professional development to improve student learning* (2nd ed.). Thousand Oaks, CA: Corwin.

Parisot, A. H. (1997). Distance education as a catalyst for changing teaching in the community college: Implications for institutional policy. *New Directions for Community Colleges, 99*, 5. doi:10.1002/cc.9901

Patton, M. (2001). *Qualitative research and evaluation methods* (3rd ed.). Thousand Oaks, CA: Sage.

Paulson, K., & Boeke, M. (2006). *Adult learners in the United States: A national profile*. Washington, DC: National Center for Higher Education Management Systems.

Pearson, W. (2005). Assuring instructional effectiveness. In Basch, L. (Ed.), *Best practices in adult learning* (pp. 129–145). Bolton, MA: Anker.

Professional and Organizational Development Network in Higher Education. (2008). *What is faculty development?* Retrieved from http://www. podnetwork.org/development.htm

Rodriquez, F. G., & Nash, S. S. (2004). Technology and the adult degree program: The human element. In Pappas, J. P., & Jerman, J. (Eds.), *Developing and delivering adult degree programs* (pp. 73–79). San Francisco, CA: Jossey-Bass. doi:10.1002/ace.150

Rogers, E. M. (1962). *Diffusion of innovations*. New York, NY: Free Press.

Rogers, E. M. (1995). *Diffusion of innovations* (4th ed.). New York, NY: Free Press.

Ross-Gordon, J. M. (1991). Critical incidents in the college classroom. *Educational Review, 55*(1/2), 14–29.

Ross-Gordon, J. M. (2003). Adult learners in the classroom. *New Directions for Student Services, 102*, 43–52. doi:10.1002/ss.88

Schön, D. (1983). *The reflective practitioner*. San Francisco, CA: Jossey-Bass.

Schön, D. (1987). *Educating the reflective practitioner*. New York, NY: Basic Books.

Schrum, L., & Hong, S. (2002). Dimensions and strategies for online success: Voices from experienced educators. *Journal of Asynchronous Learning Networks, 6*(1), 57–67.

Seaman, J. (2009). *The paradox of faculty voices: Online learning as a strategic asset (Vol. 2)*. Washington, DC: Association of Public and Land-Grant Universities.

Short, J., Williams, E., & Christie, B. (1976). *The social psychology of telecommunications*. London, UK: Wiley.

Skibba, K. (2011). *An investigation of how faculty members learn to teach adult students in a blended program*. Unpublished doctoral dissertation, University of Wisconsin, Milwaukee.

Swail, W. S. (2002). Higher education and the new demographics: Questions for policy. *Change, 34*(4), 15–23.

Swan, K., & Shea, P. (2005). The development of virtual learning communities. In Hiltz, S. R., & Goldman, R. (Eds.), *Learning together online* (pp. 239–260). Mahwah, NJ: Erlbaum.

Taylor, A., & McQuiggan, C. (2008). Faculty development programming: If we build it, will they come? *EDUCAUSE Quarterly, 31*(3), 28–37.

U.S. Department of Education, National Center for Education Statistics. (2002). *Nontraditional undergraduates (NCES 2002-012)*. Washington, DC: U.S. Government Printing Office.

Usher, R., Bryant, I., & Johnston, R. (1997). *Adult education and the postmodern challenge: Learning beyond the limits*. New York, NY: Routledge.

UW-Whitewater Learning Technology Center. (2012). *Online/blended workshop series*. Retrieved from http://geturl.uww.edu/1cg

Weimer, M. (2002). *Learner-centered teaching: Five key changes to practice*. San Francisco, CA: Jossey-Bass.

Wellington, B., & Austin, P. (1996). Orientations to reflective practice. *Educational Researcher*, *38*, 307–316.

Wenger, E. (1998). *Communities of practice: Learning, meaning and identity*. Cambridge, MA: Cambridge University Press.

KEY TERMS AND DEFINITIONS

Adult Education: The practice of educating and teaching adults when the purpose of *learning* is to acquire some form of knowledge, information, or skill (Johnstone & Rivera, 1965; Merriam et al., 2007). This study focuses on a program in the formal education of adults in higher education where the purpose of learning is to receive a degree.

Adult Learners or Students: Defined as anyone age 25 or over, married or the head of the household, who is participating in some type of formal postsecondary education (Paulson & Boeke, 2006). Adults differ from children in learning because adults have accumulated knowledge and experience that can contribute to or hinder learning experiences (Knowles, 1980; Merriam et al., 2007).

Course Delivery Format*s***:** The way in which courses are delivered to students: traditional, Web-facilitated, hybrid (partially online courses, also known as blended), and online (Allen & Seaman, 2006).

Experiential Learning: When the learner actively participates in an experience and then links what is learned from that experience to prior knowledge (Dewey, 1938, 1954, 1997; Jarvis, 1995; Knowles, 1970, 1980; Kolb, 1984; Lindemann, 1926).

Faculty Development: In this study, refers to providing instructors with instructional professional development, including training and resources, to improve teaching and learning (Millis, 1994; Professional and Organizational Development Network in Higher Education, 2008).

Faculty Learning Cycle: How faculty members learn to teach through experience by planning a course of action, acting on their plans, observing what happened, reflecting on the results, and starting the process again (Chism, 2004).

Learner-Centered Teaching: Requires that faculty members give students some control over their own learning processes (Weimer, 2002).

Managerial Role: Includes all aspects of coordinating a course, including scheduling interaction, setting due dates, and managing assignments, discussions, assessments, student roles, and workload (Berge, 1995).

Nontraditional Students: Refers to students who are not the typical 18- to 24-year-olds who attend college immediately after graduating from high school. The potential characteristics of a nontraditional student are part-time status, older than 25, delayed in college enrollment after high school, working full time while enrolled, financial independence from parents, having dependents, being a single parent, and lacking a high school degree but having completed a GED or other high school completion certificate (National Center for Education Statistics, 2002).

Online Courses: Deliver most or all of the content online and typically have no face-to-face meetings (Allen & Seaman, 2006).

Pedagogical Role: Includes both design and delivery of instructional learning activities (Berge, 1995).

Reflective Practice: The process of making judgments about complex and difficult situations based on experience and prior knowledge (Bright, 1993; Merriam et al., 2007).

Situated learning: is learning that is embedded in the situation in which a person participates (Boud & Walker, 1991; Brown, J. S., et al., 1989; Greeno, 1997; Lave & Wenger, 1991; Usher et al., 1997; Wenger, 1998).

Social Role: Involves communication between the instructor and students and among students in the course to create a friendly and nurturing environment to support a community of learners (Berge, 1995).

Technological Role: Refers to instructors utilizing technology to organize course content and to assist students with technology issues (Berge, 1995).

Chapter 15
Strategies for Online Instruction

Kim J. Hyatt
Carnegie Mellon University, USA

Michaela A. Noakes
Carnegie Mellon University, USA

Carrie Zinger
Duquesne University, USA

ABSTRACT

With diverse options for teaching and learning, continued professional development is requisite for instructors in order to meet the needs of a growing online population of students. In online learning settings, if students are not engaged through various instructional techniques, students become easily distracted and miss valuable content necessary for learning. In traditional classroom settings, instructors can easily check for levels of engagement via a visual scan of the class. In an online environment, without the use of video, a visual scan is not possible. As a result, a productive way to ensure student engagement in asynchronous or synchronous courses is for instructors to implement modeling, graphic, manipulative, and simulation strategies into the online environment. This chapter reviews a variety of best practice strategies for engaging students in an online learning environment as part of faculty professional development to improve their teaching and learning. These practice strategies will be discussed, along with examples of how they can be implemented.

INTRODUCTION

Today's students represent a culturally diverse population seeking flexibility, active engagement and a stimulating learning environment for their online educational experience. To meet this growing need, instructors are pursuing a variety of best practice strategies to enhance knowledge and skill levels regarding online learners. As this chapter identifies and defines a variety of best practice strategies that are applicable in both synchronous (instructor led) and asynchronous (individually paced study) environments, it will also outline the rationale, aims and objectives for successful implementation of these constructs.

DOI: 10.4018/978-1-4666-1963-0.ch015

The online environment is created in a non-traditional setting and designed without barriers to learning. Essentially, online instructors, in the role of lecturer, facilitator, or guide-on-the-side, provide a model of behavior they want their students to emulate. These behaviors include effective time management, good organizational skills, a collaborative attitude, and professional, interpersonal communications. Online instructors who incorporate interactive strategies, such as modeling, graphic, manipulative, and simulations, along with social networking components for online literacy, can encourage students to interact with course materials through various multimedia applications. Through this constructivist milieu, students cannot be passive learners. Carefully architecting e-learning content design is a foundational component of effective teaching and learning in our global society.

Vygotsky's (1978) theory of Social Educational Learning posits that social interaction has a fundamental role in the cognitive development process. This approach to constructivism demonstrates that each learner will bring to the environment prior knowledge and will begin to construct new knowledge from the perspectives that are shared by others through dynamic social interactions. Clark and Mayer's Segmenting principle (2008) would have the asynchronous learning process broken down into phases or manageable chunks where the students could practice independently and then synchronously interact with their group members. It is the student's ability to build upon their prior knowledge and internalize new information that will meet their psychological learning requirements and keep them engaged in an e-learning environment.

As noted by Clark and Mayer (2008), "….in asynchronous e-learning, you always allow learners control over pacing. Pacing control allows participants to progress forward or backward at their own rates. Learner control is one of the features that distinguish asynchronous from synchronous forms of e-learning" (pp. 289-290). According to Mayer (1998), there are several areas that influence problem solving and enhance critical thinking skills: (a) Cognitive skills – the facts, concepts, and guidelines unique to a skill field; (b) Metaskills – the ability to plan, monitor, and assess actions associated with problem solving; and (c) Motivation – an investment of effort to persist and solve the problem.

By subsequently increasing the potential for deep learning, interactive online environments may increase creativity, critical thinking and more effective problem solving skills for students ultimately enhancing their interest and insights as actively engaged learners. The pedagogic application of these social software tools provides a forum for students to engage in critical thinking, problem solving, ethical debates and social responsibility. In this context, learners are in control of the method of information discovery, its distribution, modification and socio-cultural collaboration in "content creation over content consumption" (McLoughlin and Lee, 2007).

MODELING

In order for students to obtain the best possible experience while participating in an online environment, it is critical for the instructor to have an established set of guidelines and instructions for students to follow. In the synchronous classroom, the guidelines and instructions establish how communication takes place. The instructor, as a demonstration, should concretely model this interaction for students. A few examples of online interactivity include making use of private and public chat functions, encouraging participants to use mark-up tools, such as agree/disagree buttons, hand raise functionality, emoticons, polling questions, etc.

Students will take cues from the instructor on how to respond and participate in this environment and adhere to the "tone" set at the beginning of the course by the instructor (Savery, 2010). The instructor should also model the use of vocalization and questioning strategies, such as speaking clearly and at an adequate pace, asking questions for clarification and making use of directed questions. As a professional development exercise, the instructor should record his/her class and critique his/her own interactions with students using the above-mentioned questioning strategies.

Because one cannot read facial expressions or make eye contact (unless using video chat), it may be more difficult to determine if students understand a concept or if they are left with residual questions. Moreover, it is worthwhile for the instructor to consider providing each student with a "Do's and Don'ts" document of online "netiquette" to follow throughout the duration of the course (Savery, 2010). The benefits of such a document are that all students are held to the same standards and they can self-monitor behaviors.

Because there are more potential distractions in the online environment, it is critical to set boundaries for what is and is not acceptable while attending an online session, and for the instructor to plan a variety of ways to elicit planned and unplanned student participation. The instructor should model good organizational and time-management skills by starting and ending the online sessions in a timely manner. One of the guidelines should including having students sign into the session fifteen minutes prior to the start time, so the actual class time can be used to cover the outlined material. This will provide adequate time to trouble-shoot with students who have technical difficulties or answer questions about upcoming assignments. Students can also be provided with a pre-class activity during this time, which can be used to engage with and practice some of the online tools while waiting for the actual class to begin. These pre-class activities can be used as an anticipatory set for the today's lesson.

The instructor also needs to model participation expectations, set clear timelines for course assignment completion and submission, and other communication guidelines, such as what to do when a class needs to be missed (Sheridan & Kelly, 2010). Just as in a traditional classroom, situations may arise which require a student to miss a course, arrive late, or leave early. Be considerate of these personal situations and talk with the participant off-line to discuss how the material should be made up. Also, from time-to-time, it may be advantageous to schedule face-to-face meetings, if possible, or one-on-one video chats, to talk about more complex subjects, present certain materials, or to simply check on students. These guidelines need to be determined at the beginning of the online course. By providing rubrics in advance for expectations, students can apply the guidelines throughout the entire course.

While many of the concepts already discussed were directed toward the synchronous classroom, many of these same techniques can be employed in the asynchronous environment. It may be even more critical to have clearly defined expectations and developed rubrics as there are far less one-on-one or small group teacher-student interactions. Setting clear expectations, reviewed at the onset of the course, will help to minimize frustration and confusion for the students and instructor alike. Included in those expectations should be specific details around how and when student-instructor communication takes place and the time-response expectations. Take advantage of a variety of online networking sites or discussion boards, such as Facebook, Twitter, LinkedIn, etc. One of the great benefits of the asynchronous environment is that instructors and students are not tied to the limited time constraints of a traditional or synchronous classroom. They can take the time they need to formulate ideas and responses, including submitting well thought-out communication pieces (Mandernach, Forrest, Babutzke, & Manker, 2009).

Incorporating social software tools such as Wikis, Blogs, Discussion Boards and online Journals into their courseware design models enables teachers to connect with their student populations through these Web 2.0 applications and collaboration tools. Evaluating Wikis and using them as an engagement tool for today's leaners presents an alternative medium to spark interest in content and enhance deep learning outcomes. As a self-paced tool, Wikis mitigate barriers to learning for those students who may be less willing to participate in a traditional setting. It also stimulates creativity and provides deep thinkers with a forum in which to express themselves. Critical thinking and problem solving skills can also be further developed when using this tool as a collaborative means for addressing complex and nebulous issues. (Clark & Mayer, 2008).

Because Wikis can accommodate multiple content formats they provide an effective technology platform to stimulate creative processes. According to Carmen and Heafner (2002), "students choose a course for its intellectual content (mind) and not for its classroom or system container (matter)" (p.28). Carmen and Heafner's (2002) *Mind over Matter: Transforming Course Management Systems into Effective Learning Environments* addressed the learning experience by defining Five Learner-Centered Principles for Deeper Learning: Active, Social, Contextual, Engaging and Student-owned (refer to Table 1).

Each of these five deeper learning principles is easily applicable to the Wiki learning environment. Clark and Mayer (2008) would again focus on the highly social interaction that is occurring with students who can download a Wiki app to their BlackBerrys and iPhones to personalize their communication with their classmates and instructors. With the Learner Control principle, students have the ability within the Wikis to conduct a self-paced review of the content by clicking on the links of interest to them and by using the navigation features within the Wiki to control the presentation format of the information being reviewed. Social software such as Wimba, Wikis,

Table 1. Applying deeper learning principles to a Wiki

Learner-Centered Principles	Evidence of Learning
Active	Cognitive Discourse
Social	Learning is anytime, all the time
Contextual	Scaffolding of Knowledge
Engaging	Community of Learners
Student-owned	Independent Learning

Blogs, Discussion Boards and Journals are all mediums through which to display and further develop these types of skills for students.

Instructional Technology content design theory encourages diversity in information presentation. Clark and Mayer (2008) caution against cognitive overload by recommending that materials be presented to the auditory and the visual channels of learners. This process is best achieved by integrating the Multimedia Principle into the design of the lesson plan.

The Multimedia Principle states that "learning gains result from combining text and relevant graphics in e-lessons". Cognitive theory contends that words (printed text) and static graphics (pictures) when used independently may result in shallow learning with those individuals who are less familiar with the subject matter (Clark & Mayer, 2008). Conversely, when the lesson material is a combination of these knowledge representations, as in a multimedia presentation, learners will use less working memory, resulting in deeper learning. Graphics should also be implemented judiciously, as they add no additional value for the learner if they are perceived to be decorative filler for screen space. Jonassen, Lee, Yang, and Laffey (2005), posit that when "tasks are complex, ill-defined or when no single correct solution exists" collaboration through Computer-supported collaborative learning (CSCL) is warranted.

Modeling the desired behaviors makes it much easier to analyze what students expect without having face-to-face interaction. It also allows the students to have a set of guidelines, especially for those students for whom this may be a new adventure.

Six general strategies for assisting student performance through teacher-student interactions were described in detail by Gallimore and Tharp (1990) as: 1) Modeling -offering non-verbal behavior for imitation, 2) Contingency Management – rewarding desired behaviors through praise/encouragement, or to control undesirable behaviors through punishment in the form of reprimand/censure, 3) Feeding Back - responding to learner performance in relation to a given standard or set of criteria including grades, 4) Instructing - direct teaching/telling and assigning of tasks. Often embedded in other means of assistance it occurs whenever the teacher assumes responsibility for assisting performance. 5) Questioning - assisting the learner as a prompt, to assess as in a test question, to stimulate thinking, or to provoke creations by the student, 6) Cognitive Structuring - to help the learner organize 'raw' experience by providing a structure for thinking/acting (Savery, 2010, pp. 148-149).

Review of Modeling: Examples for Synchronous Learning

- Model use of private and public chat
- Model use of "mark-up tools" such as check marks, "X's," hand raise function, emoticons, etc. to encourage learner participation
- Model use of vocalization and questioning strategies
- Model good organizational skills and time-line tools to accomplish tasks by due date in order to assist learners with their time-management skills

- Start and end the online sessions in the time frame communicated
- Do not allow an inordinate amount of wait-time for late learners to join out of respect for those present
- Model technology to its full capacity
- Employ a variety of instructional techniques/small group/independent activities
- Disseminate information in a timely manner, as there is more opportunity to "lose" the learner

Review of Modeling: Examples for Asynchronous Learning

- Respond to learner questions in a timely manner
- Engage in face-to-face interactions (video chat) as needed to supplement online
- Provide learners with rubrics, proper communication channels and other learning tools to lower frustration levels
- Ensure learners have job aids or access to online resources for trouble shooting technical problems in accessing course materials or using the online technology

GRAPHIC

By nature, the online learning environment lends itself to employing visually stimulating documents. Because there may be vocal or auditory limitations from time-to-time, having visuals that are easy to read, understand, and follow is one way to make best use of the online classroom environment. Hence, the instructor should familiarize him/herself with a variety of graphic options.

There are a variety of pre-fabricated interactive learning tools available for customization on the Internet through websites such as www.readwritethink.org (IRA/NCTE, 2011). Tools such as graphic organizers, story maps, semantic webs, Venn diagrams, etc. work well and can be used interactively in both synchronous and asynchronous classrooms (IRA/NCTE, 2011; Pahl & Holohan, 2009). Online instructors can use graphic organizers to outline key course topics or to summarize what was covered in a class session or unit. Additionally, students can create their own graphic organizers as a way to show what they have learned during a period of time. When presented in a synchronous session, they are useful tools to provide hands-on experiences using mark-up tools or to promote peer participation. These may also be good catalysts for the utilization of breakout rooms where students can give small-group presentations or to practice application sharing. Graphic organizers can also be used as assessment tools where students can sequence a story, provide character analysis, outline key topical concepts, etc.

When instructors or students are creating graphic organizers, they need to keep in mind the readability of the document. Proper graphic and font size guidelines should be established, as well as the amount of information on the page. Too much information may appear unprofessional, jumbled, and unreadable. If this is the case, the graphic organizer may not accomplish the intended learning goals and lead to frustration. When in doubt, in this situation err on the side of less information.

Review of Graphic Organizers: Examples for Synchronous and Asynchronous Learning

- Graphic Organizers can be used by the instructor to show an outline of key course topics in an easy to understand manner
- Graphic Organizers can be used by the instructor to re-cap or summarize what was covered in a session/class/unit/concept, etc.

- Learners can create their own Graphic Organizers as a way to show what learned in a class/session
- Graphic Organizers can be used as a form of assessment to determine students' knowledge and understanding of the concept(s) covered (i.e., sequencing a story, character analysis, etc.)

MANIPULATIVE

The online learning environment is the perfect place to implement manipulative tools. Whether utilizing a synchronous or an asynchronous environment, students can learn and retain a great deal by interacting with various media. These can be employed for practice, assessment, or simply further learning purposes.

Companies such as SMART Technologies offer "high-quality, interactive lesson activities, content, assessment material and teaching resources" (SMART Technologies, 2011). SMART Technologies available manipulatives are available on a variety of topics and concepts across the curriculum and allow instructors to build interactivity into their lessons. The National Library of Virtual Manipulatives (NLVM) at Utah State University at http://nlvm.usu.edu/en/nav/vlibrary. html houses a "collection of over 100 interactive software programs… around accelerating and deepening students' understanding of math" (Utah State University, 2010).

While there are formal pre-fabricated manipulatives available to use, students and instructors can also create their own manipulatives through their online resources and other computer-based programs. Online assessments can be created to allow students to manipulate materials via use of multiple choice, short answer, or true and false questions. Depending on the availability of resources, goals of the course, and the technologically savvy of the instructor and the students, manipulatives can be very sophisticated or more general. The goal and outcome of the manipulatives can be the same: a well-rounded learning experience, accommodating multiple learning styles with concrete interactivity with technology and peers.

Review of Manipulatives: Examples for Synchronous or Asynchronous Learning

- Online assessments can be created to allow learners to manipulate materials
- Allow students to engage in polling questions
- Encourage students to experiment with mark-up tools on whiteboards, PowerPoint slides, etc. to manipulate and interact with course material (better suited for synchronous learning)
- Utilize sources for virtual manipulatives, such as NLVM provides a variety of interactivity in the realm of mathematics in the e-classroom

SIMULATION

As with manipulatives, incorporating simulation activities into the online learning environment will provide participants with a more concrete learning experience. "Computer simulations are a form of project based learning that requires learners to discover and apply learned skills in interactive changing environments that mimic real-world situations" (Buzzetto-Moore & Mitchell, 2009). Because pre-fabricated simulation exercises are often self-paced and self-scored, these are great tools to use for assessment purposes in synchronous or asynchronous courses. Simulation exercises "allow learners to develop and apply knowledge and skills in interactive changing environments; they encourage deeper levels of learning" (Buzzetto-Moore & Mitchell, 2009). Because students interact with the mate-

rial dynamically, they will be more apt to retain information or formulate more detailed questions around points of confusion.

Through the use of resources such as those provided by SMART Technologies and ideas found on the Internet (i.e. http://blog.cathy-more.com/elearning-samples/), pre-created simulation activities or ideas can be achieved. Again, depending on the availability of resources, goals of the course, and the technologically savvy of the instructor and the students, these could be wonderful learning tools not only with which to engage, but also to create. By allowing learners to engage in simulation activities, they are able to feel confident in their strengths and identify areas of opportunity for future development. The simulations also allow learners to explore and practice skills and concepts learned in a real-world application.

Review of Simulation: Examples for Synchronous or Asynchronous Learning

- Websites such as http://blog.cathy-moore.com/elearning-samples/ provide resources to create/implement simulation exercises and provide both simple and more complex simulation activities
- Use of interactive Smart Technology provides a variety of simulation opportunities in a wide array of topics

FUTURE TRENDS

Research suggests that a transformative approach in teacher education is essential to successfully meet the diverse needs of globally integrated and culturally diverse student learners (Ambe, 2006). In this new millennium, there is an insistent need to reconsider the type of traditional delivery methods of education to those who openly embrace a society without the barriers of time, distance and cultural differences in learning. In order for students to be fully engaged as global learners and prosper in this new society, it is essential that educators commit to embracing new ideas and new applications with technology as an initiator in best practice strategies. By harnessing the power of online education, which incorporates social networking and Web 2.0 applications as innovative, collaborative and creative tools in content development, students can be empowered to become more effective critical thinkers and problem solvers.

According to Brooks-Young (2010), it is not enough for students to simply demonstrate rote memory of a subject. Students today need to be adept at information search and navigation techniques, possess evaluation and assessment skills to validate the information they find and be capable of synthesizing the results of their knowledge exploration. Introducing students to virtual simulations and manipulatives enables them to further develop and test their ideas in a whole new dimension of ubiquitous access to the multiplicity of emerging technologies.

CONCLUSION

In this chapter, educators have been provided with several best practice strategies as a pivotal approach in their professional development to insure online classroom activities remain relevant and engaging to their diverse community of learners. For best possible pedagogical effects, it is essential for educators to continually develop and adapt instruction in order to meet the ever-changing advancements in communication and collaboration strategies. As the architect of the intellectual environment, educators have a fiduciary responsibility to create motivating, inspiring and engaging online learning platform where students can connect and take ownership of their learning process and best practice strategies.

REFERENCES

Ambe, E. B. (2006). Fostering multicultural appreciation in pre-service teachers through multicultural curricular transformation. *Teaching and Teacher Education*, 22, 690–699. doi:10.1016/j.tate.2006.03.005

Brooks-Young, S. (2010). *Teaching with the tools kids really use*. Thousand Oaks, CA: Corwin.

Buzzetto-Moore, N., & Mitchell, B. C. (2009). Student performance and perceptions in a web-based competitive computer simulation. *Interdisciplinary Journal of E-Learning and Learning Objects*, 5, 73–90.

Carmen, C., & Heafner, J. (2002). Transforming course management systems into effective learning environments. *The entity from which ERIC acquires the content, including journal, organization, and conference names, or by means of online submission from the author. EDUCAUSE Review*, 37(6), 26–24.

Clark, R. C., & Mayer, R. E. (2008). *E-learning and the science of instruction: Proven guidelines for consumers and designers of multimedia learning* (2nd ed.). San Francisco, CA: Pfeiffer.

IRA/NCTE. (2011). *Student interactives*. Retrieved April 23, 2011, from http://www.readwritethink.org/classroom-resources/student-interactives/

Jonassen, D. H., Lee, C. B., Yang, C.-C., & Laffey, J. (2005). The collaboration principle in multimedia learning. In Mayer, R. E. (Ed.), *The Cambridge handbook of multimedia learning*. New York, NY: Cambridge University Press.

Mandernach, B. J., Forrest, K. D., Babutzke, J. L., & Manker, L. R. (2009). The role of instructor interactivity in promoting critical thinking in online and face-to-face classrooms. *MERLOT Journal of Online Learning and Teaching*, 5(1), 49–62.

McLouglin, C., & Lee, M. J. W. (2007). *Social software and participatory leaning: Pedagogical choices with technology affordances in the Web 2.0 era*. Paper presented at Ascilite, Singapore.

Meadows, S. (1998). Children learning to think: learning from others? Vygotskian theory and educational psychology. *Educational and Child Psychology*, 15(2), 6–13.

Moore, C. (2009, 31-January). *Elearning samples*. Making Change: Ideas for Lively eLearning. Retrieved from http://blog.cathy-moore.com/elearning-samples/

Pahl, C., & Holohan, E. (2009). Applications of Semantic Web technology to support learning content development. *Interdisciplinary Journal of E-Learning and Learning Objects*, 5, 1–25.

Savery, J. R. (2010). BE VOCAL: Characteristics of successful online instructors. *Journal of Interactive Online Learning*, 4(2), 141–152.

Sheridan, K., & Kelly, M. A. (2010). The indicators of instructor presence that are important to students in online courses. *MERLOT Journal of Online Learning and Teaching*, 6(4), 767–779.

Technologies, S. M. A. R. T. (2011). *SMART education solutions*. Retrieved from http://smarttech.com/edredirect

Utah State University. (2010). *Virtual library*. National Library of Virtual Manipulatives. Retrieved from http://nlvm.usu.edu/en/nav/vlibrary.html

KEY TERMS AND DEFINITIONS

Best Practices: Refers to strategies, activities or approaches that have been shown through research and evaluation to be effective and/or efficient.

Graphic Representations: Refers to visual representations of verbal statements; they aid understanding of concepts and conveying messages

Manipulatives: Manipulatives are defined as materials that are physically handled by students in order to help them see actual examples of mathematical principles at work.

Modeling: Educational modeling refers to the modeling of educational systems or sub-systems, such as instructional design or assessment.

Online Instruction: The provision of two-way communication via a computer network so that students may benefit from communication with each other, teachers, and staff

Professional Development: Refers to the continuous process of acquiring new knowledge and skills that relate to one's profession, job responsibilities, or work environment

Simulations: An educational simulation is based on an internal model of a real-world system or phenomena in which some elements have been simplified or omitted in order to facilitate learning.

Chapter 16
Online Education:
A Unique Opportunity to Develop Online Communication Skills while Controlling Your Personal Brand

Nicolas G. Lorgnier
Canisius College, USA

Shawn M. O'Rourke
Canisius College, USA

Patricia A. Coward
Canisius College, USA

ABSTRACT

Young people will have to change their names in order to escape their "cyber past," prophesized Eric Schmidt (Google's CEO) in August 2010. This provocative thought from the principal opponent of Facebook may be considered a strategic maneuver, but it also highlights the deep societal changes coming with the continuing development of social media. From the instructors' perspective, people may wonder if online education could help students develop their communication skills in the era of web 2.0. But others may contend that a priority has to be given to the class content, not to another use of the media, which simply provides a new channel to enhance the learning experience. This chapter proposes a first step to reconcile the two perspectives and shows that improving students' communication skills and awareness when teaching in an online environment can enhance student learning and help personal branding, i.e. developing the ability to package their skills and to showcase their distinctive attributes. To help demonstrate this, results from the authors' courses are provided.

DOI: 10.4018/978-1-4666-1963-0.ch016

INTRODUCTION

Developing Online Communication Skills, A "Must Do" in Education

In a society which has broadly been described as an Information Society (Beniger, 1986; Garnham, 2004; Webster, 2002) since the 80's, or more recently as a Network Society (Barney, 2003), it should not be a stretch to posit that online communication is not only for geeky teachers or students, but addresses society at large. Moreover, with the dramatic growth of research engine capabilities and the emerging social media phenomenon, online communication skills are at stake. The necessity to educate this skill should not be underestimated, as we were reminded by Eric Schmidt (Google's CEO) during the summer of 2010:

I don't believe society understands what happens when everything is available, knowable and recorded by everyone all the time. (...) we [Google] know roughly who you are, roughly what you care about, roughly who your friends are." He predicts, apparently seriously, that every young person one day will be entitled automatically to change his or her name on reaching adulthood in order to disown youthful hijinks stored on their friends' social media sites (Google and the Search for the Future, 2010).

So the internet – and especially social media (Facebook, Twitter, Youtube, blogs, etc.) – can be seen as a threat to privacy as it may expose the "cyber past" of young adults, endangering their reputation and their future (Fernando, 2004). This statement should be extended to what one may call the "cyber present" of a person. In fact, many companies from various industries look at prospective employees' pages on social media in order to assess potential candidates, and they can also sanction posts from current employees that involve the company.

Social media can be considered as a threat (the "dark side" of social media), but it is also a fantastic way to market one's experience and skills, in other words, to develop a personal branding strategy (the "bright side" of social media). A personal brand is sometimes described as one's most valuable asset (Alsop, 2004), and has been defined as *"the process by which individuals and entrepreneurs differentiate themselves and stand out from the crowd by identifying and articulating their unique value proposition"* (Schawbel, 2009). Needless to say, the exposure provided by the internet has been quickly identified as a determining promotion tool, notably because of its low cost and far reaching possibilities. In August 2009, LinkedIn declared that 40% of Fortune 100 companies use LinkedIn for recruiting solutions. But the phenomenon is not limited to LinkedIn, as the Social Media in Recruitment Conferences (www.socialmediainrecruitment.com, 2009, 2010, 2011) have recently shown. Thus, in the health industry, Cain, Scott & Smith (2010) show that American residency program directors from different generations use social media to aid future decisions for resident selection and hiring.

In the sport industry, one can observe similar phenomenon: social media is used for scouting promising athletes. It is also used by professional athletes to connect with their fans. For example, LeBron James was capable of getting more than 150,000 followers in less than 7 hours when opening his twitter account (becoming the most popular user of all times) and his Facebook page counts more than 4.7 million fans (results as of January 4, 2011). Nike, his sponsor, surely enjoys this type of exposure. But social media isn't only used for recruitment purposes or for professional sport players' popularity contests. Outside of the sport industry, Naslund (2010) shows that social media can be used within companies to improve creativity through discussion and to develop a sense of community. It can be used for internal branding purposes by both the company (empowerment of the employees, reinforcement of the culture) and employees (promotion of their ideas and vision inside and outside the departments). Personal branding strategies can also be used to create a "cross-cultural training of and knowledge transfer by expatriate(s)" (Kameau, 2009, p. 60).

The concept of personal branding is relatively new, as it usually is attributed to Peters' (1997). However, contemporary impression management research was initiated by Goffman's (1959) seminal book *The Presentation of Self in Everyday Life*, which describes how one's conscious or unconscious motives and strategies impact self-presentation. The theory claims that any individual must establish and maintain impressions that are consistent with the perceptions they want to convey to their public. Such a goal is constructed and measured through constant social interactions. This framework largely contributes to a reflection to measure self-conscious identity performance in social media, such as social network sites (Boyd, 2006; Livingstone, 2005), blogs (Boyd, 2006; Hodkinson and Lincoln, 2008; Reed, 2005), micro-blogs (Marwick and Boyd, 2010), dating sites (Ellison, Heino, and Gibbs, 2006), and personal homepages (Papacharissi, 2002; Schau and Gilly, 2003).

However, little has been written about teaching students to create their personal brands. In fact, only a few researchers have studied the educational potential of social media at school (Ito, M., et al., 2009; Thomas, D. & Brown, J., 2011; McLoughlin & Lee, 2007), for college students (Petrides, 2002; Rutherford, 2010) and adult learners (LeNoue, Hall, & Eighmy, 2011). However, to our knowledge, nobody has identified the necessity to teach personal branding skills at school and/or online education as an environment to favor this experience. This paper investigates the opportunity to develop such skills online, a teaching and learning environment which shares many characteristics with social media. In other words, learning about personal branding should be considered as a learning outcome and a means to enhance learning of the class content.

In order to support this idea, the authors (A) question relationships among online communication, personal branding skills and online education, then (B) present a qualitative study conducted in the Online Masters program in Sport Administration at Canisius College (NY). This research aims at discussing the first implementations of content related to personal branding in the online Masters courses and to provide a first body of evidence supporting the following hypotheses:

A. Teaching personal branding skills online enhances students' awareness of online communication issues, notably as they relate to the notion of cyber-past;

B. Teaching personal branding skills online has a positive effect on students' technological skills, as well as metacognitive, creative and critical thinking skills.

A REVIEW OF LITERATURE

Online Education and Online Communication

There continue to be controversies surrounding online education as a means to improve online communication skills. After McNeely (2005), we can affirm that in order to succeed in online education, one needs to make sure that technology isn't only the "new cool thing;" it is a learning tool. But so far, the rapid growth of online education has been led by administrative requests more related to demographics or economic considerations than students' satisfaction, learning outcomes (Betts, 2009a; McKenzie, Ozkan & Layton, 2006), empirical evidence of effectiveness (Moore & Anderson, 2003), or faculty's requests (Bolman & Deal, 2008). Convenience has also been identified as a factor of significant importance for the student (Poole, 2000). Many challenges can obstruct the way to online education excellence: financial cost, technological obstacles (Wager, 2005), faculty training (Moore, Moore, Fowler, 2005), and the need for timely interaction (Muirhead and Betz, 2002; Rovai, 2001; Song, Singleton, Hill & Koh, 2004), among others. Also, instructors need to bring relevant knowledge, regardless of the age and technological ability of the student (McNeely, 2005; Hartman, Moskal, Dziuban, 2005). As one may surmise, most challenges and issues are directly related to communication effectiveness between instructor and student(s) in online education. As a consequence, the role of the instructor increases greatly (Lorenzetti, 2003, 1; cited in Betts, 2009b).

This challenge is made more difficult by the nature of the communication in online education. On-campus programs predominantly use verbal and nonverbal communications. On the other hand, online programs are mainly based on written communication (Faharani, 2003). More precisely, a comparative review of literature conducted by Betts (2009b) affirms that unlike on-campus, online education doesn't rely on face-to-face verbal and non-verbal communications. Online education relies (a) on VoIP (Voiceover Internet protocol) through videoconferencing software like Skype but also and for most (b) computer mediated communication (blogs, emails, etc.), which is mostly text based. The latter takes a main importance in terms of communication skills as voice cues are not accessible (or with difficulty) and the need for new non-verbal cues (like Emoticons, or variations in the fonts) increases significantly for who want to communicate effectively (Tubbs & Moss, 2006; Steele, 2006).

Personal Branding: A Distinctive Set of Online Communication Skills

When looking at the skills necessary required to develop a personal branding strategy, various approaches are taken in the literature, from the introspective, step-by-step approach to the pragmatic, "to-do" list. Thus, Arruda (2007) insists on the necessity to position oneself in a brand

community (the targeted network) and then to narrate one's brand story (not the life story, the brand story). Then it's time to communicate with a targeted audience and to assess the quality of such communication. Fraser & Dutta (2008), and Dutta (2010) emphasize the need to develop self-awareness when using the social media, and advance toward a personal social media strategy by using a pragmatic "must-do" list: Google yourself, protect your identity, create a business profile, use what you have at work, and post public content. The most significant contribution to this emerging field is probably acclaimed in Schawbel (2009) "Me 2.0" (including Arruda's forewords) which propose a four step approach of personal branding including:

- Discovering your brand includes creating an introspective work leading to a personal value statement, a marketing plan to differentiate your brand.
- Creating your brand includes building attractive resumes cover letters and have the technical ability to put them online, via LinkedIn, Facebook or other social media and websites.
- Communicating your brand includes "giving before receiving" (i.e. writing recommendations, providing help and expertise on a topic, etc.) and by maintaining good blogger relations;
- Maintaining your brand includes researching (Googling) your name and control the damage, if necessary.

Such tasks involve a great variety of skills, which can be summarized as follows:

- Discovering your brand involves introspection, self awareness and critical skills (What is my brand story?);
- Creating your brand requires both technological (How to build a blog? How to em-

bed a picture? etc.) and creative thinking skills (How to narrate the brand story?).

- Communicating your brand and maintaining your brand mostly involve critical and creative skills (How should I position myself? How can I control the damages? etc.).

Personal Branding Skills and Education

From the learner's perspective it is important to understand that such actions and principles of actions are technical and require creative and critical skills. Moreover, the technical skills required evolve quickly, which will lead the instructor to adopt a more constructive and metacognitive approach to knowledge. In other words, the instructor can guide the acquisition of technical skill, but he also has the responsibility to provide students the means to build their own technical knowledge, which may quickly become obsolete; otherwise, he has to work on their metacognitive skills. Many students habitually search on Google or Wikipedia when asked to research a topic, either because they want to copy and paste the results and pretend that they came up with the idea (plagiarism) or because they are interested in the topic and they always fall back on these avenues to conduct research as they haven't been trained to use others. Regardless of their motivation, one may consider them to be inclined to search online. So it is the instructor's duty to use this natural inclination as an opportunity to develop their curiosity and their online communication skills, whether it is related to personal branding or to another specific topic related to the class content. In other words, the metacognitive skills associated with the online research can help students develop their professional competencies prior to leaving school.

In summary, it seems interesting to regroup these personal branding skills into 3 categories, or main principles: be visible (online public representation), control your image (brand protection), and bring an added value (brand promotion). Each of these categories can then be developed through 3 sets of skills: technical, creative/critical, and metacognitive (see Figure 1).

Online: The Right Place to Teach Personal Branding Skills?

In terms of teaching strategy, Web 2.0 and social media have generally been positively correlated with student engagement, especially when it comes to active and collaborative learning experiences (Petrides, 2002; McLoughlin & Lee, 2007; Rutherford, 2010), and higher engagement is usually synonymous with higher academic achievement (Kuh, et al., 2007). So, one may think that web activities can lead to higher achievement, without restriction. However, Jenner, Zhao and Foote's (2010) quantitative research shows that when it comes to online teamwork, teams may not perform as well as on-campus students (at least, it is a case when playing the "Business strategy Game," a strategy game simulation where students have to manage the strategy of an athletic footwear company). Qualitatively, Loh and Smyth (2010) also observe phenomena which may lead to lower performances (notably social loafing, free riding, limited social exchange) but note some strong benefits from online team working, especially when it comes to personal branding skills. These benefits include: self discovery, empathy and self awareness (critical thinking and introspection), setting clear role boundaries (appropriation of the means to succeed) and communication via the learning management system (use of the technology of communication).

Technology and Online Education

In online education, technology has usually been studied as something to facilitate instruction (enhance education strategies) and/or which should be facilitated (support should be provided). In fact, on the faculty side, technology is often seen as the obstacle to online education development. According to Kosak et al. (2010) faculty have historically

Figure 1. Principles of actions, actions, and related personal branding skills

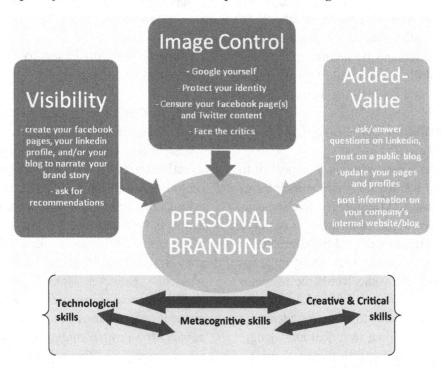

been perceived as influential and knowledgeable, but they find themselves vulnerable when expected to learn outside of their discipline and transform their teaching strategies. Moreover, faculty are already burdened with full teaching schedules, committee work, and research (McCord, 2006), "Adding to this, keeping up with technological advances, let alone changing education delivery methods, demands even more time for learning and implementation" (King, 2010). On the student side, web-based technology has historically been seen as a way to facilitate delivery of content in distance-learning environment and to increase student-to-student interaction (Eastmond, 1995; Fey, 1992; Lefor, Benke & Ting, 2003; Marantz & England, 1993; Roberts, 1987).

With these considerations in mind, we believe that online courses constitute a favorable environment for developing personal branding skills, noted above. First, online communication requires the usage of computer technology, notably the ones related to the internet 2.0 (two-way communication through internet). Many students may not realize the multiple steps needed to create two-way, online communication. For example, in order for students to setup web-based video-conferences, they need to find software such as Skype, create an account, download it and install it, then figure out how to do a name search, set up a microphone and a camera, and finally set up the call.

Basic skills (the "survival kit") will allow the student to find and download mainstream software; create and maintain an account; communicate through written communication; copy links, etc. However, when it comes to personal branding, these skills may not be present as a distinctive attribute (everyone has to know how to do these simple operations but nobody "shines" because of their use of the technology). So a more advance level of technological usage can be described by the ability to realize more complex operations such as: using professional software (MS project; SPSS, Camtasia, etc.) and advanced websites or online resources (e.g. surveymonkey.com; Google documents); record, upload and embed figures/ pictures, podcasts or videos.

Creativity and Online Education

Creativity can be described as "the ability to produce novel (original/unexpected) work that is high in quality and is appropriate (useful)" (Muirhead, 2007). And it has to be noted that online education has been described as a favorable avenue to foster creative thinking skills when instructors establish:

...a learning climate that offers students opportunities for cultivating their creative skills (e.g. problem solving). The facilitating element would involve introducing a variety of activities that represent a holistic perspective on the teaching and learning process (e.g. both individual and team work) (Muirhead, 2007, p. 11-12).

Mintu-Wimsatt, Sadler & Ingram (2007) consider that creative instruction encourages independent thinking, active participation and freedom of expression (Horng, Hong, Chankin, Chang & Chu, 2005) and should be part a management education, as "divergent thinking is essential in understanding the dynamics of any business environment." Online education has sometimes been praised for providing an environment which facilitates a student's ability to share interpretations of the course content. As Garrison (2003) points out: "online education nurtures independent thinkers in an inter-dependant collaborative community of inquiry" (47).

Critical Thinking and Online Education

Halpern (1999) defines critical thinking as what refers to the use of cognitive skills or strategies that increase the probability of a desirable outcome:

Critical thinking is purposeful, reasoned, and goal-directed. It is the kind of thinking involved in solving problems, formulating inferences, *calculating likelihoods, and making decisions. Critical thinkers use these skills appropriately, without prompting, and usually with conscious intent, in a variety of settings. That is, they are predisposed to think critically. When we think critically, we are evaluating the outcomes of our thought processes—how good a decision is or how well a problem is solved (Halpern, 1999, 70; quoted by Mandernach, Forrest, Babutzke & Manker, 2009).*

The online environment has often been considered to have a favorable impact on creative and critical thinking skills. In fact, strong correlations have been found between active learning and improvement of critical thinking skills (Mandernach, & al., 2009), and the asynchronous online setting seems to provide more opportunities for constructivist or student-led discussions (requiring active learning), as their reflection isn't time limited (Astleitner, 2002; Bruning, Zygeilbaum, Horn & Glider, n.d.; as cited by Alexander, Commander, Greenberg & Ward, 2010), and active inclusion and engagement of all students through planned, meaningful, prepared discussion (Bruning, 2005; Walker, 2005; MacKnight, 2000; Muirhead, 2002; Murchu & Muirhead, 2002; Peirce, 2003; as cited by Alexander & al., 2010) are required. However, this standpoint is becoming more controversial as non-parametric tests from Mandernach et al. (2009) did not demonstrate better critical thinking skills with online students. Such results invite to further research on the topic.

Metacognition and Online Education

Metacognition can be defined as the "knowledge of cognition and regulatory skills that are used to control one's cognition" (Schraw, 2001). In other words, it requires self-awareness – or more precisely self-evaluation – and self-management of the learning process. For Garrison (2003), metacognition is a key concept leading to effective asynchronous online learning, and the *sine qua non* is true as well: "asynchronous online learning can be extremely effective in supporting higher-order learning and creating quality" (Garrison, 2003). It can be enhanced through modeling and sharing the cognitive experience (Schraw, 2001). Thus, we believe that self-awareness, team-working and online discussions about the cognitive process could enhance such skill. This belief is supported by Petrides (2002) and Vonderwell (2003) who reported that online asynchronous learning encouraged more reflective thinking and introspection and King & Hildreth (2001) note that college students feel more comfortable discussing in this environment (Butts, 2009). Moreover, the independent learning strategies (notably online researches) experienced in the online setting seem to favor metacognitive learning (Garrison, 2003). In addition, social media is also positively correlated to differentiated instruction (Baird & Fisher, 2006; Christensen, Horn, & Johnson, 2008, cited by Rutherford, 2010).

CASE-STUDY: THE ONLINE MASTER PROGRAM IN SPORT ADMINISTRATION AT CANISIUS COLLEGE

Observations have been gathered from online students in the Master of Sport Administration at Canisius College (NYS) during courses taught between Fall 2009 and Spring 2010. The roster of each course varied from 16 to 36 students, between 23 and 33 years-old, coming from 28 US states and 4 foreign countries (Canada, Japan, Germany, and Brazil.). A total of 16 courses worth 3 US credit hours each were used for the study. Courses were fully online and taught asynchronously (each student can log in at any given time to discover the class content, post reactions, etc.). However, students are encouraged to Skype with the instructor if they need complementary support and with classmates in order to facilitate team-working in a

few given tasks. In this regard, one may argue that the courses have a synchronous component. Each course used various tools of online communication including: a study guide (video, slides, podcast and written document), announcements, course documents and other additional resources, student pages, email, discussion boards, assignment drop boxes, group discussion areas, and Skype). The learning management system used was ANGEL LMS, trademark of Blackboard.

The present research discusses major tasks involving online communication and their evolution when necessary. The main directions of the 3 chosen types of tasks are presented below:

- **Video Icebreakers:** At the beginning of 9 online courses, students are required to introduce themselves to classmates via a short video presentation. In order to do so, they need to record the video, upload it to a social media (Youtube, Screencast or others) and then embed it in a post inside a discussion board. Directions are provided by the instructor with the help of publicly accessible online content (Youtube videos created by the social media or individuals) in order to help with technical aspects of the task. Individualized support is provided on demand via email, phone call, or Skype video conference. Then students are free to welcome one another and discuss. The instructor welcomes each student individually. The activity is not graded.

- **Synthesis Group Work:** Within 7 courses, students have been asked to work in groups to create a literature review on a topic and position themselves as a group by exposing how the existing literature (and professional interviews when possible) could help them build better practices in sport administration (specifics of the topics varied depending on the course). In order to prepare for this activity, students were given 5 to 8 weeks. The instructor created a working space for each group on ANGEL. Email exchange and Skype videoconferences were strongly encouraged and directions to use Skype (mostly public Youtube videos and a Youtube video created by the instructor) were provided. The expected final product was a 10 page paper and a 10 minute oral presentation recorded with use of slides. The slides and narrations had to be uploaded and embedded in a post within a discussion forum. Student interactions were expected to comment on the products. Written presentations were submitted in a drop box and could only be seen by the instructor. The assignment is graded. Students from the same group peer-review one another and their grade impacts up to 8% of the peer's grade (of course, if found that a peer didn't contribute at all, he or she fails the activity).

- **Routine Tasks:** During each semester (total of 16 courses), students were required to participate in various activities on discussion boards involving: discovering class content (academic, professional or journalistic articles, legal cases or keywords), using critical and creative thinking to discuss the topic and provide managerial remedies or better practices. In order to do so, students had to use resources provided by the instructor on ANGEL and/or find their own resources (independent work). Then, after posting their findings, they had to discuss as a group on the discussion board. The assignments are graded.

Comments and feedback were collected during class time (emails and posts on discussion boards) by the instructors and through anonymous instructors' evaluation at the end of each semester. It is important to note that the latter remains fully

Table 1. Tasks, communication principles, and associated personal branding skills

	Video Icebreaker	Synthesis Group Project	Routine Tasks
Communication Principles			
Visibility	+	+	
Image control	+		
Added-value		+	++
Associated Personal Branding Skills			
Technical skills	+	+	(+)
Creative and Critical skills	+	+	+
Metacognitive skills	+	+	+

anonymous. Table 1 brings together the tasks and their potential impact on communication principles and associated skills.

RESULTS

Video Icebreaker

Proposed at the beginning of the semester, the video icebreaker introduced the idea of visibility and image control straightaway. Four types of reaction have been observed:

1. Most students (n=162) complied with the task without asking questions (other than technical from time to time): they recorded the video, uploaded it to Youtube, and embedded it to ANGEL (or copied the URL);
2. A minority of students (n=23) uploaded their video to social media other than Youtube (different access rights), like Screencast, that the instructor used from time to time and was recommended as an alternative to Youtube;

3. Some students (n=30) complied with the task, but when uploading the content to Youtube, they chose to publish it privately, which didn't allow other students to view the video;

4. A few students (n=16) uploaded the file directly to ANGEL because they haven't succeeded in uploading to Youtube (in this case, help from other students or from the instructor solved the problem) or – more often – because they didn't want to upload their presentation to a social media site. In the second case, a discussion was initiated by the instructor on the discussion board. If the student still wasn't comfortable with uploading his or her information (extremely rare), then the post remained unchanged. Otherwise, the student had the possibility to update it.

So far, reactions 2, 3, and 4 have occurred in almost every course. Reaction 4 is rarer since the instructor started discussing image control and online visibility in the directions for the post and a "How to-FAQ" document provided by the instructor.

Another interesting observation: many students referred to this assignment at some point during the semester in order to describe how an online learning community was born in the course. Some students even want to go further, one suggested ways to improve the assignment: "For the present yourself part of the course, call it" present your partner." Put students in pairs and have them introduce each other. Or, something like that... It would give students a chance to get to know someone in the class right away."

Synthesis Group Work

This second type of task is by far the most controversial among students. Three types of reactions

have been observed (especially in the instructor's evaluation, which is anonymous):

1. Some students enjoyed the challenge, appreciated the technical skills they learned, and understand how beneficial for their career such assignments can be. The ability to fully build a team project online were perceived as a valuable and empowering achievement.

2. Some other students didn't enjoy the activity, which they judged too technically difficult, but understand its educational value: "The group midterm was difficult to coordinate with everyone working in different areas of the country. But it is a necessary tool to learn; working with others through non-face-to-face interaction."

3. The latter didn't enjoy the activity and believe that it had no real value because the technical constraints were too strong and interfered with the acquisition of knowledge more directly related to the class content (ex: learning about sport law): "I believe what did not work was having the class divided into groups to do either a midterm or final exam. This was the hardest thing to do because the whole purpose of all of the students taking online courses for independent study and having access to continue on doing things in our lives without having to sit down in a classroom. I did not like this because we could not get together at times due to we all have different things going on in our lives. I do not think that this will work with online classes especially midterm and final."

Comparing the grades of the group assignments to the grades of individual assignments on comparable tasks (during summer session, two five-week online courses proposed similar synthesis activities but with independent work), no substantial difference in grades is observed, but the distribution is more heterogeneous for the individual assignments. However, because the assignments may vary from a semester to the next, the instructor couldn't use statistical analysis to confirm his observations (even nonparametric testing seems inadequate).

Routine Tasks

At the opposite side of the spectrum, routine tasks were very well received. If the structure of the assignments was perceived as too redundant for a few students, almost all of them thought the tasks where interesting and valuable. They enjoyed adding value to classmates' posts and receiving constructive criticism on their posts: "I really like hearing the views of other people. Being able to share views really helps me see other sides to important issues in sport. Also some of these issues most of us don't think about on a normal bases [sic] and I think the "out of site [sic] out of mind" comes into play and we really forget that these issues are in sports (…) It has been a good experience to get the different perspectives from the other students from around the country." So far, no discrimination or disaffection has been observed regarding activities requiring more personal research (full "scavenger hunt" type of tasks), but some students have complained about the overwhelming workload which can be associated with such activities.

Regarding the resources used by students, it is difficult to quantify behavioral changes because tasks are always different and it may take time for a student to fully understand the expectations of the instructor. However, it is noticeable that most students start the semester by searching information from Wikipedia and some journalistic websites and finish the semester with using more diverse web resources. Among the websites commonly used: Canisius library's website, sport law blog, Westlaw, Lexis Nexis, findarticle.com, etc. Most of them (but not all of them) are brought forward by the instructor. As a result, the improved information gathering results in a substantial im-

provement of the depth of the discussions (more variety of the point of views, more academic or statistic arguments are provided to strengthen some ideas) as well within student's posts and reactions to other posts.

It is also interesting to note that some students embed pictures and/or videos from various websites to ANGEL, technicalities which are not required (but always appreciated) for such tasks and are specific to ANGEL (which doesn't accept copy and pasted videos). However, most students didn't use such features.

DISCUSSION

Video Icebreaker

Online communication is often perceived as a threat by some students, not as an opportunity to shine, to bond or to promote oneself professionally. Complementary information regarding personal branding from the instructor prior to the recording of the videos could possibly remedy the issue and help recording videos which are more professional and useful, i.e. strongly impact the visibility of the student on the job market. Also, a study from Garrison (2003) suggests that a self-assessment activity could enhance student awareness of his online communication skills. On the positive side, some students' perceptions of the social media as a threat allowed the instructors and some students to start a discussion about image control. This discussion led to increase the awareness of students who may have not paid attention to this aspect. Finally, by creating a sense of community, the video icebreaker had a positive impact on students' engagement in team-working, collaborative inquiries and, subsequently, the student learning experience (Kuh et al., 2010).

Synthesis Group Work

It is interesting to focus on the controversy surrounding this assignment, as grades compare to an on-campus course's grades. If compared to online independent syntheses, online group syntheses probably helped students with lower technical skills and/or critical skills to perform better. In this regard, collaboration helped students in a difficult position. These considerations allow us to think that the technological aspects of the task weren't an obstacle to getting a good grade or, by extension, to receive meaningful class content.

In order to resolve the problem of the controversy, three solutions come to mind. First, more guidance was needed within the directions to limit the coordination issues related to the plan construction, which would also limit the need to coordinate and partially defeat the purpose of the task and its positive outcome.

For the second solution, more emphasis on the skills and competencies in online communications expected from 21st century managers could make the students' experience more meaningful and then limit the controversy. In fact, public representation of oneself and of one's company is an important component in today's (professional) life, and it includes online representation. Another component of one's professional life is to group work online (internally and externally); examples in sport administration: exchanging information regarding the new marketing plan (internally) before an important meeting, or coordinating (externally) with another team for a tournament (trip including flight, shuttle, hotel nights, training schedule, game schedule, etc.).

In other words, even if the task would be proven to have a negative effect on a team's overall performance (as suggested by Jenner et al., 2010), students should work towards becoming better at online team-working because this is what the industry does. In the real world, people don't build the business strategy by gathering in a room for three hours a week, they exchange email, organize phone or video conferences and (sometimes) gather for a few hours. Put in this perspective, the issue shifts from "what is the most effective environment to teamwork?" to "How can I improve my online team-working skills in order to optimize my participation to the overall work/strategy when I join the industry?"

Routine Tasks

This type of task, less technically challenging than the other two, has been enjoyed the best by all students. This result, by comparison with others, shows that not all of them are willing to struggle with technology and that being technologically skilled is seen as a bonus more than a fundamental requirement. Thus, one could argue that students may be more interested by the convenience of online education (Pool, 2000) than by one of its distinctive attributes: favoring the development of technical online communication skills. This is certainly why emphasizing this attribute is crucial. As observed in the introduction, instructors need to demonstrate that technology in the classroom isn't the new cool thing, but a valuable teaching/learning tool. Promoting online communication skills and personal branding capabilities may facilitate the acquisition of more technical skills.

On the other hand, the necessary skills to find resources to address the course content seem to improve with time and practice. These skills, which are also less technical, will aid the construction of critical and creative views of managerial practices. Thus, in this regard, the tasks impact favorably the appropriation of the class content. Moreover, by engaging the students to research online, they also encourage the creation of a more educated way to access the information, a skill that they will be likely to use in a professional environment when asked to think creatively and/or critically about a problem. In other words, they are encouraged to find the keys to solve their own problems (and others).

CONCLUSION

It is reasonable to believe that tasks proposed to students of the master of sport administration at Canisius College have engaged them to discuss the issues of online communication and helped develop a new awareness and new beneficial skills from online technologies of communication. However, it has to be mentioned that this research is a work in progress. Many improvements can be made, as stated during the discussion. Also, more data and new research design would be necessary to provide more robust evidence of a connection between personal branding and course content learning. Finally, these tasks are part of a broader teaching strategy related to management education and they interact with other activities which couldn't be added to this project. Among other aspects of the teaching strategy, personal branding is also emphasized in particular courses. For example, students are required to create a Linkedin profile and to start their network within the classroom. It may seem pushy to some readers, but as Schwabel notes, college is an excellent place to develop the personal brand (2009, 30-32). So the instructor can play an active role in this process. Another example, in contract negotiation, students are required to understand branding and personal branding principles in order to create made-to-measure negotiation strategies and tactics.

If online education is a favorable means to develop online communication skills, one may object that it may be detrimental to face-to-face communication skills, involving verbal and non-verbal communication skills. It is the duty of the instructor to prove this belief wrong, or at the least work towards that goal. A negotiation course providing basic knowledge in non-verbal communication may help, but it is important to mention that in online or in on-campus environments, life doesn't start right before the lecture and stop at the end. It is imperative that instructors help (online and on-campus) students to develop their face-to-face communication skills in the field. In order to do so, (online and on-campus) instructors must propose activities where students meet professionals. This will give students the opportunity to learn valuable knowledge from the field, to bring a new awareness to their student work, to create bridges between theoretical knowledge and professional skills, develop their professional network and develop their communication skill in a face-to-face interaction where the stakes are low (they are not coming for an internship or for a job), which is meaningful (students have questions and professionals usually like that), and which helps them network.

REFERENCES

Alexander, M., Commander, N., Greenberg, D. & Ward, T. (2010). Using the four-questions technique to enhance critical thinking in online discussions. *MERLOT Journal of Online Learning and Teaching, 6*(2).

Alsop, R. (2004). *Immutable laws of corporate reputation: creating, protecting, and repairing your most valuable asset.* New York, NY: Wall Street Journal Books.

Arruda, W. (2007). *Career distinction: Stand out by building your brand.* New York, NY: J. Wiley & Sons.

Astleitner, H. (2002). Teaching critical thinking online. *Journal of Instructional Psychology, 29*(2), 53–77.

Baird, D. E., & Fisher, M. (2006). Neomillennial user experience design strategies: Utilizing social networking media to support "Always On" learning. *Journal of Educational Technology Systems, 34*(1), 5–32. doi:10.2190/6WMW-47L0-M81Q-12G1

Barney, D. (2003). *The network society.* Cambridge, MA: Polity.

Beniger, J. (1986). *The control revolution: Technological and economic origins of the information society*. Cambridge, MA: Harvard University Press.

Betts, K. S. (2009a). Changing higher education landscape: Increasing demand for online and blended education. *Student Success,* 11-14.

Betts, K. S. (2009b). Lost in translation: Importance of effective communication in online education. *Online Journal of Distance Learning Administration, 7*(2).

Bolman, L. G., & Deal, T. E. (2008). *Reframing organizations: Artistry, choice, and leadership*. San Francisco, CA: Jossey-Bass.

Boyd, D. (2006a). A blogger's blog: Exploring the definition of a medium. *Reconstruction, 6*(4).
boyd, d. (2007). Why youth social network sites: The role of networked publics in teenage social life. In Buckingham, D. (Ed.), *Youth identity and digital media* (pp. 119–142). Cambridge, MA: MIT Press.

Bruning, K. (2005). The role of critical thinking in the online learning environment. *International Journal of Instructional Technology and Distance Learning, 2*(5).

Bruning, R., Zygielbaum, A., Horn, C., & Glider, W. (n.d.). *Online tools for enhancing student learning and extending resources in large enrollment university courses.* **Lincoln, NE**. *Center for Instructional Innovation at the University of Nebraska.*

Butts, F. (2009). Evaluations of hybrid online instruction in sport management. *Online Journal of Distance Learning Administration, 7*(2).

Cain, J., Scott, D., & Smith, K. (2010). Use of social media by residency program directors for resident selection. *American journal of health-system pharmacy, 67*, 1635–1639. doi:10.2146/ajhp090658

Christensen, C. M., Horn, M. B., & Johnson, C. W. (2008). Disrupting class: How disruptive innovation will dispositions of a critical thinker. *New Directions for Teaching and Learning, 80*, 69–7.

Dutta, S. (2010). What's your personal social media strategy? *Harvard Business Review, 88*(11), 127–130.

Eastmond, D. V. (1995). *Alone but together: Adult distance study through computer conferencing*. Cresskill, NJ: Hampton Press.

Ellison, N., Heino, R., & Gibbs, J. (2006). Managing impressions online: Self-presentation processes in the online dating environment. *Journal of Computer-Mediated Communication, 11*(2). Retrieved from http://jcmc.indiana.edu/vol11/issue2/ellison.html doi:10.1111/j.1083-6101.2006.00020.x

Faharani, G. O. (2003). *Existence and importance of online interaction*. Unpublished Doctoral dissertation, Virginia Polytechnic Institute.

Fernando, A. (2004). Big blogger is watching you! Reputation management in an opinionated, hyperlinked world. *Communication World, 21*(4), 10–11.

Fey, M. H. (1992). *Freeing voices: Literacy through computer conferencing and feminist collaboration*. Unpublished Doctoral dissertation, University of Rochester.

Fraser, M., & Dutta, S. (2008). *Throwing sheep in the boardroom: How online social networking will transform your life*. New York, NY: J. Wiley & Sons.

Garnham, N. (2004). Information society theory as ideology. In Webster, F. (Ed.), *The information society reader* (pp. 165–183). London, UK: Routledge.

Garrison, D. R. (2003). Cognitive presence for effective asynchronous online learning: The role of reflective inquiry, self-direction and meta-cognition. In Bourne, J., & Moore, J. C. (Eds.), *Elements of quality in online education: Practice and direction* (pp. 47–58). Needham, MA: Sloan Center for Online Education.

Halpern, D. F. (1999). Teaching for critical thinking: Helping college students develop the skills and dispositions of a critical thinker. *New Directions for Teaching and Learning, 80*, 69–74. doi:10.1002/tl.8005

Hartman, J., Moskal, P., & Dziuban, C. (2005). Preparing the academy of today for the learner of tomorrow. In Oblinger, D. G., & Oblinger, J. L. (Eds.), *Educating the Net generation* (pp. 6.4–6.15). Washington, DC: Educause.

Hodkinson, P., & Lincoln, S. (2008). Online journals as virtual bedrooms? Young people, identity and personal space. *Young, 16*(1), 27–46. doi:10.1177/110330880701600103

Horng, J., Hong, J., Chankin, L., Chang, S., & Chu, H. (2005). Creative teachers and creative thinking strategies. *International Journal of Consumer Studies, 29*(4), 352–358. doi:10.1111/j.1470-6431.2005.00445.x

Ito, M., Baumer, S., Bittanti, M., Boyd, D., & Cody, R. (2009). *Hanging out, messing around, and geeking out - Kids living and learning with new media*. Cambridge, MA: The MIT Press.

Jenner, S., Zhao, M., & Foote, T. H. (2010). Teamwork and team performance in online simulations: The business strategy game. *MERLOT Journal of Online Learning and Teaching, 6*(2), 416–430.

Kameau, C. (2009). Strategizing impression management in corporations: cultural knowledge as capital. In Harorimana, D. (Ed.), *Cultural implications of knowledge sharing, management and transfer: Identifying competitive advantage* (pp. 60–83). Hershey, PA: IGI Global. doi:10.4018/978-1-60566-790-4.ch004

King, K. (2010). Adaptation to pressures of changing technology and online instruction. *The LLI Review, 5*, 29–35.

Kosak, L., Manning, D., Dobson, E., Rogerson, L., & Cotnam, S. (2004). Prepared to teach online? Perspectives of faculty in the University of North Carolina system. *Online Journal of Distance Learning Administration, 7*(3).

Kuh, G., Kinzie, J., Schuh, J., & Whitt, E. (2010). *Student success in college: Creating conditions that matter*. San-Francisco, CA: Jossey-Bass.

Kuh, G. D., Kinzie, J., Cruce, T., Shoup, R., & Gonyea, R. M. (2006, July). *Connecting the dots: Multi-faceted analyses of the relationships between student engagement results from the NSSE, and the institutional practices and conditions that foster student success: Final report prepared for Lumina Foundation for Education*. Bloomington, IN: Indiana University, Center for Postsecondary Research.

Lefor, P., Benke, M., & Ting, E. (2003). Information technology and adult learners at Empire State College. *New Directions for Student Services, 102*, 35–42. doi:10.1002/ss.87

Livingstone, S. (2005). On the relation between audiences and publics. In Livingstone, S. (Ed.), *Audiences and publics: When cultural engagement matters for the public sphere* (pp. 17–42). Portland, OR: Intellect.

Loh, J., & Smyth, R. (2010). Understanding students' online learning experiences in virtual teams. *MERLOT Journal of Online Learning and Teaching, 6*(2), 335–342.

Lorenzetti, J. (2003). Getting the best out of online adjunct faculty: A guide. *Distance Education Report, 7*(4), 1–6.

MacKnight, C. B. (2000). Teaching critical thinking through online discussions. *EDUCAUSE Quarterly, 4*, 38–41.

Mandernach, B. J., Forrest, K. D., Babutzke, J. L., & Manker, L. R. (2009). The role of instructor interactivity in promoting critical thinking in online and face-to-face classrooms. *MERLOT Journal of Online Learning and Teaching, 5*(1).

Marantz, B., & England, R. J. (1993). Can CMC teach teacher training? *Educational Media International, 30*(2), 74–77. doi:10.1080/0952398930300206

Marwick, A., & Boyd, d. (2010). I tweet honestly, I tweet passionately: Twitter users, context collapse, and the imagined audience. *New Media & Society, 13*(10), 114–133.

McCord, A. (2006) Staffing and supporting a new online initiative. *Innovate, 3*(2).

McKenzie, B. K., Ozkan, B. C., & Layton, K. (2006). Tips for administrators in promoting distance programs using peer mentoring. *Online Journal of Distance Learning Administration, 9*(2).

McLoughlin, C., & Lee, M. J. W. (2007). *Social software and participatory learning: Pedagogical choices with technology affordances in the Web 2.0 era.* Singapore: Australasian Society for Computers in Learning in Tertiary Education conference.

McNeely, B. (2005). Using technology as a learning tool, not just the new cool thing. In Oblinger, D. G., & Oblinger, J. L. (Eds.), *Educating the Net generation* (pp. 4.1–4.10). Washington, DC: Educause.

Mintu-Wimsatt, A., Sadler, T., & Ingram, K. (2007). Creativity in online courses: Perceptions of MBA student. *MERLOT Journal of Online Learning and Teaching, 3*(4).

Moore, A., Moore, J., & Fowler, S. (2005). Faculty development for the Net generation. In Oblinger, D. G., & Oblinger, J. L. (Eds.), *Educating the Net generation* (pp. 11.1–11.16). Washington, DC: Educause.

Moore, M. G., & Anderson, E. G. (Eds.). (2003). *Handbook of distance education*. Mahwah, NJ: Lawrence Erlbaum Associates.

Muirhead, B. (2007). Integrating creativity into online university classes. *Journal of Educational Technology & Society, 10*(1), 1–13.

Muirhead, B., & Betz, M. (2002). Faculty training at an online university. *United States Distance Learning Association Journal, 16*(1).

Murchu, D., & Muirhead, B. (2005). Insights into promoting critical thinking in online classes. *International Journal of Instructional Technology and Distance Learning, 2*(6).

Naslund, A. (2010). Social media from the inside out. *Communication World, 27*, 36–39.

Papacharissi, Z. (2002). The presentation of self in virtual life: Characteristics of personal home pages. *Journalism & Mass Communication Quarterly, 79*(3), 643–660. doi:10.1177/107769900207900307

Peirce, W. (2003). *Strategies for teaching thinking and promoting intellectual development in online classes. Electronic communities: Current issues and best practices.* U.S. Distance Learning Association: Information Age Publishing.

Peters, T. (1997). The brand called you. *Fast Company, 10*. Mansueto Ventures LLC. Retrieved from http://www.fastcompany.com/magazine/10/brandyou.html

Petrides, L. A. (2002). Web-based technologies for distributed (or distance) learning: Creating learning-centered educational experiences in the higher education classroom. *International Journal of Instructional Media, 29*(1), 69–77.

Poole, D. M. (2000). Student participation in a discussion-oriented online course: A case study. *Journal of Research on Computing in Education, 33*(2), 162–177.

Reed, A. (2005). My blog is me: Texts and persons in UK online journal culture (an anthropology). *Ethnos, 70*(2). doi:10.1080/00141840500141311

Roberts, L. (1987). *The electronic seminar: Distance education by computer conferencing.* Paper presented at the Annual Conference on Non-Traditional and Interdisciplinary Programs, Fairfax, VA. (ERIC Document Reproduction Service, No. ED 291 358).

Rovai, A. P. (2001). Building and sustaining community in asynchronous learning networks. *The Internet and Higher Education, 3,* 285–297. doi:10.1016/S1096-7516(01)00037-9

Rutherford, C. (2010). Using online social media to support preservice student engagement. *MERLOT Journal of Online Learning and Teaching, 6*(4), 703–711.

Schau, H. J., & Gilly, M. C. (2003). We are what we post? Self-presentation in personal web space. *The Journal of Consumer Research, 30*(3), 385–404. doi:10.1086/378616

Schawbel, D. (2009). *Me 2.0: Build a powerful brand to achieve career success.* New York, NY: Kaplan Publishing.

Schraw, G. (2001). Promoting general metacognitive awareness. In Hartman, H. J. (Ed.), *Metacognition in learning and instruction: Theory, research and practice* (pp. 3–16). Boston, MA: Kluver.

Song, L., Singleton, E., Hill, J., & Koh, M. (2004). Improving online learning: Student perceptions of useful and challenging characteristics. *The Internet and Higher Education, 7*(1), 59–70. doi:10.1016/j.iheduc.2003.11.003

Steele, J. (2006). *Email: The manual: Everything you should know about email etiquette, policies and legal liability before you hit send.* Oak Park, IL: Marion Street Press, Inc.

Thomas, D., & Brown, J. (2011). *A new culture of learning: Cultivating the imagination for a world of constant change.* Lexington, KY: CreateSpace Publishing.

Tubbs, S., & Moss, S. (2006). *Human communication: Principles and contexts.* New York, NY: McGraw Hill.

Vonderwell, S. (2003). An examination of asynchronous communication experiences and perspectives of students in an online course: A case study. *The Internet and Higher Education, 6,* 77–90. doi:10.1016/S1096-7516(02)00164-1

Wager, J. (2005). Support services for the Net generation. In Oblinger, D. G., & Oblinger, J. L. (Eds.), *Educating the net generation* (pp. 10.1–10.18). Washington, DC: Educause.

Walker, G. (2005). Critical thinking in asynchronous discussions. *International Journal of Instructional Technology and Distance Learning, 2*(6).

Webster, F. (2002). *Theories of the information society.* Cambridge, MA: Routledge.

KEY TERMS AND DEFINITIONS

Communication Skills: A set of abilities and techniques that convey information so that it is received and understood.

Critical Thinking: Conceptualizing, applying, analyzing, synthesizing, and/or generated by, observation, experience, reflection, reasoning, or communication, as a guide to belief and action.

Management Education: Formal education in the principles and techniques of management and related subjects that lead to a qualification.

Online Communication: There are numerous ways people send or receive information with each other over the Internet, including e-mail, instant messages (IM), feedback on blogs, contact forms on Web sites, industry forums, chat rooms and social networking sites.

Online Education: Courses are conducted completely online in the learning management system. Student and teacher interact over the internet offering two-way communication.

Personal Branding: The process by which individuals and entrepreneurs differentiate themselves from a crowd by identifying and articulating their unique value propositions, whether professional or personal.

Social Media: The online technologies and practices that people use to share opinions, insights, experiences, and perspectives with each other.

Compilation of References

(1999). InReigeluth, C. M. (Ed.). Instructional-design theories and models: *Vol. 2. A new paradigm of instructional theory*. Hillsdale, NJ: Lawrence Erlbaum.

Abott, R., Wulff, D., & Szego, C. (1989). Review of research on TA training. In Nyquist, J. D., Abbott, R. D., & Wulff, D. H. (Eds.), *Teaching assistant training in the 1990s: New directions for teaching and learning* (pp. 111–123). San Francisco, CA: Jossey-Bass.

Adams, N. B. (2002). Educational computing concerns of postsecondary faculty. *Journal of Research on Technology*, *34*(3), 285–303.

Advisory Committee on Mathematics in Education (ACME). (2002). *Continuing professional development of teachers of mathematics: Advisory committee on mathematics in education*. Retrieved from http://tinyurl.com/3u9pcmm

Alexander, M., Commander, N., Greenberg, D. & Ward, T. (2010). Using the four-questions technique to enhance critical thinking in online discussions. *MERLOT Journal of Online Learning and Teaching, 6*(2).

Allen, E., & Seaman, J. (2008). *Staying the course: Online education in the United States, 2008*. Newburyport, MA: The Sloan Consortium.

Allen, E., & Seaman, J. (2009). *Learning on demand: Online education in the United States, 2009*. Newburyport, MA: The Sloan Consortium.

Allen, E., & Seaman, J. (2010). *Class differences: Online education in the United States, 2010*. Newburyport, MA: The Sloan Consortium.

Allen, I. E., & Seaman, J. (2006). *Making the grade, 2010. Sloan Consortium Group*. Babson Park, MA: Babson Research Group.

Allen, I. E., & Seaman, J. (2007). *Online nation: Five years of growth in online learning*. Needham, MA: Sloan Consortium.

Allen, I. E., & Seaman, J. (2010). *Class differences: Online education in the United States, 2010*. Babson Survey Research Group.

Allen, I. E., & Seaman, J. (2010). *Learning on demand: Online education in the United States, 2009*. Needham, MA: Babson Survey Research Group, The Sloan Consortium.

Allen, I. E., & Seaman, J. (2010). *Online education in the United States, 2010. Sloan Consortium Group*. Babson Park, MA: Babson Research Group.

Allen, I., & Seaman, J. (2009). *Learning on demand: Online education in the United States, 2009. Sloan Consortium Group*. Needham, MA: Sloan-C.

Alsop, R. (2004). *Immutable laws of corporate reputation: creating, protecting, and repairing your most valuable asset*. New York, NY: Wall Street Journal Books.

Ambe, E. B. (2006). Fostering multicultural appreciation in pre-service teachers through multicultural curricular transformation. *Teaching and Teacher Education, 22*, 690–699. doi:10.1016/j.tate.2006.03.005

American Association of Higher Education. Assessment Forum. (2003). *9 principles of good practice for assessing participant learning*. Brevard, NC: Policy Center on the First Year of College. Retrieved from http://www.brevard.edu/fyc/relatedlinks/aahe.htm

American Federation of Teachers (AFT). (2000). *Distance education: Guidelines for good practice*. Washington, DC: American Federation of Teachers. Retrieved from http://www.aft.org/pubs-reports/higher_ed/distancc.pdf

Anderson, T. (2003). Modes of interaction in distance education: Recent developments and research questions. In Moore, M. (Ed.), *Handbook of distance education*. Mahwah, NJ: Lawrence Erlbaum.

Anderson, T. (2006). Higher education evolution: Individual freedom afforded by educational social software. In Beaudoin, M. (Ed.), *Perspectives on the future of higher education in the digital age* (pp. 77–90). New York, NY: Nova Science.

Anderson, T., Rourke, L., Garrison, D. R., & Archer, W. (2001). Assessing teaching presence in a computer conferencing context. *Journal of Asynchronous Learning Networks, 5*(2), 1–17.

Anderson, W. G., & Moore, M. G. (2003). *Handbook of distance education*. Mahwah, NJ: Lawrence Erlbaum.

Ansah, A. O., Neill, P., & Newton, J. (2011, Spring). Who's on first in distance education? *Online Journal of Distance Learning Administration, 4*(1).

Appana, S. (2008). A review of benefits and limitations of online learning in the context of the student, the instructor, and the tenured faculty. *International Journal on E-Learning, 7*(1), 5–22.

Appel, J. (2006). *Second Life develops education following: Virtual world being used by some educators and youth groups for teaching*. Retrieved from http://www.eschoolnews.com/news/top-news/index.cfm?i=42030&CFID=8638975&CFTOKEN=21337481

Arabacz, P., Pirani, J., & Fawcett, P. (2003). *Supporting e-learning in higher education*. Boulder, CO: Educause Center for Applied Research.

Arbaugh, J. B. (2000). Virtual classrooms versus physical classrooms: An exploratory study of class discussion patterns and student learning in an asynchronous Internet-based MBA course. *Journal of Management Education, 24*(2), 207–227. doi:10.1177/105256290002400206

Arbaugh, J. B., & Benbunan-Fich, R. (2006). An investigation of epistemological and social dimensions of teaching in online learning environments. *Academy of Management Learning & Education, 5*(4), 435–447. doi:10.5465/AMLE.2006.23473204

Archambault, L. (2011). The practitioner's perspective on teacher education: Preparing for the K-12 online classroom. *Journal of Technology and Teacher Education, 19*(1), 73–91.

Archambault, L., & Crippen, K. (2009). Examining TPACK among K-12 online distance educators in the United States. *Contemporary Issues in Technology & Teacher Education, 9*(1). Retrieved from http://www.citejournal.org/vol9/iss1/general/article2.cfm

Argyris, C., & Schön, D. (1978). *Organizational learning: A theory of action perspective*. San Francisco, CA: Jossey-Bass.

Armenakis, A., Bernerth, J., Pitts, J., & Walker, H. (2007). Organizational change recipients' beliefs scale: Development of an assessment instrument. *The Journal of Applied Behavioral Science, 43*(4), 481–505. doi:10.1177/0021886307303654

Armstrong, G. (1996, May). One approach to motivating faculty to use multimedia. *T.H.E Journal, 23*, 69-71.

Armstrong, D. M. (1993). *A materialist theory of the mind*. New York, NY: Routledge.

Arruda, W. (2007). *Career distinction: Stand out by building your brand*. New York, NY: J. Wiley & Sons.

Assaf, L. (2008). Professional identity of a reading teacher: Responding to high stakes testing. *Teachers and Teaching:Theory and Practice, 14*(3), 239–252. doi:10.1080/13540600802006137

Association for Assessment in Counseling. (2003). *Responsibilities of users of standardized tests* (3rd ed.). Alexandria, VA: Association for Assessment in Counseling.

Astleitner, H. (2002). Teaching critical thinking online. *Journal of Instructional Psychology, 29*(2), 53–77.

Austin, A. E. (2002). Preparing the next generation of faculty: Graduate school as socialization for the academic career. *The Journal of Higher Education, 73*(1), 94–122. doi:10.1353/jhe.2002.0001

Austin, A. E., & Wulff, D. H. (2004). The challenge to prepare the next generation of faculty. In Wulff, D. H., & Austin, A. E. (Eds.), *Paths to the professorate: Strategies for enriching the preparation of future faculty*. San Francisco, CA: Jossey-Bass.

Axley, L. (2008). The integration of technology into nursing curricula: Supporting faculty via the technology fellowship program. *Online Journal of Issues in Nursing, 13*(3).

Bacro, T. R. (2007). Integration of Webcast lectures in a traditional gross anatomy course. *The FASEB Journal, 21*(5), 591–596.

Bain, K. (2004). *What the best college teachers do.* Cambridge, MA: Harvard University Press.

Baird, D. E., & Fisher, M. (2006). Neomillennial user experience design strategies: Utilizing social networking media to support "Always On" learning. *Journal of Educational Technology Systems, 34*(1), 5–32. doi:10.2190/6WMW-47L0-M81Q-12G1

Banas, J. R. (2007). *The impact of a tailored lesson introduction on learners' motivation and cognitive performance.* (Doctoral dissertation). ProQuest Dissertations and Theses. (3272141).

Banas, J. R. (2011). Standardized, flexible design of electronic learning environments to enhance learning efficiency and effectiveness. In Kitchenham, A. (Ed.), *Blended and mobile learning across disciplines: Models for implementation* (pp. 66–86). Hershey, PA: IGI Global. doi:10.4018/978-1-60960-511-7.ch004

Barbour, M., & Mulcahy, D. (2004). The role of mediating teachers in Newfoundland's new model of distance education. *The Morning Watch, 32*(1).

Barbules, N., & Callister, T. (2000). Universities in transition: The promise and the challenge of new technologies. *Teachers College Record, 102*(2), 271–293. doi:10.1111/0161-4681.00056

Barney, D. (2003). *The network society.* Cambridge, MA: Polity.

Barrett, K. R., Bower, B. L., & Donovan, N. C. (2007, March). Teaching styles of community college instructors. *American Journal of Distance Education, 21*(1), 37–49. doi:10.1080/08923640701298738

Bates, T. (2000). *Distance education in dual mode higher education institutions: Challenges and changes.* Retrieved from http://bates.cstudies.ubc.ca/papers/challengesandchanges.html

Bates, A. W., & Poole, G. (2003). *Effective teaching with technology: Foundations for success.* San Francisco, CA: Jossey-Bass.

Baturay, M. (2008). Characteristics of basic instructional design models. *Ekev Academic Review, 12*(34), 471–482.

Beaudoin, M. (1990). The instructor's changing role in distance education. *American Journal of Distance Education, 4*(2), 21–29. doi:10.1080/08923649009526701

Bee, H. L., & Bjorkland, B. R. (2004). *The journey to adulthood* (5th ed.). Englewood Cliffs, NJ: Prentice Hall.

Beggs, T. A. (2000). *Influences and barriers to the adoption of instructional technology.* Retrieved from http://frank.mtsu.edu/~itconf/proceed00/beggs/beggs.htm

Beijaard, D., & De Vries, Y. (1997). Building expertise: a process perspective on the development or change of teachers' beliefs. *European Journal of Teacher Education, 20*(3), 243–255. doi:10.1080/0261976970200304

Beith, L. (2006). *Hybrid faculty learning communities as a professional development strategy.* Paper presented at the "22nd Conference on Distance Teaching and Learning". Madison, Wisconsin. Retrieved from http://www.uwex.edu/disted/conference/Resource_library/proceedings/06_4229.pdf

Belenger, P. (1996). Trends in adult education policy. *Adult Education and Development, 47*, 19–29.

Beniger, J. (1986). *The control revolution: Technological and economic origins of the information society.* Cambridge, MA: Harvard University Press.

Ben-Jacob, M. G., Levin, D. S., & Ben-Jacob, T. K. (2000). The learning environment of the 21st Century. *Educational Technology Review, 13*, 8–12.

Bennett, S., Priest, A., & Macpherson, C. (1999). Learning about online learning: An approach to staff development for university teachers. *Australian Journal of Educational Technology, 15*, 207–221.

Benson, R., & Brack, C. (2009). Developing the scholarship of teaching: What is the role of e-teaching and learning? *Teaching in Higher Education, 14*(1), 71–80. doi:10.1080/13562510802602590

Benson, R., & Samarawickrema, G. (2009). Addressing the context of e-learning: Using transactional distance theory to inform design. *Distance Education, 39*(1), 5–21. doi:10.1080/01587910902845972

Bereiter, C. (1994). Constructivism, socioculturalism, and Popper's world 3. *Educational Researcher, 23*, 21–23.

Berge, Z. (2007). Motivate and manage: Key activities of online learners. In Spector, J. M. (Ed.), *Finding your online voice: Stories told by experience online educators* (pp. 73–82). Mahwah, NJ: Lawrence Erlbaum and Associates.

Berge, Z. (2009). Changing instructor roles in virtual worlds. *Quarterly Review of Distance Education, 9*(4), 407–414.

Berge, Z. L. (1995). Facilitating computer conferencing: Recommendations from the field. *Educational Technology, 35*(1), 22–30.

Berkman Center for Internet & Society. (2011). *Berkman Center meeting technology tools*. Retrieved from http://cyber.law.harvard.edu/

Bers, M. U., Ponte, I., Juelich, K., Viera, A., & Schenker, J. (2002). Teachers as designers: Integrating robotics in early childhood education. *Information Technology in Childhood Education Annual,* (1): 123–145.

Betts, K. S. (2009a). Changing higher education landscape: Increasing demand for online and blended education. *Student Success,* 11-14.

Betts, K. S. (1998). An institutional overview: Factors influencing faculty participation in distance education in postsecondary education in the United States: An institutional study. *Online Journal of Distance Learning Administration, 1*(3). Retrieved from http://www.westga.edu/~distance/betts13.html

Betts, K. S. (2009b). Lost in translation: Importance of effective communication in online education. *Online Journal of Distance Learning Administration, 7*(2).

Biggs, J. (2003). *Teaching for quality learning at university* (2nd ed.). Buckingham, UK: Open University Press/Society for Research into Higher Education.

Biggs, J. (2003). *Teaching for quality learning at university*. Berkshire, UK: Open University Press & McGraw-Hill.

Biro, S. C. (2004). *How to support faculty as they prepare to teach online*. Paper presented at the Joint International Conference for the 45th Adult Education Research Conference (AERC) and the 23rd National Conference of the Canadian Association for the Study of Adult Education, University of Victoria, Canada.

Blackburn, R. T., Boberg, A., O'Connell, C., & Pellino, G. (1980, June*). Project for faculty development program evaluation: Final report*. Ann Arbor, MI: University o Michigan, Center for the Study of Higher Education.

Blair, K., & Madigan, D. (2000). Involving faculty in faculty development: A recursive model. In D. Willis, et al. (Eds.), *Proceedings of Society for Information Technology & Teacher Education International Conference* (pp. 418-423). Chesapeake, VA: AACE.

Blanton, M. L., & Stylianou, D. A. (2009). Interpreting a community of practice perspective in discipline-specific professional development in higher education. *Innovative Higher Education, 34*, 79–92. doi:10.1007/s10755-008-9094-8

Boettcher, J. V., & Conrad, R. M. (2004). *Faculty guide for moving teaching and learning to the web*. Phoenix, AZ: League for Innovation in the Community College.

Boettcher, J. V., & Conrad, R. M. (2010). *Online teaching survival guide: Simple and practical pedagogical tips*. San Francisco, CA: Jossey-Bass.

Bolliger, D. U. (2004). Key factors for determining student satisfaction in online courses. *International Journal on E-Learning, 3*(1), 61.

Bolliger, D. U., & Wasilik, O. (2009). Factors influencing faculty satisfaction with online teaching and learning in higher education. *Distance Education, 30*(1), 103–116. doi:10.1080/01587910902845949

Bolman, L. G., & Deal, T. E. (2008). *Reframing organizations: Artistry, choice, and leadership*. San Francisco, CA: Jossey-Bass.

Bonk, C. (2002). *Online training in an online world*. Bloomington, IN: CourseShare.com.

Bonk, C. J., Kirkley, J., Hara, N., & Dennen, V. (2000). *Advances in pedagogy: Finding the instructor in post-secondary online learning*. Paper presented at the American Educational Research Association, New Orleans, LA.

Bonk, C., Wisher, R. A., & Lee, J. Y. (2004). Moderating learner-centered e-learning: Problems and solutions, benefits and implications. In Roberts, T. S. (Ed.), *Online collaborative learning: Theory and practice* (pp. 54–85). Hershey, PA: Information Science Publishing.

Border, L. B., & von Hoene, L. M. (2010). Graduate and professional student development programs. In Gillespie, K. J., & Robertson, D. L. (Eds.), *A guide to faculty development* (2nd ed.). San Francisco, CA: John Wiley & Sons, Inc.

Borko, H. (2004). Professional development and teacher learning - Mapping the terrain. *Educational Researcher, 33*(8), 3–15. doi:10.3102/0013189X033008003

Boud, D. (2001). Using journal writing to enhance reflective practice. In English, L., & Gillen, M. (Eds.), *Promoting journal writing in adult education* (pp. 9–18). San Francisco, CA: Jossey-Bass. doi:10.1002/ace.16

Boud, D., & Walker, D. (1991). *Experience and learning: Reflection at work*. Geelong, Australia: Deakin University Press.

Bower, B. (2001). Distance education: Facing the faculty challenge. *Online Journal of Distance Learning Administration, 4*(11). Retrieved from http://www.westga.edu/~distance/ojdla/summer42/bower42.html

Boyd, D. (2006a). A blogger's blog: Exploring the definition of a medium. *Reconstruction, 6*(4). boyd, d. (2007). Why youth social network sites: The role of networked publics in teenage social life. In Buckingham, D. (Ed.), *Youth identity and digital media* (pp. 119–142). Cambridge, MA: MIT Press.

Brancato, V. (2003). Professional development in higher education. In King, K., & Lawler, P. (Eds.), *New directions for adult and continuing education: New perspectives on designing and implementing professional development of teachers of adults* (Vol. 98, pp. 59–65). San Francisco, CA: Jossey-Bass.

Bright, B. (1993). What is reflective practice? *Curriculum, 16*, 69–81.

Briscoe, C. (1991). The dynamic interactions among beliefs, role metaphors, and teaching practices: A case study of teacher change. *Science Education, 75*(2), 185–199. doi:10.1002/sce.3730750204

Brockbank, A., & McGill, I. (2006). *Facilitating reflective learning through mentoring and coaching* (pp. 63–92). London, UK: Kogan Page.

Brookfield, S. D. (1995). Adult learning: An overview. In Tuinjman, A. (Ed.), *International encyclopedia of education*. Oxford, UK: Pergamon Press.

Brookfield, S. D. (1995). *Becoming a critically reflective teacher*. San Francisco, CA: Jossey-Bass.

Brooks-Young, S. (2010). *Teaching with the tools kids really use*. Thousand Oaks, CA: Corwin.

Bross, V., Beck, M., & Leffler, J. J. (2011). Like a haven in the shifting economic sands: Making the most of web conferencing tools. *The Serials Librarian, 6*(1-4), 203–205. doi:10.1080/0361526X.2011.556035

Brown, J., Sheppard, D., & Stevens, K. (2000). *Effective schooling in a tele-learning environment*. St. John's, NL, Centre for Tele-Learning and Rural Education, Faculty of Education, Memorial University of Newfoundland.

Browne, N., Maeers, M., & Cooper, E. (2000). A faculty of education as a community of learners: Growing to meet the demands of instruction and technology. In Gillan, B., & McFerrin, K. (Eds.), *Faculty development. ERIC Document (ED444497)*.

Brown, J. A. (2004). Marketing and retention strategies for adult degree programs. *New Directions for Adult and Continuing Education, 103*(Fall), 51–60. doi:10.1002/ace.148

Brown, J. S., Collins, A., & Duguid, P. (1989). Situated cognition and the culture of learning. *Educational Researcher, 18*(11), 32–42.

Brown, T. (2006). Beyond constructivism: Navigationism in the knowledge era. *Horizon, 14*(3), 108–120. doi:10.1108/10748120610690681

Brufee, K. A. (1999). *Collaborative learning: Higher education, interdependence, and the authority of knowledge* (2nd ed.). Baltimore, MD: John Hopkins University Press.

Bruning, K. (2005). The role of critical thinking in the online learning environment. *International Journal of Instructional Technology and Distance Learning, 2*(5).

Bruning, R., Zygielbaum, A., Horn, C., & Glider, W. (n.d.). *Online tools for enhancing student learning and extending resources in large enrollment university courses.* **Lincoln, NE.** *Center for Instructional Innovation at the University of Nebraska.*

Butts, F. (2009). Evaluations of hybrid online instruction in sport management. *Online Journal of Distance Learning Administration, 7*(2).

Buzzetto-Moore, N., & Mitchell, B. C. (2009). Student performance and perceptions in a web-based competitive computer simulation. *Interdisciplinary Journal of E-Learning and Learning Objects, 5,* 73–90.

Caffarella, R. S., & Zinn, L. F. (1999). Professional development for faculty: A conceptual framework of barriers and supports. *Innovative Higher Education, 23*(4), 241–254. doi:10.1023/A:1022978806131

Cain, J., Scott, D., & Smith, K. (2010). Use of social media by residency program directors for resident selection. *American journal of health-system pharmacy, 67,* 1635–1639. doi:10.2146/ajhp090658

Cambridge, D., Cambridge, B., & Yancey, K. (2009). *Electronic portfolios 2.0: Emergent research on implementation and impact.* Sterling, VA: Stylus Publishing.

Care, W. D., & Scanlan, J. M. (2001). Planning and managing the development of courses for distance delivery: Results from a qualitative study. *Online Journal of Distance Learning Administration, 4*(2).

Carlisle, Y., & Baden-Fuller, C. (2004). Re-applying beliefs: An analysis of change in the oil industry. *Organization Studies, 25*(6), 987–1019. doi:10.1177/0170840604045093

Carmen, C., & Heafner, J. (2002). Transforming course management systems into effective learning environments. *The entity from which ERIC acquires the content, including journal, organization, and conference names, or by means of online submission from the author. EDUCAUSE Review, 37*(6), 26–24.

Carnevale, D. (2000, February). Assessing the quality of online courses remains a challenge, educators agree. *The Chronicle of Higher Education, 46*(24), A59.

Carroll, J. G. (1980). Effects of training programs for university teaching assistants: A review of empirical research. *The Journal of Higher Education, 51*(2), 167–182. doi:10.2307/1981372

Carr, W., & Kemmis, S. (1986). *Becoming critical: Education, knowledge, and action research.* London, UK: Falmer Press.

Caruso, J. B., & Salaway, G. (2008, October). *The ECAR study of undergraduate students and information technology: Roadmap.* Boulder, CO: EDUCAUSE Center for Applied Research. Retrieved from http://net.educause.edu/ir/library/pdf/ers0706/rs/ERS0706w.pdf

Cary, L. J., & Mutua, K. (2010). Postcolonial narratives: Discourse and epistemological spaces. *Journal of Curriculum Studies, 26*(2), 62–77.

Cavanaugh, C. (2001). The effectiveness of interactive distance education technologies in K-12 learning: A meta-analysis. *International Journal of Educational Telecommunications, 7*(1), 73–88.

CDW-G. (2008). *The 21st-century campus: Are we there yet? Challenges and opportunities for campus technology* (21st-century campus study). Retrieved June 26, 2011 http://newsroom.cdwg.com/features/feature-10-13-08.html

Cercone, K. (2008). Characteristics of adult learners with implications for online learning design. *AACE Journal, 16*(2), 137–159.

Cherakov, L., Brunner, R., Smart, R., & Lu, C. (2009). *Virtual spaces: Enabling immersive collaborative enterprise, Part 1: Introduction to the opportunities and technologies.* IBM: DeveloperWorks. Retrieved September 18, 2011, from http://www.ibm.com/developerworks/webservices/library/ws-virtualspaces/

Chiero, R., & Beare, P. (2010). An evaluation of online versus campus-based teacher preparation programs. *Journal of Online Learning and Teaching, 6*(4), 780–790.

Chism, N. V. N. (2004). Using a framework to engage faculty in instructional technologies. *EDUCAUSE Quarterly, 2,* 39–45.

Chism, N. V. N., Lees, N. D., & Evenbeck, S. (2002). Faculty development for teaching innovation. *Liberal Education, 88*(3), 34.

Choi, I., & Lee, K. (2008). A case-based learning environment design for real-world classroom management problem-solving. *TechTrends, 52*(3), 26–31. doi:10.1007/s11528-008-0151-z

Christensen, C. M., Horn, M. B., & Johnson, C. W. (2008). Disrupting class: How disruptive innovation will dispositions of a critical thinker. *New Directions for Teaching and Learning, 80*, 69–7.

Christensen, R. (2002). Effects of technology integration education on the attitudes of teachers and students. *Journal of Research on Technology in Education, 34*(4), 411–434.

Chronicle of Higher Education. (2010, November 5). Forum. Chronicle of Higher Education, (pp. B42-46).

Cisco Systems, Inc. (2010). *Cisco video collaboration guide*. Distributed by Tandberg.com. Retrieved from http://www.tandberg.com/collateral/video_conferencing_guide.pdf

Cisco Systems, Inc. (2011). *Go green with Cisco Telepresence*. Retrieved from http://www.cisco.com/en/US/solutions/ns669/networking_solutions_products_genericcontent_green_solution.html

Clarke, L. E., & Gabert, T. E. (2004). Faculty issues related to adult degree programs. In Pappas, J., & Jerman, J. (Eds.), *Developing and delivering adult degree programs* (*Vol. 103*, pp. 31–40). San Francisco, CA: Jossey Bass. doi:10.1002/ace.146

Clarke, M., Butler, C., Schmidt-Hansen, P., & Somerville, M. (2004). Quality assurance for distance learning: A case study at Brunel University. *British Journal of Educational Technology, 35*(1), 5–11. doi:10.1111/j.1467-8535.2004.00363.x

Clark, R. C., & Mayer, R. E. (2008). *E-learning and the science of instruction: Proven guidelines for consumers and designers of multimedia learning* (2nd ed.). San Francisco, CA: Pfeiffer.

Clark, R. E. (1983). Reconsidering research on learning from media. *Review of Educational Research, 53*(4), 445–449.

Clark, R. E. (1994). Media will never influence learning. *Educational Technology Research and Development, 42*(2), 21–29. doi:10.1007/BF02299088

Coffman, T., & Klinger, M. B. (2007). Utilizing virtual worlds in education: The implications for practice. *International Journal of Sciences, 2*(1), 29–33.

Collis, B. (1996). *Telelearning in a digital world - The future of distance learning*. London, UK: Thompson Computer Press.

Collison, G., Elbaum, B., Haavind, S., & Tinker, R. (2000). *Facilitating on-line learning: Effective strategies for moderators*. Madison, WI: Atwood.

Communications News. (2004). Web meeting saves firm 1.9 M. *Communications News, 41*(9), 44–45.

comprehensive market survey. Working reports of the Learning Center. Institute of Information Management of the University of St. Gallen, Switzerland. ISSN: 1424-8557.

Conceição-Runlee, S. (2001). *Faculty lived experiences in the online environment*. Doctoral dissertation, University of Wisconsin-Madison, Madison, WI.

Conceição, S. (2006). Faculty lived experiences in the online environment. *Adult Education Quarterly, 57*(1), 26–45. doi:10.1177/1059601106292247

Conrad, D. (2004). University instructors' reflections on their first online teaching experiences. *Journal of Asynchronous Learning Networks, 8*(2), 31–44.

Cook, D. A. (2007). Web-based learning: Pros, cons and controversies. *Clinical Medicine, 7*(1), 37–42.

Cook, D., & Farmer, L. (2011). *Using qualitative methods in action research*. Chicago, IL: American Library Association.

Council for Higher Education Accreditation (CHEA). (2002). *Accreditation and assuring quality in distance learning. CHEA Monograph Series 2002, Number 1*. Washington, DC: Author.

Courtney, A. M., & King, F. B. (2009). Online dialog: A tool to support preservice teacher candidates' understanding of literacy teaching and practice. *Contemporary Issues in Technology & Teacher Education, 9*(3). Retrieved from http://www.citejournal.org/vol9/iss3/languagearts/article1.cfm

Cox, M. D. (2002). Achieving teaching and learning excellence through faculty learning communities. *Toward the Best in the Academy, 14*(4), 1-3.

Cox, M. D. (2004). Introduction to faculty learning communities. In Cox, M. D., & Richlin, L. (Eds.), *New directions for teaching and learning* (*Vol. 97*, pp. 5–23). Wiley Periodicals.

Craig, E. M. (2007). Changing paradigms: Managed learning environments and Web 2.0. *Campus-Wide Information Systems, 24*(3), 152–161. doi:10.1108/10650740710762185

Cranton, P. (1996). *Professional development as perspective transformation*. San Francisco, CA: Jossey Bass.

Cranton, P., & King, K. (2003). Transformative learning as a professional development goal. In King, K., & Lawler, P. (Eds.), *New directions for adult and continuing education: New perspectives on designing and implementing professional development of teachers of adults* (*Vol. 98*, pp. 31–37). San Francisco, CA: Jossey-Bass. doi:10.1002/ace.97

Crawford, C. M. (2002). *The design of a supportive faculty development model: The integration of technology within the university faculty's teacher candidate coursework.*

Crawford, C. M., & Cook, R. (2008). Creating and sustaining communities of learning within distance learning environments: Focusing upon making connections, creating communities of learning, and responsibilities. *International Journal of Learning, 15*(2), 179–193.

Creswell, J. (2005). *Educational research: Planning, conducting, and evaluating quantitative and qualitative research* (2nd ed.). Upper Saddle River, NJ: Pearson.

Cross, K. P. (1998). Why learning communities? Why now? *About Campus, 3*(3), 4–11.

Cuban, L. (1995). The hidden variable: How organizations influence teacher responses to secondary science curriculum reform. *Reforming Science Education, 34*(1), 4–11.

Cuper, P., & Gong, Y. (2010). Video analysis as a reflective tool. In Yamamoto, J., Penny, C., Leight, J., & Winterton, S. (Eds.), *Technology leadership in teacher education* (pp. 67–82). Hershey, PA: IGI Global. doi:10.4018/978-1-61520-899-9.ch005

D'Abate, E., Eddy, R., & Tannenbaum, S. (2011). What's in a name? A literature-based approach to understanding mentoring, coaching, and other constructs that describe developmental interactions. *Human Resource Development Review, 2*(4), 360–384. doi:10.1177/1534484303255033

Daley, B. (2001). Learning and professional practice: A study of four professions. *Adult Education Quarterly, 52*(1), 39–54.

Darby, D., & Speaker, R. (2009, October). *Under-prepared African American college students' perceptions of the impact of technology in a developmental reading course.* Paper presented at the Annual Meeting of e-Learning Association for the Advancement of Computing in Education, Vancouver, Canada.

Darling-Hammond, L. (2000). Teacher quality and student achievement: A review of state policy evidence. *Education Policy Analysis Archives, 8*(1), 1–44.

Davis, M. (2009). Creating value with online teacher training. *Education Week.* Retrieved from http://www.edweek.org/tsb/articles/2009/03/16/02onlinepd.h02.html

Davis, J. (2007). Dialog, monologue, and soliloquy in the large lecture class. *International Journal of Teaching and Learning in Higher Education, 19*(2), 178–182.

Davis, N. E., & Niederhauser, D. S. (2005). Socio-cultural analysis of two cases of distance learning in secondary education. *Education and Information Technologies, 10,* 249–262. doi:10.1007/s10639-005-3006-7

Davis, S. F., & Kring, J. P. (2001). A model for training and evaluating graduate teaching assistants. *College Student Journal, 35*(1), 45–51.

de Boer, W., & Collis, B. (2002). A changing pedagogy in e-learning: From acquisition to contribution. *Journal of Computing in Higher Education, 13*(2), 87–101. doi:10.1007/BF02940967

Dede, C. (2005). Planning for neomillennial learning styles. *EDUCAUSE Quarterly, 28*(1). Retrieved from http://net.educause.edu/ir/library/pdf/eqm0511.pdf

Dede, C. (2006). *Online professional development for teachers*. Cambridge, MA: Harvard Education Press.

Dede, C., Ketelhut, D., Whitehouse, P., Breit, L., & Mc-Closkey, E. (2009). A research agenda for online teacher professional development. *Journal of Teacher Education, 60*(1), 8–19. doi:10.1177/0022487108327554

Dennen, V., Darabi, A., & Smith, L. (2007). Instructor-learner interaction in online courses: The relative perceived importance of particular instructor actions on performance and satisfaction. *Distance Education, 28*(1), 65–79. doi:10.1080/01587910701305319

Dennis, K. B. (2009, April). Taking responsibility for your own career. *Corrections Today, 71*(2), 6.

Dermody, M., & Speaker, R. B. Jr. (2003). Multimedia literacy in the urban classroom and the reading methods course. *Journal of Reading Education, 28*(1), 24–31.

Design-based Research Collective. (2003). Design-based research: An emerging paradigm for educational inquiry. *Educational Researcher, 32*(1), 5–8. doi:10.3102/0013189X032001005

Desimone, L. (2009). Improving impact studies of teachers' professional development: Toward better conceptualizations and measures. *Educational Researcher, 38*(3), 181–199. doi:10.3102/0013189X08331140

Dewey, J. (1916). *Democracy in education.* Macmillian Publishing. Retrieved from http://www.ilt.columbia.edu/publications/digitext.html

Dewey, J. (1954). *Experience and education* (18th printing ed.). New York, NY: Macmillan.

Dewey, J. (1938). *Experience and education.* New York, NY: The Macmillan Company.

Dewey, J. (1991). *How we think.* Amherst, NY: Prometheus Books.

Dewey, J. (1997). *Experience and education.* New York, NY: Simon & Schuster.

Dick, W., Carey, L., & Carey, J. (2005). *The systematic design of instruction* (6th ed.). New York, NY: Addison-Wesley Educational Publishers, Inc.

Dillenbourg, P., Schneider, D. K., & Synteta, P. (2002). Virtual learning environments. In A. Dimitracopoulou (Ed.), *Proceedings of the 3rd Hellenic Conference "Information & Communication Technologies in Education* (pp. 3-18). Kastaniotis Editions, Greece.

Dobrovolny, J. (2006). How adults learn from self-paced, technology-based corporate training: New focus for learners, new focus for designers. *Distance Education, 27*(2), 155–170. doi:10.1080/01587910600789506

Donaldson, J. F., Flannery, D. D., & Ross-Gordon, J. M. (1993). A triangulated study comparing adult college students' perceptions of effective teaching with those of traditional students. *Continuing Higher Education Review, 57*(3), 147–165.

Dorniden, A. (2005). K-12 schools and online learning. In Howard, C., Boettcher, J. V., Justice, L., Schenk, K., Rogers, P. L., & Berg, G. A. (Eds.), *Encyclopedia of distance learning* (pp. 1182–1188). Hershey, PA: IGI Global. doi:10.4018/978-1-59140-555-9.ch176

Douglas-Faraci, D. (2010). A correlational study of six professional development domains in e-learning teacher professional development. *Journal of Online Learning and Teaching, 6*(4), 754–766.

Downes, S. (2009). *Beyond management: The personal learning environment.* Keynote address presented at the ED MEDIA Conference. Honolulu. Retrieved June 1, 2011, from http://www.downes.ca/presentation/225

Dron, J. (2005). Designing the undesignable: Social software and control. *Journal of Educational Technology & Society, 10*(3), 60–71.

Dron, J., & Anderson, T. (2009). How the crowd can teach. In Hatzipanagos, S., & Wartburton, S. (Eds.), *Handbook of research on social software and developing community ontologies* (pp. 1–17). Hershey, PA: Information Science Reference. doi:10.4018/978-1-60566-208-4.ch001

Duffee, L., & Aikenhead, G. (1992). Curriculum change, student evaluation, and teacher practical knowledge. *Science Teacher Education, 76*(5), 493–506.

Duffy, T. M., & Cunningham, D. J. (1996). Constructivism: Implications for the design and delivery of instruction. In Jonassen, D. H. (Ed.), *Handbook of research for educational communications and technology* (pp. 170–198). New York, NY: Simon & Schuster Macmillan.

Duncan, H. (2005). On-line education for practicing professionals: A case study. *Canadian Journal of Education/Revue Canadienne de L'éducation, 28*(4), 874-896. Retrieved from http://www.jstor.org

Dutta, S. (2010). What's your personal social media strategy? *Harvard Business Review, 88*(11), 127–130.

Dykman, C. A., & Davis, C. K. (2008). Online education forum: Part two-teaching online versus teaching conventionally. *Journal of Information Systems, 19*(3), 281–289.

Dziuban, C. D., Hartman, J., Moskal, P., Sorg, S., & Truman, B. (2003). Three ALN modalities: An institutional perspective. In Bourne, J., & Moore, J. C. (Eds.), *Elements of quality online education: Into the mainstream* (pp. 127–148). Needham, MA: Sloan Center for Online Education.

Dziuban, C. D., Shea, P., & Arbaugh, J. (2005). Faculty roles and satisfaction in asynchronous learning networks. In Hiltz, S. R., & Goldman, R. (Eds.), *Learning together online: Research on asynchronous learning networks* (pp. 169–190). Mahwah, NJ: Lawrence Erlbaum.

Eastmond, D. V. (1995). *Alone but together: Adult distance study through computer conferencing*. Cresskill, NJ: Hampton Press.

Ehrmann, C., & Hewett, B. L. (2005). Designing a principles-based online training program for instructors. *Distance Learning: A Magazine for Leaders, 2,* 9-13.

Ehrmann, S. C. (2010, September/October). Taking the long view: Ten recommendations about time, money, technology, and learning. *Change,* (n.d), 16–22. doi:10.1080/00091383.2010.503175

Ellison, N., Heino, R., & Gibbs, J. (2006). Managing impressions online: Self-presentation processes in the online dating environment. *Journal of Computer-Mediated Communication, 11*(2). Retrieved from http://jcmc.indiana.edu/vol11/issue2/ellison.htmldoi:10.1111/j.1083-6101.2006.00020.x

Ertl, H., & Plante, J. (2004). *Connectivity and learning in Canada's schools*. Ottawa, Canada: Government of Canada.

Ertmer, P. A. (1999). Addressing first- and second-order barriers to change: Strategies for technology integration. *Educational Technology Research and Development, 47,* 47–61. doi:10.1007/BF02299597

Eunjoo, O., & Suhong, P. (2009). How are universities involved in blended instruction? *Journal of Educational Technology & Society, 12*(3), 327–342.

Exter, M. E., Korkmaz, N., Harlin, N. M., & Bichelmeyer, B. A. (2009). Sense of community within a fully online program. *The Quarterly Review of Distance Education, 10*(2), 177–194.

Facing History and Ourselves. (2011). *Café conversations*. Retrieved from http://www.facinghistory.org/resources/strategies/caf%C3%A9-conversations

Faharani, G. O. (2003). *Existence and importance of online interaction*. Unpublished Doctoral dissertation, Virginia Polytechnic Institute.

Fang, B. (2007). A performance-based development model for online faculty. *Performance Improvement, 46*(5), 17–24. doi:10.1002/pfi.129

Farmer, L. (2003). Facilitating faculty incorporation of information literacy skills into the curriculum through the use of online instruction. *RSR. Reference Services Review, 31*(4), 307–312. doi:10.1108/00907320310515220

Fenwick, T. (2008). Workplace learning: Emerging trends and new perspectives. *New Directions for Adult and Continuing Education, 119,* 17–26. doi:10.1002/ace.302

Fenwick, T. J. (2003). *Learning through experience: Troubling orthodoxies and intersecting questions*. Malabar, FL: Krieger Publishing Company.

Fernando, A. (2004). Big blogger is watching you! Reputation management in an opinionated, hyperlinked world. *Communication World, 21*(4), 10–11.

Fey, M. H. (1992). *Freeing voices: Literacy through computer conferencing and feminist collaboration*. Unpublished Doctoral dissertation, University of Rochester.

Finaly-Neumann, E. (1994). Course work characteristics and students' satisfaction with instructions. *Journal of Instructional Psychology, 21*(2), 14–19.

Finkelstein, J. (2006). *Learning in real time: Synchronous teaching and learning online*. San Francisco, CA: Jossey-Bass.

Finley, L., & Hartman, D. (2004). Institutional change and resistance: Teacher preparatory faculty and technology integration. *Journal of Technology and Teacher Education, 12*, 319–337.

Flanagan, B., & Calandra, B. (2005). Podcasting in the classroom. *Learning and Leading with Technology, 33*(3), 20–22.

Flint, T. A. (2005). *How well are we serving our adult learners? Investigating the impact of institutions on success and retention*. Chicago, IL: Council for Adult and Experiential Learning (CAEL).

Frankman, M. (2004). The developers' apprentices. In Saroyan, A., & Amundsen, C. (Eds.), *Rethinking teaching in higher education* (pp. 153–167). Sterling, VA: Stylus.

Fraser, M., & Dutta, S. (2008). *Throwing sheep in the boardroom: How online social networking will transform your life*. New York, NY: J. Wiley & Sons.

Fresen, J. (2005). *Quality assurance practice in online (web-supported) learning in higher education: An exploratory study*. Unpublished Master's thesis, University of Pretoria, Pretoria, South Africa, Africa.

Frey, B. A., & Alman, S. W. (2003). Applying adult learning theory to the online classroom. *New Horizons in Adult Education, 17*(1), 4–12.

Frost & Sullivan. (2001). *The European web conferencing market* (pp. 3989-74). New York, NY: Frost & Sullivan. FIT&L. (2002). Some best practices in online teaching and learning. *Online: RIT Online Learning*. Retrieved from http://www.edpath.com/images/RITWorkshop.pdf

Fulton, C., & Licklider, B. L. (1998). Supporting faculty development in an era of change. *To Improve the Academy, 19*, 51-66.

Furey, D., & Stevens, K. (2008). New systemic roles facilitating the integration of face-to-face and virtual learning. *Online Journal of Distance Learning Administration, 11*(4).

Gagné, R. M. (1985). *The conditions of learning* (4th ed.). New York, NY: Holt, Rinehart, and Winston.

Gagne, R. M., Briggs, L. J., & Wager, W. W. (1992). *Principles of instructional design*. Fort Worth, TX: Harcourt Brace Jovanovich.

Gallant, G. (2000). Professional development for Web-based teaching: Overcoming innocence and resistance. In Burge, E. J. (Ed.), *New directions for adult and continuing education* (pp. 69–78). San Francisco, CA: Jossey-Bass. doi:10.1002/ace.8807

Galley, M. (2002). E-training offers options. *Education Week, 21*(35), 41–44.

Garnham, N. (2004). Information society theory as ideology. In Webster, F. (Ed.), *The information society reader* (pp. 165–183). London, UK: Routledge.

Garrison, D. R. (2003). Cognitive presence for effective asynchronous online learning: The role of reflective inquiry, self-direction and metacognition. In Bourne, J., & Moore, J. C. (Eds.), *Elements of quality in online education: Practice and direction* (pp. 47–58). Needham, MA: Sloan Center for Online Education.

Garrison, D. R., Anderson, T., & Archer, W. (2001). Critical thinking, cognitive presence, and computer conferencing in distance education. *American Journal of Distance Education, 15*(1), 7–23. doi:10.1080/08923640109527071

Garrison, R., & Cleveland-Innes, M. (2005). Facilitating cognitive presence in online learning: Interaction is not enough. *American Journal of Distance Education, 19*(3), 133–148. doi:10.1207/s15389286ajde1903_2

Geertz, C. (1983). *Local knowledge*. New York, NY: Basic Books.

Germain-McCarthy, Y., Haggerty, D., Buxton, C., & Speaker, R. B., Jr. (2003). Crafting the technological solutions in high school science and mathematics teaching and learning: Matthew effects and the digital divide (pp. 1041-1048). In C. P. Canstantinou, & Z. C. Zacharai (Eds.), *Computer Based Learning in Sciences: Conference Proceedings 2003 Volume 1 New Technologies and their Applications in Education.* Nicosia, Cyprus: University of Cyprus.

Gibson, J. J. (1977). The theory of affordances. In Shaw, R., & Bransford, J. (Eds.), *Perceiving, acting and knowing.* Hillsdale, NJ: Erlbaum.

Ginsburg, A., Gray, T., & Levin, D. (2004). *Online professional development for mathematics teachers: A strategic analysis.* Washington, DC: National Center for Technology Innovation, American Institutes for Research.

Glaser, B. G., & Strauss, A. L. (1967). *The discovery of grounded theory.* Chicago, IL: Aldine.

Glasersfeld, E. V. (1996). *Radical constructivism: A way of knowing and learning.* London, UK: Falmer Press.

Glick, D. B. (2005). K-12 online learning policy. In Howard, C., Boettcher, J. V., Justice, L., Schenk, K., Rogers, P. L., & Berg, G. A. (Eds.), *Encyclopedia of distance learning* (pp. 1175–1181). Hershey, PA: IGI Global. doi:10.4018/978-1-59140-555-9.ch175

Glowa, E. (2009, March). *Guidelines for professional development of online teachers.* Southern Regional Education Board. Retrieved from http://publications. sreb.org/2009/09T01_Guide_profdev_online_teach.pdf

Golde, C. M., & Dore, T. M. (2004). The survey of doctoral education and career preparation: The importance of disciplinary contexts. In Wulff, D. H., & Austin, A. E. (Eds.), *Paths to the professorate: Strategies for enriching the preparation of future faculty* (pp. 19–45). San Francisco, CA: Jossey-Bass.

Goodyear, P. (2002). Teaching online. In Hativa, N., & Goodyear, P. (Eds.), *Teacher thinking, beliefs and knowledge in higher education* (pp. 79–101). The Netherlands: Kluwer Academic Publishers. doi:10.1007/978-94-010-0593-7_5

Gordon, T. J., & Pease, A. (2006). RT Delphi: An efficient, "round-less", almost real time Delphi method. *Journal of Technological Forecasting and Social Change, 73*(4), 321–333. doi:10.1016/j.techfore.2005.09.005

Gorsky, P., & Caspi, A. (2005). Dialogue: A theoretical framework for distance education instructional systems. *British Journal of Educational Technology, 36*(2), 137–144. doi:10.1111/j.1467-8535.2005.00448.x

Government of Newfoundland and Labrador. (2000). *Supporting learning: Report on the ministerial panel on educational delivery in the classroom.* St John's, Canada: Department of Education.

Graham, S. W., & Gisi, S. L. (2000). Adult undergraduate students: What role does college involvement play? *NASPA Journal, 38*(1), 99–121.

Greenberg, G. (1998). Distance education technologies: Best practices for K-12 settings. *IEEE Technology and Society Magazine,* (Winter): 36–40. doi:10.1109/44.735862

Greeno, J. G. (1997). On claims that answer the wrong questions. *Educational Researcher, 26*(1), 5.

Grubaugh, S., Levitt, G., Speaker, R., & Rector, P. (2010). Supporting, motivating and engaging all learner in online learning: Literacy and critical thinking in virtual school content area courses. *Proceedings of NSSA Conference.*

Guerrero, S. (2010). The role of teacher thinking in technology-based reform: A multiple case study. *Journal of the Research Center for Educational Technology, 6*(2), 18.

Guldberg, K. (2008). Adult learners and professional development: Peer-to-peer learning in a networked community. *International Journal of Lifelong Education, 27*(1), 35–49. doi:10.1080/02601370701803591

Gunawardena, C. N., & McIsaac, M. S. (2003). Distance education. In Jonassen, D. H. (Ed.), *Handbook of research on educational communications and technology* (2nd ed., pp. 113–142). Mahwah, NJ: Lawrence Erlbaum Associates, Inc.

Guskey, T. (1995). *Results-orientated professional development: In search of an optimal mix of effective practice.* NCREL Literature Review. Retrieved from http://www. ncrel.org/sdrs/areas/rpl_esys/pdlitrev.htm

Gustafson, K., & Maribe Branch, R. (2002). *Survey of instructional design models* (4th ed.). Washington, DC: Department of Education.

Halpern, D. F. (1999). Teaching for critical thinking: Helping college students develop the skills and dispositions of a critical thinker. *New Directions for Teaching and Learning*, *80*, 69–74. doi:10.1002/tl.8005

Hanna, M., Salzman, J. A., Reynolds, S. L., & Fergus, K. B. (2010). Engaging teachers as learners: Modeling professional development for adult literacy providers. *Adult Basic Education and Literacy Journal*, *4*(3), 173–177.

Hansen, S., Kalish, A., Hall, W. E., Gynn, C. M., Holly, M. L., & Madigan, D. (2004, Spring). Developing a statewide faculty learning community program. *New Directions for Teaching and Learning*, (n.d), 97.

Harasim, L., Hiltz, S. R., Teles, L., & Turroff, M. (1995). *Learning networks: A field guide to teaching and learning online*. Cambridge, MA: MIT Press.

Hardré, P. L. (2005). Instructional design as a professional development tool-of choice for graduate teaching assistance. *Innovative Higher Education*, *30*(3), 163–175. doi:10.1007/s10755-005-6301-8

Hardré, P. L., Ferguson, C., Bratton, J., & Johnson, D. (2008). Online professional development for TAs: What they need, what they have, what they want. *Journal of Faculty Development*, *22*(1), 11–23.

Hargreaves, A. (1997). *Rethinking educational change: going deeper and wider in the quest for success*. Alexandria, VA: Association for Supervision and Curriculum Development.

Hargreaves, A. (2005). Educational change takes ages: Life, career and generational factors in teachers' emotional responses to educational change. *Teaching and Teacher Education*, *21*(8), 967–983. doi:10.1016/j.tate.2005.06.007

Hartman, H. (2001). Teaching metacognitively. In H. J. (Ed.), *Metacognition in learning and instruction: Theory, research, and practice*. Dordrecht, The Netherlands: Kluwer Academic Publishers. Retrieved from ttp://condor.admin.ccny.cuny.edu/~hhartman/tchmtlyhjh.html

Hartman, J., Dziuban, C., & Moskal, P. (2000). Faculty satisfaction in ALNs: A dependent or independent variable? In J. Bourne (Ed.), *Online Education Volume 1: Learning Effectiveness and Faculty Satisfaction: Proceedings of the 1999 Sloan Summer Workshop on Asynchronous Learning Networks* (pp. 151-172). Needham, MA: Sloan Center for OnLine Education.

Hartman, J., Otte, G., & Niemiec, M. (2006). *Blended learning institutional strategies for success*. Paper presented at the 12th Sloan-C International Conference on Asynchronous Learning Networks, Orlando, FL.

Hartman, J., Moskal, P., & Dziuban, C. (2005). Preparing the academy of today for the learner of tomorrow. In Oblinger, D. G., & Oblinger, J. L. (Eds.), *Educating the Net generation* (pp. 6.4–6.15). Washington, DC: Educause.

Hawkes, M., & Halverson, P. (2002). Technology facilitation in the rural school: An analysis of options. *Journal of Research in Rural Education*, *17*(3), 162–170.

Healey, D., & Stevens, K. (2002). Student access to information technology and perceptions of future opportunities in two small Labrador communities. *Canadian Journal of Learning and Technology*, *28*(1), 7–18.

Heinrich, T. (2006). Web conferencing 101. *OfficePro*, *66*(1), 24.

Henri, F., & Pudelko, B. (2003). Understanding and analyzing activity and learning in virtual communities. *Journal of Computer Assisted Learning*, *19*, 472–487. doi:10.1046/j.0266-4909.2003.00051.x

Herrington, J., McKenney, S., Reeves, T., & Oliver, R. (2007). Design-based research and doctoral students: Guidelines for preparing a dissertation proposal. In C. Montgomerie & J. Seale (Eds.), *Proceedings of World Conference on Educational Multimedia, Hypermedia and Telecommunications 2007* (pp. 4089-4097). Chesapeake, VA: AACE.

Herrington, A., Herrington, J., Hoban, G., & Reid, D. (2009). Transfer of online professional learning to teachers' classroom practice. *Journal of Interactive Learning Research*, *20*(2), 189–213.

Hillman, D. C., Willis, D. J., & Gunawardena, C. N. (1994). Learner-interface interaction in distance education: An extension of contemporary models and strategies for practitioners. *American Journal of Distance Education, 8*(2), 30–42. doi:10.1080/08923649409526853

Hiltz, S. R., & Shea, P. (2005). The student in the online classroom. In Hiltz, S. R., & Goldman, R. (Eds.), *Learning together online* (pp. 145–168). Mahwah, NJ: Lawrence Erlbaum Associates.

Hmelo-Silver, C. E., & Barrows, H. S. (2006). Goals and strategies of a problem-based learning facilitator. *Interdisciplinary Journal of Problem-based Learning, 1*, 21–39.

Hodge, E. M., Tabrizi, M. H. N., Farwell, M. A., & Wuensch, K. L. (2007). Virtual reality classrooms strategies for creating a social presence. *International Journal of Sciences, 2*(1), 105–109.

Hodkinson, P., & Lincoln, S. (2008). Online journals as virtual bedrooms? Young people, identity and personal space. *Young, 16*(1), 27–46. doi:10.1177/110330880701600103

Hofmann, J. (2004). *The synchronous trainer's survival guide: Facilitating successful live and online courses, meetings, and events.* San Francisco, CA: Pfeiffer.

Hogan, R., & McKnight, M. (2007). Exploring burnout among university online instructors: An initial investigation. *The Internet and Higher Education, 10*, 117–124. doi:10.1016/j.iheduc.2007.03.001

Hogarth, K., Day, I., & Dawson, D. (2004). Online professional development in support of online teaching: Some issues for practice. *International Journal of Instructional Technology & Distance Learning, 1*(9). Retrieved from http://www.itdl.org/Journal/Sep_04/article05.htm

Horgan, B. (1998, August). Faculty, instruction and information technology. *The Technology Source.* Retrieved March 25, 2011 from http://ts.mivu.org/default.asp?show=article&id=75

Horng, J., Hong, J., Chankin, L., Chang, S., & Chu, H. (2005). Creative teachers and creative thinking strategies. *International Journal of Consumer Studies, 29*(4), 352–358. doi:10.1111/j.1470-6431.2005.00445.x

Hovorka, D., & Rees, M. (2009). Active collaboration learning environments - The class of web 2.0. In *Proceeding of the 20ᵗʰ Australasian Conference on Information Systems Active Collaboration Learning Environments.* Melbourne, Australia: ACIS

Howell, S. L., Williams, P. B., & Lindsay, N. K. (2003, Fall). Thirty-two trends affecting distance education: An informed foundation for strategic planning. *Online Journal of Distance Learning Administration, 6*(3).

Hughes, G. (2009). Using videos to bring lecture to the online classroom. *College Quarterly, 12*(1), Retrieved from http://www.collegequarterly.ca/2009-vol12-num01-winter/hughes.html

Hu, R., Caron, T., Deters, F., Moret, L., & Swaggerty, E. A. (2011). Teacher educators teaching and learning together: A collaborative self-study of support within an online literacy learning community. *Journal of Online Learning and Teaching, 7*(1), 57–67.

Hutchins, H. (2003, Fall). Instructional immediacy and the seven principles: Strategies for facilitating online courses. *Online Journal of Distance Learning Administration, 6*(3). Retrieved from http://www.westga.edu/~distance/ojdla/fall63/hutchins63.html

Hyslop-Margison, E., & Strobel, J. (2008). Constructivism and education: Misunderstandings and pedagogical implications. *Teacher Educator, 43*(1), 72–86. doi:10.1080/08878730701728945

iLinc Communications, Inc. (2011). *State of Arizona relies on web and video conferencing to cut costs and CO² emissions.* Retrieved from http://www.ilinc.com/pdf/case-studies/ilinc-state-of-arizona-case-study.pdf

Illinois Online Network. (2010). *Instructional strategies for online courses.* Retrieved from http://www.ion.uillinois.edu/resources/tutorials/pedagogy/instructionalstrategies.asp

Information Highway Advisory Council. (1997). *Preparing Canada for a digital world.* Ottawa, Canada: Author.

Ingalls, J. (1972). *A trainer's guide to andragogy* (rev. ed.). Waltham, MA: Data Education.

Ingram, A. (2005). Kent State offers learning communities for online instructors. *Distance Education Report, 9*(13), 8.

Innes, R. B. (2007). Dialogic communication in collaborative problem solving groups. *International Journal for the Scholarship of Teaching and Learning, 1*(1), 1–17. Retrieved from http://academics.georgiasouthern.edu/ijsotl/2007_v1n1.htm

Institute for Higher Education Policy. (2000). *Quality on the line: Benchmarks for success in Internet-based distance education.* A report prepared for The Institute for Higher Education Policy, Washington, DC.

IRA/NCTE. (2011). *Student interactives.* Retrieved April 23, 2011, from http://www.readwritethink.org/classroom-resources/student-interactives/

Issenberg, S., & Scalese, R. (2008). Simulation in health care education. *Perspectives in Biology and Medicine, 51*(1), 31–46. doi:10.1353/pbm.2008.0004

Ito, M., Baumer, S., Bittanti, M., Boyd, D., & Cody, R. (2009). *Hanging out, messing around, and geeking out - Kids living and learning with new media.* Cambridge, MA: The MIT Press.

Jacobsen, M. (1997). Bridging the gap between early adopters' and mainstream faculty's use of instructional technology. *Information Analysis.* Retrieved from http://eric.ed.gov/ERICDocs/data/ericdocs2sql/content_storage_01/0000019b/80/16/ed/23.pdf

Jacobs, R., & Osman-Gani, A. (1999). Status, impacts and implementation issues of structured on-the-job training: A study of Singapore-based companies. *Human Resource Development International, 2*(1), 17.

Jamieson, J., Chapelle, C., & Preiss, S. (2004). Putting principles into practice. *ReCALL, 16*(2), 396–415. doi:10.1017/S0958344004001028

Janik, D. S. (2007). *What every language teacher should know about the brain and how it affects teaching.* Paper presented at Wikipedia 2007 Conference on Foreign Language Pedagogy, University of Helsinki, Finland.

Jarvis, P. (1987). *Adult learning in the social context.* London, UK: Croom Helm.

Jarvis, P. (1995). *Adult & continuing education. Theory and practice* (2nd ed.). New York, NY: Routledge.

Jaworski, B. (1993). Professional development of teachers - The potential of critical reflection. *British Journal of Inservice Education, 19*, 37–42. doi:10.1080/0305763930190307

Jenner, S., Zhao, M., & Foote, T. H. (2010). Teamwork and team performance in online simulations: The business strategy game. *MERLOT Journal of Online Learning and Teaching, 6*(2), 416–430.

Johnson, L., Smith, R., Levine, A., & Haywood, K. (2010). *The 2010 horizon report: K-12 edition.* Austin, TX: The New Media Consortium.

Johnstone, J. W. C., & Rivera, R. J. (1965). *Volunteers for learning: A study of the educational pursuits of American adults.* Chicago, IL: Aldine.

Jonassen, D. H. (1997). Instructional design models for well-structure and ill-structured problem-solving learning outcomes. *Educational Technology Research and Development, 45*(1), 65–94. doi:10.1007/BF02299613

Jonassen, D. H. (2000). Toward a design theory of problem solving. *ETR&D, 48*(40), 63–85. doi:10.1007/BF02300500

Jonassen, D. H., Lee, C. B., Yang, C.-C., & Laffey, J. (2005). The collaboration principle in multimedia learning. In Mayer, R. E. (Ed.), *The Cambridge handbook of multimedia learning.* New York, NY: Cambridge University Press.

Jonassen, D. H., & Reeves, T. C. (1996). Learning with technology: Using computers as cognitive tools. In Jonassen, D. H. (Ed.), *Handbook of research for educational communications and technology.* New York, NY: Simon & Schuster Macmillan.

Jones, M. G., Harmon, S. W., & O'Grady-Jones, M. K. (2005). Developing the digital mind: Challenges and solutions in teaching and learning. *Teacher Education Journal of South Carolina, 2004-2005,* 17–24.

Jones, S. (2006). Evaluation of instructor knowledge on structuring and facilitating effective online discourse. *The Journal of Educators Online, 3*(2). Retrieved from http://www.thejeo.com/Volume3Number2/JonesFinal.pdf

Jordan, H. R., Mendro, R., & Weerasinghe, D. (1997). *Teacher effects on longitudinal student achievement: A preliminary report on research on teacher effectiveness.* Paper presented at the National Evaluation Institute, Indianapolis, IN.

Joseph, P. B., Bravmann, S. L., Windschitl, M. A., Mikel, E. R., & Green, N. S. (2000). *Cultures of curriculum.* Mahwah, NJ: Lawrence Erlbaum Associates.

Kameau, C. (2009). Strategizing impression management in corporations: cultural knowledge as capital. In Harorimana, D. (Ed.), *Cultural implications of knowledge sharing, management and transfer: Identifying competitive advantage* (pp. 60–83). Hershey, PA: IGI Global. doi:10.4018/978-1-60566-790-4.ch004

Kasworm, C. E., & Blowers, S. S. (1994). *Adult undergraduate students: Patterns of learning involvement. (Final research report to U.S. Department of Education).* Knoxville, TN: College of Education, University of Tennessee.

Kasworm, C. E., Polson, C. J., & Fishback, S. J. (2002). *Responding to adult learners in higher education.* Malabar, FL: Krieger Publishing Company.

Kaufman, D. M. (2003). ABC of learning and teaching in medicine: Applying education theory in practice. *British Medical Journal, 326,* 213–216. doi:10.1136/bmj.326.7382.213

Kearsley, G. (2000). *Online education: Learning and teaching in cyberspace.* Belmont, CA: Wadsworth.

Keegan, D., Schwenke, E., Fritsch, H., Kenny, G., Kismihók, G., & Bíró, M. … Nix, J. (2005). *Virtual classrooms in educational provision: Synchronous elearning systems for European institutions.* Hagen, Germany: FernUniversitaet (ZIFF). Retrieved February 18, 2009 from: http://www.fernuni-hagen.de/ZIFF/synchronous.pdf.

Keengwe, J., Kidd, T., & Kyei-Blankson, L. (2009). Faculty and technology: Implications for faculty training and technology leadership. *Journal of Science Education and Technology, 18*(1), 23–28. doi:10.1007/s10956-008-9126-2

Keller, B. (2005, July 27). Teachers flocking to online sources to advance and acquire knowledge. *Education Week, 24,* 22–24.

Keller, J. M. (2008). First principles of motivation to learn and e³-learning. *Distance Education, 29*(2), 175–185. doi:10.1080/01587910802154970

Kerka, S. (1988). *Strategies for retaining adult students: The educationally disadvantaged.* Columbus, OH: ERIC Clearinghouse on Adult Career and Vocational Education.

Kester, L., Kirschner, P. A., & Corbalan, G. (2007). Designing support to facilitate learning in powerful electronic learning environments. *Computers in Human Behavior, 23,* 1047–1054. doi:10.1016/j.chb.2006.10.001

Kezar, A. J. (2000). *Teaching and learning: ERIC trends, 1999-2000. Eric Clearinghouse on Higher Education.* Washington, DC: George Washington University Graduate School of Education and Human Development.

Kieff, J., & Speaker, R. B., Jr. (2003). Teaching sciences and mathematics concepts in the early grades: K-3 teachers engaging developmentally appropriate practice which incorporated technologies (pp. 1049-1054). In C. P. Constantinou, & Z. C. Zacharai (Eds.), *Computer Based Learning in Sciences: Conference Proceedings 2003 Volume 1 New Technologies and their Applications in Education.* Nicosia, Cyprus: University of Cyprus.

Kim, B. (2001). Social constructivism. In M. Orey (Ed.), *Emerging perspectives on learning, teaching, and technology.* Retrieved from http://projects.coe.uga.edu/epltt/

Kim, K., & Bonk, C. (2006). The future of online teaching and learning in higher education. *EDUCASE Quarterly, 29*(4). Retrieved from http://www.educause.edu/EDUCAUSE+Quarterly/EDUCAUSEQuarterlyMagazineVolum/TheFutureofOnlineTeachingandLe/157426

Kim, K., & Bonk, C. (2006). The future of online teaching and learning in higher education: The survey says. *EDUCAUSE Quarterly, 29*(4), 22–30.

Kincheloe, J. L. (2005). *Critical constructivism primer.* New York, NY: Peter Lang.

King, K. (2000, June 2-4). *Educational technology that transforms: Educator's transformational learning experiences in professional development.* Paper presented at the Adult Education Research Conference, Vancouver, Canada.

King, K. (2001). The tail of the comet: Helping faculty focus on their pathway of discovery in learning and using technology. *Journal of Faculty Development, 18*(4), 123–129.

King, K. (2002a). Identifying success in online teacher education and professional development. *The Internet and Higher Education, 5*, 231–246. doi:10.1016/S1096-7516(02)00104-5

King, K. (2002b). Technology catalyzing change in how faculty teach and learn. *Journal of Continuing Higher Education, 50*(2), 26–37.

King, K. (2003). Learning the new technologies: Strategies for success. *New Directions for Adult and Continuing Education, 98*, 49. doi:10.1002/ace.99

King, K. (2010). Adaptation to pressures of changing technology and online instruction. *The LLI Review, 5*, 29–35.

King, K. P. (2002). Educational technology professional development as transformative learning opportunities. *Computers & Education, 39*, 283–297. doi:10.1016/S0360-1315(02)00073-8

King, K., & Lawler, P. (2003). Trends and issues in the professional development of teachers of adults. In King, K., & Lawler, P. (Eds.), *New directions for adult and continuing education: New perspectives on designing and implementing professional development of teachers of adults* (*Vol. 98*, pp. 5–13). San Francisco, CA: Jossey-Bass. doi:10.1002/ace.94

Kirkpatrick, D. L. (1994). *Evaluating training programs: The four levels.* San Francisco, CA: Berrett-Koehler Publishers, Inc.

Kleiman, G. M. (2004). *Meeting the need for high quality teachers: E-learning solutions.* A paper presented at the U.S. Department of Education Secretary's No Child Left Behind Leadership Summit (July 12–13). Retrieved from http://www.ed.gov/about/offices/list/os/technology/plan/2004/site/documents/Kleiman-MeetingtheNeed.pdf

Kleiman, G. M., & Treacy, B. (2006). EdTech leaders online: Building organizational capacity to provide effective online professional development. In C. Dede (Ed.), *Online professional development for teachers: Emerging models and methods* (pp, 31-47). Cambridge, MA: Harvard Educational Press.

Kluge, S., & Riley, L. (2008). Teaching in virtual worlds: Opportunities and challenges. *Issues in Informing Science and Information Technology, 5*, 127–135.

Knapper, C. K. (1995). Understanding student learning: Implications for instructional practice. In Wright, W. A. (Eds.), *Teaching improve practices: Successful strategies for higher education* (pp. 58–75). Boston, MA: Anker.

Knobel, M., & Lankshear, C. (2009). Wikis, digital literacies, and professional growth. *Journal of Adolescent & Adult Literacy, 52*(7), 631–634. doi:10.1598/JAAL.52.7.8

Knowles, M. S. (1970). *The modern practice of adult education: Andragogy vs. pedagogy.* New York, NY: Cambridge Books.

Knowles, M. S. (1984). *Andragogy in action.* San Francisco, CA: Jossey-Bass.

Knowles, M. S., Holton, E. F. III, & Swanson, R. A. (2005). *The adult learner: The definitive classic in adult education and human resource development* (6th ed.). Burlington, MA: Elsevier.

Knowlton, D. S. (2002). *Technology-enhanced courses versus traditional instruction: Empirical evidence, reflections from practice, and designing for maximum learning. The CyberPeer Newsletter.* Memphis, TN: Crichton Distance Education.

Kolb, D. A. (1984). *Experiential learning: Experience as the source of learning and development.* Englewood Cliffs, NJ: Prentice-Hall.

Koopman, B. (2011). From Socrates to wikis: Using online forums to deepen discussions. *Phi Delta Kappan, 92*(4), 24–27.

Kosak, L., Manning, D., Dobson, E., Rogerson, L., & Cotnam, S. (2004). Prepared to teach online? Perspectives of faculty in the University of North Carolina system. *Online Journal of Distance Learning Administration, 7*(3).

Kosak, L., Manning, D., Dobson, E., Rogerson, L., Cotnam, S., Colaric, S., & McFadden, C. (2004, Spring). Prepared to teach online? Perspectives of faculty in the University of North Carolina System. *Online Journal of Distance Learning Administration, 7*(3). Retrieved from http://www.westga.edu/~distance/ojdla/fall73/kosak73.html

Kramarae, C. (2003). Gender equity online, when there is no door to knock on. In Moore, M. G., & Anderson, W. G. (Eds.), *Handbook of distance education* (pp. 261–272). Mahwah, NJ: Lawrence Erlbaum Associates.

Kuh, G. D., Kinzie, J., Cruce, T., Shoup, R., & Gonyea, R. M. (2006, July). *Connecting the dots: Multi-faceted analyses of the relationships between student engagement results from the NSSE, and the institutional practices and conditions that foster student success: Final report prepared for Lumina Foundation for Education.* Bloomington, IN: Indiana University, Center for Postsecondary Research.

Kuh, G., Kinzie, J., Schuh, J., & Whitt, E. (2010). *Student success in college: Creating conditions that matter.* San-Francisco, CA: Jossey-Bass.

Kurubacak, G., & Yuzer, T. (2004). The building of knowledge networks with interactive radio programs in distance education systems. In G. Richards (Ed.), *Proceedings of World Conference on E-Learning in Corporate, Government, Healthcare, and Higher Education 2004* (pp. 2360-2367). Chesapeake, VA: AACE.

Kyei-Blankson, L. (2009). *Learning to teach and teaching online: Faculty-faculty interactions in online environments.* Paper presented at the Society for Information Technology & Teacher Education International Conference, Chesapeake, VA.

Laird, D. (1985). *Approaches to training and development.* Reading, MA: Addison-Wesley.

Lane, D. (2002). *Theory and research methods.* Lexington, KY: University of Kentucky.

Lao, T., & Gonzales, C. (2005). Understanding online learning through a qualitative description of professors and students' experiences. *Journal of Technology and Teacher Education, 13*(3), 459–474.

Lau, L. K. (2003). Institutional factors affecting student retention. *Education, 124*(1), 126–136.

Lave, J., & Wenger, E. (1991). *Situated learning: Legitimate peripheral participation.* Cambridge, UK: University of Cambridge Press.

Lave, J., & Wenger, E. (1991). *Situated learning: Legitimate peripheral participation.* New York, NY: Cambridge Press.

Lawler, P. A. (2003, Summer). Teachers as adult learners: A new perspective. In K. P. King & P. A. Lawler (Eds.), New directions for adult and continuing education (pp. 15–22). San Francisco, CA: Jossey-Bass. doi:10.1002/ace.95doi:10.1002/ace.95

Lawler, P., & King, K. (2000). *Refocusing faculty development.* Paper presented at the Adult Education Research Conference (AERC), Vancouver, British Columbia, Canada.

Lawler, P., & King, K. (2001, March). *Refocusing faculty development: The view from an adult learning perspective.* Paper presented at the Pennsylvania Adult and Continuing Education Research Conference, Indiana, PA.

Lawler, P., King, K., & Wilhite, S. C. (2004). *Living and learning with technology: Faculty as reflective practitioners in the online classroom.* Paper presented at the Joint International Conference of the 45th Adult Education Research Conference (AERC) and the 23rd National Conference of the Canadian Association for the Study of Adult Education, University of Victoria, Canada.

Lawler, P. (2003). Teachers as adult learners: A new perspective. In King, K. P., & Lawler, P. A. (Eds.), *New directions for adult and continuing education* (pp. 15–22). San Francisco, CA: Jossey-Bass. doi:10.1002/ace.95

Lee, J. A., & Busch, P. E. (2005). Factors related to instructors' willingness to participate in distance education. *The Journal of Educational Research, 99*(2), 109–115. doi:10.3200/JOER.99.2.109-115

Lefor, P., Benke, M., & Ting, E. (2003). Information technology and adult learners at Empire State College. *New Directions for Student Services, 102*, 35–42. doi:10.1002/ss.87

Lesser, E. L., & Storck, J. (2001). Communities of practice and organizational performance. *IBM Systems Journal, 40*(4). Retrieved from http://www.research.ibm.com/journal/sj/404/lesser.htmldoi:10.1147/sj.404.0831

Levy, S. (2003). Six factors to consider when planning online distance learning programs in higher education. *Online Journal of Distance Learning Administration, 6*(1). Retrieved from http://www.westga.edu/~distance/ojdla/spring61/levy61.htm

Lewin, K. (1952). *Field theory in social science. Selected theoretical papers*. London, UK: Travistock Publications.

Lewis, C. C., & Abdul-Hamid, H. (2006). Implementing effective online teaching practices: Voices of exemplary faculty. *Innovative Higher Education, 31*(2), 83–98. doi:10.1007/s10755-006-9010-z

Lincoln, Y., & Guba, E. (1985). *Naturalistic inquiry*. New York, NY: Sage.

Lindeman, E. C. (1926). *The meaning of adult education*. New York, NY: New Republic.

Littlejohn, A. H. (2002). Improving continuing professional development in the use of ICT. *Journal of Computer Assisted Learning, 18*, 166–174. doi:10.1046/j.0266-4909.2001.00224.x

Livingstone, S. (2005). On the relation between audiences and publics. In Livingstone, S. (Ed.), *Audiences and publics: When cultural engagement matters for the public sphere* (pp. 17–42). Portland, OR: Intellect.

Loh, J., & Smyth, R. (2010). Understanding students' online learning experiences in virtual teams. *MERLOT Journal of Online Learning and Teaching, 6*(2), 335–342.

Lorenzetti, J. (2003). Getting the best out of online adjunct faculty: A guide. *Distance Education Report, 7*(4), 1–6.

Lorenzo, G., & Moore, J. C. (2002). *The Sloan Consortium report to the nation: Five pillars of quality online education*. The Alfred P. Sloan Foundation.

Lowes, S. (2008). Online teaching and classroom change: The trans-classroom teacher in the age of the Internet. *Innovate: Journal of Online Education, 4*(3). Retrieved from http://innovateonline.info/index.php?view=article&id=446

Lowry, P., & Bush, R. (2009). *Technologies and delivery methods*. Paper presented at the International Conference on e-Learning, Academic Conferences.

Lowther, D., Ross, S., & Morrison, G. (2003). When each has one: The influences on teaching strategies and student achievement of using laptops in the classroom. *Educational Technology Research and Development, 51*(3), 23–44. doi:10.1007/BF02504551

MacKnight, C. B. (2000). Teaching critical thinking through online discussions. *EDUCAUSE Quarterly, 4*, 38–41.

Mager, R. (1984). *Developing attitude toward learning*. Belmont, CA: David S. Lake Publishers.

Maki, P. (2002). Developing an assessment plan to learn about student learning. *The Journal of Academic Leadership, 28*(1), 8–13.

Malopinsky, L., Kirkley, J. R., Stein, R., & Duffy, T. (2000). An instructional design model for online problem based learning (PBL) environments: The learning to teach with technology studio. In *Proceedings of the Association for Educational Communications and Technology*. Denver, CO: AECT.

Maloy, R., Verock-O'Loughlin, R., Edwards, S., & Woolf, B. (2011). *Transforming learning with new technologies*. Boston, MA: Pearson.

Mancuso, S. (2001). Adult-centered practices: Benchmarking study in higher education. *Innovative Higher Education, 25*(3), 165. doi:10.1023/A:1007647531576

Mandel, M., Hamm, S., Matlack, C., Farrell, C., & Palmer, A. (2005). The real reasons you're working so hard and what you can do about it. *Bloomberg Businessweek*. Retrieved from http://www.businessweek.com/magazine/content/05_40/b3953601.htm

Mandernach, B. J., Forrest, K. D., Babutzke, J. L., & Manker, L. R. (2009). The role of instructor interactivity in promoting critical thinking in online and face-to-face classrooms. *MERLOT Journal of Online Learning and Teaching, 5*(1).

Mandernach, B. J., Forrest, K. D., Babutzke, J. L., & Manker, L. R. (2009). The role of instructor interactivity in promoting critical thinking in online and face-to-face classrooms. *MERLOT Journal of Online Learning and Teaching, 5*(1), 49–62.

Marantz, B., & England, R. J. (1993). Can CMC teach teacher training? *Educational Media International, 30*(2), 74–77. doi:10.1080/0952398930300206

Marek, K. (2009). Learning to teach online: Creating a culture of support for faculty. *Journal of Education for Library and Information Science, 50*(4), 275–291.

Marienau, C., & Reed, C. (2008). Educator as designer: Balancing multiple teaching perspectives in the design of community based learning for adults. *New Directions for Adult and Continuing Education, 118*, 61–74. doi:10.1002/ace.296

Marwick, A., & Boyd, d. (2010). I tweet honestly, I tweet passionately: Twitter users, context collapse, and the imagined audience. *New Media & Society, 13*(10), 114–133.

Mathiasen, H. (2004). Expectations of technology: When the intensive application of IT in teaching becomes a possibility. *Journal of Research on Technology in Education, 36*(3), 273–294.

Mayer, R. E. (2001). *Multi-media learning*. Cambridge, MA: Cambridge University Press.

Maykut, P., & Morehouse, R. (1994). *Beginning qualitative research*. Philadelphia, PA: The Falmer Press.

Mayrhofer, D., Back, A., & Hubschmid, R. (2004). *Web-conferencing software tools: A*

McAnuff-Gumbs, M. (2011). "Virtually There": Making online training 'real' for Caribbean literacy coaches – What government can do. *Journal of Online Learning and Teaching, 7*(1), 134–146.

McCarthy, S., & Samors, R. (2009). *Online learning as a strategic asset, Vol. 1: A resource for campus leaders*. Washington, DC: Association of Public and Land-Grant Universities. Retrieved from http://www.aplu.org/NetCommunity/Document.Doc?id=1877

McCombs, B., & Vakili, D. (2005). A learner-centered framework for e-learning. *Teachers College Record, 107*, 1582–1600. doi:10.1111/j.1467-9620.2005.00534.x

McCord, A. (2006) Staffing and supporting a new online initiative. *Innovate, 3*(2).

McDaniels, M. (2010). Doctoral student socialization for teaching roles. In Gardner, S., & Mendoza, P. (Eds.), *On becoming a scholar: Socialization and development in doctoral education* (pp. 29–44). Sterling, VA: Sylus Publishing.

McDermon, L. (2005). Distance learning. It's elementary. *Learning and Leading with Technology, 33*(4), 28–34.

McFarlane, D. A. (2011, Spring). The leadership roles of distance learning administrators (DLAs) in increasing educational value and quality perceptions. *Online Journal of Distance Learning Administration, 4*(1).

McKenzie, B. K., Ozkan, B. C., & Layton, K. (2006). Tips for administrators in promoting distance programs using peer mentoring. *Online Journal of Distance Learning Administration, 9*(2).

McLoughlin, C., & Lee, M. J. W. (2007). *Social software and participatory learning: Pedagogical choices with technology affordances in the Web 2.0 era*. Singapore: Australasian Society for Computers in Learning in Tertiary Education conference.

McLoughlin, J. A., & Wang, L.-C. C. (2008). Transforming the college through technology: A change of culture. *Innovative Higher Education, 33*, 99–109. doi:10.1007/s10755-008-9065-0

McNamara, J., & Brown, C. (2009). Assessment of online discussion in work-integrated learning. *Campus-Wide Information Systems, 26*(5), 413–423. doi:10.1108/10650740911004822

McNamara, K. P., Duncan, G. J., McDowell, J., & Marriott, J. L. (2009). Community pharmacists' preferences for continuing education delivery in Australia. *The Journal of Continuing Education in the Health Professions, 29*(1), 52–57. doi:10.1002/chp.20006

McNeely, B. (2005). Using technology as a learning tool, not just the new cool thing. In Oblinger, D. G., & Oblinger, J. L. (Eds.), *Educating the Net generation* (pp. 4.1–4.10). Washington, DC: Educause.

McQuiggan, C. (2007). The role of faculty development in online teaching's potential to question teaching beliefs and assumptions. *Online Journal of Distance Learning Administration, 5*(3). Retrieved from http://www.westga.edu/~distance/ojdla/fall103/mcquiggan103.htm

Meadows, S. (1998). Children learning to think: learning from others? Vygotskian theory and educational psychology. *Educational and Child Psychology, 15*(2), 6–13.

Means, B., Toyama, T., Murphie, R., Bakia, M., & Jones, K. (2010). *Evaluation of evidence-based practices in online learning: A meta-analysis and review of online learning studies.* Research Report, U.S. Office of Planning, Evaluation and Policy Development (OPEPD). Retrieved from the www.ed.gov/about/offices/list/opepd/ppss/reports.html

Merriam, S. B. (2002). *Qualitative research in practice: Examples for discussion and analysis* (1st ed.). San Francisco, CA: Jossey-Bass.

Merriam, S. B., & Caffarella, R. S. (1999). *Learning in adulthood* (2nd ed.). San Francisco, CA: Jossey-Bass.

Merriam, S. B., Caffarella, R. S., & Baumgartner, L. M. (2007). *Learning in adulthood: A comprehensive guide* (3rd ed.). San Francisco, CA: Jossey-Bass.

Merrill, H. S. (2003). Best practices for online facilitation. *Adult Learning, 14*(2), 13–16.

Merrill, M. D. (2002). First principles of instruction. *Educational Technology Research and Development, 50*(3), 43–59. doi:10.1007/BF02505024

Meyer, K. A. (2003). The web's impact on student learning. *T.H.E. Journal, 30*(10), 14.

Michaelsen, M. S. (2009). *Team-based learning: Small group learning's next big step. New Directions for Teaching and Learning, 116.* Hoboken, NJ: Jossey-Bass.

Miller, T., & King, F. (2003). Distance education: pedagogy and best practices in the new millennium. *International Journal of Leadership in Education: Theory and Practice, 6*(3), 283–297. doi:10.1080/1360312032000118225

Millis, B. J. (1994). Faculty development in the 1990s: What it is and why we can't wait. *Journal of Counseling and Development, 72*(May/June), 454–464. doi:10.1002/j.1556-6676.1994.tb00974.x

Mintu-Wimsatt, A., Sadler, T., & Ingram, K. (2007). Creativity in online courses: Perceptions of MBA student. *MERLOT Journal of Online Learning and Teaching, 3*(4).

Mishra, P., & Koehler, M. (2008). *Introducing technological pedagogical content knowledge.* Paper presented at the AERA Annual Meeting, March 2008, New York.

Mishra, P., & Koehler, M. (2006). Technological pedagogical content knowledge: A framework for teacher knowledge. *Teachers College Record, 108*(6), 1017–1054. doi:10.1111/j.1467-9620.2006.00684.x

Mitra, A. (2005, June). Weaving a new web. *Parks and Recreation.* Retrieved from http://www.nrpa.org/content/default.aspx?documentId=2298

Molenda, M. (2011). Historical perspectives. In Spector, M., Merrill, D., Van Merrienboer, J., & Driscoll, M. (Eds.), *A handbook of research for educational communications and technology* (3rd ed., pp. 12–14). Bloomington, IN: Association for Educational Communications and Technology.

Molenda, M., & Boling, E. (2008). Creating. In Januszewski, A., & Molenda, M. (Eds.), *Educational technology: A definition with commentary* (pp. 81–139). New York, NY: Lawrence Erlbaum Associates.

Monaghan, C. H., & Columbaro, N. L. (2009). Communities of practice and students' professional development. *International Journal of Teaching and Learning in Higher Education, 20*(3), 413–424.

Moon, J. A. (1999, 2004). *Reflection in learning & professional development: Theory & practice.* New York, NY: Routledge Falmer.

Moore, C. (2009, 31-January). *Elearning samples.* Making Change: Ideas for Lively eLearning. Retrieved from http://blog.cathy-moore.com/elearning-samples/

Moore, A., Moore, J., & Fowler, S. (2005). Faculty development for the Net generation. In Oblinger, D. G., & Oblinger, J. L. (Eds.), *Educating the Net generation* (pp. 11.1–11.16). Washington, DC: Educause.

Moore, M. (1989). Editorial: Three types of interaction. *American Journal of Distance Education, 3*, 1–6. doi:10.1080/08923648909526659

Moore, M. (1993). Theory of transactional distance. In Keegan, D. (Ed.), *Theoretical Principles of Distance Education* (pp. 22–38). London, UK: Routledge.

Moore, M. G., & Anderson, E. G. (Eds.). (2003). *Handbook of distance education.* Mahwah, NJ: Lawrence Erlbaum Associates.

Moore, M. G., & Kearsley, G. (1996). *Distance education.* Wadsworth Publishing Company.

Moreno, R. (2006). Does the modality principle hold for different media? A test of the method-affects learning hypothesis. *Journal of Computer Assisted Learning, 22,* 149–158. doi:10.1111/j.1365-2729.2006.00170.x

Morrison, G. R., Ross, S. M., & Kemp, J. E. (2004). *Designing effective instruction* (4th ed.). New York, NY: John Wiley & Sons, Inc.

Moser, P. K. (1986). Perception and belief: A regress problem. *Philosophy of Science, 53*(1), 120–126. doi:10.1086/289297

Mowl, G. (1996). *Innovative assessment.* Newcastle, UK: University of Northumbria. Retrieved fdrom http://www.city.londonmet.ac.uk/deliberations/assessment/mowl_fr.html

Muirhead, B., & Betz, M. (2002). Faculty training at an online university. *United States Distance Learning Association Journal, 16*(1).

Muirhead, B. (2007). Integrating creativity into online university classes. *Journal of Educational Technology & Society, 10*(1), 1–13.

Mullen, L., Beilke, J., & Brooks, N. (2007). Redefining field experiences: Virtual environments in teacher education. *International Journal of Social Sciences, 2*(1), 22–28.

Murchu, D., & Muirhead, B. (2005). Insights into promoting critical thinking in online classes. *International Journal of Instructional Technology and Distance Learning, 2*(6).

Naslund, A. (2010). Social media from the inside out. *Communication World, 27,* 36–39.

National Center for Education Statistics. (2002). *Nontraditional undergraduates (NCES 2002-012).* Washington, DC: U.S. Government Printing Office.

National Center for Education Statistics. (2010). *Digest of educational statistics.* Retrieved from http://nces.ed.gov/pubsearch/pubsinfo.asp?pubid=2011015

National Staff Development Council. (2001). *E-Learning for educators: NSDC-NICI. Implementing standards for staff development. NSDC, 1128 Nottingham Road* (p. 49230). MI: Grosse Pointe Park.

Nespor, J. (1987). The role of beliefs in the practice of teaching. *Journal of Curriculum Studies, 19*(4), 317–328. doi:10.1080/0022027870190403

New Media Consortium and EDUCAUSE. (2010). *The 2010 horizon report.*

Newell, T. (2004). Thinking beyond the disjunctive opposition of information literacy assessment in theory and practice. *School Library Media Research, 7.*

Nicolle, P. S., & Lou, Y. (2008). Technology adoption into teaching and learning by mainstream university faculty: A mixed methodology study revealing the "how, when, why, and why not.". *The Journal of Educational Research, 39*(3), 235–265.

Norman, D. A. (1988). *The design of everyday things.* New York, NY: Basic Books.

North Central Association of Colleges and Schools, Higher Learning Commission. (2007). *Best practices for electronically offered degree and certificate programs.* Retrieved from http://www.ncahlc.org/download/Best_Pract_DEd.pdf

Northrup, P. T. (2002). Online learners' preferences for interaction. *Quarterly Review of Distance Education, 3*(2), 219–226.

Nye, B., Konstantopoulos, S., & Hedges, L. V. (2004). How large are teacher effects? *Educational Evaluation and Policy Analysis, 26,* 237–257. doi:10.3102/01623737026003237

Nyquist, J. D., & Wulff, D. H. (1996). *Working effectively with graduate assistants.* Thousand Oaks, CA: Sage Publications.

Oblinger, D., Barone, C. A., & Hawkins, B. L. (2001). *Distributed education and its challenges: An overview.* American Council on Education (ACE). Retrieved from http://www.acenet.edu/bookstore/pdf/distributed-learning/distributed-learning-01.pdf

Onwuegbuzie, A. J., & Leech, N. L. (2007). A call for qualitative power analyses. *Quality & Quantity, 41,* 105–121. doi:10.1007/s11135-005-1098-1

Orland-Barak, L. (2005). Cracks in the iceberg: Sufacing the tensions of constructivist pedagogy in the context of mentoring. *Teachers and Teachers: Theory and Practice, 11*(3), 293–313.

Orr, R., Williams, M. R., & Pennington, K. (2009). Institutional efforts to support faculty in online teaching. *Innovative Higher Education, 34,* 257–268. doi:10.1007/s10755-009-9111-6

Ostashewski, N. (2010) Online technology teacher professional development courselets: Design and development. In D. Gibson & B. Dodge (Eds.), *Proceedings of Society for Information Technology & Teacher Education International Conference 2010* (pp. 2329-2334). Chesapeake, VA: AACE.

Ostashewski, N., & Reid, D. (2010a) Online teacher professional development: Redesign and delivery of a technological pedagogical courselet within a social networking site. In *Proceedings of World Conference on Educational Media, Hypermedia and Telecommunications 2010* (pp. 1111-1116). Chesapeake, VA: AACE.

Ostashewski, N., & Reid, D. (2010b). Networked teacher professional development: Applying the networked learning framework to online teacher professional development. In *Proceedings EDGE 2010 e-Learning: The Horizon and Beyond Conference.* St. John, NL.

Osterman, K. F., & Kottkamp, R. B. (2004). *Reflective practice for educators: Professional development to improve student learning* (2nd ed.). Thousand Oaks, CA: Corwin Press.

Padavano, D., & Gould, M. (2004, December). Best practices for faculty who teach online. *DEOSNews, 13*(9). Retrieved from http://www.ed.psu.edu/acsde/deos/deosnews/deosnews13_9.pdf

Page, M., Wilhelm, M., & Regens, N. (2011). Preparing graduate students for teaching: Expected and unexpected outcomes from participation in a GK-12 classroom fellowship. *Journal of College Science Teaching, 40*(5), 32–37.

Pahl, C., & Holohan, E. (2009). Applications of Semantic Web technology to support learning content development. *Interdisciplinary Journal of E-Learning and Learning Objects, 5,* 1–25.

Pajares, M. F. (1992). Teachers' beliefs and educational research: Cleaning up a messy construct. *Review of Educational Research, 62*(3), 307–332.

Palloff, R., & Pratt, K. (2001). *Lessons from the cyberspace classroom: The realities of online teaching.* San Francisco, CA: Jossey-Bass.

Palloff, R., & Pratt, K. (2002). Beyond the looking glass: What faculty and students need to be successful online. In Rudestam, K., & Schoenholtz-Read, J. (Eds.), *Handbook of online learning: Innovations in higher education and corporate training* (pp. 171–184). Thousand Oaks, CA: Sage Publications.

Palloff, R., & Pratt, K. (2008). *Assessing the online learner: Resources and strategies for faculty.* San Francisco, CA: Jossey-Bass.

Palmer, S. R., & Holt, D. M. (2009). Examining student satisfaction with wholly online learning. *Journal of Computer Assisted Learning, 25,* 101–113. doi:10.1111/j.1365-2729.2008.00294.x

Papacharissi, Z. (2002). The presentation of self in virtual life: Characteristics of personal home pages. *Journalism & Mass Communication Quarterly, 79*(3), 643–660. doi:10.1177/107769900207900307

Papert, S. (1992). *The children's machine.* New York, NY: Basic Books.

Papert, S., & Harel, I. (1991). Situating constructionism. In Harel, I., & Papert, S. (Eds.), *Constructionism* (pp. 1–11). Norwood, NJ: Ablex Publishing Corporation.

Parisot, A. H. (1997). Distance education as a catalyst for changing teaching in the community college: Implications for institutional policy. *New Directions for Community Colleges, 99,* 5. doi:10.1002/cc.9901

Park, Y. (2011). A pedagogical framework for mobile learning: Categorizing education applications of mobile technologies into four types. *International Review of Research in Open and Distance Learning, 12*(2).

Parsad, B., Lewis, L., Tice, P., & National Center for Education Statistics. (2008). *Distance education at degree-granting postsecondary institutions: 2006-07: First look.* Washington, DC: National Center for Education Statistics, Insitute of Education Sciences, U.S. Dept. of Education.

Parscal, T., & Riemer, D. (2010, Summer). Assuring quality in large-scale online course development. *Online Journal of Distance Learning Administration, 13*(2).

Partlow, K., & Gibbs, W. (2003). Indicators of constructivist practices in internet-based courses. *Journal of Computing in Higher Education, 14*(2), 68–97. doi:10.1007/BF02940939

Patton, M. (2001). *Qualitative research and evaluation methods* (3rd ed.). Thousand Oaks, CA: Sage Publications.

Paulson, K., & Boeke, M. (2006). *Adult learners in the United States: A national profile National Center for Higher Education Management Systems*. NCHEMS.

Pearson, W. (2005). Assuring instructional effectiveness. In Basch, L. (Ed.), *Best practices in adult learning* (pp. 129–145). Bolton, MA: Anker Publishing Company.

Pedler, M., & Abbott, C. (2008). Am I doing it right? Facilitating action learning for service improvement. *Leadership in Health Services, 21*(3), 185–199. doi:10.1108/17511870810893010

Peirce, W. (2003). *Strategies for teaching thinking and promoting intellectual development in online classes. Electronic communities: Current issues and best practices*. U.S. Distance Learning Association: Information Age Publishing.

Pellegrino, J., Chudowsky, N., & Glaser, R. (Eds.). (2001). *Knowing what students know: The science and design of educational assessment. Committee on the Foundations of Assessment, Board on Testing and Assessment, Center for Education, Division on Behavioral and Social Sciences and Education, National Research Council Washington.* DC: National Academic Press.

Pelz, B. (2004). My three principles of effective online pedagogy. *Journal of Asynchronous Learning Networks, 8*(3), 33–46.

Perlman, C. (2003). Performance assessment. In Nettles, A., & Nettles, M. (Eds.), *Measuring up: Assessment issues for teachers, counselors, and administrators*. Boston, MA: Kluwer Academic.

Peters, T. (1997). The brand called you. *Fast Company, 10*. Mansueto Ventures LLC. Retrieved from http://www.fastcompany.com/magazine/10/brandyou.html

Petrides, L. A. (2002). Web-based technologies for distributed (or distance) learning: Creating learning-centered educational experiences in the higher education classroom. *International Journal of Instructional Media, 29*(1), 69–77.

Petty, R. E., & Cacioppo, J. T. (1981). Epilog: A general framework for understanding attitude change processes. In *Attitudes and persuasion: Classic and contemporary approaches* (pp. 255–269). Dubuque, IA: William C. Brown Company.

Phillips, D. C. (1995). The good, the bad, and the ugly: The many faces of constructivism. *Educational Researcher, 24*(7), 5–12.

Picciano, A., & Seaman, J. (2008). *K–12 online learning: A 2008 follow-up of the survey of the U.S. school district administrators*. Newburyport, MA: The Sloan Consortium.

Pillai, P. (2009). *Creating an online community of teachers and the librarian for*

Pinar, W. F. (1998). Understanding curriculum as gender text: Notes on reproduction, resistance, and male-male relations (pp. 221-243). In W. F. Pinar (Ed.), *Queer theory in education.* Mahwah, NJ: Erlbaum Associates. Retrieved June 1, 2011 from www.questia.com

Pinar, W. F. (1994). *Autobiography, politics, and sexuality: Essays in curriculum theory, 1972-1992*. New York, NY: Peter Lang.

Pinar, W. F. (2004). *What is curriculum theory?* Mahwah, NJ: Lawrence Erlbaum.

Poole, D. M. (2000). Student participation in a discussion-oriented online course: A case study. *Journal of Research on Computing in Education, 33*(2), 162–177.

Price, H. B. (May 12, 1993). Teacher professional development: It's about time. *Education Week.* Retrieved from http://www.edweek.org/ew/articles/1993/05/12/33price.h12.html

Professional and Organizational Development Network in Higher Education. (2008). *What is faculty development?* Retrieved May 8, 2008, from http://www.podnetwork.org/development.htm

Professional Development through Social Networking Tools. Paper presentation at the International Conference on Academic Libraries (ICAL), October 5, 2009, Vice Regal Lodge, University of Delhi, Delhi India.

Purdue, K. (2003). Web-based continuing professional education: Uses, motivations, and deterrents to participation. In Moore, M. G., & Anderson, W. G. (Eds.), *Handbook of distance education* (pp. 615–630). Mahwah, NJ: Lawrence Erlbaum Associates Inc.

Pursel, B. K., & Bailey, K. D. (2007). *Establishing virtual learning worlds: The impact of virtual* worlds and online gaming on education and training. Retrieved from http://citeseerx.ist.psu.edu/viewdoc/download?doi=10.1.1.121.1959&rep=rep1&type=pdf

Reed, A. (2005). My blog is me: Texts and persons in UK online journal culture (an anthropology). *Ethnos*, *70*(2). doi:10.1080/00141840500141311

Reid, D. (2002). A classification schema of online tutor competencies. *Conference Proceedings, International Conference for Computers in Education 2002*. Auckland, New Zealand.

Reid, D. (2003). "Was she smiling when she typed that?": An exploratory study into online tutor competencies and the factors which affect those competencies. *Conference Proceedings, ASCILITE 2003* (pp. 684-690). Adelaide, Australia.

Reiser, R. A., & Dempsey, J. V. (Eds.). (2007). *Trends and issues in instructional design and technology*. Boston, MA: Pearson.

Renes, S. L., & Strange, A. T. (2011). Using technology to enhance higher education. *Innovative Higher Education*, *36*, 203–213. doi:10.1007/s10755-010-9167-3

Rice, J. K. (2003). *Teacher quality: Understanding the effectiveness of teacher attributes*. The Economic Policy institute.

Richardson, M. (2007). Constructivism in education: An overview of contributions to the literature and to the JPACTe annotated bibliography. *JPACTe*, *2*(1), 1–16.

Richardson, V. (1990). Significant and worthwhile change in teaching practice. *American Educational Research Association*, *19*(7), 10–18.

Richlin, L., & Cox, M. D. (2004). Developing scholarly teaching and the scholarship of teaching and learning through faculty learning communities. *New Directions for Teaching and Learning*, *97*, 127–135. doi:10.1002/tl.139

Rivkin, S. G., Hanushek, E. A., & Kain, J. F. (2005). Teachers' schools, and academic achievement. *Econometrica: Journal of the Econometric Society*, *73*(2), 417–458. doi:10.1111/j.1468-0262.2005.00584.x

Roberts, L. (1987). *The electronic seminar: Distance education by computer conferencing*. Paper presented at the Annual Conference on Non-Traditional and Interdisciplinary Programs, Fairfax, VA. (ERIC Document Reproduction Service, No. ED 291 358).

Roblyer, M., & Doering, A. (2009). *Integrating educational technology into teaching*. Boston, MA: Allyn & Bacon.

Rodriguez, M. A., & Anicete, R. C. R. (2010). Students' views of a mixed hybrid ecology course. *Journal of Online Learning and Teaching*, *6*(4), 791–798.

Rodriquez, F. G., & Nash, S. S. (2004). Technology and the adult degree program: The human element. In Pappas, J. P., & Jerman, J. (Eds.), *Developing and delivering adult degree programs* (pp. 73–79). San Francisco, CA: Jossey-Bass. doi:10.1002/ace.150

Rogers, E. M. (1962). *Diffusion of innovations*. New York, NY: Free Press.

Rogers, E. M. (1995). *Diffusion of innovations* (4th ed.). New York, NY: Free Press.

Rogers, P. L. (2000). Barriers to adopting emerging technologies in education. *Journal of Educational Computing Research*, *22*(4), 455–472. doi:10.2190/4UJE-B6VW-A30N-MCE5

Ronkowski, S. A. (1998). The disciplinary/departmental context of TA training. In Marincovich, M., Prostko, J., & Stout, F. (Eds.), *The professional development of graduate teaching assistants*. Bolton, MA: Anker Publishing.

Ross-Gordon, J. M. (1991). Critical incidents in the college classroom. *Educational Review*, *55*(1/2), 14–29.

Ross-Gordon, J. M. (2003). Adult learners in the classroom. *New Directions for Student Services*, (102): 43–52. doi:10.1002/ss.88

Rovai, A. P. (2001). Building and sustaining community in asynchronous learning networks. *The Internet and Higher Education, 3*, 285–297. doi:10.1016/S1096-7516(01)00037-9

Rowlands, I., Nicholas, D., Huntington, P., Gunter, B., Withey, R., Dobrowolski, T., et al. (2008). *Information behaviour of the researcher of the future.* Retrieved from http://www.jisc.ac.uk/whatwedo/programmes/resource-discovery/googlegen.aspx

Rutherford, C. (2010). Using online social media to support preservice student engagement. *MERLOT Journal of Online Learning and Teaching, 6*(4), 703–711.

Rutherford, L., & Grana, S. (1995). Retrofitting academe: Adapting faculty attitudes and practices to technology. *Technical Horizons in Education Journal, 23*(2), 82–86.

Salden, R. J. C. M., Paas, F., & van Merriënboer, J. J. G. (2006). Personalised adaptive task selection in air traffic control: Effects on training efficiency and transfer. *Learning and Instruction, 16*, 350–362. doi:10.1016/j.learninstruc.2006.07.007

Santovec, M. L. (2004, October 15). Training the people who train the teachers. *Distance Education Report,* (pp. 3-6). Retrieved from http://www.magnapubs.com/newsletter/issue/444/

Santovec, M. (2004). Training the people who train the teachers. *Distance Education Report, 8*(20), 3–6.

Saroyen, A., Amundsen, C., McAlpine, L., Weston, C., Winer, L., & Gandell, T. (2004). Assumptions underlying workshop activities. In Saroyen, A., & Amundsen, C. (Eds.), *Rethinking teaching in higher education* (pp. 15–29). Sterling, VA: Stylus.

Sauer, J. (2007). *Employment planning for an aging workforce.* A report for Knowledge Management AARP. Retrieved from http://assets.aarp.org/rgcenter/econ/ca_employer.pdf

Savery, J. R. (2010). BE VOCAL: Characteristics of successful online instructors. *Journal of Interactive Online Learning, 4*(2), 141–152.

Schau, H. J., & Gilly, M. C. (2003). We are what we post? Self-presentation in personal web space. *The Journal of Consumer Research, 30*(3), 385–404. doi:10.1086/378616

Schawbel, D. (2009). *Me 2.0: Build a powerful brand to achieve career success.* New York, NY: Kaplan Publishing.

Schmidt, M., & Datnow, A. (2005). Teachers' sense-making about comprehensive school reform: The influence of emotions. *Teaching and Teacher Education, 21*(8), 949–965. doi:10.1016/j.tate.2005.06.006

Schneckenberg, D. (2009). Understanding the real barriers to technology-enhanced innovation in higher education. *Educational Research, 51*(4), 411–424. doi:10.1080/00131880903354741

Schöen, D. (1995). The new scholarship requires a new epistemology. *Change, 27*(6), 26–34.

Schön, D. (1983). *The reflective practitioner.* San Francisco, CA: Jossey-Bass.

Schön, D. (1987). *Educating the reflective practitioner.* New York, NY: Basic Books.

Schraw, G. (2001). Promoting general metacognitive awareness. In Hartman, H. J. (Ed.), *Metacognition in learning and instruction: Theory, research and practice* (pp. 3–16). Boston, MA: Kluver.

Schrum, L. (2005). E-learning and K-12. In Howard, C., Boettcher, J. V., Justice, L., Schenk, K., Rogers, P. L., & Berg, G. A. (Eds.), *Encyclopedia of distance learning* (pp. 737–742). Hershey, PA: IGI Global. doi:10.4018/978-1-59140-555-9.ch107

Schrum, L., & Hong, S. (2002). Dimensions and strategies for online success: Voices from experienced educators. *Journal of Asynchronous Learning Networks, 6*(1), 57–67.

Schwen, T. M., & Hara, N. (2003). Community of practice: A metaphor for online design? *The Information Society, 19*, 257–270. doi:10.1080/01972240309462

Schwille, J., Dembélé, M., & Schubert, J. (2007). *Global perspectives on teacher learning- Improving policy and practice. Fundamentals of Educational Planning, 84.* Paris, France: UNESCO.

Seaman, J. (2009). *The paradox of faculty voices: Online learning as a strategic asset (Vol. II).* Washington, DC: Association of Public and Land-Grant Universities.

Seels, B. B., & Glasgow, Z. (1998). *Making instructional design decisions* (2nd ed.). Upper Saddle River, NJ: Prentice-Hall, Inc.

Seels, B. B., & Richey, R. C. (1994). *Instructional technology: The definitions and domains of the field.* Washington, DC: Association for Educational Communications and Technology.

Segrave, S., & Holt, D. (2003). Contemporary learning environments: Designing e-Learning for education in the professions. *Distance Education, 24*(1), 7. doi:10.1080/01587910303044

Selwyn, N. (2007). E-learning or she-learning? Exploring students' gendered perceptions of education technology. *British Journal of Educational Technology, 38*(4), 744–746. doi:10.1111/j.1467-8535.2006.00659.x

Senge, P., Cambron-McCabe, N., Lucas, T., Smith, B., Dutton, J., & Kleiner, A. (2000). *Schools that learn. A fifth discipline fieldbook for educators, parents, and everyone who cares about education.* New York, NY: Doubleday/Currency.

Serdiukov, P., Niederhauser, D., & Reynolds, R. (2000, February). *Teachers' distance professional development and support model.* Paper presented at the Society for Information Technology & Teacher Education International in San Diego, CA. (ERIC Document Reproduction Service No. ED444497)

Sherer, P. (2005). Web-based technology improves faculty development. *Academic Leader, 21*(1), 2–8.

Sheridan, K., & Kelly, M. A. (2010). The indicators of instructor presence that are important to students in online courses. *MERLOT Journal of Online Learning and Teaching, 6*(4), 767–779.

Short, J., Williams, E., & Christie, B. (1976). *The social psychology of telecommunications.* London, UK: John Wiley & Sons.

Shrivastava, P. (1999, December). Management classes as online learning communities. *Journal of Management Education, 23,* 691–702. doi:10.1177/105256299902300607

Shulman, G. M., Cox, M. D., & Richlin, L. (2004). Institutional considerations in developing a faculty learning community program. *New Directions for Teaching and Learning, 97,* 41–49. doi:10.1002/tl.131

Siemens, G. (2004). *Connectivism: A learning theory for the digital age.* Retrieved from http://www.elearnspace.org/Articles/connectivism.htm

Sierra, J. (2010). Shared responsibility and student learning: Ensuring a favorable educational experience. *Journal of Marketing Education, 32*(1), 104–111. doi:10.1177/0273475309344802

Simmons, S., Jones, W. Jr, & Silver, S. (2004). Making the transition from face-to-face to cyberspace. *TechTrends: Linking Research & Practice to Improve Learning, 48*(5), 50–85.

Sinha, H., Rosson, M. B., Carroll, J., & Du, H. (2010). Toward a professional development community for teachers. In D. Gibson & B. Dodge (Eds.), *Proceedings of Society for Information Technology & Teacher Education International Conference 2010* (pp. 2390-2397). Chesapeake, VA: AACE.

Skibba, K. (2011). *An investigation of how faculty members learn to teach adult students in a blended program.* Unpublished doctoral dissertation, University of Wisconsin, Milwaukee.

Sloan Consortium. (2002). *The 5 pillars: Sloan-C quality framework.* Retrieved from http://sloanconsortium.org/5pillars

Sloan-C. (n.d.). *A quality scorecard for administration of online education programs.* Retrieved from http://sloan-consortium.org/quality_scoreboard_online_program

Smith, M. K. (2003). Communities of practice. *The Encyclopedia of Informal Education.* Retrieved from http://www.infed.org/biblio/communities_of_practice.htm

Smith, A. D. (2001, March). Perception and belief. *Philosophy and Phenomenological Research, 62*(2), 283–309. doi:10.1111/j.1933-1592.2001.tb00057.x

Smith, P., & Ragan, T. (1999). *Instructional design* (2nd ed.). New York, NY: John Wiley & Sons, Inc.

Snyder, M. M. (2009). Instructional-design theory to guide the creation of online learning communities for adults. *TechTrends, 53*(1), 45–57. doi:10.1007/s11528-009-0237-2

Song, L., Singleton, E., Hill, J., & Koh, M. (2004). Improving online learning: Student perceptions of useful and challenging characteristics. *The Internet and Higher Education*, 7(1), 59–70. doi:10.1016/j.iheduc.2003.11.003

Southern Regional Education Board. (2004). *Standards for online professional development: Guidelines for planning and evaluating online professional development courses and programs*. Atlanta, GA: Author.

Speaker, R. B., Jr., Dermody, M., Knighten, B., Suzuki, T., Wan, C., & Parigi, A. (2001). Student/faculty relationships, methods courses and K-12 classrooms: Examples of integration of technology in teacher education. In C. Spirou (Ed.), *Proceedings of the 2nd International Conference on Technology in Teaching and Learning in Higher Education* (307-313). Athens, Greece: National and Kapodistrian University of Athens.

Speaker, R., Graveline, L., Johnson, M., Darby, D., & Heath, P. (2010, May). *Shaping distance education in a virtual world: A case of a university developing its virtual campus within a state-wide network*. Paper presented at the Annual Meeting of the Athens Educational Research Conference, Athens, Greece.

Speaker, R., Johnson, M., & Graveline, L. (2009). Toward understanding student and faculty perceptions of teaching, learning and disaster resilience in Second Life. In C. Fulford & G. Siemens (Eds.), *Proceedings of ED-MEDIA 2009: World Conference on Educational Multimedia, Hypermedia and Telecommunications* (pp. 585-590) Chesapeake, VA: Association for the Advancement of Computing in Education. (CD version; Abstract volume: p. 101 Retrieved from http://www.aace.org/conf/edmedia/sessions/index.cfm/fuseaction/PaperDetails?CFID=1055 6463&CFTOKEN=72042024&presentation_id=38776

Speaker, R., Johnson, M., Scaramella, L., & Cashner, R. (2008). Technology failures and successes with Hurricane Katrina: Voices from the University of New Orleans tell stories of the disaster and rebuilding. In J. Luca & E. Weippi (Eds.), *Proceedings of ED-MEDIA 2008: World Conference on Educational Multimedia, Hypermedia and Telecommunications* (pp. 857- 862). Chesapeake, VA: Association for the Advancement of Computing in Education.

Speaker, R. B. Jr. (2007). Technologies for teaching science and mathematics in the K-12 schools: Review, observations and directions for practice in the southern United States. In Hirschbuhl, J. J., & Kelley, J. (Eds.), *Computers in education* (12th ed., pp. 123–128). Dubuque, IA: McGrawHill.

Speaker, R. B. Jr, & Barnitz, J. G. (1999). Electronic and linguistic connections in one 21st-century classroom. Column on linguistic perspectives in literacy education. *The Reading Teacher*, *53*, 874–877.

Speaker, R. B. Jr, Laskowitz, R., Thompson, C., Speaker, P., Chauvin, B., Darby, D., & Willis, E. (2005). Collections, critical selections and the teaching repertoire: Examples from autobiographical memoirs and multimedia teaching units. In Griffin, R. E., Chandler, S. B., & Cowden, B. D. (Eds.), *Visual literacy and development: An African experience* (pp. 187–196). Loretto, PA: International Visual Literacy Association.

Spillane, J., Reiser, B., & Reimer, T. (2002). Policy implementation and cognition: Reframing and refocusing implementation research. *Review of Educational Research*, *72*(3), 387–431. doi:10.3102/00346543072003387

Stanford Center for Teaching & Learning (2007). *Speaking of Teaching Newsletters*.

Starkey, L. (2010). Teachers' pedagogical reasoning and action in the digital age. *Teachers and Teaching*, *16*(2), 233–244. doi:10.1080/13540600903478433

Starkey, L. (2011). Evaluating learning in the 21st century: A digital age learning matrix. *Technology, Pedagogy and Education*, *20*(1), 19–39. doi:10.1080/14759 39X.2011.554021

State Educational Technology Directors Association. (2005). Making the case for online professional development. *National Leadership Institute's toolkit 2005: Professional development* (pp. 11-19). Retrieved from ttp://tinyurl.com/md8g99

State Educational Technology Directors Association. (2008). *Class of 2020: Action plan for education*. Retrieved from http://tinyurl.com/69lndb

Steele, J. (2006). *Email: The manual: Everything you should know about email etiquette, policies and legal liability before you hit send.* Oak Park, IL: Marion Street Press, Inc.

Steffe, L. P., & Thompson, P. W. (Eds.). (2000). *Radical constructivism in action: Building on the pioneering work of Ernst Von Glasersfeld.* London, UK: Routledge Falmer.

Stevens, K. J. (2000). Télé-enseignement et éducation en milieu rural en Nouvelle Zélande et à Terre Neuve. *Géocarrefour - Revue de Geographie de Lyon - Espaces Ruraux et Technologies de L'Information, 75*(1), 87 – 92.

Stevens, K. J. (2005). The integration of virtual and actual classes in sparsely populated regions. In Kinshuk, G. Sampson, & P. Isaias (Eds.), *Cognition and exploratory learning in the digital age* (pp. 517-520). Lisbon, Portugal: IADIS Press.

Stevens, K. J. (1999a). A new model for teaching in rural communities – The electronic organisation of classes as intranets. *Prism – Journal of The Newfoundland and Labrador Teachers'. Association, 6*(1), 23–26.

Stevens, K. J. (1999b). Telecommunications technologies, telelearning and the development of virtual classes for rural New Zealanders. *Open Praxis, 1,* 12–14.

Stevens, K. J. (2001). The development of digital intranets for the enhancement of education in rural communities. *Journal of Interactive Instruction Development, 13*(3), 19–24.

Stevens, K. J. (2002a). Minnkandi heimur -Rafrænt net smárra skóla- Óvænt tengsl Íslenska menntanetsins við Nýja Sjáland og Kanada, (Making the world smaller -The electronic networking of small schools –Some unseen connections of the Icelandic Educational Network in New Zealand and Canada). [Icelandic translation by Karl Erlendsson]. *Skólavarðan, 2*(2), 22–24.

Stevens, K. J. (2002b). The expansion of educational opportunities in rural communities using web-based resources. In Santana Torrellas, G. A., & Uskov, V. (Eds.), *Computers and advanced technology in education* (pp. 221–225). Anaheim, CA: ACTA Press.

Stevens, K. J. (2007). A matrix for e-collaboration in rural Canadian schools. In Kock, N. (Ed.), *Encyclopedia of e-collaboration* (pp. 444–449). Hershey, PA: IGI Global. doi:10.4018/978-1-59904-000-4.ch068

Stevens, K. J., & Moffatt, C. (2003). From distance education to telelearning -The organization of open classes at local, regional and national levels. In Bradley, J. (Ed.), *The open classroom – Distance learning in and out of schools* (pp. 171–180). Sterling, VA: Kogan.

Stevens, K. J., & Stewart, D. (2005). *Cybercells – Learning in actual and virtual groups.* Melbourne, Australia: Thomson-Dunmore Press.

Stevens, K., Sandalov, A., Sukhareva, N., Barry, M., & Piper, T. (1999). The development of open models for teaching physics to schools in dispersed locations in Russia and Canada. In Grementieri, V., Szucs, A., & Trukhin, V. I. (Eds.), *Information and communication technologies and human resources development: New opportunities for European co-operation* (pp. 148–154). Budapest, Hungary: European Distance Education Network.

Stover, C. (2005, April 15). The four stages of faculty development at Empire State. *Distance Education Report,* 3-6. Retrieved from http://www.magnapubs.com/newsletter/issue/498/

Swail, W. S. (2002). Higher education and the new demographics: Questions for policy. *Change, 34*(4), 15–23.

Swan, K., & Shea, P. (2005). The development of virtual learning communities. In Hiltz, S. R., & Goldman, R. (Eds.), *Learning together online* (pp. 239–260). Mahwah, NJ: Lawrence Erlbaum Associates.

T&D. (2008). What does it cost to host web conferences and webcasts? *T&D, 62*(9), 88.

Tabata, L. N., & Johnsrud, L. K. (2008). The impact of faculty attitudes toward technology, distance education, and innovation. *Research in Higher Education, 49,* 625–646. doi:10.1007/s11162-008-9094-7

Tallent-Runnels, M. K., Thomas, J. A., Lan, W. Y., Cooper, S., Ahern, T. C., & Shaw, S. M. (2006). Teaching courses online: A review of the research. *Review of Educational Research, 76*(1), 93–135. doi:10.3102/00346543076001093

Tarr, T., & McDaniel, R. (2005). IUPUI 'Jump Start' program for new faculty. *Distance Education Report, 9*(2), 8.

Taylor, A., & McQuiggan, C. (2008). A faculty development survey analyzed what faculty want and need to be successful teaching online. *EDUCAUSE Quarterly, 31*(3). Retrieved from http://www.educause.edu/EDUCAUSE+Quarterly/EDUCAUSEQuarterlyMagazineVolum/FacultyDevelopmentProgrammingI/163099

Taylor, A., & McQuiggan, C. (2008). Faculty development programming: If we build it, will they come? *EDUCAUSE Quarterly, 31*(3), 28–37.

Taylor, E. W. (2008). Transformative learning theory. *New Directions for Adult and Continuing Education, 119*, 5–15. doi:10.1002/ace.301

Taylor, S. (2010). Negative judgments: Reflections on teaching reflective practice. *Organization Management Journal, 7*, 5–12. doi:10.1057/omj.2010.1

Technologies, S. M. A. R. T. (2011). *SMART education solutions.* Retrieved from http://smarttech.com/edredirect

Tella, S. (1995). *Virtual school in a networking learning environment.* Helsinki: University of Helsinki, Department of Teacher Education.

Tharp, R. G., & Gallimore, R. (1988). *Rousing minds to life.* New York, NY: Cambridge University Press.

Thomas, D., & Brown, J. (2011). *A new culture of learning: Cultivating the imagination for a world of constant change.* Lexington, KY: CreateSpace Publishing.

Thomas, D., & Brown, J. S. (2009, January). Why virtual worlds can matter. *International Journal of Media and Learning, 1*(1).

Thoms, K. J. (2001, April). They're not just big kids: Motivating adult learners. *Proceedings of the Annual Mid-South Instructional Technology Conference, Murfreesboro, TN.* (ERIC Document Reproduction Service No. ED463720)

Thornton, K. (2009). *Blended action learning: Supporting leadership learning in the New Zealand early childhood education sector.* Unpublished PhD thesis, Victoria University of Wellington, Wellington.

Thornton, K., & Yoong, P. (2011). The role of the blended action learning facilitator: An enabler of learning and a trusted inquisitor. *Action Learning Research and Practice, 8*(12), 129–146. doi:10.1080/14767333.2011.581021

Timperley, H., Wilson, A., Barrar, H., & Fung, I. (2007). *Professional learning and development: Best evidence synthesis iteration (BES).* Wellington, New Zealand: Ministry of Education.

Traphagan, T., Kucsera, J. V., & Kishi, K. (2010). Impact of class lecture webcasting on attendance and learning. *Educational Technology Research and Development, 5*(1), 19–37. doi:10.1007/s11423-009-9128-7

Treacy, B., Kleiman, G., & Treacy, K. P. (2002). Successful online professional development. *Learning and Leading with Technology, 30*(1), 42–47.

Trenton, G. (2006). The Xanadu project: Training faculty in the use of information and communication technology for university teaching. *Journal of Computer Assisted Learning, 22*, 182–196. doi:10.1111/j.1365-2729.2006.00168.x

Tsunoda, J. S. (1992, Fall). Expertise and values: How relevant is preservice training? *New Directions for Community Colleges, 79*, 11–20. doi:10.1002/cc.36819927904

Tubbs, S., & Moss, S. (2006). *Human communication: Principles and contexts.* New York, NY: McGraw Hill.

U.S. Army Field Artillery School. (1984). *A system approach to training* (Course Student textbook; ST - 5K061FD92).

U.S. Department of Education National Center for Education Statistics. (2002). *Nontraditional undergraduates (NCES 2002-012). National Center for Education Statistics.* Washington, DC: U.S. Government Printing Office.

U.S. Department of Education. (2010). *Evaluation of evidence-based practices in online learning: A meta-analysis and review of online learning studies.* Retrieved from http://www2.ed.gov/rschstat/eval/tech/evidence-based-practices/finalreport.pdf

U.S. News & World Report. (2011). *US News rankings.* Retrieved from http://www.usnews.com/rankings

US Department of Education. Office of Planning, Evaluation, and Policy Development Policy and Program Studies Service. (2010). *Evaluation of evidence-based practices in online learning: A meta-analysis and review of online learning studies.* Retrieved from http://www.ed.gov/about/offices/list/opepd/ppss/reports.html#edtech

US Department of Education. Office of Postsecondary Education. (2006). *Evidence of quality in distance education programs drawn from interviews with the accreditation community.* Retrieved from http://www.ysu.edu/accreditation/Resources/Accreditation-Evidence-of-Quality-in-DE-Programs.pdf

Usher, R., Bryant, I., & Johnston, R. (1997). *Adult education and the postmodern challenge: Learning beyond the limits.* New York, NY: Routledge.

Utah State University. (2010). *Virtual library.* National Library of Virtual Manipulatives. Retrieved from http://nlvm.usu.edu/en/nav/vlibrary.html

UW-Whitewater Learning Technology Center. (2011). *Online/blended workshop series.* Retrieved September 8, 2011, from http://www.uww.edu/icit/instructional/showcase/2/index.html

Valentine, D. (2002, Fall). Distance learning: Promises, problems, and possibilities. *Online Journal of Distance Learning Administration, 5*(3).

Van der Klink, M., & Streumer, J. N. (2002). Effectiveness of on-the-job training. *Journal of European Industrial Training, 26,* 196–199. doi:10.1108/03090590210422076

Van Hook, S. R. (2006). *Access to global learning: A matter of will.* University of California – Santa Barbara. Extension Language and Culture Program.

van Manen, M. (2002). The pedagogical task of teaching. *Teaching and Teacher Education, 18*(2), 135–138. doi:10.1016/S0742-051X(01)00058-0

Varvel, V. (2007, Spring). Master online teaching competencies. *Online Journal of Distance Learning Administration, 10*(1). Retrieved from http://www.westga.edu/~distance/ojdla/spring101/varvel101.htm

Velez, A. M. (2010). *Creating and sustaining virtual communities of practice by operationalizing constructs of preparation, collegiality, and professional development.* (Doctoral dissertation). Retrieved from ProQuest Dissertations and Theses. (3409364).

Vision, G. (2009). Fixing perceptual belief. *The Philosophical Quarterly, 59*(235), 292–314. doi:10.1111/j.1467-9213.2008.566.x

von Glasersfeld, E. (1989). Cognition, construction of knowledge, and teaching. *Synthese, 80*(1), 121–140. doi:10.1007/BF00869951

Vonderwell, S. (2003). An examination of asynchronous communication experiences and perspectives of students in an online course: A case study. *The Internet and Higher Education, 6,* 77–90. doi:10.1016/S1096-7516(02)00164-1

Vrasidas, C., & Glass, G. V. (Eds.). (2004). *Online professional development for teachers.* Greenwich, CT: Information Age Publishing.

Vrasidas, C., & McIsaac, M. S. (1999). Factors influencing interaction in an online course. *American Journal of Distance Education, 13*(3), 22–36. doi:10.1080/08923649909527033

Vrasidas, C., & Zembylas, M. (2004). Online professional development: lessons from the field. *Education + Training, 46*(6/7), 326–334. doi:10.1108/00400910410555231

Vygotsky, L. S. (1978). *Mind and society: The development of higher mental processes.* Cambridge, MA: Harvard University Press.

Wager, J. (2005). Support services for the Net generation. In Oblinger, D. G., & Oblinger, J. L. (Eds.), *Educating the net generation* (pp. 10.1–10.18). Washington, DC: Educause.

Wagner, E. D. (1994). In support of a functional definitions of interaction. *American Journal of Distance Education, 8*(2), 6–26. doi:10.1080/08923649409526852

Wainhouse. (2002). *Survey results: Usage trends of collaboration technology by business travelers.* Wainhouse Research.

Walker, G. (2005). Critical thinking in asynchronous discussions. *International Journal of Instructional Technology and Distance Learning, 2*(6).

Wallace, R. (2003). Online learning in higher education: A review of research on interactions among teachers and students. *Education Communication and Information, 3*(2), 241–280. doi:10.1080/14636310303143

Wang, H. (2009). Best practices: Preparing faculty for online teaching. In I. Gibson, et al. (Eds.), *Proceedings of Society for Information Technology & Teacher Education International Conference 2009* (pp. 1339-1343). Chesapeake, VA: AACE.

Wang, L., & Speaker, R. B., Jr. (2002). Investigating education faculty perspectives of their experiences technology project: Issues and problems related to technology integration (pp. 2011-2016). In P. Baker, & S. Rebelsky (Eds.), *Proceedings of ED-MEDIA 2002: World Conference on Educational Multimedia, Hypermedia & Telecommunications*. Norfolk, VA: Association for the Advancement of Computing in Education.

Wang, P., Huh, J., & Zygouris-Coe, V. (2007). Key factors affecting participant satisfaction of course facilitators in a large-scale online professional development context. *Proceedings of the 13th Sloan-C International Conference on Online Learning.* Orlando, FL: The Sloan Consortium.

Waugh, R., & Punch, K. (1987). Teacher receptivity to system wide change in the implementation stage. *Review of Educational Research, 57*(3), 237–254.

Weaver, D., Robbie, D., & Borland, R. (2008). The practitioner's model: Designing a professional development program for online teaching. *International Journal on E-Learning, 7*, 759–774.

Webster, F. (2002). *Theories of the information society.* Cambridge, MA: Routledge.

Weimer, M. (2002). *Learner-center teaching: Five key changes to practice.* San Francisco, CA: Jossey-Bass.

Weistra, H. (2000). *E-Learning, waar zijn we mee bezig? (E-learning, what are we doing?).* Keynote at the Best Practices E-Learning Conference, Nijrnegen, November 2000. Retrieved from http://www.sbo.nl/

Wellington, B., & Austin, P. (1996). Orientations to reflective practice. *Educational Researcher, 38*(3), 307–316.

Wenger, E. (1998). *Communities of practice: Learning, meaning and identity.* Cambridge, MA: Cambridge University Press.

Whitehouse, P., Reynolds, R., & Caperton, I. (2009). Globaloria pilot year one: New directions for 21st century Teacher professional development. In I. Gibson et al. (Eds.), *Proceedings of Society for Information Technology & Teacher Education International Conference 2009* (pp. 1590-1597). Chesapeake, VA: AACE.

Whitehouse, P. (2010). Networked teacher professional development: The case of Globaloria. *Journal of Interactive Learning Research, 21*(4).

Whitehouse, P., Breit, L. A., McCloskey, E. M., Ketelhut, D. J., & Dede, C. (2006). An overview of current findings from empirical research online teacher professional development. In Dede, C. (Ed.), *Online professional development for teachers: Emerging models and methods* (pp. 17–20). Cambridge, MA: Harvard Educational Press.

Wiley, D. A. (2000). Connecting learning objects to instructional design theory: A definition, a metaphor, and a taxonomy. In D. A. Wiley (Ed.). *The instructional use of learning objects.* Retrieved from http://reusability. org/ read/

Willard, N. E. (2006). *A briefing for educators: Online social networking communities and youth risk.* Retrieved from http://www.csriu.org/cyberbully/docs/youthriskonlinealert.pdf

Williams, W. M., & Ceci, S. J. (1997). "How am I doing?" Problems with student ratings of instructors and courses. *Change, 29*, 12–23. doi:10.1080/00091389709602331

Wittrock, M. C. (1992). Generative learning processes of the brain. *Educational Psychologist, 27*(4), 531–541. doi:10.1207/s15326985ep2704_8

Wolf, P. (2006). Best practices in the training of faculty to teach online. *Journal of Computing in Higher Education, 17*(2), 47–78. doi:10.1007/BF03032698

Wood, L. W. (2010). *Faculty perceptions about virtual world technology: Affordances and barriers to adoption.* Unpublished Doctoral dissertation, Middle-Secondary Education and Instructional Technology Dissertations, Georgia State University, Atlanta. Retrieved from http://digitalarchive.gsu.edu/msit_diss/70

Wood, C. (2005). Highschool.com. *Edutopia, 1*(4), 32–37.

Wright, A. (2005). *From ivory tower to academic sweatshop.* Retrieved from http://dir.salon.com/tech/feature/2005/01/26/distance_learning/index.html

Wright, S. P., Horn, S. P., & Sanders, W. L. (1997). Teacher and classroom context effects on student achievement: Implications for teacher evaluation. *Journal of Personnel Evaluation in Education, 11*, 57–67. doi:10.1023/A:1007999204543

Yang, S. C., & Liu, S. F. (2004). Case study of online workshop for the professional development of teachers. *Computers in Human Behavior, 20*, 733–761. doi:10.1016/j.chb.2004.02.005

Yontz, E., & de la Pena McCook, K. (2003). Service-learning and LIS education. *Journal of Education for Library and Information Science, 44*, 55–68. doi:10.2307/40323942

Zhang, D., Zhou, L., Briggs, R. O., & Nunamaker, J. F. Jr. (2006). Instructional video in elearning: Assessing the impact of interactive video on learning effectiveness. *Information & Management, 43*(1), 15–27. doi:10.1016/j.im.2005.01.004

Zheng, R., Stucky, B., McAlack, M., Menchana, M., & Stoddart, S. (2005). WebQuest learning as perceived by higher education learners. *TechTrends: Linking Research & Practice to Improve Learning, 49*(4), 41-49. Retrieved from http://www.eric.ed.gov

Zhu, E., Groscurth, C., Bergom, I., & Hershock, C. (2010). Assessing and meeting TA's instructional technology training needs: Research and practice. *Journal of Faculty Development, 24*(3), 37–43.

Zull, J. E. (2002). *The art of changing the brain: Enriching teaching.* Sterling, VA: Stylus.

About the Contributors

Jared Keengwe is an Associate Professor in the Department of Teaching and Learning at the University of North Dakota. His primary research interests are focused on computer technology integration and constructivist pedagogical approach to teaching and learning. He facilitates, Technology for Teachers, Social Studies in Elementary Schools, and Multicultural Education undergraduate courses and Diversity in Higher Education, and Scholarly Writing graduate courses. Dr. Keengwe's research has resulted in more than 100 refereed publications in journals, book chapters, and conference proceedings. He is the co-editor of "*Adult Learning in the Digital Age: Perspectives on Online Technologies and Outcomes*" – a premier reference source for computer science and information technology management.

Lydia Kyei-Blankson is a faculty member at Illinois State University. Dr. Lydia Kyei-Blankson has expertise in research methods, applied statistics, and psychometrics. She teaches graduate courses in research methods and statistics at Illinois State University. Her research interests investigate the underlying factors associated with student academic achievement. She is especially interested in technology use in education to improve student learning and achievement and has co-authored a number of articles in this area.

* * *

Sheri Anderson is the Faculty Liaison/Instructional Designer for the Office of e-Learning at the University of North Carolina Wilmington. She collaborates with colleagues to deign faculty professional development for online and web-enhanced course design and delivery. She also disseminates information regarding pedagogy for online and web-enhanced courses to the faculty through print and web media. Sheri has taught both web-enhanced and fully online for UNCW for the last 4 years. Her prior experience includes e-Learning Instructional Support Specialist and special education teacher and department chair. Sheri earned a Bachelor of Arts in Art History and a teaching certificate in special education.

Jennifer Banas is an Assistant Professor in the College of Education at Northeastern Illinois University. Dr. Banas earned her Doctorate in Instructional Design & Technology from Northern Illinois University. She has previously served as an online course designer and dean for the American College of Education. Other career experience includes teaching high school health education, working as a county health educator, and serving as a visiting research project coordinator for the Survey Research Laboratory at the University of Illinois-Chicago. Her areas of research include the application of learning, behavior, and communication models and theories to effectively and efficiently teach and motivate learners.

Carol A. Brown is Associate Professor of Instructional Technology. Dr. Brown earned her doctorate (Ed.D. in Curriculum and Instruction) from the University of Memphis. With over ten years of faculty experience, her work with distance education through the online degree programs and in-service teachers for technology integration in K12 classrooms have provided rich experiences with professional and continuing education. Her research interests include professional development for teachers and best practices in teaching with digital resources. She is currently working with faculty at North Carolina State University to implement game based learning for teaching English Language Arts in middle school classrooms.

Patricia Coward is the Director of the Center for Teaching Excellence and Faculty Development at Canisius College in Buffalo, NY. She earned her PhD in English, and Rhetoric and Composition from Bowling Green State University, and has held faculty appointments at Frostburg State University and Canisius College. Since 2005, Dr. Coward has directed the CTE, guiding and mentoring faculty in the Scholarship of Teaching and Learning (SoTL), Assessment of Student Learning, and Teaching for Justice. Dr. Coward has given presentations at teaching conferences in the USA and Japan, on topics ranging from student engagement to responding to student writing.

Lesley Farmer, Professor at California State University Long Beach, coordinates the Librarianship program. She earned her M.S. in Library Science at the University of North Carolina Chapel Hill, and received her Doctorate in Adult Education from Temple University. She has worked in K-12 school settings and public academic libraries. She serves as CSLA Research Committee Chair, International Association of School Librarianship Vice-President of Association Relations, and Editor for the IFLA School Libraries and Resource Centers Section. Her research interests include information literacy, assessment, collaboration, and educational technology. Her most recent book is *Instructional Design for Librarians and Information Professionals* (Neal-Schuman, 2011).

Steven Grubaugh received his Doctorate in Literacy Education from the University of Northern Colorado. Dr. Grubaugh is a Professor of Education at UNLV with a specialty in literacy, new literacies and online and blended education. He teaches courses in new literacies, content area literacy, and young adult and children's literature. He has published numerous professional articles in refereed journals, authored funded grant proposals and presented professional papers at regional and international conferences. He believes in and practices the core principles that inform the iNACOL National Standards of Quality for Online Courses and the IRA/NCTE Standards for the English Language Arts, revised 2010.

Denice Ward Hood is tenure-track faculty member in the Department of Education Policy, Organization and Leadership at the University of Illinois (Urbana-Champaign). Her research focus is on online teaching and learning in higher education. Specifically, Dr. Hood investigates online access and achievement in STEM fields, the intersection between adult learning, cognitive and social factors that contribute to academic success, cultural aspects of online pedagogy, program evaluation and the policy implications. Prior to her present appointment, Dr. Hood was an Associate Professor in the Department of Educational Psychology at Northern Arizona University where she taught online courses for 6 years.

Wenhao David Huang currently holds a tenure-track faculty position at Department of Education Policy, Organization and Leadership at University of Illinois at Urbana-Champaign. His research interests mainly focus on cognitive as well as motivational issues in technology-enhanced learning and performance settings across organizations. Specifically, D. Huang investigates the empirical relationship between cognitive and motivational processing afforded by highly interactive learning environments such as digital game-based learning systems (DGBLS). His projects also focus on the design differences between genders (and other social variables) in the context of game-enabled learning. His primary goal is to promote learner- and instructor-friendly online instructional practices.

Kim J. Hyatt is an Associate Teaching Professor at Carnegie Mellon University's Heinz College. She teaches Strategic Writing for the School of Information Systems & Management and Strategic Presentation Skills for the School of Public Policy & Management. Dr. Hyatt is an Associate Editor for the *International Journal of Information and Communication Technology Education*. She is also a member of China Links, an international consulting firm that specializes in creating and implementing professional development workshops. She specializes in literacy education, instructional technology and assessment. Dr. Hyatt's previous appointment was at Duquesne University as the Director of the Graduate Elementary Leading Teacher Program.

Greg Levitt is a Professor of Education at the University of Nevada Las Vegas. Dr. Levitt graduated from The Ohio State University with a Ph.D. in Global Education and Asian Studies. He served as Department Chair and Assistant Dean in the College of Education. He also served as a Technology Coordinator for the College. Dr. Levitt worked at the Andre Agassi College Prep Academy as a university consultant where he helped start the urban teacher-training program with the University of Nevada, Las Vegas. He also worked with public schools to establish technology programs and field experience sites for college students.

Nicolas Lorgnier has been teaching at the university level in the US and in France for 5 years. He currently teaches contemporary issues in sport, risk management, and contract negotiation at Canisius College (Buffalo, NY), and project management in sport tourism for University of Lille (France). The aforementioned courses are online, blended, and hybrid. His research focuses on organizational behaviors and the impact of new technology on organizational strategy.

Allie McDonald is an elementary school teacher currently engaged in post-graduate study in Christchurch, New Zealand. She is an Associate Teacher and Research Associate for the University of Canterbury and is currently working alongside school staff to implement school-wide E-learning spaces. Her primary research interests include e-learning and teacher professional development.

Lex McDonald is Head of the Educational Psychology and Pedagogy School at Victoria University, Wellington, New Zealand. He has worked as a teacher and psychologist in New Zealand and overseas. His particular interest is in instructional psychology and has had a number of papers published on adult learner motivation and professional development. Over the years he has worked in e-learning programmes for trainee teachers, teachers, police, psychologists, social workers, and training of the trainers. The intersection of theory with practice and phenomenological research approaches have been pivotal concerns in his work.

Renée E. Weiss Neal is Teaching Assistant Professor of Instructional Technology at East Carolina University. She received her Doctorate in Instructional Technology from The University of Memphis in 1999. Since then she has worked as the Interim Director for the Center for Academic Excellence at The University of Memphis and Assistant Professor at Southern Illinois University Edwardsville where she taught instructional systems technology and performance improvement. She has been an Editor of a book on online pedagogy. She has also worked at FedEx Corporation, Time Warner Communications, and Edward Jones Investments where her focus was on performance improvement and leadership development.

Michaela A. Noakes is a Doctoral candidate and Research Assistant in Instructional Technology in the School of Education at Duquesne University. She serves as a data analysis consultant, and also an Adjunct Faculty member at Duquesne University, Point Park University and Butler County Community College. She was recently inducted into Pi Lambda Theta, the International Honor Society for Educators. She has co-authored a paper titled Learning by Wandering: A Framework for Transformative e-Learning (in press) and accepted for presentation at the International Conference on E-Learning. Other scholarly works include co-authored conference proceeding papers, co-authored book chapters, and research manuscripts (in press).

Shawn M. O'Rourke has over ten years of administrative experience at the university level and over twenty years teaching in the sport administration field. He teaches courses in Leadership, Philosophy and Ethics and Financial Aspects of the sport industry. He is also been a Faculty Athletic Representative (FAR) for the past six years at Canisius College and Director of the Sport Administration program and Institute for Research in Sport (IRIS). '

Nathaniel Ostashewski has been a K-20 educator for over 25 years and has spent the past 15 years helping teachers integrate technology into their teaching practices. He has worked as a multimedia and instructional designer of many courses for colleges and universities in Canada. His expertise is in the utilization of social media and Web 2.0 tools to support online courses. He has presented at many International conferences on iPads in education, networked and online learning, media in online education, and Lego robotics in the classroom. Nathaniel is completing his Doctorate in Distance Education with Athabasca University in Alberta, Canada.

Beth Allred Oyarzun is an Instructional Designer for the Office of e-Learning at the University of North Carolina Wilmington. She collaborates with colleagues to design, develop, and deliver professional development for faculty teaching web-enhanced or fully online courses. Her research interests involve effective instructional strategies for online teaching and learning. She also teaches online sections of undergraduate education courses in Instructional Design and Instructional Technology. Her prior experience includes serving as the technology liaison for the school of education at UNCW and teaching high school mathematics. She is pursuing her Ph.D. in Instructional Design and Technology from Old Dominion University.

Doug Reid is a career educator with a wide variety of experiences. Doug has been a school teacher, tenured professor, coach, mentor, instructional designer, and educational coordinator. Dr. Reid is an innovative professional and has used cutting edge technology to support student learning for 20 years. Most recently, he has been using mobile technology to promote digital storytelling in K-12 aboriginal classrooms. He is also working with social networking technologies to develop non-traditional teaching and learning opportunities for students and professionals. Dr. Reid is a Canadian who has taught and presented his research work at professional conferences around the globe.

Brenda Service is Programme Director of the Graduate Diploma of Teaching (Secondary) in the Faculty of Education at Victoria University of Wellington in New Zealand. Prior to working at Victoria, she taught and held leadership positions in a number of secondary schools and facilitated courses for aspiring and experienced principals. In addition to her programme director role, Brenda contributes to a number of undergraduate and post graduate courses. Brenda's research interests are curriculum and the implementation of pedagogical change. Her Doctoral study focuses on implementation of the New Zealand curriculum in secondary schools.

Karen Skibba is an instructional design specialist at the University of Wisconsin-Whitewater's Learning Technology Center where she consults with faculty on developing online and hybrid courses and using technology to enhance student learning. Dr. Skibba received her Doctorate in Adult and Continuing Education from the University of Wisconsin-Milwaukee. Her research focuses on instructional design and online and blended teaching and learning. She has co-authored a chapter on blended learning published by the Sloan-Consortium. Karen has presented her research at national conferences including EDUCAUSE, Sloan Consortium, Professional and Organizational Development, and the Distance Teaching and Learning Conference in Madison.

Richard B. Speaker, Jr. is Graduate Studies Coordinator and Associate Professor of Curriculum and Instruction at the University of New Orleans (UNO). Dr. Speaker earned his Doctorate in Language and Literacy Studies from the Graduate School of Education at University of California, Berkeley. His interests include integrated instructional programs across the curriculum (literacy, science, mathematics, and social studies), curriculum theory and development, international studies, and technology integration into instruction. He also maintains the Second Life site for UNO and Louisiana under the auspices of the Louisiana Regents Second Life Estate as part of the Louisiana Board of Regents SELECT project.

Louise Starkey is the Associate Dean of Primary and Secondary Teacher Education at Victoria University of Wellington, New Zealand. She has previously taught and held leadership positions in a number of secondary schools. Dr. Louise's research focus on teaching and learning in the digital age and include exploring theories, policies, and practice within schools and university systems. From this research she has developed thinking about the future of teaching in the schooling sector shared in the book *"Teaching and Learning in the Digital Age."* Louise's contribution to educational research has been recognized through being named in the Routledge class of 2011.

Ken Stevens is a Professor of Education at Memorial University of Newfoundland where he was appointed to a chair in e-learning, funded by Industry Canada. His previous appointments were at James Cook University in Queensland, Australia, and at Victoria University of Wellington, New Zealand. In Australia, New Zealand, and Canada he has specialized in the provision of education in rural communities and the application of information technologies for teaching and learning in schools located in sparsely populated areas. He has been cross-appointed as an Adjunct Professor of Education at Victoria University of Wellington and lives in Canada and New Zealand.

Kate Thornton is a Senior Lecturer in the School of Education Policy and Implementation at Victoria University of Wellington, New Zealand. Dr. Thornton's research interests include educational leadership, leadership development, mentoring and coaching, and online professional learning. She teaches both undergraduate and post graduate courses. Her publications include articles arising from her doctoral research into the use of blended action learning to support leadership development. She is currently national president of the New Zealand Educational Administration and Leadership Society (NZEALS) and was recently awarded a Fulbright scholarship to study mentoring and coaching programmes in the United States.

Linda Wood is the Department Chair of Graphic Design and Photographic Imaging at The Art Institute of Atlanta. She earned her Ph.D. in Instructional Technology from Georgia State University; a M.S. in Instructional Technology from Western Illinois University; and a B.F.A. in Graphic Design from The University of Georgia. Dr. Wood has been teaching at the college level since 1992. In addition, she has over 30 years experience as a graphic designer, art director, and creative professional in the field of visual communications.

Angela Velez-Solic is the Instructional Design Specialist at IU Northwest. She received a Doctorate (Ph.D.) in Adult Education. She presently trains faculty to teach online, provides technology workshops for faculty and staff, assists faculty with instructional design, and is helping the campus develop their online program protocol. Prior to this position, Dr. Velez-Solic was the Coordinator of Learning Technologies at Northeastern Illinois University and helped transform the faculty from instructors who feared technology to instructors who embrace it. Her areas of interest are online course quality, training, and support for faculty who teach online and hybrid and innovative instructional design.

Carrie L. Zinger is a graduate of Duquesne University's Master of Science in Education Program. She possesses two teaching certifications in the state of Pennsylvania: English and elementary education. Her work experience includes twelve years as a Learning & Development Specialist, delivering synchronous and asynchronous training programs for professionals in the financial sales and service industry.

Vassiliki Zygouris-Coe is an Associate Professor of Education at the University of Central Florida, College of Education. Her research focuses in literacy in the content areas, online learning, and professional development. Dr. Zygouris-Coe has impacted reading instruction in the state of Florida through the Florida Online Reading Professional Development project—Florida's first online large-scale project for preK-12 educators. Her work has been published in multiple refereed journals including, *The Reading Teacher, The Journal of Technology and Teacher Education*, and *The International Journal of E-Learning*. She serves in several editorial roles, including Co-Editor of the *Literacy Research and Instruction* journal.

Index